Why Do You Need this New Edition?

If you're wondering why you should buy this new edition of *American Military History*, here are six good reasons!

1. Each chapter has been updated and revised to provide stronger analysis and conciseness.

2. The end-of-chapter bibliographies have been updated.

3. The illustrations in every chapter are new to this edition.

4. There are now review questions at the end of each chapter in a new section called **Research and Explore**.

5. A new Web site, **MySearchLab with Pearson e-Text**, provides a wealth of online resources related to the content of the text and to the research and writing process.

6. New **MySearchLab Connections: Sources Online** sections at the end of each chapter list primary source documents and other resources that are part of the new MySearchLab Web site that is now available with the second edition.

PEARSON

American Military History

American Military History

A Survey from Colonial Times to the Present

SECOND EDITION

William T. Allison
Georgia Southern University

Jeffrey G. Grey
Australian Defence Force Academy

Janet G. Valentine
United States Army Command and General Staff College

PEARSON

Boston   Columbus   Indianapolis   New York   San Francisco   Upper Saddle River
Amsterdam   Cape Town   Dubai   London   Madrid   Milan   Munich   Paris   Montreal   Toronto
Delhi   Mexico City   São Paulo   Sydney   Hong Kong   Seoul   Singapore   Taipei   Tokyo

Editor-in-Chief: Dickson Musslewhite
Publisher: Charlyce Jones Owen
Senior Assistant: Maureen Diana
Associate Editor: Emsal Hasan
Media Editor: Andrea Messineo
Vice President, Director of Marketing: Brandy Dawson
Marketing Manager: Maureen Prado Roberts
Production Manager: Laura Messerly
Senior Art Director: Jayne Conte
Cover Designer: Suzanne Behnke
Cover Image: Library of Congress Print and Reproductions Division [LC-DIG-cwpb-03156]; Library of Congress Print and Reproductions Division [LC-DIG-pga-01669]; Library of Congress Print and Reproductions Division [LC-USZ62-90239]; Photo Courtesy of U.S. Army and SFC James K.F. Dung
Composition and Full Service Project Management: Jogender Taneja, Aptara®, Inc.
Printer/Binder/Cover Printer: R.R. Donnelley & Sons/Crawfordsville

Credits and acknowledgments for materials borrowed from other sources and reproduced, with permission, in this textbook appear on the appropriate page within text.

Copyright © 2013, 2007 by Pearson Education, Inc., Upper Saddle River, New Jersey, 07458. All rights reserved. Manufactured in the United States of America. This publication is protected by Copyright, and permission should be obtained from the publisher prior to any prohibited reproduction, storage in a retrieval system, or transmission in any form or by any means, electronic, mechanical, photocopying, recording, or likewise. To obtain permission(s) to use material from this work, please submit a written request to Pearson Education, Inc., Permissions Department, One Lake Street, Upper Saddle River, New Jersey 07458, or you may fax your request to 201-236-3290.

Library of Congress Cataloging-in-Publication Data
Allison, William Thomas.
   American military history: a survey from colonial times to the present/
William T. Allison, Jeffrey G. Grey, Janet G. Valentine.—2nd ed.
    p. cm.
   ISBN-13: 978-0-205-89850-3
   ISBN-10: 0-205-89850-5
   1. United States—History, Military.   I. Grey, Jeffrey.   II. Valentine,
Janet G. III. Title.
   E181.A33 2012
   355.00973—dc23   2012019797

10 9 8 7 6 5 4 3 2

PEARSON

ISBN-10:   0-205-89850-5
ISBN-13: 978-0-205-89850-3

Contents

MySearchLab Connections

Chapter 16

Jimmy Carter, The "Malaise" Speech (1979)
George Bush, Allied Military Action in the Persian Gulf (1991)
Bill Chappell, Speech to the American Security Council Foundation (1985)

Chapter 17

George W. Bush, Address to the Nation (2001)
Notes from Donald Rumsfeld on Iraq War Planning (2001)
Oral History of Colonel Terry L. Sellers (2007)

Preface

The American military experience is so distinctly woven into American history that it is at times difficult to separate the two. Such a notion is perhaps uncomfortable for some historians, but the fact remains that although American history has been shaped by race, ethnicity, economy, regionalism, power, and myriad other influences, so, too, has this experience been tremendously shaped by war and the struggle to define the role of a military in a democratic society.

Since colonial times, the people of America, including Native Americans, have spent a great deal of time at war. Well over one million Americans have perished in these wars. Americans have fought for land, trade, freedom, slavery, prestige, empire, democracy, and humanity, to list but a few. Over time, the American people and their government have developed a distinctive way of thinking about, preparing for, and fighting wars.

This textbook is meant to serve as a foundation for undergraduate courses in American military history. The content and style are meant to appeal to undergraduate students who may or may not be history majors. In providing such fundamental themes and content, the text is designed to allow instructors flexibility in their own course design, be it through lecture, supplemental readings, or other methodologies. The text is organized chronologically, beginning with European conflict with Native Americans and concluding with military affairs in the early twenty-first century. Each chapter offers a brief chronology, subheadings, and terms (such as concepts, people, places, and events) to provide the reader a pedagogical framework for understanding the central themes and events in the American military experience and their relation to American history.

Each chapter also includes a primary document relating to the time period covered in that particular chapter. These documents provide the student with a glimpse into a variety of issues and experiences in American military history. Each chapter also includes a brief list of books for further student reading. Obviously, the selection of such documents and additional reading is subjective, and the book lists are not meant to be authoritative or definitive, but rather representative and appropriate for undergraduates. Individual instructors would certainly add to, or delete from the documents and books offered in each chapter. Again, the purpose is to offer the student a foundation and give the instructor flexibility. Appropriate maps and illustrations are added to provide further context for the student.

War, naturally, plays a central role in this textbook, and in several instances chapters are devoted solely to conflict. Other issues and events beyond war, however, also characterize the American military experience. The struggle between the tradition of militia and the need for a standing army, the evolution of civil-military relations, the advent of professionalism in the military, the nonmilitary uses of the military, and the military's role in democratic society as a tool of international and domestic power, a social institution, and symbol of American prestige abroad are all also part of this experience. In order to gain a holistic appreciation of American military history, these themes and others must be examined in the context of American history.

This textbook is influenced by the great wealth of scholarship on a wide range of topics and issues that comprise the historiography of American military history. Alan Millett and Peter Maslowski's *For the Common Defense: A Military History of the United States*, Russell Weigley's *The American Way of War: A History of United States Military Strategy and Policy*, Millett's *Semper Fidelis: The History of the United States Marine Corps*, Stephen Howarth's *To Shining Sea: A History of the United States Navy*, and the many publications of the historical offices of the various branches of the American Armed Services were especially helpful in putting together this textbook.

What's New in the Second Edition

The new edition features a revised illustration program, with new images in every chapter. The bibliography has been updated in every chapter as well. A new feature, *MySearchLab Connections: Sources Online*, ends each chapter with a list of documents available to complement the chapter discussions. These documents are part of a new website available with the second edition, **MySearchlab with Pearson eText** (www.mysearchlab.com). A full description of the site is included on page xx. Also included are new review questions that can be used as study aids or as possible topics for research papers.

CHAPTER 1

- Updated "Virginia and the Powhatan" and "New England's Pequot War" sections
- New primary document, *John Smith's Proposal to Subjugate the Powhatan*

CHAPTER 2

- Updated "Great War for Empire (1756–1763)" section

CHAPTER 3

- Updated "The Southern Phase (1778–1781)" and "The Constitution and the Military" sections

CHAPTER 5

- Updated entire War of 1812 content

CHAPTER 6

- Updated "The Army and the West," "The Naval Expeditions," and "Frontier Constabulary and Indian Affairs" sections

CHAPTER 7

- Updated "Napoleon and A Revolution in Warfare," and "War with Mexico" sections

CHAPTER 8

- Updated "The Eastern Theater (1861–1863)," "The Western Theater (1861–1863)," and "Reconstruction" sections

CHAPTER 9

- All sections updated
- Updated chapter chronology

CHAPTER 10

- Strengthened discussion of the 92nd Division

CHAPTER 11

- Broadened discussion of the evolution of amphibious doctrine

CHAPTER 12

- Expanded discussion of black divisions and internment

CHAPTER 13

- Updated "Integration of the Armed Forces" (added information on the Women in Military Service Act) and "The Korean War" (throughout all sections on the war); revised "Conclusion"

CHAPTER 14

- Updated chapter chronology

CHAPTER 15

- Added a new section on antiwar activism

CHAPTER 16

- Added discussion of Desert One and outcomes

CHAPTER 17

- Entire chapter substantially revised and updated to include developments in Iraq and Afghanistan since 2006

MySearchLab

The Moment You Know

www.mysearchlab.com

MySearchLab with eText delivers proven results in helping individual students succeed. Its automatically graded assessments and interactive eText provide engaging experiences that personalize, stimulate, and measure learning for each student. And, it comes from a trusted partner with educational expertise and a deep commitment to helping students, instructors, and departments achieve their goals.

PERSONALIZE LEARNING

Writing, Research, and Citing Sources

- Step-by-step tutorials present complete overviews of the research and writing process.
- Instructors and students receive access to the EBSCO ContentSelect database, census data from Social Explorer, Associated Press news feeds, and the Pearson bookshelf. Pearson SourceCheck helps students and instructors monitor originality and avoid plagiarism.

eText and more

- **Pearson eText**—An e-book version of *American Military History, Second Edition* is included in MySearchLab. As with the printed text, students can highlight and add their own notes as they read their interactive text online.
- **Chapter quizzes and flashcards**—Chapter and key term reviews are available for each chapter online and offer immediate feedback.
- **Primary and Secondary Source Documents**—A collection of documents, organized by chapter, is available on MySearchLab. The documents include head notes and critical thinking questions.
- **Gradebook**—Automated grading of quizzes helps both instructors and students monitor their results throughout the course.

MySearchLab Connections

At the end of each chapter in the text, a special section, *MySearchLab Connection: Sources Online*, provides a list of the documents included on the MySearchLab website that relate to the content of the chapter. See page xiii for a full list of the sources listed in the text.

Acknowledgments

We would like to thank the following reviewers for their thoughtful reviews that have helped us shape this new edition.

Lesley J. Gordon, *University of Akron*
Alan M. Osur, *University of Colorado*
Steven J. Rauch, *Augusta State University*
Mackubin Thomas Owens, *Naval War College*

The authors wish to thank the very generous and patient people at Pearson, especially Charlyce Jones Owen, Maureen Diana, Debra Wechsler, and the production staff for their patience, support, and hard work. Many reviewers offered insightful and constructive suggestions; any oversights and errors, however, are ours alone. Of course, the support of friends and family is appreciated beyond measure.

About the Authors

William Thomas Allison is Professor of History at Georgia Southern University. He earned his Ph.D. in history at Bowling Green State University in 1995, and has taught as Visiting Professor at the Air War College and the School for Advanced Air and Space Studies. He is author of *Military Justice in Vietnam: The Rule of Law in an American War* (Kansas, 2007), *The Tet Offensive* (Routledge, 2008), *My Lai: An American Tragedy* (Johns Hopkins, 2012), and *The Gulf War, 1991* (Palgrave, 2012), among other works. He has served on the editorial board of the *Journal of Military History* and as a member of the Department of the Army Historical Advisory Committee.

Jeffrey G. Grey is Professor of History in the School for Humanities and Social Sciences at the Australian Defence Force Academy. He earned his Ph.D. at the University of New South Wales in 1986, and has held several professorships, including the Major General Matthew C. Horner Chair of Military Theory at the United States Marine Corps University. His numerous publications include *The Commonwealth Armies and the Korean War: An Alliance Study* (Manchester, 1988), *A Military History of Australia* (Cambridge, 1990), *Australian Brass: The Career of Lieutenant General Sir Horace Robertson* (Cambridge University Press, 1992), *"Up Top": The Royal Australian Navy in Southeast Asian Conflicts 1955–1972* (Allen & Unwin, 1998), *The Australian Army: Volume I: The Australian Centenary History of Defence* (Oxford, 2006), as well as several authored and co-authored volumes on Australian military history for the Australian Army History Unit and Australian Military History Publishing. He has served as a trustee for the Society for Military History and on the editorial boards of the *Journal of the Australian War Memorial*, *Journal of Military History*, *Scientia Militaria*, *War in History*, and *Australian Army Journal*, and is editor for the journal *War and Society*.

Janet G. Valentine is Assistant Professor in the Department of Military History at the United States Army Command and General Staff College, Fort Leavenworth, Kansas. She earned her Ph.D. at the University of Alabama in 2002 and has worked as a historian for the United States Army Center of Military History, the Air National Guard History Office, and the Joint History Office. She has served on the advisory board for H-WAR and the editorial board of the *Journal of Military History*. She has taught at the University of North Florida and Mississippi State University. Her current research focuses on the Korean War, and citizenship and military obligation.

American Military History

The First American Way of War

◆ INTRODUCTION

When English settlers arrived to colonize the Atlantic seaboard of North America in the early 1600s, they found a most threatening and inhospitable environment against which they would struggle for decades to establish permanent settlements. From the English viewpoint, strange diseases, a dramatically diverse climate, and a primitive indigenous people haunted the shores and estuaries of New England, the Chesapeake

Bay region, and the Carolinas. These early colonists arrived with no promise of royal protection from hostile natives or encroaching armies of competing European powers. From the standpoint of the English crown and Parliament, the colonists were on their own and would have to provide for their own defense. These circumstances gave colonists plenty of cause to be conscious of military matters. The warfare that developed in North America was not European in style or purpose, and it forced colonists to move away from military concepts of the Old World and open their minds to new but brutal ideas about warfare and military affairs that suited their unique situation.

◆ THE AMERICAN COLONIES AND THE BRITISH MILITARY TRADITION

It was only natural that English settlers would bring with them to the New World their ideas and traditions from home. This concept of transplanting one's customs, beliefs, and traditions is called cultural mimesis. To the American wilderness English colonists brought their traditional notions on social order, localized representative government, basic rights, loyalty to the King, civic obligation, and military affairs. From the time of their initial settlement in Virginia and Massachusetts, English colonists became entangled in a paradoxical trinity of trade, alliance, and warfare that resulted in frequent conflict with Native Americans throughout the seventeenth century. In their adaptation to the unique circumstances of North America, English colonists developed their own attitudes toward military affairs and gradually created their own style of war. It was the beginning of what became the American military tradition. This included an adapted English militia system that grew throughout the colonies and varied widely in form, regulation, and effectiveness compared to its counterpart back in England. At first, conflict with Native Americans over trade and land and then wars against rival European powers, particularly France, influenced colonists to adopt, then adapt, this institution.

The English had developed two principal values concerning military affairs. First, the idea of a militia had become an English tradition in and of itself. Militia in England had been an institution with which all Anglo colonists would have been familiar. Each county in England was obligated to keep and train militia units, known as trainbands, under the leadership of a lord lieutenant. Only about one-tenth of Englishmen participated in these local training units, whose discipline and ability varied widely. Rarely called to muster, few militiamen in England expected actually to be called into service because the very idea of defending England's shores from an invader seemed so remote (except in 1588, of course). Militia service and training also had become a sort of informal social control mechanism that helped regulate class relationships and bonded county to country. In times of war militia units would not *per se* integrate with the English army. Rather, recruits who often had militia experience would augment already existing localized army units. Remember that England had been principally a naval power during the sixteenth century, and as a result, comparatively little money from the royal treasury had been expended to maintain a large standing professional army.

This leads to the second value—the English looked upon a standing professional army with grave suspicion, because many feared such an army might violate basic liberties that were guaranteed under Parliament and crown. Standing armies also cost money, which England's coffers could ill afford, especially with so much of the national budget spent on naval power. Militia service in England was also a nationwide obligation with centralized standards that applied equally to all county militia units. But this was on paper, and periodic drill was insufficient to lessen the contempt felt by professional army officers toward county militia.

In England, these values shifted during the 1600s. The English Civil War of 1640–1649 and the Thirty Years' War (1618–1648), among other conflicts, exposed the weaknesses of militia training and the shortcomings of temporary armies. Oliver Cromwell's New Model Army, officered mainly by Puritans, became a well-trained, well-disciplined force that soundly defeated the armies of Charles I in the English Civil War. Cromwell's army also avoided needless casualties among noncombatants and rarely employed terror as a tactic or strategy, recognizing the risks of alienating the population. The large, standing professional armies of the latter years of the devastating Thirty Years' War also gravitated toward more limited notions of warfare, employing discipline and training while avoiding terrorizing noncombatant populations.

Because of these and other destructive and costly conflicts, by the end of the seventeenth century the scale and risk of war on the imperial stage made a constant, prepared armed force a national necessity. National political objectives in war had also become limited because of the expense and risk of state-on-state warfare. The colonies, however, did not reach such conclusions. Their enemies were indeed different, and their political objectives and strategic concerns retained a significant bias toward total destruction. Somewhat detached from European conflict and military advancements, the English colonists developed their own security system and concept of warfare based upon their inherent traditions, geopolitical circumstances, and brutal attitudes toward noncombatants.

This wilderness in which the settlers had planted themselves was indeed wild and hostile. The nascent settlements carved out of the forests of Massachusetts and the Chesapeake Bay region were in constant danger of Indian attack and within striking distance of rival French and Spanish settlements in Canada and Florida. For the English colonists, even the Dutch settlement at New Amsterdam was a possible threat. As the decades passed, the settlements grew in population and size, pushing more Native Americans off their lands.

More imperial competition also accompanied this growth. Mercantilism became the means to imperial dominance, which required a strong navy to protect sea lanes between the mother country and colonies scattered literally around the world. French, Spanish, Portuguese, and Dutch fleets battled England's Royal Navy for maritime supremacy, pouring money into fleets while often neglecting armies at home. Only when war broke out on the European continent did these imperial powers attempt to modernize their armies. Colonies, however, were often left to their own devices, as few regular troops could be spared for colonial service. In North America, England had neither the means nor the money to provide regulars to defend English settlements, thus leaving the colonists to defend themselves for most of the seventeenth century.

◆ COLONIAL MILITIA AND MILITARY ORGANIZATION

The colonists proved quick learners and adapted to their surroundings with violent alacrity. They had not come to America wholly unprepared. Quite to the contrary, settlers in Virginia and Puritan colonists in Massachusetts brought with them their preconceived attitudes toward war and defense as well as weapons of war. The Virginia Company hired the English soldier, explorer, and adventurer Captain John Smith to shape a mostly defenseless Jamestown into a militarized outpost and train a militia company for its defense. Miles Standish and John Underhill were among the men with military background and experience who accompanied the Puritan Separatists to Massachusetts, helping them build defensive perimeters and organize militia. This was typical among the early colonizers—to establish defensive fortification of some sort and organize militia based upon the English tradition while adapting both to the unique circumstances of colonial America.

Early colonial fortifications were rather simple; most consisted of either a stockade fence or a central blockhouse as a defense against Indian raids. In an emergency, a general alarm would gather colonists from surrounding farms into the settlement's stronghold. Once inside, militiamen and other colonists would take up positions on ramparts and behind loopholes to fend off attackers. This strategy often worked well against small Indian raids, but anything more substantial in size and longer in time put the settlers at a disadvantage. Scarce arms and valuable supplies had to be centralized at the stronghold. Food and water would run out quickly under any sort of siege, leaving the besieged colonists in dire straits unless soon relieved. Fortunately, the nature of Indian warfare allowed for few organized, lengthy assaults, much less for any sort of siege. Fleeing to the relative safety of the stronghold, colonists left homes and other property unprotected. Indians contented themselves with leaving the settlers in the blockhouse while they looted and burned homesteads and farms, having little patience or incentive for an organized siege.

Lines of small forts along the frontier did not fare much better. Forts were expensive, often making up the largest single expense in a colony's budget. Construction was costly, especially for the ring of forts that Virginia built along its frontier in the 1600s. Maintenance cost even more, as wood rotted and cannon rusted. Moreover, the men assigned to these outposts faced incredible boredom and idleness, which often led to breakdowns in discipline and poor morale. Forts on the frontier rarely proved effective, as Indians easily passed between the forts, which were tens of miles apart in many spots and nonexistent in most others. Pure chance more often than not brought native raiding parties in contact with ranger patrols from the forts. Most of the time, raiding parties avoided the patrols through superior reconnaissance or both groups simply missed each other unawares. Over time, blockhouses and garrisons in more established settlements fell into disuse and disrepair as the Indian threat moved further inland.

In theory, well-trained and organized militia would have made this defensive system work against supposedly primitive Indians, but such was not usually the case. In scattered settlements and even more scattered farms across the countryside, gathering militia to respond to a sudden raid or attack was inefficient at best. Nevertheless, the militia was an integral part of early colonial society, though its form and regulation varied from colony to colony. It served three primary purposes: to defend settlements; to act as a police force; and to provide a trained pool from which a colony could draw soldiers for extended campaigns and wars.

Militia units became centralized agents of social cohesion in many settlements, much like the local church or congregation. In fact, in many places, particularly in New England, the two often were tied together. Normally, colonial law obligated all

FIGURE 1-1   Militia training on village common in Massachusetts.

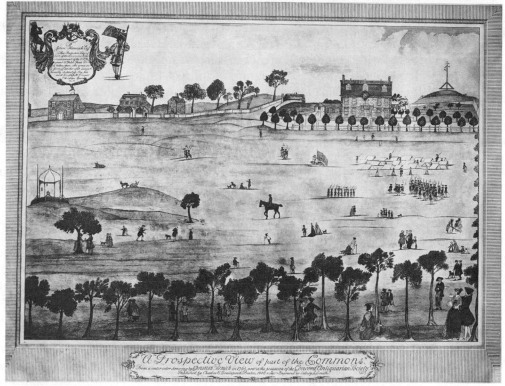

Source: Library of Congress Print and Reproductions Division

able bodied males to serve. Age limits varied, usually from 16 or 18 to 45, or even up to 60. Virginia's militia system required that all members provide their own weapons, which had to be clean and in good working condition. All males in Virginia from age 16 to 60 were required to serve, participate in drill, and, when not in service, protect the property of neighbors who were fulfilling their militia obligation. This system operated under the auspices of the Virginia Company administration in the colony and continued when Virginia became a royal colony. By 1634, due to Virginia's growth its militia was organized by county instead of settlement. Although the militia was under the direct control of the royal governor it also could be called out by local commanders in emergencies. As the colony grew in size and population and the Indian threat lessened, the militia actually grew smaller. Indentured servants were no longer required to serve. Slaves, of course, were always exempted. The colony also began to pay militiamen when on active duty. Appointed by the governor, officers came almost exclusively from the gentry class.

Militia in New England was organized along similar lines but had the significant added dimension of religion. Like Virginia, Massachusetts and other New England colonies organized their militia at the county level, thus each county regiment was made up of smaller units from villages and hamlets in the county. All males fulfilled their militia obligation or faced a small fine. Of course, the wealthy could afford the fine and often did not serve. Unlike other English colonies in America, in New England substitutes were illegal. All men, including servants, had to provide for their own weapon, and each village had to keep a store of powder and shot. Each trainband unit consisted of members of the local congregation. Because the local militia unit was so closely tied with the local church, pressure within the congregation to serve and serve well was indeed great. One did not want to let his friends and neighbors, and pastor, down. New England militia developed a deep sense of martial spirit that was often enhanced by inspiring sermons from church ministers. The social contract established by the Mayflower Compact applied equally to militia service in Puritan New England. Such a system was consistent with Puritan ideology. Although Puritan social strictures were often rigid, Puritans valued democratic processes and participation in the congregation at all levels. Since ministers, sheriffs, magistrates, and the like were elected, it should come as no surprise that militia officers were also popularly chosen. Though militia officers were elected locally, a colony's general court or assembly usually reserved final approval of militia commissions.

This integrated system resulted in a militia with tight local bonds built around religion, choice, and deference, so much so that military organization and social structure were basically one and the same. Such a system valued decentralization and instilled a reluctant attitude toward centralized control. Under such systems, then, militias functioned as both an initial reaction force and a social stabilizer. Militia service provided a sense of security, established and maintained social parameters, and satisfied the expectations of civic duty.

Much overshadowed by its defensive purpose was the effective job militia performed as police, functioning as an overseer of internal order in a colony. Troubled times frequently brought riots and, as in the case of Virginia in 1676, occasional rebellion. Theft and violent crime plagued port cities. Economically displaced vagrants passed through towns and villages, rousing the suspicion of residents. Some drifters were actually impressed into militia service. To protect themselves from these threats, many communities impressed small numbers of militia to serve as watch patrols. Like militia, the colonial watch had its origins in England and was also transported to America by English colonists.

In the southern colonies, militias and the watch evolved into slave patrols, which roamed the countryside on the lookout for runaway slaves and signs of slave insurrection, much as the old ranger patrols had against the Indian threat. Even in New York City, militia helped put down a slave revolt in 1741. In essence, militia came to serve more as a "hue and cry" response force. Occasionally, militia could not be used to quell disorder because militiamen themselves made up much of the disturbing party. Such was the case in the Carolinas when roving militia patrols known as regulators grew into a law unto themselves and had to be reined in by legitimate legal authority. Indeed, militia came to epitomize the precarious balance between civil order and the abuse of military authority.

Militia also served as a training mechanism and manpower reservoir for colonial expeditionary forces. Training was important for several reasons, but in the broad context its most important function was to provide a ready pool of citizen soldiers to fill county quotas for larger armies. Because militia units could not serve outside their home colony, colonial governments organized expeditionary forces to fight more serious conflicts, such as Indian wars and wars against other European colonial powers. Under such a system in the 1630s, Virginia could muster about 2,000 decently equipped men for a military expedition while leaving a bare minimum of militia in reserve to defend more populated settlements. In 1690, Massachusetts was able to put together a force of over 700 militiamen under the leadership of the daring Sir William Phips to overwhelm the well-defended French garrison at Port Royal.

Plucking men from local militia units to form a colonial expeditionary force was, however, not a straightforward process. Politics at both the local and colonial levels had to be considered. Additionally, all of the English colonies in America had economically diverse settlements. Port cities often had robust economies and larger populations while frontier regions were sparsely populated and less advanced economically. Merchants tended to dominate coastal politics while gentlemen farmers exercised greater influence inland. Whenever a colonial governor or assembly needed to organize a military force, these diverse relationships had to be considered.

Moreover, such expeditions were costly. Outfitting expeditions with weapons, powder and shot, and other necessary supplies strained colonial coffers and forced assemblies and governors to raise taxes or risk crippling deficits. These circumstances were not unique to colonial America by any means, but the governmental process of preparing a military force helped establish long-standing principles such as civilian control of the military and power sharing in American political culture. For example, a colonial governor often acted as commander-in-chief of all militia and military forces of the colony while the assembly exercised exclusive fiscal control over funding these enterprises. As such, the principle of power sharing in military affairs was set long before the Constitution outlined similar civil-military controls.

Under the expeditionary model, local militia deferred to expeditionary commanders appointed by the governor and assembly. Individual militiamen would be singled out or would volunteer to serve in an expeditionary force. Rarely would an entire unit be drafted into service, since that would leave that unit's homes and loved ones unprotected and cause discontent among the troops. Such discontent would not only hamper the unit's effectiveness, but would also put the local assemblyman in a precarious political situation. Thus, it was in the interest of the assembly and the governor to be certain of the need for an expedition and, if so, to ensure its proper supply and command to avoid jeopardizing their political position. Not surprisingly, however, such was often not the case.

The politics of colonial civil-military affairs impeded efforts toward intra-colonial military cooperation because it was difficult to muster support for expeditions that would take men away from their homes, leave their families unprotected, and put their own lives in jeopardy in faraway places for what appeared to be little direct benefit for one's home colony. Moreover, getting a colony to surrender control of its force to another colony infringed upon its sovereignty. Arguments over sovereignty plagued leaders during the American War for Independence, but it was a frequent concern as far back as the 1660s. As in most politics, colonial military affairs were, in the end, determined by political expediency.

Although the militia concept suited colonial security needs for the first few decades of settlement in the New World, in the long run militias outlived their practical usefulness.

Their experience as amateur citizen soldiers in the Indian wars of the 1600s left militiamen ill prepared for the broader imperial conflicts of the 1700s. While the militia concept worked well for local security needs, the changing geopolitical conditions of North America required broader military institutions and redefined relationships in civil-military affairs at the intra-colonial as well as the imperial level.

◆ A CLASH OF CULTURES

Much has been written about the clash of cultures that was initiated when Europeans first stepped upon North American shores. Economy, religion, worldview, technology, and other facets of cultural differentiation represented major obstacles to finding common ground for common existence. A major difference between the Europeans, English settlers in particular, and the native peoples they encountered involved approaches and attitudes toward warfare. The military culture of Native Americans was vastly different from that of Europeans. Through violent encounters, including several near-catastrophic wars, English colonists and Native Americans were forced to alter their concepts of warfare. For the one, this change allowed the Europeans to conquer land and secure settlements on the east coast of North America. For the other, this change so drastically altered cultural norms that as a people Native Americans would never be the same again—and in some cases faced outright extinction.

English colonists brought to the New World their own acculturated ideas about military service, purpose, and practice. A well-trained and equipped militia based upon the English model provided protection from whatever dangers were lurking in the dense forests of North America. Classic European battlefield practices at first ruled the colonial warring style. Partly because of tradition but also in part because of financial limitations, many militiamen were armed with inexpensive pikes with which they maneuvered in tight, lined formations. Matchlock and later flintlock muskets were used in the same fashion—lines of moving troops, maneuvering to the command officers usually on horseback. These single-shot, muzzle-loading muskets required intensive training to fire properly and quickly, not to mention accurately. Smooth-bore muskets weighed in excess of 15 pounds and could be as long as 4-1/2 feet, plus the added length of a large bayonet.

The vast majority of colonists had never fired a weapon of any sort, much less handled one, before coming to America. Whatever militia training they had in England most likely had been accomplished with long wooden pikes rather than more expensive and complicated muskets. With its wooden shaft or pole plus a large steel or iron tip, a pike could be as long as 15 feet. In the thickly wooded hills of English North America, such weapons and line formations quickly proved ineffective against Indian tactics. In Europe, pikes were often used to defend against cavalry attacks but could also be used in formation to attack infantry. Native Americans in colonial North America, however, neither had cavalry nor employed massed infantry, preferring instead ambush and other stealthy tactics that left many a colonial force frustrated by their failure to draw native warriors into a European-style decisive battle.

Native Americans' tactics reflected their strategic objectives. Unlike Europeans, many Indians had little cultural attachment to material goods or territorial conquest. Taking and holding territory was a truly foreign concept to them. Warfare for Native

Americans was more an individual or kin-group activity than an act that involved whole societies, and it usually entailed righting perceived wrongs or forcing small tributes from weaker tribes. Contemporary Europeans frequently attested to the few casualties and lack of destruction in battles pitting native against native. Native Americans preferred quick, tactical raids rather than pitched battles in open fields, and war parties often dwindled as individuals reconsidered their commitment to hostilities. Spilling blood over largely symbolic matters did not make much sense in native societies. Bows and arrows, tomahawks, and deadly looking knives made the Native American warrior seem fierce indeed, but these weapons rarely met such horrific expectations in native battles.

Native codes of honor on the battlefield were in some respects remarkably similar to those of Europeans. In native warfare, women and children rarely suffered at the hands of an enemy. Declarations of war were used to formally commence hostilities. Torture, however, was another matter. While Europeans eschewed the practice in warfare but seemed to delight in it in jurisprudence, it was not uncommon for Native Americans along the eastern coast of North America to ritually torture and kill male prisoners of war. Torture served two purposes. First, it allowed for an emotional release that probably made restraint in combat possible. Second, in tribal society tortured captives gained stature and esteem with their captors by courageously accepting their horrific fate. Colonists, who began to see the Native American as less a noble and more a barbarous savage, easily misconstrued this notion of torture. The alternative to torture was adoption of defeated or captured combatants and their families into the victorious tribe, a practice that became more common as European diseases decimated native groups. The Iroquois in particular practiced this custom to replenish growing losses among their own tribes from disease and battle with European settlers.

◆ VIRGINIA AND THE POWHATAN

Colonists' dire circumstances had more to do with their rejection of the view that Native Americans were noble savages than anything the natives actually did. Jamestown settlers had the first serious encounters with Native Americans, and the rapidity with which they changed their strategic approach toward warfare with natives was indeed extraordinary. Context is important in this case, as the Jamestown colony suffered tremendously during its first two decades of existence. From 1607 through the early 1620s, only around 20 percent of the colonists who came to Jamestown from England survived. The vast majority died from starvation and disease, while only a comparative few died in skirmishes with local natives.

At first, these conflicts centered on food. Native Americans normally had only enough for themselves but nonetheless had generously given any meager but valuable surplus to starving colonists, who had largely expected the local Indians to feed them in the first place. If the natives did not offer foodstuffs, hungry colonists raided native villages and stole food. When natives resisted, the colonists responded with astonishing brutality, as in 1610, when Captain George Percy led a small group of men against a Paspahegh village up the James River. The attack was for the natives a brutal introduction to what became the colonial style of warfare. Percy laid waste to the village, burning homes and destroying crops. His men killed over 65 men, women, and children, and took the village chieftain's wife and children captive. As they traveled by boat back to the settlement, Percy allowed the men to throw the children overboard and shoot them for sport. When Percy presented the chieftain's wife to the governor as a prize, the governor was offended, not because of the massacre but because Percy had not also killed the woman. She was executed immediately. The strategic objective of the entire operation had not been to destroy these natives in particular; it was, rather, to send a clear signal to the other villages in the region that the same fate awaited them if they did not contribute to the feeding of Jamestown.⌋

To the surprise of Jamestown's leaders, more than a few men abandoned the settlement to live with the comparatively better off Indians, who welcomed them if the desperate colonists brought guns, powder, knives, and anything else of value that the natives could not produce themselves. Violating the strict ban on selling arms and munitions to natives resulted in harsh punishments for offenders, usually death.

⌈Thus, the stage was set for over sixty years of on-and-off warfare between the English colonists of Virginia and their Indian neighbors. The most serious of these conflicts were the so-called Powhatan Wars, also known as the Tidewater Wars. The first war occurred in 1622, after several years of minor skirmishes and individual acts of vengeance committed by both sides. The catalyst in this case was a group of indentured servants seeking revenge for the apparent death of their master, a man named Morgan, who had disappeared on an inland trek to trade with area natives. His men blamed a Powhatan named Nemattanow, whom they found and summarily killed⌋

Opechancanough, chief of the confederacy of Algonquin tribes that the colonists collectively called the Powhatans, boisterously vowed to avenge the murder. But equally belligerent colonists threatened to punish the Powhatans if they made the attempt, resulting in what appeared to be a stalemate. The appearance, however, proved deceptive. On March 22, 1622, after personally serving as a sociable guide for a group of Virginia planters only two days before, Opechancanough unleashed a string of well-coordinated attacks on Virginia settlements and farms, catching colonists and their militia completely off guard. Three hundred and forty-seven colonists, almost a third of the Anglo population, were dead by the end of the day.⌋

For the next ten years, the Powhatan and Virginia colonists warred on each other, committing ghastly atrocities on both sides. At one point, the governor invited Opechancanough and his warriors to a peace conference and had over 200 natives poisoned through intentionally tainted drink—most of the desperately ill natives were slaughtered, but Opechancanough somehow managed to get away.

JOHN SMITH'S PROPOSAL TO SUBJUGATE THE POWHATAN

After the Powhatan attack of March 1622, John Smith resubmitted a proposal to the Virginia Company that he had first offered during his earlier tenure in the new colony. Though the Virginia Company's board of governors failed to act on it, the proposal reveals Smith's organizational and military skills and his own ambitions in the Virginia colony. Smith recorded his proposal in his *Generall historie of Virginia*, first published in 1624 just as King James I revoked the Virginia Company's charter, making Virginia the first English royal colony in North America.

> If you please, I may be transported with a hundred Souldiers and thirty Sailers by next Michaelmas, with victual, munition, and such necessary provision; by Gods assistance, we would endeavour to inforce the Salvages to leave their Country, or bring them in that feare and subjection that every man should follow their businesse securely. Whereas now halfe their times and labours are spent in watching and warding, onely to defend, but altogether unable to suppresse the Salvages: because every man now being for himselfe will be unwilling to be drawne from their particular labours, to be made as pack-horses for all the rest, without any certainty of some better reward and preferment then I can understand any there can or will yet give them.
>
> These I would imploy onely in ranging the Countries, and tormenting the Salvages, and that they should be as a running Army till this were affected; and then settle themselves in some such convenient place, that should ever remained a garrison of that strength, ready upon any occasion against the Salvages, or any other for the defence of the Countrey, and to see all the English well armed, and instruct them their use. But I would have a Barke of one hundred tunnes, and meanes to build sixe or seven Shalops, to transport them where there should bee occasion.
>
> Towards the charge, because it is for the generall good, and what by the massacre and other accidents, Virginia is disparaged, and many men and their purses much discouraged, however a great many doe hasten to goe, thinking to bee next heires to all the former losses, I feare they will not finde all things as they doe imagine; therefore leaving those gilded conceits, and dive into the true estate of the Colony; I thinke if his Majestie were truly informed of their necessitie, and the benefit of this project, he would be pleased to give the custome of Virginia; and the Planters also according to their abilities would adde thereto such a contribution, as would be fit to maintaine this garrison till they be able to subsist, or cause some such other collections to be made, as may put it with all expedition in practice: otherwise it is much to be doubted, there will neither come custome, nor any thing from thence to England within these few yeares.
>
> Now if this should be thought an imploiment more fit for ancient Souldiers there bred, then such new comers as may goe with me; you may please to leave that to my discretion, to accept to refuse such voluntaries, that will hazard their fortunes in the trials of these events, and discharge such of my company that had rather labour the ground then subdue their enemies: what releefe I should have from your Colony I would satisfie,

and spare them (when I could) the like courtesie. Notwithstanding these doubts, I hope to feede them as as well as defend them, and yet discover you more land unknown then they all yet know, if you grant me such priviledges as of necessity must be used.

For against any enemy we must be ready to execute the best can be devised by your state there, but not that they shall either take away my men, or any thing else to imploy as they please by vertue of their authority: and in that I have done somewhat for New-England as well as Virginia, so I would desire liberty and authority to make best use I can of my best experiences, within the limits of those two Patents, and to bring them both in one Map, and the Countries betwixt them, giving alwaies that respect the Governors and government, as an Englishman doth in Scotland, or a Scotchman in England, or as the regiments in the Low-countries doe to the Governors of the Townes and Cities where they are billeted, or in Garrison, where though they live with them, and are as their servants to defend them, yet not to be disposed on at their pleasure, but as the Prince and the State doth command them. And for my owne paines in particular I aske not any thing but what I can produce form the proper labour of the Salvages.

Source: John Smith, *The Generall Historie of Virginia, New England, and the Summer Isles: Together with the True Travels, Adventures, and Observations, and a Sea Grammar* (Glasgow: J. McLehose, 1907), 295–97.

At the beginning of the Powhatan Wars the Virginia militia was disorganized because of neglect, sickness, and poor equipment, but it recovered enough to mount a nominal defense and carry out several haphazard campaigns against Powhatan villages. Adopting a European tactic, the Powhatan at first attempted to lay siege against the handful of Virginian strongholds. Though at first effective, these sieges fell apart as militiamen broke out to attack Powhatan villages, burning them to the ground while seizing stores of food. Still, neither side could gain advantage. Exhaustion on both sides brought the first Powhatan War to an end in 1632, as neither the Powhatan nor the colonists could continue the fight after years of neglected crops and economic degradation.

Twelve years of uneasy peace followed, allowing Virginia to recover and grow in population as, despite native troubles, hundreds of colonists arrived to take their chances in what appeared to be a land of unparalleled opportunity. Feeling the pressure of Virginia's population growth and the colonists' thirst for land, Opechancanough, now nearly 100 years old, ordered another campaign against the Virginians. In coordinated assaults along the James River, warriors again attacked with stealthy surprise. This time 500 colonists were killed in the first hours of the attack, but their counterattack was much quicker and better organized. Virginia militia staged several attacks on Powhatan villages, again destroying crops and homes. Sensing the colony was now simply too big for them to fight, the Powhatan capitulated in 1646. What was once a grand alliance of

Algonquin tribes, numbering some 10,000 people, was now a shell of its former self. Only around 4,000 Powhatan remained. For the natives, political disorganization, the incapacity to produce powder, and the inability to maintain sustained military campaigns doomed any long-term effort against the Virginia colonists.

For the colonists, a way of war had developed that struck at the heart of the enemy—his homes, villages, crops, and families. It was brutal, but the colonists convinced themselves that fighting savages demanded savage strategies. Moreover, the apparent success at arms had come via the citizen soldier, the militia. This convinced many in the colony that the militia system worked and could repel attack without the assistance of regular, professional troops. It was a false lesson.

◆ NEW ENGLAND'S PEQUOT WAR

Aware of what was happening in Virginia, the New England colonies hoped to avoid bloody conflict with their native neighbors. The colonies of Plymouth, Massachusetts Bay, and Connecticut all shared borders with a variety of tribal groups, including the Narragansett, Mohegan, and Pequot. [As in Virginia, conflict exploded after years of territorial pressure, population decline, and cultural misunderstanding. The Pequot War of 1636–1637 and King Philip's War (also known as Metacom's War) of 1675–1676, the two major conflicts that occurred in this region, are illustrative of the New England experience with native warfare.]

The death of two traders set in motion what would erupt into the Pequot War. A powerful tribe that occupied much of the land along the Thames River in southeastern Connecticut, the Pequot reigned over several tributary tribes that traded with Dutch and English settlers. The murders were committed by a Pequot tributary tribe, the Niantic, and the rival Narragansett. Authorities in Massachusetts Bay and Connecticut, however, ignored what seemed only semantics and went on the offensive against the Pequot.

Both colonies disputed rights to the Connecticut Valley, and whichever colony defeated or concluded peace with the Pequot would have the inside edge in securing the territory. In August 1636, Massachusetts Bay sent Captain John Endicott and a small militia expeditionary force to Block Island, where they hoped to draw the Pequot into a decisive engagement. The natives, however, would not be baited and withdrew into the swamps. Endicott tried another attack from Pequot Harbor and again failed to bring the natives to battle. Frustrated, he let loose his militia on the countryside to destroy Pequot homes and crops. The colonists then withdrew to Fort Saybrook at the mouth of the Connecticut River, where the Pequot promptly attempted a siege. Keeping the colonists penned down at Fort Saybrook, Pequot reinforcements raided Wethersfield, killing several colonists.

In May 1637, Connecticut militia entered the fray with their new Narragansett allies. Attempts to stage a cooperative effort with Massachusetts Bay had stumbled, but circumstance would bring militia from both colonies together. Under the command of John Mason, the Connecticut militia and their Narragansett comrades fell upon a sleeping Pequot camp on the Mystic River. Mason's original orders had been to attack the fortified camp of the Pequot leader Sassacus, but upon hearing that hundreds of Pequot were concentrated at the Mystic River camp, Mason turned his force toward that new objective. Mason and his men may have deliberately moved on Mystic to massacre women and children in hope of bringing the warriors under control. Along with Captain John Underhill, Mason struck the sleeping Mystic encampment early on the morning of May 26. After encircling the sleeping Indians, the colonists set fire to the primitive fortifications and camp, shooting those who tried to escape, a tactic that would be used by whites against natives time and time again into the nineteenth century. Within an hour, over 700 Pequot had perished. Only seven escaped, while another seven were taken captive.

Massachusetts militia under the command of Daniel Patrick and Israel Stoughton united with the Connecticut expedition in June to deliver the final blow to the Pequot. Narragansett warriors played the false role of protector, bringing the Pequot out of hiding. Pequot warriors then found themselves surrounded by the combined militia force. Another slaughter ensued; hundreds of natives died. In July, the few remaining Pequot were rounded up near New Haven. A treaty formally ended what colonial tactics had almost made extinct. The Pequot nation ceased to exist, and the surviving members were given away as slaves to native allies. Neighboring tribes captured those who had tried to escape, returning their severed heads as a sign of tribute to the colonists.

The Pequot War had been expensive and ruthless, but for the colonists of both Massachusetts and Connecticut, it had been worthwhile. At the cost of fewer than 50 colonists, the Pequots had been literally wiped out and their tribal lands opened to exploitation. The colonists were fine-tuning a way of war that used death and destruction to bring an enemy to bear. The natives were slow on the uptake and, in the eyes of the colonists, had wasted opportunities. In truth, however, the perceived opportunities were little more than the natives adhering to their customary restraint in war. This would change during subsequent decades. As a point of comparison, as the Thirty Years' War continued to rage in Europe, the Battle of Wittstock in October 1636 featured almost 40,000 troops and cavalry engaged in a day-long fight that cost over 8,000 dead and wounded on both sides. While colonists could not bring natives into full battle as was the practice in Europe, like their European counterparts in the Thirty Years' War they brought death and destruction upon noncombatant populations. Europe would move away from such devastation; the English colonists in North America would not, as their next major native conflict made the Pequot War seem like a series of small skirmishes.

◆ KING PHILIP'S WAR

King Philip's War engulfed New England beginning in spring 1675 and before the conflict's conclusion brought the New England colonies together militarily and solidified the colonial way of war. King Philip's War began with the murder of a native, supposedly by three Wampanoag. Ordinarily, the death of a native would not matter much to the Puritan colonists of New England, but this particular man was a resident of one of the missionary prayer towns and, more importantly, was an informer for colonial authorities. Colonial authorities caught the three offenders and promptly executed them. The executions unexpectedly sparked an Indian uprising, led at first by young Wampanoag warriors who attacked isolated farms and homesteads. The war soon devolved into a civil war as colonists united with Indian allies against Indians and other

Indian allies in a conflict that very nearly destroyed the unique mesh of colonial and native societies in New England.

The Puritans conducted reprisal attacks against several tribes that were completely innocent in the matter, thus alienating potential native allies. Even the Narragansett, the region's largest tribe after the demise of the Pequot, found themselves on the receiving end of Puritan raids. The Puritans blamed the Wampanoag leader Metacom, whom they had earlier dubbed King Philip as a sign of honor, for instigating his and other area tribes to rebel against the colonists. Metacom was the son of the beloved Massasoit, who had helped keep an uneasy peace with the Puritans for several decades. Metacom was not his father, however, and clearly felt threatened by the ever-encroaching colonists. He never became involved in the level of conspiracy that the colonists assumed, but he nonetheless became for the colonists the symbolic leader of the native revolt.

King Philip's War serves as an excellent example of the results of decades of acculturation through economic, religious, and military contact while continuing the tradition of misunderstanding. Illegal arms trading lessened the technological disadvantage Indians suffered in the Pequot War. They had now mastered the flintlock musket and

FIGURE 1-2   Phillip [sic] alias Metacomet of Pokanoket.

Source: Library of Congress Print and Reproductions Division [LC-USZ62-96234]

had plenty of them. Many of the native casualties in the war came from colonial attacks on the Indians who were easily located—those in the several prayer towns that dotted Massachusetts. When they first arrived in America, the Puritans did not attempt to convert the natives, but beginning in the 1640s they turned to missionary work as a means to pacify local tribes and avoid repeating the terrible slaughter of the Pequot War. The great irony, of course, was that this very effort now provided the colonists with an accessible killing ground.

Fearing annihilation, the natives adopted colonial military methods. They burned settlements, attacking 52 of 90 settlements in 1675 alone and completely destroying 12. Entire families were massacred, and churches burned to the ground. So great was native success in the beginning of the war that the Narragansett boldly proclaimed that the English god had abandoned the Puritans and was now with them. By the end of 1675, the Puritan colonists were in severe trouble. Frontier settlements lay empty as the population fled to the relative safety of more densely populated coastal areas. The flood of refugees squeezed food supplies, because few farmers were willing to risk their lives to bring in the crops needed to feed the burgeoning population. New England was in a state of shock and denial—could God really have forsaken the Puritans, and was he punishing them for failing in their dedication? It appeared so. The question now was how to right the situation and reclaim God's favor. Militant revenge with God's blessing was the answer.

Unable to bring the raiding Indians to battle, colonists turned instead on the peaceful natives in the prayer towns and noncombatants in native villages. An intra-colonial force of soldiers massacred over 500 Narragansett, mostly women and children, in what the colonists called the Great Swamp Fight of December 1675. After formally declaring war on Philip the previous September, colonists in Plymouth, Massachusetts, Rhode Island, and Connecticut came together in November to establish the Army of the United Colonies. Under the command of Plymouth governor Josiah Winslow, this force of 1,000 slogged its way through a heavy snowstorm to attack a Narragansett fort and encampment in a frozen swamp near Kingston, Rhode Island. On December 19, the Army of the United Colonies attacked in bitter cold across a landscape covered with deep snow. Winslow's men set fire to wigwams and then waited to shoot down helpless men, women, and children as they tried to escape the flames. As many as 600 of the estimated 3,000–4,000 Indians were killed that cold day, while Winslow's force lost a not inconsequential 80 men, including 14 company commanders. Despite the lopsided affair, Winslow ordered a withdrawal, as the now disorganized Army of the Unified Colonies, low on supplies and suffering from cold, retreated, taking over a month to recover from its "victory."

By the spring of 1676, the natives were out of food, low on powder, and unable to repair broken muskets. In exchange for a multitude of gifts, the Mohawk gladly attacked Algonquian villages in New England, further pushing New England's native enemies toward complete collapse. A second but much smaller Army of the United Colonies, this time commanded by the able Benjamin Church, finally tracked down Philip after several skirmishes in summer 1676. Philip was killed in battle on August 12, effectively ending the war. His head was severed and taken to Plymouth, where it was prominently displayed for years.

Considering the ratio of casualties to population, it had been a costly, bloody war. Indeed, it was among the deadliest in the history of North America. Over 1,000 colonists lost their lives in the conflict, while over 3,000 natives died. Once again, however, the colonists could recover while the natives could not. Several chiefs and their families were executed as traitors, as were some colonists who had taken native wives. Many natives, including Philip's nine-year-old son, were sold into slavery in the Caribbean or to New England tribes that had fought alongside the colonists, while the remaining survivors either escaped to New France or eked out a meager existence surrounded by growing colonial settlements.

Having lost over a third of their population in the war and with another third having fled the region or been forced into foreign slavery, the natives of New England could not recover from such attrition. In 1670, Native Americans accounted for 25 percent of the population of New England; by 1680, they made up only 10 percent. The colonial population increased from 52,000 to 68,000 during the same ten-year period. Contemporary estimates placed the war's cost at £100,000, an amount closer to £13 million today. Colonists suffered property losses in excess of £150,000—an enormous amount for the time period. Even though the colonists came out better in the end, the victory had a Pyrrhic touch, as it would take New England years to financially recover and rebuild what had been destroyed in less than two years of war.

Though costly in blood and treasure, the New England victory in King Philip's War was perhaps the most significant of all the colonial wars with Native Americans. The colonies unified in common purpose and never lost governmental control of the war. Militia provided ample decently trained recruits to fill quotas for colonial regiments. Troops, arms, and ammunition were plentiful throughout the conflict. The social strength of the Puritan community often acted as a centralizing force for militia training and filling quotas. The local meeting house and its congregation provided more than a headquarters for building morale and encouraging the troops; it also served as a barracks, an advanced base in some cases, and offered a largely reliable support system that often fed troops passing through the region.

The colonists benefited from what could be called a civil war among the region's Native Americans and were able to take advantage of their own efforts at intra-colonial cooperation in prosecuting the war. New England forces also willingly adapted native tactics, such as ambush and stealthy raids, to the colonial strategy of total war, and they realized that threats to colonial security could not be handled by one colony alone—cooperation and unity were now critical to security and military success. While King Philip's War was not the only factor that forced England to reorganize its imperial administration, it certainly removed whatever obstacles there were to creating the Dominion of New England. Still, the New England colonies were in shambles despite the victory, and they had driven many surviving tribes into the open and waiting arms of England's enemies, the French.

There were, of course, dozens of other wars and hundreds of skirmishes pitting colonists against Native Americans, all the way up to the American War for Independence. The Algonquian fought the Dutch from 1639 to 1645 in Keift's War and again in 1655–1657 in the Peach War. The Iroquois and French squared off intermittently from 1642 to 1696 while colonists in Maryland warred on the Susquehannock from 1643 to 1652. Colonists in northwest New England fought the Abnaki in 1675–1678, 1702–1712, and again in 1722–1727. Virginia found itself simultaneously in conflict with natives and in rebellion in 1676, just as King Philip's War was ending. North Carolina defeated the Tuscarora in 1712, while South Carolina warred on the Yamasee from 1715 to 1716.

◆ CONCLUSION

Native Americans slowly recognized that war with colonists meant war to the death. To have a chance at survival, they too had to burn and destroy as the colonists did. Colonists came to believe that militia worked, that the expeditionary model could defeat native uprisings, and that cooperation with other colonies was necessary to fight natives whose lands and tribal allies did not recognize colonial political boundaries. Moreover, colonial governments realized that exploiting native political fissures to form alliances with rival tribes could tip the balance in these wars. New England certainly would have had a much more difficult fight on its hands had it not formed alliances with other tribes against Philip and the Narragansett.

The American military experience got off to a violent start. For the American colonists, the native wars of the 1600s had transformed their European concepts of warfare into a uniquely American way of war that emphasized destruction of property and the annihilation of noncombatants as well as combatants. Success in these wars also gave the colonists an overblown sense of their own military capabilities, convincing them that their notion of the citizen soldier was much more militarily effective and less threatening to personal liberties than were large, standing armies. War in North America was about to broaden, however, to encompass more than conflict with Native Americans. Now that the various colonies of North America had matured and become more profitable, integral cogs in the imperial machines of England and France, they would be drawn into—and in some cases be the cause of—the wars of empire.

Further Reading ●

Ahearn, Marie L. *The Rhetoric of War: Training Day, the Militia, and the Military Sermon.* Westport, Connecticut: Greenwood Press, 1989.

Axtell, James. *The Invasion Within: The Contest of Cultures in Colonial America.* New York: Oxford University Press, 1986.

Chet, Guy. *Conquering the American Wilderness: The Triumph of European Warfare in Colonial New England.* Amherst: University of Massachusetts Press, 2003.

Cress, Lawrence Delbert. *Citizens in Arms: The Army and the Militia in American Society to the War of 1812.* Chapel Hill: University of North Carolina Press, 1982.

Drake, James D. *King Philip's War: Civil War in New England, 1675–1676.* Amherst: University of Massachusetts Press, 1999.

Ferling, John E. *A Wilderness of Miseries: War and Warriors in Early America.* Westport, Connecticut: Greenwood Press, 1980.

Grenier, John. *The First Way of War: American War Making on the Frontier, 1607–1814.* Cambridge: Cambridge University Press, 2005.

Jennings, Francis. *The Invasion of North America: Indians, Colonialism, and the Cost of Conquest.* Chapel Hill: University of North Carolina Press, 1975.

Kupperman, Karen Ordahl. *Indians and English: Facing Off in Early America.* Ithaca: Cornell University Press, 2000.

Leach, Douglas Edward. *Flintlock and Tomahawk: New England in King Philip's War.* New York: Norton, 1966.

Lee, Wayne E., ed. *Empires and Indigenes: Intercultural Alliance, Imperial Expansion, and Warfare in the Early Modern World.* New York: New York University Press, 2011.

Shea, William L. *The Virginia Militia in the Seventeenth Century.* Baton Rouge: Louisiana State University Press, 1983.

Steele, Ian K. *Warpaths: Invasions of North America.* New York: Oxford University Press, 1995.

Whisker, James Biser. *The American Colonial Militia.* Lewiston, New York: Edwin Mellon Press, 1997.

mysearchlab Connections: Sources Online ● ● ● ● ● ● ● ● ● ● ●

READ AND REVIEW

Review this chapter by using the study aids and these related documents available on MySearchLab.

Study Plan

Chapter Test

Essay Test

Documents

The Journal of Samuel de Champlain (1609)

The French explorer Samuel de Champlain offers one of the earliest accounts of warfare with Native Americans in North America.

Remarks by Chief Powhatan to John Smith (c. 1609)

Chief Powhatan expresses his concerns about relations between his people and the Virginia colonists.

An Account of King Philip's War (1685)

Edward Randolph reports on the causes of King Philip's War and assesses the damage from this destructive conflict.

RESEARCH AND EXPLORE

Explore the following review questions using the research tools available on www. mysearchlab.com.

1. What ideas concerning warfare and civil-military relations did the English colonists bring with them from England?
2. How did the English colonists adapt their ideas about war to fighting Native Americans?
3. What advantages and disadvantages did Native Americans have in conflict with the English colonists?

The Colonies and Wars for Empire

◆ INTRODUCTION

The colonial wars that culminated in the Great War for Empire had a profound effect on the American colonies, shaping colonial attitudes toward civil-military relations, civil liberties, and intra-colonial cooperation, indeed, even unity. Colonial wars also influenced already maturing concepts of colonial warfare, relations with Native Americans, and American exceptionalism. These wars were unique, as the strategic objectives of the warring powers in the Old World often did not match those of English ("British" after the 1707 Acts of Union), French, and Spanish colonists in the New World. In essence, although they were often fighting the same war, their reasons for doing so just as often differed.

◆ THE COLONIES: STRATEGIC CONTOURS

As far-flung settlements became permanently settled colonies, their role in imperial trade and security systems became invaluable to their respective home countries. Throughout the seventeenth and eighteenth centuries, imperial competition between Great Britain and France, and to a lesser extent Spain, for control of North American trade created fluid alliances with Native Americans, who had become dependent upon trade with colonists for manufactured goods and gunpowder. By the beginning of the eighteenth century, the North American colonies were indeed worth fighting for. For Britain and France in particular, such heavy investments in the North American settlements represented the importance of these colonies to their imperial systems. Fishing, the fur trade, and timber, pitch, and tar for shipbuilding made the New England and Middle colonies lucrative imperial possessions. In the Chesapeake and southern colonies, tobacco, indigo, rice, and other labor-intensive crops created an equally lucrative credit-based trade system between the colonies and the mother country. For the colonies, such a situation required military organization, support, and participation, all of which evolved with violent effect throughout the colonial period in American history.

For the French in Canada and British colonists in the frontier regions of New England and western New York, the fur trade was king, and it was the fur trade that perhaps caused more mischief in the colonies than any other factor. Key to the fur trade were various Native American tribes, in particular the Algonquian, who traded with the French, and the Iroquois, who often traded with the British. In exchange for profitable pelts, British and French traders quickly addicted the Indians to metal utensils, steel knives, axes, mirrors, muskets, powder, lead for bullets, and a host of other goods with which natives were unfamiliar before European contact. With the natives dependent on European goods and the British and French just as dependent on profits from the fur trade, the stakes for controlling the trade skyrocketed.

It is important to realize that for the British and French this situation took place within greater empires that incorporated possessions in the Caribbean, Africa, and southern Asia. Trade among these possessions created an elaborate financial network that required centralized regulation to balance regional deficits as well as increasingly costly navies and land forces to defend critical ports and far-flung colonies. The prevailing notion of imperial competition held that the only way to increase one's imperial might was to do so at the expense of one's imperial competitors. In other words, the imperial pie was finite; increasing one's share of the pie meant taking slices from somebody else's empire.

In colonial North America, geography played a crucial role in the imperial game. The St. Lawrence River provided the only waterway to French settlements at Quebec and Montreal, the Great Lakes, and the Canadian interior. Guarding the entrance to the St. Lawrence River was the impressive French fortress at Louisbourg on Cape Breton Island. Whoever controlled Louisbourg easily controlled the river. Of more direct importance for the colonists of New England and New York was the Hudson River Valley, its northern lakes, and the Richelieu River, which connected the British colonies to French Canada. To the west lay the Appalachian Mountains, through which only a precious few gaps, the main one along the Mohawk River, allowed armies to pass.

Consequently, the wars fought between the British and French and their Native American allies tended to concentrate around these natural invasion routes. For the French, an invasion through the Appalachian Mountains or down Lake Champlain could split New England from New York—a classic example of divide and conquer. For the British, controlling the St. Lawrence River would sever New France from its Atlantic lifeline. Geography lent itself to a strategy of conquest, and for both British and French colonists, the urge to expand territory and control trade proved too great to resist. The Spanish, increasingly a pretender in the imperial contest, found themselves subject to similar British restlessness in the Carolinas, Georgia, and the Caribbean.

◆ KING WILLIAM'S WAR

The first major colonial conflict coincided with the Glorious Revolution of 1689 in England. What became King William's War began in 1688 in North America with French-supported Abnaki (a French corruption of the Algonquian name Wabanaki) raids on English settlements in Maine. New England governor Edmund Andros had ordered an expeditionary force of 1,000 volunteers and draftees to drive the Abnaki back into French Canada; but the expedition fell victim to winter, and Andros fell victim to the Protestant revolt against the Catholic King James II. The accession of William of Orange to the throne of England as a result of the Glorious Revolution of 1688 and the expansionist tendencies of Louis XIV of France initiated war in Europe and intensified the colonial conflict between Protestant England and Catholic France in North America.

France hoped to capitalize on what it assumed was administrative chaos in English North America because of the Glorious Revolution and the war in Europe. With Andros gone, France dispatched the aged but ambitious Count de Frontenac to Canada to oversee the conquest of New York. Frontenac had served as governor of New France once before and was familiar with colonial political and physical geography. His plan was straightforward—to attack New York via Lake Champlain and take Albany, and hope that the Iroquois would as a result abandon their English friends and side with the victorious French. From that point, the French assumed the entire colony of New York would collapse as a matter of course.

As is common, the plans looked grand on paper but lost their appeal when actually implemented. When Frontenac finally reached the French capital at Quebec in late 1689, he found instead a French colony in disarray. As was often the case for European possessions in the New World, there was a rather wide gap between what European imperial ministries supposed and what actually existed in the colonies. The French Canadians were in no condition to wage offensive campaigns against the English colonies.

[Instead, Frontenac mounted several raiding expeditions using small units on multiple fronts to harass and indeed terrorize the English. His so-called *la petite guerre* would soon be commonly known as guerrilla warfare. In the winter of 1690, Frontenac sent a force of 160 Canadians along with over 100 native allies on a three-prong attack against New England. From Montreal, the combined force would hit New York, New Hampshire, and Maine. As had become the custom in colonial warfare, the French and natives slaughtered their enemies. At Schenectady, they killed over 60 men, women, and children. Similar fates befell English colonists at Salmon Falls, New Hampshire, and Falmouth, Maine, where over 100 people were killed after having been granted safe passage.]

[On May 1, 1690, representatives from the now-defunct Dominion of New England met in Albany to organize a joint campaign to invade Canada in response to Frontenac's attacks. Two land forces, from New York and New England, would simultaneously invade Canada. A naval force would support these attacks by driving down the St. Lawrence River. Once again, great plans had disappointing results. The assault on Port Royal led by William Phips was the highlight, but his march on Quebec met not only French resistance but also smallpox. Neither side could marry its strategically ambitious objectives to its extremely limited resources. Phips lost Port Royal and for the next five years, both sides resorted to guerrilla war, staging raids and counter-raids that further exhausted both sides. Colonists lived in constant fear of sudden attack by native raiding parties, who burned their farms and often took captives. Upon return to their families, captives, such as those taken at Deerfield and Haverhill in Massachusetts, often, but not always, told of horrific ordeals and brutal atrocities. To encourage terror, all of the English colonies paid bounties for scalps.]

The war in Europe and North America ended in September 1697 with the Treaty of Ryswick, through which all gains reverted to *status quo ante bellum*. In North America, casualties were relatively light compared to those in earlier conflicts with Native Americas. Approximately 300 French were killed, along with 100 of their native allies. The English colonists suffered approximately 650 dead from battle, disease, or captivity, while their Iroquois allies sacrificed more than 1,300 to battle and disease. Fighting along the frontier continued sporadically for the next few years, mainly between the native allies of the French and the Iroquois nations. In the end, the Iroquois were badly mauled and significantly weakened, while the English colonies took years to recover.

Heavy debt and a realization that individual colonies could no longer act unilaterally in military matters against the French, defensive or otherwise, forced the English colonies to reassess their strategic situation. Intra-colonial cooperation proved necessary for any future military adventure. With so much now at stake in the imperial game, the colonies also realized that they needed more financial and military help from their mother country. Additionally, imperial growth and more permanent territorial security required that the French be removed from the North American scene, forcibly or otherwise.

The English colonies had learned a hard lesson. Despite their loyalty to the king, they could not count on the crown to protect them. Only a small handful of troops from England made their way to English North America. Their contribution was negligible.

The colonists believed that the stakes were high in North America and their new monarch had let them down. The colonists had to defend themselves, and whatever offensive campaigns they deigned to attempt had to come from colonial rather than crown resources. In London, members of the Board of Trade saw the situation in exactly the same way, except for the important difference that the board viewed the colonists as English subjects who were duty bound to take care of themselves. From the standpoint of observers in London, excessive and irritating bickering among the colonies had stifled attempts to take Canada. With respect to colonial warfare, Frontenac's concept of *la petite guerre* and the value of native allies grew in strategic importance, even though such strategies would prove time and again to be fundamentally flawed. They would soon again be put to the test.

◆ QUEEN ANNE'S WAR

Known in North America as Queen Anne's War, the conflict that broke out in the colonies in September of 1702 was again part of a broader European conflict known as the War of the Spanish Succession. In North America, the French also again indirectly initiated hostilities. The French pursued a strategy of encirclement, hoping to strangle the English colonies along the Atlantic seaboard. Geographically, France was well on its way to achieving this objective *de facto*. From Port Royal near the mouth of the St. Lawrence River, around the Great Lakes to Fort Michilimackinac, and southward to the Gulf of Mexico at Biloxi and Mobile Bay, New France essentially surrounded the British colonies and cut off the Spanish colony of Florida from New Spain (Mexico).

With Spain and France allied against England, the South Carolina legislature formed an expedition to seize St. Augustine in September 1702. The expedition failed to take the formidable fortress there, but contented itself with burning and destructive looting in the town, then withdrew. For the next few years, various expeditions from South Carolina, along with Chickasaw allies, raided with sporadic success along the Florida panhandle, threatening French Louisiana. These raids tended to avoid Spanish and French strongholds and concentrated instead on weakly defended Catholic missions. The French, however, had reliable native allies of their own, including the Choctaw and Creek, who prevented a force led by South Carolina Governor James Moore from invading Louisiana in July 1704.

A combined Spanish-French force attempted to take Charleston in 1706, but was beaten back by South Carolina militiamen manning strong fortifications. South Carolina's attempts to take Spanish Pensacola met with failure in 1707, as did forays into Alabama to engage the French garrison at Mobile. Logistical requirements limited whatever chance of success these expeditions had, and without the full support of local natives, they really had no chance at all.

New York managed to stay out of harm's way in this war, concluding an uneasy peace with the Iroquois Confederation. New England was not so fortunate and, as was becoming customary, suffered the brunt of conflict because of its geographic position. Stirred by Puritan sermons, New Englanders lashed out at the local native population, often disregarding attempts to discern friend from foe. Leadership failed early. Massachusetts Governor Joseph Dudley, for example, alienated remaining local tribes and made little effort to find peace with the dangerous Abnaki. A conference in June

1703 promised peace, but English contempt toward Native Americans drove them again into the waiting arms of the French.

Dudley's attempts to recruit a strong militia force met with equal ineptitude, as only a few hundred were willing to leave their homes and communities unprotected to serve in an expeditionary force. All along the New England frontier, the French and their native allies attacked with vicious ferocity. Despite improvements in fortification, Deerfield was once again hit hard in February 1704 by a combined French-Abnaki force of over 300, killing 50 colonists and taking over 100 captive.

Benjamin Church, the veteran of many a conflict with Native Americans, was commissioned again in 1704 to raise a force of 550 to pursue the Abnaki and also take Port Royal. Typical of colonial warfare, Church's force fell into predictable patterns of guerrilla war, raiding here and there as it made its way toward Port Royal. Church failed to take Port Royal, however, and was forced to return to Massachusetts at the end of the summer with little to show for the effort.

Dudley was not to be deterred and doggedly pushed for another expedition to Port Royal. He petitioned England for troops to take the strategically important fort, but was denied. England remained convinced that colonial enterprises were just that — colonial. In 1707, Dudley gained permission from the Massachusetts General Court to try for Port Royal one more time. Under the command of Colonel John March, an intra-colonial expedition of 60 from New Hampshire, 80 from Rhode Island, and two regiments from Massachusetts departed on May 13. The force of nearly 1,100 men approached Port Royal in two groups, forcing the French into the confines of the fortress. A well-coordinated siege appeared the obvious tactic, but the inexperienced and impatient colonial commanders badly bungled things, so much so that the militiamen lost all sense of discipline. They were not, after all, professional soldiers. They had not come all this way to sit and wait for victory through a lengthy siege.

With no plunder, no action, and little to occupy the troops' idle time, conditions quickly deteriorated. March decided to abandon the siege, but Dudley commanded him to return and engage the French. With an additional 100 men from Maine and a frigate, the expedition attacked Port Royal in August. The French had also received reinforcements and were able to hold off the New Englanders' disorganized attacks. March withdrew again. Officers on the expedition blamed one another for the adventure's failure. It was not a model intra-colonial effort by any means.

It took only until 1709 for Dudley and Lord Lovelace, the new governor of New York (which had finally decided to enter the fray), to convince the Board of Trade that the only chance for success against Canada was a combined colonial-regular campaign. It was the first time the crown would send regular troops in force to British North America. Two battalions of regulars along with six warships would join 1,500 men from New York, New Jersey, and (for the first time) Pennsylvania. New England promised to send a 1,000-man force. The plan was for a two-prong attack on Canada: the first prong, which included the 1,500 from New York, New Jersey, and Pennsylvania under the command of former governor of Virginia Colonel Francis Nicholson, would leave from Albany and attack Montreal; the other prong, made up of New Englanders, would embark from Boston to join the British regulars against Quebec.

What looked so grand on paper quickly fell apart in the field. The Pennsylvania men never showed up. The British fleet carrying the regulars failed to appear. Nicholson departed Albany in May, slowly cutting a road to Lake Champlain. By September, with no sign of the promised British troops, Nicholson was ordered to stand down and demobilize. In October, word reached the colonies that the decision had been made in England in late May to abandon the expedition; thus, no British troops would be sent to the colonies. Unfortunately, the colonies did not learn this significant bit of information until August. Had the colonies kept an agent or representative in London, they would certainly have received this incredibly vital news much sooner. They would not make this mistake again.

The colonies tried again, this time meeting in Rhode Island. New York did not take part, but representatives from Massachusetts, New Hampshire, Connecticut, and Rhode Island agreed to petition for an attack on Port Royal. They wanted to move immediately to take advantage of the coincidental presence of a few Royal Navy ships nearby, but the captains of these vessels refused to help without orders from Nicholson's superiors. Instead, the colonies sent Nicholson to London to ask again for help.

In 1710, Nicholson was ordered to command colonial forces and 500 British Marines to take Port Royal. Finally, this time, the expedition was successful. The French had downsized the garrison at Port Royal and as a consequence they surrendered in October. A British regiment was sent to garrison the key fortress. The colonies, elated with their success, wanted more. Canada seemingly lay before them. Nicholson returned to London to push the old Montreal-Quebec plan and was armed further with an offer from the colonial governors that the colonies would pay for British regulars. Nicholson would command the colonials against Montreal, and the British regulars would attack Quebec. London agreed.

For the first time, then, Britain finally landed regulars in force in the North American colonies. Sixty ships with 5,000 regulars arrived in Boston in June 1711. The colonists were overjoyed at the sight; the British commanders, Admiral Sir Hovenden Walker and General John Hill, seemed less enthusiastic. They departed for the St. Lawrence River at the end of July. Then disaster struck. The fleet sailed into a deadly storm at the mouth of the St. Lawrence and foundered. As many as 1,600 troops and sailors lost their lives as the ships crashed aground. General Hill wanted to continue toward Quebec, but the Royal Navy overruled him. The surviving vessels sailed for home, bypassing a return to Boston. Nicholson, by this time again at Lake Champlain, could hardly believe his ears upon receiving the devastating news. Once again, the two-prong attack had to be abandoned. Two expeditions had failed—two large investments of scarce colonial resources and money lost. A third attempt was out of the question.

Events in Europe outweighed those in America. Peace came by treaty in 1713, although the fighting on both continents had halted by truce in August 1712. This time *status quo ante bellum* did not rule the day, which gave the colonists some cause to rejoice. Great Britain gained Hudson Bay, Acadia (Port Royal), Newfoundland in North America, and St. Kitts and Nevis in the Caribbean, as well as strategically imperative Gibraltar from Spain. The Peace of Utrecht also preserved the Protestant throne in Great Britain, permanently separated the French and Spanish crowns, and gave Great Britain the massive monopoly on the slave trade, known as the *Asiento*, for 30 years. The balance of power in the New World now favored Great Britain, but only slightly. Without their knowledge or approval, the Iroquois became subjects of the British crown. France still held Cape Breton Island and its fortress at Louisbourg.

Ironically, casualties for the British colonials were extremely light while the British Navy and Army suffered great losses, mostly on the St. Lawrence River.

For the British colonies, initial euphoria gave way to a more mixed reaction to this apparent victory. Indeed, the colonies had shown they could cooperate, though unevenly. Their militia-trained expeditions had successfully defended the region against the French and, combined with British regulars, had provided significant and able forces. Yet, they again felt let down, even betrayed, by their home government. The perceived folly of British participation in the colonial war left the colonies with a feeling of disillusionment. Their strategic interests seemed growing apart from that of Great Britain, which held to a strategy of balance of power in Europe combined with a conservative approach to colonial affairs. The colonies, on the other hand, wanted to eliminate France and Spain from North America. Canada was the great prize. After two wars, France seemed just as entrenched as ever before in Canada, the Great Lakes, and Louisiana. The colonists would get another chance to gain at the expense of Britain's imperial rivals.

◆ KING GEORGE'S WAR

King George's War, named for King George II of Great Britain, was an extension of what was known as the War of Jenkins' Ear (1739) between England and Spain and the War of the Austrian Succession (1740–1748) pitting Great Britain and Austria against France, Prussia, and Spain. To kick off this convoluted conflict in America, Georgia's ambitious founder James Oglethorpe led an invasion of Florida in 1740. Native allies, as was the norm, played a significant role, as Chickasaw, Creek, and Cherokee attacked Spanish missions and settlements in western Florida while Oglethorpe's force attempted to take St. Augustine. The plan resulted in stalemate. For three years, raids and counter-raids resulted in little progress for the Georgians. South Carolina offered no help. Oglethorpe withdrew his force from near St. Augustine in 1743 when a Spanish fleet threatened his long and tenuous line of communication back to his Georgia colony.

Also as part of this conflict with Spain, there occurred one of the worst disasters involving American arms. The Royal Navy developed an elaborate plan to take the Spanish port at Cartagena with a fleet of Royal Navy warships and a large force of colonials to supplement ground operations. The call for volunteers went out in 1740, with most colonies offering bounties and promises of pirate-like loot. Eleven colonies sent 36 companies of 100 men each, making up what was called the American Regiment, commanded by Virginia Governor William Gooch. Since most of the officers were also American colonists, military relations between the colonists and British professionals were taking an unprecedented approach. The regiment met the fleet, commanded by Admiral Edward Vernon, and British Army units, commanded by General Thomas Wentworth, at Jamaica. Their combined forces totaled over 9,000.

The British professionals treated their American comrades in arms with unabashed contempt, assigning them the worst duties, poorest quarters, and most putrid rations. The campaign was a complete and utter disaster, encountering not only fierce Spanish opposition but also spring rains. Soldiers who survived the assaults against Spanish positions met an even stiffer foe in yellow fever, which killed hundreds. In mid-April, the expedition left Cartagena and foolishly tried to attack Cuba. By the time the American Regiment returned home, only 600 men were alive. Bitter resentment deepened as colonial governments blamed British incompetence for the disaster, which left the colonies much weakened against Spanish or French encroachments. In yet another irony of the colonial wars, Captain Lawrence Washington survived only barely to return to his plantation along the Potomac River in Virginia in pitiful health. He renamed his farm Mount Vernon, honoring the admiral who so incompetently led the ill-fated expedition.

These events took place amidst yet another European conflict over royal succession, this time over the Austrian throne. It did not take much for this conflict to spill over into North America. Once again, Great Britain was pitted against Spain and France, and for the British colonies, Canada again was the strategic objective. For the most part, King George's War was a guerrilla war that inflicted only light casualties, conducted mildly destructive raids, and mounted small but failed campaigns. Even poor Deerfield, Massachusetts, was again on the receiving end of a raid. The strategic contours were similar to those in previous wars, including a British desire to conquer Canada, a French desire to divide and weaken the British colonies, and the desire of both to exploit native alliances against the other.

The major conflict of the war, not surprisingly, centered on the entrance to the St. Lawrence River. The French failed in an attempted assault on Port Royal, which the British had renamed Annapolis Royal, in late 1744. In 1745, the British set their sights on Louisbourg, the principal thorn in their side that had long ensured the survival of French Canada. At the behest of Governor William Shirley, Massachusetts organized a huge—by colonial standards—expedition to take Louisbourg. Under the command of William Pepperell, 3,000 Massachusetts militia—500 from Connecticut, 450 from New Hampshire—along with cannon from New York, a ship from Rhode Island, and provisions from Pennsylvania and New Jersey, made up the largest intracolonial expeditionary force to date. The Royal Navy provided one 60-gun warship and three 40-gun warships. Their target was the fortress at Louisbourg, which was now a well-built, formidable Vauban fortification that some called the "Gibraltar of the New World." Its 30-foot-high walls were lined with over 250 cannon. Intelligence reports, however, noted weaknesses, namely that only 100 of the cannon were actually in place. Moreover, poor food, tedious duty, and homesickness infected the garrison's morale. The high hills to the west of the town provided an unhindered line of fire down onto the fortress. Despite its reputation and impressive fortifications, Louisbourg was vulnerable to attack, especially siege.

Pepperell's force laid siege on Louisbourg for 49 days. The French apparently never suspected an attack from the landward side of the fort; thus, they had faced their guns out to sea to defend against naval bombardment and protect the entrance to the bay and river. The New Englanders captured the Grand Battery, exploiting two unrepaired breaches in the battery's otherwise strong wall. With cannon they peppered the town and fort. In mid-June, Pepperell and his Royal Navy counterpart Commodore Peter Warren planned a joint land-sea assault to take the fortress, but the French preempted these plans by surrendering on June 17. Low on supplies and food, the garrison could carry on no more. Louisbourg was in British hands at last.

It was a great victory, to be sure, but one tainted by events that reinforced the stereotypes that colonial militia and British professional military men held regarding

FIGURE 2-1   Defeat of General Braddock, in the French and Indian War, in Virginia in 1755.

Source: Library of Congress Print and Reproductions Division [LC-USZ62-1473]

each other. On at least two occasions, land assaults had to be redirected or terminated because large numbers of militiamen were drunk. In another instance, militia successfully stormed an island battery without drawing artillery fire from the fort, but their drunken cheers awoke the French cannon. Sixty militiamen were killed and 119 captured in the French counterattack. From the standpoint of the Royal Navy, such behavior was preposterous and typical of the poorly trained and poorly led colonial rabble.

The Royal Navy, however, also let down the colonials. After taking the fort, Commodore Warren insisted on leaving the French flag flying at Louisbourg to trick French ships into entering the harbor. It worked. Prizes quickly totaled over £1 million, half of which went to the English crown and the other to the Royal Navy's officers and crews that captured the ships. None trickled down to the colonials who helped capture the fort and make such loot possible. Thus, while taking Louisbourg was a significant feat of arms and a long awaited dream of the colonials, it did little to improve relations and perceptions between colonials and British regulars. Casualties were relatively light. The French lost 53 regulars killed out of a force of 600. How many of the 1,300 civilians in Louisbourg lost their lives is unknown. The colonials lost approximately 140 men during the entire campaign, plus another 30 or so to disease, which is remarkable considering that at one point over 1,500 men were down with dysentery and other camp diseases.

For the British, the war began to go badly despite the victory at Louisbourg. Colonial legislatures failed to regularly pay their militias, causing some to mutiny in protest. The Iroquois joined the fight against the French in the west, but received little meaningful support from their British allies, leaving them feeling ill-regard toward their British "Father." The French took and destroyed the British fort at Saratoga. The Royal Navy showed its complete lack of colonial understanding by sending press gangs into Boston in November 1747. Governor Shirley suddenly had a violent mob on his hands, one that had actually accosted and held as prisoners several naval officers. Shirley and the mob made an exchange—the officers for those who had been impressed, and then the Royal Navy rather hastily left Boston. No one seemed happy with this war.

In addition to conventional military operations, privateering was another important part of strategy in this war. The lure of windfall profits from capturing enemy transports and supply ships made it very easy to bring daring sailors and ship owners on board for the war effort. Such practice had a long tradition in the colonial game. The famous and mysterious English settlement at Roanoke (1585–1590), never intended to be permanent, was actually a base to support operations of the Sea Dogs against Spanish shipping. Hundreds of colonial, British, French, and Spanish ships prowled the Caribbean and other waters in search of prey. Investors poured money into what they believed would offer an easy return. In fact, a single prize could bring an average return of 130 percent on the original investment. Ports such as New York and Charleston financially benefited from privateering efforts during the war. For the British, the success and popularity of privateering was a double-edged sword. On the one hand, privateering hurt the enemy and brought riches into increasingly strained colonial coffers. On the other, this same success and popularity took able seamen out of the available pool of sailors serving the crown; for the Royal Navy, privateering meant increasing difficulty in finding experienced, worthy seamen to crew His Majesty's vessels. In the long term, the tradition of privateering helped give birth to an American navy during the War for Independence, and privateering's objective of individual gain for individual effort fit neatly into the independent attitude growing among many colonials.

The Treaty of Aix-la-Chapelle ended hostilities in October 1748, which for North America meant early spring 1749 due to communication delays. To the shock and disappointment of the colonists, Great Britain traded Louisbourg and Cape Breton Island to France to regain Madras in India. The one thing that seemed to secure the inevitable end of French Canada, control of the St. Lawrence River, had been lost in some faraway negotiation. New Englanders felt betrayed, to put it mildly. They had, after all, taken the fort without the help of the British Army and in their minds with only nominal help from the British Navy. For the home government simply to return the fort as if it were of little consequence only reinforced among colonists already deep suspicions about their mother country.

Despite this setback, events had inflated the colonists' sense of their own military prowess and deepened the contempt in which they held professional armies. The colonists also now firmly understood that the strategic contours of colonial wars demanded control of the St. Lawrence River. They knew they would have to fight to take Louisbourg again. Another 1,600 colonials, 3,000 French, and untold hundreds of Spanish and Indians died from battle and disease in King George's War, yet another colonial war that once again gave none of the three powers a clear advantage in North America.

The drain on imperial treasuries from these wars took longer and longer to recover, leading some among the British and French governments to urge a lasting military resolution to the imperial game. Believing the continuation of these colonial wars too costly in the long term, what was needed, they argues, was a final war for all of the pie rather than another fight for a mere slice.

◆ THE GREAT WAR FOR EMPIRE (1756–1763)

The Great War for Empire was the first worldwide war involving the imperial powers, and it began in North America. While fought for the same strategic reasons as the previous colonial conflicts, this war—known as the French and Indian War in America and as the Seven Years War in Europe—would be fought in an entirely different way while confirming old assumptions and prejudices. For Great Britain, nothing less than the complete decapitation of the French empire in North America would suffice. Whereas in the previous wars the colonies provided the bulk of manpower, material, financial support, and leadership, professional regulars from Great Britain would take the lead in this new conflict. While earlier battles in North America were essentially a sideshow for continental operations, North America was the primary theater of operations in this war. Consequently, the scale of the French and Indian War dwarfed all previous conflicts in North America. While colonial forces would continue their tradition of guerrilla war, the European professional armies warred in European style at places such as the Plains of Abraham, Fort William Henry, and Montreal. And finally, unlike previous wars, this conflict produced a clear and triumphant victor. The long-term repercussions of this major war could not have been told at its end, but in little more than a decade afterwards the colonials rose up in rebellion against mother Britain.

Conflict began in North America in 1754, well before general war broke out in Europe and elsewhere between Britain and France. King George's War had left Britain in tenuous control of the lucrative and fertile Ohio Valley, using its sovereignty over the Iroquois as a pretext to lay claim to the extravagant colonial charters that asserted ownership of territory all the way across the continent. France, of course, laid claim to these same lands. With few troops and fewer outposts, both played a game centered on who could establish and hold a fort deeper into the other's claimed territory. In British North America, this time the Chesapeake colonies, Pennsylvania, and New York played the role of antagonists, instead of New England. Speculators from these colonies began exploring in earnest into the Ohio Valley, forcing the French, who clung to the strategy of encirclement, to establish forts to stem British intrusion and lure the Indians caught in between into the French camp.

The French built a series of forts, erecting each one progressively southward from Lake Erie. Fort Presque Isle, Fort Le Boeuf, and Fort Machault followed French Creek to the Allegheny River. Virginians built a small stockade where the Allegheny and Monongahela rivers met to form the great Ohio River. The French could not let such a strategic post stand; they promptly ousted the Virginians and built Fort Duquesne. Virginia's Robert Dinwiddie took great umbrage at this insulting show of bravado and with the blessing of the British government sent a young militia officer named George Washington and a regiment of Virginia militia to force the French to withdraw. The expedition ultimately was defeated by the French after a brief battle at a crudely constructed Fort Necessity in a clearing known as the Great Meadows in southwestern Pennsylvania. Surrounded, soaked by heavy rains, and with many wounded, Washington surrendered. Washington's not-so-glorious introduction to military command helped set in motion a series of events that started a war.

In response to French advances along the Ohio frontier, the representatives from the various colonies met at Albany in 1754 to discuss military unification and the establishment of a centralized native affairs bureau to coordinate pushing the French out of the Ohio Valley. The Albany Plan of Union outlined such a collaborative effort, including the raising of regiments and commissioning of officers, but failed to receive the blessing of any of the colonial assemblies. Like previous efforts, this try at unification also failed.

The French would not leave, forcing Dinwiddie and the British government to take the initiative in 1755. This time London would not leave the matter to the colonials, sending Major General Edward Braddock and two under-strength Irish regiments to Virginia to take Fort Duquesne. According to the plan, volunteers drawn in part from Virginia militia would augment the weak regiments. Ultimately, a force of 2,500—including three independent companies of regulars, the two Irish regiments, units of Virginia, Maryland, and North Carolina militia, and some native allies—slowly set off from Fort Cumberland, Maryland, in June 1755 for Fort Duquesne.

The experienced Braddock came to North America with preconceived notions of colonials, their military prowess, and how to deal with the French and Native Americans. He considered his colonial colleagues amateur adventurers who had no clue as to how to organize and command a military campaign. Not surprisingly, Braddock got off on the wrong foot with colonial administrations when they refused to provide a common defense fund to cover Braddock's military expenses despite their offer to do so at the Albany conference in 1754. Pennsylvania provided no money at all, while the others offered disproportionate amounts at irregular intervals. Not without some justification, Braddock and his officers found the colonial expeditionary units lazy, poorly trained, and undisciplined—a rabble that slowed his progress and would lose the baggage were it not for the presence of the seasoned professional British Army officers. The British also did not like their colonial counterparts, refusing to accept colonial militia and volunteer officers as equals. Clearly, ill feelings worked both ways, as egos got in the way of good sense. Indeed, George Washington, now a colonel in the Virginia militia, refused a temporary captain's commission from Braddock because he was, after all, a colonel. Still hoping for a more fitting commission in the British army, Washington served with Braddock as a civilian volunteer, hoping to earn the British general's good graces and be rewarded with the coveted officer's commission. Braddock, however, held no high opinion of colonial military capabilities, particularly those of militia officers, and loathed having to come out to the wilderness to clean up what he considered the colonists' mess.

It took weeks for Braddock's force and its long baggage train to cut a path through the thick forests. After slogging his way through miles of densely wooded hills—on its own a significant feat of logistics—Braddock ordered and accompanied part of his force forward to cross the Monongahela above Fort Duquesne. Poor reconnaissance

General Wolfe killed at the Siege of Quebec September 14.1759.

Source: Library of Congress Print and Reproductions Division [LC-USZ62-53]

allowed this advance force to walk right into an advance party of French regulars, Canadian militia, and their native allies. The British, in a tight but lengthy marching formation, were completely surprised by the smaller French force that had enveloped them. Because of the narrow path, the British rear bunched up against the forward position, causing panic and confusion. Braddock fell, mortally wounded. With many British officers killed and wounded, George Washington stepped in to coolly help much of the British force get out of the debacle and make its retreat.

Braddock's defeat was a disaster of major proportions for the British, who lost 63 officers and 914 men killed or wounded against French losses of 23 killed and a handful of wounded. The French and their native allies stayed hidden in the thick brush, firing into the British mass with deadly effectiveness. As they had been trained to do, the British regulars stood and fought but many of the Americans fled. This was an inauspicious beginning to a war that for any hope of success would require cooperation between the British regulars and the colonials. After hastily burning most of the wagons and supplies, the British and American survivors retreated to Fort Cumberland, leaving Braddock's newly cut path wide open to the French and Washington sorely disappointed.

GEORGE WASHINGTON DESCRIBES BRADDOCK'S DEFEAT TO ROBERT DINWIDDIE, JULY 18, 1755

In his report to Governor Robert Dinwiddie, Washington admits that Braddock was surprised by the Indian attack; however, he praises the British officers and his own Virginians for their courage in this most desperate situation. Note that Washington mentions that he escaped being wounded despite having four bullet holes in his coat and two horses shot out from under him.

Fort Cumberland, July 18, 1755.

Honbl. Sir: As I am favour'd with an oppertunity, I shou'd think myself inexcusable was I to omit giv'g you some acct. of our late Engagem't with the French on the Monongahela the 9th. Inst.

We continued our March from Fort Cumberland to Frazier's (which is within 7 Miles of Duquisne) with't meet'g with any extraordinary event, hav'g only a stragler or two picked up by the French Indians. When we came to this place, we were attack'd (very unexpectedly I must own) by abt. 300 French and Ind'ns; Our numbers consisted of abt. 1300 well arm'd Men, chiefly Regular's, who were immediately struck with such a deadly Panick, that nothing but confusion and disobedience of order's prevail'd amongst them: The Officer's in gen'l behav'd with incomparable bravery, for which they greatly suffer'd, there being near 60 kill'd and wound'd. A large proportion, out of the number we had! The Virginian Companies behav'd like Men and died like Soldiers; for I believe out of the 3 Companys that were there that day, scarce 30 were left alive: Captn. Peyrouny and all his Officer's, down to a Corporal, were kill'd; Captn. Polson shar'd almost as hard a Fate, for only one of his Escap'd: In short the dastardly behaviour of the English Soldier's expos'd all those who were inclin'd to do their duty to almost certain Death; and at length, in despight of every effort to the contrary, broke and run as Sheep before the Hounds, leav'g the Artillery, Ammunition, Provisions, and, every individual thing we had with us a prey to the Enemy; and when we endeavour'd to rally them in hopes of regaining our invaluable loss, it was with as much success as if we had attempted to have stop'd the wild Bears of the Mountains. The Genl. was wounded behind in the shoulder, and into the Breast, of w'ch he died three days after; his two Aids de Camp were both wounded, but are in a fair way of Recovery; Colo. Burton and Sir Jno. St. Clair are also wounded, and I hope will get over it; Sir Peter Halket, with many other brave Officers were kill'd in the Field. I luckily escap'd with't a wound tho' I had four Bullets through my Coat and two Horses shot under me. It is suppose that we left 300 or more dead in the Field; about that number we brought of wounded; and it is imagin'd (I believe with great justice too) that two thirds of both [?] received their shott from our own cowardly English

Soldier's who gather'd themselves into a body contrary to orders 10 or 12 deep, wou'd then level, Fire and shoot down the Men before them.

I tremble at the consequences that this defeat may have upon our back settlers, who I suppose will all leave their habitations unless there are proper measures taken for their security.

Colo. Dunbar, who commands at present, intends so soon as his Men are recruited at this place, to continue his March to Phila. into Winter Quarters: so that there will be no Men left here unless it is the poor remains of the Virginia Troops, who survive and will be too small to guard our Frontiers. As Captn. Orme is writg. to your honour I doubt not but he will give you a circumstantial acct. of all things, which will make it needless for me to add more than that I am, etc.

Source: The George Washington Papers, Library of Congress.

Braddock's failed approach to Fort Duquesne was part of a three-prong British strategy to push the French back into Canada. By taking Fort Duquesne in the Ohio Valley, Fort Niagara and Fort St. Frederic in New York, and Fort Beausejour off the Bay of Fundy in Nova Scotia, the British hoped to put the French on the defensive and open their offensive campaign to finally take Canada. The British navy would harass French troop ships bound for Canada, which had already received 78 companies of French reinforcements.

While Braddock met disaster at Fort Duquesne, a Massachusetts force of 2,000 militia under John Winslow and some British regulars under the command of Brigadier General Robert Monckton set sail in May 1755 for Nova Scotia to secure Fort Beausejour. The force landed at Fort Lawrence, on the British side of the vague boundary that separated British Nova Scotia from French Acadia. When Winslow and Monckton arrived at Fort Beausejour, they found the fort ready to give up. A British agent provocateur named Thomas Pinchon had convinced the French garrison that resistance was futile. After a brief and mostly phony siege of four days, the French capitulated. On June 17, the British easily took nearby Fort Gaspereau. The British now controlled Nova Scotia, except for the perennial thorn that was Louisbourg.

What followed in Nova Scotia eerily resembled ethnic cleansing concepts of the nineteenth and twentieth centuries. Many French Acadians refused to take a loyalty oath to the British crown. The British governor of Nova Scotia, Charles Lawrence, distrusted Acadians who did accept allegiance and ordered the entire population deported. Close to 7,000 were eventually dispersed among other colonies and Louisiana. They were allowed to take only what they could carry, sometimes nothing at all. The British destroyed their homes, and the dikes they had built to restrain the saltwater tides, and then went after the Micmac tribe who had been friendly to the French. Many issues motivated the expulsion of the Acadians, including thinning out Catholic influence amongst the British Protestant majority and opening Acadia to fresh British colonization. Nevertheless, removing an entire civilian population was an unprecedented act by one European colonial power against another.

Papers found in the smoldering remains of Braddock's baggage train near Fort Duquesne revealed to the French the nature of his plan to attack French Canada. As a result, Fort Niagara and Fort St. Frederic were reinforced, and plans were made to move on Fort Oswego on Lake Ontario. The Native American allies that Braddock had counted on to rally to the British never materialized once word spread of his death and defeat. Instead, they joined the French and raided up and down the Virginia, Maryland, and Pennsylvania frontiers, killing over 700 settlers. Pennsylvania again failed to organize militia and opted to pay settlers in the far reaches to defend themselves. Things looked bleak, indeed. Other than the success in Nova Scotia, reverse after reverse hit the colonies and the British Army.

Governor Shirley, who took over as commander-in-chief after Braddock's death, failed to attack Fort Niagara. Under temporary major general and superintendent of native affairs for the northern colonies William Johnson, a force of 1,200 that was supposed to take Fort St. Frederic narrowly escaped a Braddock-like disaster at the southern end of Lake George in September 1755 to earn a minor victory in the Battle of Lake George. Rather than following up to destroy the French opposition and take his objective, however, Johnson regrouped and began building Fort William Henry. He quickly lost control of his ill-disciplined colonial troops, who wanted higher pay and to return home, costing Shirley opportunity and initiative.

Governor Shirley then tried to reinforce Fort Oswego in early March 1756. The first attempt to get much-needed supplies and men to the fort was met by a French-native ambush and the destruction of Fort Bull, whose inhabitants were put to the sword by the French. Lieutenant Colonel John Bradstreet led another expedition to Fort Oswego, reaching the beleaguered post in late May to deliver desperately needed food and ammunition. On his return, however, Bradstreet and his relief expedition were ambushed but managed to recover and inflict heavy casualties on their French attackers. However, this proved only a flickering bright spot for the British, for Bradstreet's commander, Governor Shirley, was relieved in late March and replaced by a new commander-in-chief, Lord Loudoun, who had little sympathy for colonial concerns. Major General James Abercromby, a British regular, took command of all colonial forces. Abercromby promptly ignored all counsel from his colonial officers and the colonial governors, creating more antagonism between the colonies and Great Britain.

The French also received a new commander that May. The Marquis de Montcalm arrived in Canada to take over French regular and colonial forces just as England formally declared war on France. Like Frontenac years before, Montcalm was appalled at what he found in Canada—corruption in the colonial administration, incompetence at all levels, and no strategic direction for the hostilities in North America. Montcalm's hands would always be tied, however, because he was subordinate to Canada's corrupt and ambitious governor, the Marquis de Vaudreuil.

Ignoring Bradstreet's warning that Oswego was highly vulnerable, Abercromby was slow in sending Major General Daniel Webb to reinforce the garrison. Montcalm took the initiative and captured Oswego in August 1756 with little resistance. Native allies of the French ambushed the British survivors who had been promised safe passage back to Albany. All of Lake Ontario was now under French control, as was the line of communication down to Fort Duquesne.

FIGURE 2-3   The French and Indian War.

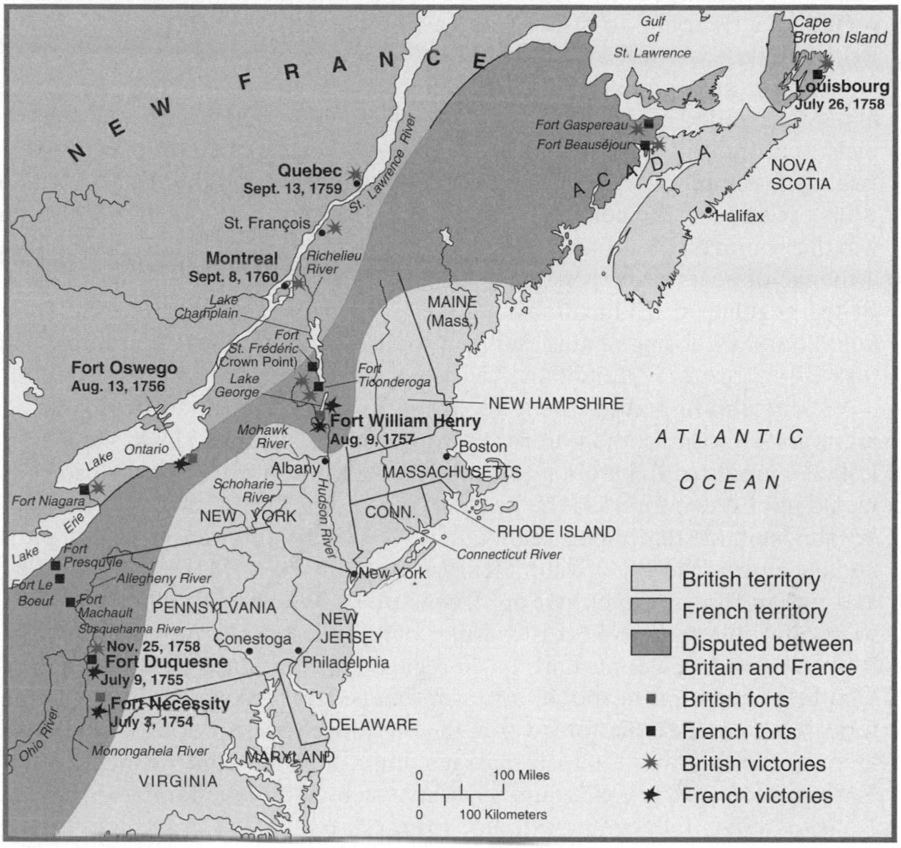

Despite alienating the colonials, Lord Loudoun demanded more colonial regiments, greater material support, and more money from the colonies he had been sent to defend. The situation had long since reached the crisis point, yet to his great frustration the colonies failed to cooperate. Colonial experience held that militia stayed close to home to defend their own frontiers. British authorities had confused local militia units with colonial expeditionary units and thus could not grasp why the colonies would not provide more men. The answer was simple—militiamen defended frontier settlements; expeditionary units were drafted from militia, but only under the proviso that enough men remained to defend the home colony.

Virginia and Pennsylvania spent their money in building defensive forts along their frontiers to defend against French-native raids. These forts, which were expensive to build, garrison, and maintain, left little money to contribute to the overall effort. New York and New England were ordered to use their own militia for defense and fill large quotas for expeditionary forces. Only New York managed to fulfill the quota, and even then superficially, since men deserted or quit service as soon as their brief enlistments expired. Officers had their problems, too—even the highest-ranking colonial officer had to answer to captains in the British army. Nonetheless, overall command of colonial forces remained with Lord Loudoun, even after he violated colonial enlistment regulations by trying to disband colonial units and enlist the individuals into regular British units.

Amidst these troubles, Webb dawdled, never making it to Fort Oswego, and in fact blatantly avoided its defense. Loudoun ordered General Edward Winslow and his colonials to abandon an attack on Fort Ticonderoga on Lake George and return to defend Albany from an enemy that, in reality, was nowhere nearby. Loudoun then relieved Winslow and left the colonials behind, deciding that only regular British forces could win this war in North America. Manpower shortages, however, forced Loudoun to have a change of heart, as he personally led an American force from New York to link with British regulars at Halifax to assault the grand prize, Fort Louisbourg. The expedition failed horribly, losing almost 300 men to disease in an effort that never assaulted the fort. By August 1757, Loudoun abandoned the plan and returned to New York.

Montcalm hoped to finally realize a principal French strategic aim of the colonial wars—to control the waterways from the St. Lawrence, down the Richelieu River, Lake Champlain, Lake George, on to the southern end of the Hudson River, which would put French forces in the heart of New York. The ineptness of British commanders almost made this hope a reality. In early 1757, Webb went back out with 4,000 men and encamped at Fort William Henry, sitting idly by as Montcalm built up his French and Indian forces at nearby Fort Ticonderoga. When he finally decided to move, he went down the road to Fort Edward, leaving Lieutenant Colonel George Monro with 2,400 men to face Montcalm's 9,000 regulars and Indian allies. On August 9, Monro had little choice save capitulation, as his men were wracked with disease and without food. Webb made no effort to trek the ten miles to save Monro. Once again, natives ignored the guarantee of safe passage and attacked Monro's men as they left Fort William Henry. The exact number of massacred soldiers, families, and camp followers is unknown, but estimates range from 200 to 1,500. The French stood by and did nothing to stop the murder. They may, in fact, have encouraged it, using the natives to spread terror in the northern British colonies.

Incredibly, more than 4,000 hastily mobilized New England militia, requested in panic by Webb, suddenly arrived at Fort Edward just after Fort William Henry fell. In deciding not to move, Webb had little extra to feed and house this militia force. Ultimately, he sent the militia home. For New England, mustering this large force was yet another wasteful expense of money and manpower and only deepened the fissures between the British Army and the colonies. It was the low point of the British war in North America.

Meanwhile, in England, Lord Cumberland's government collapsed, enabling the very able and energetic William Pitt to take power and dramatically change British imperial strategy. Until that time, England took a Europe-first approach to imperial conflict. Pitt, however, had other ideas. Beginning in December 1756, when he came to power, and carrying through until late 1757, Pitt worked to change the strategic outlook of Great Britain's war plan despite strong opposition in Parliament (Pitt actually lost power in April 1757 before regaining control in June of that year). The result was a complete turnaround in the way Great Britain prosecuted the war. Pitt recognized that North America, rather than the European continent, was the key to the war if not the entire British imperial system. Holding France where it was strongest—on the European continent—would allow Great Britain to shift its might to strike France where it was weakest—Canada.

The Royal Navy would have to take firm control of the Atlantic and thereby strangle French supply lines to North America. Additionally, the British Army would have to be reinforced in North America. Moreover, Great Britain would have to rely much more heavily than ever before on the cooperation of volunteer colonial forces in joint campaigns aimed at conquering French Canada. By attacking the sources of French wealth—Canada, French colonies in Africa, India, and the West Indies—Pitt saw a way to bring France to its knees. Victory over France would leave Great Britain as lord and master of the world's imperial system.

To achieve his strategic aims, Pitt first had to repair the damaged relationship between Great Britain and its North American colonies. Knowing that the colonies had been regarded as unruly and undisciplined subordinates, Pitt began to treat them as valued allies in a common cause. He rescinded military authority over colonial governors and assemblies, restoring the traditional administrative chain of command that came from the British secretary of state for colonial affairs down to the governors and assemblies. In addition to acquiring financial subsidies from the colonies to support the colonial war effort instead of forcing the colonies to contribute levies, Pitt hoped that restoring a degree of autonomy to the colonies would induce rather than compel colonial cooperation and, indeed, patriotism. In 1758, he went even further to address poor relations between colonial forces and the British army by decreeing that all colonial officers would be treated as equals to their British regular equivalents rather than as subordinates. This was a major change for the colonists, and Pitt's recognition of the problem went a long way toward rebuilding colonial trust and confidence in his plan for victory over France.

The colonists certainly desired a change in the crown's attitude toward them after the failed attempt on Louisbourg and the loss of Fort William Henry in 1757. Pitt recalled Loudoun in December 1757, replacing him with General Abercromby. Massachusetts Governor Thomas Pownall praised Pitt's new approach to colonial affairs and, with the enthusiastic support of the Massachusetts Assembly, authorized a new army of 7,000 volunteers. New campaigns signaled renewed offensives against French Canada in 1758. General Geoffrey Amherst carried Pitt's banner to take Louisbourg, while Brigadier General John Forbes was entrusted with an attack on Fort Duquesne. Abercromby led a force of 16,000 in July 1758 to invest Fort Ticonderoga. Abercromby split his force, failed to wait for his artillery, and showed little imagination in his repeated frontal assaults against Montcalm's well-entrenched and well-reinforced French fort. What appeared to be assured defeat for the French—they were prepared to beat a hasty retreat to Fort St. Frederic—turned out to be a stunning victory. Abercromby turned tail and retreated to Albany.

Amherst's campaign against Louisbourg, however, brought the British effort out of what must have seemed its lowest point. While Abercromby was meeting with self-inflicted disaster at Ticonderoga, Amherst and a force of 9,000 regulars and 500 colonials, ferried by a fleet of 40 vessels, began a textbook siege on Louisbourg. Beginning June 8, British troops under James Wolfe began digging the trenches that signaled the beginning of a siege. Louisbourg could be overcome—according to the military architect, Vauban, who originated the fort's style—by the principles of siege warfare. With no relief from the outside, a besieged fortress could not hold out against a well-supplied siege.

Siege warfare required the attacker to patiently dig a series of alternating parallel and approach trenches, slowly moving to within cannon range of the fortress walls. Once within range, siege cannon pounded the fortress walls, creating numerous breaches. The perfect siege, however, would not require a dangerous infantry attack into these breaches, for the besieged fortress would surrender, realizing that breached walls made defense futile. Typically, however, defenders did whatever they could to delay the unavoidable; musket and artillery fire and small harassing raids on the "sappers" could only temporarily stop the digging. Vauban had concluded that a properly invested siege would bring a fortress to its knees in forty days. Louisbourg took six weeks. By July 26, Louisbourg had fallen. Amherst and Wolfe had conducted one of the more effective Vauban sieges in history.

With Fort William Henry in fresh memory, however, Amherst and Wolfe refused the honors of war to the Louisbourg defenders. Wanting to avoid revenge for those slaughtered after the fall of Fort William Henry, Amherst closed Louisbourg to plunder. In addition, although Amherst deported Louisbourg's residents to France—a fate similar to the Acadians' in 1755—he allowed them to keep their possessions. French soldiers were made prisoners and sent to England to sit out the rest of the war. Pitt wanted Louisbourg as much as any other prize in North America. He had every intention of keeping the fort in postwar treaty negotiations, a much easier task with the fortress in British hands. Pitt also wanted to end French harassment of British shipping and open the Grand Banks to the British fishing industry. With Louisbourg under British control, the Prime Minister could achieve all of these objectives.

Not wanting to incur Pitt's wrath for his failure at Ticonderoga, Abercromby sensibly gave Bradstreet the go-ahead to lead an oddly mixed force of fewer than 135 regular troops with well over 2,000 colonials and 70 Iroquois warriors for an attack on Fort Frontenac on Lake Ontario. Bradstreet was no genius; nevertheless he understood speed and logistics. Badly outnumbered and poorly supplied, the French had no chance against Bradstreet's force. Warned of the impending British approach, the French capitulated. Taking Fort Frontenac helped soften the disaster at Fort Ticonderoga, for without Fort Frontenac, the French supply line to Fort Niagara and Fort Duquesne was cut. For the first time, the British controlled Lake Ontario.

The fall of Fort Duquesne topped off the remarkable British turnaround in 1758. The French garrison at Fort Duquesne, under the command of Francois-Marie le Marchand de Lignery, was small, poorly supplied, and under strained relations with its native allies. Brigadier General John Forbes had been charged to lead the British expedition to Fort Duquesne. Forbes had to overcome many obstacles just to get the expedition on its way. Basing the campaign in Pennsylvania, Forbes and the Pennsylvania assembly butted heads over logistical and manpower matters. They finally reached a compromise that opened the colony's store of arms and ammunition to the British and required the Pennsylvania to raise a regiment of 2,700 volunteers for the campaign. Native troubles also hampered Forbes' preparations as well-intentioned, Quaker-supported peace initiatives muddied negotiations with Iroquois, Cherokee, and Catawba aimed at convincing the tribes to join the campaign. In the end, the Treaty of

Easton settled few issues except to ease relations among the rival Indians and secure their allegiance to the British crown.

To add to his troubles, Forbes fell desperately ill and had to be carried by litter to Carlisle. There, he found confusion: the supply train was in disarray; colonial "volunteers" from Pennsylvania and Virginia were the most ragged lot Forbes had ever seen; and an emboldened Colonel George Washington of Virginia pleaded with Forbes to use Braddock's Road to approach Fort Duquesne. Instead, Forbes decided to cut his own road through western Pennsylvania.

Once again, the colonials failed to endear themselves to the British army. In addition to the ragged Pennsylvanians and Virginians, North Carolina sent an ill-equipped group of 300 men, while South Carolina and Maryland, seeing no advantage to participating in such an expedition, sent none. Once again, the colonies presented independent self-interest that highlighted their disunity in the face of crisis. Taxation, manpower, and regional security limited broader colonial vision, leaving the British army, and Forbes in particular, with a reinforced prejudice against colonial provincialism.

Under these circumstances Forbes forged ahead, as his men painstakingly cut a road toward the French outpost. Rain, mud, desertions, and supply problems harried Forbes and his men throughout the campaign. The French were in equally bad straits, but found brief success on the battlefield by defeating a British reconnoitering party of 800 men, which was surprised that the French attacked instead of remaining inside the fort. Still, French commander Lignery had to take excessive risks to defend the post. He tried a preemptive raid on Forbes' advance column on October 12, but the raid failed and lost Lignery his Indian allies, who saw little point in the endeavor. Fewer than 1,000 French soldiers remained to face the 5,000 British. Low on supplies and morale, the French decided to withdraw on November 24, burning Fort Duquesne to the ground before moving to Fort Machault.

Forbes occupied the ruins on November 25, thankful that an assault against the formidable fortress had not been required. He rebuilt the fort, renaming it Fort Pitt, and he named the new settlement Pittsburgh—both in honor of the headstrong British prime minister. Taking Fort Duquesne was an achievement of immense importance for Pitt's strategic plan and further served to soften Braddock's defeat in 1755. However, not all was serene. Forbes' army of colonials rapidly disintegrated through desertion and expired enlistments. At the end of December 1758, fewer than 200 men garrisoned Fort Pitt. Fortunately, trade goods arrived in January 1759 to improve relations with area natives, and Forbes' replacement, Brigadier General John Stanwix, eventually brought over 3,000 troops to keep the Ohio Valley free of the French.

With success won, Pitt had vital political support for the final conquest of Canada. He proposed a tidy plan to isolate western Canada from the St. Lawrence River by taking Fort Niagara and reinforcing Fort Oswego. British and colonial forces would simultaneously drive into the St. Lawrence Valley via Lake Champlain, a movement that would place the British at the gates of Quebec. By July 1759, British forces under Brigadier General John Prideaux were laying siege to the French garrison at Fort Niagara. In June, a force of over 9,000 under the command of British General Wolfe approached Quebec from the north shore of the St. Lawrence River, probing for weaknesses in the city's defenses. Montcalm, in command at Quebec, began a lengthy and tedious game of cat and mouse with Wolfe, trying to outwit and outlast his British opponent. Wolfe initiated a siege that lasted until September.

Meanwhile, at Fort Niagara, an impatient Lieutenant Colonel Eyre Massey, in command following the untimely death of Prideaux, ordered a hasty but successful assault. Participation by young Joseph Brandt and several hundred warriors from the Iroquois Confederacy played a significant role in Massey's victory. The fort surrendered on July 23. Western Canada had now been cut from the St. Lawrence River. On the Lake Champlain front, the French abandoned Fort Ticonderoga and Fort St. Frederic to General Amherst in late July and retreated toward Quebec. By late summer, only Quebec remained, a symbolic heart keeping French Canada alive.

Quebec was the decisive theater for the war in North America, and the battle there placed Wolfe and Montcalm at the forefront of the pantheon of great generals of Anglo-French conflict. Both died during the climactic, European-style battle on the Plains of Abraham outside the city. Wolfe used stealth and amphibious operations to land a large force above Quebec, completely surprising Montcalm, who assumed the British would assault the city proper. On the Plains of Abraham, Montcalm hastily organized his French soldiers into line to meet the British head-on. Montcalm ordered a charge that was received by a well-disciplined British line that held its fire until the very last moment. The effect was devastating. Montcalm's attack was repelled within fifteen minutes. Out of an initial force of 4,500, two hundred French and French colonial troops lay dead, while another 1,200 were wounded. The British lost 60 killed with another 60 wounded. Quebec formally surrendered on September 18. Over 80 years of colonial warfare for control of North America had culminated in a European battle lasting little more than a quarter of an hour. France was finished in North America.

While a few more battles occurred—namely, along Lake Champlain and, incredibly, a failed French siege of Quebec—the British were content to consolidate their hard-won gains during the winter of 1759–1760. Amherst assaulted Montreal in September 1760, forcing Governor Vaudreuil to surrender the whole of Canada. Detroit fell to Major Robert Roger's famous Rangers that same month, solidifying Britain's hold on the French province and swiftly gaining the allegiance of Native Americans who had forsaken the French.

Not all of the Indians, however, remained pacified. In what is the somewhat misnamed Pontiac's Rebellion, Ottawa, Seneca, Delaware, Iroquois, and Shawnee violently attacked the new British outposts in the west to take advantage of the French defeat. Before finally being put down, these loosely connected attacks killed over 2,000 civilians as well as 400 British and colonial troops, and cost Native Americans untold losses from battle and disease.

The Treaty of Paris (1763) formally ended the Great War for Empire. The French imperial system was neutered, losing all its possessions in North America. Great Britain was now the unquestioned ruler of the high seas and an imperial superpower. Spain's late entry into the war against France was rewarded with French Louisiana. But the initial euphoria of victory soon wore thin for the crown's loyal subjects in both Britain and the colonies. Taxes had reached unprecedented levels, yet the British treasury lay barren. His Majesty's army and navy now had to defend an empire twice as large as it had been in 1754.

For the colonies, Parliament's new interest in colonial matters began to intrude on what had been a tradition of salutary neglect. Postwar depression hit the colonial economy hard. A policy of taxation from the crown caused colonial rumblings of reform if not independence. Victory in a war that had been fought to solidify and strengthen the British imperial system now threatened the system it was intended to preserve. As an example of these difficulties, Pontiac's Rebellion caused Parliament to pass the Proclamation Line of 1763, prohibiting settlement west of the Appalachian Mountains. The arbitrary move infuriated colonists, who felt they had fought and sacrificed for the right to capitalize on these vast and fertile lands. Parliament was trying to prevent future conflict in North America, but the colonists wanted to claim what they considered their just reward for the victory they helped achieve. Parliament and the colonies seemed to be headed in opposite directions.

In colonial and military matters, the war had profound and lasting results. Pitt's attempt at reconciliation with the colonial administrations failed in part because the colonial assemblies took advantage of Pitt's generosity to further their own independence in military affairs. Colonial assemblies argued with Parliament over money, control, and prerogative concerning British regulars, whom they considered under their jurisdiction. This was especially the case with regard to quartering troops, an issue on which the assemblies gradually took the lead. Since British regulars had rarely visited the American colonies before this conflict, few barracks existed. As a result, British commanders occasionally forced colonists to quarter troops in their homes. Quartering troops in private homes without the owner's consent violated the spirit of English law and tradition, and colonists would not soon forget the presence of British troops on their property. When Parliament attempted to impose quartering, the assemblies resisted.

The presence of large numbers of British troops, particularly in New England and the Middle Colonies, brought colonists unaccustomed to a military presence into close contact with regular British forces. The British army relied heavily upon recruiting colonials into regular regiments, but questionable recruiting methods made service distasteful to many colonists and caused petty but long-lasting rifts between British authorities and the communities from which they recruited. Indentured servants were a prime target of recruiters, a fact that aggravated colonists who considered indentures to be legally binding contracts. The British army, in essence, was undermining a contractual obligation and a long-standing, although dwindling, source of labor.

Moreover, the continuing conflict between British military authorities and colonial assemblies over enlistment quotas, money, material, and common purpose left a bitter taste on both sides. Colonial assemblies felt threatened by what they perceived as an overt military threat to their governing prerogative, while British commanders such as Loudoun and Amherst were insulted by the impudent if not treasonous lack of deference to their command and judgment. British regulars stereotyped colonial volunteers as disorganized, undisciplined, and cowardly militia. Such a characterization completely misunderstood the American colonial militia system and its purpose of local defense.

In attempting to fulfill their enlistment obligations, many colonies resorted to impressing vagabonds, thieves, and other undesirables to clear out their towns and cities of an unwanted population. While many volunteers served with sincere distinction, the bad apples at the bottom of the barrel polluted the entire lot in the eyes of the British regulars. From the viewpoint of the colonials, the British regular army treated them unfairly in almost every military arena—colonists tended to get the most undesirable duty, poorest equipment, most uncomfortable quarters, most rotten food, and perhaps most significantly the harshest end of military justice.

Despite victory, the British perception of the colonists as unruly, ungrateful, and ill-mannered children hardened, while the colonists grew to see Britain as an overbearing, threatening, and unsympathetic parent who failed to appreciate the value of traditional liberties in the colonies. Although victory had come and benefited both Britain and colonies, the aftermath left discord festering in the British imperial house.

◆ CONCLUSION

These perceptions were all but confirmed for the colonists during the colonial wars, in which colonists proved their mettle against French and Spanish regulars, demonstrated an ability to think strategically, and established concrete notions of civil-military relations under colonial conditions. Their rare but disappointing experience fighting alongside their British brethren left the colonies with lingering resentment. Selective memory held the citizen soldier in much higher esteem than the professional regular. Still, the American colonists generally never fully appreciated that the security interests of the British Empire extended beyond the colonies' own immediate security needs.

It is indeed ironic that the colonies came away from the Great War for Empire thinking that their way of war had stood the test when it was in fact the British professional regulars who had organized an effective strategy, commanded the campaigns, and fought most of the battles. The victory that so greatly benefited the colonies had, in truth, been won by British know-how and experience. In fact, this same British army ultimately served as the model for the new American army that was born in 1775.

Further Reading

Anderson, Fred. *Crucible of War: The Seven Years War and the Fate of Empire in British North America, 1754–1766.* New York: Knopf, 2000.

Anderson, Fred. *George Washington Remembers: Reflections on the French and Indian War.* Lanham, Maryland: Rowman & Littlefield, 2004.

Barr, Daniel P. *Unconquered: The Iroquois League at War in Colonial America.* Westport, Connecticut: Greenwood Press, 2006.

Brumwell, Stephen. *Redcoats: The British Soldier and War in the Americas, 1755–1763.* Cambridge: Cambridge University Press, 2002.

Dederer, John Morgan. *War in America to 1775: Before Yankee Doodle.* New York: New York University Press, 1990.

Dowd, Gregory Evans. *War Under Heaven: Pontiac, the Indian Nations, and the British Empire.* Baltimore: Johns Hopkins University Press, 2002.

Ferling, John. *Struggle for a Continent: The Wars of Early America.* Arlington Heights, Illinois: Harlan Davidson, 1993.

Fowler, William. *Empires at War: The French and Indian War and the Struggle for North America, 1754–1763.* New York: Walker & Company, 2005.

Jennings, Francis. *Empire of Fortune: Crown, Colonies, and Tribes in the Seven Years War in America.* New York: W. W. Norton, 1988.

Leach, Douglas Edward. *Roots of Conflict: British Armed Forces and Colonial Americans, 1677–1763.* Chapel Hill: University of North Carolina Press, 1986.

Peckham, Howard H. *The Colonial Wars, 1689–1762.* Chicago: University of Chicago Press, 1964.

Swanson, Carl E., and William E. Still, eds. *Predators and Prizes: American Privateering and Imperial Warfare, 1739–1748.* Columbia: University of South Carolina Press, 1991.

mysearchlab Connections: Sources Online

READ AND REVIEW

Review this chapter by using the study aids and these related documents available on MySearchLab.

Study Plan

Chapter Test

Essay Test

Documents

The Schenectady Massacre (1709)

Richard Ingoldsby outlines grievances against the French in North America during Queen Anne's War, noting their use of brutal native attacks against noncombatants.

Queen Anne's War (1708)

Thomas Oliver describes to his sovereign the harsh realities of war in New England.

The Albany Plan of Union (1754)

Benjamin Franklin and Thomas Hutchinson proposed that the colonies formally unify for purposes of trade and defense, including raising an army, establishing a navy, and commissioning officers.

The Capture of Quebec (1759)

Captain John Knox describes in his journal his experience in the climactic battle for Quebec.

RESEARCH AND EXPLORE

Explore the following review questions using the research tools available on www.mysearchlab.com.

1. What did British colonists hope to gain through these colonial wars?
2. What disconnects occurred between colonists and leaders in Britain?
3. Why did the British resort to the expensive use of regulars in North America instead of relying on colonial expeditionary forces?

CHAPTER 3

Independence and the Birth of a National Military

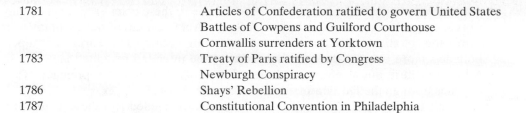

1781	Articles of Confederation ratified to govern United States
	Battles of Cowpens and Guilford Courthouse
	Cornwallis surrenders at Yorktown
1783	Treaty of Paris ratified by Congress
	Newburgh Conspiracy
1786	Shays' Rebellion
1787	Constitutional Convention in Philadelphia

◆ INTRODUCTION

While the Great War for Empire had left Great Britain the primary global imperial power, the cost of the war and of now defending a larger empire placed even greater demands on a nearly empty British treasury. In an effort to raise revenue, station British regulars permanently in the American colonies, and restrict colonial settlement west of the Appalachian Mountains, Parliament inadvertently sparked a revolution that would cost the British crown thirteen of its North American colonies.

Born of this revolution, the United States of America and its fledgling military successfully fought a war for independence and then experienced postwar economic and political problems that forced the new nation to reconfigure its governing administration and its military establishment. Achieving this was difficult because the colonial traditions of loathing centralized authority, abhorring a standing military, and regarding militia highly survived the revolution and greatly influenced the way the new nation approached military affairs and national security.

◆ TOWARD A BREAK WITH GREAT BRITAIN

Despite victory over the French in the Great War for Empire, Great Britain faced serious financial and strategic problems. The need for revenue to pay for the war and to sustain a permanent military presence in North America led Parliament to pass a series of revenue acts aimed at the colonists, who until then had rarely paid taxes directly to Great Britain. Having managed their own affairs for several decades, the colonists took for granted that Parliament's salutary neglect would continue. Beginning in 1763, however, this lax attitude toward the colonies came to an abrupt halt. A preemptive measure, the Proclamation Line of 1763 prohibiting colonial settlement west of the Appalachians, aimed to prevent further conflict with Native Americans. The colonists, considering western settlement as a spoil of victory over the French, considered the Line an arbitrary restriction of their right to pursue their happiness.

Parliament then embarked upon a series of similar restrictive measures and revenue acts, each causing varying degrees of reaction from the colonies. The hundreds of thousands of pounds expended annually to maintain several thousand British troops in the colonies, Parliament rightly asserted, was a cost that should be absorbed by the colonists themselves. Clinging to their militia tradition and distrust of standing armies, the colonists believed that the presence of British regulars was unnecessary and intrusive.

As revenue generators, the Sugar Act of 1764 and the Stamp Act of 1765 elicited fervent protest among some segments of the colonial populace. With a stagnant postwar economy and resentment against Parliamentary intrusion into what had been the purview of colonial legislatures, colonial resistance to these taxes erupted in a string of riots and attacks against tax collectors. A Stamp Act Congress of representatives from across the colonies met to formally protest the hated Stamp Tax. Parliament repealed both acts more because the taxes did not raise the intended revenue than because of colonial protest, but also reminded the colonies of Parliament's supremacy over the colonies through the Declaratory Act of 1766.

With tax revenue still far short of the amounts needed to relieve the debt and pay for British troops in America, Parliament tried again to tax the colonies through the so-called Townshend Duties. The colonists responded with nonimportation and boycotts of British goods. Outside the Boston customs house in 1770, British soldiers guarding the building squared off against an angry mob. Shots were fired and several Bostonians lay dead. Defended by the able John Adams, the soldiers involved in the incident were mostly exonerated of any wrongdoing or malicious misconduct. This, however, did not stop the Sons of Liberty from turning this minor incident into the infamous Boston Massacre. Heightened tensions in Boston and severe losses for British businesses because of the nonimportation movement convinced Parliament to repeal the Townshend Duties in 1770.

The passage of the 1773 Tea Act placed the American colonies squarely on the path toward independence. Previous parliamentary measures and colonial reaction to them had been relatively contained, but the Tea Act sparked more passionate widespread protest. Showing their enthusiasm for destroying private property, the Sons of Liberty led a mob in dumping hundreds of pounds of the East India Tea Company's tea overboard from company ships anchored in Boston Harbor in December 1773. Faced with wanton destruction of private property and angry stockholders, Parliament now had to respond with a firm hand.

The following year Parliament passed a series of acts that the colonists called collectively the Coercive Acts. Through the acts, Parliament closed the port of Boston, limited freedom of assembly across Massachusetts, and moved out of the colony trials that involved British officials and soldiers. Moreover, the new Quartering Act allowed Great Britain to force colonists in Massachusetts to do what British subjects in England had been doing for decades—house British troops in their own homes.

Boston already had a large garrison of British regulars, but now hundreds more poured into New England's main port. Finally, Boston was placed under martial law. While Parliament considered the rebellious colonists of Massachusetts primarily a localized problem, across the colonies many wondered how far Parliament would go to regain control not only of Massachusetts, but of all the colonies.

The answer came in 1775. For over a year, the Sons of Liberty and Committees of Correspondence had been working feverishly to build colonial support for armed resistance against British intrusion into colonial affairs. The First Continental Congress met in Philadelphia to alleviate the crisis with the mother country and hesitantly began to prepare for the worst while hoping to find a peaceful resolution. Militias trained, gathered and stored arms, and listened to impassioned sermons and political tracts urging the colonists to stand firm in defense of their rights as subjects of the British crown.

In 1775, King George III declared Massachusetts to be in a state of rebellion and ordered the colony's militia to stand down. It did not, forcing the British military governor of Massachusetts, General Thomas Gage, into a showdown with the militia. In

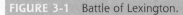

FIGURE 3-1   Battle of Lexington.

Source: Library of Congress Print and Reproductions Division [LC-DIG-ppmsca-05483]

April, Gage sent 700 men to secure stores of arms held by militia near Concord. At Lexington, along the route to Concord, an advance party of British regulars found several dozen militiamen with muskets primed and at the ready awaiting them on the village green. The British ordered the colonials to disperse, after which shots rang out. It is not known who fired the first shot, but regardless of which side fired first, volleys were exchanged, killing ten Massachusetts militiamen. The British wisely withdrew from Lexington and doggedly fought their way to Concord, where they found several hundred militia also at the ready. After a brief skirmish, the British withdrew—in orderly fashion at first, then falling into mass panic as militiamen took potshots at the retreating force all the way back to Boston. The British suffered over 20 percent casualties among their total force of over 1,500.

In a matter of days, over 20,000 militiamen besieged Gage and his garrison of regulars in Boston. The Second Continental Congress (1775–1776) formally reorganized the ragtag force surrounding Boston as a national or "continental" army. On June 14, 1775, it created the Continental Army. The "shot heard 'round the world" had now pushed the colonies past the point of no return. The first phase of the American Revolution had ended, as the national political institutions that had evolved since

1765 were now in place to conduct a war for independence. The second phase of the Revolution, the war itself, had now begun.

◆ THE WAR FOR INDEPENDENCE

It is extraordinary that the colonies ultimately managed to unify themselves in common cause enough to build an army, attract the support of France, and defeat the greatest military power in the world. At first, the Continental Congress simply wanted Parliament to restore the rights of the colonies, but as this objective became less obtainable, Congress decided upon independence as the only alternative. With no professional army, no navy, no money, no support from an outside power, a divided populace (many of whom did not want independence), and many mislearned lessons in their collective military past, the colonies warred against the most powerful nation-state in the world.

In 1775, the colonies had a population of about 2.5 million, including almost half a million slaves. Great Britain, on the other hand, could boast a population several times that of the colonies as well as a professionally trained army of at least 50,000 men and a navy second to none in quantity and quality. Bookmakers would certainly have placed the British as heavy favorites in this obvious mismatch.

The advantages and disadvantages for each side, however, did not stop at mere numbers of population and troops. Consider that the American revolutionaries (or rebels from the British point of view) had the benefit of knowing the land, the waterways, and the political mood of people across the colonies. This localism was a distinct advantage over the British, who often did not have as good a grasp of local conditions. The Americans also had the benefit of fighting a defensive war. In essence, they did not necessarily have to win—all they had to do was avoid losing. They fought for liberty, freedom, and rights that they had always assumed as British subjects. Still, they were not professional soldiers, had little money, and did not enjoy the total popular support. Moreover, the colonies were united only in the cause for independence; beyond that they bickered amongst themselves over resources, men, and money throughout the conflict.

Despite their overwhelming military might, the British found themselves in a delicate spot. On the one hand, Parliament certainly had to preserve its control over the American colonies and could not let these rebels set the dangerous precedent of getting away with flouting the mother country's authority over the empire. On the other hand, the economic and philosophical arguments supporting the rebellion rang with some truth for many in Great Britain. How far should the British go to crush a rebellion of fellow subjects of the British crown? And once crushed, then what? Moreover, the sheer logistical requirements of a military campaign in North America were well known to the British. A war against American rebels could be an extremely costly war. Parliament never fully addressed these problems nor did it form a cohesive strategy in North America.

Both sides nonetheless attempted to develop strategies that played to their strengths and took advantage of the other side's weaknesses. For the Americans, forming an army that could survive British attack was paramount. Since there were no centers of gravity in the American colonies, such as a pivotal city that if captured would cause the entire movement to collapse, such an army could move about the colonies and stay alive. It was imperative that the new army avoid a decisive battle with British forces. The Americans also needed the support of a foreign power. France was the obvious candidate. Having lost its North American possessions in the last war, France was eager to get back into the imperial game and break up the British mercantile system in North America.

At first, the British followed a strategy of containment. By containing the rebel cancer in and around Boston, the British army hoped to excise it before it spread to other parts of the colonies. After this strategy failed, the British then tried to lure the American army into a traditional set-piece battle in which the rebel force could be totally destroyed; such a decisive victory would end the rebellion. The problem was in determining exactly how to do this. Logistical needs tied the British to a base of operations, which in this case would have to be a deepwater port. Conducting operations away from such an important base was risky, as supply lines would get strung out and become vulnerable to rebel attack. With few roads and an uncertain knowledge of the land, the British could not afford long campaigns deep into the American interior.

Of equal importance for both the British and the American revolutionaries was winning the support of unaligned colonists. Traditionally, historians have estimated that approximately one-third of the population supported independence, another third remained loyal to the crown, and the remaining third did not lean either way. Convincing these unaligned people to join the cause for independence or remain loyal greatly influenced the way both sides fought the war.

◆ THE NORTHERN PHASE (1775–1777)

As more colonial militia descended upon the outskirts of Boston to contain British forces, the Continental Congress made its most monumental decision of the war. Even though there would be an army, each state demanded to retain its respective militia. Having a coexistent army and militia unintentionally created a dual army tradition in the new nation. An army was necessary, requiring not only soldiers to fill its ranks but someone to lead them. The Continental Congress would simultaneously have to build the army while using it to fight the British. Moreover, Congress also had to find a commanding general to both form the militias into a usable force and lead the new army. Few in the colonies had that sort of military experience and fewer still were willing to place their lives on the line for the cause.

George Washington, however, wanted the job and Congress gave it to him. He had been a delegate to both Continental Congresses and wore his Virginia militia uniform while Congress was in session. He was capable, commanding, had limited but important military experience, and served a broader political purpose for Congress, which needed to shape the rebellion into more of a "continental" movement. As a Virginian, Washington was not part of the radical Massachusetts revolutionary crowd. But some feared that as a Virginian Washington would defend only Virginia's interests in the conflict. Washington promised that he would do what was best for the colonies as a whole, favoring no region or special interest. He kept his word.

Washington's first task was to go to Boston and take control of colonial forces. Militia enlistments were expiring and many men simply returned home. Washington had to recruit a new army in the field and keep the British contained in Boston at the same time. Washington's first big break came in early 1776 when a force under the command of Henry Knox brought fifty cannon from recently captured Fort Ticonderoga—a Herculean task considering the snow-covered terrain of the 300 miles to Boston. Washington had the cannon placed on Dorchester Heights, where the barrels looked down upon the city, placing the British in an untenable situation. The new British commander, Major General William Howe, decided to withdraw from Boston in March 1776 to the safe confines of Nova Scotia where he planned his next move.

From Nova Scotia Howe decided to relocate his primary base of operations to New York City in August 1776. The previous month the colonies unanimously declared their independence from Great Britain, making an official and hopefully permanent break with the mother country. Sensing that strong loyalist sentiment among New Yorkers would provide better accommodations for his growing force than would the uninviting citizens of Boston, Howe sent over 30,000 men—supported by a large Royal Navy fleet commanded by Howe's brother Vice Admiral Richard Howe—to invest Manhattan Island. A smaller force of British regulars made their way down Lake Champlain from Canada to recapture Fort Ticonderoga and link with Howe in New York City.

In the meantime, Washington struggled to form an army and recover from Benedict Arnold's ambitious but unsuccessful invasion of Canada that had been undertaken in the vain hope of enlisting Britain's northernmost colony's support for the revolution. Taking a two-prong pincer-like approach, one wing managed to take Montreal; but Arnold's men suffered tremendously from cold and exposure before reaching Quebec in December 1775. An assault on the fortified city failed, not the least because of wretched weather and Arnold being severely wounded. The rebels lay siege on Quebec until the spring of 1776, when the arrival of British reinforcements forced them to withdraw. Battered and exhausted, Arnold's force turned back southward, ending the gamble to make Canada part of the revolution.

Among his Continentals and militia Washington now had almost 20,000 troops. He took them to New York to defend the city against Howe's invasion. Recruiting men for the new Continental Army had been and remained extremely difficult. Fear of a standing army was the least of Washington's recruiting problems. Militia service carried more prestige, short enlistments, and often better supplies. Service in the new army, on the other hand, offered lengthy privation, poor supplies, and little else. Still, despite a host of deferments and other ways to avoid serving, many men chose to serve in Washington's army. The Continental Army never reached more than half its authorized strength, and while men from all segments of American society served as soldiers, most came from the lower rungs of the colonial social ladder.

With his motley force of Continentals and militia, Washington set up to defend New York City by splitting his forces between Long Island and Brooklyn Heights. Howe coolly teased the rebels with the real threat of annihilation while offering amnesty for those who returned to the loyalist fold before the British launched the assault. In late August Howe attacked, all but wiping out the Americans on Long Island. Washington's forces on Brooklyn Heights barely escaped destruction by retreating to Manhattan. Howe may have allowed Washington to slip away in a fruitless effort to convince the Americans to give up the fight before the Continental Army was physically destroyed. Additional battles occurred in New York City, Forts Washington and Lee, and White Plains. Despite heavy losses due to combat, capture, and desertion, Washington managed to get a small portion of his original force out of New York and into New Jersey. He now had less than 3,000 men. It was, perhaps, the low point of the war for the Americans.

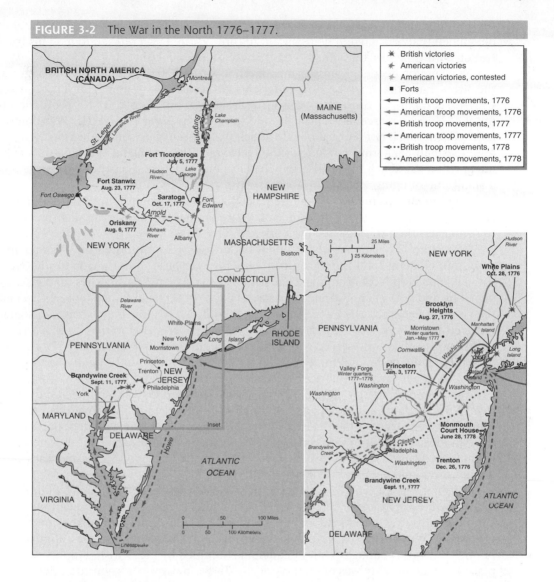

FIGURE 3-2 The War in the North 1776–1777.

Although Arnold had managed to stop the British approach down Lake Champlain, Howe comfortably occupied New York City. Washington laid low in New Jersey throughout the fall and winter of 1776–1777 so that he could rebuild his fading army. Making no progress in his efforts to get the rebels to surrender, Howe reluctantly sent the able General Lord Charles Cornwallis into New Jersey in pursuit of Washington. In a bitter winter campaign during which the Americans more frequently employed guerrilla tactics than they fought conventional war, Cornwallis and Washington dueled across the New Jersey countryside, fighting for food and forage and inflicting as much damage upon the other's force as possible. In Congress, some delegates argued that Washington should be sacked for incompetence. This was not the last time that Congress and Washington were at odds; fickle delegates repeatedly demanded that Washington be replaced. In turn, Washington refused to hide his frustration with Congress for failing to adequately supply the army.

Washington needed a success, no matter how trivial, to boost morale in Congress, the army, and the thirteen now-independent states. He found it at Trenton on Christmas night, 1776. Facing expiring enlistments, bitter cold, and a professional army of Hessian mercenaries brought into the fight by King George III, Washington hatched a daring if not reckless plan to attack the Hessian garrison at Trenton. Making a tedious and dangerous crossing of the Delaware River at night, Washington's men managed not so much to surprise the Hessians but rather to overwhelm them. It was a small but stunning victory for a victory-less army. It was the shot in the arm that Washington and his men so desperately needed. Washington followed this success in January 1777 with an attack on Princeton that ultimately forced Cornwallis and Howe to reconsider their strategy in New York and New Jersey.

When the 1777 campaign season got under way, Howe ordered the dashing and ambitious General John Burgoyne to attempt another push from Canada to split New England and New York. Burgoyne knew little of the American wilderness and insisted on a long and heavy supply train. His army of about 8,000 regulars and loyalists hacked their way through the thick forests, literally building a road as they advanced, sometimes covering only yards in a day. American Major General Horatio Gates, a former British army officer who served with Braddock in the previous war, harassed Burgoyne with his small Continental force and large number of militia until finally baiting the British to attack strong American defensive positions around Saratoga in the fall of 1777. In a series of battles during September and October, Gates maintained the initiative. With supplies running out and no hope of reinforcement, Burgoyne had to surrender. The victory over the British at Saratoga became the turning point of the war for the American cause, as France considered the victory a definite sign that the Americans might indeed have a chance of winning, and, thus, decided to support the Americans with money, arms, and ultimately troops.

Washington huddled his meager force at Valley Forge in Pennsylvania during the winter of 1777–1778. Lacking adequate shelter, provisions, and clothing, the Continentals suffered tremendous hardship from freezing temperatures and harsh winter storms. Washington badgered Congress for help. Congress was doing all it could, but this was rarely enough. With Philadelphia occupied by the British, simply finding a place to meet in safety was often the priority. In the meantime, troops deserted, died, and talked of mutiny. But the men who stayed, and survived, became an army that the British would not recognize when compared to their own. Whereas the British soldier often was forced into service, the Continental soldier volunteered often for little more reason than peer pressure and a desire to not let down comrades in arms. Bounties and the promise of pay no doubt encouraged many to enlist as well. With the help of a former Prussian officer, Friedrich Wilhelm von Steuben, Washington slowly turned the bedraggled men into soldiers. In Congress, Robert Morris used creative financing to better supply the army. From what should have been the demise of Washington's army grew a stronger, better-trained force, bonded in common cause and suffering.

This revitalized force had its baptism by fire at the Battle of Monmouth in New Jersey in June 1778. General Henry Clinton, who had replaced Howe as British commander in North America, withdrew most British forces in the North to New York City to consolidate and reorganize. Along the way, Washington, with a combined force of Continentals and militia, hit Clinton's flank near Monmouth Courthouse. Just as General Charles Lee's assault on the British began to fall apart, Washington arrived to rally the men. Monmouth was a European-style battle in which Washington's army could not have engaged the year before. Darkness halted the action, and Clinton withdrew during the night. From this point, Clinton had to change the British strategic approach to the war. As the Americans and British warily eyed each other in New York, the British regrouped, intending to take advantage of loyalist support in the southern colonies.

◆ THE SOUTHERN PHASE (1778–1781)

Failing to destroy the rebellion at its heart in Massachusetts and missing more than a few opportunities to wipe out Washington's small but determined army in New York and New Jersey, the British tried another tack. The face of the war had changed dramatically in 1778 when France entered the fray as both ally of the American rebels and worldwide belligerent against Great Britain. Holland and Spain also joined the war, which now had become a world war with combat operations in India, the Mediterranean, the South Atlantic, and elsewhere. North America, in some respects, became a secondary theater. Now, in addition to fighting a war in North America and coping with its increasing cost, Great Britain had to consider its own security against French attack. More members of Parliament began to question the war in America and British public opinion seemed to be swinging against this expensive and lengthy war.

Some fighting had already occurred in the Carolinas, mostly to the advantage of the British. Without strategic guidance in the south, however, the British failed to take full advantage of these small successes. Clinton believed that loyalists in the southern colonies would rally to the crown, and he thought that the prominence of slavery in the southern colonies could be used to British advantage. All this talk of freedom might place slavery in jeopardy and thus, the reasoning went, more southerners might stick with the British in the long run. Clinton also hoped that regiments of volunteer loyalists would augment his shrinking army in North America. Battle and disease were taking their toll on the British just as they had on the Americans, and with a wider war fewer reinforcements would be coming to America. Moreover, with an increased French naval presence in the Caribbean the British needed a base of operations south of New York to augment naval stations in the West Indies. Charleston on the coast of South Carolina was perfect. From there, Clinton planned to gain control of the Carolinas and then move up to Virginia.

Clinton made his move in December 1778. He secured Savannah with rapidity and ease, a fact that makes his year-long sojourn there before moving on Charleston seem remarkable. This delay allowed the Americans to form a southern Continental army and raise militia and irregular forces in the Carolinas. Clinton laid siege to Charleston, taking the port city along with Major General Benjamin Lincoln's force of over 5,000 Continentals a month later. It was indeed a disaster for the Americans, perhaps the greatest of the war.

In June, British Lieutenant Colonel Banastre Tarleton and his Loyalist British Legion defeated a force of Virginia militia at the Waxhaws near Lancaster, South Carolina. Known for his ruthlessness and hatred of those he considered traitors against the crown, Tarleton apparently gave no quarter, as over 100 Virginians were killed despite throwing down their muskets in surrender. The way the war was being fought began to matter. Washington had already mandated that all surrendering British troops be treated as prisoners of war in the European tradition of warfare—with the utmost respect and best possible care. The British, on the other hand, treated American prisoners as well as noncombatants inconsistently and often brutally.

Assuming that the southern colonies were under British control, Clinton departed for New York, leaving mopping-up operations to General Cornwallis. Meanwhile, in Morristown, New Jersey, Washington and his army endured an even worse winter than they had at Valley Forge. Mutinies, desertion, sickness, and death once again threatened to defeat the cause, for if Washington's army disintegrated, so too would the rebellion.

Without Washington's consent, Congress authorized a new Continental army in the south, giving it to the hero of Saratoga, General Horatio Gates. Gates was arrogant, overconfident, and careless, and quickly met with disaster. In August 1780, Gates' 1,500 Continentals and several hundred militiamen collided with Cornwallis at Camden, South Carolina. Entrusting his left flank to undisciplined militia, Gates kept his trained Continentals together on the right. Recognizing this unwise division of force, Cornwallis hit the militia hard. They fled in panic, leaving Gates and his Continentals outnumbered and exposed. Gates and the regulars were all but destroyed.

With Gates in the south with virtually no army, Benedict Arnold plotting treason at West Point in the North, and Washington's army barely managing to keep Clinton entrenched in New York, prospects indeed looked bleak for the American cause. The situation, however, began to turn in the Americans' favor. Significant help from France finally arrived. The first French troops to join the fight landed in Newport, Rhode Island, in July 1778, under the command of the Comte de Rochambeau. Washington convinced Congress to relieve the incompetent Gates, replacing him with Nathaniel Greene, a courageous commander but one whose battlefield success came at great risk. In the south, loyalist support for the British eroded as Cornwallis either allowed or ignored the brutality of his troops against noncombatants. British troops pillaged, raped, and managed to alienate many among the one-third of nonaligned colonists, as well as some loyalists.

Greene used irregular bands of mounted troops to harass the British and interdict their supply lines. The British, in response, adopted similar tactics, which, combined with the use of loyalists, inadvertently caused what amounted to a civil war in the Carolinas. Often, it was colonist fighting against colonist in the South, such as at King's Mountain in North Carolina in October 1780, where rebel militia wiped out loyalists under British command. Clinton had left Cornwallis with only 8,000 regulars, thus he had to recruit from loyal colonists to augment his inadequate force. To both pacify the Carolinas and destroy Greene's force, Cornwallis needed significantly more troops.

The turning point for the Americans in the South came at the Battle of the Cowpens in South Carolina in January 1781. Brigadier General Daniel Morgan and his combined force of Continentals and militia capitalized on the increased discipline

FIGURE 3-3 The War in the South 1778–1781.

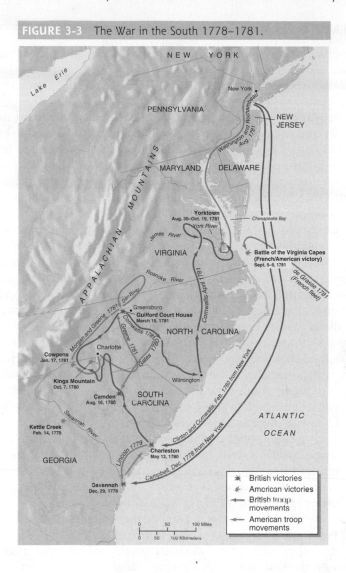

of his regulars and superior tactical use of terrain to draw Tarleton's overconfident British into a costly defeat. Despite this enormous loss, Cornwallis pursued Greene and Morgan deeper into the North Carolina wilderness, stretching the British supply line to Charleston dangerously thin.

At Guilford Courthouse in March, Greene and Cornwallis clashed in a huge, disorganized battle that left both sides badly battered. Even though the British commanded the field, they had again suffered debilitating casualties. Greene escaped with the remnants of his army, and Cornwallis, short of men and supplies, decided to move into Virginia in the hope of getting help from Clinton in New York. With French land and naval assistance finally available, Washington seemed to have the edge as the war entered its climactic moment.

◆ THE NAVAL WAR

Naval operations during the American War for Independence are often overshadowed by the land war. Facing the mightiest navy in the world, the American rebels had woefully little with which to face the British at sea. Still, the diminutive American navy, formally created in October 1775, played a key role in the war.

The Royal Navy blockaded much of the Atlantic seaboard throughout the war but kept its own shipping lanes open to allow limited trade and to enable resupply. To combat this situation, Congress created a navy and also granted letters of marque to privateers. During the colonial wars, American seamen had learned that privateering was often lucrative and thus many seamen forwent service in the new navy to instead pursue privateering. By the end of the war, American privateers (more than 1,500 of them) had captured more than 600 British ships.

The Continental Navy, on the other hand, was pitiably small and on paper hopelessly outgunned and inexperienced when compared to the Royal Navy. At its height during the war, the Navy had fewer than 60 ships, including 13 frigates, 10 of which were either destroyed or captured by the British. To support the navy, Congress established a Naval Committee under the leadership of Robert Morris and ordered the states to recruit men for naval service. None of the states reached their recruitment goals, in part because many seamen opted for serving aboard a privateer. All of the states, save New Jersey and Delaware, however, formed navies of their own, made up mostly of small ships to defend coastlines and ports; all of the states authorized privateering.

As mighty as the Royal Navy was, it, too, had challenges to overcome. Many of the great ships of the line built during the 1756–1763 war had to be refurbished due to poor maintenance or mothballing at the end of that war. Unlike the previous war, in this one the Royal Navy had to maintain its principal logistical line back to Portsmouth in England. American naval stores, pitch and tar, and most importantly timber for masts and spars were no longer available, forcing the British to seek these vital supplies elsewhere and often in inferior form. And unlike the American navy, manned by volunteers, the Royal Navy still relied on impressments to man its fleet. Personal motivation for service, be it greed, liberty, or both, simply did not resonate in the Royal Navy, which relied heavily on impressing men into service, as it did among the American navy and privateers.

Not yet mature enough to engage in fleet actions against the Royal Navy, the Americans followed their privateering tradition and went after defenseless merchantmen on the high seas. This strategy actually proved effective, forcing the Royal Navy to take valuable ships away from blockade duty—and later, from fighting the French navy—and reassign them to convoy duty to protect British merchantmen from American raiders. In the young U.S. Navy, bold captains, such as Nicholas Biddle and John Paul Jones, had better success in harassing British trade than in engaging ships of the line. Jones even operated with successful effect near the British coast. So effective was this strategy that the British suffered tremendous commercial losses during the war, which greatly displeased business interests in Parliament. Over the course of the war, American privateers and the U.S. Navy accounted for over $60 million in losses for the British merchant fleets.

The many actions fought by the Navy during the war included an assault on Nassau by Esek Hopkins. Inexperienced and rash, Hopkins disobeyed orders to patrol the

Chesapeake Bay area and instead attempted to capture the British port at Nassau in the Bahamas. While the raid was partly successful, HMS *Glasgow* found Hopkins and his twenty-four-gun frigate USS *Alfred* off the coast of Connecticut making its way back to port. Hopkins lost his ship and was subsequently court-martialed for disobeying orders.

The U.S. Navy used the first submarine in a combat operation in 1776. The *Turtle*, a single-man underwater craft operated by Ezra Lee, unsuccessfully attempted to attach an underwater mine to HMS *Eagle*, flagship of the British fleet at New York. Western navies would continue to experiment with underwater craft over the course of the nineteenth century before perfecting their use during the two World Wars of the twentieth century.

Britannia ruled the seas until France entered the war in 1778. Now, with the French navy harassing the Royal Navy in the Caribbean and elsewhere, the American navy and privateers had greater latitude in commercial raiding. Because such a large French naval presence now operated in American waters, it was easier for Washington to keep Clinton in New York. Clinton could ill afford to sail with his army out of New York to reinforce Cornwallis in the south lest he get caught on the open seas by the French fleet.

◆ **THE FINAL CAMPAIGN**

With Cornwallis in southern Virginia, Clinton still bottled up in New York, and the French Caribbean fleet willing to sail northward to escape hurricane season in the Caribbean, Washington finally had an opportunity to deliver a decisive blow to the British. Effectively abandoning Georgia and the Carolinas, Cornwallis left only token forces to hold strategic centers in the south. Nathaniel Greene was able to reclaim the southernmost states for the rebel cause, even though he himself did not command a single victorious battle. As Cornwallis's forces gathered at Yorktown in Virginia, Washington ordered American forces under the Marquis de Lafayette to trap them there. Following with his army and the Comte de Rochambeau's 7,000 French troops, Washington abandoned his original hope to converge his land force and the French fleet of the Comte de Grasse on the British at New York. Now, with de Grasse sailing toward the Chesapeake and Cornwallis on the Yorktown peninsula, Washington decided instead to bag Cornwallis.

Cornwallis understandably found Yorktown a strategically advantageous location. It afforded access to the sea for resupply or rescue but because it lay on a peninsula, Yorktown was also easily cut off from a land escape route. Sea access disappeared in early September, however, when the British fleet was soundly defeated by de Grasse and his French fleet in the Battle of the Chesapeake. Miscommunication between British Admirals Alexander Hood and Samuel Graves allowed de Grasse to seize the initiative and win the day.

With siege equipment thoughtfully included in the French expeditionary arsenal, Washington and his French allies dug in and began pounding Cornwallis in late September. Washington had 6,000 Continentals and over 3,000 militia combined with de Rochambeau's 7,000 French, to Cornwallis' 8,000 men who were under siege at Yorktown.

Source: National Archives and Records Administration

For three weeks, the Americans and French hammered away at Cornwallis, who now had no hope of rescue or resupply. He formally surrendered on October 19, 1781.

First Saratoga, and then Yorktown—the British could not tolerate such losses. The British people were already divided on the war and Parliament had been split over how to pursue the conflict after Burgoyne's surrender and French entry into the conflict. Lord North's ministry fell on 1782. Now, after Yorktown and still facing an increasingly stronger French enemy and determined rebel army, the British made the difficult decision to let the colonies in America go their separate way.

Great Britain had certainly underestimated the problems posed by the American interior with its deep forests, hills, valleys, rivers, and rugged landscape. Logistical challenges plagued the British effort to end the rebellion, as did the lack of a coherent strategy and poor generalship. Perhaps their greatest mistake was in failing to convince the one-third of nonaligned American colonists to join the loyalist cause as well as a failure effectively to use the one-third who were indeed loyal; instead, bumbling policies and inept commanders managed to alienate both groups. Carrying on a war in such a place and in such a manner for six years to an inglorious conclusion would shake any nation to its core, as it did Great Britain during the American War for Independence.

For the Americans the war had been a bloody affair, one of the bloodiest in relation to population in American history. Over 25,000 soldiers lost their lives, mostly from disease and privation; the death toll amounted to just under 1 percent of the population (the Civil War, by comparison, cost the lives of just over 1.6 percent of the population). Victory had been hard won. Indeed, the Americans took advantage of localism and of their familiarity with the terrain, and they fought the war in a way that did not alienate the bulk of the population. Despite bickering among the states and Congress, and Washington's seemingly insurmountable problems of supply, enlistment, mutiny, and the overall poor condition of the Continental Army, America prevailed.

Victory could not have been achieved without France, which played the odd role of monarchy helping to create a republic with not only no king but without hereditary titles. France had much to gain from seeing the American rebellion succeed: revenge for the total defeat in the previous conflict, delivering a severe blow to the British mercantile system through the loss of its colonies in America, and establishing a primary trade relationship with the new United States. All of these achievements would benefit France and its power on the European continent and abroad.

Important as France was to the American victory, so too was the role of George Washington as commander-in-chief of the Continental Army. Washington proved himself adaptive, flexible, and a skilled strategist who kept the army, and thus the revolution, alive. He channeled the varied motives of his volunteers into creating a European-style army that could ultimately face the British army on its own terms. As commander-in-chief he managed to find subordinate commanders, such as Henry Knox and Nathaniel Greene, who could lead men in battle and maintain a broad strategic view of the war. Washington overcame discontent, hardship, and even mutiny among his troops and some of his officers to persevere against a weak and often ineffective Congress and uncooperative states. While he did not overcome his disdain for the militia, he learned how best to employ them on the battlefield.

Finally and perhaps most importantly, Washington came to embody the ideals of the revolution. He was an elitist who expected deference but he also genuinely practiced public virtue. While it would have been easy for him to abandon the rebel cause and defend the interests of his native Virginia, he did not. Even at the expense of Virginia's security, throughout the conflict Washington managed to retain perspective and see the revolution as a national movement.

◆ THE END OF THE CONTINENTAL ARMY

Following the victory at Yorktown, Washington and his army nervously kept watch on the remaining British troops that continued to occupy New York and Charleston as peace negotiations commenced in Paris. Washington by no means took it for granted that the war was actually over, for much of the British army in America and Canada remained undefeated. French attempts to influence the new United States stalled the peace talks, until finally the American negotiators abandoned the French and made a deal directly with the British. Among other things, the Treaty of Paris, ratified by Congress in 1783, guaranteed American independence, established American control of all territory west to the Mississippi River, and promised British withdrawal from posts west of the Appalachian Mountains.

With his charge from Congress accomplished, Washington sought nothing more than to retire from public life and return to his wife Martha and his beloved Mount Vernon. But as word came of the Treaty of Paris, Washington's officers were in the midst of what could have been a most shameful ending to a most honorable achievement. Having fought a long and costly war, Washington's men awaited promised pay from Congress for their service to the new nation. In 1780, Congress had passed legislation that promised officers of the Continental Army a pension of half pay for life that was consistent with pensions granted by European states to their armies. Impatient and prone to ambitious talk, Washington's officers anxiously awaited word at their winter camp in Newburgh, New York, that this promise would be carried out before Congress disbanded the army.

At issue among these officers was more than just back pay and promised pensions, however. Many nationalist officers and like-minded members of Congress wished to increase the power of Congress to strengthen the central government over the growing power of the individual states, which had plagued national governance during the war. General Alexander McDougall presented a petition to Congress from these officers that demanded the pension in one lump-sum payment. Despite strong support among nationalists in Congress and implied threats that the army might not obey a congressional order to disband, Congress refused the petition. The old fear of a standing army still held prominence despite the Continental Army's vital role in achieving independence; it had fulfilled its duty and was no longer needed. At Newburgh, gossip and idle talk escalated; various circulars were passed around the officer corps in camp, including one that called for a meeting to respond to Congress' refusal to meet their demands and another that outright threatened mutiny against congressional authority.

Washington sympathized with the officers' frustrations but did not support their threats against Congress. To Washington, civil-military relations were paramount to the survival of the young American nation. He already had made plans to return his commission to Congress and had ideas about the establishment of a permanent military structure to defend the security of the new nation. But such talk of mutiny and defiance of civilian authority could gravely taint not only Washington's reputation, which he certainly held most dear, but also that of the United States as a new country.

When Washington got wind of a pending meeting where the discontented officers were to air their grievances and plan what they would do about Congress's failure to act, he called a preemptive meeting. In the officers' barracks in Newburgh, Washington reminded them of their service and obligation to their country. He appealed to their sense of duty and patriotism then promised to ensure that their sacrifice would not go unrewarded by Congress. When pleading his case before them, Washington took from his pocket a letter suggesting that Congress would address their concerns. He began to read it but then stopped, putting on a pair of eyeglasses. His men had never seen him wear glasses. Washington told them he had not only grown gray in their service, he was now growing blind. He left the building, leaving some officers in tears. They passed a resolution pledging their support of Congress. The so-called Newburgh Conspiracy had collapsed, affirming civilian control of the first national army in American history and setting the precedent of military noninterference in government affairs. Although Washington had prevented what would have been a disastrous movement, less than a month later Pennsylvania troops in the Continental Army marched against Congress, meeting in the Pennsylvania statehouse in Philadelphia and demanding discharge and back pay. Congress refused their demands and the crisis abated, but as Washington feared, such action fueled concerns about a standing army in a republic.

With the navy all but dissolved, Congress debated what to do with the army it had created back in 1775. To avoid more mutinies and disaffection among the officer corps, Robert Morris, a financial wizard, worked out a way to pay the troops as Congress slowly furloughed and then discharged them. By 1784, only a handful of troops remained, most at Continental Army headquarters at West Point along the Hudson River in New York. The Continental Army that had won American independence ceased to exist. Although its tradition remained strong as an organization, the Continental Army was only a temporary structure created to fight the British in a war. It was never meant to be a permanent fixture of American security.

With independence won, many in Congress saw no need for a permanent military establishment. State militias could ably defend the United States against foreign enemies, as they had done in the past. Congress, however, seriously considered the problem and appointed a committee—chaired by one of Washington's staff officers, Alexander Hamilton of New York—to study the issue of a permanent standing army. Hamilton and other New Yorkers had earlier balked provisions in the Articles of Confederation that had governed the states since 1781 prohibiting individual states from creating permanent armies. With the British still occupying forts in predominantly native lands west of the Appalachian Mountains, New York wanted to use its contingent of Continentals to relieve the British and keep watch over Native Americans and settlers along the frontier. Other states had similar concerns, and many in Congress came to accept that the westward growth of the new nation combined with its unique security needs required some sort of permanent military establishment.

Hamilton's committee solicited the opinion of Washington, who in turn asked his senior generals, including Knox and von Steuben, to weigh in on the matter. All supported creating a national army to police the western frontier, establishing a navy, building coastal fortifications and arsenals to equip this force, and founding military schools to promote the study of the military arts. All agreed that militia was inadequate for these functions.

The problem was, however, to create such an establishment without arousing traditional fears of a standing army, without creating an elite military class, and without giving the new government the power to tax. To make the concept more appealing to the states, Washington and his colleagues proposed reforming the traditional militia system by making it uniform from state to state, improving training, and improving the quality of the militia officer corps. With such improvements a standing national army of militia numbering perhaps around 25,000 could be at the ready to defend the nation from any outside attack.

In his final report to Hamilton, Washington recommended these proposals and additionally suggested that active duty militia should serve as a real national army to discourage foreign attack and defend the western frontier. Four infantry regiments and one artillery regiment, some 2,600 officers and men, could protect New England against an attack from Canada, defend the Great Lakes region, patrol the Ohio River Valley, and protect the Georgia and Carolina frontier. Arsenals, a military staff, and even a military academy to train artillerists and engineers rounded out Washington's plan for a national military establishment.

Hamilton liked the proposals, not the least because they suited his nationalist political leanings. He accepted Washington's ideas in principle but went further to centralize the new military in the national government rather than in the states, as had been the militia tradition. Hamilton proposed that Congress rather than the states appoint officers, recruit and pay the troops, and supply the army. He also wanted to make the national army the core for an expansible army during a national emergency. Finally, the committee recommended that the new national army be an army of citizen volunteers rather than made up of state militia.

While both Washington's and Hamilton's proposals made sense as a means to provide security for the new nation, convincing a Congress with little money and a people who held fast to a strong anti-standing army tradition to accept these ideas was another matter. Although Hamilton's report to Congress coincided with the Pennsylvania mutiny, Congress still approached these radical ideas with extreme caution if not hesitancy. Worse still for Hamilton and his committee was that under the Articles of Confederation, Congress could not raise an army during peacetime. Politically, too many in Congress continued to think regionally. They abhorred centralized government at the expense of state power and understandably convinced themselves of plots by nationalists, ambitious military men, and others to use a national army to seize control of Congress. While many of Hamilton's proposals ultimately found their way into the nation's military establishment in the early nineteenth century, doing so just after the end of the War for Independence made Congress unenthusiastic about meddling with what they perceived as a sound military policy that had brought success in the war.

The national government did not yet have the legal structure or the political will to create a permanent military structure. As it stood in 1784, the best Congress could do was to raise a temporary force of 700 state militiamen to defend the frontier against Indian attack. The next year, Congress transformed this hodgepodge creation into a regular army unit called the 1st American Regiment. Under the command of Pennsylvanian Josiah Harmar, the 1st American Regiment never had the strength or the support to effectively deal with either natives or the British on the frontier.

WASHINGTON RETURNS HIS COMMISSION TO CONGRESS

On December 23, 1783, George Washington did something rather extraordinary for one who held so much popularity and power at the end of the American War for Independence—he resigned his commission, returning it to Congress, the body that had originally given him this power. Washington knew this act would set a precedent for civil-military relations in the new nation. He also thought he could retire to his farms at Mount Vernon to never again be called to public service. Congress accepted the commission, and gave a letter of thanks to its commander-in-chief.

Annapolis, Maryland 23 December 1783

Mr. President:

The great events on which my resignation depended having at length taken place; I have now the honor of offering my sincere Congratulations to Congress and of presenting myself before them to surrender into their hands the trust committed to me, and to claim the indulgence of retiring from the Service of my Country.

Happy in the confirmation of our Independence and Sovereignty, and pleased with the oppertunity afforded the United States of becoming a respectable Nation, I resign with satisfaction the Appointment I accepted with diffidence. A diffidence in my abilities to accomplish so arduous a task, which however was superseded by a confidence in the rectitude of our Cause, the support of the Supreme Power of the Union, and the patronage of Heaven.

The Successful termination of the War has verified the most sanguine expectations, and my gratitude for the interposition of Providence, and the assistance I have received from my Countrymen, encreases with every review of the momentous Contest.

While I repeat my obligations to the Army in general, I should do injustice to my own feelings not to acknowledge in this place the peculiar Services and distinguished merits of the Gentlemen who have been attached to my person during the War. It was impossible the choice of confidential Officers to compose my family should have been more fortunate. Permit me Sir, to recommend in particular those, who have continued in Service to the present moment, as worthy of the favorable notice and patronage of Congress.

I consider it an indispensable duty to close this last solemn act of my Official life, by commending the Interests of our dearest Country to the protection of Almighty God, and those who have the superintendence of them, to his holy keeping.

Having now finished the work assigned me, I retire from the great theatre of Action; and bidding an Affectionate farewell to this August body under whose orders I have so long acted, I here offer my Commission, and take my leave of all the employments of public life.

Source: The George Washington Papers, Library of Congress.

◆ A NEW CONSTITUTION

In September 1786, a mob of angry farmers in western Massachusetts descended upon Springfield to protest requirements that property taxes be paid in specie rather than with paper currency. A struggling postwar economy, high taxes, restrictive requirements for voting and office holding, foreclosures, and the threat of debtor's prison made life for many in rural Massachusetts difficult. It seemed that the divide between the political and financial power of Boston versus the poor economic conditions of the Massachusetts hinterland had reached a breaking point. Instigated by Samuel Ely and Luke Day, what became known as Shays' Rebellion started as a farmer's protest but turned into an armed rebellion.

The event's namesake, Daniel Shays, was a veteran of the War for Independence. After fighting at Bunker Hill, Saratoga, and Stony Point, Shays fell on hard times upon returning to his farm in Pelham, Massachusetts. Shays had attended several town meetings to air farmers' grievances, and when the Massachusetts legislature adjourned in the summer of 1786 without addressing these concerns the farmers decided to shut down court proceedings in Northampton and Worcester. With his military experience, Shays was chosen to lead the "army" of farmers against the militia that Massachusetts governor James Bowdoin sent to quell the uprising. Shays led his band of rebels to Springfield in January 1787 to capture the arsenal there but were turned back by Bowdoin's militia, under the command of Benjamin Lincoln and Rufus Putnam. Lincoln chased Shays and his army of about 1,200 to Petersham, where he defeated the rebels and ended the rebellion. Shays escaped. Newly elected governor John Hancock addressed many of the farmers' concerns and pardoned all of the rebels except for Shays and other leaders of the uprising. Shays was tried and convicted in absentia for treason and sentenced to death, but was later pardoned.

Congress attempted to send a force of over 2,000 men under General Henry Knox to defend the arsenal at Springfield and stop the rebellion, but raised only a token force and was thus left powerless to do much of anything. The Articles of Confederation made Congress impotent to deal with such domestic crises. Shays' Rebellion alerted many, including Washington, to the weaknesses of the Confederation. If Congress could not put down an uprising of Massachusetts farmers, how could it defend the country against a foreign attack? Although it was just one of many reasons that political leaders from across the states agreed to attend a convention that would reconsider the Articles of Confederation, Shays' Rebellion underscored the need to address the absence of adequate military power at the national level.

◆ THE CONSTITUTION AND THE MILITARY

As what became the Constitutional Convention convened in Philadelphia during the summer of 1787, few of those present doubted that the principal purpose of a national government was to provide for the security of the nation and its citizens. Exactly how to provide that security without also creating a potentially oppressive centralized government that could endanger the rights of those same citizens was a question that occupied much of the ensuing debate that long hot summer. One of the first decisions made by the delegates reflected the importance of military matters in reforming the national government. George Washington, convinced to come out of retirement to return to public life as a delegate from Virginia, was chosen to preside over the convention. Who else but the man who epitomized public virtue despite having exercised supreme military power could symbolically assure the American people that the secret meetings in the Pennsylvania statehouse were for the public good?

Deciding to scrap the old Articles of Confederation, the delegates created instead a new government structure based upon balance and separation of powers to provide for the security of the new nation while at the same time protecting the power of the states and individual rights from burdensome government intrusion. It was a delicate process that required compromise and forethought, for the nation would surely change and grow with coming generations.

In military matters, the new Constitution provided for the creation of a national military establishment, the power over which was shared between the new Congress and the chief executive, or president. Article 1 authorized Congress to establish an army and navy and collect taxes to provide for the maintenance of both. It could also regulate and provide for militia and use state militia in national service. Funding for the army was limited to two years, so that every two years Congress could determine whether to continue the existence of a standing army via new budgetary appropriations.

While Congress had the supreme power and authority to declare war in the new Constitution, Article 2 made the president the commander-in-chief of national military forces and gave him authority to commission officers with the consent of the upper house of Congress, the Senate. Authority for military affairs was shared, then, between Congress and the executive branch, both civilian bodies. Such power sharing was designed to prevent despotic abuse of whatever national military power might be created.

The states reserved the right to maintain their own militias, which would serve as a check against the national standing army. But they lost all other sovereign uses of military power. They could not declare war, enter into alliances, or maintain an army or navy in peacetime. States appointed their own militia officers, but training, procurement, and organization were mandated by Congress to assure uniformity and effectiveness.

Great debate surrounded the new document. The ratification process stirred nationalist and antinationalist emotions alike. Those against a strong national government created by the Constitution argued that the document gave excessive military power to the national government and to the president in particular. Nationalists countered that checks and balances made it extremely unlikely that any government body or individual would be able to undertake such an abuse of power. In the end, the Constitution was ratified by the summer of 1788, putting a new government in place in 1789.

As part of the compromise to attain ratification, however, the first Congress that met in 1789 was obliged to enumerate rights not listed in the Constitution. These first amendments to the Constitution collectively became known as the Bill of Rights, and included important protections against abuses by a standing military. The Second Amendment firmly embedded the militia as a sort of failsafe measure against abusive federal power by granting citizens the right to bear and maintain arms. Mindful of the uproar caused by the Quartering Act, the Third Amendment prohibited the quartering of troops in people's homes.

◆ CONCLUSION

The War for Independence made the American Revolution possible, a revolution that was realized in the drafting and ratification of the Constitution in 1787–1789. The United States had been born through the force of arms. A dual citizen army made up of both militia and volunteers made it possible to break the link binding the colonies with Great Britain, but the hardships of that process did not go unnoticed when the framers of the Constitution considered how to provide for the security of the United States. Civilian control over the military was maintained throughout the process of securing independence and establishing a national government. No hereditary military class grew out of this experience, as many had feared might occur.

With an ocean discouraging European intervention into the affairs of the new republic, security seemed assured. But such was not the case; the United States faced threats from within and abroad, threats that forced the nation to continue to consider its military establishment and use of military power in a democracy.

Further Reading

Allen, Thomas B. Tories: Fighting for the King in America's First Civil War. New York: Harper, 2010.

Black, Jeremy. *War for America: The Fight for Independence, 1775–1783*. New York: St. Martin's Press, 1991.

Bobrick, Benson. *Angel in the Whirlwind: The Triumph of the American Revolution*. New York: Simon and Schuster, 1997.

Coakley, Robert W., and Stetson Conn. *The War of the American Revolution*. Washington, D.C.: United States Army Center for Military History, 2004.

Countryman, Edward. *The American Revolution*. Revised ed. New York: Hill and Wang, 2003.

Ferling, John. *Almost a Miracle: The American Victory in the War of Independence*. New York: Oxford, 2009.

Fischer, David Hackett. *Washington's Crossing*. New York: Oxford University Press, 2004.

Flexner, James Thomas. *Washington: The Indispensable Man*. Boston: Little Brown, 1974.

Frey, Sylvia R. *The British Soldier in America: A Social History of Military Life in the Revolutionary Period*. Austin: University of Texas Press, 1981.

Griffith, Samuel B. *The War for Independence*. Chicago: University of Chicago Press, 2002.

Hibbert, Christopher. *Redcoats and Rebels: The American Revolution through British Eyes*. New York: W.W. Norton, 2002.

Higginbotham, Don. *The War of American Independence: Military Attitudes, Policies, and Practice, 1763–1789*. New York: Macmillan, 1971.

Kohn, Richard H. *Eagle and Sword: The Federalists and the Creation of the Military Establishment in America, 1783–1802*. New York: The Free Press, 1975.

MacKesy, Piers. *The War for America, 1775–1783*. Reprint ed. Lincoln: University of Nebraska Press, 1993.

McCullough, David. *1776*. New York: Simon & Schuster, 2005.

Morgan, Edmund S. *The Birth of the Republic, 1763–1789*. 3rd ed. Chicago: University of Chicago Press, 1992.

Patterson, Benton Rain. *Washington and Cornwallis: The Battle for America, 1775–1783*. New York: Taylor, 2004.

Randall, Willard Sterne. *George Washington: A Life*. New York: Henry Holt, 1997.

Richards, Leonard L. *Shays's Rebellion: The American Revolution's Final Battle*. Philadelphia: University of Pennsylvania Press, 2003.

Royster, Charles. *A Revolutionary People at War: The Continental Army and American Character, 1775–1783.* New York: W.W. Norton, 1975.

Shy, John. *A People Numerous and Armed: Reflections on the Military Struggle for American Independence.* Revised ed. Ann Arbor: University of Michigan Press, 1990.

mysearchlab Connections: Sources Online ● ● ● ● ● ● ● ● ● ● ●

READ AND REVIEW

Review this chapter by using the study aids and these related documents available on MySearchLab.

Study Plan

Chapter Test

Essay Test

Documents

Joseph Warren, "Account of the Battle of Lexington" (1775)

Dr. Joseph Warren, president of the Massachusetts Provincial Congress, gave this account of the first battle of the American War for Independence in an open letter to the people of Great Britain.

Letter from a Revolutionary War Soldier (1776)

Thomas Rodney's letter to his brother Caesar describes his experience in crossing the Delaware River on Christmas night 1776.

William Dobein James, The Rise of Partisan Warfare in the South (1778)

William Dobein James recounts the battles at Waxhaws and King's Mountain.

Military Reports on Shays' Rebellion (1787)

Officers of the Massachusetts militia report to Governor James Bowdoin their preparations to put down Shays' Rebellion.

RESEARCH AND EXPLORE

Explore the following review questions using the research tools available on www.mysearchlab.com.

1. What advantages and disadvantages did the American rebels and British forces have to contend with during the American War for Independence?

2. How and why did British strategy change during the war? What was the American strategy?

3. What weaknesses in military affairs under the Articles of Confederation did the new Constitution attempt to address?

CHAPTER 4

The Young Nation and Its Young Military Challenged

◆ INTRODUCTION

Despite the significant improvement of the new Constitution over the ineffective Articles of Confederation, the new nation remained nonetheless weak and vulnerable. The idealism of the anti-Federalists, or Republicans, held that the new nation could defend itself by rallying citizen militia that would patriotically answer the call to arms in a crisis. The Federalists on the other hand had taken a much more realistic view, maintaining that nothing short of a regular army and strong navy could adequately defend the new nation against foreign designs.

Threats to the young United States were indeed real. Great Britain retained control of Canada. Various confederations of Native American tribes held sway along much of the frontier. Spain held Florida, and republican France had regained the vast Louisiana Territory. Despite the ocean separating the United States from the European continent, events in Europe would have a great impact upon the new nation. Great Britain and Napoleonic France would war on each other during much of this period for the United States. A sound military policy was essential, but competing partisan visions of the new nation's future made creating such a policy difficult. Instead, the United States took a compromising and reactionary course that placed its very existence in jeopardy as it fended fend off a variety of predators to survive its fledgling years.

To meet these national security challenges, the United States had to overcome the traditional politicization of its military affairs. Reaction to unforeseen threats guided a patchwork military policy. The Quasi War with France, troubles with the tribes of the Northwest Territory, Barbary pirates, and the Napoleonic Wars forced the United States to defend its ill-concealed craving for economic growth and territorial expansion.

◆ BUILDING AN ARMY

The traditional fear of a standing army and support for a citizen militia blocked President George Washington's efforts to establish a viable regular army at almost every turn. The various states jealously guarded their long-standing militias and control over them. The federal government had little money to support state militias, much less for a national army. Few Americans wanted to serve in the regular army anyway, preferring instead the prestige associated with many local militia units that had come to resemble social clubs more than effective military forces. Washington's vision of a national militia or reserve force was infeasible in the climate of the new Republic. Instead, the states clung precariously to their militia traditions.

Congress only reluctantly passed legislation regulating state militias. The Calling Forth Act of 1792 authorized the president as commander-in-chief to exercise his Constitutional prerogative to call out the militia to enforce the law or suppress rebellion, but only if a federal judge had certified that local authorities no longer exercised civil control. It said nothing about using the militia to stop an invasion by a foreign power.

The Uniform Militia Act, passed the same year by Congress, required all able-bodied men from the ages of 18 to 45 to enroll in local militia units and provide their own weapons and equipment. No militiaman would be required to serve more than three months in a 12-month period. To Washington the law was an utter failure. He wanted standardized militia across the nation, well trained and equipped to meet a national emergency. What he got was a law that failed to punish states for noncompliance; the response by many states was to simply ignore the law and continue to organize militia along regionalized models just as they had as colonies. Officers continued to be appointed locally, training remained inconsistent, and politics infested militia issues at every level.

Still Congress could not ignore the potential threats to American security. A standing army, no matter how distasteful, was necessary. In 1790, the United States Army consisted of the 1st American Regiment and an artillery battalion to total just over 1,200 men. In response to Indian trouble in the Ohio River Valley and Kentucky, Congress authorized the formation of the Legion of the United States in 1792. The creation of Secretary of War Henry Knox, the Legion of the United States had its organizational roots in the old Roman legion system. As a mixed force of infantry, cavalry, and artillery, the legion system allowed for flexibility in balance and organization, enabling a legion to meet whatever crisis it was sent to face. Perhaps more important politically, Congress liked the idea of a "legion" because it did not bring to mind unpleasant visions of a standing army. Four sublegions of 1,800 troops each comprised the Legion of the United States. Congress reorganized the Legion into the 1st, 2nd, 3rd, and 4th Regiments of Infantry and a Corps of Artillerists and Engineers. In 1798 the cavalry was reconfigured into the Regiment of Light Dragoons, and in 1808 a light artillery regiment was created along with a regiment of riflemen. As the tensions between the United States and Britain and France escalated from 1807 to 1812, more regiments were authorized. Increasing the size of the Legion was a contentious issue because Congress was always strapped for funds and Republicans resisted the growth of the standing army.

◆ FIGHTING INDIANS AND INSURRECTION

Much of the reorganization occurred while the Army was in the field engaged against native tribes in the Old Northwest Territory. Often at British instigation but certainly prompted by threats to their own autonomy and territorial integrity, the tribes of the lower Great Lakes and the Ohio River Valley were forced to stand against the slowly growing tide of settlers from east of the Appalachians. Although the War for Independence was over and the British had agreed to withdraw from their posts in the west, they had not done so; nor had Native Americans ceased to resist encroaching settlers. The Delaware, Miami, Ottawa, Cherokee, Shawnee, Chippewa, and others intimidated, raided, and killed settlers who ventured into what the natives considered their lands and the settlers considered American territory. Resolving these conflicts could happen in one of two ways—by treaty or by force. Often, settlers failed to respect the provisions of treaties, thus virtually guaranteeing the use of force to reach a final solution.

Initial efforts to deal with Native Americans in the Old Northwest Territory offered little promise and said much about the poor organization and leadership of the Army and a lack of national direction for policy. Responding to raids that President Washington and Secretary of War Knox thought had been staged by renegade bands of Shawnee and Cherokee, Washington ordered territorial governor Arthur St. Clair and General Josiah Harmar, commander of the 1st Regiment, to organize a punitive expedition into Indian territory to deal with what was then considered a nuisance. Washington's instructions seemed fairly clear—punish the renegade raiders, respect legitimate tribal authority, and offer peace whenever possible. St. Clair and Harmar had other ideas; both wanted an intense campaign to end the problem once and for all.

Initial peace efforts made no progress, leading St. Clair to call for militia from Kentucky to join the 1st Regiment at Fort Washington (Cincinnati) for a campaign against Wabash and Miami villages in Indiana and Ohio. President Washington ordered levies of 2,000 volunteers to augment the regulars and militia in part to establish federal control at the expense of state militias. Levies were not militia; thus, the administration did not have to worry about the political consequences of calling state militias to serve outside their home areas on a long dangerous campaign.

[Washington had decided to use force to ensure peace between settlers and Native Americans. St. Clair planned a two-prong campaign that divided his force to raid the villages, then establish a post on the Maumee River to ensure the security of the region. Washington, Knox, and General Harmar approved the plan less the establishment of the Maumee post. It possibly never occurred to Washington or Knox, or St. Clair, that the expedition might meet defeat and start a larger war, perhaps even the British. St. Clair had planned a difficult 2,000-man campaign against an uprising that probably could have been quelled with a quick raid conducted by light cavalry.

FIGURE 4-1 Indian Resistance 1790–1816.

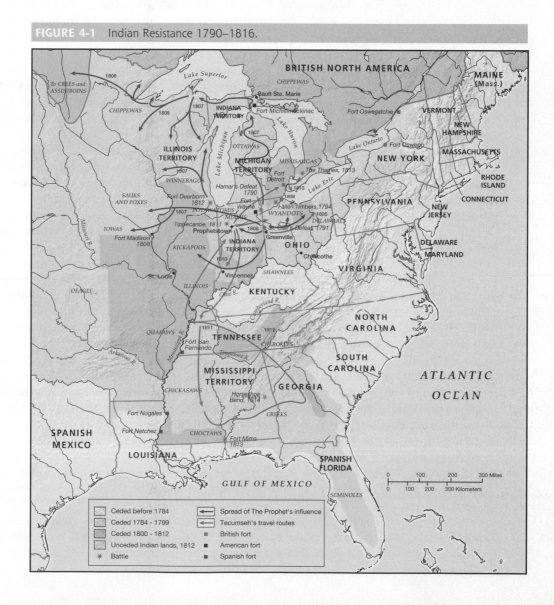

Harmar took his force toward the Maumee River in October. Discipline suffered, militia and regulars did not get along, and a long cumbersome baggage train slowed the expedition's pace to about ten miles a day. Although the force destroyed several native villages, when it faced the natives in battle it suffered embarrassing defeats. Harmar insisted on splitting his force and further allowed his subcommanders to divide their forces in a strategy that played into the natives' hands by allowing them to engage smaller American units rather than being drawn into a set-piece battle against the entire expedition. By the end of October Harmar turned back, having lost 200 men. One hundred and fifty years of warfare with the Indians had taught the Americans very little, it seemed. Harmar and St. Clair tried their best to put a positive spin on a near-disastrous campaign, but Washington and Knox were not fooled.

St. Clair organized another effort for 1791. This time he commanded the expedition as a major general. The War Department approved his plan for a force of 3,000 men, including a new regiment of regulars, volunteer cavalry, and another levy to serve for four months. However, such shortcuts did not guarantee better troops, and the levies were often poorly trained, lacked discipline, and generally displayed low morale. As part of the campaign, a string of posts was established northward from Fort Washington to keep tribes in the region under control. Knox was explicit in his instructions to St. Clair and insisted upon constant communication between Fort Washington and Philadelphia.

Nothing went right. Logistics broke down, leaving many soldiers without adequate clothing and ammunition. The levies often had only a few muskets with which to train, much less fight. Discipline among the levies became a serious problem, and even the regulars sank into undisciplined disarray. Smallpox also ravaged the camps. St. Clair absented himself from the preparations to run frivolous errands to Fort Washington or Kentucky. His lack of leadership caused infectious dissent among his officer corps. The expedition finally set off in early October with less than 1,500 troops and traveled only about five miles a day. Because of the delays in getting started, the three-month enlistments for many of the levies began to expire. They understandably wanted to go home.

The ultimate disaster hit St. Clair's force on November 4. St. Clair knew his army was not prepared to face a large force of Indian warriors, a fact the Indians knew as well from their own scouts and American deserters. As the expedition camped under full alert along the Wabash River the night of November 3, over 1,000 Miami and allied warriors, including a young Shawnee named Tecumseh, prepared to attack under the able generalship of Little Turtle. Early in the morning of November 4, just as many of the soldiers and levies assumed that the height of danger had passed, the warriors made their move to overrun the camp. The levies and militia broke, then ran for their lives but were cut down by native warriors as they fled. Regulars formed a line and held out for nearly three hours before breaking through to flee southward. Over 600 Americans had been killed and another 300 wounded in the attack. It was an unmitigated disaster of American arms. St. Clair, however, was cleared of any negligence, as Washington and Knox could not politically afford to admit they had placed the wrong general in command.

St. Clair's Defeat, as it is known, brought down a rain of criticism upon Washington's administration. Many in the eastern parts of the United States claimed that land-hungry settlers and frontiersmen had initiated the conflict by violating already-established treaties and informal agreements with the Indians. Others worried that the costly campaigns were destroying what little of the Army was left and pushing the young nation toward financial ruin. Still others voiced concerns that such intense focus on the native problem ignored threatening developments in Europe. Washington made an earnest effort to make negotiations with the Indians work, but he also made plans for a proper punitive campaign to bring the tribes of the northwest finally under government control.

With suspicion of standing armies still strong in the United States, Washington's plan to enlarge the Army and not use levies or militia in the coming campaign was politically if not militarily risky. To command this new expanded force Washington chose aggressive and courageous General "Mad" Anthony Wayne. Diplomatic efforts gave Wayne almost two full years to train and equip his new army, and he used the time to mold it into a well-disciplined fighting force. But Wayne was eager, and the two-year wait frustrated him despite his recognition that having the extra time had given him a much better army than he would have had if the campaign had begun in 1792. While negotiations took place and made little headway, Wayne received often conflicting orders that did not allow him properly to pave the way for an invasion into native lands. Knox did not want to provoke the tribes by making an overtly offensive movement, yet Wayne's idea of preparing an offensive campaign made unconcealed offensive preparations necessary. When talks seemed to have stalled in the fall of 1793, Knox ordered Wayne to move out. The force did not get far before disease, low numbers of recruits, and lack of supplies forced a discouraged Wayne to abort the campaign. He stopped in October to winter at newly built Fort Greenville. Native warriors raided and sniped at his posts, knowing that Wayne could do little in retaliation while talks took place.

Meanwhile, it became clear to Washington and others in the United States that the British indeed supported and encouraged native attacks on the United States. Long suspected, the proof came when Chief Joseph Brant publicly claimed that British Indian agents in the west were paying off natives to make attacks on American settlements and outposts. This was further confirmed when the British built Fort Miamis on the north bank of the Maumee River just above the rapids from Lake Erie.

The tribal alliance, however, had begun to crumble despite the leadership of Chiefs Little Turtle and Blue Jacket. Wayne was ordered to destroy the tribal alliance and eject the British from American territory. In July 1794, Wayne's force reached the confluence of the Auglaize and Maumee Rivers to establish Fort Defiance. His movements thus far had been peaceful as several tribes bowed to his superiority in numbers and strength. Little Turtle nonetheless refused to surrender.

In August Wayne moved his force closer to the British fort where Little Turtle also was encamped. Early in the morning on August 20, Wayne's scouts ran into a line of native warriors and Canadian militia in an area of fallen trees and undergrowth. In what became known as the Battle of Fallen Timbers, Wayne slowly pushed the Indians back toward Fort Miamis. The natives finally broke and ran for the fort only to find the gate shut and barred. The British faced a choice—support their native allies and risk war with the United States or abandon their friends and avoid a broader conflict. They chose the latter. Little Turtle's force disintegrated. For several days Wayne and his troops razed Native American villages and storehouses around the fort and burned nearby fields of crops. The British did not reply despite Wayne's overtly aggressive attempts to goad them into battle.

By November Wayne was back at Fort Greenville. In 1795 he concluded the Treaty of Greenville with the tribal confederation to give the United States complete control of the region and pave the way for the Jay Treaty with Great Britain to finally remove the British from American territory. Wayne's triumph erased four years of misguided, poorly implemented, and strategically failed military and political policies to return peace to the Northwest Territory and restore some honor to the United States Army.

While Wayne was advancing up the Maumee River toward Fort Miamis to deal with the native problem in the Northwest Territory, another threat to the stability of the new nation erupted in western Pennsylvania. The Whiskey Rebellion was the most serious internal challenge the new nation had faced to that time. Farmers in western Pennsylvania responded violently to the new federal excise tax on whiskey passed by Congress as part of Secretary of the Treasury Alexander Hamilton's plan to reduce the national debt. Farmers often used homemade whiskey as a medium of exchange in rural areas; thus, the tax hit these farmers hardest.

As in the early days of the Revolution, citizens resisted government attempts to collect a legally authorized tax. Mobs of farmers attacked tax collectors and interfered with other government business. Much of western Pennsylvania government ceased to

FIGURE 4-2   General Anthony Wayne.

Source: Library of Congress Print and Reproductions Division
[LC-DIG-pga-02142]

function. Supreme Court Justice James Wilson certified that the courts in the region no longer operated, thus allowing President Washington to declare a state of emergency and send troops and militia into the area to restore order.

Washington's decision to use force after the rebels ignored his order to disperse is intriguing. The authority of the new government had been directly and violently challenged. Because of Wayne's campaign in the Northwest, Washington had little military force available and was left with only militia. He was hesitant to use the Army in any case since doing so would make it easy for Republicans to contend that the "true nature" of the Federalist army had been revealed—could this be a Federalist plot? Washington concluded that only militia could deal with the crisis and the militia had to be under control of the federal government in order for the government to retain its authority.

Washington put out the call for militia, to which Pennsylvania, New Jersey, Virginia, and Maryland responded with 13,000 troops. Washington actually commanded the force for a few weeks before turning it over to Henry Lee and Hamilton. As it marched on Pittsburgh, which the rebels had threatened to burn to the ground, the rebellion collapsed. Only a handful of rebels were arrested; only two were tried for treason and they were subsequently pardoned.

Using force against the Indians of the Northwest Territory and the rebels in western Pennsylvania were decisions crucial to the development of the new Republic. Washington had made it clear that the national government would use executive power to enforce the laws of the land and protect Americans on the frontier. After the "successes" of Wayne's campaign and putting down the Whiskey Rebellion, Federalists could argue with some ease that the nation needed a permanent standing army to garrison frontier posts and guard against internal rebellion. Republicans countered that such an army could just as easily be used against the people of the United States in an abuse of power that could destroy the Republic. Besides, now that the British finally had agreed to quit their posts on the American frontier, a large army no longer seemed necessary. Republicans argued that settlers on western lands could defend themselves through the American tradition of organized militia.

In 1796 Congress disbanded the Legion of the United States, leaving only four infantry regiments and some dragoons. It was a clear signal that standing armies were still viewed with suspicion. Although the Army still existed, it did so in a tenuous state. Yet, the fact remained that there was a standing, though very small army that could be expanded upon during crisis to meet threats against the Republic. This would remain the model and policy for American military organization for the next 100 years.

◆ AN ACADEMY AT WEST POINT

Of equal symbolic importance in the political conflict between Federalists and Republicans over the establishment of a permanent military was the founding of the United States Military Academy at West Point. As headquarters for the Corps of Artillerists and Engineers, the old fort on the Hudson River had been the site of an earlier attempt to formalize officer training under the tutelage of foreign officers in the 1790s. It seems that no American officers had the knowledge or training to skillfully teach gunnery; thus, foreign officers were commissioned to do the job. Young lieutenants and captains deeply resented being taught by foreigners, and the foreign officers themselves soon got crossways with fellow American officers—so much so that in one case an argument led to a duel (without injury to either party, thankfully). Using foreign officers to train American artillerists stopped in 1798.

In the meantime, Washington had called for a military academy to train new officers during peacetime. By 1800 the various models for such an academy under consideration did not include what the Corps of Artillerists and Engineers had attempted. Alexander Hamilton pushed one model in 1799 that included an academy of five schools, beginning with a basic school for all cadets followed by schools for specific branches of service as well as for naval service. Hamilton's plan was watered down to include only the basic school and a school for artillery and engineers. The plan went to Congress but was defeated. Republicans saw it as a Federalist plot to further that party's domination of the small officer corps, and many Federalists voted against the idea because it originated with the controversial Hamilton.

In 1800, Secretary of War Samuel Dexter reintroduced the idea of a military academy for artillerists and engineers. Dexter presented his plan as organizationally efficient, and proposed combining training for artillerists and engineers in a single location. Because these regiments already existed, Congressional approval was not needed save for appropriation. It was a good idea to circumvent the bitter politics of Congress, but the timing fell flat as President John Adams' term ended before the school could be formally established.

Thomas Jefferson—long an opponent of a military academy, claiming that such an institution was not provided for in the Constitution—entered office in 1801 and quickly established just such an institution. After barely a month in office, Jefferson and his Secretary of War, Henry Dearborn, hired a mathematics teacher to conduct classes for artillerists and engineers at West Point. Carlisle and Springfield had been considered as suitable sites for an academy, but Dearborn decided upon West Point. By 1801, Carlisle was a dismal post and Springfield Arsenal was just a few small buildings. West Point, on the other hand, was an established post and a well-maintained fortification. Through the Peace Establishment Act of 1802 Congress formally established the academy.

The Peace Establishment Act not only gave congressional approval for a military academy, it also dramatically reshaped the Army. It authorized Jefferson as Commander-in-Chief to discharge many Federalist officers and replace them with Republicans. The academy provided an easy means to introduce Republican officers to the lower ranks. It is odd that Jefferson, so long an opponent of a military academy and an enemy of a permanent military force, would support—let alone establish—such an institution. Some historians suggest that Jefferson wanted a top-notch school of science and mathematics to train engineers for civil use but the engineering curriculum was mediocre at best, comprising little beyond basic instruction and a few courses on military fortifications. Others more convincingly argue that establishing the academy was part of Jefferson's attempt to bring the Army and the government into closer harmony with Republican ideology and partisan goals.

Federalists had governed the nation since its founding; now it was the Republicans' turn, and Jefferson used his power as president to make sweeping social and political changes in all areas of government rather than just the military. His appointments to the academy clearly show favoritism toward the sons of loyal Republicans and an obvious intent to make Republicans into military officers. What should have been an attempt to depoliticize the officer corps served only to further politicize the Army's officers.

◆ BUILDING A NAVY

The Navy also increased in size and strength in reaction to world events. From the ratification of the Constitution to the end of the War of 1812 two competing naval policies characterized American maritime security strategy. Expanding American maritime trade demanded a deepwater fleet presence, while defending American shores from sea-borne threats required a naval presence beyond coastal fortifications. Politics, of course, weighed in on these strategic issues as Federalists supported a more outward-looking national security policy while Republicans looked inward to avoid provoking the European powers.

The Constitution had indeed authorized the creation and maintenance of a navy, and events at sea in the late 1780s warranted such an authorization. American merchant ships in the Mediterranean fell victim to the well-organized extortion racket of the Barbary pirate states of North Africa. Tensions between Great Britain and France brought on by the French Revolution also endangered American merchant ships since Americans traded with both of the belligerents. At the end of the War for Independence the United States Navy had been demobilized, and by 1785 it had all but ceased to exist. For over 100 years American merchants had depended upon, and expected the protection of the Royal Navy. Now, as the newly independent nation had no navy, American seagoing trade had become dangerously vulnerable.

Such circumstances made the U.S. government a ripe target for the North African pirate states of Morocco, Tripoli, Algiers, and Tunis. Each demanded and received ransom from the United States in exchange for the release of hostages and tribute in return for leaving American ships unmolested. Paying bribes also encouraged France and Britain to blatantly ignore the sovereign maritime rights of the new nation. The American flag on the high seas commanded little respect from either pirates or other seafaring nations.

Without a navy to protect its shipping, the young nation quickly found itself entangled in the conflict between its helpful ally France and its recent enemy Great Britain. Tensions between the two nations erupted in overt warfare in 1793, which further exacerbated the American shipping situation. The United States maintained that as a sovereign neutral nation it could trade with either belligerent while accepting that both nations had every right to confiscate war contraband. Through Orders in Council Great Britain added more and more goods to its contraband list with each passing month. The Royal Navy blockaded the French coast and declared that any goods bound for France were subject to seizure—neutrality be damned.

France grew embittered toward its former ally because the United States allowed trade with Great Britain. Still, French and British warships stopped and boarded American merchantmen to impress sailors who could not prove their citizenship. More than 300 impounded American merchant ships sat idle in British ports and hundreds of impressed American crewed Royal Navy ships. The United States government seemed powerless to do anything but offer the mildest protest.

A navy, however, might bring respect for the flag, and Congress began debating authorization for a fleet of first-rate warships. The debate was intense as critics condemned the establishment of a permanent navy and increased taxation to pay for the new ships. The current crisis, however, lent weight to the argument for a navy, and in March 1794 Congress authorized the creation of a six-frigate navy. The frigates were to be first-rate ships, a bold signal to Great Britain and France that the United States meant business.

Congress appropriated close to $700,000 to pay for ship construction and eagerly recognized the political benefit of building the new vessels, as contracts were handed out from New Hampshire to Virginia. Portsmouth, New Hampshire, built the 38-gun USS *Congress*; in Philadelphia, Joshua Humphreys designed and built the 44-gun *United States*; the famous 44-gun *Constitution* was built in Boston; Forman Cheesman built USS *President* with its 44 guns in New York; Baltimore laid the 38-gun *Constellation*; and the Norfolk shipyard produced the *Chesapeake* with its 38 guns. These were truly American ships—slaves cut down huge pines, cedars, and oaks along the Gulf Coast for framing, masts, and timbers, and Paul Revere made the brasswork for the *Constitution*.

In an attempt to resolve outstanding issues with Great Britain left over from the War for Independence, Washington sent Supreme Court Chief Justice John Jay to London to negotiate a treaty. As Jay left for London, the Republican faction in Congress managed to pass an embargo on American trade to British ports. This congressional effort to impress the British fell flat as Jay had no intention of being so firm with the British. In the end, Great Britain agreed to evacuate its forts in the American Northwest—which it was supposed to have done under the Treaty of Paris of 1783—and open trade in India to American merchant ships. Additionally, the British gained navigation rights on the Mississippi River, a concession that had the direst potential strategic consequences for the United States. Southern states complained bitterly that Jay had not secured financial compensation for slaves taken by the British in the War for Independence.

Jay's efforts achieved little. The British continued the practice of impressment, refused to recognize American neutrality in the war with France, and, in keeping with its rejection of American neutrality, Parliament also refused to let American ships pass through the Royal Navy's blockade of the French coast. Although the treaty sneaked through the Senate in 1795, Jay's work pleased no one. Protesters burned Jay in effigy, and the House of Representatives threatened to delay appropriations to enforce the treaty's provisions.

◆ THE QUASI WAR

France was incensed by the Jay Treaty and severed diplomatic relations with the United States in 1796. President Washington urged continuing the naval building program to increase the size of the Navy. Upon assuming the presidency in 1797, John Adams echoed his great predecessor but noted that the strength and size of the navy the United States required could not be built to meet the present crisis—it would be a long and laborious process that might take decades.

In April 1798 Congress established a Navy Department separate from the War Department and in July formally established the Marine Corps. Also, in July Congress appropriated money for twenty-four warships in addition to the six frigates already under construction. Tensions with France increased dramatically that same summer when the infamous XYZ Affair exposed French attempts to bribe American negotiators to begin talks on a new treaty with France. With President Adams' blessing, Congress nullified all existing treaties with France. The break with France appeared complete.

Thus began what became known as the Quasi War with France that lasted until late 1800. Neither side formally declared war nor were land forces ever used, although Federalists took the opportunity to enlarge the Army just in case. The Quasi War was a naval war fought mainly by privateers and in scattered ship-to-ship actions, taking place primarily in the West Indies. The U.S. Navy, however, was now much stronger than it had been in the War for Independence. Officers had some experience, and the new frigates were first-rate, fast, well-armed ships. Perhaps more importantly, American strategy also had matured. With much of its fleet trapped by the British blockade in harbors around the coast of France, the French navy could not mass a large force against the United States, much less the American navy. With the French fleet bottled up in home ports, the United States chose to hit France in the West Indies, the location of some of the most valuable French imperial possessions. Patrolling in four small squadrons across the Caribbean, the U.S. Navy achieved some spectacular successes.

Two of these involved the Navy's most promising officer, Thomas Truxtun. He not only captained the *Constellation* but had also overseen its construction. Truxtun was unusual among officers in the American navy. He wrote on naval tactics and practices and insisted that his subordinate officers study them. Truxtun was a consummate officer who viewed his naval service as a profession. In February 1799 Truxtun brought *Constellation* southeast of Nevis and engaged the French Frigate *L'Insurgente*. The French warship initially tried to mask its identity but then raised the French tricolor to bring on the fight. Both ships exchanged numerous broadsides in less than an hour as they headed toward St. Christopher. Truxtun concentrated his fire on the *L'Insurgente*'s gun decks to wreak horrific destruction upon the French crew. The French captain chose to follow standard French tactics and aimed for *Constellation*'s rigging. The American gunners proved superior in aim and rate of fire, forcing the *L'Insurgente* to surrender. Truxtun's crew suffered only five casualties, while the French lost as many as seventy.

Truxtun and the *Constellation* faced off against a larger French warship, the *Vengeance*, in February 1800. This time Truxton did not come away victorious, as the two ships squared off for over four hours in intense combat. Both were badly damaged, and as Truxtun maneuvered *Constellation* to board *Vengeance* the mainmast toppled to suddenly render his ship useless. *Vengeance* escaped but only to run aground four days later, never to sail again. Despite losing the prize, Truxtun firmly established himself as one of the best American naval commanders.

Diplomacy ended the Quasi War. France was forced to accept that it was no longer the principal ally of the United States and that the Jay Treaty between the United States and Great Britain was legal and binding. The United States was finally free of all obligations to France. Although at great political cost, Adams had kept the United States out of a full-scale war. Federalists and Republicans had become deeply divided over the Quasi War, a division that carried forward into the Jefferson administration. The fact remained, however, that the United States had gone toe-to-toe with France, a major power, and had emerged arguably in a better position.

◆ JEFFERSON'S GUNBOATS

Upon taking office as president, Thomas Jefferson began one of his most controversial military programs. Many in Congress agreed that coastal defense was a primary concern for the young United States, but opinion was sharply divided on how the coast should be defended. As president, Jefferson came to support a blue-water fleet as an important part of the overall American defensive strategy, but he doubted such a fleet's ability to defend the American coast and its all-important ports. Just before Jefferson took office the Federalist Congress slashed the Navy, leaving only a handful of frigates to patrol American shipping lanes and protect American interests abroad.

⌈To address the gap in the coastal defense system Jefferson proposed a fleet of shallow-draft gunboats⌋ These small craft, not more than 80 feet long and 20 feet across, seven feet of draft, and armed with a couple of 24- or 32-pounders, could move through coastal waters with relative ease. These one- or two-mast boats were part of Jefferson's coastal defense strategy complemented by floating gun platforms and coastal fortifications. Gunboats were cheap, which pleased Jefferson and Secretary of the Treasury, Albert Gallatin. With his gunboats Jefferson attempted to beef up coastal defense while decreasing the public debt and tax burden.⌋

⌈Gunboats were not a new idea. Most coastal European nations employed them for coastal defense, many with good success, and they had been used in the American War for Independence. Wherever gunboats had been used they had served as a complement to an overall naval strategy rather than as a replacement for seagoing vessels or permanent coastal fortifications. Cost savings were important as well. Not only did a $12,000 gunboat fall well below the cost of a new $300,000 frigate, a gunboat required only a small crew. Jefferson planned to recruit from the naval militias that manned fortifications at American ports and harbors. These citizen sailors would operate a few gunboats during times of peace and would also crew the many boats that could be brought out of mothballs during war. Maneuverable, versatile, economical, and, for the Republican Jefferson, egalitarian—on paper the gunboats seemed to have it all for a president of distinct political philosophy faced with complicated defense issues⌋

Similar to the construction of the frigates, the construction of the gunboat fleet offered an appropriations boom for several congressional districts. Jefferson wisely dispersed the contracts for individual boats around the nation to increase popular support for Republican policies other than the gunboat program and national security in Republican states and perhaps inspire modest gains in Federalist strongholds. From 1804 through 1808, contracts for 257 gunboats, of which 177 were actually built, were issued to contractors in 11 of the 17 states. Many of the contracts went to shipbuilders in New York, Massachusetts, Connecticut, South Carolina, and Virginia, while several were also awarded to builders along the Ohio River in Ohio and Kentucky as well as Lake Champlain and Lake Ontario. Some of these contracts went directly to congressmen and senators themselves—arms procurement and congressional politics have a long intimate history, indeed.

Politics also broadened the actual use of the gunboats. Jefferson did not hesitate to utilize these controversial craft for duties other than coastal defense. Gunboats Nos. 2–10 were sent to the Mediterranean to support American naval action against the Barbary pirates in 1805. Although none of the boats engaged in direct combat, one—No. 7—was lost at sea during the crossing. Gunboats were sent to New Orleans to patrol the mouth of the Mississippi River during the Burr conspiracy and afterward to scare privateers away from American shipping into and out of New Orleans. The 1807 Embargo Act brought gunboats to the fore of a failed national policy as the small craft served as the primary though ill-fitted tool for enforcing the embargo. Smugglers always used the fastest ships they could lay their hands on and they easily outran the lethargic gunboats, which were built for neither speed nor the open sea. In 1810, gunboats around Charleston vainly tried to put a dent in the now-illegal slave trade.

During the War of 1812, gunboats were used primarily for their original purpose—coastal defense. Their actual record, however, was mixed. Gunboats often discouraged British warships from entering harbors but they could do nothing to prevent British fleet operations up the Chesapeake. Far more significant was their contribution to the war effort in other ways—as transports, convoy escorts, and hospital and prison ships, as well as a means to gather intelligence and boost local morale. Only during the naval actions preliminary to the Battle of New Orleans did Jefferson's gunboats fulfill their intended mission. By 1825, most of the gunboats had been retired with only a few surviving as tenders.

The gunboats' record is indeed mixed. They certainly served a practical purpose in defending a nation with hundreds of miles of coast line and navigable inland waterways and they also fit Jeffersonian politics. As naval vessels, however, they handled poorly and were often cheaply constructed. Jefferson's idealized view of the citizen sailors who would crew these craft never really took hold. Naval officers shunned service on gunboats, preferring the much more high-profile billets aboard frigates and other warships, and the naval militia remained small and stagnant. Critics charged that the boats stood idle much of the time, promoting vice and poor discipline among both crew and officers. Still, the gunboats are an excellent example of how arms procurement, national security, and national politics meld to determine how a nation provides for its security.

◆ THE TRIPOLITAN WAR

During this period the United States fought its longest war between the War for Independence and Vietnam. From 1801 through 1805 (actually a little past 1805) the young nation attempted to regain honor lost to the pirate kingdoms of the Barbary Coast. Often overlooked, the Tripolitan War was small in cost, casualties, and scope but tells much about the relationship between the use of force, diplomacy, and national identity in the early American experience.

The Tripolitan War erupted after years of tension between the United States and the Barbary kingdoms of Morocco, Tripoli, Tunis, and Algiers. After the British Royal Navy stopped protecting American shipping in the Mediterranean in 1783, the United States had little choice but to pay the bribes demanded by the Barbary States in exchange for not harassing American merchant ships. Paying tribute, however, undermined the United States as a sovereign, independent nation that desperately needed respect abroad. As presidents, both Washington and Adams swallowed their pride and paid tribute through negotiated agreements that freed captured sailors in exchange for an annual payment. Jefferson, a member of both administrations, contradicted his long-held pacifist views and urged building a large fleet and using force to subdue the

Barbary pirate states. Jefferson remained a voice in the wilderness until he was elected president in 1800. By then the Barbary States' rulers had played into Jefferson's hands.

[In July 1800 Captain William Bainbridge, in command of the *George Washington*, brought the annual cash tribute to the Dey of Algiers only to be told to transfer the Dey's annual tribute to the sultan in Constantinople. Although this was humiliating for the United States, Bainbridge had little choice. Shortly afterward, in October, the pasha of Tripoli repudiated the Treaty of 1797 with the United States.]

Tripoli demanded more substantial tribute from the United States. The United States could not afford to pay, prompting Tripoli to announce that it would commence war against the United States in six months' time if the additional tribute was not forthcoming. Five months later, the United States learned of this brazen announcement, leaving little time to respond. Jefferson had anticipated this breakdown in relations and upon taking office ordered a small squadron under the command of Commodore Richard Dale to the Mediterranean. In the meantime Tripoli captured more American ships and held several crews hostage. Jefferson ordered Dale, with his frigates *President* and *Philadelphia* and the sloop of war *Enterprise*, to take offensive action if provoked.

In May 1801, Tripoli made good its threat by chopping down the flagpole at the American consulate. Dale's squadron arrived in Gibraltar where he left USS *Philadelphia* to contain two Tripolitan ships, reaching Tripoli in June. Once there the squadron promptly established a leaky blockade. After "showing the flag" for six weeks Dale returned his squadron to the United States. His only real success had been to bottle up two of Tripoli's best ships at Gibraltar.

Dale's successor, Commodore Richard Morris, headed to the Mediterranean with six ships in 1802. Cautious, if not timid, Morris left three ships, all frigates, at Gibraltar and took the remainder to Malta. Only the *Constellation* would reach Tripoli, where it would weakly blockade the port for several weeks. Morris ended up in Tunis in January 1803 because of foul weather. He then found himself in jail because of debts owed by William Eaton, the American consul there. Twenty-two thousand dollars later, Morris was freed and the consul sent home. Morris finally got to Tripoli in May 1803 where he employed a strategy of fighting while negotiating, shelling the port and landing a raiding party that destroyed some grain barges. Morris and the pasha talked—Morris offered $15,000 for ten years, which further entrenched the hated tribute system. The pasha had much larger aspirations—he wanted $200,000 for the treaty then $20,000 a year. Obviously at an impasse, Morris was recalled and dismissed from the Navy in disgrace.

Enter here the very able Edward Preble. An already successful and highly regarded naval officer with combat experience in the War for Independence and the Quasi War, Preble was finally the right commander for the situation. A man of action and intellect, Preble became the first in a "who's who" of Navy officers who served in the Mediterranean during the first half of the nineteenth century. Stephen Decatur, William Bainbridge, and Isaac Hull are some of the most important officers who succeeded Preble. With seven ships under his command, including the venerable *Constitution*, Preble made his way west to east across the coasts of the Barbary States. He captured two Moroccan ships, including one towing an American prize behind it. In Tangiers, Preble staged a serious show of force that included three frigates. Convinced of American naval might, the Moroccan regency quickly agreed to renew the 1786 treaty with the United States and dropped the demand for more tribute. Preble's tour had started with a bang.

⌈With things well in hand at Tangiers, Preble ordered Bainbridge to take *Philadelphia* and *Vixen* to Tripoli. In late October disaster struck when the *Philadelphia* grounded on an uncharted reef while pursuing a corsair into Tripoli's harbor. Bainbridge could not get the frigate free of the reef, and owing to the position of the stranded ship he could not effectively use most of the *Philadelphia*'s guns. He was forced to surrender the ship and its crew of 300, a shocking loss for the young U.S. Navy. The pasha demanded $3 million for ransom and a new treaty, which Preble rejected without hesitation. In February 1804 a daring and audacious attack by Stephen Decatur and the *Intrepid*, a refitted captured Tripolitan ketch, used deception and stealth to approach the insecurely guarded *Philadelphia*. After boarding and quickly subduing the handful of guards on the moored frigate, Decatur had the *Philadelphia* put to the torch, then quickly made his escape from Tripoli Harbor. It was the high point of the war for the Americans, and Decatur became a household hero back in the United States.⌋

The loss of the *Philadelphia* convinced Preble that only shallow-draft boats could make an effective attack on Tripoli Harbor. Acquiring six gunboats and a couple of bomb vessels from nearby Sicily, Preble gathered the largest American fleet to date and attacked Tripoli in August 1804. Over the next four weeks he launched five attacks

FIGURE 4-3 Burning of the frigate Philadelphia, Tripoli, Feb. 16, 1804.

BURNING OF THE FRIGATE PHILADELPHIA, TRIPOLI, FEB. 16TH 1804

Source: Library of Congress Print and Reproductions Division [LC-USZ62-67510]

but made little progress. His patience running out, Preble took the drastic measure of using a fire ship to attack the harbor. Loading the brave *Intrepid* full of powder and explosives, a volunteer crew took the ship into the harbor on the night of September 4. At about 10:00 P.M. the ship prematurely ignited in a huge explosion that killed the volunteer crew on board. It is not clear if the explosion was accidental or if the crew ignited the ship after being boarded. Regardless, the *Intrepid* did little damage to the harbor. Preble's desperate gamble had failed and now he too was finished in the Mediterranean.

CONGRESSIONAL RESOLUTION PRAISING COMMODORE PREBLE

Congressional recognition of courageous deeds and distinguished service was a delicate matter. In keeping with its egalitarian traditions the military had no awards, but Congress felt it necessary and appropriate in some cases to offer formal recognition to officers and men who had behaved meritoriously. What better way to laud a soldier serving a republic than through the people's representatives?

Resolutions Expressive of the Sense of Congress of the Gallant Conduct of Commodore Edward Preble, the Officers, Seamen, and Marines of His Squadron

Resolved by the Senate and the House of Representatives of the United States of America in Congress assembled, That the thanks of Congress be, and the same are hereby presented to Commodore Edward Preble, and through him to the officers, petty officers, seamen, and marines attached to the squadron under his command, for their gallantry and good conduct, displayed in the several attacks on the town, batteries, and naval force of Tripoli, in the year one thousand eight hundred and four.

Resolved, That the President of the United States be requested to cause a gold medal to be struck, emblematical of the attacks on the town, batteries, and naval force of Tripoli, by the Squadron under Commodore Preble's command, to present it to Commodore Preble, in such manner as in his opinion will be most honourable to him. And that the President be further requested to cause a sword to be presented to each of the commissioned officers and midshipmen who have distinguished themselves in the several attacks.

Resolved, That one month's pay be allowed exclusively of the common allowance to all petty officers, seamen, and marines of the squadron, who so gloriously supported the hour of the American flag, under the orders of their gallant commander in the several attacks.

> Resolved, That the President of the United States be also requested to communicate to the parents or other near relatives of Captain Richard Somers, Lieutenants Henry Wadsworth, James Decatur, James R. Caldwell, Joseph Israel, and Midshipman John Sword Dorsey, the deep regret which Congress felt for the loss of those gallant men, whose names ought to live in the recollection and affection of a grateful country, and whose conduct ought to be regarded as an example to future generations.
> *APPROVED, March 3, 1805.*
>
> *Source:* United States Statutes at Large, Avalon Project, Yale Law School. Reprinted with permission.

Commodore Samuel Barron replaced Preble, but Barron was ill and therefore participated little in events. The former consul to Tunis, William Eaton, had come from the United States with Barron. Eaton was a veteran of the War for Independence and the campaigns in the Northwest Territory. As "Navy Agent of the United States for the Several Barbary Regencies," Eaton had an ambitious plan to topple the pasha of Tripoli. First he would capture the city of Derna, about 800 miles east of Tripoli, from land rather than by sea. To do this he assembled a motley crew of Greeks, Egyptians, and other mercenaries along with a handful of Marines. Setting out from Egypt, the force made a perilous trip across 500 miles of desert, picking up a large Bedouin tribe along the way. At Derna Eaton attacked, and aided by two American naval vessels that shelled Tripoli from the sea he took and held the city despite several counterattacks from Tripolitan troops. In June, Eaton learned that a peace agreement had been reached with Tripoli. He and the Americans in the expedition, along with Ahmed Quaramanli—the pasha's brother with whom they hoped to replace the pasha—abandoned their allies and Derna to certain retribution.

Tobias Lear, former personal secretary to George Washington turned diplomat, was the one who finally concluded an agreement with Tripoli. A rival of Eaton's, Lear wanted to end the war and preempt Eaton's grand plan of attack across the desert. Lear understood the complexities of Barbary politics and knew that the pasha would never surrender the crew of the *Philadelphia* without tribute of some sort. Captain John Rodgers had now established a firm blockade and was eager to shell the city as Preble had months earlier. Lear believed that the pasha was close to surrender and interested in making a deal. The pasha first asked for $200,000, then $130,000. Rodgers, unimpressed, rejected both offers. Lear countered with $60,000 and a promise that the United States also would withdraw from Derna and abandon support of Ahmed. If the pasha rejected this offer, Lear promised that Rodgers would be let loose to shell the city. The pasha realized his precarious position and accepted the new treaty to end the war but left the question of future tribute unresolved.

Tunis remained a problem for a short time but it too found common ground with the Americans after threat of bombardment. Once again, Rodgers yielded to Lear, who found a peaceful resolution to the standoff. The treaty, however, ran into stiff resistance in the Senate. The United States had both paid off the pasha and failed to use its military resources in defense of national honor, so went the arguments against the treaty. The fact remained, however, that what had been done was done. Lear had paid off the Pasha and freed the *Philadelphia* prisoners, who now returned home as heroes. The Mediterranean Squadron also returned home while Barbary pirates continued to harass American shipping through the 1810s, although at nowhere near the levels of intensity that they had between the 1780s and 1805.

The Tripolitan War had been a convoluted affair—inconsistent leadership, lack of strategy, and a confused political objective hampered American effectiveness. Was the war fought to end tribute, lessen it, or simply to strike a better deal for the Americans? In national security policy, the diplomatic and military tools of strategy must complement each other. For much of the Tripolitan War it seemed that the one was completely unaware of the other.

Still, Jefferson had made a bold statement to the rest of the world—the United States would fight a war not only for practical economic reasons, it would also fight for an ideal, in this case the principle of unhindered sovereign trade. Moreover, the young United States had stood up to extortion and terror, thus sending what should have been a clear signal to Britain and France that America would also resist interference from them. Militarily the United States had fought its first war on foreign soil, used allies and mercenaries, and established foreign bases. The war provided the Navy with invaluable experience. America soon faced a much more serious and deadly threat to shipping on the high seas, and the Navy would need every bit of experience it could muster to meet the challenge.

◆ THE *CHESAPEAKE–LEOPARD* AFFAIR

On June 22, 1807, the 40-gun USS *Chesapeake* commanded by Commodore James Barron sailed from Hampton Roads, Virginia, to take up station in the Mediterranean. Waiting off the Chesapeake Bay was HMS *Leopard*, a 50-gunner with orders to stop and board the *Chesapeake* to search for deserters from the Royal Navy. Based in Halifax, the Royal Navy's North American squadron patrolled up and down the Atlantic seaboard in the hope of catching French prizes trading in American ports. The Royal Navy suspected that deserters from British ships could be found in most major American ports. These deserters crewing American vessels risked being returned by force to Royal Navy duty or, worse, possible execution. With gun ports open, the *Leopard* stopped the *Chesapeake* and sent aboard a dispatch demanding that any Royal Navy deserters be returned to the *Leopard*. Completely surprised by the encounter, Barron steadfastly denied he had any deserters among his crew and refused to allow the British to board his ship.

At this point things went terribly wrong for Barron and the *Chesapeake*. Surprised by the British boldness at stopping an American naval vessel just off the Virginia coast, Barron had not cleared for action. Angered by the American refusal of what the Royal Navy considered just demands, the *Leopard* opened fire, raking the *Chesapeake* with three horrific broadsides. Barron managed one ineffective shot before surrendering. Four crew members were taken from the *Chesapeake*, one of whom was later executed for desertion. Barron was subsequently court-martialed for failure in the face of the enemy and permanently relieved of command—an outcome that caused division among the Navy's officers.

The young "Hawks" in Congress demanded a declaration of war against Great Britain to avenge what they considered an egregious affront to American sovereignty. Jefferson would not be goaded into a war against the supreme naval power in the world that his country was not politically, economically, nor militarily prepared to fight. The encounter between the two ships was the near-inevitable culmination of numerous meetings on the high seas between Royal Navy ships and American merchant and naval vessels since hostilities had broken out between Great Britain and France in the 1790s. The Royal Navy contended that it had the right to "impress" British sailors into service aboard Royal Navy vessels regardless of the flag of their ship. The United States maintained that as a sovereign nation, as well as a neutral nation in the conflict between Great Britain and France, impressing sailors who served on American-flagged ships was a violation of its sovereignty and neutrality. American sea captains, however, clearly and regularly recruited British deserters to serve aboard American ships. Yet the Jefferson administration did next to nothing to stop either the British or the American practice. That is, until the *Chesapeake-Leopard* encounter.

Jefferson could not agree to war, but he could vigorously protest to the British government. He demanded that Great Britain renounce impressment and rescind Orders in Council, a demand that the British found impossible to accept. As if the British Orders in Council were not bad enough, Napoleon put in place his continental system, which also restricted American shipping and challenged American neutrality. Jefferson, followed by his successor James Madison, implemented controversial and ill-advised embargoes, including the Embargo Act of 1807, the Non-Intercourse Act of 1809, and Macon's Bill Number 2, none of which proved effective at changing British, or for that matter French policy. Both Britain and France stopped American vessels on the high seas, searched them, and seized cargo they considered war contraband. As the principal belligerents in an increasingly costly and widening war, Great Britain and France appeared to be forcing the United States to choose one side or the other.

War in 1807 or 1808, however, was out of the question. The Army was still small, although Congress approved a modest expansion in response to the *Chesapeake* crisis. The Navy was also equally minute, having just one gun to every Royal Navy ship. Although British military and naval resources were engaged across the world they could still rally plenty of force against the American nuisance. As Congress debated whether to pour money into coastal fortifications or more of Jefferson's gunboats the diplomatic situation stalemated, for both sides had made demands that the other could never accept.

The *Chesapeake-Leopard* affair itself did not directly lead to the War of 1812, but it was certainly among several incidents that point to the poor state of American military preparedness, lack of national strategy and clear policy objectives, and the overall disrespect that the major powers exhibited toward the young United States. For five long years Great Britain and France played what they thought was a relatively low-stakes game of poker, using American trade, sovereignty, and neutrality as cheap chips.

◆ THE HUNGER FOR EXPANSION

While American merchantmen and naval vessels struggled on the high seas, the increasing population west of the Appalachians found itself embroiled in related troubles. In the west prices on everyday goods increased because of the embargoes on the coast. While the price increases had some legitimate foundation, westerners could not help thinking that some old-fashioned eastern price gouging was at play. A firm response against Great Britain, they claimed, would stop the nonsense on the high seas and restore normal pricing. Moreover, more people were heading across the Appalachians, creating what they perceived as a need for more land. Settlers wanting the rich lands in Ohio and Indiana ignored the Treaty of Greenville before the ink had dried, once again giving tribes cause to band together.

Tecumseh and his brother the Prophet brought together another federation to fight white encroachment. At a new settlement along the Tippecanoe River called Prophet's Town, Tecumseh gathered over 1,000 warriors. William Henry Harrison, whom Jefferson appointed governor of the new Indiana Territory in 1801, feared Tecumseh's movement would get in the way of his ability to uphold the Treaty of Greenville and his own ambitious land schemes. At Harrison's behest, in 1809 Little Turtle agreed to sell more than three million acres of land in northern Indiana to the United States. Harrison wanted statehood for Indiana, and native land stood in the way. Tecumseh met with Harrison at Vincennes in the spring of 1810 to discuss the unfavorable land sale that Harrison had negotiated. The two leaders found themselves at an impasse. Tecumseh left to visit southern tribes to invite them to join his confederation while Harrison remained at Vincennes to plan a punitive expedition for the following year.

Harrison had been a young lieutenant on "Mad" Anthony Wayne's staff at the Battle of Fallen Timbers. He had experience in "punitive" expeditions and probably planned all along to war against Tecumseh. During the winter of 1810–1811 President Madison approved Harrison's campaign plans. By the summer of 1811 Indiana militiamen, the 4th U.S. Infantry Regiment, and Governor Harrison were ready to hunt down the Prophet. Once again the regulars were well trained and, although lacking combat experience, were mostly disciplined, while the militia was undisciplined but eager to clear away native resistance to open northern Indiana to settlement.

Harrison's force of 900 militia and regulars left Vincennes on September 26, 1811, heading up the Wabash River to an abandoned Wea village to build an outpost that Harrison unabashedly named Fort Harrison. By early November they were only a few miles from Prophet's Town. A delegation of chiefs met with Harrison to arrange a parley and offered Harrison and his army a place to make camp that Harrison suspiciously accepted. Tecumseh was away, still south visiting the major tribes on his recruiting tour. Without Tecumseh's superior military leadership on the other side, Harrison knew he had the advantage. The Prophet, himself no military genius, conjured up visions and spells to take Harrison's encampment by surprise. He also promised his warriors that the American bullets would harmlessly bounce off them. The Prophet's mysticism seemed to almost work, but then while attempting to encircle the camp under cover of darkness, a sentry saw movement and fired. The Prophet's warriors charged toward the camp as weary soldiers pulled themselves out of their bedrolls and into line. On the northwest side of the encampment the fighting was hand to hand. By daybreak the natives had reorganized on the left and right flanks of Harrison's bloodied line. Major Samuel Wells led a reckless but effective charge on the north flank to drive the Prophet's warriors back in disarray. The southern flank broke as well, reeling back into a swampy wood to shield itself from a punishing charge of cavalry.

Despite the Prophet's assurances, hundreds of warriors had been killed and wounded by the supposedly harmless American bullets. The day after the battle, November 7, Harrison found Prophet's Town deserted. The tribes abandoned the Prophet and Tecumseh to return to their villages. Harrison ordered the village put to the torch. His victory was stupendous in effect, breaking the confederation and opening the Old Northwest Territory to settlement. Harrison talked of annexing part of Canada to the United States and blamed British agents for the native troubles, although in this exceptional case they were innocent in the matter. Such bold talk came at a great price—Harrison had lost over 180 killed and wounded in the Battle of Tippecanoe, but the cost was overlooked as congressmen and settlers west of the Alleghenies applauded Harrison's ambition and cheered for war against England to expand American territory.

◆ CONCLUSION

Security concerns over both the West and the Atlantic had forced the new Republic to reconsider its defense needs, often at the expense of previously held high ideals about standing armies and centralized authority. Molding effective defense policy out of domestic political disputes, regional interests, republican ideals, and military capabilities proved extremely difficult; yet, as evidenced by Jefferson's gunboat program, the United States was willing to at least try radical ideas to address its unique security needs. It is ironic that the conflict with Native Americans along the frontier, British harassment of American shipping on the Atlantic, and the American thirst for expansion would come together in 1812 in a general war with Great Britain. The new nation was ill prepared for such a conflict, one that would in essence be a second war for its independence.

Further Reading

Bird, Harrison. *War for the West, 1790–1813.* New York: Oxford University Press, 1971.

Crackel, Theodore J. *Mr. Jefferson's Army: Political and Social Reform of the Military Establishment, 1801–1809.* New York: New York University Press, 1987.

Fowler, William M. *Jack Tars and Commodores: The American Navy, 1783–1815.* Boston: Houghton Mifflin, 1984.

Gaff, Alan. *Bayonets in the Wilderness: Anthony Wayne's Legion in the Old Northwest.* Norman: University of Oklahoma Press, 2004.

Kohn, Richard H. *Eagle and Sword: Federalists and the Creation of the Military Establishment in America, 1783–1802.* New York: The Free Press, 1975.

McKee, Christopher. *A Gentlemanly and Honorable Profession: The Creation of the U.S. Naval Officer Corps, 1794–1815.* Annapolis: Naval Institute Press, 1991.

McKee, Christopher. *Edward Preble: A Naval Biography, 1761–1807.* Annapolis: Naval Institute Press, 1972.

Morris, John D. *Sword of the Border: Major General Jacob Jennings Brown, 1775–1828.* Kent, Ohio: Kent State University Press, 2000.

Parker, Richard B. *Uncle Sam in Barbary: A Diplomatic History.* Gainesville: University Press of Florida, 2004.

Peskin, Allan. *Winfield Scott and the Profession of Arms.* Kent, Ohio: Kent State University Press, 2003.

Skaggs, David Curtis. *Thomas Macdonough: Master of Command in the Early U.S. Navy.* Annapolis: Naval Institute Press, 2003.

Skelton, William B. *An American Profession of Arms: The Officer Corps, 1784–1861.* Lawrence: University Press of Kansas, 1999.

Smith, Gene A. *"For the Purposes of Defense": The Politics of the Jeffersonian Gunboat Program.* Newark: University of Delaware Press, 1995.

Sword, Wiley. *President Washington's Indian War: The Struggle for the Old Northwest, 1790–1795.* Norman: University of Oklahoma Press, 1993.

Tucker, Spencer C. *The Jeffersonian Gunboat Navy.* Charleston: University of South Carolina Press, 1993.

Tucker, Spencer C., and Frank T. Reuter. *Injured Honor: The Chesapeake-Leopard Affair, June 22, 1807.* Annapolis: Naval Institute Press, 1996.

Wheelan, Joseph. *Jefferson's War: America's First War on Terror, 1801–1805.* New York: Carroll and Graf, 2003.

Whipple, A.B.C. *To the Shores of Tripoli: The Birth of the U.S. Navy and Marines.* New York: William Morrow, 1991.

^{PEARSON}mysearchlab Connections: Sources Online • • • • • • • • • •

READ AND REVIEW

Review this chapter by using the study aids and these related documents available on MySearchLab.

Study Plan

Chapter Test

Essay Test

Documents

President George Washington's Proclamation Regarding the Whiskey Rebellion (1794)

Washington explains why and how he intends to use force troops to put down the Whiskey Rebellion.

The Militia Act (1792)

This document contains both the Calling Forth and Uniform Militia Acts passed by Congress in 1792 and reveals the delicate political nature of a standing army, the reliance upon militia, and the executive power of the president as commander-in-chief.

Decatur's Report to Preble on the Destruction of the Frigate *Philadelphia* **(1804)**
In this document, Decatur provides an after-action report on the assault, capture, and firing of the *Philadelphia*, moored in Tripoli Harbor, on February 16, 1804.

RESEARCH AND EXPLORE

Explore the following review questions using the research tools available on www. mysearchlab.com.

1. What advantages and disadvantages did a standing military offer compared to continuing to rely upon militia?
2. What factors influenced the development of the new United States Navy during this time period?
3. How did the United States define the many threats against its national security during this time period?

The Second War of Independence

◆ INTRODUCTION

The War of 1812 was both a war of expansion and a second war of independence for the young United States. American economic and strategic desires in Canada and Spanish Florida were widely known and even popular among the American people. Indeed, the United States had embarked on a policy of expansion long before the War with Mexico in 1846. On the high seas American merchant vessels and naval ships ran into far more trouble with the British and French navies than they had ever met against the Barbary pirates. With Napoleon's domination of Europe in the balance, the United States found itself caught in an untenable situation that threatened its sovereignty and notions of neutrality. Bumbling and inexperience showed in ineffective American diplomacy and inadequate military preparedness, both of which made the War of 1812 an exceptionally dangerous conflict for the young nation. Yet the threats to the United States by Great Britain demanded defense of the nation's honor if not its liberty.

◆ A DECLARATION OF WAR

On June 1, 1812, President Madison delivered a message to Congress declaring that a state of war existed between the United States and Great Britain. The impressment of American citizens into the Royal Navy; the unlawful search and seizure of American ships, sometimes just off the coast of the United States; the Orders in Council; and the assumed British agitation of native tribes in the west made for a wide-ranging list of reasons that the United States had to go to war to defend its sovereignty.

Congress approved the declaration on June 18 by a vote of 79–49 in the House of Representatives and 19–13 in the Senate. Opposition came from representatives of New England, New York, and New Jersey, while strong support for war came those representing western and southern states, led by War Hawks Henry Clay and John C. Calhoun. While geographic splits in the vote were apparent, so too were partisan lines, with Federalists holding most seats in New England and Republicans dominating the West and South. Mr. Madison's War, as it was known, was for some Americans exactly that.

While war fever ran high, financial support for the war was limited. Congress initially offered no appropriation for expanding the Navy and allowed the Army to increase from around 10,000 to only 35,000. Madison could call out volunteers, up to 100,000 for six months, to supplement the meager regular force. In 1812 the War Department had a Secretary, William Eustis, and eleven clerks. Many senior officers were aged and owed their appointments to politics rather than merit. While many had served in the War for Independence, they had since grown soft intellectually—and in some cases physically—from inactivity. Younger officers had little if any experience. Among the troops desertion and poor discipline were the norm. Pay was poor, and because of equally poor administration it was also rare—sometimes as much as six months behind. Volunteers were enticed to enlist with bounties of up to $124 and 320 acres of land. Enlistees, however, did not equate to an effective fighting force. Militia units were in worse condition. Jeffersonians had always resisted a large standing army in the expectation that in crisis the militia would rally to the nation's defense.

Now, the crisis was at hand, and the militia was almost universally in complete confusion. The Uniform Militia Act of 1792 had not worked, mainly because of neglect rather than flawed policy. On the eve of the War of 1812, Congress hoped to use state militias as an inexpensive auxiliary force to fill out the small regular Army, but the poor condition and initial performance of the militia quickly convinced commanders and Congress alike that a national volunteer system was a better option. Congress responded with a call for 50,000 volunteers to serve essentially as a national militia, while the Army was increased by 25,000 men.⌉

American political objectives far outstretched American military capacity and capability. With a weak navy the United States did not dare to punish Great Britain for the litany of offenses committed against America on the high seas. As an alternative means of inflicting some harm against Great Britain, the United States turned its sights on Great Britain's most vulnerable point in North America—Canada. In order to wed American political objectives to an appropriate military strategy, an offensive plan seemed the only alternative. Yet American political leadership failed to make the war's objectives clear to its military leadership, resulting in a muddled if not deeply flawed military strategy. In a war that was apparently about maritime rights and foreign support of native tribes, the United States chose to invade Canada as its first military move. Even with Great Britain embroiled in the struggle against Napoleon on the European continent, the American strategy was bold indeed, considering the young nation's economic and military limitations.

The logistical, natural, and strategic problems that had plagued the colonial wars in North America and the War for Independence resurfaced in the War of 1812. The British would have to ship men and supplies across the Atlantic—a rough and often uncertain journey of six to eight weeks. Draft animals were always in short supply. Moreover, the Americans had only one arsenal at Springfield. The geography offered limited and mostly poor roads, so rivers and other waterways would once again play a pivotal role in the strategy of both armies. The St. Lawrence River, Lake Champlain and the Richelieu River, Lakes Ontario and Erie, the Mississippi River, and Chesapeake Bay each played leading roles in this war just as they had in the past. Moreover, the clear lesson of the previous wars showed that the key to breaking Canada was control of the St. Lawrence River. Achieving that objective required naval superiority.

Two days before Congress voted to approve the declaration of war, the British government withdrew its Orders in Council to nullify many American grievances. But Great Britain failed to publicize its increasingly ad hoc policy changes, and since the United States had no ranking diplomat in London at the time, it remained mostly in the dark as to British intentions. By the time news reached Washington that the British had changed their tack, it was too late. Yet the United States remained deeply divided on war, so much so that violent riots broke out in Baltimore between Republican proponents and Federalist opponents of the war. Because the Republicans received most of the blame for starting the riots, Federalists were able to sweep the November congressional elections, leaving Madison with a Congress strongly opposed to his war.

◆ FIRST MOVES—WESTERN CANADA

⌈For the divided United States, little strategy existed beyond an invasion of Canada via Montreal in the hope of splitting western Canada from the more populous and accessible eastern half. Once western Canada fell to American forces, so the thinking went, the remainder of Canada also would collapse.⌉

Major General William Hull attacked Canada from his base at Detroit. Hull's campaign excited war supporters in the West, but the effort proved disastrous as Hull's army was forced back into American territory before the year was out. Hull crossed the river from Detroit into Canada in July with about 1,200 regulars and militia. General Isaac Brock knew that Hull was coming. Hull's papers had been found aboard a captured transport on Lake Erie just days before he crossed into Canada. With his own assorted lot of regulars and militia, Brock moved to counter the invasion. Meanwhile, a small British force with 400 native allies took Fort Michilimackinac, without a shot being fired, on July 17. The native warriors proved to be the counter that Brock really needed. Wyandots left the Detroit area and joined the British. Tecumseh swung into action as well, surprising 200 men that Hull had sent as escort for supplies from Ohio at Brownstown. More of Hull's reports fell into Brock's hand as a result. When Hull learned that Brock and Tecumseh were on the move toward his force, he abandoned his plan to attack Fort Malden, the principal British post on the northern shore of Lake Erie, and retreated back to Detroit.

Brock and Tecumseh approached the fort at Detroit, using deception to convince Hull that he faced a huge force of British regulars and hundreds of Indians when in reality Brock's force outnumbered Hull's by about two to one. Based on the captured letters, Brock gambled that Hull had lost his nerve—he was right. After an early morning cannonade into Fort Detroit and a brazen show of force outside its thin walls, Brock got what he wanted: Hull surrendered without firing a shot. Fort Dearborn, near modern Chicago, promptly followed suit. British native allies fell upon helpless families and soldiers as they abandoned Fort Dearborn; the assault was reminiscent of the native attack on British forces leaving Fort William Henry in the Great War for Empire.

With Detroit and Fort Dearborn in their hands, the British easily advanced as far south as the Maumee River. Hull faced court-martial and was convicted of cowardice before the enemy and sentenced to death. Taking into consideration Hull's service in the War for Independence, President Madison pardoned him.

William Henry Harrison replaced Hull and tried to right the western disasters. Hoping to retake Detroit and avenge Fort Dearborn, Harrison left Fort Wayne with a large force of regulars and militia in September 1812. He split his army into three divisions, each taking a slightly different route toward Detroit. In January 1813 Harrison lost part of his force in a very one-sided affair at Frenchtown on the River Raisin near modern-day Monroe, Michigan. General James Winchester, with whom Harrison did not get along and for whom he had little respect as a commander, staged two attacks on Frenchtown, badly losing the second. Another native massacre took place, as warriors murdered over fifty captured Kentuckians.

By this time weather and expired enlistments forced Harrison to halt his campaign. Near the site where Anthony Wayne had defeated Tecumseh at the Battle of Fallen Timbers almost twenty years before, Harrison established Fort Meigs on the Maumee River as a base of operations. Other than personnel, logistics proved his greatest challenge, as supplies had to be wheeled by wagon across hundreds of miles of poor roads, many of which were nothing more than trails. Because the British controlled Lake Erie, supply from ship was spotty at best. Harrison's resolution of this problem turned the corner for his western campaign.

FIGURE 5-1 War of 1812.

Louisiana

[Like Hull, Harrison believed that the only way to defeat the British in the west was to control Lake Erie. While Harrison fretted at Fort Meigs, Commodore (Captain) Oliver Hazard Perry put in motion a plan to make Lake Erie an American lake. Only twenty-seven years old, Perry was young, bright, and ambitious—and apparently scared to death of cows. A professional sailor, he read every naval and military work he could find. He had commanded a small squadron of gunboats at Rhode Island and feared he might miss the war. When the campaign went sour in the west, Perry offered to command a squadron to gain control of Lake Erie. At Erie, Pennsylvania, in February 1813, Perry arrived to find work already started on two brigs and plans laid out for gunboats.]

Commander Robert H. Barclay commanded the British squadron that dominated Lake Erie and kept British forces in Michigan well supplied. Although he could not mount an amphibious assault on the American shipyard at Erie, Barclay could try to keep whatever the Americans were building bottled up. By July, Perry's small fleet was ready to sail but he lacked the skilled sailors to handle the tricky waters of Lake Erie. Finally, hurriedly assembling skeleton crews for the vessels, Perry took advantage of Barclay's unexplained absence on August 1 to sneak out onto Lake Erie in force. Barclay suddenly found himself outnumbered. With Perry on the water, control of the lake was up for grabs. The British could no longer assume the proper supply of Forts Malden and Detroit.

Perry and Harrison held a council of war and came up with a daring plan. Perry first had to destroy Barclay's squadron to give his own squadron and Harrison's men the ability to maneuver freely, which would allow Perry to ferry Harrison's force across the lake to attack Fort Malden. Barclay came out to challenge Perry, who had stationed his squadron near Bass Island, on September 10. Barclay had six ships with 63 guns against Perry's nine vessels and 54 guns. The British ships were armed with long-range cannon, while Perry had mostly short-range carronades.

Aboard his flagship *Lawrence*, Perry hoisted a blue ensign decorated with "Don't Give Up The Ship." Just before noon, Perry led the *Lawrence* and four other ships straight at the British. Lieutenant Jesse Elliott, commanding the large *Niagara*, failed to engage the British *Queen Charlotte*. Nevertheless, Perry continued the attack. British and American ships exchanged intense fire that eventually forced Perry to abandon the *Lawrence* and take command of the *Niagara*. When Barclay fell wounded, the British *Detroit* surrendered, followed by most of the British squadron.

Meanwhile, Harrison crossed his army to the Canadian side of the lake. British commander Henry Proctor studied the strategic situation and declared it hopeless, allowing Harrison to take both Fort Detroit and Fort Malden unopposed. Tecumseh and his large band of Shawnee warriors and their families found themselves virtually abandoned by the British, just as they had at Fallen Timbers. At Moraviantown near the Thames River, Harrison engaged Tecumseh and what remained of Proctor's army. Proctor fled in panic, leaving his men with no option other than surrender. Tecumseh was killed while making a last stand with his 600 warriors, who, like their erstwhile British counterparts, found themselves leaderless. The Battle of the Thames, over in less than an hour, permanently weakened the native tribes of the Northwest. Moreover, with Harrison's victory the Niagara frontier became the primary theater of war.

"WE HAVE MET THE ENEMY AND THEY ARE OURS"— THE BATTLE OF LAKE ERIE

Oliver Hazard Perry's bold proclamation of his "signal victory" to General William Henry Harrison has been firmly carved in the history and tradition of the United States Navy. The after-action reports of Perry and his erstwhile foe Robert H. Barclay clearly indicate that Perry maintained the initiative to win the battle. Note the descriptions of the action from the British and American perspectives, in particular Perry's reasons for winning and Barclay's excuses for losing. Also note Perry's vague mention of Elliott and the *Niagara*. After the battle, Elliott was cleared of any misconduct by a board of inquiry. In 1818, however, when Elliott was promoted to captain, his conduct at Lake Erie surfaced again. Elliott challenged Perry to a duel, which Perry wisely refused. Instead, Perry accused Elliott of incompetence and requested that court-martial charges be brought against Elliott. President Monroe rejected the request, not wanting to bring bad publicity on the Navy that had done so well in the War of 1812.

> Lieutenant Robert H. Barclay to Commodore
> Sir James Lucas Yeo
> His Majesty's late ship *Detroit*
> Putin Bay, Lake Erie, 12 Sept. 1813

Sir,

… it now remains for me, the most melancholy task, to relate to you the unfortunate issue of that Battle, as well as the many untoward circumstances that led to that event.

No intelligent seamen having arrived, I sailed on the 9th Inst. Fully expecting to meet the Enemy next morning as they had been seen among the Islands, nor was I mistaken, soon after daylight they were seen in motion in Putin Bay, the Wind then at SW, and light, given us the Weather gage, I bore for them, in hopes of bringing them to Action amongst the Islands, but that intention was soon frustrated by the Wind suddenly shifting to the South East, which brought the Enemy directly to Windward.

The Line was formed according to a given plane, so that each Ship might be supported against the superior Force of the two Brigs opposed to them. About then the Enemy had cleared the Islands and immediately bore up under easy sail in a line abreast, each Brig being also supported by the small Vessels; At a quarter past the American Commodore, also supported by two Schooners, one carrying four long twelve Prs., the other a long thirty two and twenty four pr. Came to close action with the *Detroit*, the other Brig of the Enemy apparently destined to engage the *Queen Charlotte*, supported in the like manner by two Schooners, kept so far to Windward as to render the *Queen Charlotte's* 24 pr. Carronades useless, while she was with the *Lady Prevost*, exposed to the heavy destructive Fire of the *Caledonia* and four other Schooners armed with heavy Guns like those I have already described… .

The Action continued with great fury until half past two, when I perceived my opponent drop astern and a Boat passing from him to the *Niagara*, … the American Commodore seeing that as yet the day was against him and also the very defenseless state of the *Detroit*, which Ship was now a perfect Wreck, principally from the Raking Fire of the Gun Boats, and also that the *Queen Charlotte* was in such a situation that I could receive very little assistance from her and the *Lady Prevost* being at this time too far to Leeward from her Rudder being injured, made a noble, and alas, too successful an effort to regain it, for he bore up and supported by his small Vessels passed within Pistol Shot and took a raking position on our Bow, nor could I prevent it, as the unfortunate situation of the *Queen Charlotte* prevented us from wearing, in attempting we fell onboard her. My Gallant Lieut. Garland was now mortally wounded and myself so severely that I was obliged to quit the deck.

Manned as the Squadron was with not more than Fifty British Seamen, the rest a mixed Crew of Canadians and Soldiers, and who were totally unacquainted with such Service, rendered the loss of Officers more sensibly felt—And never in any Action was the loss more severe, every Officer Commanding Vessels and their Seconds was either killed or Wounded so severely as to be unable to keep the deck... .

The Weather Gage gave the Enemy a prodigious advantage, as it enabled them, not only to choose their position, but their distance also, which they did in such a manner as to prevent the Carronades of the *Queen Charlotte* and *Lady Prevost* from having much effect, while their long Guns did great execution, particularly against the *Queen Charlotte*, But the great cause of losing His Majesty's Squadron on Lake Erie was the want of a competent number of Seamen: until the thirty six arrived from the *Dover*, I had not more than ten or fifteen, and those you know Sir, were of the very worst quality, the rest consisted of Canadians, who could not even speak English, and Soldiers, who except crossing the Atlantic, had never seen a ship... .

Such was the means I had to defend the Squadron entrusted to my charge against a Force superior in itself and dully equipped and manned, and in a situation where an Action was inevitable, or probably we must have last surrendered for want of Provisions... .

I trust that although unsuccessful you will approve of the motives that induced me to sail under so many disadvantages, and that may be hereafter proved that under such circumstances the Hour of His Majesty's Flag has not been tarnished.

> R.H. Barclay
> Commander and late Senr. Officer

> Captain Oliver H. Perry to Secretary of the Navy Jones
> U.S. Schooner *Ariel*
> Put in Bay
> 13th Septr. 1813

Sir,

In my last I informed you that we had captured the Enemy's Fleet on this Lake. I have now the honour to give you the most important particulars of the Action.

On the morning of the 10th. Inst., at sunrise, they were discovered from Put in Bay, where I sat at anchor with the Squadron under my command. We got under way, the wind light at S.W., and stood for them. At 10 A.M. the wind hauled to S.E., and brought us to windward; formed the Line, and bore up. At 15 minutes before twelve, the Enemy commenced firing; at 5 minutes before twelve, the action commenced on our part. Finding their fire very destructive, owing to their long guns, and its being most directed at the *Lawrence*, I made sail, and directed the other vessels to follow, for the purpose of closing with the Enemy. Every brace and bowline being soon shot away, she became unmanageable, notwithstanding the great exertions of the Sailing Master. In this situation, she sustained the action upwards of two hours, within canister distance, until every gun was rendered useless, and the greater part of the crew either killed or wounded. Finding she could no longer annoy the Enemy, I left her in charge of Lieut. Yarnall, who, I was convinced, from the bravery already displayed by him, would do what would comport the honour of the Flag. At half past two, the wind springing up, Capt. Elliott was enabled to bring his vessel, the *Niagara*, gallantly into close action. I immediately went on board of her, when he anticipated my wishes, by volunteering to bring the Schooners, which had been kept astern by the lightness of the wind, into closer action. It was with unspeakable pain that I saw, soon after I got on board the *Niagara*, the Flag of the *Lawrence* come down; although I was perfectly sensible that she had been defended to the last, and that to have continued to make a shew [sic] of resistance would have been a wanton sacrifice of the remains of her brace crew. But the Enemy was not able to take possession of her, and circumstances soon permitted her Flag again to be hoisted. At 45 minutes past two the signal was made for closer action. The *Niagara* being very little injured, I determined to pass through the Enemy's line; bore up, and passed ahead of their two Ships and a Brig, giving a raking fire to them from the Starboard Guns, and to a large Schooner and Sloop from the Larboard side, at half Pistol shot distance. The smaller vessels, at this time, having got within Grape and Canister distance, under the direction of Captain Elliott, and keeping up a well directed fire, the two Ships, a Brig, and Schooner, surrendered, a Schooner and Sloop making a vain attempt to escape.

O.H. Perry

Source: William S. Dudley, ed., *The Naval War of 1812: A Documentary History* (Washington, D.C.: Naval Historical Center, 1985), 2:555–58.

The campaign into western Canada exposed the Americans' strategic weakness and questionable military leadership. Instead of a concerted push on the vulnerable St. Lawrence River to strike the heart of British Canada the Army chose to spread its already meager forces even thinner, hitting weakly at various points from Lake Erie eastward. While it may have been an ill-advised plan, the United States hoped that, by spreading itself thin with major campaigns against three points, including western Canada, it would force the British to spread their equally meager British force equally thin.

◆ THE NIAGARA CAMPAIGN

With the failed effort in the west, the Army turned its attention toward the Niagara River frontier and Lake Ontario. The Army made several attempts on the Niagara region in 1812 but all failed because of poor planning and a general lack of will both on the part of planners and commanders. In October Major General Stephen Van Rensselaer planned to lead his mostly militia force across the Niagara River against Queenston. However, many militia units refused to cross the river and fight on foreign soil. The attack failed miserably and highlighted the lack of cooperation between militia and regular forces. Van Rensselaer's militia lacked even the most basic supplies, and regulars under the command of General Alexander Smyth failed to support the attack. British general Brock was killed in the defense of the town.

As a young lieutenant colonel of regulars Winfield Scott provided the single bright spot in the campaign. With 300 troops Scott managed to hold on to a bit of ground on Queenston Heights, but no reinforcements came. When he tried to retreat he found no boats to take him and his men back across the Niagara, forcing Scott to surrender. In addition to Scott's 300 troops, over 600 other Americans were captured and over 100 killed in the battle.

Van Rensselaer resigned to leave Smyth to take overall command. Smyth failed to move, however, claiming that his army was not ready and that the militia were unreliable. Both regulars and militia deserted in droves. After two aborted campaigns, Smyth released the militia, an action that prompted accusations that he was a coward. The Niagara River frontier remained weakly defended on the American side, a great irony since it was the Americans who had originally intended to take offensive action there.

In 1813, new Secretary of War John Armstrong made plans for an ambitious campaign to sever Upper Canada from the eastern half. He wanted to separate Kingston from Montreal, forcing the British to withdraw from the western areas and concentrate at Montreal. In a two-part campaign, former Secretary of War and now Major General Henry Dearborn would take the excellent harbor and well-fortified town of Kingston on the north shore of Lake Ontario. After Kingston, Dearborn would subdue the capital of Upper Canada, York (Toronto). Last, he would secure the Canadian side of the Niagara River. Dearborn, however, failed to stage an earnest campaign on Montreal in late 1812. Poor recruitment, undisciplined militia, disease, and a confused command structure forced Dearborn to give up his campaign and retire to winter quarters.

Dearborn got started again in April once the ice had cleared and the weather had improved. Convinced that Kingston was too well defended, Dearborn instead concentrated on York and the Niagara River region. In a joint operation, Commodore Isaac Chauncey's Lake Ontario squadron escorted Brigadier General Zebulon Pike's attack force from Sackett's Harbor across the lake to York, which was surprisingly and easily captured on April 27. Pike, however, was killed when the British exploded the powder magazine. As York was put to the torch, Kingston was left unmolested.

Bad weather and disease forced the Americans to delay the next step in the campaign—an attack against Fort George on the Niagara Peninsula, which was taken on May 27. On paper it was a stunning success, but Dearborn did not pursue the escaping British ranks. Winfield Scott, paroled and now full colonel, commanded the amphibious assault that actually captured the fort. But his pursuit of the fleeing British came to naught because he was ordered to halt. Scott searched for the British the following day, but they were long gone. Although the fort had been taken, a great opportunity to destroy a British army had been lost. The failure to capture the British forces on the peninsula contributed to the low morale and worsening conditions among American troops at Fort George. In one of the few attempts to hunt down the British, two American generals were captured in a disorderly battle at Stony Creek in June. Another American force of 600 surrendered in an ambush at Beaver Dams. Many lower-ranking officers resigned their commissions in disgust over poor conditions and frustration with the War Department. Armstrong relieved Dearborn and sent him into retirement.

While Dearborn was making a mess of the Niagara campaign, the British staged an offensive of their own. In a daring amphibious operation, Sir George Prevost, the Governor General of Canada, took a force of 900 men across Lake Ontario from Kingston to attack Sackett's Harbor. Jacob Brown, a major general of militia, with his 400 regulars and nearly 800 militia—including a detachment of Albany Volunteers— waited for the assault. Still winds prevented the British from landing just west of Horse Island early in the morning of May 28, forcing a delay of one day because landing at dawn was critical to the success of the operation. British ships first intercepted several boats of American reinforcements, about 140 men in all, on their way to Sackett's Harbor. With freshening winds restoring confidence in their attack plan, the British loaded their assault boats the night of the 28th. Brown arrived at Sackett's Harbor on the morning of the 28th to take command of the garrison. Anticipating the attack, Brown reasoned that the only suitable landing place for the British attackers was either on or just near Horse Island, which was connected to the mainland by a narrow causeway. Brown placed his Albany Volunteers on Horse Island to meet the landing. Expecting that they would break and flee, he made plans for reassembling the militia on the mainland to attack the British right flank. Brown's regulars would stage a fighting retreat to Fort Tompkins. That night Brown made out his will; clearly he had little confidence in his force's ability to defend Sackett's Harbor.

The British landed on the northern tip of Horse Island amid heavy fire from the New York militia and their six-pounder. But once the British were ashore, the Albany Volunteers had to retreat. Following his plan, Brown gathered what militia and remaining Albany men he could to volley fire into the approaching British. He managed a few volleys before the remaining militia broke and ran. The British now divided into two forces—one advancing along the shore and the other deeper inland on a parallel path. Brown, again sticking to his plan, staged a fighting retreat back to Fort Tompkins. From the fort's palisades and barracks Brown's regulars and his remaining militia leveled devastating fire upon the advancing British. Brown was absent during the battle, having gone to rally the militiamen who had fled from Horse Island. After almost an hour Brown reappeared, having managed to convince only eighty men under Captain Samuel McNitt to man a line intended to delay the British advance.

After two hours of fighting Prevost thought his force had achieved its mission. Burning barracks lit up the dawn sky while one of the naval stores exploded into a great ball of fire. A large dust cloud seemed to indicate American reinforcements. Prevost prematurely ordered a withdrawal, thinking his work done but not wanting to engage American reinforcements. Prevost lost 26 percent of his landing force, including 48 killed and almost 200 wounded. Brown lost 21 dead and 85 wounded in his successful defense of Sackett's Harbor.

For the Americans, the uninspiring year of 1813 closed with a failed campaign against Montreal. Major General James Wilkinson, a veteran of the War for Independence and Dearborn's replacement, planned a two-prong advance against Montreal for November. With the British threat in the west apparently gone after the Battle of the Thames in October, Wilkinson believed that the time was right for such an attack. Wilkinson himself would lead the western advance of 8,000 regulars from Sackett's Harbor up the St. Lawrence River, while Major General Wade Hampton would lead his force of 5,000 from Plattsburg with the two wings converging on Montreal. Hampton and Wilkinson, however, despised each other—a sad fact that grossly affected their command.

Wilkinson's force ran into trouble just as it left Sackett's Harbor, hitting foul weather and driving sleet. The men were crammed into hundreds of small boats to cross the St. Lawrence, which swamped the tiny vessels with its turbulent waters. Over 50 sank, taking much of their human cargo with them to the bottom. To make matters worse, a British force of 800 shadowed the fleet from shore. At the Long Sault Rapids, Wilkinson disembarked his troops; he then ordered Jacob Brown and Winfield Scott with their respective brigades to occupy the village of Cornwall. Brigadier General John Boyd's brigade guarded the boats but abandoned them when Wilkinson learned that the British force was encamped at nearby Chrysler's Farm.

On the morning of November 11, Boyd attacked, sending wave after wave into repeated British repulses. Boyd's losses were high—over 100 killed, 230 wounded, and another 100 missing. The British lost only 22 killed and less than 150 wounded. The Battle of Chrysler's Farm convinced Wilkinson to abandon his part of the campaign. Hampton fared no better as his New York militia refused to cross the border into Canada. With only 4,000 troops remaining, Hampton pressed on, only to hit a smaller but determined force of British regulars in the Battle of the Châteauguay on October 26. After two hours of repeated assaults on the British entrenchment, Hampton gave up and went back to Plattsburg. The 1813 campaign for Montreal was over.

The year 1813 had exposed several critical weaknesses in the American effort. Militia had proven unreliable. Generalship lacked imagination and determination. Political maneuvering between Federalists and Republicans not only affected decision making on the national level but also infected the officer corps, particularly in the upper ranks. Politics aside, the overblown egos of the likes of Hampton, Wilkinson, Scott, and others caused all sorts of dissent, and petty personal feuds hindered thoughtful command.

The campaign of 1813 suffered from a near complete disconnect between political objectives and military objectives, and more so between political objectives and military capabilities. Joint operations on the Great Lakes showed some promise, but the naval war on the high seas had not gone well. Heavily outnumbered, the American navy largely remained blockaded in ports up and down the Atlantic seaboard. The British blockade was also having its desired effect on prices in the United States, which began to climb dramatically.

While the British had also missed opportunities, by December 1813 they had retaken Fort George and captured Fort Niagara on the American side of the river. To top it all off, the Prussians and their allies scored a tremendous victory over Napoleon at Leipzig in October, thus forcing Napoleon to withdraw from Germany and allowing the British to free up forces for duty in North America. Despite the British having the initiative as 1814 began, the United States controlled Lake Erie and Tecumseh's confederation had been destroyed, developments that left the Americans with at least a few offensive options.

◆ THE CAMPAIGN OF 1814

Following the failures of 1813, President Madison made momentous command changes. After another disastrous defeat by a British force that he outnumbered 8 to 1 at La Colle Mill in March 1814, Wilkinson was relieved of command. Hampton also resigned over what he considered incompetent prosecution of the war. Madison commissioned Jacob Brown as a brigadier general in the regular Army and gave him command of the Niagara frontier. Brown had Winfield Scott, also now a brigadier general, in command of one of his brigades. Major General George Izard took up command in the Lake Champlain/Plattsburg area, along with Brigadier General Alexander Macomb as his subordinate.

Brown granted Scott's request for time to formally train the Left Division of Brown's army. Scott, a voracious reader on military affairs, did not disappoint Brown. For three months, Scott drilled and trained the Left Division, whipping it into fighting shape. With so few soldiers reenlisting, Scott had little choice but to drill new recruits hard to replace the experienced troops the army had lost. He ordered and personally conducted frequent inspections, instructed on proper drill, and read aloud to officers from various military texts—including Alexander Smyth's *Regulations for the Field Exercises, Manoeuvre, and Conduct of the Infantry*, a basic abridgment of the standard French regulations. Scott used discipline, drill, and motivation to teach his men how to operate in unit formations and convince them that doing so in strict obedience to their officers would likely save their lives. The standard-issue blue uniform of the regular Army was unavailable, so Scott commandeered gray and white cloth for uniforms. Impressively, Scott eradicated common camp diseases through proper sanitation and discipline.

Secretary Armstrong hoped to move on the Niagara frontier and gain control of Lake Ontario, thereby opening the door to attacking Kingston and Montreal. On the Niagara front, Brown crossed the Niagara River in yet another amphibious operation and took Fort Erie with little fighting. Two days later, as the army advanced toward the Chippewa River, American militia encountered British-supported Indians and attacked. Quickly, however, the small force hit a strong line of British regulars and broke and fled. Winfield Scott stepped into the breach with his 1,500 regulars. Well-disciplined and well-trained, the gray-clad regulars held their line as they advanced into withering British fire. British General Phineas Riall, convinced that the gray soldiers must be militia, suddenly realized that indeed they were regulars. Scott boldly ordered a bayonet charge that broke the British right flank, forcing Riall to withdraw his entire force back across the Chippewa River.

At the Battle of Chippewa, Riall lost 500 killed, wounded, and missing to Scott's 325. Although the battle was strategically indecisive, Scott had notched his belt with yet another admirable example of combat command and gave Brown's army a substantial morale boost. In honor of Scott's "Grays" success, the United States Military Academy at West Point adopted the gray tunic as its official uniform.

Just a few weeks later, the American army was engaged again, this time in a large affair near Niagara Falls at a spot called Lundy's Lane. With only 1,000 troops, Scott struck at a British force of 1,800. Reinforcements increased Scott's force to 2,100 and the British numbers to over 3,000 by the end of the day. Fighting continued into the night. A battery at the British center was overrun by the Americans, who in turn had to repulse several bloody British assaults to retake the battery. Some veterans of earlier battles in the War of 1812 and the Napoleonic Wars claimed that this was the fiercest fight they had ever witnessed. Both Scott and Brown received serious wounds. As the fighting subsided out of sheer exhaustion, Brown ordered his men from the field and detailed wagons to collect the wounded.

Learning that cannon may have been left on the field, Brown ordered General Eleazer Ripley to re-form the division to retrieve the cannon and to destroy the British army should it reappear. Ripley had no intention of carrying out the weakened Brown's order. Exhaustion, lack of water, and low ammunition made such a prospect unfeasible. After heated argument, Brown finally acquiesced to Ripley's request to withdraw. Brown's army returned to Fort Erie, where it had started. Hard-fought battles had come to naught; and now the initiative, which Brown and Scott had so brilliantly exercised, seemed to pass back to the British. Casualties amounted to over 800 for each side, but the Americans felt they had won the day by voluntarily withdrawing from the field in good order. The British, however, could equally claim victory in this, the bloodiest battle of the war.

Now the British took the offensive. In August a British force of 2,100 attacked Fort Erie. After a two-day artillery barrage the British assaulted the fort with bayonets fixed at 2:00 a.m. on August 15. Hand-to-hand combat raged during a driving rainstorm. After two hours the affair was decided by an exploding magazine, which killed and wounded many more British than Americans. The British withdrew, leaving behind over 500 killed, wounded, and missing to the Americans' 130. The British did not give up completely. They placed three batteries some 500 yards from the fort and opened a continuous fire. Jacob Brown did not want to abandon Fort Erie, but neither could he allow his men to be shelled into submission. Brown ordered two brigades of New York militia to assault the batteries. On the night of September 17, the New Yorkers performed well, taking two of the three batteries in fierce fighting. The British withdrew. On November 5, so too did the Americans, destroying the fort as

FIGURE 5-2 Battle of Lake Erie. September 1813. Oliver Hazard Perry, standing. Copy of engraving by Phillibrown after W.H. Powell, published in 1858.

Source: National Archives and Records Administration

they evacuated. The bloody fighting achieved little of strategic importance, but the Americans had clearly shown they could go toe-to-toe with the British army.

While Fort Erie lay under siege, Prevost set his sights on taking control of Lake Champlain as part of a broad British strategy to attack into American territory from Canada as well as to hit strategic points along the American coast. Prevost hoped to put the Americans on the defensive and maintain initiative by destroying the American naval squadron on Lake Champlain and defeating land forces at Plattsburgh. His force of 8,000 crack British troops, many just arrived after defeating Napoleon, crossed into the United States on September 3. Brigadier General Alexander Macomb abandoned Plattsburgh to Prevost on September 6, withdrawing across the Saranac River to earthworks on the high ground opposite Plattsburgh. Prevost's attempts to cross the Saranac River via two bridges were repulsed by determined American regulars and militia.

Prevost then decided to let Captain George Downie's flotilla of 93 guns take care of Captain Thomas Macdonough's squadron of 86 guns formed for battle in Plattsburgh Bay. By defeating Macdonough's squadron, Prevost hoped to starve out Macomb's land force. In a two-hour, bitterly fought battle that killed Downie, Macdonough prevailed by using difficult anchor maneuvers that allowed his ships to swing quicker and at shorter distance and thus to outmaneuver the British vessels. The British hauled down their colors and surrendered. Meanwhile, Prevost delayed what was supposed to be a simultaneous attack across the Saranac River. Although a brigade had crossed the river, when Prevost saw that Downie's squadron had been defeated he lost his nerve and recalled the attacking force. Arguably, Prevost could have taken the field. Had he defeated Macomb's force and taken the earthen forts on the hill overlooking Plattsburgh and Plattsburgh Bay, Macdonough assuredly would have been forced to leave the protective confines of the bay and expose himself on Lake Champlain, where Downie's larger ships might have had a better chance to defeat Macdonough. Alas, this was not the case and Prevost withdrew from Plattsburgh in disgrace.

While the British attempt to invade via Plattsburgh had failed, joint operations in the Chesapeake Bay region came very close to decisive success. British activity in the Chesapeake Bay had been limited to sparse but effective raids, such as the unusually brutal British attack on Hampton, Virginia, in June 1813. Two thousand troops, mostly French prisoners of war known as the Chasseurs Britannique, quickly chased off 450 militiamen defending the town. British operations in the Chesapeake also affected slavery; as in the War for Independence the British offered captured slaves the opportunity for freedom and resettlement in exchange for service in His Majesty's forces. An estimated 600 slaves enlisted.

In 1814, however, the British decided to make a more determined diversionary campaign in the Chesapeake region in the hope of forcing the Americans to redeploy

FIGURE 5-3 Bird's-eye view of the battle near New Orleans, January 8, 1815. Copy of engraving from a sketch by Latour, Jackson's chief engineer.

Source: National Archives and Records Administration

forces from the Niagara front to the Chesapeake. Moreover, taking Washington, Baltimore, or Philadelphia would certainly give the British a large advantage in peace negotiations. By July 1814, Madison had become increasingly alarmed that the British would indeed invade up the Chesapeake Bay and destroy the American capital, much as the Americans had razed York earlier in the war.

Remarkably, before July 1814, the United States had no established defense strategy for the Washington–Baltimore area. Madison made Brigadier General William Winder, a Federalist, commander of the new 10th Military District for the defense of Washington and Baltimore. Three thousand regulars and over 10,000 militia would do the job with the help of various natural obstacles, not the least of which were the dense undergrowth and swampy bogs of the Tidewater region. Secretary of War Armstrong, who disagreed with Madison's fear for Washington, neglected Winder's requests for staff, material, and ammunition. The governors of Maryland, Virginia, and Delaware, among other states, acted slowly to fulfill Madison's requests for more militia. The nation's capital was exceptionally vulnerable to attack.

British General Robert Ross eagerly took command of the British effort, knowing what taking the American capital would mean for British morale both in North America and at home. Admiral Alexander Cochrane shared Ross's enthusiasm for the campaign, hoping to cash in on prize money from the rich port of Baltimore. On August 20, Ross and Cochrane sailed up the Patuxent River and landed 4,500 troops at Benedict, Maryland. By August 22, the British had advanced to Upper Marlborough, Maryland, just sixteen miles away from Washington. Pandemonium struck the capital city, and the Army command structure, never efficient to begin with, began to break down at the most critical moment.

Winder had about 7,000 troops of mostly hastily trained militia under his command. With his force formed in three lines between the British and the capital, Winder lost operational control. Secretary of State James Monroe, who had volunteered as a cavalry scout and was nominally acting Secretary of War, personally ordered the second line to redeploy to a position where it could not support the front line. The third line had already been placed in a position where it could not support the second. General Tobias Stansbury, commander of Maryland militia in the second line, obeyed the order, assuming that it had come from Winder. It had not—Monroe had no authority whatsoever.

On August 24, British troops easily crossed the Potomac River via a poorly defended bridge near Bladensburg. The first American line was quickly outflanked. British rockets did little harm but scared the daylights out of the Americans. Militia ran rearward, while the few regulars manning the defenses staged a largely orderly retreat. The retreating militia ran pell-mell into the second line, causing widespread panic—the infamous Bladensburg Races were under way.

Holding the third and last line was Navy Captain Joshua Barney, who had commanded the gunboat flotilla on the Chesapeake Bay. With naval guns positioned on high ground, Barney hit the advancing British lines with devastating grapeshot. Still, the British managed to overrun Barney's militia-defended flank, putting the British in a strong position to overrun the guns. They promptly took advantage of the opportunity. Americans who could walk left the field. Although the British suffered over 250 casualties to the Americans' 70, they had won the Battle of Bladensburg. The road to Washington was now wide open for the British advance.

By 8:00 p.m. that same day, the British marched into Washington. Ross searched in vain for anyone with authority to arrange for the surrender of the city. The executive mansion, the capitol, and the Treasury, War, and State Departments were looted and burned. The American navy captain in command of the Washington Navy Yard followed his orders and set fire to the Navy's best-supplied shipyard and two frigates moored there. The sacking of Washington was a bitter pill indeed for the United States.

Baltimore lay next in the path of the seemingly unstoppable British onslaught. Ross left Washington on August 25 and headed back to Benedict. Meanwhile, a British naval force raided Alexandria, taking twenty-one prize ships fully loaded with flour, tobacco, cotton, sugar, wine, and other valuable commodities. In Baltimore the alarm had been sounded. Senator and Major General of Maryland militia Samuel Smith organized over 10,000 militia to defend the city from a land attack. Fourteen miles from Baltimore at North Point, Ross landed his 4,500 troops. There a force of 3,200 militia tried unsuccessfully to stop the British advance. Although the British prevailed in the Battle of North Point, the victory came at a high price—340 British casualties, including Ross, who was killed by a sharpshooter.

Lacking naval support, the British had to stop just short of Baltimore on September 13. To get to Baltimore, Ross first had to pass Fort McHenry, a Vauban-style fortification built as part of the coastal defense program. Admiral Cochrane's guns fired over 1,500 shells at the fortification but did little damage. Fort McHenry held, an event immortalized by Georgetown lawyer and artillery volunteer Francis Scott Key in his poem "The Star Spangled Banner."

September 1814 had been a good month for the American war effort. Victories at Plattsburgh, Lake Champlain, and now Baltimore should have given the Americans a sense of relief and newfound confidence. Baltimore had been successfully defended by militia and the local community—a fact that somehow masked the repeated failures of militia, most recently at Bladensburg. The British had been repulsed, and peace negotiations at Ghent seemed to be making headway.

Partisan politics in Congress and deep divisions in the Madison administration, however, overshadowed the short-lived sense of optimism. Congressional committees immediately began investigations into the loss of Washington. The secretaries of War, the Treasury, and the Navy resigned. James Monroe ambitiously, if not recklessly, tried to be Secretary of State and War at the same time. New Englanders began their controversial meetings in Hartford and openly talked of secession unless the war was ended. By November Ross's army had rendezvoused with the British fleet in Jamaica to refit for the next campaign. British plans for what had originally been another diversionary campaign turned into hopes for a decisive strike at arguably the most strategic, important American possessions—the Mississippi River and New Orleans.

President Madison earlier approved of plans to ignite an uprising in Spanish Florida supported by American troops and naval forces. The United States had taken similar action in Spanish West Florida in 1810 and Congress had approved a secret act to occupy and acquire all of Spanish Florida in 1811. By 1812 as the war with Britain got under way, American filibusters, or private adventurers, supported by Georgia militia and with the blessing of the Madison administration secured Amelia Island just off the Florida coast and were preparing to lay siege against St. Augustine. Americans in Georgia and South Carolina strongly supported expansion into Florida, while New

Englanders denounced the plan as Republican aggression. President Madison had to play an extremely delicate role by publicly denying the effort while privately cheering it on. Strategically Madison claimed that American aggression in East Florida was a preemptive move to counter British possession of the region. The so-called Patriot War failed in the end but cleared the path for the United States to acquire Florida through the Adams-Onis Treaty of 1819.

General Andrew Jackson had just triumphed in the Creek War. The great warrior chieftain Tecumseh visited the Creek in 1811 in a vain attempt to gather Creek support for his united front against Anglo encroachment upon native lands. Tecumseh was a long way from home and arguably had little influence on the Creek who were in the nascent stages of their own civil war. But like Tecumseh many Creek found the idea of returning to their native ways appealing as European customs seemed about to forever bury the old ways. The Red Sticks surfaced as leaders of this resistance movement. Conflict broke out among the Creek in 1813 after some Upper Creek warriors killed several white settlers. The Creek Council condemned the warriors to death, but Upper Creek and Red Sticks protested and raided several Lower Creek towns, killing several hundred men, women, and children, including over 500 in the massacre at Fort Mims in Alabama.

This complex intertribal conflict quickly erupted into a full-fledged war with the United States, which feared the Creek might be lured into an alliance with the British to assist British operations in the South, perhaps even against New Orleans. The massacre at Fort Mims occurred in the midst of these concerns and easily persuaded the Madison administration to send Federal troops and militia from Tennessee, Georgia, and Mississippi to deal with the Creek. Among these was a large force from Tennessee that was later reinforced to total some 5,000 troops led by the rugged Jackson. A harsh disciplinarian, Jackson kept his Army well trained and supplied, and it grew more disciplined as the campaign continued.

Jackson and the Red Sticks fought several engagements, with neither side gaining a sustainable advantage. Red Stick causalities in these battles were high, numbering in the hundreds in some instances. Finally, in March 1814, Jackson attacked a large Red Stick encampment at Horseshoe Bend along the Tallapoosa River in Alabama. The Creek had a well-entrenched position but were easily diverted by a small unit of Jackson's force. Jackson took advantage of the opportunity, and his forces overwhelmed the battlement. Few Red Sticks surrendered or had the opportunity to do so, resulting in almost 1,000 Creek deaths. Over 300 Creek men, women, and children were captured. Jackson lost fewer than 30 troops killed. It was a stunning and complete victory in what had become a very bloody small war within the War of 1812. Sam Houston and Davy Crockett, among several participants, later capitalized on fame from the conflict. Jackson was given a regular Army commission and promoted to major general, then ordered to New Orleans to take command of the 7th Military District. The Creek were finished as a political-military force in the American South as the Treaty of Fort Jackson forced them to cede much of their 20 million acres of land to the United States.

Jackson did not yet know if he should defend New Orleans or Mobile. After dispensing with the Creeks, Jackson had occupied Mobile and garrisoned Fort Boyer on the eastern shore of the mouth of Mobile Bay with a force of 160 men. In September

1814 a British force of 225 Royal Marines from Pensacola landed nine miles east of Fort Boyer, while a small British squadron of 78 guns approached the mouth of Mobile Bay. Major William Lawrence, commander of Fort Boyer, exchanged fire with the British ships and managed to shoot away the rigging of HMS *Hermes*, which had to be abandoned by the British. The weather favored the Americans, as calm winds made naval maneuver dangerously risky under the accurate fire of American artillery on the walls of Fort Boyer. The British squadron withdrew to Pensacola, while the Royal Marines attempted a brief assault and then also withdrew upon learning that the squadron was gone. Taking Fort Boyer had been key to British plans for taking Mobile, which in turn was the key for mounting an invasion against Louisiana. The British had failed to appreciate the shallow waters of Mobile Bay and the well-disciplined force of regulars that manned Fort Boyer.

Instead of waiting for the British to return with a larger force, Jackson took the initiative against the British base of operations at Pensacola. Joining forces with General John Coffee's 2,000 cavalry from Tennessee, Jackson amassed an army of 4,000, including several hundred Indians and 1,000 regulars. Pensacola was still a Spanish possession, yet the Spanish had allowed the British to garrison Fort Barrancas. Two other forts, St. Rose and St. Michael, were weakly manned by a few hundred Spanish soldiers. Jackson arrived at Pensacola and camped on the west side of the small village and the Spanish forts.

The Spanish rejected Jackson's terms for surrender; then, on November 7, Jackson attacked the town. A small demonstration on the west side of Pensacola fooled the Spanish as well as the British squadron in the bay into believing that the American attack would come from that direction. Instead, Jackson attacked with his main body from the east, easily investing the town. The Spanish commander quickly surrendered the forts, but officers in the forts delayed surrendering in the vain hope that the British ships would be able to reposition to support them. Furious, Jackson was forced to delay his assault on the British at Fort Barrancas. Fortunately, he would not have to take Fort Barrancas by force as on the next day the British withdrew from the fort, destroying it in a tremendous explosion. The British soldiers sailed away, their commanders having decided that Pensacola was not worth defending.

With the British gone, Jackson returned Pensacola to the Spanish and headed back to Mobile, arriving there on November 19. With the expeditionary force back from the Chesapeake and further reinforcements arrived from Plymouth, the British made sail from Jamaica to take New Orleans. Lieutenant General Sir Edward Pakenham, a seasoned veteran of the Peninsula Wars, commanded the force in place of General Ross, who had been killed. Jackson, still not completely certain that New Orleans was the target, took the gamble and set out with 2,000 men for the Crescent City.

New Orleans possessed impressive natural defenses. The turbulent Mississippi River bordered its southern edge, while Lake Pontchartrain provided a formidable barrier north of the city. To the west and east as well as the north, hundreds of creeks, bayous, and swamps made New Orleans a daunting objective for an invading force. Man-made levies in and around the city itself added further protection. Two forts, St. Leon nearer the city and St. Philip 60 miles further south, guarded the southern approaches along the river. Pakenham concluded that the northern and eastern approaches would be the least defended.

Jackson found help in New Orleans, and more help was on the way from Tennessee. Militia and two battalions of free blacks combined with 3,000 militia from Tennessee under General William Carol and Jackson's 2,000 men to give Jackson a force of almost 6,000 to defend against Pakenham's 14,000 troops. Even the pirate Jean Laffite, whose men had for years been notorious for raiding ships near the mouth of the Mississippi River, contributed his services in exchange for Jackson's promise that the pirate and his men would be pardoned for their past deeds. On December 16 Jackson declared martial law in New Orleans, risking the support of Louisiana's state government and causing no end of legal problems for his command.

The British had already landed near Lake Borgne, where a Royal Navy squadron defeated the American gunboat fleet to clear the way for Pakenham's troops. A British advance force of 1,600 came within seven miles of the city on December 22. The next day, in a daring night attack, Jackson and 2,000 men managed to stall the advance. He then retreated three miles to the Rodriguez Canal, a fine defensive position with the Mississippi River on the west, the dense Cypress Swamp on the east, and a ten-foot-wide canal connecting the two. Three ditches also ran west to east in front of the Rodriguez Canal. Jackson's men feverishly dug to build a rampart along the canal but found another enemy in the wet Louisiana soil. Fences, slave cabins, cotton bales, and whatever else his men could tear down and transport to the canal were used to shore up the breastworks. Pakenham assaulted this position on December 28 but deadly artillery fire from the American line and the *Louisiana* from the river forced him to withdraw.

Pakenham tried again on January 1, 1815, launching a massive artillery assault on the Rodriguez Canal. Jackson replied in kind. For over ninety minutes the two sides pounded each other, but the British failed to make a dent in Jackson's line. Pakenham then resolved to take the position by frontal assault. In the early hours of January 8, Pakenham sent a force of 600 across the river to the west bank to engage the force of 1,200 that Jackson had positioned there to prevent a British attempt to simply go around on the other side of the river. Jackson held his main force on the canal. Pakenham sent 3,500 men directly at Jackson's line at about 7:00 a.m. On their left lay the mighty Mississippi River; on their right was the Cypress Swamp. They had nowhere to go but forward into the well-entrenched American line. Jackson laid down a murderous wall of musket fire and canister shot that decimated the British ranks, most of whom were veterans of the Napoleonic wars. Pakenham fell dead. In just over an hour the British suffered almost 300 killed, 1,200 wounded, and 480 captured to Jackson's 13 dead and 39 wounded. The Battle of New Orleans was a stunning defeat for the British and an extraordinary victory for the Americans.

◆ THE WAR ENDS

On February 8, 1815, a British force launched a final assault against Fort Boyer in an attempt to renew the offensive to take Mobile. Fort Boyer fell, but just afterward news reached both sides that a peace treaty had been signed at Ghent on Christmas Eve, 1814. The war had been over for six weeks and for two weeks before the Battle of New Orleans. News of Jackson's victory reached Washington just before the word of the treaty.⌈The Treaty of Ghent restored the geopolitical situation to *status quo ante bellum*. With the war against Napoleon finished, there was no longer any need to harass American shipping and impress American sailors. With Tecumseh's confederation broken in the Old Northwest Territory and the Creeks under control in the south, the native threat and British irritation had apparently vanished. Canada had not fallen to America, but neither had New England seceded from the Union. The United States had survived an apparent "second war of independence" by fighting the world's foremost military power to what amounted to a draw.⌋

The war had touched people all across the young nation. Over 450,000 militia had been mustered and tens of thousands of volunteers had been recruited. Over 50,000 served in the regular Army during the war and another 20,000 had served in the Navy and Marines. According to official records, only 2,260 had been killed in battle with another 4,500 wounded, but perhaps as many as 17,000 men died from nonmilitary causes, mostly disease. The war had cost $158 million, including Army and Navy expenditures, interest on war loans, and veterans' benefits. The national debt had risen from $45 million in 1812 to over $127 million at war's end.⌈The economy was slow to recover, hitting rock bottom in the Panic of 1819–1820.⌋

Despite the euphoric celebrations at war's end,⌈problems that had plagued American foreign and military policy since the founding of the Republic had become more serious. The war had exacerbated the spirit of factionalism and sectionalism to further divide the nation. The military faced a critical crossroads—would it remain small and weak, reliant upon the militia, or would it begin the long process of becoming a professional peacetime standing army? Would the naval successes in 1814 justify a larger, more powerful permanent fleet? For the United States to capitalize on its newfound respect abroad and continue its territorial and commercial growth, it would have to address these and many additional issues. As is often the case, the end of a war may resolve some problems but create others.

◆ THE BEGINNINGS OF A PROFESSIONAL MILITARY

Efforts to assess the successes and failures of the military after the war had already become clouded by selective memory and political purpose. Junior officers who had risen through the ranks, such as Scott, had been frustrated by incompetent generalship, glacial bureaucracy, nightmarish logistical shortcomings, and other maladies that had plagued an unprepared nation and its military during the war. Although they had not completely forgotten these problems, many junior officers had come to sugarcoat them because of the way they remembered, with great pride, the exaggerated success of the regular Army during the war—Lundy's Lane, Chippewa, and Plattsburgh, among others, highlighted for these officers the increasing professionalism of the regular Army and cast grave doubt upon the unmanageable militia. Granted, the militia had failed on numerous occasions, but so too had had the regulars. Many officers had conveniently forgotten that it had been mostly militia that defeated Tecumseh and Brock in 1813 and gave Jackson victory at New Orleans. Career officers easily formulated an argument promoting their own military prowess and denigrating the shameful failures of the militia, quickly convincing themselves that the United States could no longer depend upon a citizen-led army. Only a large, disciplined army led by professional officers could save the nation from the total disintegration it nearly faced in 1812 and 1813.

Winfield Scott went immediately to work at the end of the war to rectify the gross shortcomings of the Army. He had learned that not only did field armies need organized staffs, so too did the generals in Washington. Moreover, politically appointed officers had to be driven out in favor of an officer corps that saw military service as a career and a profession. The lack of recruiting, training, and operational standards had created a force that suffered from poor morale, inconsistent performance, and high rates of attrition. Many frustrated officers left service after only a few years due to the lack of opportunity for promotion, inferior quality of life, and general corruption that had seized the officer corps. Scott, Jackson, Brown, and Macomb, among others, would lead this effort to reorganize the officer corps and make the best of an Army reduced from its authorized wartime strength of 65,000 to just 10,000. While much dead weight was cut away from the Army, demobilization caused thousands of men with few prospects to be put out on the streets. No pensions or bonuses were immediately available to ease the financial pain.

Scott and his compatriots faced a Congress and a nation that retained a fear of standing armies; once again, most people wanted to hastily dismantle the wartime military and return to a militia-based peacetime establishment. Officers who remained in the Army and earnestly wanted to make it a professional standing force believed that too much dismantling would risk the valuable experience that had been gained from the war.

Scott and others proposed instead to implement George Washington's original idea from 1783. Using a skeleton structure, the current regimental organization would be retained but at less strength. In a crisis, the skeleton could be filled out with volunteers or conscription rather than state militia. Scott and Secretary of War Monroe suggested a similar plan in 1815. Scott actually wanted an army of 65,000 troops, then realizing the political climate of the time he proposed 20,000. Through the Army Reduction Act of 1815, Congress allowed only 10,000. Over the next several years the skeleton or expansible army plan gained support in Congress.

In 1821, now President Monroe and Secretary of War John C. Calhoun considered a plan wherein each company maintained a full complement of officers but only fifty-five enlisted men. With a severe economic depression wracking the nation, money could not be found to support a force structure of even that size. Instead, in 1821 Congress reduced the Army to 6,000 men. By 1823, the ratio of officers to enlisted men dropped to 1 to 8, down from 1 to 16 in 1814.

Nonetheless, by getting the expansible army idea accepted and thereby protecting the officer corps from dismemberment, Scott and his colleagues had achieved an astounding success in professionalization. Professional skills had been saved and dispersion prevented so that in the next crisis, the theory went, these officers could quickly train and command an expanded force. Still wary of a standing army, many in Congress eagerly voted to limit the size of the regular Army.

Career officers also wanted to solve recruitment, training, and quality of life problems for the officer corps. Scott helped write a new uniform manual for tactical drill, based upon French models of the day. While criticized for being merely a translation of French drill manuals, slightly adapted for American conditions, Scott's manual was significant. For the first time, it provided uniformity and consistency for Army drill and infantry tactics. Several officers, including Scott, took advantage of leaves of absence and official assignments to visit Europe and discuss military matters with their British and French comrades in arms.

American officers considered the European continent the center of progressive military thought and cutting-edge military technology, the professional benefits of two decades of near-constant war. Captain Sylvanus Thayer, for example, spent invaluable time observing at French military schools and brought home books, manuals, and ideas to strengthen instruction at the U.S. Military Academy. His efforts resulted in a revised curriculum, more demanding admission standards, and much better professionally prepared graduates. In 1818, Thayer's reforms helped get the academy's first independent appropriation from Congress. Scott spent two years on a personal leave of absence to tour Europe to hobnob with military leaders in Prussia, Russia, Great Britain, and France. Officially an observer with the French army, Scott found that the mostly pleasurable sojourn across the Atlantic influenced his ideas on military thought and strengthened his commitment to professionalization. Still, European ideas often encountered resistance among American officers. Foreign ideas were, after all, foreign—and therefore suspect. Moreover, many European officers tended to treat their American counterparts as inferiors on the grounds that Americans lacked a true officer class and had not, of course, fought a Napoleonic war.

Although Congress reluctantly maintained a very small professional force, it was less hesitant to pass legislation to better organize that force. In April 1816, Congress authorized the Army to adopt wartime staff organization in peacetime. In 1816, only three generals heading staff departments had headquarters in Washington—the Adjutant General, the Paymaster General, and the Chief of Ordnance. In 1818, Calhoun convinced Congress to authorize three additional positions—the Quartermaster General, Surgeon General, and Commissary General. In addition to the already existing chief of the Corps of Engineers, the new departments also had headquarters in Washington. On paper this staff organization looked effective, however, as an unintended consequence it created not only conflict between staff and line officers but also a system that became disconnected and increasingly bureaucratic and decentralized.

Moreover, the war provided motivation for expanding and enhancing the coastal defense system. Madison established a board of engineers to study the nation's seacoast defenses. Their 1821 report found serious gaps and highlighted the need for major additions that would better secure the United States from foreign attack. Congress had provided a paltry $800,000 in 1816 to repair aging fortifications, but more was needed. Since the Navy remained relatively small, coastal fortifications would have to serve as the true first line of defense. The board suggested fifty sites for new fortifications, but recommendations and Congressional appropriations to fulfill those suggestions often proved to be two different things.

The Navy also received a much-needed boost from the war. Having performed well considering its size and the enemy it faced in battle, the expanded fleet of frigates had scored several brilliant one-on-one victories during the war. Organizationally, a Board of Navy Commissioners was created to advise the Navy Department. Made up of three captains, the first board included John Rodgers, David Porter, and Stephen Decatur. How well it worked over the next several decades depended upon the management style of the Secretary of the Navy and the makeup of the board. Often, as in the case of the first board, the advice was limited to logistical and administrative matters.

As for the fleet, Congress passed an act in 1816 that provided a generous $1 million per year for six years for naval construction. Twelve 44-gun frigates and nine 74-gun ships of the line were planned, but only the frigates were completed in a timely manner (one of the 74s was still under construction when the Civil War began in 1861). Congress had been convinced that a stronger peacetime navy was necessary in the postwar environment, especially with Great Britain still in command of the seas.

Debate continued about how best to employ the Navy. Sticking to traditional strategies, the Navy continued to use its frigates in squadrons that really amounted to a few ships acting independently under a commodore who exercised regional command. By 1821 the Navy, like the Army, came under the budgetary and ideological knife of men who wanted to limit severely the peacetime military establishment. The Navy's annual appropriation dropped from $3.7 million for the years 1817–1821 to $2.9 million for the years 1822–1825. Navy personnel also declined, from 5,500 in 1816 to 4,000 in 1821.

◆ CONCLUSION

The young republic survived serious challenges to its sovereignty, indeed its very existence. In military affairs it had learned much but still had much to learn. Experience was shaping the way the nation approached military matters and warfare and it was changing the ideological landscape that governed the way the American military would be organized, manned, and used. Experience also gradually better defined American national interests. Sea-borne trade, territorial integrity and expansion, and defense of liberty at home evolved from basic ideals to real national strategic objectives.

The military strategy to achieve and maintain these objectives had also matured to include fortified coastal defense, an established navy, a peacetime army of some size, and continued reliance upon militia to expand both the Army and Navy in times of danger. The nation had survived birth. It next had to face the growing pains of an ambitious and expanding people. The military would be at the forefront of such national movements as Manifest Destiny, the Market Revolution, the beginnings of industrialization, and the expansion of democracy in America.

Further Reading ●

Barbuto, Richard V. *Niagara 1814: America Invades Canada.* Lawrence: University Press of Kansas, 2000.

Elting, John R. *Amateurs to Arms! A Military History of the War of 1812.* Chapel Hill: Algonquin Books, 1991.

Graves, Donald E. *Field of Glory: The Battle of Chrysler's Farm, 1813.* Toronto: Robin Brass, 1999.

Graves, Donald E. *Lords of the Lake: The Naval War on Lake Ontario, 1812–1814.* Annapolis: Naval Institute Press, 1998.

Hickey, Donald R. *The War of 1812: A Forgotten Conflict.* Urbana: University of Illinois Press, 1989.

Pitch, Anthony S. *The Burning of Washington: The British Invasion of 1814.* Annapolis: Naval Institute Press, 1998.

Quimby, Robert S. *The U.S. Army in the War of 1812: An Operational and Command Study.* East Lansing: Michigan State University Press, 1997.

Remini, Robert V. *The Battle of New Orleans.* New York: Viking, 1999.

Skaggs, David Curtis. *A Signal Victory: The Lake Erie Campaign, 1812–1813.* Annapolis: Naval Institute Press, 1997.

Skeen, C. Edward. *Citizen Soldiers in the War of 1812.* Lexington: University Press of Kentucky, 1999.

Skelton, William B. *An American Profession of Arms: The Army Officer Corps, 1784–1861.* Lawrence: University Press of Kansas, 1992.

Stagg, J. C. A. *Mr. Madison's War: Politics, Diplomacy and Warfare in the Early Republic, 1783–1830.* Princeton: Princeton University Press, 1983.

Sugden, John. *Tecumseh's Last Stand.* Norman: University of Oklahoma Press, 1985.

Turner, Wesley. *The War of 1812: The War That Both Sides Won.* Toronto: Dundurn Press, 1990.

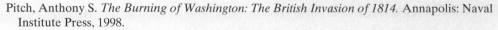 **Connections: Sources Online** • • • • • • • • • • • •

READ AND REVIEW

Review this chapter by using the study aids and these related documents available on MySearchLab.

Study Plan

Chapter Test

Essay Test

Documents

Petition from Citizens of Boston (1812)

This petition from citizens of Boston outlines their fears of possible war with Great Britain, revealing the lack of enthusiasm of many New Englanders for another war.

Ephraim Hubbard Foster to William Graham (1814)

This letter from Tennessee Senator Ephraim Hubbard Foster praises Jackson's victory over the Creek at the Battle of Horseshoe Bend.

Broadside Announcing Jackson's Victory at New Orleans (1815)

The broadside from Essex, Massachusetts, details the American victory over British forces at the Battle of New Orleans for a public eager for news of the battle.

The Taking of the City of Washington in America (1814)

The British engraving depicts the burning of Washington by British forces in August 1814.

RESEARCH AND EXPLORE

Explore the following review questions using the research tools available on www.mysearchlab.com.

1. How did militia perform in the War of 1812 compared to regulars?
2. What issues of professionalism arose during and after the war?
3. How did the United States try to marry its military strategy in the War of 1812 to its political objectives in the conflict?

Agents of Empire

◆ INTRODUCTION

From the early 1800s through the Civil War, the United States experienced great territorial, economic, and democratic growth. Settlers occupied lands that few had thought habitable as well as other lands already claimed by native peoples. Oregon, the Louisiana Territory, Texas, and the Mexican Cession lands became organized territories and states. The Market Revolution broadened economic opportunity, just as political reforms expanded the electorate and egalitarianism shaped democratic values during the Age of Jackson. At the same time, the beginnings of an industrial revolution changed labor patterns and made material goods more widely available than ever before. New technology, such as the steam engine, challenged traditional ways of doing things. While stunning in scope and effect, such change and growth had disadvantages. Territorial expansion brought contact with indigenous peoples and Hispanics, as well as more territory to defend. Economic growth and opportunity did not reach all levels of society. More often than not, immigrants provided the unskilled labor that supported the expansion of transportation, manufacturing, and capitalism. Explosive population growth brought crowding and other problems to American cities.

◆ THE MILITARY AND A CHANGING NATION

Because the oceans continued to protect the growing nation from external threats, the American military remained small and technologically behind the times. Yet, during this period the Army performed many nonmilitary tasks for which it had no training and little experience. At the same time, the Army continued to prepare for war to defend the United States.

From the beginning of the nineteenth century through well after the Civil War, the U.S. Army and Navy used the experience gained from their nonmilitary duties to improve their military knowledge and skills. Officers found professional stimulation in exploration and science, and in studying the Napoleonic Wars that had engulfed the European continent from 1799 to 1815. Internal matters, such as Indian removal and frontier garrison duty, however, often interfered with the pursuit of professionalism because such duties required that the Army function more as a constabulary than as a military force preparing for war. Nonetheless, when war against Mexico came in 1846, the United States had an Army and Navy much better prepared and led than they had been in 1812. The frontier duties and the officer corps' efforts toward professionalism paid off in a military that, although far from perfect, had successfully carried out difficult and distant campaigns against a formidable enemy.

With relative peace from the War of 1812 through the early 1840s, military officers eagerly volunteered for exploring expeditions on land and sea. These expeditions contributed valuable knowledge to various scientific fields, produced improved maps and charts, and brought prestige and pride to the military and the United States. Moreover, exploring gave the Army an opportunity to improve upon and learn new skills, practice organizing large deployments, and develop a sense of purpose. A greater sense of professionalism accompanied the improvement in knowledge and skill level. During the pre-Civil War period, the United States experienced significant territorial expansion, commercial growth, and a surge in diplomatic prestige. As the only government entity with the organization, resources, and leadership skills to carry out such missions, the military became the "pointy end" in the expansionist movement.

◆ THE ARMY AND THE WEST

On March 31, 1804, U.S. Army Captain Meriwether Lewis and Lieutenant of Artillery William Clark conducted a brief ceremony to formally enlist twenty-two soldiers into the "Detachment destined for the Expedition through the interior of the *Continent* of North America." Also known as the Corps of Discovery, the Lewis and Clark expedition to find a water route from the Missouri River to the Pacific Ocean and to explore the lands acquired through the Louisiana Purchase in 1803 was first and foremost a military operation. President Thomas Jefferson had little choice but to look to the Army to carry out this important and dangerous assignment because no other department in the federal government had the organizational and logistical ability, the training and discipline, or the resources needed to put together, equip, man, and conduct an exploration of such extended length covering such enormous space.

Jefferson ordered captains Lewis and Clark (Lewis gave his good friend an informal brevet promotion to captain so that the two men could co-command the expedition) to locate a water route to the Pacific, and explore the new territory. The president also ordered the explorers to record the types of flora and fauna found along the way, to make extensive notes on the native peoples encountered, and to map rivers and possible trade routes. The expedition carried the latest scientific equipment to assist in drawing maps, and in recording and preserving the plants, animals, rocks, and minerals collected.

Despite failing to find a water route to the Pacific Ocean—because none existed—the Lewis and Clark expedition successfully reached the Pacific and returned to St. Louis two years later, with only one fatality among the expedition's company. The Corps of Discovery maintained strict organization and discipline for the duration of the expedition, and, when necessary, overawed many of the native peoples it encountered by displaying the weapons and wearing the dress uniforms it had packed in anticipation of just such events. Only rarely did the expedition members have to shift from scientist to soldier in order to defend themselves against potentially hostile Indians, often the Teton Sioux or the Blackfoot. Lewis and Clark met Jefferson's many objectives save one—they had not found the desired all-water route to the Pacific. However, the native peoples of the northern Louisiana Purchase territory had been largely peacefully introduced to the federal government and the U.S. Army.

The wealth of scientific information in the form of specimens, maps, measurements, and other data provided more in quantity and quality than Jefferson had dared to hope. Moreover, the expedition sent a subtle but clear signal to the British and Russians, who had interests in the Pacific Northwest, and to the Spanish, who owned the territory south and west of the Louisiana Purchase, that the United States not only held claim to this territory but also possessed it. Lewis and Clark realized that only a military presence could keep hostile Indians subdued, regulate the movements of traders and other whites, and check the intrigues of foreign powers. With that in mind, Clark recommended a chain of forts at strategic points along the Missouri and other major rivers in the region, while Lewis suggested nonmilitary approaches to creating order in the explored, but untamed region.

Even before Lewis and Clark emerged from the Missouri River country, Jefferson had ordered more exploration. Nationalism, security, diplomacy, and science motivated Jefferson's desire to know more about the expanded Republic. Again, he turned to the military, which had several ambitious young officers who considered themselves gentlemen scientists and were eager to make a name for themselves through exploration. Thus began a tradition of scientific and exploratory service in the American military that indirectly promoted national security and professionalism.

Jefferson ordered exploration of the Red River and Arkansas River in 1804. The first expedition, led by civilian scientists under military escort, was forced to change course because of threats from nearby Spanish troops and Osage Indians. Congress authorized another attempt up the Red River in 1805 under civilian surveyor Thomas Freeman and botanist Dr. Peter Custis.

The Freeman Expedition left Fort Adams, near Natchez, Mississippi, in April 1806, accompanied by a reinforced military escort in response to rumors of Spanish troops patrolling the Red River area. Nevertheless, after encountering a large Spanish patrol, Freeman's group returned to Fort Adams in July 1806. Although neither of the Red River expeditions was successful, the efforts are noteworthy in that they demonstrated that Jefferson and the War Department considered the military essential to exploration.

In 1805, General James Wilkinson, governor of the Louisiana Territory, sent Lieutenant Zebulon Pike up the Mississippi River to discover its source. Like Lewis and Clark, Pike had orders to note flora and fauna, record geographic features, map possible sites of settlement, collect weather data, and identify strategic locations for military posts. British traders still worked the upper reaches of the Mississippi, and Pike had to warn several that they were not welcome in what was now American territory. While the nearly year-long expedition temporarily placed an American presence in the north country, Pike did not find the source of the Mississippi River, nor did he force British traders to scale back their activities on American soil. His expedition report described what is now called the Great Plains as unsuitable for agriculture, and fit only for the native tribes that lived there. This description discouraged serious white settlement of that region until after the Civil War.

Pike set out again in July 1806 on a much bolder expedition into the heart of the Spanish borderlands. Splitting his force of twenty men, Pike sent a small party to explore the Arkansas River while he took the rest of the company up the Red River into Colorado. There, he and his men spent a difficult winter. In February 1807, Spanish officials in New Mexico heard rumors of Pike's presence in Colorado and sent a patrol to locate the Americans. Upon finding Pike's group, the Spanish escorted them to the provincial capital at Chihuahua. The Spanish treated the Americans with courtesy and generosity, but confiscated Pike's notes and journals. Finally, in July 1807, the Spanish delivered Pike and most of his men to the Texas border with the United States. The Pike Expedition sorely tested the United States' relations with Spain for little scientific gain. However, publication of his expedition journal in 1810 stimulated popular interest in the American Southwest and initiated white settlement of that area via the Santa Fe Trail that opened in 1821. Pike did not live to see his legacy. During the War of 1812 he died while leading an attack against a British force.

Obviously, establishing friendly relations with Indians was paramount to the success of both expeditions. During his first expedition, Pike attempted to assure the Indians of the United States' good intentions. He also informed the tribes that America had replaced Great Britain as the power in the region. Many tribes accepted the change and surrendered the flags and other symbols the British had given them. Unfortunately, failure to carry through on promises to replace surrendered British decorations with American medals and flags was an oversight that disturbed the Indians. Similarly, during the 1807 expedition Pike found that Spanish gifts and medals to the Pawnee and Osage tribes impeded his efforts to sway them into transferring their allegiance to the American government.

The War of 1812 temporarily halted military expeditions, but the surge of nationalism after the conflict spurred renewed effort. In the 1820s, Secretary of War John C. Calhoun developed a plan to link military posts along the Missouri River with those along the Mississippi in order to create a cohesive western defense system. Although his defense system plan failed, his effort resulted in several expeditions.

Perhaps the most of famous of the Calhoun-sponsored enterprises was the Yellowstone Expedition. It was certainly the most successful for Major Stephen H. Long. In addition to Long and his fellow soldiers (including two military topographers), the company included a botanist, a geologist, a zoologist, and an artist. After spending the winter of 1818–1819 at Council Bluffs, Iowa, Long and his party headed west across the plains along the Platte River. Reaching the Rockies, the expedition discovered Long's Peak, climbed and measured Pike's Peak, and descended what they thought was the Red River but was instead the Canadian River. After a grueling journey during which he and his fellows nearly starved, Long's group reunited with the rest of the Yellowstone Expedition at Fort Smith, Arkansas. Long's published report and maps solidified the myth that the Great Plains was unfit for farming, declaring it useful only as a barrier between U.S. and Spanish territory. His expedition map identified the region as the "Great Desert," inspiring the term "Great American Desert," the name used to describe the Great Plains until the 1870s.

In the 1830s, Army expeditions mapped the Great Basin, an area that encompasses most of Nevada, large portions of Utah, and parts of California, Idaho, Oregon, and Wyoming. An Army expedition also mapped the Trans-Mississippi West for likely railroad routes, a task that was possibly the most important cartographic achievement in the United States before the Civil War.

In 1838, the quality of exploration and mapping improved with the establishment of the Army Topographical Corps, and an improved engineering curriculum at West Point. Of the seventy-two officers who served as topographical engineers from 1838 to 1863, sixty-four graduated from West Point. The Military Academy's new curriculum gave future officers the scientific training that provided skills compatible with the expanding nation's needs. Earlier Army explorers had to learn many of these skills on their own, but now the core curriculum at West Point was geared to preparing young officers for exploration as well as war.

John C. Fremont was, perhaps, the most famous Army explorer. He did not attend West Point, and owed his prominence to his father-in-law, Missouri Senator (and proponent of Manifest Destiny) Thomas Hart Benton. Because of Benton's influence, Lieutenant Fremont commanded a secret reconnaissance to the Rocky Mountains in

FIGURE 6-1 Exploration of the West.

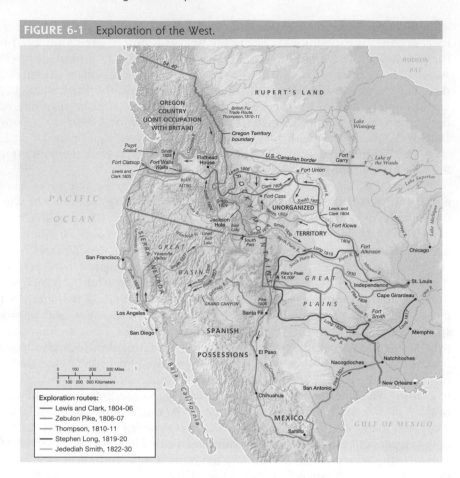

1842. With several fur trappers and mountain men—including Kit Carson, who became Fremont's closest friend—Fremont led his party up the Platte River and west to the Rockies. He mapped the South Pass in Wyoming, climbed the Wind River Mountains, and then turned for home. Along the way, he lost many of his personal notes and journals when his boat capsized in the Sweetwater River. Enough remained, however, to complete a report providing latitude and longitude readings, meteorological information, geological description, and a map of the area from Fort Laramie to the Wind River Mountains. These meager scientific observations paled, however, in comparison to the nationalistic sentiment his report inspired. Congress and people eager to settle in Oregon country mistakenly thought that Fremont's report showed a practical route to Oregon.

In 1843, Fremont received orders to lead another reconnaissance to find a pass across the central Rockies and then to California. Science took a back seat to politics, as Benton and other Manifest Destiny proponents wanted to build on Fremont's first expedition and popularize Oregon and California. Only Fremont and surveyor-cartographer Charles Preuss had any degree of scientific training. The expedition carried few scientific instruments and collected only a smattering of specimens. Fremont's 1843–1844 route took him from the central Rockies, where he found no pass, back north to South Pass, then to the Great Salt Lake, north to Fort Hall in Idaho, and then overland to Fort Vancouver in Washington. There, his official mission ended; his orders dictated returning east via the Oregon Trail. Fremont had other plans, however, and he began an extraordinary and difficult journey from Fort Vancouver, south into eastern California, across the Sierra Nevada mountains through Carson Pass, and on to Sutter's Fort, in California. He then found the Old Spanish Trail to southern California, and traveled back across the Great Basin, the Wasatch Range, and across the Continental Divide. He continued down the Arkansas River, until he reached St. Louis.

Fremont's report on the expedition was a sensation. He promoted the mouth of the Columbia River as the best potential port for trade with Asia, and claimed that the agricultural potential of Oregon could rival that of the eastern United States. Most importantly, he detailed the geography of the West. Emigrant trains along the Oregon Trail found Fremont's information indispensable. Fremont was feted by Congress and the president, and he was promoted to captain. Although much of the region he traveled had already been explored and, in some cases, well-traveled by others, and his maps contained errors (as most maps then did), the expedition's nationalist and expansionist effect was beyond measure. Fremont's report of his second expedition was the most comprehensive on the American West at that time.

Fremont's third expedition in 1845 was controversial. With increasing interest in western settlement, expansionists' eyes on Texas and Mexican California, and growing tensions with Mexico, Fremont had little difficulty getting orders to make a third journey west. The War Department ordered Fremont to confirm river routes and drainages for rivers running east of the Rockies. Fremont himself planned to go back to California for what he claimed were scientific reasons but were more likely commercial ones. Fremont had stretched orders before, and with Benton's protection, he would do so again. At Bent's Fort, Idaho, Fremont gathered his men, including several trappers, soldiers, scientists, and officers. Rather than surveying rivers east of the Rockies, Fremont headed across the Rockies and into the Great Basin and the southern shore of the Great Salt Lake. After spending some time resting the horses and gathering specimens, Fremont led his party across the desert toward California. Fremont's path across the desert would later be known as the Hastings Cutoff, the same trail that the ill-fated Donner Party would later follow.

Fremont's presence in California, of course, irritated and frightened Mexican authorities. Once in California, Fremont met with Mexican General Don Jose Castro, telling the general that his expedition hoped to further the cause of science and explore commercial opportunities. Fremont's well-armed force made it difficult for Castro to accept the explorer's explanation. After resupplying at Sutter's Fort early in 1846, Fremont led his men into the Salinas Valley; there, Mexican authorities ordered his arrest. Fremont held out for several days in a hastily built fort and then retreated toward Oregon. On his way north in May, Fremont learned that war had broken out with Mexico. He then turned his men southward, ending his expedition. He and his comrades joined the fight against Mexico as a detachment of mounted rifles. When the war ended, Commodore Robert F. Stockton appointed Fremont as governor of California. However, Fremont refused to give up the position when ordered to by

President James K. Polk, and so was court-martialed and dishonorably discharged. Although Polk commuted the sentence, Fremont resigned and returned to live in California.

Fremont's expedition was only one of three staged by the Army in 1845. Colonel Stephen W. Kearny took a company of dragoons along the Oregon Trail to South Pass and then down the east slope of the Rockies to Bent's Fort, Colorado. In addition to keeping Indians in line, Kearny surveyed and mapped the region and took the opportunity to experiment with dragoon movements on the open plains. Another expedition, smaller, travelled up the Canadian River into Comanche territory. Like Fremont's, both of these expeditions had a thinly veiled military purpose.

The "high point" of Army expeditions came in the 1850s with the transcontinental railroad route surveys. Weighing options for the best route for a railroad to the Pacific, the Corps of Topographical Engineers produced a thirteen-volume report that included volumes on natural resources, topography, zoology, and botany. The report rivals any of those produced by the military during the nineteenth century. It was natural for the Army to lead this effort—only it had the organization, experience, and skills to conduct such a large undertaking. Moreover, the Army had a strategic stake in a transcontinental railroad.

Army exploration achieved many political, diplomatic, scientific, and military objectives. The Army had become a willing tool of proponents of expansionism, because expeditions of discovery established the territorial integrity of the western United States, although often at the cost of blatantly violating the borders of the northern Mexican frontier. Native tribes had been contained or at least monitored. In the realm of science and discovery, the Army explorations contributed substantially to geographic, botanical, zoological, and meteorological knowledge. By far, the most important contribution was the updated and more accurate maps of the vast expanse of the American West. The Army had been on the "pointy end" of expansion in many ways, and it gained a reputation as a professional force possessing the knowledge and skills to perform tasks that were nationally useful beyond maintaining the security of the United States.

◆ THE NAVAL EXPEDITIONS

Naval exploration grew out of the concerns and conflicts that plagued American sea trade from the beginning of the Republic. Protecting the merchant fleet, securing access to ports in China and other places, instilling respect for the flag, protecting American citizens, and simply promoting an American presence on the high seas sparked conflict with France in the Quasi War, the Barbary pirates in the Tripolitan War, and the British in the War of 1812. By the 1830s, the dramatic increase in American sea-borne trade and the growth of the seal and whaling industries demanded not only a better navy, but also a navy with a sense of mission.

Traders, whalers, and sealers increasingly journeyed to poorly charted or uncharted waters in the western and southern Pacific, the northwestern Pacific coast of North America, and the Antarctic (where it was rumored an entire continent might exist), in search of profit. For example, the whaling industry relied heavily on whaling in the Pacific, accounting for a $5 million per year industry with a fleet of whaling vessels valued at over $225 million. Scientists also had interests in naval exploration and charting, including discovering new lands, mapping currents, and understanding weather patterns. The United States had clear strategic, scientific, and economic reasons for better understanding the world's oceans and distant lands.

Even before the Navy officially sponsored expeditions of discovery, American naval vessels had done some remarkable exploring. The *Vincennes* traveled to ports in the Pacific Islands and the Far East in 1829, sailed around the Cape of Good Hope in 1830, and became the first American naval ship to circumnavigate the globe. The *Potomac* accomplished the same feat between 1831–1834, making several stops in the East Indies, including the first American intervention in Asia at Sumatra. One member of that cruise, Jeremiah Reynolds, pushed for congressional support of an Antarctic expedition to confirm the existence of an Antarctic continent, to map whaling and sealing routes, and to conduct general scientific observation. Through the efforts of Reynolds and others, Congress finally agreed to appropriate $300 thousand for an expedition to the South Atlantic and Pacific, the United States Exploring Expedition of 1838–1842.

It is remarkable that the U.S. Navy was able to undertake this expedition because the Navy and Congress concurred that a peacetime navy's only task was to protect merchant shipping, and had shaped the Navy for that purpose. The Navy Board of Commissioners, with congressional approval, expanded the "squadron" system. Thus, the West Indian (1822), the Pacific (1822), the Brazilian (1826), the Mediterranean (1835), the Home (1841), the East Indian (1835), and the African (1843) Squadrons patrolled ocean regions to protect American shipping and strategic interests. Depots at Key West and San Francisco (after 1848) in the United States, and abroad at places like Hong Kong and Rio de Janeiro, kept these small groups of ships supplied. The concept of fleet operations, however, had not yet developed and ships in the squadrons typically did not operate as fleets, but rather as individual ships patrolling an assigned area.

Senior naval officers and Congress seemed content with a sailing navy versus one powered by new steam technology, thus falling behind other navies. After brief flirtations with steam power, the United States stuck doggedly to sail, while the British and French navies continued experimenting with steam vessels. While Robert Fulton's steam-powered warship *Demologos* (1814) and David Porter's *Seagull* (1823) were put through trials, the Navy was not given funding for a steam-powered vessel for permanent sea duty until 1839. After intense lobbying from Captain Matthew C. Perry and Secretary of the Navy Abel P. Upshur, Congress funded two paddle-wheeled steamers, USS *Mississippi* and USS *Missouri* (completed in 1842), and the first screw-propeller-powered warship in the world, USS *Princeton* (completed in 1841). Tragically, Upshur (appointed Secretary of State by President John Tyler in 1844) and Secretary of the Navy Thomas W. Gilmer were killed when one of the *Princeton*'s new guns exploded during a demonstration firing. To design, build, maintain, and operate these steam vessels, the Navy had to establish a Naval Corps of Engineers. Still, the Navy lagged behind Great Britain and France. By 1854, Britain had 141 steamships while the French had 68, compared to the U.S. Navy's 18.

The Navy and merchant marine also needed accurate charts and maps, better navigation instruments, and the ability to use both in order to compete with their British and European counterparts. The Navy established the Depot of Charts and Instruments in 1830 to correct this weakness. In 1842, the Navy built the Naval Observatory to update astronomical data for navigation books. Young naval officers took brief courses to learn how to use new instruments, translate new data to charts, and get up to date on the latest advancements in meteorology, oceanography, geography, biology, and other sciences. The Naval Observatory gained a reputation among young naval officers as a center for professional education, and among foreign navies as a center for naval science. In 1849, the Navy established the Nautical Almanac Office to publish advancements in naval sciences and the latest astronomical, oceanographic, and meteorological data. Headquartered at Cambridge, Massachusetts, the Nautical Almanac Office employed some of the leading mathematicians and astronomers in the United States.

To better manage the Navy's mission, Secretary of the Navy Upshur abolished the Navy Board of Commissioners in 1842, replacing it with a bureau system similar to that of the Army. Although the Navy still lacked an academy like the one that the Army had at West Point, technology, science, and education had become important to the U.S. Navy well before the outbreak of the Civil War.

Amidst these developments, the United States Exploring Expedition got under way in 1838. Lieutenant Charles Wilkes, typical of the Navy's junior officers in the high value he placed on science and education, and adventure, commanded the expedition. Wilkes, an expert navigator and chart maker, actively sought the command. The Navy's imagination had been captured by the eighteenth-century exploits of the likes of Captain James Cook and his Pacific voyages. Now, with the Wilkes expedition, the U.S. Navy could join Cook in the pantheon of naval exploration.

Secretary of the Navy James Paulding ordered Wilkes to explore and chart the South Pacific and the Antarctic region, then return northward to chart shores in and around Puget Sound. Along the way, he and his contingent of scientists made extensive studies of the oceans, weather, animal and plant life, geology, and astronomy. Wilkes set sail on August 22, 1838, with four ships: the sailed schooner *Seagull*, which sank off Cape Horn in 1839; the schooner, *Flying Fish*, sold in Singapore in 1842 because it was too worn out to repair; the sloop *Peacock*, which had seen action in the War of 1812 and had to be abandoned off the coast of Oregon in 1841; and the brigantine *Porpoise*, the only vessel from the original squadron that completed the entire voyage. The *Vincennes*, which had already circumnavigated the globe, joined the expedition in Rio de Janeiro.

Wilkes's expedition was nothing short of extraordinary. The expedition explored the Society Islands, stopped briefly at Samoa, and then sailed on to Australia. Wilkes then sailed due south, where he charted over 1,000 miles of previously unmapped ice and coastline. This part of the journey tested Wilkes's command and his officers and crew. His strict discipline and questionable decisions left many officers doubting his ability, but none mutinied. In addition, during a four-month stay in the Fiji Islands, where Wilkes meticulously charted reefs and shoals, two of his officers were murdered by Fijians. Wilkes killed over fifty islanders in retribution. After wintering in Hawaii, Wilkes led his expedition to the American Northwest, where it surveyed the northern California and Oregon coastlines and Puget Sound. He then headed across the Pacific

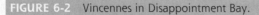

FIGURE 6-2   Vincennes in Disappointment Bay.

Source: Library of Congress Print and Reproductions Division [LC-USZ62-79706]

to the Philippines, on to Singapore, around the Cape of Good Hope, and home to New York in June 1842.

Wilkes returned a hero, but public charges against him by some of his officers clouded the expedition's achievements. The Navy cleared Wilkes of the serious charge of conduct unbecoming an officer, but convicted him on seventeen charges of illegal punishment. The Navy reprimanded Wilkes, and then hailed him as a great explorer.

Wilkes and his men had sailed over 85,000 thousand miles and surveyed over 280 islands. The Antarctic coastline explored and mapped by the expedition is still known as Wilkes Land. Wilkes's condensed public report on the expedition aided whalers, sealers, commercial shippers, and the Navy alike. The official report comprised over twenty volumes, some of which were not completed until after the Civil War, while others were never published. The U.S. government kept some parts of his final report secret, however, due to concern that his description of San Francisco Bay and his recommendation that the United States claim Oregon might cause increased tension with Great Britain and Spain.

Thousands of the new species and specimens collected by the expedition's scientists were haphazardly displayed in the National Gallery in the Patent Office, causing several of the scientists to resign in disgust. Wilkes ultimately reorganized the exhibition himself. Despite Wilkes's court martial and the scientists' resignations, the first official exploring expedition of the U.S. Navy had been a stunning success. The Navy was still using Wilkes's meticulous charts and maps when war broke out with Japan 100 years later.

More expeditions followed as the Navy rode the wave of the Wilkes Expedition's success. From 1847 to 1849, Lieutenant William F. Lynch and the store ship USS *Supply* explored the River Jordan and the Dead Sea and even attempted sailing up the Euphrates. Lynch's primary task was gathering scientific information, but he also had orders to ascertain the commercial situation in the region.

The Navy sponsored an expedition to the Amazon from Lima, Peru to the Brazilian coast in 1851–1852. With pack mules loaded with boxes of scientific instruments, notebooks, tents, weapons, and other necessities, the expedition departed Lima on May 21, 1851. In addition to the usual scientific tasks, the expedition was ordered to discover which Brazilian waterways could be navigated, to note Brazilian trade goods, the economic condition of the people encountered, and any undeveloped commercial resources. The journey was arduous, with the explorers enduring bouts of jungle fever, close calls with South American Indians, and daunting river obstacles. Yet, the men survived, becoming the first white men to descend from the source of the Madeira River to the Amazon. Expedition reports were detailed, offering insightful observations about economic, political, and social conditions. Unfortunately, the many specimens the men had collected sat unstudied in the Patent Office for years before being transferred to the Smithsonian Institution.

Other naval expeditions established an observatory in Chile that operated from 1846 to 1852 to study the movement of Mars and Venus, and to make other astronomical observations; explored the Rio de la Plata and Rio Paraguay from 1853 to 1856; conducted a reconnaissance of Liberia in 1852; and explored the Bering Strait and China Sea from 1852 to 1863. Diplomatically and commercially, the most important of these expeditions was Commodore Matthew Perry's mission to Japan from 1852 to 1854. American commercial and naval vessels had made contact with the isolationist Japanese Islands before Perry's mission in 1852. But, aside from rescuing stranded American whalers or foiled attempts to establish relations, the United States had made little headway in opening Japan to American commerce. Fearing that Great Britain, its main trading rival in the Asian market, would be first to get a trade agreement with the very cautious Japanese, the United States dispatched Perry to open relations with Japan.

Perry was also tasked with conducting what had become standard scientific activities. The mission was at once commercial, diplomatic, and scientific. Perry was the obvious choice to lead the mission. He had just been named commander of the East India squadron, and had conducted successful negotiations with Naples, Turkey, and Mexico. Much respected by his fellow naval officers, Perry had a reputation for hard work, leadership, and endurance. In preparation for his mission he read logs and reports from previous voyages to Japan, talked with officers from some of these voyages, and tried to learn as much as he could about Japanese history and culture. He knew that Japan had not completely sealed off outside contact, and that the Japanese were aware of Western medicine, military affairs, and technology. Perry took a fleet of four ships—the *Susquehanna, Plymouth, Saratoga*, and the steamer *Mississippi,* arriving in Tokyo Bay in July 1853. In 1854, several other naval vessels joined Perry's fleet.

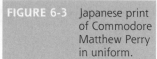

FIGURE 6-3   Japanese print of Commodore Matthew Perry in uniform.

Source: Library of Congress Print and Reproductions Division [LC-USZ62-519]

PERRY DESCRIBES BURIAL OF A MARINE IN JAPAN

In a March, 1854, journal entry, Commodore Matthew Perry described the burial of Marine Private Robert Williams. Note how this normal occurrence presents not only a diplomatic problem but also a diplomatic opportunity for Perry. Still, with pivotal negotiations in the balance and the expedition continuing its busy work, it is easy to forget that this was a naval expedition under naval command— the routine occurrences, such as discipline, daily duties, and death, sometimes preempt the grand schemes of diplomacy.

March 9, 1854

As it would happen, a Marine belonging to the Mississippi had died two days before this conference, and the very first matter to be discussed was the suitable interment of the body. I had apprehended much difficulty upon this point, and had in my own mind determined—if the Japanese persisted in forbidding the interment within either of their numerous burial places—to have effected the object, let what might occur, upon the small island called in our charts Webster Island and lying convenient to the American Anchorage. I was pretty well satisfied that once the body was in the ground it would not be disturbed, and as others of the squadron might die during our stay, it would be a very appropriate place of interment for all. I was moreover anxious for special reasons to acquire an interest in this island to subserve some ulterior objects.

The proposition seemed to perplex the Japanese commissioners, and after some consultation they retired to discuss the question alone. On leaving they requested that in their absence we might partake of a few Japanese dishes.

I observed that we should be most happy to do so, but it would be more consonant to our notions of hospitality if the commissioners were to join us, as the breaking of bread together was amongst many nations considered an evidence of friendship. They replied that they were unacquainted with foreign customs but would cheerfully join us. Upon this they all retired, but shortly after, the second and third in rank of the number returned, and the collation was served, and all went off in apparent kindness and good nature.

It was not long before the entire board was again in session and a written reply to my request respecting the interment was presented by the chief commissioner. Its purport was that as a temple had been set apart at Nagasaki for the interment of strangers it would be necessary that I should send the body to Uraga, whence at a convenient season it might be conveyed in a Japanese junk to the former named place.

To this I objected, remarking that undisturbed resting places for the dead were granted by all nations, and then proposed to send boats and inter the body at Webster Island. To this they evinced strong objections, and after considerable discussion amongst themselves finally consented to allow the interment to take place at Yokohama, at a spot adjoining one of their temples, and in view of the ships. They observed that as the novelty of the scene might attract an inconvenient crowd, the authorities would send on board Mississippi in the morning an officer to accompany the funeral party.

Accordingly on the following day one of the interpreters made his appearance and corpse was taken on shore in the usual manner and placed in a grave near to a Japanese temple with all religious ceremony, conformably to the forms of the Episcopal Church, since which a neat enclosure of bamboo has been put up by the Japanese authorities.

Source: Roger Pineau, ed., *The Japan Expedition, 1852–1854: The Personal Journal of Commodore Matthew C. Perry* (Washington, D.C.: Smithsonian Institution Press, 1968), 105–106.

Perry understood the delicate diplomacy required to conclude an agreement with the shogunates of Japan. On March 31, 1854, Perry and the Japanese signed the Treaty of Kanagawa, which gave the United States access to the ports of Shimoda and Hakodate, arranged for future transfers of stranded American seamen, established an American consulate at Shimoda, and gave Japan trade status equivalent to most favored nation. What should have been a significant moment for Japan instead turned dark; over the next few years, deep division between Japanese open to Western contact and those opposed erupted in a long civil war that lasted until 1868. For Perry, however, the treaty was a success; he returned to the United States a hero and Congress voted him a $20,000 bonus for his achievement.

Part of the expedition's mission was scientific, and Perry did not disappoint in this regard either. His ships had explored and charted the China Sea and much of the coastline of the Japanese Islands. Several volumes of the expedition's findings were published, primarily sailing directions and harbor charts, but also details of Japanese currents and wind directions. Perry published a personal narrative of the voyage, and several other officers and scientists on the voyage also published recollections. The many gifts received from the Japanese, as well as specimens collected by scientists on the voyage, were given to the Smithsonian Institution.

The pre-Civil War Navy had indeed shown a willingness to undertake expeditions that delicately balanced commercial, scientific, military, and diplomatic objectives. Naval officers proved enthusiastic and adept in organizing, carrying out, and reporting the results of these expeditions. Although the Navy undertook fewer such missions after the Civil War, letting organizations such as the Smithsonian Institution and the National Geographic Society sponsor scientific expeditions, the Navy retained the capability and eagerness required to do so when it was called upon. For officers, the experience, knowledge, and overall growth gained from organizing and participating in these expeditions contributed to a growing sense of naval professionalism.

◆ FRONTIER CONSTABULARY AND INDIAN AFFAIRS

Frontier duty remained the Army's primary task after the War of 1812. Although this role was ill fitted to the service's principal mission of defending the United States from foreign enemies, the Army was the natural agency for maintaining order along the frontier and regulating relations between settlers and native peoples. As before the War of 1812, regulating relations between whites and Indians often placed the Army in a difficult position. Although civilian Indian agents normally represented the federal government to Indian tribes, military officers often assumed the role of agent in the absence of the civilian official. In addition, the president had the authority to order a military officer to take over as agent. Indian agents were often housed on Army posts on the frontier, and disputes between commanders and agents frequently erupted over the implementation of federal Indian policy. Agents, officers, settlers, and the Indians themselves made plenty of mistakes, both honest and otherwise, for there to be enough blame to go around for the tragedies of U.S. –Indian relations before, as well as after, the Civil War.

Few officers subscribed to the noble-savage idea so prominent in antebellum American literature. Military officers, more often than not, were realists in their approach to, and outlook on, Indians. Experience shaped their opinions. Words like "treachery," "indolence," and "savage" frequent officers' writings about Indians. Yet, their writings also reflect a grudging respect for Native Americans as human beings. Officers did not attribute Indian behavior, as they observed it, to race, but rather to environmental determinism.

Army officers often saw the native tribes of the Southeast as the most civilized and socially complex. The Cherokees in particular impressed them. The Plains Indians and the tribes of the Southwest ranked in the middle, as officers admired their warrior skills but found their tendency toward brutality uncivilized. Few officers saw much hope of assimilation for these mostly nomadic tribes. The Indians of the Rocky Mountains and California ranked at the bottom of the scale. Officers saw these peoples as nothing more than diggers and beggars; many officers compared them to animals, because their societies were not highly organized, and their living conditions were poor.

Despite having such a negative attitude toward Indians, the officers' views moderated when the tribes were at peace. Because of their own sense of professionalism and their disdain for greedy white settlers—and often, their sincere concern for the plight of Indian peoples as human beings—officers frequently adopted a paternalistic attitude toward Native Americans. The United States, according to these officers, had an obligation to protect Indians. Many officers supported the assimilation policy, which up to the 1830s had practical application because white settlers had not headed West in large numbers, nor had there been major conflict between whites and Indians in the West. Many officers, including then Colonel Zachary Taylor, defended Native American rights and tried to enforce treaties. There was a sense among military men that the tribes had been taken advantage of, and that they were owed protection from further humiliation. Such ideas were indeed noble, but sympathetic officers found it increasingly difficult to transfer noble thoughts into practical reality.

Because of the constant reductions in the size of the military and the expansion of its duties during the 1820s through the 1850s, the Army never had enough troops on the frontier to adequately maintain order. As a result, conflict broke out with increasing frequency along the Trans-Mississippi frontier, in Georgia, Alabama, Mississippi, and Florida. Army posts had the difficult responsibilities of keeping white settlers from encroaching upon Indian lands and prohibiting the trade of illegal goods, such as whiskey and arms, to Indians. Military men generally did not like frontiersmen and overzealous traders. In the early 1830s, Captain William R. Jouett, commander of Fort Snelling on the upper Mississippi River in Wisconsin, frequently seized illegal liquor from Indian traders in his jurisdiction. In one instance, the American Fur Company even charged Jouett with illegal trespass and assault, but lost the case. Captain John Stuart, the commander at Fort Smith in Arkansas, tried in vain to stop the illegal liquor trade with Indians but did not have the men to police his huge jurisdiction.

Soldiers spent just as much time keeping whites out as they did keeping Indians in. Illegal settlement forced the Army to send out frequent patrols that sometimes forcibly removed settlers and occasionally destroyed their homes. Major David E. Twiggs forced loggers to leave the upper Wisconsin River area in 1829, only to be charged with trespassing by the company in question and actually arrested by the local sheriff. The district court in Green Bay made no judgment against Twiggs. When Twiggs tried to sue the loggers and their company for his legal expenses, his case was dismissed.

Frontier officers often found themselves on the unpopular side of the law, as well as of local law enforcement. Fear of extensive legal ramifications for what they considered carrying out the letter of the law left many officers hesitant to act as law enforcement. The strong political power of the American Fur Company in Washington made the officers' and Indian agents' jobs harder to carry out. Many officers supported declaring martial law in Indian country in order to curb the power of the traders and their power over local courts. The War Department, however, proved unhelpful. Commanders at such posts as Fort Armstrong, Illinois, and Fort Des Moines, Iowa, found themselves helpless to control illegal trade with Indians and encroachment upon tribal lands.

During the 1830s, frontier tensions erupted into major conflict between the federal government and Native Americans over the government's Indian removal policy. As one example, the Black Hawk War of 1832 started as a series of misunderstandings that turned into a bloody conflict during which hundreds on both sides were killed.

Beginning in the 1820s, increasing numbers of white settlers in Illinois had pushed the Sauk and Fox Indians out of their territory and across the Mississippi River. In 1832, Chief Black Hawk led a large band back into Illinois. Governor John Reynolds called out more than 1,500 militia to confront Black Hawk, and force his band back across the Mississippi. The first engagement took place along the Rock River when Black Hawk and forty warriors attacked a force of 300 militiamen in retaliation for the murder of two peace envoys. The undisciplined militia fled, forcing Governor Reynolds to call for help from the federal government. In June, dissatisfied with the progress of the war, President Andrew Jackson ignored the chain of command and directly ordered Brevet Major General Winfield Scott to take command of the war, and to defeat Black Hawk's augmented force of Sauk, Fox, Potawatomi, and Winnebago warriors. It was, after all, an election year. Cholera, however, ran rampant throughout Scott's force, killing more than 200 of his men and preventing him from taking the field.

After raiding isolated settlements and killing over 200 whites, Black Hawk decided to retreat back across the Mississippi River but was hit by regular forces under General James D. Henry in the Battle of Wisconsin Heights. Suffering heavy losses, Black Hawk continued to retreat. While the band was crossing the Mississippi at its confluence with the Bad Axe River on August 1, regular troops hit the Indians again and killed more than 300, half of whom were women and children. Black Hawk was captured on August 25, and taken hostage to ensure that his surviving followers met the terms of the Treaty of Fort Armstrong ending the war. The war had been a badly managed affair. Nonetheless, none of the tribes involved ever again threatened the peace in the region. Now, Wisconsin and Iowa were open to white settlement.

In the midst of the Black Hawk War, the Jackson administration tasked the Army with carrying out the Indian Removal Act of 1830. While tribes originally had been treated as nations, and thus the federal government had concluded treaties with them as nations, this interpretation of tribal status had changed by the 1820s. Constitutional questions about a national status within the boundaries of the United States convinced the Supreme Court to nullify these arrangements. Jackson, concerned for the welfare of the tribes in question and giving up on regulating white encroachment, could think of only one solution—remove the tribes to western lands, where they would be safe from illegal white settlement. Such a policy had been discussed for decades, but now it became law. The only federal organization large enough and strong enough to carry out the task was the Army. The Army wanted no violence, hoping instead that careful organization would be sufficient to provide for and protect tribes as they emigrated westward. Responsibility for the removal was placed with the Commissary General of Subsistence, and civilian superintendents supervised the emigration.

First to move were the Choctaws. They signed over all of their lands east of the Mississippi River in 1830, and had three years to move out, but impatient whites illegally squatted on Choctaw land. The Army provided escort for Choctaw officials to scout out possible settlement sites west of Arkansas in what became known as Indian Territory, posting companies of troops along the emigration route as well as in Indian Territory to help the Choctaw during their sad journey. The Army repaired Fort Smith to serve as a supply station, reestablished Fort Towson (in what is now Oklahoma) to keep whites out of Indian Territory, and helped locate water and livestock sources in the area designated for Choctaw settlement. While passing through Arkansas, the tribes encountered white settlers who charged the Indians and the government outrageous prices for basic goods. By 1834, nearly 13,000 Choctaws had made the trek to Indian Territory.

At first, the Creek Indians peacefully resisted removal, but by 1831 white squatters had begun to overrun Creek lands. Moreover, the government of the state of Alabama began enforcing state laws over the Creeks. Because of this increased pressure, in March 1832, the Creeks signed over their lands and agreed to move west. Although the agreement allowed individual Creeks to farm a parcel of land for five years and at the end of that period receive title to it, the treaty nonetheless strongly encouraged the Creeks to move west. Moreover, the federal government failed to keep whites out of Creek lands and prevent land speculators from defrauding individual Creeks of their allotments. The emigrant agents assigned to remove the Creeks had been the same individuals who had earlier tried to swindle them. Many Creeks fled into Cherokee territory in Georgia and Alabama. As the federal investigation into the fraudulent dealings wallowed in bureaucratic morass, the Creeks began to suffer from poor conditions brought on by economic stagnation. Georgia militia attacked Creek refugee camps, while bands of Creeks raided white farms and settlements in retaliation.

Secretary of War Lewis Cass ordered the Army to remove the Creeks without delay. General Thomas S. Jesup first had to subdue the renegade bands and then organize the removal. Thus began the Creek War of 1836. Jesup placed Winfield Scott in overall command of the campaign. At the time Scott had been dealing with the Seminoles in Florida, where things had gone badly for him. With more than 1,000 regulars augmented by more than 8,000 Georgia and Alabama volunteers, Scott divided his force in a bid to catch the Creeks from two directions. Scott delayed his movements, claiming he needed more time to get his force ready for the field. Fearing that the Creeks might flee to Florida, Jesup moved ahead without Scott, capturing the main Creek encampment along with 400 warriors and their leader, Eneah Micco. This rapid success impressed the Creeks so much that they lost their enthusiasm for further resistance. Jesup wrote to Scott that the Creeks had been pacified, but Scott insisted on capturing all Indians who had escaped Jesup's attack. After a few weeks, the Creeks had been rounded up and completely subdued.

Removal began in July 1836. Over 2,500 Creeks traveled by wagon to Montgomery, then by water to their designated lands. The journey took a month. Creek warriors were chained together for the entire journey. The peaceful Creeks followed in August and September under military escort. Over 14,000 Creeks immigrated to Indian Territory in 1836. In 1837, the Chickasaw left their homeland in a comparatively uneventful removal. The Cherokee removal, however, remains the most infamous of the removal policy.

The Army played the largest and most controversial role in the removal of the Cherokee in 1836. By far the most advanced of what the colonists called the civilized tribes, the Cherokee stubbornly resisted removal despite the white settlers in Georgia, Alabama, Tennessee, and North Carolina who were already squatting on Cherokee lands. The discovery of gold there brought still more illegal settlement. By using legal challenges and stubborn negotiations, the Cherokee held out for almost eight years before signing a removal treaty in 1835. Even then, many Cherokee resisted. They had two years to move west to their new lands in Indian Territory, by which time Martin Van Buren had assumed the presidency.

Van Buren ordered the Cherokee to move. The Georgia militia, poorly led and poorly trained, forced Cherokee families from their homes at bayonet point. Scavengers ransacked their houses and farms. Hastily constructed stockades (in effect concentration camps) held 17,000 Cherokee while their removal west was organized. Horrid conditions in the camps killed more than 4,000 Cherokee while they were under the charge of Georgia militia. As the Army escorted the survivors of the camps along what came to be known as the Trail of Tears, more perished. Winfield Scott commanded the trek west, but he and his troops received little support from the government and even less from local citizens along the route. A horde of greedy agents, speculators, lawyers, and other profit seekers cheated the Cherokee. The Army also conducted itself badly; several soldiers disgraced themselves during the removal by robbing, abusing, and raping Cherokee. The Cherokee removal proved to be a serious blemish on the Army's record of Indian affairs.

The Black Hawk War of 1832 and the long and bloody Second Seminole War of 1835–1842 cost hundreds of lives and forced removal of the involved tribes from their lands. Of the available options, all of which seemed inhumane, the most humane was removal. The Indians were the losers in this policy; more than 45,000 Native Americans were uprooted from their homes and crowded onto lands already inhabited by other native peoples. In exchange, the U.S. government gained nearly 100 million acres of land at the cost of $68 million. Despite this poor record, Jackson maintained until his death that he had saved the tribes from extinction.

Even as Indian removal commenced, the U.S. government looked ahead, planning how it would protect both Indians and settlers in the West. Despite removal, Indians still lived in close proximity to white settlements, which steadily pushed westward to the Mississippi River and beyond. British interests in Oregon and the upper Mississippi River region threatened to cause conflict, while the Spanish borderlands presented potential security problems that were in turn made more threatening by the 1836 Texas Revolution. The United States needed a frontier military policy to secure the dual objectives of regulating settlement and Indian relations, and maintaining national security.

To meet these objectives, mounted dragoons patrolled a string of outposts manned by infantry. Located along the frontier between white settlement and Indian lands, the outposts gave the Army the ability to strike quickly, and served as a haven for settlers during Indian uprisings. These "forts," which usually amounted to little more than tented settlements, also allowed the Army to regulate white movement in frontier areas. With limited troop numbers covering a cordon hundreds of miles long, dispersing units in the most efficient manner became the primary goal of military planners.

In 1836, Jackson's Secretary of War Lewis Cass presented a plan for frontier military policy. Cass maintained that Indians had no concept of the military might of the United States, and that they measured American military power solely by what they could see. Thus, it was necessary to station sufficient numbers of troops along the frontier to overawe the Indians. In case of a major uprising or Indian attack on a settlement, the Army needed a way quickly to concentrate large forces in the area in question. According to Cass, the answer was a military road that ran roughly south to north from Fort Towson on the Red River to Fort Snelling along the upper Mississippi River. Because the frontier had moved west, posts east of this line could be abandoned in the hope of saving money and using troops more efficiently. Each post was garrisoned by a minimum number of troops and augmented by so-called disposable forces that could move from post to post or respond to emergencies, using the road and waterways for transportation. The post and road system that Cass proposed was similar to the frontier defensive outpost system used by the ancient Romans.

Congress appropriated $100,000 for the road in 1836. Troops would build the road and the outposts. Just when the program got going, however, it changed direction. Benjamin Butler replaced Cass as Secretary of War, serving only briefly from 1836 to 1837. Where Cass had focused on the Indian threat to whites, Butler saw an equal threat of whites against Indians and was worried about conflict between tribes caused by the Indian removal policy. He, therefore, added posts in interior areas, including Indian Territory. Butler's successor, Joel R. Poinsett, altogether rejected Cass's idea of a single north-south road. Lines of communication could be compromised easily, thus Poinsett recommended establishing two lines of posts. The first line, the exterior, would place advanced posts deep into Indian lands; the second line, the interior, would establish positions closer to settlements. A large force of troops would be placed in reserve at Jefferson Barracks, Missouri and Baton Rouge.

Manning these posts posed a challenge. The Army recommended 30,000 troops, but had to settle for fewer than 10,000. Poinsett's plan got congressional backing, but Congress also insisted on completion of the road, a task that the Army finished in 1845. While the Army and various secretaries of war discussed these ambitious strategies for frontier security, the actual implementation of these schemes was much more piecemeal. The establishment of outposts and the strength of garrisons had more to do with local conditions than any plan. Indian removal that increased emigrant traffic on the Oregon Trail, and war with Mexico each demanded unique strategies no matter which national plan was in vogue at any particular time.

◆ CONCLUSION

During the first half of the nineteenth century, the American military was the only federal entity adequately organized and disciplined, and sufficiently funded to support America's compulsion toward expansion. The Army and the Navy explored and mapped tens of thousands of miles, adding to scientific knowledge, opening doors for American trade, and building a sense of prestige and professionalism within the American military. Not all was grand and glorious, however, for the Army was saddled with frontier constabulary duties and the unpleasant task of implementing the Indian removal policy. Nonetheless, a precedent was set. The American military could, and would, be used by the federal government to carry out tasks beyond providing for the security of the United States. This precedent continues, remaining a hallmark of the flexibility of American military forces.

Further Reading

Chaffin, Tom. *Pathfinder: John Charles Fremont and the Course of American Empire.* New York: Hill and Wang, 2002.

Ehle, John. *Trail of Tears: The Rise and Fall of the Cherokee Nation.* New York: Doubleday, 1988.

Goetzmann, William H. *Army Exploration in the American West, 1803–1863.* New York: Macmillan, 1969.

Green, Michael D. *The Politics of Indian Removal: Creek Government and Society in Crisis.* Lincoln: University of Nebraska Press, 1982.

Hogan, David W. Jr., and Charles E. White. *The United States Army and the Lewis and Clark Expedition.* Washington, D.C.: United States Army Center of Military History, 2003.

Philbrick, Nathaniel. *Sea of Glory: America's Voyage of Discovery, The U.S. Exploring Expedition, 1838–1842.* New York: Viking, 2003.

Pronko, Vincent Jr. *Ships, Seas, and Scientists: U.S. Naval Exploration and Discovery in the Nineteenth Century.* Annapolis: Naval Institute Press, 1974.

Prucha, Francis Paul. *The Sword of the Republic: The United States Army on the Frontier, 1782–1846.* New York: Macmillan, 1968.

Remini, Robert. *Andrew Jackson and His Indian Wars.* New York: Viking, 2001.

Ronda, James P. *Finding the West: Explorations with Lewis and Clark.* Albuquerque: University of New Mexico Press, 2001.

Stanton, William. *The Great United States Exploring Expedition of 1832 1842.* Berkeley: University of California Press, 1975.

Tate, Michael L. *The Frontier Army in the Settlement of the West.* Norman: University of Oklahoma Press, 1999.

Van DeVelder, Paul. *Savages and Scoundrels: The Untold Story of America's Road to Empire through Indian Territory.* New Haven: Yale University Press, 2009.

Wiley, Peter Booth. *Yankees in the Land of the Gods: Commodore Perry and the Opening of Japan.* New York: Penguin, 1990.

mysearchlab Connections: Sources Online

READ AND REVIEW

Review this chapter by using the study aids and these related documents available on MySearchLab.

Study Plan

Chapter Test

Essay Test

Documents

Jefferson's Description of Discoveries Made by Lewis & Clark (1806)

In this document, President Jefferson praises the accomplishments of the Voyage of Discovery, the famous expedition led by two military officers.

Treaty of Kanagawa (1854)

This treaty concluded between the Tokugawa shogunate and Commodore Matthew Perry highlights the dual diplomatic-military role of American naval officers in the nineteenth century.

Jackson's Message to Congress on Indian Removal (1830)

This document outlines President Jackson's policy on moving native tribes out of the Southeastern United States for relocation to what became known as Indian Territory.

RESEARCH AND EXPLORE

Explore the following review questions using the research tools available on www.mysearchlab.com.

1. How did military exploration affect American expansion?
2. Describe America's policy toward Native Americans during the 1830s and 1840s.
3. What role did the Army play on the frontier in the first half of the nineteenth century?

Toward a Professional Military

◆ INTRODUCTION

The impact of the Napoleonic Wars, the experience of the War of 1812, and the changing roles of the American military moved many in the officer corps to begin seeing their craft not merely as a job, but as a profession and a career. Education and the study of the art of warfare became important to the officer corps not only in the Army but also in the Navy. Over time, officers came to see the principal role of the military as the defense of the United States. To fulfill this role, the officer corps believed the military had to prepare itself, and the nation, for war.

The War with Mexico gave the military, especially the Army, the chance to exhibit the progress of its initial professionalization. Ironically, many of the officers who fought against Mexico would, just more than a decade later, fight each other in one of the bloodiest wars in American history, the Civil War.

◆ NAPOLEON AND A REVOLUTION IN WARFARE

The Wars of the French Revolution and Napoleonic Wars (1792–1815) caused a revolution in military affairs, one that continues to influence the practice of warfare and the way many nations approach military organization and purpose. The establishment of the French Republic in 1792 reflected and encouraged an intense sense of nationalism among the French people. The French government obligated all citizens to join the armed service in order to form huge armies with which France conquered neighboring countries, established republican governments in those subjugated states, and tried to make a republican empire out of the European continent. The monarchies that had escaped France's initial conquest, however, developed their own sense of nationalist energy that they could channel toward a massive effort to contain the French state. If victory came with breaking the enemy's will to fight, then nationalism made that objective all the more difficult for both sides by the time of the Napoleonic Wars. Warfare became an intense, year-round endeavor that harnessed the total resources of the nation state. These resources included conscription, which gave states an almost inexhaustible pool of manpower to maintain such large armies. With seemingly unlimited numbers of men, generals became bolder in their willingness to accept larger casualties in pursuit of victory.

Napoleon Bonaparte became the master practitioner of this new style of warfare. Napoleon took control of the French Republic, declared himself emperor in 1804, and accelerated French expansion during the first years of the nineteenth century. His hallmark strategy involved seeking a climactic battle that would completely destroy the enemy's army. Employing overwhelming force and swift maneuver, Napoleon inflicted huge casualties and extracted a devastating psychological toll on the enemy.

With such large national armies facing him, however, Napoleon's strategy required him to sacrifice large casualties of his own, which he willingly did. Tactically, more mobile artillery allowed him to employ cannon at close range without increasing the risk of losing them to enemy fire. Case shot at close range fired by artillery batteries that could so swiftly shift positions made Napoleonic battles a holocaust of gunfire. Moreover, Napoleon's organization and placement of divisions before and during battle gave him a strategic advantage. Even in the United States, military officers took note of this intensified way of war.

Napoleon's way of war gave birth to modern military thought. A new generation of military thinkers examined Napoleon's successes and failures and wrote about this new approach to warfare. Antoine Henri Jomini, a French officer born in Switzerland, and the Prussian Karl von Clausewitz were the most prominent of these thinkers. Their writings helped solidify Napoleon's influence on modern warfare.

Jomini had the most immediate effect on American military thought. He was a major general in Napoleon's army and later served in the Russian army of Alexander I. During the Napoleonic Wars, Jomini held staff positions that permitted him to closely observe Napoleon's methods. His position also gave him experience in logistics and troop movements during battles, but he never personally commanded troops in combat. He wrote prolifically, publishing twenty-seven books on modern warfare. His most influential work was his 1838 *Précis de l'art de la guerre* (Summary of the Art of War). Jomini was influenced by Enlightenment thought and found the human and financial cost of Napoleonic battle disturbing. As a result, Jomini found perfection in the less costly tactics and strategy of Frederick the Great, who ruled Prussia from 1740 until 1772. Still, Jomini admired the brilliance of Napoleon's offensive capabilities and sought to interpret them for professional military study. Jomini argued that warfare had universal fundamental principles that military strategists could understand and apply.

Jomini suggested four primary rules for battle: maneuver one's forces to bear upon the enemy's most important points and disrupt his communications without placing one's own forces in a vulnerable position; concentrate one's forces on only part of the enemy's force rather than bringing them to bear on all of the enemy's force; determine the decisive point of the battlefield and the enemy's force to maneuver one's forces against it; and when concentrating mass upon decisive points, do so swiftly and in a well-timed and coordinated maneuver. To conduct these moves required forethought and planning. The strategically intelligent general could plan and carry out such a campaign to bring his mass against the decisive point of the enemy's force in a climactic battle, thus achieving military victory.

Key to Jominian thought was the idea of maintaining the initiative. The general who had control of his forces and who, therefore, could force his opponent to react to his wishes had the strategic initiative. Ideally, according to Jomini, when a general conducted this sort of campaign, dominating the battlefield through superior maneuver, the enemy would capitulate without a battle of annihilation. Departing from Napoleon, Jomini contended that gaining territory, not annihilating the enemy's force, would achieve the overall political objectives of the war. In the 1830s, Jomini's ideas became central to the curriculum at the U.S. Military Academy at WestPoint. His principles dominated U.S. Army thinking until after World War II.

Although his writings did not enjoy much influence in the United States until the middle of the twentieth century, Clausewitz, like Jomini, also sought to discover universal principles of warfare based upon the Napoleonic experience. Clausewitz served in both the Russian and Prussian armies during the Napoleonic Wars. Afterward, he served as superintendent of the Prussian *Kriegsakademie* until 1830, when he returned to field service as Chief of Staff of the Prussian Army. He died in 1830. Clausewitz's single great work was *Vom Krieg* (On War), an enormous, posthumously published tome that outlined his concepts of the universal principles of war. Unlike Jomini, Clausewitz understood war as a violent act that was not subject to a set of strategic principles. Rather, factors beyond human control—what he termed "fog" and "friction"—determined the course of war. For Clausewitz, war was a "continuation" of diplomacy, a tool used to force an adversary to concede to your demands. Much like Napoleon, Clausewitz argued that such coercion worked by destroying the opposing military force and the enemy's will to use military force, rather than by taking territory. Thus war, according to Clausewitz, was not an end in itself but rather a means to an end. Perhaps his most important concept is what students of military theory call the "trinity"—the three forces that determine a war's development. According to Clausewitz, the forces are primordial violence, chance, and reason. Following the Vietnam War, *On War* gained a wider audience within the U.S. military.

Clearly, Jomini was the source of theoretical discussion among pre-Civil War American officers. Even before Jomini's *Précis* was published, however, American officers had begun to explore the significance of the Napoleonic Wars, with the U.S. Military Academy at West Point serving as the center of that study. West Point-educated officers increasingly dominated the officer corps. In 1817, West Point accounted for 14.8 percent of Army officers. By 1830, 63.8 percent of Army officers graduated from the military academy, and by 1860, West Point produced 75.8 percent of U.S. Army officers. The appointment formula for West Point broadened significantly by the 1830s, giving each congressional and territorial district one appointment and providing for additional at-large appointments. In addition to making each class geographically balanced, if not diverse, the formula gave Congress a political interest in the academy, which helped soothe Jacksonian Era complaints about the non-egalitarian nature of the military. As a result of this system, most of the American officer corps shared a common educational foundation and military ethos.

West Point Superintendent Sylvanus Thayer began the process of making strategic theory part of the curriculum after the War of 1812. His travels in Europe after the war exposed him to the new literature on military thought, convincing him that Europe was indeed leading the new field of military studies. Thayer strove to establish an overall, integrated military strategy for the United States, bringing together the maritime defense tradition with the new strategic thought on land war. Although Thayer added strategic theory to the academy curriculum, external factors limited how much class time could be devoted to such studies. Several factors limited Thayer's progress and kept West Point primarily a school of engineering, including the traditional fear of a standing army, a reduction in the Army's size, a lack of funds, the subsequent small number of cadets, and, not surprisingly, peace. Moreover, President Andrew Jackson's harsh criticism and high-handed interference with the academy prompted Thayer to resign the superintendency in 1833.

Upon Thayer's resignation, his protégé, Denis Hart Mahan, became the leading proponent of Jominian thought at West Point. Mahan, an 1824 graduate of the academy, studied in France before joining the faculty. As primary instructor on warfare and engineering, Mahan influenced dozens of West Point graduates. Mahan taught warfare as both science and art, focusing on strategy, fortification, logistics, and tactics as well as on the role of warfare as a tool of statecraft. Mahan used S. F. Gay de Vernon's

Treatise on the Science of War and Fortification as his textbook. Gay de Vernon's work focused on engineering and fortification, but included a chapter on Jomini's ideas.

One of Mahan's students, Lieutenant Henry W. Halleck, became the first American military officer to write a book on military thought and strategy. Published in 1846, just as the war with Mexico began, Halleck's *Elements of Military Art and Science* applied Jominian thought to the American strategic situation. On the surface, Halleck promoted the Jominian principle of offensive warfare and concentration of mass on decisive points. The book, however, gradually strays from this bold approach to a more cautious one. In applying these precepts to the United States, Halleck backed away even further from offensive war, focusing instead on the necessarily defensive nature of American military policy. Despite its territorial and commercial growth, the United States, according to Halleck, had no need for an aggressive military policy because of its unique geostrategic situation. In his mind, the primary role of the American military was to defend the nation against foreign attack and to protect American resources in the continental United States.

Halleck strongly supported the traditional policy of fixed coastal fortifications intended to help repel foreign invasion. Major ports and cities had to be denied to the enemy, and the threatened cities' populations had to be protected. Yet, Halleck cautioned against becoming too dependent on such a static fortification system. Offensive warfare still had a role, although Halleck never seemed comfortable in fully endorsing it. In the end, Halleck's prescription was largely Jominian in that he supported the defense of places rather than the Napoleonic preference for the destruction of enemy forces.

In 1847, Mahan published *An Elementary Treatise on Advanced-Guard, Out-Post, and Detachment Service of Troops, and the manner of Posting and Handling Them in Presence of an Enemy. With a Historical Sketch of the Rise and Progress of Tactics, &c., &c.*—more simply referred to as *Out-Post*. Mahan believed that Napoleon had discovered all there was to know about the art of war; thus, by studying Napoleon and his campaigns, one could learn the art of war. Nevertheless, like Halleck, Mahan was cautious in his discussion of the movement of forces and the security of defensive positions. As for the offensive, Mahan, like Halleck, cautioned against recklessness, instead suggesting that the best offensive is the one that gains position through deception and maneuver at the least cost to one's own forces. This was not, however, an endorsement of a Napoleonic willingness to accept tremendous losses in order to destroy the enemy's forces. And, again like Halleck, Mahan believed in strong defensive fortifications as the best long-term military policy for the United States.

Neither soldier-scholar attempted to apply the principles of Napoleonic warfare to frontier constabulary duties or to the Indian problem. In trying to apply Napoleonic ideas to the United States, both men had to compromise those ideas to make them fit the American strategic situation. Both Halleck and Mahan seemed to confirm a preference for George Washington's defensive strategy in the War for American Independence or Winfield Scott's strategy of limited territorial gain to achieve political objectives in the War with Mexico, both of which are more Jominian in principle than Napoleonic.

It is important to understand the strategic context that influenced these men. The United States did not have serious concerns about a foreign invasion from the 1820s through the Civil War. Nor did American military officers spend much time studying Jomini, Halleck, and Mahan. The strategy course at West Point represented only a small portion of the overall curriculum, which remained dedicated to engineering and mathematics. As educated military men, officers thus had only a rudimentary understanding of Napoleonic warfare—mainly that a climactic battle to annihilate the enemy's force would bring victory.

Studying strategic thought was an important step toward professionalism. Over the course of the pre-Civil War decades, a growing number of officers wrote books, articles, and reports on a wide range of mostly military subjects. They had certainly been influenced by similar trends in Europe. While the tradition of using European military officers as expert teachers in the United States slowed after the War of 1812 and ended by the 1830s, American officers traveled to Europe to learn about European military strategy, education, and training techniques. Despite some resistance to European military ideas among some senior officers, scores of junior officers spent time abroad to learn. They witnessed military operations; visited military schools, fortresses, and ports; brought back hundreds of books and treatises; and examined what they could of the latest European military technological developments.

Lieutenant Daniel Tyler visited France in 1828–1829 and somehow gained access to secret plans for new weapons designs and field maneuvers for French artillery units. Tyler translated the plans into English and produced a report that heavily influenced American artillery development before the Civil War. Many officers translated other French, Austrian, and Prussian infantry, cavalry, and artillery studies and manuals into English for American study. In 1840, a group of ordnance officers toured munitions factories, arsenals, and proving grounds across Europe, gaining invaluable knowledge about European munitions production and capabilities. Several officers spent as long as two years in Europe touring the continent, and meeting with their European counterparts. Even Thayer made a return trip in 1844 for a two-year tour of fortifications and schools, bringing back books, knowledge, and experience to the Corps of Engineers. Some American officers attended European military schools. For example, six cavalry officers attended the French cavalry school in 1839, while some artillerists attended the French artillery school at Metz.

Another trend in budding American military professionalism involved assigning American officers as observers with European armies in training or on actual operations in the field. Many officers who visited European armies, their schools, and installations noted the camaraderie and the common sense of purpose and dedication among officers, especially in the Prussian and Austrian officer corps. As a lieutenant, Philip Kearney observed and even participated in French military operations in Algeria. Lieutenant Colonel Edwin V. Summer observed British and French cavalry maneuvers in 1854. During the 1859 War of Italian Unification, several American officers observed combat operations.

The Crimean War of 1855–1856 presented the most important opportunity to see modern European military forces in action. Secretary of War Jefferson Davis, a veteran of the War with Mexico, sent Major Richard Delafield of the Corps of Engineers, Major Alfred Mordecai of the Ordnance Department, and Captain George B. McClellan of the 1st Cavalry Regiment to observe the action. Arriving too late to witness the major battles, the officers nevertheless conducted extensive studies of battlefields, logistics, and transportation. Their reports offered valuable information on the organization of field armies, forts, arms design and manufacture, basic field equipment, and field hospitals.

Early professionalization also involved standardization of training, ordnance, and equipment. Secretary of War John C. Calhoun established the Artillery School of Practice at Fort Monroe in Virginia in 1824 and an Infantry School of Practice at Jefferson Barracks in St. Louis in 1826. Using the French "schools of practice" concept, units rotated through these schools to receive standardized training and drill. Lack of funding from Congress hampered the mission of these schools.

During the Jackson administration, egalitarianism and a need for troops during the Second Seminole War forced closure of both schools. In the early 1840s, however, the War Department established four regimental schools of practice at regimental posts across the country. In 1858, the artillery school reopened at Fort Monroe with an expanded mission to study the theoretical use of artillery. A cavalry school of practice informally operated at Jefferson Barracks before being formally established at Carlisle Barracks in Pennsylvania in 1855. At West Point, Mahan created a two-year postgraduate course for engineers. The schools of practice improved the Army's use of light artillery and infantry tactical maneuver and, although the Civil War placed many of these schools on hiatus, the movement toward specialized, advanced military education gained even more momentum after the Civil War.

Standardizing fortification and ordnance received much attention during the 1840s and 1850s. The Corps of Engineers proposed hundreds of projects to strengthen and diversify fixed fortifications. Among the ideas put forward were floating batteries powered by steam (a favorite of Secretary of War Lewis Cass), and fortress design and placement that used railroads for logistics and troop movement. Individual engineers debated the merits and flaws in the coastal fortification system. At the same time, the Ordnance Department standardized munitions and equipment. Artillery design, the percussion rifle, breech-loading weapons, and other equipment and weapons received the Board of Ordnance's stamp of approval. The board also considered proposals for new technologies from both military officers and civilian inventors. Its method of testing and approving new weapons and equipment for standardized use by the Army made the Board of Ordnance the Army's first real research and development program.

Finally, any profession needs a means of sharing information, raising questions and discussing issues that affect the ability of that profession to fulfill its purpose. Before the Civil War, the American military already had developed such a process. Through various revisions of field manuals for artillery, infantry, and cavalry, officers discussed not only different methods and tactics for defense against foreign invasion, but also how best to deal with the Indian problem, maintain frontier security, and incorporate new technology. Journals, such as the *Army and Navy Chronicle* and the *Military and Naval Magazine of the United States,* became *de facto* professional publications in which officers could express concerns, raise issues, and share ideas. Some officers wrote military history. Congress published a wide range of military reports. The topics ran the gamut from military pay to infantry tactics, or from the diplomatic implications of exploratory expeditions to sanitation. Pre-Civil War era officers had a range of publications available to promote discussion about their profession at arms.

The Navy lagged behind the Army in professionalism. The establishment of the Depot for Charts and Instruments, the Naval Observatory, and the Nautical Almanac Office initiated some standardization, but resistance to new technology, especially steam, remained entrenched among senior officers. Naval education was inconsistent and mostly relied on the traditional midshipmen apprentice system. As a challenge to this system, Matthew Perry established what he called the Naval Lyceum at the Brooklyn Navy Yard in 1833, but there was no formalized curriculum—only loosely directed independent study. A Naval School had also been established at Philadelphia for midshipmen, but it hardly qualified as a military academy.

Secretary of the Navy (and historian) George Bancroft finally formalized midshipmen education in 1845, and moved the Naval School from Philadelphia to Annapolis, Maryland. Congress, which had been in recess when Bancroft made the switch, turned a blind eye once it learned that Bancroft had saved money by moving the school. Congress approved the move, and appropriated funds for its operation, thus officially creating the U.S. Naval Academy.

Nevertheless, the Navy had serious problems. Inconsistency in quality of command resulted in even more inconsistency in the administration of discipline. Questionable hangings for mutiny on the *Somers* in 1842, and other dubious executions and floggings brought naval justice and officership into question. It took decades before these and other issues addressed adequately.

For the Army, at least, education, thought, and standardization in the pre-Civil War era put the American military on the path to professionalism. Army officers came to see themselves as part of a unique subculture with a sense of purpose and mission. The ideal of the educated, well-mannered, and courageous officer who was intellectually involved in the development of his craft gradually became the norm rather than the exception. The Navy did not catch up until after the Civil War.

◆ WAR WITH MEXICO

American expansion encroached upon Mexican lands primarily via expeditions and illegal settlement. The exception to this pattern was the permission that Spanish authorities gave to Americans to settle in Texas in 1821. Shortly thereafter, Mexico gained independence from Spain, and disagreements between Texans and the Mexican government immediately ensued. When Mexico outlawed slavery in 1835, Texans rebelled. The Texas Revolution ended in April 1386 with a treaty granting independence from Mexico, and recognizing the Rio Grande River as the southern border of the new republic. When the United States annexed Texas in 1845, Mexico severed diplomatic relations with the United States. Historically, Mexico considered the Nueces River as Texas's southern boundary, and saw the American annexation of Texas as a grab at Mexican territory. The Mexican government also worried that the U.S. wanted California. In fact, President James K. Polk was interested in annexing California, and offered to buy the territory from Mexico, and to settle the border dispute over the Texas-Mexico boundary.

Polk anticipated a Mexican invasion of Texas and, perhaps, hoped that negotiations would break down. In preparation, the president ordered Brevet Brigadier

General Zachary Taylor to position 1,500 troops along the Nueces River in July 1845. In February 1846, negotiations with Mexico indeed collapsed. Polk ordered Taylor to move his force to the Rio Grande. Supplied by sea at Point Isabel, Taylor established Fort Texas, near modern-day Brownsville, Texas, as a defensive stronghold to repel a Mexican attack, which he assumed would come from Matamoras, directly across the border from Brownsville.

On April 23, an American patrol sent to intercept a large force of Mexican troops crossing the Rio Grande was ambushed by a Mexican patrol. Of the sixty American dragoons, eleven were killed and the rest captured. Taylor informed President Polk of the hostile action. The American press proclaimed that "American blood had been shed on American soil." Polk asked for a declaration of war, which Congress over-whelmingly approved on May 11, 1846. Taylor called on the state of Texas to provide four regiments of volunteers rather than state militia. Militia could not leave American territory, but volunteers could.

Even before Congress formally declared war, Taylor fought the Mexicans at Palo Alto, north of the Rio Grande River, on May 8. Lieutenants Ulysses S. Grant and George Meade saw their first combat there. After suffering more than 300 killed and 300 more wounded, the Mexicans retreated to a dry riverbed called Resaca de la Palma, where they dug in to await Taylor's advance. On May 9, Taylor again prevailed over the Mexicans in a fierce hand-to-hand contest. By the next day, the remaining Mexican forces had retreated across the Rio Grande. Without supplies, however, Taylor was unable to move his army across the river in pursuit until May 18.

Polk had a clear objective in going to war with Mexico. He wanted Mexican territory north of the Rio Grande and west to the Pacific, including California. Polk and Major General Winfield Scott developed a three-prong strategy to achieve this objective. Taylor, now a brevet major general and in command of all armies in Mexico, would drive west from Matamoras to Monterey, then south toward Mexico City. From San Antonio, Brigadier General John Wool would move south into Mexico toward Saltillo. From Fort Leavenworth, in present-day Kansas. Colonel Stephen W. Kearny would move southwest to take Santa Fe and then San Diego. By taking these places, Polk would have the advantage in negotiating an expansionist peace with Mexico.

Both Polk and Congress hoped for a quick war. Congress gave Polk $10 million and raised the authorized strength of the Army to 15,540 troops by filling out 64-man companies to 100 men with new recruits. Congress also authorized 50,000 volunteers with a term of one year. Militia units were not called. Instead, the idea of an expansible army prevailed as volunteers augmented many existing units.

West Point graduates played their greatest role yet in an American war. Jefferson Davis, Robert E. Lee, Ulysses S. Grant, George B. McClellan, and Thomas J. Jackson, among many others, learned a great deal from their Mexican War experience that influenced their leadership in the Civil War just over a decade later. The Mexican War, however, was commanded by generals who had not graduated from West Point, and who held to pre-Napoleonic concepts of warfare. And, despite the growing influence of West Point in depoliticizing the officer corps, political disputes among officers influenced conduct of the war. Polk disliked both Taylor and Scott, because each of them was interested in being president. Seeing Scott as the greater political threat, Polk gave Taylor overall command. Polk could not keep Scott out of action for long, however,

FIGURE 7-1   Zachary Taylor, Major General of the U.S. Army, drawn by Edward Clay, 1847.

Source: Library of Congress Print and Reproductions Division [LC-DIG-pga-02187]

because his successes in northern Mexico had made him very popular. Maneuvering by important political figures such as Thomas Hart Benton, who wanted Polk to appoint him a general, and Polk's direct interference in command issues further complicated relations among the leadership.

CONGRESSMAN ABRAHAM LINCOLN SUPPORTS GENERAL TAYLOR FOR PRESIDENT IN 1848

A Whig representative from Illinois, Abraham Lincoln did not have a solid position on the war in Mexico before he joined Congress, where together with other Whigs he strongly criticized Polk's war policy. In the House of Representatives, Lincoln introduced the famous "spot" resolutions, which questioned Polk's reasons for going to war against Mexico. Lincoln was an astute politician and had his ear to the political ground during the 1848 presidential election year. In this letter to Elihu B. Washburne, Lincoln notes that although Henry Clay had announced he would seek the Whig Party's presidential nomination in 1848 and that General Scott and Supreme Court Justice John McLean also had presidential aspirations, General Taylor would be the better candidate for the Whigs. Lincoln encourages his friend Washburne, a fellow Whig and lawyer in Galena, Illinois, to build support for General Taylor in his district. The Mexican War certainly gave some military men political ambitions.

Washington, April 30, 1848

Dear Washburne:

I have at this moment received your very short note asking me if old Taylor is to be used up, and who will be the nominee. My hope of Taylor's nomination is as high—a little higher—than it was when you left. Still, the case is by no means out of doubt. Mr. Clay's letter has not advanced his interests here. Several who were *against* Taylor, but not *for* anybody particularly, before, are since taking ground, some for Scott and some for McLean. Who will be nominated neither I nor any one else can tell. Now, let me pray to you in turn. My prayer is, that you let nothing discourage or baffle you; but that, in spite of every difficulty, you send us a good Taylor delegate from your Circuit. Make [Edward D.] Baker, who is now with you I suppose, help about it. He is a good hand to raise a breeze . . . .

Yours Truly,
A Lincoln

Source: Abraham Lincoln Papers, Library of Congress.

Taylor began his advance on Monterey in June 1846, with over 3,000 regulars and 3,000 more volunteers after several weeks of preparation during which disease and desertion ravaged his army. At Monterey, a well-armed force of 7,000 Mexican troops awaited Taylor's army in well-fortified positions. On September 20, Taylor sent a force of regulars and Texas Rangers to secure the Saltillo road to the west. Batteries of American howitzers shelled the Monterey citadel and other fortifications in and around the city. On September 23, the Americans converged on the city from east and west in fierce house-to-house fighting. By the next day, the Mexicans were trapped around the main plaza of the city and forced to surrender. Taylor, hoping to show his generosity and sway the Mexican government toward peace negotiations, allowed the Mexican army at Monterey to withdraw under an eight-week armistice.

Polk, however, canceled the armistice and ordered an offensive against the Mexican capitol, Mexico City, through the port of Veracruz. The president hoped that capturing the enemy capitol would raise sagging popular support for the war, and force the Mexican government into peace negotiations. General Scott commanded the forces destined for Veracruz. In preparation for the invasion, Scott ordered Taylor to remain on the defensive at Monterey, and to send a large portion of his army to support the Veracruz operation. Angry at what he perceived as Scott's attempt to undermine his political ambitions, Taylor advanced his remaining 6,000 troops south to an indefensible position at Agua Nueva. Meanwhile, former Mexican dictator General Antonio de Santa Anna had returned from exile and accepted command of a large army at San Luis Potosi that was intended to repel the American invaders. Learning of Taylor's weak position and small force of mostly volunteers, Santa Anna advanced north, hoping to smash Taylor's army.

In February, Taylor's lead force of 5,000 troops met Santa Anna's army of more than 20,000 soldiers just outside Saltillo at Buena Vista. Santa Anna quickly gained the initiative through superior artillery placement, but his cavalry was almost useless in the rough terrain. A regiment of Indiana volunteers broke and ran, leaving the field open to the Mexicans. Taylor then arrived with Jefferson Davis's Mississippi Dragoons, headed off a Mexican cavalry assault, and ordered American artillery into the fight. This turned the tide of the battle, and Santa Anna, having lost nearly 2,000 killed and wounded, fell back to San Louis Potosi under cover of darkness on September 23. Taylor had lost 264 killed and about 450 wounded, but he could have lost many more. The terrain, weather, and deadly use of artillery made the Battle of Buena Vista one of the fiercest fights of the war. Santa Anna had to abandon the north to the Americans. Taylor, motivated by political ambition, had, with almost stunning battlefield courage, led his men well. But now the focus shifted toward Scott in Mexico, and Kearny's advance in the west.

From Fort Leavenworth, Kearny set out for Santa Fe with 300 Army dragoons and 1,000 Missouri volunteer mounted infantry. Arriving near Bent's Fort in July 1846, Kearny's men had suffered tremendous deprivation on their journey. The heat, lack of potable water, sunburn, and vicious mosquitoes plagued them. Kearny lost several men to sun-induced madness and dozens of horses to the heat. In late August, Kearny occupied Santa Fe, where the Mexican territorial governor had fled before the Americans' arrival. Kearny encountered no resistance among the local population, which included several American traders. He then set up a provincial government, writing a new constitution that combined American and local Hispanic governing organization, which came to be known as the Kearny Code.

Having taken Santa Fe without firing a shot, Kearny then set out for San Diego—a long, grueling journey. Along the way he met Kit Carson from whom he learned that the Navy and John Fremont had all but secured much of northern California. With his mission now changed, Kearny sent back the bulk of his dragoons, and took 100 men across the desert into California to San Diego. He suffered a setback against a force of Californios (the Spanish speaking settlers of California) at the Battle of San Pascual; his force was saved only by a contingent of sailors and Marines sent by Commodore Robert Stockton, who unbeknownst to Kearny had already taken San Diego. In 1847, Stockton's and Kearny's combined force defeated a small Californio army near Los Angeles, taking the town on January 10. Fremont's California Battalion, made up mostly of Americans from Sutter's Fort, arrived days later. At this point, Fremont signed the Treaty of Cahuenga with the defeated army, granting terms that Stockton had earlier refused. Stockton, angry, but eager to conclude affairs approved the treaty on January 13. California was now in American hands. The California campaign had benefited from the poor state of Mexican and Californio forces, but was almost derailed by inter- as well as intra-service bickering between Kearny, Stockton, and Fremont.

With California and northern Mexico under American control, all that remained for Polk was to force the Mexican government to the peace table. With the defiant

FIGURE 7-2   The Mexican War.

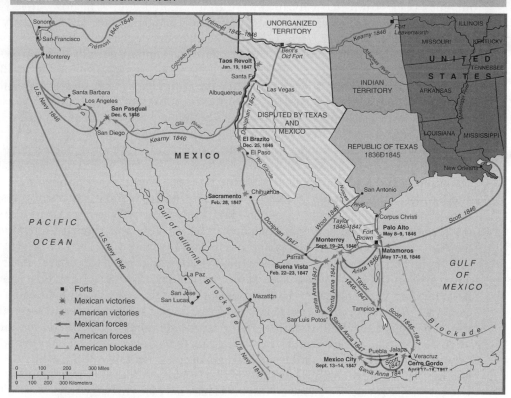

Santa Anna in command, however, the prospect seemed unlikely. Scott had to proceed with his campaign against Mexico City. On March 9, 1847, Scott landed 10,000 troops just three miles south of Veracruz in the first major amphibious landing in American military history; specially built surfboats ferried troops and supplies to the beach. Facing a Mexican force of over 4,000 behind Veracruz's formidable walls, Scott took his time preparing artillery positions for siege guns to bombard the city. On March 22, ten-inch mortars began firing on Veracruz from just half a mile away. Commodore Matthew C. Perry, in command of the naval force off Veracruz, loaned Scott several naval guns, which had even greater effect in shelling the city. Veracruz surrendered on March 27. Scott occupied the city, declaring martial law, which applied to his own troops as much as it did to the civilian population. He had a soldier hanged for rape, making it clear that no depredations would be tolerated.

Scott now faced the long and difficult 200 miles to Mexico City. He chose to use the National Highway, which led out of the malaria-bearing, mosquito-infested coastal lowlands into the high mountains. Poor transportation plagued his effort from the beginning, as there were never enough wagons or draft animals to keep his army moving as a single unit. Still, he needed to get his army off the coast before fever destroyed it and before the Mexicans could organize defenses.

Santa Anna had lost almost half of his army in fights with Taylor and his forced marches back to Mexico City to thwart an attempted coup. He now moved east along the National Highway to stop Scott. Santa Anna positioned his small army in a series of cliffs just outside Cerro Gordo to block Scott's advance, down the National Highway. While Scott did come that way, a daring reconnaissance by Captain Robert E. Lee found a route around the cliffs to even higher ground that, with artillery, commanded Santa Anna's positions. After the Herculean effort of moving artillery up and down steep ravines and cliffs, Scott opened fire on the morning of April 18, forcing the Mexicans into a chaotic retreat and leaving Scott to deal with over 3,000 prisoners of war.

Now it seemed that the highway to Mexico City was wide open. Scott's good fortune, however, was soon overshadowed by new challenges. At Puebla, Scott had to rest his men and await resupply and reinforcements. Over 2,000 of his men were sick, and to make matters worse, 3,000 volunteers returned to Veracruz to await transport home when their enlistments expired in May. It took over 600 wagons to carry the sick, the former volunteers, and their equipment back to Veracruz, forcing Scott to make the risky decision to cut his supply line and live off the land.

To further complicate Scott's situation, Polk's appointed negotiator, Nicholas Trist, arrived while Scott was at Veracruz. Trist did not like Scott, and Scott had no need for Trist or his mission. The two men got off on the wrong foot, but Scott's concern for Trist, who became very ill in Vera Cruz, helped bridge the gap between these two enormous egos. Polk ordered Trist to negotiate an end to the fighting, and to offer the Mexican government $1 million dollars for a treaty. Trist failed to make any headway in negotiating with the Mexican government, notably because Santa Anna had forced the Mexican congress to pass a law making it illegal to negotiate with the United States. As a consequence, Scott made his final plans for assaulting Mexico City.

By August 10, Scott's isolated force had advanced within fourteen miles of Mexico City. Santa Anna had manned several well-fortified positions to the east of the city, forcing Scott to approach from the west. The route was narrow, confined by lakes, mountains, and apparently impassable lava fields known as the Pedregal. The Pedregal did indeed seem impassable to everyone—except Robert E. Lee. Lee found a path through the challenging terrain that could be widened to a road. Supporting Brevet Major General Gideon J. Pillow's road crews, Brigadier General David E. Twiggs's division and light artillery served as a covering force. Before long, both Twiggs and Pillow had a fight on their hands against well-placed Mexican howitzers near Contreras. The next day, reinforced American units sneaked through a path in the Pedregal to hit the Mexican rear. The Battle of Contreras was brief but deadly for the Mexicans, who lost over 700 killed and 800 captured to the Americans' 60 killed and wounded. Scott, however, did not rest.

Scott ordered his forces to go after Santa Anna, chasing the Mexican forces through San Angel and then to Churubusco. The battle went back and forth all afternoon, but subsided as the Mexicans ran low on ammunition. Santa Anna had lost another 4,000 killed and wounded while Scott suffered 1,000 casualties. A unit of over 200 American deserters—mostly Irish Catholic immigrants who sided with the Mexican Catholics—had fought against the Americans since the Battle of Monterey. Many among this unit, known as the San Patricios, were captured at Churubusco; now, their fate lay in Scott's hands. Just as American forces raised the flag over Chapultepec Castle, the U.S. Army carried out the execution of 35 of these deserters.

Both sides were exhausted and agreed to a brief armistice for negotiations. Trist and the Mexican government, however, could not find common ground. Santa Anna used the break to rebuild his beleaguered forces. Scott, knowing that time only made the Mexicans stronger, terminated the armistice and prepared to make a final assault on the city.

Two strong positions threatened to stop Scott's assault—Chapultepec Castle, and El Molino del Rey. Recognizing their significance, Santa Anna personally oversaw deployment of troops to those strongholds. Located high on a bluff, the castle served as the Mexican equivalent to West Point. Chapultepec blocked Scott's approach to the city. Below, the castle's causeways and steep slopes made for a difficult approach. When intelligence suggested the Mexican Army was casting cannon at El Molino del Rey, Scott determined to attack it. Curiously, Scott anticipated little resistance. To his surprise, the Battle of Molino del Rey (September 8, 1847) was a violent, bloody affair, one of the bloodiest in the War with Mexico. It cost Scott 700 casualties, while the Mexicans suffered 2,000. After taking El Molino del Rey, Scott's forces discovered only a few cannon. Scott launched his attack against Chapultepec on September 13. His plan called for a three-prong assault supported by heavy artillery. After a horrific few hours of fighting the castle fell, but the work was not done for the Americans. Scott kept the momentum going, pushing deep into the city. After enduring a day of house-to-house fighting, the Mexicans surrendered their capitol. Santa Anna fled with what little was left of his army, leaving Scott to occupy Mexico City and declare martial law.

Trist and Scott pursued negotiations with the defeated government, which concluded in February 1848. Interestingly, Trist had been recalled by an angry President Polk in October 1847. Trist had learned of the recall in November but, with Scott's counsel, had ignored it. By the time Washington learned of the current situation in Mexico City, Trist reasoned, the war might be over and the treaty signed. After several weeks of negotiations, the Mexican government finally agreed to terms. The Treaty of Guadalupe Hidalgo gave the United States modern-day New Mexico, Arizona, Nevada, Utah, and California, and parts of Wyoming and Colorado. Both sides agreed to the Rio Grande as the southern boundary of Texas. The United States assumed American claims against Mexico and gave Mexico $15 million. The American occupation force left Mexico in August 1848.

The Mexican War of 1846–1848 in reality had not been a very glorious affair. For the Americans, disease and hardship took many more lives than did battle. Of the 13,780 American dead, only one in eight died as the result of combat. Over 2,000 regulars and 3,000 volunteers had deserted during the war. The war also had a high financial cost—close to $100 million.

Despite the human and financial cost, the U.S. military had prevailed in a difficult war. Leadership was key to the American victory. Both Taylor and Scott, despite their personal and political rivalry, exhibited strategic creativity and daring. Scott's decision to cut his supply line from Veracruz remains studied to this day. Cooperation between Navy and Army commanders continued to improve, as it had in the War of 1812. The war had been a proving ground for the professional military education provided at West Point, whose graduates dominated junior-officer ranks in the regular army.

FIGURE 7-3   Landing of the American forces under General Scott, at Vera Cruz, March 9, 1847.

Source: Library of Congress Print and Reproductions Division [LC-USZ62-14216]

Yet, the very public postwar bickering among Army commanders—particularly Scott (who had to face a court of inquiry after the war), Fremont, and Stephen Kearny—over alleged affronts and charges of incompetence tarnished the military's achievement in carrying out a limited war in support of clear national objectives. Ironically, these very national objectives caused other problems. The addition of such a vast territory to the United States irritated the festering wound of slavery and territorial expansion, ultimately leading to civil war. Mexico, arguably, never recovered from the 1846–1848 war.

◆ CONCLUSION

By the 1850s, the American military had made great strides in professionalism, training, and, to a lesser extent, technology. Both the Army and Navy had developed a sense of *esprit d'corps* among their officers, especially the junior grades. Along with the *esprit,* there developed a sense of professional ethics and an understanding of the military as a career. More officers stayed in service for several years, even decades. The military had also found purpose beyond defending the territory of the United States. The War with Mexico had given it wartime experience, though there were still lessons to learn. War remained a romantic and glorious affair for many officers, who openly promoted a new, heroic tradition of American military prowess. While the war had been a great success for American combat arms, officers tried to compare the achievement to Napoleonic conflicts earlier in the century.

The American military had improved dramatically since the War of 1812. Despite success in the War with Mexico, serious issues remained. Civil-military relations continued to be tense despite the desire of officers to accept civilian authority over them. The Indian dilemma left a bitter taste in the mouths of Army officers. Significantly, sectionalism began to divide the officer corps. The regional crisis over slavery and expansion that erupted in civil war provided the supreme test for the American military, one that would force it to come of age.

Further Reading

Bauer, Jack. *The Mexican War, 1846–1848.* Annapolis: Naval Institute Press, 1974.

Crackel, Theodore J. *West Point: A Bicentennial History.* Lawrence: University Press of Kansas, 2003.

De Voto, Bernard A. *Year of Decision: 1846.* Boston: Houghton Mifflin, 1950.

Dugard, Martin. *The Training Ground: Grant, Lee, Sherman and Davis in the Mexican War, 1846–1848.* New York: Little Brown and Company, 2008.

Eisenhower, John S. D. *Agent of Destiny: The Life and Times of General Winfield Scott.* Norman: University of Oklahoma Press, 1997.

Eisenhower, John S. D. *So Far from God: The U.S. War with Mexico, 1846–1848.* New York: Random House, 1989.

Foos, Paul. *"A Short, Offhand, Killing Affair": Soldiers and Social Conflict during the Mexican-American War.* Chapel Hill: University of North Carolina Press, 2002.

Henderson, Timothy J. *A Glorious Defeat: Mexico and its War with the United States.* New York: Hill and Wang, 2008.

Johnson, Timothy D. *A Gallant Little Army: The Mexico City Campaign.* Lawrence: University Press of Kansas, 2007.

Lewis, Felice Flanery. *Trailing Clouds of Glory: Zachary Taylor's Mexican War Campaign and his Emerging Civil War Leaders.* Tuscaloosa: University of Alabama Press, 2010.

McCaffrey, James M. *Army of Manifest Destiny: The American Soldier in the Mexican War, 1846–1848.* New York: New York University Press, 1992.

Peskin, Allan. *Winfield Scott and the Profession of Arms.* Kent: Kent State University Press, 2003.

Singletary, Otis. *The Mexican War.* Chicago: University of Chicago Press, 1960.

Skelton, William B. *An American Profession at Arms: The Army Officer Corps, 1784–1861.* Lawrence: University Press of Kansas, 1992.

Waugh, John. *The Class of 1846: From West Point to Appomattox—Stonewall Jackson, George McClellan, and Their Brothers.* New York: Ballantine, 1999.

Winders, Richard Bruce. *Mr. Polk's Army: The American Military Experience in the Mexican War.* College Station: Texas A&M University Press, 1997.

mysearchlab Connections: Sources Online • • • • • • • • • • • • •

READ AND REVIEW

Review this chapter by using the study aids and these related documents available on MySearchLab.

Study Plan

   Chapter Test

   Essay Test

Documents

Zachary Taylor Proclamation (1847)
This document reveals the problems inherent in military occupation duties, very similar to those experienced by American forces in Iraq from 2004–2011.

First-Hand Account of the Capture of Mexico City (1847)
This document details the assault and capture of Mexico City by American forces under the command of General Winfield Scott.

Letter from Mexican War Soldier to His Parents (1848)
This letter relays the day-to-day concerns of a typical soldier, not unlike those in other wars.

RESEARCH AND EXPLORE

Explore the following review questions using the research tools available on www. mysearchlab.com.

1. Who was Jomini? What was his influence on the American military?
2. What role did the U.S. Military Academy play in the professionalization of the American officer corps?
3. Why was the War with Mexico important to the growth of the American military profession?

CHAPTER 8

Civil War & Reconstruction

◆ CHRONOLOGY

1860	Abraham Lincoln elected President
	South Carolina secedes from the Union
1861	Jefferson Davis sworn in as President of the new Confederate States of America
	Fort Sumter falls
	Battle of First Bull Run
1862	Union captures Forts Henry and Donelson
	Monitor and *Virginia* clash off Hampton Roads
	Battle of Shiloh
	Battle of Seven Pines
	Robert E. Lee takes command of Army of Northern Virginia
	Battles of the Seven Days
	Battle of Second Bull Run
	Battle of Antietam
	Emancipation Proclamation issued by Lincoln
	Battle of Fredericksburg
1863	Congress passes Enrollment Act
	Battle of Chancellorsville
	Stonewall Jackson killed
	Siege of Vicksburg
	Battle of Gettysburg

	Draft riots in New York City
	Battle of Chickamauga
	Battle of Chattanooga
1864	Lincoln names Ulysses S. Grant General-in-Chief of all Union armies
	Battle of the Wilderness
	Battle of Spotsylvania
	Battle of Cold Harbor
	Battle of Atlanta
	Sherman's "March to the Sea"
1865	Siege of Petersburg
	Freedmen's Bureau established by Congress
	Lee surrenders at Appomattox Courthouse
	Lincoln assassinated
1867	Reconstruction Acts
	Tenure of Office Act
	Command of the Army Act
1868	Grant elected President of the United States
1876	Rutherford B. Hayes elected President of the United States
1877	Reconstruction formally ends

◆ INTRODUCTION

As America's bloodiest conflict, the Civil War is integral to not only American history but also the American cultural tradition. Divided into North and South, the nation warred on itself for four years, with each side bringing a near-total commitment of not only military forces but also of government and the whole of American society to the fight. The delicate issue of slavery was at the conflict's core. What began for the North as a war to restore the Union also became a war to finally end slavery. In the southern Confederacy, the war was perceived as akin to the War for Independence in some respects. From the viewpoint of many southerners, an oppressive government was close to taking away basic rights, among which was the right to own other human beings as property. Only by having their own country, Southerners reasoned, could they continue to maintain slavery as the primary labor system to support the South's economy and its unique society.

Militarily, the Civil War was a Jominian conflict in part because West Point graduates versed in Jomini's writings commanded the largest armies ever seen in North America. Over the course of the war, however, a new way of war evolved—one with its roots in the colonial conflicts of the seventeenth century. This total war concept not only included making relentless war upon armies but also involved mobilizing and attacking industry, agriculture, transportation, and other war-making capacities. The goal of total war was to destroy the will of both military forces and the noncombatant population to carry on the fight by depriving both of needed food and other materials.

The Civil War remains a topic of the most intensive study among historians. The war's significance to American military history emerges through studying the strategies of the Union and Confederacy, reviewing the main theaters of operations and major battles, and examining the effects of the war on the future development of the American military.⌋

◆ YANKS AND REBS

Regionalism, in this case a sense of allegiance to either the North or the South, developed because of westward territorial expansion and the War with Mexico, the growth of Northern manufacturing, and the expansion of the South's cotton economy. By the 1850s, regionalism had manifested itself most intensely in the debate over slavery. Since 1820, successive compromises had failed to resolve the issue to either side's satisfaction, and with the election of Republican Abraham Lincoln in 1860 it seemed apparent to Southerners that slavery and their unique society were about to be destroyed by Northern abolitionists in Congress. Successive Southern states subsequently seceded from the United States to form the Confederate States of America. The United States that remained, the Union, faced few alternatives: either let the Southern states go or bring them back into the Union by force, if necessary.

⌈When hostilities broke out in April 1861, the Union had over 20 million people to the Confederacy's nine million, of whom almost half were slaves who at least initially would not be allowed to serve in the Confederate army. In the North over one million people worked in over 100,000 factories, while in the South fewer than 110,000 people worked in about 20,000 factories. The total industrial output of the Confederacy equaled that of the state of New York alone. The Northern rail network had over 31,000 miles of track—over 70 percent of the track in the United States. Among other industrial resources the North dominated in steel production and coal mining. The South had comparatively little with which to fuel and supply its comparative handful of factories. Based on these facts alone, odds makers would have heavily favored the North in any armed conflict against its southern neighbor.⌋

Union victory in the Civil War nevertheless was not assured. Like the patriot rebels in the War for Independence the Confederates did not have to win; rather, they had only to not lose. ⌈The South could fight a defensive war, hope for foreign intervention, and perhaps achieve a decisive victory that would force the Union to negotiate a settlement preserving Southern independence. The Union, on the other hand, barring a decisive victory against the Confederacy, would have to fight an offensive war without the benefit of interior lines of communication. Such a war would require large armies, extraordinarily long and complex logistical lines, and immense industrial output. The Confederacy might be able to hold on just long enough to break the will of the Northerners to fight such a protracted and costly war. ⌋

⌈It is ironic that Lincoln, a man with little military experience—he served 36 days of militia duty in the Black Hawk War (1832)—was a better war president than Jefferson Davis, who was a graduate of West Point, veteran of the War with Mexico, and former Secretary of War. Both men served as commanders-in-chief of their respective nations during the Civil War. Davis was perhaps at a disadvantage from the beginning of the war because the Confederate constitution limited his presidential powers. As in the old Articles of Confederation, states retained power over a relatively weak central government. Lincoln had much more leeway as commander-in-chief and arguably overstepped his power by suspending habeas corpus during the war. Lincoln nonetheless had to contend with more partisan bickering throughout the war than did Davis, as both Democrats and Republicans constantly criticized, questioned, and interfered with Lincoln's war effort.]

◆ STRATEGIC AND TECHNOLOGICAL CONTOURS

[Civil War grand strategy essentially evolved around two ideas. First, many believed that capturing the opponent's capital city would end the fighting and force a peace settlement. Such an approach clearly required defending one's own capital from capture. Second, Napoleonic tradition held that destroying the enemy's armies could achieve the same goal. With so many West Point graduates among the Confederate and Union officer corps, all having studied the Napoleonic Wars and Jomini, and in many instances having served in the War with Mexico, it is not surprising that these ideas held so much prominence in Civil War strategy.]

 When the war began, [Lieutenant General Winfield Scott, the experienced and aged head of the Union Army, proposed a tight naval blockade against Southern ports that was intended to deny the rebels support from abroad. Meanwhile Union armies would seize control of the Mississippi River with simultaneous approaches along the Ohio River from the north and from New Orleans in the south. Scott then planned to let the Confederacy slowly suffocate. The so-called Anaconda Plan] however, did not satisfy public demands in the North that the rebellion be put down quickly. [Thus, the Union attempted to capture Richmond as well as destroy Confederate armies — initially through attempts to fight decisive battles but later through a strategy of attrition. This grand strategy more or less guided Union strategic thinking throughout the war. Confederate strategy remained simply to fight a defensive war until the Union tired of the conflict or a foreign power intervened to help guarantee Confederate independence.

Neither Union nor Confederate strategy changed much until the spring of 1864. In March of that year, Lincoln appointed Lieutenant General Ulysses S. Grant as commander of all Union forces. Under Grant, [the strategic landscape changed. General Grant held strategic notions that went far beyond the decisive battle and slow strangulation. By fighting a total war, Grant aimed to utterly destroy the Confederacy's war-making capacity. He hoped to erode the political will of the people of the Confederacy by ruining the civilian economy. Additionally, Grant relentlessly pursued Confederate armies in the field, especially the Army of Northern Virginia, forcing its commander General Robert E. Lee into a war of attrition that the Confederacy could not win. As an experienced commander, Lee also coveted the decisive battle, even though it arguably did not fit with the overall Confederate strategy. Lee strategically and tactically took the defensive while looking for the critical decisive victory, which often required taking the offensive instead. The Confederacy was indeed caught in a strategic dilemma — it had to outlast the Union, but could it last that long without seeking the decisive battle to bring quick victory?]

Civil War armies began the fight expecting to use Napoleonic practices but they were forced to adjust tactics because of technological advancements in shoulder arms.

During the War with Mexico the U.S. Army had largely replaced smoothbore muskets with more accurate and deadly percussion-lock rifled muskets that used a conical bullet. The French Army officer Claude Etienne Minié in the 1840s designed a new bullet with a cone-shaped nose and a hollow base to replace the traditional round ball. When fired from Minié's new rifled musket, the base expanded into the rifling of the barrel, causing the bullet to spin horizontally and driving it outward faster, farther, and more accurately. Minié's new bullet made reloading quicker, which meant that each soldier could fire more often and expect the bullet to strike the enemy at greater distances. The .58 caliber muzzle-loading rifled muskets issued to most soldiers during the Civil War were not the best weapons available, but they were still sufficiently advanced over previous arms to force tactical changes on the battlefield. Other weapons, such as the breech-loading .52 caliber Sharps carbine and the .52 caliber Henry and .52 caliber Spencer repeating rifles, also had great impact on the battlefield.

More rapid, accurate fire made possible by the new rifles and the new bullet meant that the traditional tight attack formations had to give way to less dense battle lines of soldiers at greater distances opposite each other. Larger intervals between men created lines sometimes three-fourths of a mile long, if not longer. In addition, armies increased the distances between them when they met for battle. As a result, battles tended to last much longer and the decisive battle became more elusive. Rifled muskets and conical bullets also shifted the advantage from the attack to defense. Increased firepower spurred defending soldiers to seek shelter behind quickly constructed earthworks, a development that also eased distribution of ammunition. Thus, attacking soldiers were forced to advance across expanses of open ground against punishing rifle fire often delivered by enemy soldiers in well-protected defenses.

Assaulting forces also faced deadly fire from opposing artillery batteries. The smoothbore Napoleon 12-pound cannon was a mainstay for both armies and it could fire canister, shrapnel, or case shot, depending on what the battlefield situation warranted. Napoleons had an effective range of about 1,200 yards. The advent of rifled artillery, however, dramatically changed the battlefield as had rifled musketry. With a range of over 2,500 yards, rifled artillery provided greater accuracy at a greater distance. New and improved percussion fuses also gave artillery shells more lethality.

Extensive rail networks gave the railroad a pivotal transportation role for moving armies and supplying them in the field. Steam-powered riverboats allowed for greater mobility along inland waterways. The telegraph also played a prominent role, for now commanders could be in almost instant communication on the battlefield as well as with political leaders in Richmond and Washington.

◆ CIVIL WAR ARMIES

Army organization was essentially the same for both the Union and Confederate armies, with each comprising the three combat arms: infantry, artillery, and cavalry. The regiment was the basic unit in Civil War armies. Infantry, long the "queen of battle," was the centerpiece of both Union and Confederate forces. Brigades were composed of four to six regiments, with three to four brigades making up a division, of which three to four would make up a corps. When fully manned, the ten companies in an infantry regiment totaled 1,000 men, but as the war dragged on unit rolls listed fewer and fewer troops. By 1863, as men died, enlistments expired, and recruiting lagged, regiments typically carried fewer than 350 soldiers. These units would assault enemy positions in lined formations in successive waves in the face of deadly artillery and rifle fire.

Cavalry troops (a troop of cavalry was the same as a regiment) had twelve companies, with the same command structure as infantry. Improved firepower made traditional cavalry charges too costly, so most cavalrymen functioned as scouting or screening parties. In combat, cavalry more often than not functioned as dragoons, riding to the battlefield to fight while dismounted. Due primarily to this development, cavalry largely discarded the romantic but impractical saber early in the war in favor of the Spencer repeating rifle, and generally became highly effective fighters.

Similarly, artillery batteries were about the size of an infantry company and were attached to units from infantry corps down through to brigades. Artillery was used mostly in defensive positions and once dug in, artillery emplacements became formidable obstacles. Artillery could, however, function in a more mobile manner. Lighter cannon with smaller horse-drawn caissons could quickly be run into place, manned, and fired, then just as quickly moved to a new location.

To build these massive armies, both the Union and Confederacy used a variety of mobilization methods. The Union did not rely upon state militia, instead once again using volunteers in the expansible army concept. Each state was obligated to fulfill a quota of volunteers to be formed into units from that particular state. By 1863, however, volunteerism waned as the war dragged on and Union troop needs increased. Congress passed the Enrollment Act, which put in place conscription or, as it was known, a draft. This unprecedented expansion of federal authority caused riots in protest of the draft, the most infamous of which occurred in New York City during July 1863. The Confederacy earlier instituted a draft in April 1862. In both the Union and Confederacy, a myriad of exemptions and replacement provisions allowed many who were financially able to escape the draft, thus leaving the poorer adult male population available for conscription. Still, the threat of being drafted and the social stigma attached to it motivated many to volunteer for service. Even though conscription was controversial and drew a great deal of attention, it was not the primary means to raise forces.

◆ THE EASTERN THEATER (1861–1863)

Lincoln ordered most federal posts abandoned except for a small few, including Fort Sumter in Charleston harbor. When Confederate artillery under General P. G. T. Beauregard began bombarding the fort on April 12, 1861, Major Robert Anderson and his small garrison of men could offer little in reply. The following day a barracks caught fire, prompting Anderson to concede. Although hardly a great military victory, Anderson's surrender along with Lincoln's call for 75,000 volunteers to suppress the rebellion was enough to rally rebel spirits and spur Arkansas, North Carolina, Tennessee, and Virginia to join the Confederacy, thereby providing the new Confederacy with much needed resources and more troops. Most importantly,

Virginia's entry into the Confederacy convinced Lee to resign his U.S. Army commission and remain loyal to his home state. Fort Sumter's capitulation also united the North in support for war against the rebels. Now that the Confederacy had fired the first shot, state governments in the Union responded enthusiastically to Lincoln's April 15 call for 75,000 ninety-day volunteers to put down the rebellion.⌐

⌐Lincoln believed that the rebellion could be crushed by taking the Confederate capital at Richmond, some 100 miles to the south of Washington⌐From Washington, Union forces under Brigadier General Irvin McDowell headed toward Richmond in July 1861. At an important railroad junction at Manassas along Bull Run Creek, McDowell's force encountered Confederate forces in the first major battle of the war. Poorly trained and not well led, McDowell's force of mostly volunteers, over 30,000 troops, set out from Alexandria on July 16. They took four days to reach Manassas where Beauregard's force of 22,000 rebels awaited them. Reinforced by Brigadier General Joseph E. Johnston's 11,000 Confederates brought by railroad from the Shenandoah Valley, Beauregard now had at least a numerical advantage.⌐

⌐McDowell hoped to flank the Confederate battle line, then destroy the Confederate force in total. Not surprisingly, things did not go as planned. As prominent Northern politicians and other Washingtonians watched the action from what they thought was a safe distance, the Union attack began to falter. The long march, the July heat, and a courageous stand made by Brigadier General Thomas J. Jackson—which earned him the nickname "Stonewall"—at first caused the Union line to waiver and then break into a chaotic retreat all the way back to Washington. What was supposed to have been an easy Union rout of rebel forces had turned into a Union disaster. Fortunately for McDowell, the Confederates were too elated with victory or perhaps too exhausted to maintain the initiative and give chase to the fleeing Union troops. The Battle of First Bull Run, or Manassas, cost the Union 3,000 casualties and the Confederacy almost 2,000. Such a decisive Confederate victory shocked the North while bringing great hope for a swift victory across the South.⌐

Lincoln promptly relieved McDowell and named Major General George B. McClellan to command the new Army of the Potomac. "Little Mac," as his troops affectionately called him, refused to take his men into battle until he thought they were absolutely trained and ready. It took months but McClellan managed to build a disciplined army of over 150,000 men. Once he built this fine army, however, McClellan proved reluctant to use it.

Meanwhile, Confederate General Johnston and his rapidly growing army of 50,000 men stood between the Army of the Potomac and Richmond. Finally, in early 1862, Lincoln ordered McClellan to move on Richmond. McClellan moved his army at a glacial pace, landing on the Virginia Peninsula to approach Richmond from the east. Always fearing that the Confederate army was larger than it really was and angry that Lincoln had forced him to keep over 40,000 of his men near Washington to protect the capital from Jackson's small but mobile Confederate force, McClellan hesitated, giving Johnston time to reinforce and plan for the defense of Richmond. Finally, on May 31, the two armies met in a battle at Seven Pines near Richmond, where Johnston was severely wounded. President Davis replaced Johnston with Robert E. Lee.

Lee attacked the Army of the Potomac's right flank in what became known as the Battles of the Seven Days between June 25 and July 1, 1862. Despite poor coordination of attacks at places like Mechanicsville and Gaines Mill, Lee managed to drive McClellan away from Richmond. Now, with great confidence, Lee attempted to stage the decisive battle at Malvern Hill. Well-entrenched and fortified, the Army of the Potomac repulsed wave after wave of assaulting Confederates. Of Lee's 20,000 casualties during the Seven Days, over 5,000 occurred at Malvern Hill.

Impatient at McClellan's lack of progress, Lincoln decided to make yet another change. The president had learned, however, that he could not personally direct the war. Although a gifted organizer, McClellan was too timid in the field, and Lincoln needed a fighting general. Henry W. Halleck replaced McClellan as General-in-Chief of the Union Army, though McClellan retained command of the Army of the Potomac and Major General John Pope took command of the new Army of Virginia, which was scattered about the Shenandoah Valley. Though Halleck proved a disappointment in coordinating field armies, he did provide a useful conduit between the field armies and Lincoln.

McClellan and Pope converged their armies at Fredericksburg in northern Virginia. Fearful that the combined armies might be too much for his Army of Northern Virginia, Lee struck Pope as the Army of Virginia slowly made its way toward Fredericksburg. With McClellan nowhere near Fredericksburg, Pope was left to fight Lee on his own. In the Second Battle of Bull Run, or Manassas, Lee and Pope clashed where Confederate and Union armies had battled the previous year. Lee distracted Pope by bringing Jackson's force behind the Army of Virginia. Jackson's troops then led Pope's army right into Lee's hands at Bull Run on August 29–30, 1862. Pope suffered over 16,000 casualties while Lee had 9,000.

Infuriated at the failure to trap the Army of Northern Virginia, Lincoln fired Pope and incorporated the Army of Virginia into the Army of the Potomac to restore McClellan to overall field command. The bold Lee again chose to seek a decisive battle by invading Maryland with the hope of drawing the Army of the Potomac into the open where he could destroy it. Doing so would leave Washington, Baltimore, even Philadelphia open to Confederate attack. With Major General J. E. B. Stuart's cavalry screening his right flank, Lee crossed his army into Maryland to march into Hagerstown.

What happened next was one of those odd twists of luck that often occur in wars. Union troops investigating an abandoned Confederate camp found several cigars, one of them wrapped in a copy of Lee's orders for the march into Maryland. McClellan now knew exactly where the Army of Northern Virginia was headed and where it would converge. McClellan, however, squandered the opportunity by hesitating again—this time he delayed for over half a day. He could have attacked Lee's forces before they had converged. Instead, the delay and Lee's discovery that Union soldiers had found his plan prevented such a move. Lee abandoned the invasion and gathered his army at Sharpsburg near Antietam Creek. With little room to maneuver, but with the advantage of interior lines, Lee made his stand in the Battle of Antietam—the bloodiest day in American history—that became a turning point in the war.

On September 17, Lee's army of 40,000 faced off against McClellan's 70,000 near Sharpsburg. McClellan believed he had the chance to wipe out the Army of Northern Virginia and gain a Napoleonic-style decisive victory. All day long at places like the Cornfield, Bloody Lane, and Burnside's Bridge, the two massive armies clashed.

Neither one could gain the advantage. McClellan failed to put in his reserve corps when doing so might have won the day for the Union. Battered and bloodied, the two armies warily eyed each other throughout the following day, then Lee withdrew back into Virginia. Between the two armies almost 5,000 men had been killed with another 21,000 wounded or missing. Neither side could afford such casualties.⌉

Still,⌈the Army of the Potomac held the field in what had been a tactical draw. McClellan did not pursue Lee. Arguably, his force was so bloodied that it simply could not do so. Lincoln was able to put enough political spin on the Battle of Antietam to change the objective of the war. Preserving the Union had not sold well among the Northern public as casualties mounted. Now Lincoln added a new objective—in addition to preserving the Union he wanted to end slavery once and for all. It was a brilliant political stroke that changed not only the Union's war aims but also how the Union would fight the war.⌉

⌈Lincoln issued an Emancipation Proclamation that freed slaves only in states that were in rebellion against the United States. Border states still in the Union could retain their slaves, but Lincoln's announcement served as notice that slavery even in those states would soon end. In order to carry out the proclamation Union armies would have to occupy the Confederacy. Otherwise, the order had no standing since the Confederacy considered itself an independent and sovereign nation. Diplomatically, Lincoln's proclamation preempted possible recognition of the Confederacy by Great Britain, which had abolished slavery in the British Empire in 1833, and also made it more difficult for France to recognize the Confederacy. Both countries briefly considered intervening because they feared that emancipation would expand the conflict into an all-out race war. By broadening Union war aims to include the eradication of slavery, however, Lincoln convinced both Great Britain and France to reconsider intervention. As word of emancipation spread, thousands of slaves abandoned their owners to seek Union lines and freedom. The principal labor source of the South had been irrevocably undermined.⌉

⌈The Emancipation Proclamation had another significant effect. Now African-Americans, both free and slave, wanted to join the Union ranks and fight to end slavery.⌉The War Department had already recruited African Americans into the Army, but they had been relegated to noncombat duties. In May 1863, the War Department established the Bureau for Colored Troops, and before long colored regiments officered by whites, such as in the immortalized 54th Massachusetts, served in combat roles. Close to 180,000 African Americans served in the Union Army during the war, plus another 19,000 in the Navy. As many as 40,000 died, including approximately 30,000 from disease, in the conflict that ultimately ended slavery in the United States.⌉

⌊Lincoln replaced McClellan with Major General Ambrose E. Burnside on November 7, 1862. Burnside had shown promise as a combat commander, serving with distinction at Antietam and other battles. Lincoln wanted Richmond and Burnside sought to give it to him. Burnside marched his Army of the Potomac, now over 120,000 strong, southward from Washington to get between Lee and Richmond before Lee could block him. Burnside attempted to cross the Rappahannock River at Fredericksburg, but before he could do so Lee arrived with the Army of Northern Virginia's now 70,000 troops to occupy the high ground on the south side of the river. Burnside still managed to cross to attempt a series of futile frontal assaults on Lee's entrenched lines. The idea of hitting weak points in the enemy's line with overwhelming mass still guided battlefield tactics.

[The Battle of Fredericksburg began in earnest on December 13, 1862. Along Marye's Heights, Major General James Longstreet's Confederates unleashed devastating rifle fire from behind a stone wall as Union troops attempted to cross a mile of open ground to assault Longstreet's position. As at Antietam, the casualties were horrendous. Burnside lost over 12,000 killed and wounded, while Lee lost a not-insignificant 5,300. Although he had initially planned a second attack on December 18, Burnside reconsidered and withdrew the Army of the Potomac back across the Rappahannock.]

[As 1862 drew to a close in the east, the massive armies had bloodied each other badly but made no strategic progress. Stalemate seemed to be the best way to characterize the situation. Lincoln fired Burnside, whose subordinates had lobbied for his removal. Burnside's replacement was Major General Joseph Hooker, yet another proven combat leader given the chance to guide the Army of the Potomac to Richmond. Hooker used the winter to restore morale and improve discipline and training. He gave each corps distinctive insignia to help build unit identity, beginning a tradition that remains in the American armed forces to this day.]

As the weather improved, [Hooker was still faced with Lee's army firmly entrenched at Fredericksburg. Learning from Burnside's mistakes, Hooker planned a double envelopment to dislodge Lee from Fredericksburg and divided his force of 130,000 to hit the right and left flanks of the Army of Northern Virginia. Of course, in battle the best-laid plans often fall apart, which is why a combat commander must be creative, flexible, and coolheaded. Realizing what was happening, Lee divided his force, leaving part on Marye's Heights and withdrawing the rest to nearby Chancellorsville.]

[The Battle of Chancellorsville is often considered the finest example of Lee's combat command ability. During this engagement Lee utilized economy of force, surprise, offensive maneuver, and basic daring to again defeat the Army of the Potomac.[First contact was made in a wooded area of thick undergrowth called the Wilderness. Having hacked its way through this dense forest, on May 1 Hooker's army was surprised by Stonewall Jackson's smaller force. Hooker withdrew back through the Wilderness to Chancellorsville.]

Lee again divided his force, using defensive screens and quick but long marches to surprise Hooker. On May 2, just outside Chancellorsville, Union Major General Oliver O. Howard mistook Confederate movements for a retreat and ordered his men forward just before dusk. It was a trap in which Jackson's men very nearly destroyed Howard's force. That same night Jackson was mistakenly shot by a sentry as he returned from a reconnaissance of Union lines. He died eight days later. Lee's army never fully recovered from the loss of Stonewall Jackson.

On [May 3, Lee struck Chancellorsville and drove Hooker out of the city. Meanwhile, in Fredericksburg, Major General John Sedgwick broke through the Confederate lines in an effort to reach Chancellorsville. On May 4, Lee again divided his force to stop Sedgwick's advance. Near Salem Church, Lee and Sedgwick clashed in a fierce fight. Hooker refused to send reinforcements to help Sedgwick. Incredibly, over one-third of the Army of the Potomac had yet to be engaged. With Sedgwick thwarted and Hooker uncertain, Lee had another opportunity to destroy the Army of the Potomac. Before he could pull it off, however, Hooker withdrew back across the Rappahannock. Hooker's grand plan to take Richmond had miscarried, resulting in over 17,000 Union casualties to Lee's 13,000. Lee had also failed to crush the Army of the Potomac despite his brilliant tactical movements during the battle.

Lee then planned his boldest campaign—an invasion deep into Northern territory, perhaps as far as Philadelphia. Among his many objectives Lee hoped to relieve Richmond by forcing the Army of the Potomac out of Virginia and destroying it, much as he had tried to do in 1862. Such a victory might entice foreign recognition or at least foreign aid, as well as aggravate Lincoln's troublesome political situation in the North. The risk was huge. If the Army of Northern Virginia itself was destroyed, then the Confederate cause would be lost.

By June 30, 1863, Lee had his three corps across the Potomac and into Maryland. Using the Shenandoah Valley and the hills of western Maryland to screen his movements, Lee was able to move his 75,000 men deep into Union territory before the Army of the Potomac realized what was happening. Hooker proposed hitting Richmond while Lee was absent. Lincoln rejected the idea, wanting instead to protect Washington and Baltimore and destroy Lee's army. One problem was that for several days neither side seemed to know exactly where the other was. Lee's cavalry under the command of Stuart failed in its mission to act as Lee's eyes and ears. Stuart lost contact with Lee, instead riding his cavalry on admittedly daring raids that were otherwise of little use to Lee as he entered Pennsylvania for the first time in the war. Hooker headed north, keeping the Army of the Potomac between Lee and Washington.

Knowing that Hooker was on the move, Lee ordered his far-flung corps to regroup in southern Pennsylvania near Gettysburg. On the same day, June 28, Lincoln replaced Hooker with Major General George Meade. Gettysburg was a crossroads, as major roads from almost every direction came together there like the hub of a spoked wheel. It was there that the largest battle in the history of North America and arguably the most important battle of the Civil War took place—the Battle of Gettysburg.

Advance units of Union cavalry under the command of Brigadier General John Buford literally ran into advance units of Confederate infantry belonging to Lieutenant General A. P. Hill's Confederate corps to the west of Gettysburg on July 1. Major General John Reynolds and his more than 20,000 Union troops arrived to support Buford. By late afternoon both Hill's and Lieutenant General Richard Ewell's Confederate corps were engaged, pushing Reynolds' men back through Gettysburg to Culp's Hill and Cemetery Hill southeast of the town. Reynolds preferred the defensive advantage of the hills; thus, from his viewpoint, being pushed through Gettysburg was not catastrophic. Before Reynolds could move to the hills, however, he was killed. Meade replaced him with the very able Major General Winfield Scott Hancock. Lee ordered Ewell to take Cemetery Hill lest the Union troops get entrenched in a solid defensive position, but Ewell's advance failed. Throughout the night, the main bodies of the two armies converged on Gettysburg, with Meade placing his men on the hills as well as along a slight ridge to the south called Cemetery Ridge.

On July 2, Lee tried to flank the hills in order to get around to the Union rear. Longstreet's advance division did not arrive until early afternoon, thus delaying Lee's plan to launch a coordinated attack on both flanks while attacking the center of the Union line. The Confederates held a long exterior line along Seminary Ridge to the south and west of Gettysburg. It took Longstreet until late afternoon to get his men in position to make the attack on the Union's left flank. The immediate objective was an unoccupied

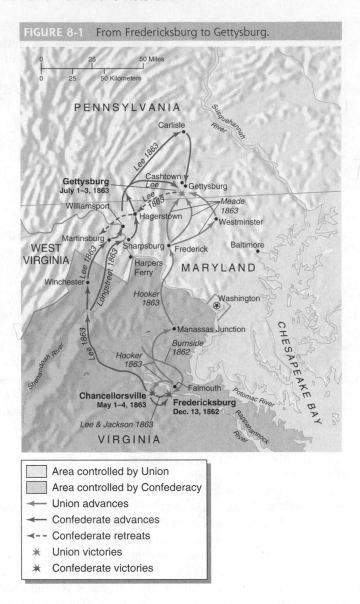

FIGURE 8-1 From Fredericksburg to Gettysburg.

Area controlled by Union
Area controlled by Confederacy
◀— Union advances
◀— Confederate advances
◀- - Confederate retreats
✳ Union victories
✳ Confederate victories

rocky hill known as Little Round Top, from which the Confederates could flank the entire Union line on Cemetery Ridge. Noticing the Confederate movement, Brigadier General Gouverneur Warren managed to get two brigades on the hill just before the assault began.

By this point the coordination of the Confederate flanking attacks had failed, so each attack occurred in relative isolation from the other. Ewell's assaults on Culp's Hill were unsuccessful as were the Confederate attacks on the Union center. At Little Round Top Longstreet's repeated assaults also failed. At the end of the second day's fighting, Lee was convinced that although he had not pushed Meade's men off the high ground, the flanks must be weak from the repeated assaults. He logically thought that Meade would have to weaken his center line to reinforce the flanks on the hills.

FIGURE 8-2 Confederate dead behind stone wall. The 6th Main Infantry penetrated the Confederate lines at this point. Fredericksburg, Virginia, ca. 1860–1865.

Source: Library of Congress Print and Reproductions Division [LC-DIG-ppmsca-11747]

[July 2 had been an extraordinary day of battle at Gettysburg. Colonel Joshua Lawrence Chamberlain's 20th Maine managed to hold the extreme left end of the Union line at Little Round Top despite repeated Confederate charges and almost running out of ammunition. Fierce fighting immortalized places on the expansive battlefield such as the Peach Orchard, the Wheat Field, and Devil's Den. Casualties had been enormous on both sides. The heat sapped the troops' strength as much as did the fighting. Meade did not think Lee would attack again on the next day.]

On [July 3, Lee did attack. Lee took the approach opposite to what he had done the previous day by planning a coordinated attack that feinted this time at both Union flanks then struck sharply against the Union center line. Lee believed that a massive infantry assault supported by an artillery bombardment would split the Army of the Potomac in two. Of course, the timing did not work. Units took too long to get into position, and Ewell renewed his attack on Culp's Hill too early. The movement alerted Union lines to the plan of attack, allowing them to prepare for the assault on their center. The Confederate artillery barrage proved ineffective despite its scale and ferocity. Lee sent Major General George Pickett's division along with brigades from other divisions to make the frontal assault on the Union center—across a mile of open field and up a slight rise—where Union forces waited, firmly dug in.

JOSHUA LAWRENCE CHAMBERLAIN'S AFTER-ACTION REPORT FROM LITTLE ROUND TOP

A professor at Bowdoin College in Maine, Joshua Lawrence Chamberlain believed in the Union and believed as well that the war was about slavery, which he abhorred. At Little Round Top Chamberlain's 20th Maine held the very end of the entire Union line, and on July 2, 1863, the Confederates attempted to flank his position. Chamberlain was later awarded the new Medal of Honor for his actions on Little Round Top. What follows is Chamberlain's after-action report describing the engagement of July 2.

Field Near Emmitsburg, July 6, 1863

Sir:

In compliance with the request of the colonel commanding the brigade, I have the honor to submit a somewhat detailed report of the operations of the Twentieth Regiment Maine Volunteers in the battle of Gettysburg, on the 2d and 3d instant.... .

Rations were scarcely issued, and the men about preparing supper, when rumors that the enemy had been encountered that day near Gettysburg absorbed every other interest, and very soon orders came to march forthwith to Gettysburg.

My men moved out with a promptitude and spirit extraordinary, the cheers and welcome they received on the road adding to their enthusiasm. After an hour or two of sleep by the roadside just before daybreak, we reached the heights southeasterly of Gettysburg at about 7 a.m., July 2.... .

Somewhere near 4 p.m. a sharp cannonade, at some distance to our left and front, was the signal for a sudden and rapid movement of our whole division in the direction of this firing, which grew warmer as we approached. Passing an open field in the hollow ground in which some of our batteries were going into position, our brigade reached the skirt of a piece of woods, in the farther edge of which there was a heavy musketry fire, and when about to go forward into line we received from Colonel Vincent, commanding the brigade, orders to move to the left at the double-quick, when we took a farm road crossing Plum Run in order to gain a rugged mountain spur called Granite Spur, or Little Round Top.

The enemy's artillery got range of our column as we were climbing the spur, and the crashing of the shells among the rocks and the tree tops made us move lively along the crest. One or two shells burst in our ranks. Passing to the southern slope of Little Round Top, Colonel Vincent indicated to me the ground my regiment was to occupy, informing me that this was the extreme left of our general line, and that a desperate attack was expected in order to turn that position, concluding by telling me I was to "hold that ground at all hazards." This was the last word I heard from him... .

The line faced generally toward a more conspicuous eminence southwest of ours, which is known as Sugar Loaf, or Round Top. Between this and my position intervened a smooth and thinly wooded hollow. My line formed, I immediately detached Company B, Captain Morrill commanding, to extend from my left flank across this hollow as a line of skirmishers, with directions to act as occasion might dictate, to prevent a surprise on my exposed flank and rear.

The artillery fire on our position had meanwhile been constant and heavy, but my formation was scarcely complete when the artillery was replaced by a vigorous infantry assault upon the center of our brigade to my right, but it very soon involved the right of my regiment and gradually extended along my entire front. The action was quite sharp and at close quarters.

In the midst of this, an officer from my center informed me that some important movement of the enemy was going on in his front, beyond that of the line with which we were engaged. Mounting a large rock, I was able to see a considerable body of the enemy moving by the flank in rear of their line engaged, and passing from the direction of the foot of Great Round Top through the valley toward the front of my left. The close engagement not allowing any change of front, I immediately stretched my regiment to the left, by taking intervals by the left flank, and at the same time "refusing" my left wing, so that it was nearly at right angles with my right, thus occupying about twice the extent of our ordinary front, some of the companies being brought into single rank when the nature of the ground gave sufficient strength or shelter. My officers and men understood wishes so well that this movement was executed under fire, the right wing keeping up fire, without giving the enemy any occasion to seize or even to suspect their advantage. But we were not a moment too soon; the enemy's flanking column having gained their desired direction, burst upon my left, where they evidently had expected an unguarded flank, with great demonstration.

We opened a brisk fire at close range, which was so sudden and effective that they soon fell back among the rocks and low trees in the valley, only to burst forth again with a shout, and rapidly advanced, firing as they came. They pushed up to within a dozen yards of us before the terrible effectiveness of our fire compelled them to break and take shelter.

They renewed the assault on our whole front, and for an hour the fighting was severe. Squads of the enemy broke through our line in several places, and the fight was literally hand to hand. The edge of the fight rolled backward and forward like a wave. The dead and wounded were now in our front and then in our rear. Forced from our position, we desperately recovered it, and pushed the enemy down to the foot of the slope. The intervals of the struggle were seized to remove our wounded (and those of the enemy also), to gather ammunition from the cartridge-boxes of disabled friend or foe on the field, and even to secure better muskets than the Enfields, which we found did not stand service well. Rude shelters were thrown up of the loose rocks that covered the ground... .

It did not seem possible to withstand another shock like this now coming on. Our loss had been severe. One-half of my left wing had fallen, and a third of my regiment lay just behind us, dead or badly wounded. At this moment my anxiety was increased by a great roar of musketry in my rear, on the farther or northerly slope of Little Round Top, apparently on the flank of the regular brigade, which was in support of Hazlett's battery on the crest behind us. The bullets from this attack struck into my left rear, and I feared that the enemy might have nearly surrounded the Little Round Top, and only a desperate chance was left for us. My ammunition was soon exhausted. My men were firing their last shot and getting ready to "club" their muskets.

It was imperative to strike before we were struck by this overwhelming force in a hand-to-hand fight, which we could not probably have withstood or survived. At that crisis, I ordered the bayonet. The word was enough. It ran like fire along the line, from man to man, and rose into a shout, with which they sprang forward upon the enemy, now not 30 yards away. The effect was surprising; many of the enemy's first line threw down their arms and surrendered. An officer fired his pistol at my head with one hand, while he handed me his sword with the other. Holding fast by our right, and swinging forward our left, we made an extended "right wheel," before which the enemy's second line broke and fell back, fighting from tree to tree, many being captured, until we had swept the valley and cleared the front of nearly our entire brigade... .

Having thus cleared the valley and driven the enemy up the western slope of the Great Round Top, not wishing to press so far out as to hazard the ground I was to hold by leaving it exposed to a sudden rush of the enemy, I succeeded (although with some effort to stop my men, who declared they were "on the road to Richmond") in getting the regiment into good order and resuming our original position.

Four hundred prisoners, including two field and several line officers, were sent to the rear. These were mainly from the Fifteenth and Forty-seventh Alabama Regiments, with some of the Fourth and Fifth Texas. One hundred and fifty of the enemy were found killed and wounded in our front... .

We went into the fight with 386, all told—358 guns. Every pioneer and musician who could carry a musket went into the ranks. Even the sick and foot-sore, who could not keep up in the march, came up as soon as they could find their regiments, and took their places in line of battle, while it was battle, indeed. Some prisoners I had under guard, under sentence of court-martial, I was obliged to put into the fight, and they bore their part well, for which I shall recommend a commutation of their sentence.

The loss, so far as I can ascertain it, is 136—30 of whom were killed, and among the wounded are many mortally... .

On the 4th, we made a reconnaissance to the front, to ascertain the movements of the enemy, but finding that they had retired, at least beyond Willoughby's Run, we returned to Little Round Top, where we buried our dead in the place where we had laid them during the fight, marking each grave by a head-board made of ammunition boxes, with each dead soldier's name cut upon it. We also buried 50 of the enemy's dead in front of our position of July 2. We then looked after our wounded, whom I had taken the responsibility of putting into the houses of citizens in the vicinity of Little Round Top, and, on the morning of the 5th, took up our march on the Emmitsburg road.

I have the honor to be, your obedient servant,

Joshua L. Chamberlain,
Colonel, Commanding Twentieth Maine Volunteers

Source: *War of the Rebellion: A Compilation of Official Records of the Union and Confederate Armies.* Series 1, Volume 27, Part 1: Gettysburg Campaign (Washington, D.C.: Government Printing Office, 1886), 622–626.

What followed was perhaps the best-known moment in American military history. After a long bombardment that placed supporting Confederate artillery in danger of not being able to support the actual assault before the assault began because of low ammunition, over 13,000 Confederates marched out of the woods along Seminary Ridge in long lines, moving toward the Union line on Cemetery Ridge. Mostly undamaged by the preparatory bombardment, Union artillery began punching large holes in the Confederate lines with canister shot. As the Confederates crossed the Emmitsburg Road just in front of the Union line, Yankee musketry unleashed a deadly barrage of fire that mowed the Confederates down by the hundreds. Only a handful of Confederates actually reached the Union line, where they were promptly killed or captured.

Pickett's men fell back to Seminary Ridge, where a horrified Lee met them, telling them that the attack had been his idea, his decision, and therefore his fault. He waited for Meade to counterattack, but Meade did not—and arguably could not. Both armies were low on supplies and ammunition, and they were simply worn out. Almost half of the Confederates who made the charge against the Union center became casualties. Over the three days of fighting, both sides had roughly 51,000 men killed, wounded, or listed as missing. The Army of the Potomac suffered over 3,000 killed, 14,000 wounded, and 5,000 taken prisoner or missing. Lee's Army of Northern Virginia lost almost 4,300 killed, over 18,500 wounded, and had at least 5,400 missing or taken prisoner.

Lee retreated back through Maryland and across the Potomac into Virginia. Much to Lincoln's irritation, Meade did not pursue Lee's army, but Meade's army also had been bloodied and arguably could not effectively pursue the retreating Confederates. Still, heavy casualties like those suffered at Gettysburg could be absorbed by the Union, while the Confederacy simply did not have the reserve to replace such huge losses. Lee had failed, catastrophically.

◆ THE WESTERN THEATER (1861–1863)

For the Union's grand strategy, the western theater of operations (encompassing the region extending from west of the Appalachians to west of the Mississippi River) was just as important as the eastern theater. Control of the Mississippi River had been a major objective for the North, and extensive combat operations were directed toward that end. From a Union perspective, one of the more unique aspects of the campaigns to gain control of the Mississippi was joint operations involving both Army and Navy units.

In addition to controlling the Mississippi River, the Union had to retain control of as much of Kansas, Missouri, and Kentucky as possible. Existing posts, supplies, and telegraph communications made it doubly important to keep the Confederacy out of this region. Union troops kept an uneasy eye out for Confederate activity along the Ohio River, eastern Kansas, and Missouri. One of the earliest major engagements occurred in August 1861 at Wilson's Creek in Missouri, resulting in a nominal Confederate victory that gave the South control of southern Missouri. Soon after, Union commander Major General John C. Fremont was relieved as head of the Department of the Missouri and replaced by Henry Halleck. Under Halleck were Brigadier General Ulysses S. Grant and Major General Samuel Curtis, commanding corps of 20,000 and 30,000, respectively. The Department of the Ohio, under the command of Brigadier General Don Carlos Buell, had only 45,000 troops. The Confederate commander was Major General Albert Sydney Johnston, who had a force of over 40,000.

Much of 1861 and early 1862 were consumed with occupying strategic locations. Grant occupied Paducah and Smithland at the confluence of the Tennessee and Cumberland rivers, while other Union forces under Buell occupied Louisville. Johnston took Bowling Green and Columbus in Kentucky. To protect his interior lines of communication that ran along rivers and bisecting railroads, Johnston established Fort Henry on the Tennessee River and Fort Donelson on the Cumberland River. Because of organizational issues, Buell and Halleck had a difficult time coordinating efforts in the region, especially since practicality called for operations that would violate arbitrary borders established between the Departments of the Missouri and the Ohio. Buell made an effort to secure eastern Tennessee, while Halleck focused on taking the new Confederate forts on the Tennessee and Cumberland rivers.

Halleck sent Grant with 15,000 troops supported by Navy river-gunboats under Flag Officer Andrew H. Foote to take Fort Henry. Grant easily took Fort Henry on February 6, 1862, and then set his sights on nearby Fort Donelson. Johnston reinforced

Fort Donelson with 12,000 troops as Foote arrived to begin a naval bombardment of the heavily fortified Confederate position on February 14. Confederate gunners forced Foote to withdraw, but not before Grant was able to stage an assault on Fort Donelson. Inside the fort, a divided command argued about what to do next. Sensing that the fort was untenable, Brigadier General John B. Floyd and Major General Gideon J. Pillow sneaked away in the night with their forces, leaving Brigadier General Simon Bolivar Buckner to deal with Grant. Buckner surrendered unconditionally to Grant on February 15. Grant and Foote had now secured the Cumberland and Tennessee rivers, and with the fall of Nashville just days later to Buell's army, western Tennessee was under Union control.

Lincoln then unified these disparate departments into a single western command under Halleck. Halleck sent Grant and Buell down the Tennessee River to secure Corinth in northern Mississippi. The two generals and their armies planned to meet at Pittsburgh Landing in southern Tennessee near Shiloh Church. Meanwhile, Johnston tried to get his force up past Corinth to hit Grant before Buell joined him. On April 6, Johnston attacked a surprised Grant at Shiloh.

Johnston nearly pushed Grant's force back into the Tennessee River, but the Confederate commander was mortally wounded at the moment when victory seemed at hand. Grant rallied the next morning, reinforced by some of Buell's advance units. The Confederates, now under the command of Beauregard, fell back in disarray all the way to Corinth. The Battle of Shiloh foreshadowed the high cost of Civil War combat—out of 63,000 Union troops engaged, over 13,000 were casualties. The Confederates suffered 11,000 killed, wounded, and missing. In what seemed to become the theme of the early years of the war, Halleck did not pursue Beauregard. It was not until the end of April that Halleck occupied Corinth. Still, the Union now controlled the Mississippi River southward to Memphis where Foote and John Pope had captured Island No. 10. With the occupation of New Orleans by Major General Benjamin Butler and Navy Captain David G. Farragut, all that remained was to link the two port cities.

Union forces thwarted confederate counteroffensives in 1862. The Battle of Pea Ridge secured Missouri for the Union, and Union victories at Perryville and Stone's River ended Confederate attempts to invade Kentucky. A halfhearted attempt to regain Corinth also met with no success. In 1863, the key to Union control of the Mississippi was the river port of Vicksburg, Mississippi. Grant made four attempts from December 1862 to March 1863 to take Vicksburg, but the well-fortified bluffs and swampy approaches made assaulting the Gibraltar of the Mississippi River extremely difficult and costly.

Finally, in late March, Grant gathered his three corps, marching them past Vicksburg on the west side of the river on a swampy road they themselves cut. Appropriately, they were headed toward the town of Hard Times, Louisiana, to make a crossing well below Vicksburg so that they could then approach the fortified port from the south and east. Grant used intrepid Flag Officer David Porter and his small fleet of river-gunboats and transports to get his men across to the Mississippi side of the river. Porter had to pass Vicksburg twice, once going up river from New Orleans and again going down river to link with Grant at Hard Times. He lost only one boat to the intense Confederate fire.

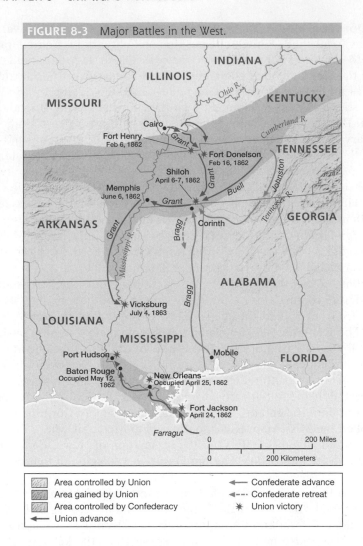

FIGURE 8-3 Major Battles in the West.

Grant then moved on the state capital at Jackson instead of striking directly at Vicksburg, which Lieutenant General John C. Pemberton and his force of 30,000 at Vicksburg fully expected. Grant sent the corps of Major Generals William Tecumseh Sherman and James B. McPherson on to Jackson, which they took on May 14. Sherman's corps held Jackson to prevent Joseph Johnston from relieving Vicksburg from the east. McPherson and Major General John McClernand's army turned back toward Vicksburg from where Pemberton had come out of the city to block Grant's advance. After engagements at Champion's Hill and Black River Ridge, Pemberton withdrew into his defenses around Vicksburg.

Grant tried a direct assault on Vicksburg from the east on May 18, and again on May 22, but then wisely decided to instead besiege the city. Grant's force slowly dug its way toward the Confederate works, while Pemberton's troops along with the remaining inhabitants of Vicksburg began to run out of food. By July 1, after six weeks of siege, the Confederates were in dire straits. Pemberton surrendered to Grant, who took control of Vicksburg on July 4, the day after the great battle at Gettysburg ended.

The Union now controlled the Mississippi River and had repulsed Lee's invasion of Maryland and Pennsylvania. The Confederates had lost a significant army at Vicksburg—it was a loss they could ill afford. Later that summer, the Army of the Cumberland under Union General William Rosecrans advanced toward Chattanooga, where Lieutenant General Braxton Bragg abandoned the town without a fight on September 9. With reinforcements from Longstreet, Bragg regrouped and tried to retake Chattanooga. On September 18 Rosecrans and Bragg clashed along Chickamauga Creek just south of Chattanooga. For two days the armies battered each other until a gap opened in the Union lines. Exploiting the opening, the Confederates would have defeated Rosecrans in detail were it not for the gallant efforts of Major General George H. Thomas, who fought a rear-guard action that protected the remaining Union forces as they withdrew to Chattanooga. The Battle of Chickamauga resulted in over 16,000 Union casualties and at least 18,000 Confederate dead, wounded, or missing.

Bragg positioned his victorious Confederates on a line running from Lookout Mountain to Missionary Ridge, hoping that Rosecrans would withdraw completely from Chattanooga. Meanwhile, Lincoln placed Grant in command of the new Division of the Cumberland. Grant immediately relieved Rosecrans, replacing him with Thomas, and went to Chattanooga to take personal command of the situation. As Grant arrived, Longstreet left with his two divisions to attack Knoxville. Beginning November 23, Grant attacked Bragg on Lookout Mountain and Missionary Ridge. On November 25, a charge led by Major General Philip H. Sheridan broke the Confederate line to force Bragg to withdraw from the field to retreat into Georgia.

◆ THE NAVAL WAR

The U.S. Navy grew to record levels during the Civil War and played an important role in blockading Southern ports and conducting river operations in conjunction with Union armies. The fledgling Confederate Navy had little success in the war. Always undermanned and with few ships, Confederate naval policy relied upon commerce raiding and blockade running.

Lincoln's Secretary of the Navy Gideon Wells rapidly built up Union naval capacities with Congress' record appropriations. With only 42 ships operating in 1860, by 1864 the Navy had over 650 vessels, including more than 70 ironclads. Wells included numerous steam-powered ships in his building program. The Confederate Navy, on the other hand, never matched its Northern counterpart. With only a few ships, a small number of which were ironclads, and the famous submarine *Hunley*, Southern naval abilities were negligible.

As the U.S. Navy attempted to make the announced blockade of the Confederacy real, the Confederacy turned to commerce raiders and blockade runners as a means to keep supplies coming in by sea. At ports like Wilmington, Mobile, and Charleston, the South hoped to maintain a lifeline to Europe. At first, Southern blockade runners were effective, using fast ships that could easily outrun the Union blockade squadrons.

By 1864, however, the blockade was having greater effect, severely distressing the Southern economy and war production capacity.

With so many Union naval vessels on blockade duty, fewer were available to protect Northern merchant ships on the high seas. The Confederate raider *Alabama* had great success, capturing more than 60 merchant ships before being sunk in 1864 by USS *Kearsarge* off Cherbourg in the English Channel. The commerce raider *Shenandoah* focused its efforts on the lucrative Yankee whaling fleet and was never captured. While Confederate commerce raiding had little negative impact upon Northern trade, the fear of raiders increased insurance rates to record high levels.

In addition to blockade duties and river operations such as that at Fort Donelson and Vicksburg, the U.S. Navy played a major role in securing Confederate ports for Union use. The Navy either captured or helped capture every major Southern port except for Galveston, which remained under Confederate control until the war's end. Union naval officers such as Samuel F. DuPont and David Porter helped establish the Navy's reputation as a versatile and effective fighting force.

The most famous Civil War naval engagement took place on March 9, 1862, as the ironclad gunboats USS *Monitor* and the Confederate *Virginia* battled off Hampton Roads, Virginia. The *Virginia* had been rebuilt from the hull of the burned-out steamship USS *Merrimack*, while the *Monitor* had been designed and built from the keel up at Long Island. Both were literally iron clad, with the *Virginia* boasting ten guns to the *Monitor*'s turreted two. The two odd-looking vessels battered each other for hours. Each vessel's shots simply glanced off the other's armored sheeting, and neither did much harm to the other. The battle between the *Monitor* and the *Virginia* ended in a tactical draw, but the *Virginia* no longer had free rein in Chesapeake Bay. In May 1862, the *Virginia* was scuttled to prevent its capture when Union forces occupied Norfolk. The *Monitor* also met an inglorious end, foundering while under tow off Cape Hatteras in December of the same year.

◆ GRANT TAKES COMMAND

As 1864 began, Lincoln believed that victory was in sight. He lacked, however, a commander who he believed could deliver victory. Lincoln had noticed Grant's successes in the West and in March 1864 gave him command of all Union armies. As General-in-Chief, Grant had two objectives—divide the Confederacy further by driving south and east from Chattanooga, taking Atlanta, which was probably the most important city in the South; and destroy Lee's Army of Northern Virginia. Progress toward winning the war was critical for Lincoln, who faced political criticism of his approach to the war and perhaps possible defeat in the 1864 presidential election.

Grant ordered Sherman to drive toward Atlanta. With 100,000 troops, Sherman began his march to Atlanta in early May. Joseph Johnston stood between Sherman and the Georgia city with over 50,000 Confederate troops. They clashed at several places, including New Hope Church and Kennesaw Mountain, with Johnston withdrawing steadily toward Atlanta. Finally, President Jefferson Davis could no longer tolerate Johnston's withdrawal and replaced him with Lieutenant General John Bell Hood of Texas in July. The Battle of Atlanta began July 22, lasting over six weeks until Hood finally had to abandon the city to Union forces on September 1.

FIGURE 8-4   Ulysses S. Grant, who became the 18th president of the United States, outside his tent. Grant served in the American army during the Mexican War, and was appointed general and commander of the Union armies during the Civil War. He was elected to two terms in office, beginning in 1868.

Source: Library of Congress Print and Reproductions Division [LC-USZ61-903]

From Atlanta, Sherman began his "March to the Sea" to take Savannah on December 21. Sherman brought total war to the people of Georgia as his forces destroyed any structure deemed integral to the Southern economy. Living off the Land, Sherman's force foraged with impunity, leaving little food or livestock for the inhabitants. The Confederacy had been split again. Hood's army tried taking Nashville but failed, retreating to the relative safety of Mississippi. From this point forward, Confederate action in the western theater was severely limited. Now Sherman could move northward through the Carolinas and into Virginia, where Grant planned to trap Lee between Sherman's army and the Army of the Potomac to end the war.

In May 1864, Grant ordered Meade, nominally in command of the Army of the Potomac since Grant traveled with it, to begin the move on Richmond. With 120,000 troops to Lee's 63,000 (probably much less, considering desertion and sickness), Meade struck Lee's army in the Wilderness. From May 5 through May 7, the two armies battled in the dense growth where they had fought the year before. Casualties again were horrendous—17,500 for the Army of the Potomac and 7,500 for the Army of Northern Virginia. Unlike previous Army of the Potomac commanders who either withdrew in defeat or refused to give chase, Grant forced Meade and the Army of the Potomac to press on in what became a relentless almost year-long pursuit of Lee and his Army of Northern Virginia.

From May 9 through May 19, Grant repeatedly hit Lee at Spotsylvania, where the Army of Northern Virginia had dug in to prevent Grant from directly assaulting Richmond. Wanting to get Lee off the defensive, Grant began maneuvering to the Confederate left toward Richmond on May 20, forcing Lee to counter him at every move. At Cold Harbor on June 3, an impatient Grant tried to punch through Lee's defenses. It was a bloodbath, with several thousand Union troops falling in a matter of minutes. Grant's push on Lee's army had cost him 55,000 casualties in less than a month. Lee had suffered 32,000 causalities that he could not afford, while Grant could absorb such heavy losses. By June 18, Grant accepted that he would have to begin a siege to starve Lee's army into submission. Petersburg became the central point of siege operations until the spring of 1865.

A brief Confederate foray into Maryland that threatened Washington convinced Grant that unity of command was paramount if he was to conclude the war successfully. He accordingly abolished the various departments in the eastern theater and created a single command. In February 1865, Davis appointed Lee commander of all Confederate armies, although by that point the Army of Northern Virginia was really the only remaining force of consequence. Meanwhile, Sherman made his way toward Richmond, cutting a path of devastation as he took Columbia, South Carolina, and Wilmington, North Carolina. In March, Grant decided to end the siege and force Lee out of his defenses around Richmond. Capturing Richmond undoubtedly would have been a great prize, but no matter who controlled the city, the Army of Northern Virginia still had to be destroyed.

Grant began his final assault on Lee's lines on April 2. The Confederates collapsed, forcing President Davis to flee Richmond. Lee abandoned both Petersburg and Richmond and tried to get to Lynchburg's railroad in order to link with Joseph Johnston's remaining forces. With Lee now in the open, Grant gave chase and by April 6 had enveloped the Army of Northern Virginia near Appomattox Courthouse. Lee's troops were ragged, exhausted, and hungry, and many were shoeless. The Confederate commander decided that further resistance was futile. He cared for his men too much to carry on the fight. Meeting on April 9 at the McLean House, Grant and Lee agreed to terms that were generous toward the Confederates. The men of the Army of Northern Virginia were paroled and allowed to keep their horses. Grant understood that the terms of surrender were the first steps toward unifying the broken nation. Johnston surrendered to Sheridan on April 26, and the last Confederate holdouts capitulated by late June.

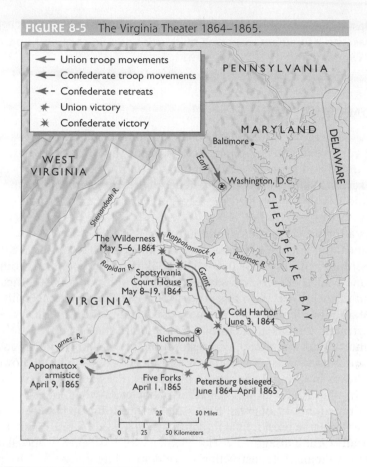

FIGURE 8-5   The Virginia Theater 1864–1865.

Preserving the Union and ending slavery had cost the Union over 350,000 dead, including more than 130,000 killed in battle. Over 280,000 Union troops had been wounded. Because of still-primitive battlefield medicine, many of the wounded were amputees. The Confederacy lost over 160,000 dead from battle and disease with at least 250,000 wounded. Perhaps as many as 50,000 Confederate and Union prisoners of war died in squalid prison camps, the most infamous of which was at Andersonville, Georgia. Battles of varying size and importance had been fought from as far north as Maine to as far west as New Mexico. The Civil War truly engulfed the American nation.

Other dimensions of the conflict are worthy of note. Civilian aid organizations such as the U.S. Sanitary Commission and the U.S. Christian Commission helped organize clean camps to stave off camp diseases and provide troops with moral support and guidance. Women played larger roles than they had in previous wars, including serving in military hospitals as nurses and organizing clubs and other organizations to provide troops with clothing, fresh food, and books. Some women even passed themselves off as men and served in armies on both sides. The American Civil War was also the first war to be extensively photographed. Portrait photographers followed the armies wherever they went, producing a treasure trove of faces—most of which remain nameless—that provide a personal connection with the conflict. Battlefield photography was also prominent, exposing millions of people then and now to the horrors of Civil War combat.

◆ RECONSTRUCTION

Jubilation at the war's end was brief. President Lincoln was assassinated just days after Lee surrendered at Appomattox, plunging the Northern states, at least, into deep mourning. The former Confederate states had to be militarily occupied to enforce whatever reconstruction policy the federal government decided upon to fully restore the Union. This duty placed the Army in yet another nontraditional role as nation builders.

As after previous wars, demobilization was quick. By 1866 most volunteers had been mustered out to leave the Army with only 57,000 troops. By 1876 it had an authorized strength of only 27,000. The Navy likewise demobilized, going from over 700 ships and 60,000 officers and sailors to just 48 ships and 8,000 officers and sailors by the end of the 1870s. With this downsized force the American military had to patrol the Mexican border, garrison frontier posts, defend the American coast, and carry out Reconstruction duties in the former Confederate states.

Lincoln had wanted a quick restoration, establishing civilian governments in the rebel states as soon as practicable. With Lincoln's assassination, however, the Radical Republicans in Congress dismissed this policy. President Andrew Johnson attempted to put in place an even more lenient policy than what Lincoln had proposed, but quickly ran afoul of Congress. Both Lincoln and Johnson believed that reconstruction in the South was a presidential rather than congressional prerogative. The Army, more specifically Grant, disagreed with the leniency of Johnson's proposals and thus courted Congress to make Reconstruction more demanding on the Southern states. Johnson was a weak president and as such he left the Radical Republicans in Congress an open door to take control of Reconstruction.

Before the war ended, Congress established the Bureau of Refugees, Freedmen, and Abandoned Lands, more commonly known as the Freedmen's Bureau, to handle the huge numbers of newly freed slaves, perhaps as many as four million, who had little to no means of subsistence. The War Department administered the Freedmen's Bureau until its termination in 1871. Under the leadership of General Oliver O. Howard, the Freedmen's Bureau provided food, medical assistance, and most notably education for freed slaves across the South. Resistance to the Freedmen's Bureau among many white Southerners grew fierce after the end of the war and in part contributed to the resurgence of Black Codes in the many Jim Crow laws adopted by several states following Reconstruction.

The Radical Republicans passed several measures to enforce a long and demanding process in the former rebel states. The Command of the Army Act of 1867 established a chain of command from the president as commander-in-chief, to the general-in-chief of the Army, and then to field commands. The general-in-chief could be removed only with the approval of the Senate. The Tenure of Office Act, also passed in 1867, declared that the Senate had to approve removal of cabinet officers. Both of these acts were directed at President Johnson, who wanted to fire several of Lincoln's appointees and take power away from Grant and Secretary of War Edwin M. Stanton. As it was, Grant and Stanton rather than President Johnson essentially controlled the Army through Congress. This was an interesting twist in the evolution of civil-military relations in the United States.

The Reconstruction Acts passed by the Radical Republicans created five military districts to govern the now-defunct Confederacy. A major general commanded each district, thus this period of Reconstruction became known as the "Rule of the Major Generals." These commanders administered martial law that superseded all civilian law in each of the Southern states. Congress also authorized each of the military governments to register all recently freed male slaves to vote. Acting outside his authority, Grant as general-in-chief ordered each of the five major generals to accept orders only from Congress. President Johnson angrily resisted such usurpation of executive authority, thus openly ignoring both the Command of the Army Act and the Tenure of Office Act. Johnson's response led to his impeachment in the House of Representatives and a trial in the Senate that ended only one vote short of convicting Johnson. If convicted, Johnson would have been removed from office.

Reconstruction under military rule in the South was harsh. Lawlessness and resistance to military rule and the Freedmen's Bureau in particular inspired violent reaction from white Southerners. Clandestine terrorist organizations, such as the Ku Klux Klan and the Knights of the White Camellia, terrorized free blacks as well as the whites who tried to help them, especially those working with the Freedmen's Bureau. With only about 17,000 troops to occupy the South and administer Reconstruction policies, the Army was ill equipped to carry out these nation-building duties. State militias composed in part of freed slaves were restored across the South as part of Reconstruction to help establish law and order, but because the new militias were tied to the Radical Republicans, many Southerners violently resisted the efforts of state militias to return federal control in the former Confederacy.

Reconstruction ended with a political bargain as a result of the election of 1876. Grant had been elected in 1868, serving two controversial terms to allow the Radical Republicans a free hand in Reconstruction. By 1876, however, both North and South had grown weary of Reconstruction and simply wanted the whole thing to end. In a contested election, Rutherford B. Hayes, a Civil War veteran, promised to end Reconstruction as soon as he took office. The promise worked, and Congress gave the election to Hayes. In 1877, occupation troops withdrew from the South and were reassigned to other posts, many on the western frontier where conflict with Native American tribes in the region had already begun. Without strong federal authority in the South, old habits returned, as blacks were subjected to Jim Crow laws and other state policies that made them second-class citizens. Reconstruction had been a failure, and although it was not solely at fault, the Army received a great deal of the public blame.

◆ CONCLUSION

Many historians consider the Civil War as the first modern war, foretelling the horrific industrialized conflicts of the late nineteenth and twentieth centuries. The impact of new technology and the harnessing of industrial production in the North certainly support this view. The tactics and strategies, however, harkened backward instead of into the future as both Union and Confederate military and political leaders drew upon the Napoleonic Wars and other conflicts of the early nineteenth century as their guide to conducting operations in the Civil War. The Civil War was a major turning point in the political and social history of the United States. It was also a turning point in American military history, for mass mobilization, civil-military relations, officership, professionalization, and centralized planning and control all evolved dramatically during and after this fratricidal war. Perhaps most important for future warfare, the Civil War formally introduced the United States to the concepts of total war and nation building; practices that became part of the strategic toolbox of the evolving American way of war.

Further Reading

Boritt, Gabor S., ed. *Why the Confederacy Lost.* New York: Oxford University Press, 1993.

Cozzens, Peter. *This Terrible Sound: The Battle of Chickamauga.* Urbana: University of Illinois Press, 1992.

Foner, Eric. *Reconstruction: America's Unfinished Revolution, 1863–1877.* New York: Harper and Row, 1988.

Foote, Shelby. *The Civil War.* 3 vols. New York: Random House, 1958–1974.

Fowler, William M. *Under Two Flags: The American Navy in the Civil War.* New York: Norton, 1990.

Gallagher, Gary W., ed. *The Third Day of Gettysburg and Beyond.* Chapel Hill: University of North Carolina Press, 1994.

Glatthaar, Joseph. *General Lee's Army: From Victory to Collapse.* New York: Free Press, 2009.

Goodheart, Adam. *1861: The Civil War Awakening.* New York: Knopf, 2011.

Griffith, Paddy. *Battle Tactics of the Civil War.* New Haven: Yale University Press, 1989.

Hagerman, Edward. *The American Civil War and the Origins of Modern Warfare.* Bloomington: Indiana University Press, 1988.

Luraghi, Raimondo. *The Southern Navy: The Confederate Navy and the American Civil War.* Annapolis: Naval Institute Press, 1995.

McMurray, Richard M. *Two Great Rebel Armies: An Essay in Confederate Military History.* Chapel Hill: University of North Carolina Press, 1989.

McPherson, James. *Battle Cry of Freedom: The Civil War Era.* New York: Oxford University Press, 1982.

McPherson, James. *What They Fought For, 1861–1865.* Baton Rouge: Louisiana State University Press, 1994.

Nolan, Alan T. *Lee Considered: General Robert E. Lee and Civil War History.* Chapel Hill: University of North Carolina Press, 1991.

Perret, Geoffrey. *Ulysses S. Grant: Soldier and President.* New York: Random House, 1997.

Reardon, Carol. *Pickett's Charge in History and Memory.* Chapel Hill: University of North Carolina Press, 1997.

Reid, Brian Holden. *America's Civil War: The Operational Battlefield, 1861–1863.* Amherst, New York: Prometheus Books, 2008.

Rhea, Gordon C. *The Battle of the Wilderness.* Baton Rouge: Louisiana State University Press, 1994.

Royster, Charles. *The Destructive War: William Tecumseh Sherman, Stonewall Jackson, and the Americans.* New York: Knopf, 1991.

Sears. Stephen W. *Gettysburg.* Boston: Houghton Mifflin, 2003.

Sears, Stephen W. *Landscape Turned Red: The Battle of Antietam.* Boston: Houghton Mifflin, 1993.

Stoker, Donald. *The Grand Design: Strategy and the U.S. Civil War.* New York: Oxford University Press, 2010.

Thomas, Emory M. *Robert E. Lee: A Biography.* New York: Norton, 1995.

Trudeau, Noah Andre. *Southern Storm: Sherman's March to the Sea.* New York: Harper Perennial, 2009.

Waugh, John C. *The Class of 1848: From West Point to Appomattox: Stonewall Jackson, George McClellan, and Their Brothers.* New York: Warner Books, 1994.

Weigley, Russell F. *A Great Civil War: A Military and Political History, 1861–1865.* Bloomington: Indiana University Press, 2000.

Wert, Jeffrey D. *General James Longstreet: Lee's Most Controversial Soldier.* New York: Simon & Schuster, 1993.

Woodworth, Steven E. *Jefferson Davis and His Generals: The Failure of Confederate Command in the West.* Lawrence: University Press of Kansas, 1990.

Woodworth, Steven E. *The Art of Command in the Civil War.* Lincoln: University of Nebraska Press, 1998.

mysearchlab Connections: Sources Online

READ AND REVIEW

Review this chapter by using the study aids and these related documents available on MySearchLab.

Study Plan

Chapter Test

Essay Test

Documents

Joseph E. Johnston, A Confederate General Assesses First Bull Run (1861)

In his memoir written after the Civil War, Confederate General Joseph E. Johnston describes the Battle of First Bull Run from his perspective.

Charles Harvey Brewster, Three Letters from the Front (1862)

A 27-year-old store clerk from Northampton, Massachusetts, Charles Harvey Brewster enlisted in the 10th Massachusetts Volunteers when the war began. His letters to his mother and sisters describe daily life in the Union Army.

John Dooley, Passages from His Journal (1863)
Confederate soldier John Dooley fought with Pickett at Gettysburg. His journal entries describe his experience in that pivotal battle.

James Henry Gooding, Letter to President Lincoln (1863)
An African American in the famous 54th Massachusetts Infantry Regiment, James Henry Gooding describes the inequities among black and white soldiers in the Union Army.

RESEARCH AND EXPLORE

Explore the following review questions using the research tools available on www.mysearchlab.com.

1. How did Union and Confederate strategic approaches to the war differ?
2. How do Grant and Lee compare as Civil War commanders?
3. How did the Civil War affect the delicate balance of civil-military relations?

Becoming a Modern Military

◆ INTRODUCTION

In 1877, Henry O. Flipper, of Thomasville, Georgia, became the first African American to receive a commission from the U.S. Military Academy at West Point. The Army assigned Flipper to the 10th Cavalry, one of two all-black, but mostly white-officered cavalry regiments—the mounted counterparts to the two all-black infantry regiments in service since 1869. Flipper joined an Army that was entering one of the most unusual periods in its history. Between the Civil War and the Great War, the Army returned to frontier duties, including long, brutal wars against Native Americans; put down domestic disorders; and fought the Spanish in a brief conflict that exposed serious problems within the Army that limited its ability to conduct operations outside the United States. Despite these challenges, the Army continued to professionalize.

Similarly, the Navy found the post-Civil War years challenging. While struggling to incorporate modern technology into its fleet, Navy intellectuals sought a doctrine to guide planning for defense of the United States and its newly acquired American possessions overseas. In 1890, Captain Alfred Thayer Mahan provided that guidance when he published *The Influence of Sea Power Upon History*. Mahan's work helped transform naval thought not only in the United States, but throughout the Western world and Japan. Congressional support for the Navy further assisted the service's advancement. As a result of the Navy's pivotal role in the Spanish-American War in 1898, Congress supported building a modern battleship fleet rivaling that of the Royal Navy.

Developments during the period between the Civil War and the Great War of 1914–1918 largely determined the character of the twentieth-century American military. The old and new often clashed in a period during which the military attended to familiar problems while trying to adjust to increased responsibilities, new technologies, and the United States' growing involvement in world affairs.

◆ INDIAN WARS

From the end of the Civil War to 1890, the U.S. Army undertook a long, arduous, and harsh war against Indians. After Reconstruction ended in 1877, Congress reduced the authorized strength of the Army from more than 57,000 to only 27,000 men. With this small force, the Army was responsible for manning not only frontier posts but also coastal fortifications. West of the Mississippi River, wagons and now new railroad routes were flooded with waves of migrants hoping to farm, mine, or otherwise cash in on the explosion of western development following the Civil War. White settlers increasingly encroached upon land already occupied by Indians.

Native American tribes on the Plains and in other areas resented the intrusion of whites onto lands the tribes understood as theirs in perpetuity by treaty with the U.S. government. Because of the pressure brought to bear on Native Americans by westward migration, tribes faced difficult and calamitous choices. They could either assimilate into white society or resist white encroachment upon their lands. Either option held the threat of extinction. While some Indians looked for peaceful ways to deal with the competition for land, others chose to fight. As settlers and Indians clashed, the Army once again found itself in the role of a frontier constabulary tasked with maintaining an uneasy peace. While the frontier Army spent a great deal of time and energy fighting what it deemed hostile Indians, it also had its hands full protecting peaceful tribes from harassment and encroachment by settlers.

The federal government's attempts to prevent conflict between Native Americans and whites typically favored the settlers. The Indian Bureau, part of the Department of the Interior, tried to force assimilation of Indian tribes. For example, the bureau encouraged railroads and white hunters to destroy the massive buffalo herds that were central to the Plains tribes' economy, and then tried to turn the Plains Indians into farmers. Farming was an occupation more compatible with white settlement. In addition, the War Department used force to keep tribes on reservations by policing tribal lands, and returning renegade bands to the reservations. Combined with frequent military campaigns against the tribes, these efforts ended Indian resistance by 1890.

Returning to the rudimentary and neglected pre-Civil War frontier post-and-road network, the Army reorganized its administrative structure in the West into two divisions: the Division of the Missouri, and the Division of the Pacific. A separate Department of the Gulf administered military affairs in Texas. Without an extensive rail network like that in the East, logistics and communication rivaled the Indians as the Army's principal problem. In addition, the extremes in climate from season to season, and the rough and varied terrain in the West made campaigning over great distances extremely difficult.

The Army invested a good portion of its small budget into new posts along major wagon trails and the new railroads, as well as into housing for the military detachments on reservations. Most frontier posts were not the large stockades often seen in Hollywood westerns, but tent encampments with only a few permanent structures. Most frontier posts were manned for only a few years before the units moved to new posts closer to whichever tribe was most troublesome. With limited manpower and other resources, this was the best the Army could do.

Most officers, such as Lieutenant Colonel George Armstrong Custer, and soldiers who served in the Indian Wars had little frontier experience because they entered the Army during the Civil War. A few, like General George Crook, had pre-Civil War frontier experience. Thus, the frontier force had to alter its understanding of campaigning and combat developed on Civil War battlefields to fit the altogether different conditions of the Indian Wars.

Despite these difficulties, the frontier Army carried out extensive military campaigns against the Comanche, Kiowa, Arapaho, Cheyenne, Apache, and the Sioux tribes, among others. Facing a cunning and resourceful—and often well-armed— native enemy, the Army found that as in the early Indian wars, winter campaigns that destroyed encampments and wiped out native supply stores were particularly effective in subduing recalcitrant Indians. The Army also used Indians in the fight against Indians. Friendly Indians, however, were employed largely as scouts rather than as fighters. When chasing renegade bands, the Army tried to converge multiple units and maneuver the Indians into a corner to force a decisive action.

Clashes began between white settlers and Native Americans before the Civil War ended. Migrant trails through Wyoming and Montana brought thousands of white settlers and gold miners into contact with the Sioux, Cheyenne, and Arapaho tribes.

Responding to Indian raids against mining camps and settlers along the Oregon and Bozeman trails, the Army ordered the Powder River campaign in 1865. When the campaign ended in disaster for the Army, the federal government began treaty negotiations at Fort Laramie with the tribes in the Powder River region. Some Indian leaders agreed to terms, but others refused. Chief Red Cloud, a Sioux, was notable among those who rebuffed government terms.

While at Fort Laramie, the Native American representatives learned that the Army was sending an infantry column under Colonel Henry B. Carrington to establish forts along the Bozeman Trail. Angry, Red Cloud and his followers left Fort Laramie in 1866 without signing a treaty with the U.S. government. Red Cloud's band retaliated against government actions by harassing the outposts that Carrington established, particularly Fort Phil Kearny.

In December 1866, one of Red Cloud's most talented warriors, Crazy Horse, led a band of Sioux in attacking a small wood-gathering party outside the fort in the hope of drawing a large column of troopers into an ambush. Eighty men under Captain William J. Fetterman were organized to relieve the beleaguered wood party. Just a few miles outside—and out of sight—of the post, the Indians fell upon Fetterman and his men, completely wiping them out. Acting as decoys, warriors led by Crazy Horse lured Fetterman and his men into a trap. Fetterman ordered his column to give chase as the decoys disappeared behind a ridge. As the troopers crested the ridge, they encountered hundreds of Indian warriors. The battle was over in a matter of minutes.

The Fetterman Massacre gave the Army an excuse to launch a punitive campaign against the Sioux and their Cheyenne allies; but as it developed, only minor engagements took place. Without the manpower or the political will to mount a serious offensive campaign against the Sioux and Cheyenne in Montana, the United States chose to abandon Fort Kearny and the other outposts in 1868.

Meanwhile, in the Southern Plains, commander of the Division of the Missouri Lieutenant General William Tecumseh Sherman complained that he would need an army of more than 100,000 to satisfy the demands for protection of every settlement, isolated rancher, and farmer along thousands of miles of frontier and desolate trails. Instead, he had to thinly spread his meager force in small units across a vast territory. Comanches, Kiowas, Cheyennes, and Arapahos raided settlements, ranches, and farms, and ambushed travelers along the trails. Mindful of white encroachment on their treaty lands and the memory of such tragedies as the Sand Creek Massacre in 1864, these bands had little interest in living on reservations.

Major General Philip H. Sheridan, one of Sherman's subordinates, ordered a bold campaign of three converging columns to attack Indian winter camps in the Red River region near the Texas Panhandle. On November 19, 1868, one of these three columns, the 7th Cavalry under the command of George Armstrong Custer, surprised Chief Black Kettle's Cheyenne encampment on the Washita River. Custer himself was surprised, however, when he discovered that several bands of Cheyenne, Kiowa, Comanche, and other tribes also had winter camps along the river. During a hard day's fighting Custer burned the village, slaughtered hundreds of Indian ponies, and killed Black Kettle and his wife. The 7th Cavalry then withdrew under cover of darkness. Although Custer had something of a narrow escape, evidence found at the camp convinced many white Americans that Sheridan's campaign was both necessary and effective.

Sheridan's campaign began a six-year-long struggle to bring the Plains tribes under control. Although living on reservations in Indian Territory, the Kiowas, for example, raided into northern Texas in 1871. By 1874, with Sherman now General of the Army and Sheridan in command of the Division of the Missouri, a full-fledged war broke out between the Army and the loosely organized Comanche, Kiowa, Arapaho, and Cheyenne tribes along the Red River. In the ensuing Red River War, Sheridan again ordered a multicolumn attack on the Indians' winter campgrounds along the Red River. Under the command of Colonel Nelson A. Miles, five columns converged on the area, trapping the remaining Indians in Palo Duro Canyon. As a result, the Army forced the Indians back to their reservations.

In the Northwest, the Army fought Indians across a wide range of territory, from Utah to Idaho, in Oregon, and as far south as California. The Modoc War of 1872–1873 began when the Modocs left their reservation in Oregon to return to their homeland near the Lost River in California. Four major battles involving hundreds of troops and Modocs gave neither side a clear advantage. Peace negotiations also were fruitless until the federal government's primary negotiators, General Edward Canby and Reverend Eleaser Thomas, were murdered while meeting with Modoc leaders. Fearing extreme reprisals, the Modocs gave up the fight and returned to the reservation. Four Modoc leaders were tried and executed for the murders.

In the Southwest, the Army faced what may have been its most challenging enemy in the most expansive and difficult of theaters. Across Arizona, New Mexico, western Texas, and even into Mexican territory, the Army spent more than twenty years trying to bring the fierce Apache under government control. Cochise, chief of the Chiricahua Apache, kept General Crook and the Army occupied in Arizona; but through relentless campaigning, using mule pack trains instead of wagons, establishing the equivalent of modern small rapid reaction forces, and making administrative improvements on reservation lands, Crook brought relative peace to Arizona by the time he was reassigned in 1875.

Crook's departure, however, ended the uneasy peace. Corruption among the agents representing the Bureau of Indian Affairs was common; Indian agents in Arizona took advantage of Crook's absence to line their pockets by selling the region's best land and prime beef to speculators, leaving the worst of both for the Indians. Divided authority made the situation worse. By leaving administrative authority with the Bureau of Indian Affairs in the Department of the Interior, and law enforcement authority with the War Department, the federal government had created a dual authority over Indian affairs that simply did not work.

By the early 1880s, the Apaches began leaving the reservations in Arizona. The War Department sent Crook to repair the damage done by corrupt administrators and return the renegade bands that had fled the reservations. Crook worked long and hard on both assignments, until the Apache leader Geronimo was the only holdout. Crook tracked Geronimo and his band into the Sierra Madre Mountains of northern Mexico and arranged their surrender; but the federal government reneged on the terms, leaving Crook embarrassed and appearing as untrustworthy to the remaining Apache holdouts. In protest, Crook asked to be relieved.

FIGURE 9-1 Conflicts in the West.

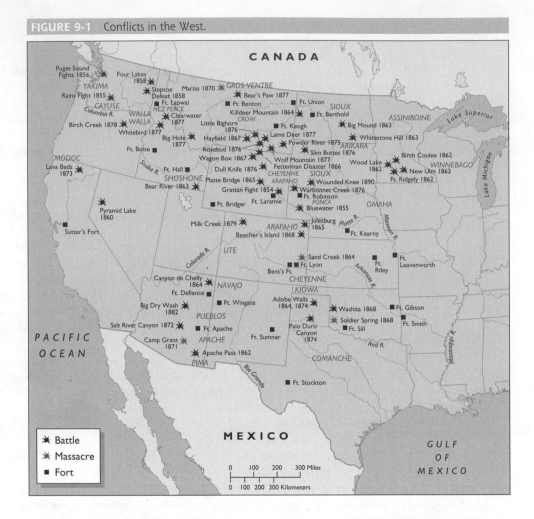

Nelson Miles replaced Crook and vowed to capture Geronimo, sending a small force under Captain Henry W. Lawton after Geronimo. Throughout the summer of 1886, Lawton's force chased the Apache band deep into Mexico, traveling over 2,000 miles. Lawton lost over two-thirds of his command to desertion or being unfit for duty because of sickness and exhaustion. The chase also took its toll on Geronimo's band, and in August he stopped running. Agreeing to terms that included his incarceration in a federal prison at Fort Pickens in Florida, Geronimo formally surrendered to General Miles in a ceremony complete with a regimental band. Geronimo rode in President Theodore Roosevelt's 1905 inaugural parade, and in 1909, at the age of eighty, he died at Fort Sill, Oklahoma.

By far the most famous of the Indian Wars was the great Sioux War of 1876. Conflict began with disputes over the Northern Pacific Railroad's right of way through Sioux lands in 1873 and the discovery of gold by Custer's expedition into the sacred Black Hills in 1874. Despite the Army's best effort, it could not prevent prospectors from pouring into the Black Hills region. White encroachment once again made previous treaties meaningless, and efforts to negotiate a new settlement with the Sioux failed. Following the example of the Sioux leader Sitting Bull, the Sioux and Cheyenne left their reservations. The federal government issued an ultimatum demanding that they return by January 1, 1876. It is doubtful that many of the bands ever heard of the ultimatum, because they were in winter encampments scattered across Dakota Territory, Wyoming, and Montana. In any event, few returned to the reservation.

General Sheridan ordered three columns—one under Brigadier General Alfred Terry from Fort Lincoln in Dakota Territory, one from Fort Ellis in Montana under the command of Colonel John Gibbon, and the last from Fort Fetterman in Wyoming under General Crook—to converge on the largest concentration of Sioux and Cheyenne in the Powder River area. Crook's force of 1,000 men and 300 Indian scouts clashed with 1,500 Sioux and Cheyenne warriors at the Battle of Rosebud Creek in June 1876. After an intense, six-hour-long engagement, Crook finally ordered a retreat to a supply base.

Unaware of Crook's retreat, Terry and Gibbon met at the confluence of the Yellowstone and Powder Rivers. Scouts found evidence that pointed to a large Indian encampment somewhere along what the Indians called the Greasy Grass and what the Army referred to as the Little Bighorn River. Aboard the steamer *Far West* on the Powder River, Terry, Gibbon, and other officers, including Custer, planned to find and attack the encampment. Terry and Gibbon were supposed to march up the Yellowstone and Little Bighorn to prevent the Indians from escaping to the north. Custer and the 7th Cavalry would approach from the south to complete a pincer-like movement to trap the Sioux and Cheyenne. The column that made contact first was to engage and drive the Indians into the other column.

At least 7,000 Sioux and Cheyenne, probably nearer 12,000 and including at least 3,000 warriors, were camped on the banks of the Little Bighorn. On June 15, 1876, Custer's 7th Cavalry made contact with what it assumed was an isolated, small village of Sioux. Custer did not realize, nor did he bother to ascertain, that this was the first camp of a longer string of camps along the river. Believing that he had the advantage of surprise, and fearing that if his force was discovered the Sioux would break into numerous small parties and flee, Custer decided to press the attack.

Custer ordered Captain Frederick W. Benteen and three companies to scout a few miles to the west of the 7th Cavalry's main column. A couple of hours later, Custer then ordered Major Marcus A. Reno and three more companies to cross the Little Bighorn and charge the south end of the village. Custer then moved five companies along a ridge, where they took cover in several ravines and gullies that formed folds in the landscape. Perhaps hoping to flank the Indians while they were tied down defending against Reno's attack at the bottom end of the village, Custer rushed to get into an attacking position before he could be discovered by Sioux and Cheyenne scouts. Custer sent messengers back to Benteen directing him to bring up the pack train.

Custer had divided his already outnumbered force of about 600 troopers. He did not know the terrain, nor, apparently, did he realize the size of the village along the river below him; he had apparently either ignored intelligence or simply failed to gather this vital information. It proved his undoing. Reno's force ran directly into a large force of warriors who attacked with skill and overwhelming force. Reno's detachment had no choice but to halt its charge, dig in, and fight for survival. Reno conducted at least three fighting retreats, losing half his men. Seeing Reno's force engaged, Custer, still four miles away, began to advance, but not before being spotted by the Indians below. From the South, Chief Gall led a large force of warriors toward Custer's command, while Crazy Horse bore down on Custer from the north. Outnumbered by at least 20 to 1, and outgunned, Custer and his 230 troopers perished in less than an hour.

When Reno and Benteen finally reunited, they heard the gunfire from over the ridge, but knowing neither their own position nor exactly where Custer was, they decided to remain where they were and attempt to hold out. Throughout the remainder of June 25, and well into June 26, the remaining 350 or so men of the 7th Cavalry fought for their lives. Finally, on June 27, Sitting Bull ordered the village to move south as scouts warned that Terry's and Gibbon's columns were advancing from the north. Custer's men, strewn about his own naked but otherwise unmolested body, were found mutilated. The Battle of the Little Bighorn was an unqualified disaster for the Army and its campaign to bring the Indians of the Northern Plains under control. Custer's death shocked the nation—he was a well-known and popular figure. In the end, Crazy Horse and Sitting Bull and their Sioux and Cheyenne warriors outmaneuvered and outfought Custer and his brave 7th Cavalry. It is a great irony that as the nation celebrated its centennial of independence with expositions highlighting the industrial progress and modern advancements of the still-young United States, the nation's military forces suffered such a tremendous defeat at the hands of people whom many at the time considered "savages."

Custer's defeat was also a disaster for the Indians because it spurred the federal government into stronger action. The War Department sent more than 2,500 men into the Powder River area to chase down the Little Bighorn Indians. By 1877, a lack of provisions began to tell on the Sioux and Cheyenne. Desperate, Sitting Bull escaped with his band of Sioux into Canada. Spotted Tail and other leaders gained power over the war factions and sued for peace. Crazy Horse brought his band into the Red Cloud agency and was later arrested by Crook, who feared that the great leader would foment a rebellion at the agency. In September 1877, Crazy Horse died in a fight between some Indians and their cavalry guards. By 1879, after several more skirmishes and intense negotiations, the Sioux and Cheyenne surrendered. Sitting Bull finally returned to the United States in July 1881.

The Nez Perce War of 1877 was one of the more remarkable of the Indian Wars. Evicted from the Wallowa Valley in Oregon, their homeland, guaranteed by treaty since the early 1800s, the Nez Perce resisted the federal government's order that they be removed to a reservation in Idaho. Under Chief Joseph, the Nez Perce led the Army on a winding chase of over 1,700 miles. In major engagements at places such as White Bird Canyon and Bear Paw Mountain, and in fights across recently established Yellowstone National Park (where Army units, stationed to administer the nation's first national park, gave chase), both sides suffered significant casualties.

Living off the land, the Indians maintained the initiative throughout the campaign; for its part, the Army had to rely on long, exposed logistical lines across incredibly challenging terrain. Technology, however, turned the tide toward the Army. Gatling guns and artillery finally overcame the Nez Perce. Unrelentingly pursued by the Army, the Nez Perce had difficulty gathering food. Low on provisions, with many of the band's

FIGURE 9-2 In Search of Crazy Horse. Despite efforts by Crazy Horse to make peace, General Miles decided to make war. Late in December, 1876, the soldiers set out to find the camp of Crazy Horse, and bring the warriors in, or take their scalps. Among the soldiers was the group above. Left to right: Luther S. "Yellowstone" Kelly, mounted; Lt. Oscar F. Long, Dr. Henry R. Tilton, Lt. J. W. Pope, General Nelson A. Miles, Lt. F. D. Baldwin, Lt. Charles E. Hargons, Lt. H. K. Bailey. This picture was taken on January 2, 1877.

Source: National Archives and Records Administration

women and children sick, Chief Joseph finally surrendered. After a battle at Bear Paw Mountain, just forty miles from the Canadian border and refuge with Sitting Bull, Joseph agreed to terms. In the end, Chief Joseph vowed to "fight no more, forever."

The final tragedy of the Indian Wars grew out of the Ghost Dance movement in 1890. Believing that returning to traditional ways would bring back the buffalo and their old life, a Sioux shaman named Wovoka began the Ghost Dance movement on Sioux reservations. At the Pine Ridge Reservation in particular, the Ghost Dance took a fanatical turn, as its adherents preached the total destruction of the white man. Even Sitting Bull became enthralled with the Ghost Dance and was arrested at the Standing Ridge Reservation. Negotiations broke down between the Army and Sioux leaders Short Bill and Kicking Bear. During the arrest of Sitting Bull, carefully conducted by reservation police, things went horribly wrong and Sitting Bull died at the hands of a fellow Indian.

The final act of the Ghost Dance occurred along Wounded Knee Creek in December 1890. Nelson Miles misunderstood Chief Big Foot's decision to come into the reservation to persuade the Ghost Dancers to put an end to what he considered useless mysticism. Miles thought that Big Foot was planning to join forces with the

Ghost Dance leaders and start a widespread rebellion. More than 500 troops, mostly from the 7th Cavalry, found Big Foot and his band of 300 encamped at Wounded Knee Creek. Colonel James W. Forsyth had orders to disarm the Indians and transport them to a safe area on the reservation. Forsyth surrounded the camp, trained four Hotchkiss guns on the camp, and ordered his men to move in and disarm the Indians. As the soldiers searched for and collected weapons, some Indians began performing the Ghost Dance and taunted the soldiers. One Indian boldly held his Winchester rifle above his head and challenged the soldiers to take it from him. When they did, a shot rang out. The heavily armed soldiers and lightly armed Indians opened fire on each other. The Hotchkiss guns opened up on women and children fleeing the melee in the camp. In less than an hour, Big Foot and 150 Indian men, women, and children lay dead. More than fifty troops had been killed or wounded, many by friendly fire. At least another 150 Indians died of exposure after escaping the camp.

The massacre at Wounded Knee, along with similar massacres at Sand Creek, Bear River, and other sites, has come to epitomize the Indian Wars. The Army and the Indians had been placed in a no-win situation by unfortunate timing and circumstances. For the Indians, the choice was to accept assimilation on reservations or to fight for their independence. Neither choice offered hope for a happy outcome. For the Army, a poorly coordinated and often conflicting policy of pacification and military action placed the Army in an unpopular situation. For many soldiers and officers, forcing a people to give up their native ways and live on squalid reservations held no honor, nor did fighting an enemy who most of the time was outgunned and outmanned. Despite the well over 1,000 engagements during the Indian Wars, frontier duty was boring and tedious in the extreme, leading to poor morale, glacial promotion rates, and high turnover among the thousands of immigrants, former slaves, and other underclass men who served in the Army during the latter half of the nineteenth century.

◆ THE NATIONAL GUARD

Labor unrest during the late nineteenth century aided the development of the modern National Guard. With industrialization under way in the northeastern United States and cities bulging with foreign immigrants and rural newcomers, labor disputes and other domestic disturbances often erupted in violence. Factory owners usually turned to private security forces, such as that provided by the Pinkerton Agency, to maintain order in and near their factories during strikes. Occasionally, violence from strikes became widespread. In such cases, local and state authorities relied first on local police and then on state National Guard units to restore order. After the Civil War, the National Guard Movement gained rapid popularity among Civil War veterans who had served in units raised by the states. In continuation of the militia tradition, National Guard units remained state-run organizations. The National Guard Association, founded in 1879, lobbied Congress for federal funding to support state Guard units. By 1892, every state had a National Guard in place, and several had established naval equivalents. The National Guard promoted itself as an at-the-ready militia that could respond to domestic crises that the regular Army could not because of Constitutional and Congressional restraints. By the end of the nineteenth century, the aggregate manpower of National Guard units across the United States surpassed the total enlistment for the regular Army.

Both the National Guard and the Army were called upon to restore order because of strike-related violence. The national railroad strike in 1877 forced President Rutherford B. Hayes to use soldiers and marines to protect private property, and to run rail lines that were shut down because employees had walked out. In 1894, President Grover Cleveland used troops commanded by Indian fighter Nelson Miles to restore order in Chicago during the violent Pullman Strike. Cleveland resorted to using regular Army soldiers because Illinois Governor John Peter Altgeld refused to call out Illinois National Guard units.

Frequently, issues of state versus federal authority led several of the industrial states to rely on their own Guard units rather than the regular Army to restore law and order during labor unrest. National Guard units mobilized to deal with more than 300 separate incidents from 1877 through the early 1900s. Putting down labor unrest was unpopular duty with both regulars and guardsmen. Most significantly, however, using the Guard in this manner had the unintended consequence of establishing the National Guard as part of the national defense apparatus. This development forced the War Department to rethink national mobilization plans as well as reconsider training for this new iteration of citizen soldier.

In 1903, Congress passed the Militia Act, officially establishing a National Guard system under the War Department, complete with guidelines for mobilization and training in accordance with standards set by the War Department. With federal funding, the Militia Act created a National Guard of Organized Militia and a Reserve Militia. National Guard units trained at least twice a month, and participated in maneuvers with regular Army units. Regular Army officers served periodically with Guard units. Shortcomings in Guard service on the Mexican border and less-than-efficient Guard mobilization in 1917 prompted Congress to continue reform measures. By the 1920s, the War Department had both the National Guard and the newly formed Reserves under more centralized control and authority, which helped address traditional problems between the regular Army establishment and the "militia."

◆ RENEWED PUSH TOWARD PROFESSIONALISM

With the industrialization in the United States and Western Europe, the advent of new weapons technology, and lessons learned from the Civil War, the American military engaged in another push toward professionalization similar to what it had experienced in the decades following the War of 1812. Progressives in both the Army and Navy struggled to bring their respective services up to date with modern military technology and military thought.

Studying military developments in England and Germany, Army Progressives argued that in the modern industrialized world, relying on a skeletal standing army filled out by militia would no longer suffice to defend American security and national interests. Moreover, they contended, the inefficiency caused by the traditional rivalry between staff and line officers had to be fixed with a staff system based on the German model, which promoted officers by merit rather than by seniority. For the Army, such reform was indeed radical.

In 1903, the Army adopted a general staff model that promoted better cooperation between the various bureaus and field commands. Secretary of War Elihu Root, serving under President Theodore Roosevelt, strongly supported such reforms in the interest of professionalization and national security. In addition, the Dodge Commission's (named for its chairman, Major General Grenville M. Dodge) criticism of the Army's organization and command structure during the Spanish-American War made reform seem imperative. Under Root's tenure as Secretary of War, Congress passed the General Staff Act of 1903, which replaced the General of the Army position with a chief of staff to oversee war planning and conduct of combat operations.

To have such a staff system led by professional officers, the Army had to invest in professional military education, a concept that it had haltingly accepted over the course of the nineteenth century. General of the Army William T. Sherman, one of the original Army Progressives, kick-started the movement. He established engineering and artillery schools, as well as schools for the Signal Corps and the Medical Corps. In 1881, he established The School of Application for Infantry and Cavalry, the forerunner of the Command and General Staff College at Fort Leavenworth, as the senior service school for the Army until the creation of the Army War College in 1903. Sherman intended that the Army War College would educate senior officers on the new staff structure, and reduce the influence of the traditionally strong bureaus.

Emory Upton provided the energy behind much of the Army reform movement. An 1856 graduate of West Point, Upton served as an officer in the Union Army during the Civil War, seeing action at Antietam, Gettysburg, and Cold Harbor, among other major battles. By the end of the war, he had risen to the rank of brevet major general. After the war, Upton served as commandant at West Point and at the Presidio and instructed at the Army Artillery School. Perhaps his most significant scholarly experience was a two-year-long trip across Europe and Asia to study military organization.

Upton had an immediate and direct effect upon the reform debate even after his death in 1881. He wrote a controversial and extensive study of American military policy after his trip abroad that offered for the first time a strong and well-supported argument against the American militia tradition. The militia was political, poorly led, and poorly trained, all of which contributed to an overall poor combat record. In the modern, industrialized world of the post-Civil War era, reliance upon such a force was foolhardy. Upton instead supported an expansible army concept similar to that promoted by John Calhoun after the War of 1812. Upton envisioned a professional, highly trained and educated army, with a general staff that could mobilize and train a ready reserve of militia under federal rather than state control. Most controversially, Upton called for the complete independence of the Army from meddlesome political control.

As much sense as most of Upton's plan made, and as popular as his ideas were among Progressive reformers in the Army, Congress remained tied to the pro-militia fear of a standing army and anti-professional officer corps traditions that had characterized American military policy since the colonial era. Moreover, Congress had no intention of eliminating civilian control of the Army. While "Uptonians" may have been vindicated in the General Service Act of 1903, the Militia Act of 1903 did not fulfill Upton's original vision of the organization and role of a national guard. Military policy in America had always been, and remains, highly politicized. Arguments supporting an all-volunteer officer corps, for example, like that of retired Major General

John A. Logan, even went so far as to recommend closing the academies at West Point and Annapolis to prevent the creation of an elite officer corps.

Technology and tactics also received some overdue attention in the Army; nonetheless, the Army remained technologically backward compared to its European counterparts. Only in 1892 did the Army replace the old black-powder, breech-loading 1872 and 1873 Model Springfields with the more modern .30 caliber, smokeless-cartridge-firing Krag-Jörgensen rifle. In 1903, the Army began replacing the Krag-Jörgensen with the new clip-loading, high-velocity Springfield. Machine guns designed by Hiram Maxim, Isaac Lewis, and John Browning were adopted by armies in Europe, but the U.S. Army did not procure a modern machine gun until 1917. The Colt .45 caliber pistol replaced the weak .38 caliber revolvers as the Army's sidearm of choice in 1911. The Army continued to lag behind European armies in artillery and in using smokeless powder. Likewise, the Army was slow to invest in motorized vehicles and airplanes, despite purchasing a few 1909 Wright Flyers, before entering the Great War in 1917.

◆ BUILDING A MODERN NAVY

Naval modernization also occurred in fits and starts. The great advances in naval technology so eagerly adopted by the U.S. Navy during the Civil War were unceremoniously pushed aside after the conflict. The "old salts" and "mossbacks" of the Navy, its sail-loving admirals, looked upon steam-powered ships with suspicion. They argued that these modern vessels wasted valuable space for fuel that sailing ships more efficiently used for guns, crew, and storage. Steam engines could break down, but a sail could easily be replaced. With so little enthusiasm for modern naval ships at the top of the Navy, it is little wonder that the Navy nearly foundered on its sail-based fleet in the 1870s.

Industrial growth and its corresponding increase in American trade abroad, however, demanded a larger, modern fleet of naval vessels to protect American shipping and trade interests beyond the waters of the United States. Moreover, as European navies, particularly the Royal Navy, eagerly adopted coal-fueled, steam-powered vessels complete with steel hulls and huge guns, the coast of the United States seemed at greater risk of foreign attack than ever before. In order to address these very real security concerns, the Navy had to modernize.

In 1882, a naval board recommended a bold program of modern shipbuilding. Unwilling to make such a large investment in expensive ships, Congress would authorize only the ABCD steel-hulled, steam-powered ships—the *Atlanta*, *Boston*, *Chicago*, and *Dolphin*—in 1883. Without a strong ethic of professionalism and little in the way of a reform movement, the Navy could not make much progress against such a strong budgetary headwind and traditionalist tide.

When Secretary of the Navy William E. Chandler established the Naval War college in 1885, the Navy began to reform more steadily. Two notable proponents of modern American naval thought, Rear Admiral Stephen B. Luce and Captain Alfred Thayer Mahan, found that the War College was the perfect environment to promote their bold views on naval reform.

Luce was instrumental in establishing the Naval War College. Inspired by what Sherman and Upton were doing in the Army reform movement, Luce had earlier helped establish the U.S. Naval Institute in 1873 as the center for professional naval education. Professionalism reigned at the Naval Institute, as officers studied naval strategy and tactics and published articles in the Institute's *Proceedings*, which remains one of the leading naval journals in the world. When the Naval War College opened in 1885, Luce was named its first president. For Luce, the principal and direct objective of the Naval War College was to create a doctrine for steam-powered naval warfare.

Luce found his greatest disciple in a naval officer who abhorred sea duty—Captain Mahan. Mahan was the son of Dennis Hart Mahan, and the namesake of Sylvanus Thayer, both of whom were influential military thinkers at West Point before the Civil War. When Luce asked Mahan to lecture at the Naval War College, it was an offer the intellectual Mahan could not refuse.

Mahan's lectures were collectively published in *The Influence of Sea Power upon History, 1660–1782* in 1890, and ultimately translated into several languages, including German and Japanese. Mahan suggested that the genuinely great maritime empires of the world achieved such status through supreme naval power. For the United States to break out of its continental shell and become a true world power, it had to marry trade and naval superiority. In other words, the United States had to invest in a modern battleship fleet and naval bases to support the new fleet in strategic locations around the globe.

To accomplish this, Mahan concluded, the United States had to enter the imperialist race—a competition that had been going full bore among European powers for much of the nineteenth century. Accordingly, he recommended annexing Hawaii, and building and controlling a Central American canal. Most importantly, however, he urged the creation of a battleship fleet. Disavowing commerce raiding, Mahan suggested that only a fleet of capital ships, acting in concert in a decisive naval battle against a rival's fleet, could guarantee American superiority on the high seas.

Little of what Mahan said was original. Several American naval officers and other naval thinkers had expressed similar opinions since the Civil War. To draw naval lessons from the British experience of the seventeenth and eighteenth centuries and apply them to the American situation in the late nineteenth century was a stretch, at best. His concept of a decisive battle at sea was drawn from Napoleonic land warfare ideas and from the rare instances when such an event occurred at sea, such as at Trafalgar in 1805.

Still, Mahan helped give big-navy thinking a popular voice. A young New Yorker named Theodore Roosevelt, who had given a guest lecture for Mahan based on his recent history of naval action in the War of 1812, was greatly influenced by Mahan's work. Under the guidance of Mahanian Secretaries of the Navy, such as William C. Whitney and Benjamin F. Tracy, Congress cautiously authorized a handful of modern ships. By the early 1900s, the U.S. Navy boasted a modern fleet that included the 6,000-ton cruiser *Maine*; the battleships *Texas*, *Oregon*, *Indiana*, and *Massachusetts*; and the still larger *Kentucky*, *Illinois*, *Alabama*, and *Wisconsin*, each with modern guns and solid armament. It is important to remember, however, that American naval building barely kept pace with that of Great Britain, Germany, and Japan over the course of the late 1890s through the 1920s.

Battleships, however, were not the only naval advancement. Navy recruiting began targeting young men from the interior of the nation, giving the Navy a more national flavor. With the Naval Personnel Act of 1899 the old seniority promotion system gave way to a merit-based system. The Navy invested personnel and funds into new cutting-edge fields, such as scientific management and hydro-electronics. One of the first agencies of its kind, the Office of Naval Intelligence was created in 1882.

By 1898, the U.S. Navy was on the verge of becoming a world-class sea power. Progressive officers or Young Turks who strongly supported and carried out naval reform, were having a revolutionary impact. When war broke out with Spain, the Navy was much better prepared and equipped for war than was the Army.

◆ WAR WITH SPAIN

The Spanish-American War of 1898 is considered a major turning point in American military and diplomatic history. In this brief but important conflict, the United States enforced the old Monroe Doctrine, became the unquestioned master of the Western Hemisphere, exhibited its new naval strength, exposed weaknesses in mobilization and preparedness in the Army, gained possessions in the Caribbean and the western Pacific, and solidified its role as a major player in the Far East. With victory in the Spanish-American War, the United States began its steady rise to world power status, and overall took a major step onto the world stage. The swiftness and suddenness of success led many in the United States to become overconfident of American military prowess. In the Philippines, this led to one of the more regrettable military experiences in American history.

President William McKinley asked Congress for a declaration of war against Spain in April 1898, which Congress readily granted. The war began over Cuba, a poverty-stricken remnant of the once-great Spanish empire in the Western Hemisphere. Americans had long coveted the island just off the southern Florida coast. Southern filibusters had tried to take it before the Civil War. As president, Ulysses S. Grant tried unsuccessfully to buy it from Spain. President Grover Cleveland had offered mediation to end the widespread rebellion that had enveloped the island since 1895. During President McKinley's first two years in office, Spanish policy to end the rebellion in Cuba took a brutal turn.

Public outcry to end the suffering of the Cuban people, promoted by "yellow journalism" and a vociferous Cuban community in the United States, came to a head in 1898. McKinley seemed reluctant to go to war over Cuba; he gave diplomacy every chance in order to avoid a war with Spain. Hoping to find a solution that would grant Cuba at least nominal independence from Spain, McKinley worked untiringly to bring an end to Cuba's troubles. Such a settlement, however, became increasingly unlikely, as the American public grew more outraged at each Spanish atrocity, whether alleged or genuine. Captain-General of Cuba Valeriano Weyler committed an act that particularly aroused American sympathies. In an effort to finally destroy the Cuban rebels, Weyler rounded up Cubans from the countryside and resettled them in concentration camps, where tens of thousands perished from disease, starvation, and exposure. Declaring people who remained outside the camps rebels, Weyler initiated what was essentially a "search and destroy" campaign against rebel bands.

In a show of "gunboat diplomacy," McKinley ordered the cruiser *Maine* to Havana in February 1898. Ostensibly there to evacuate American citizens if the need arose, the presence of the great American naval vessel increased the tension substantially. On February 15, the *Maine* exploded, sinking to the bottom of Havana harbor in a matter of minutes, taking 250 American sailors and marines with it. American newspapers quickly claimed that Spanish agents had planted a mine or a torpedo to destroy the ship. Investigations by the Navy and the Spanish government followed; both failed to find the cause of the explosion, but the Navy concluded that the explosion had been external. Later investigations confirmed that an internal explosion, probably caused by spontaneous combustion in the coal room, sank the *Maine*. That conclusion came decades too late, however, as the press had already convinced the American public that Spain was to blame.

When Spain failed to respond satisfactorily to his peace offers, McKinley reluctantly asked for a declaration of war. Congress passed the declaration, but added the Teller Amendment stipulating that the United States would not annex Cuba. McKinley immediately ordered the Navy to blockade Cuba and signed into law a mobilization act to get the Army ready for action. Initially, the Army wanted only 100,000 men to occupy Cuba after the Navy's Atlantic Squadron destroyed Spanish naval reinforcements in a Mahan-style decisive sea battle.

Congress, however, dashed the Army's hopes for speedy mobilization by allotting volunteer slots to National Guard units from the states. States protested that their Guard units could not by law serve overseas, so instead guardsmen were allowed to volunteer to form new units within the regular Army. The Army itself expanded from a scattered 27,000 troops to 59,000 men plus more than 200,000 volunteers (whom the Army had not requested in the first place). Politics played a hand in the mobilization, catching the Army completely unprepared for a force of that size. With inadequate equipment and supplies even for training that number of men, and with inadequate rail stock for transporting them to Tampa, Florida, for embarkation to Cuba, the Army experienced a logistical nightmare during the brief four-month war.

Americans reasonably assumed that Cuba would be the primary theater of operations. Few anticipated that the Pacific, particularly the Philippine Islands, would also become a major theater. Speculating that war with Spain was imminent, Assistant Secretary of the Navy Theodore Roosevelt, heavily influenced by Mahan's writings, had earlier ordered the commander of the American Asiatic Squadron, Commodore George Dewey, to refuel his fleet in Hong Kong for possible action in the Philippines. When Congress declared war, the Navy Department ordered Dewey to steam to Manila and destroy the Spanish fleet there. On May 1, Dewey struck the still-anchored Spanish fleet, literally destroying it in a matter of hours. Dewey lost only one man to heat exhaustion, while the Spanish lost 7 ships and 350 killed. Although the Spanish fleet was dilapidated, Dewey's victory in the Battle of Manila Bay was nonetheless a triumph of the new modern Navy.

Dewey controlled Manila Bay and occupied the Cavite Navy Yard, across the bay from Manila. Manila, however, remained in Spanish hands, forcing Dewey to wait until Army reinforcements arrived to take the Spanish-controlled city. Dewey became an overnight sensation in the United States—perhaps more popular than any other

FIGURE 9-3 The Spanish-American War.

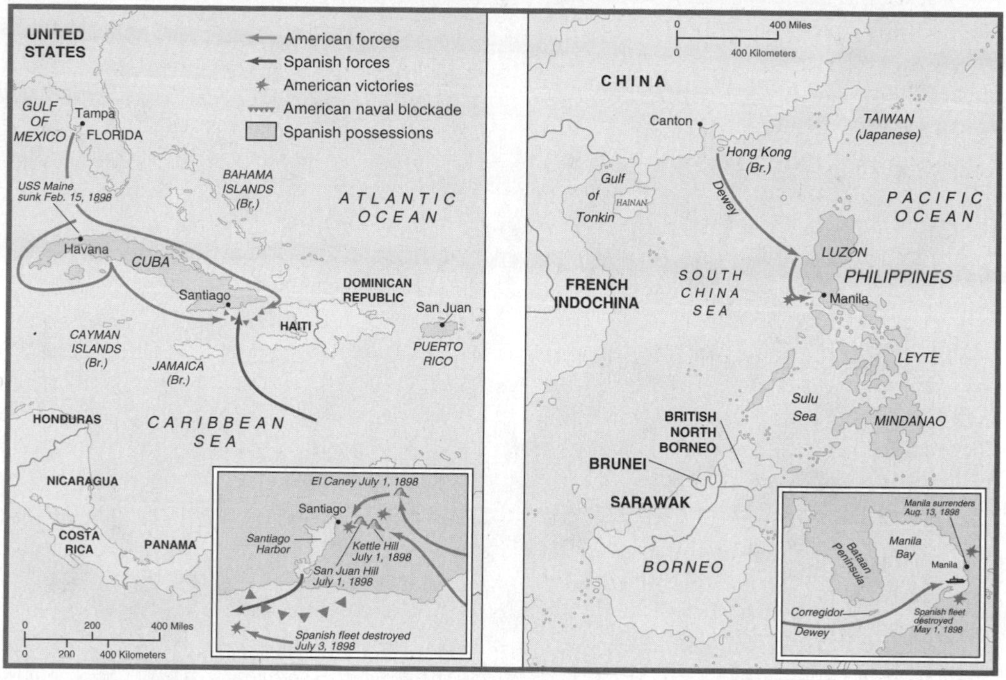
UNITED STATES
American forces
Spanish forces
American victories
American naval blockade
Spanish possessions
GULF OF MEXICO
Tampa
FLORIDA
USS Maine sunk Feb. 15, 1898
BAHAMA ISLANDS (Br.)
ATLANTIC OCEAN
Havana
CUBA
Santiago
DOMINICAN REPUBLIC
San Juan
HAITI
CAYMAN ISLANDS (Br.)
JAMAICA (Br.)
PUERTO RICO
HONDURAS
CARIBBEAN SEA
NICARAGUA
COSTA RICA
PANAMA
El Caney July 1, 1898
Santiago Harbor
Kettle Hill July 1, 1898
San Juan Hill July 1, 1898
Spanish fleet destroyed July 3, 1898
0 200 400 Miles
0 200 400 Kilometers
CHINA
Canton
Hong Kong (Br.)
TAIWAN (Japanese)
Gulf of Tonkin
HAINAN
Dewey
PACIFIC OCEAN
LUZON
FRENCH INDOCHINA
SOUTH CHINA SEA
PHILIPPINES
Manila
LEYTE
Sulu Sea
BRITISH NORTH BORNEO
MINDANAO
BRUNEI
SARAWAK
BORNEO
Manila surrenders Aug. 13, 1898
Manila Bay
Bataan Peninsula
Manila
Corregidor
Dewey
Spanish fleet destroyed May 1, 1898

military officer in American history to that point. He was even lauded as a possible candidate for the 1900 presidential election.

Meanwhile, on the Cuban front, action progressed more slowly. The Spanish Atlantic fleet had left the Cape Verde Islands for the Caribbean at the end of April. Not knowing the fleet's location or ultimate destination, Rear Admiral William Sampson guessed that Spanish Admiral Pascual Cevera would take his fleet to San Juan, Puerto Rico. Learning that Sampson was waiting for him off Puerto Rico, Cevera instead went to Santiago Bay on the southeastern coast of Cuba. Santiago Bay was heavily fortified with shore batteries, thus giving the Spanish fleet protection. This protection, however, came at the cost of freedom of movement. Once Sampson found Cevera, he bottled up the Spanish fleet in Santiago Bay while staying out of range of Santiago's shore batteries.

Sampson understood that he could not destroy Cevera's fleet unless the shore batteries were knocked out, a task that required the Army's help. Commanding General of the Army Nelson Miles originally wanted to assault Havana with a 70,000-man force in October, after the rainy season, when the roads would be dry and tropical fevers less virulent. Spanish men under arms on the island numbered more than 200,000, although many were Cuban conscripts. The American public and Secretary of War Russell M. Alger, along with Admiral Sampson, prodded Miles for more-immediate action. Mobilizing such a large force in June, however, was impossible. Under such pressure, Miles canceled his Havana plan and instead agreed to cooperate with Sampson to assault Santiago.

FIGURE 9-4 Battle of El Caney. Capron's battery firing on the stone fort at El Caney, Cuba, 1898.

Source: Library of Congress Print and Reproductions Division [LC-USZ62-85573]

Departing from Tampa, where the logistical problems reached unprecedented levels of confusion and incompetence (even Theodore Roosevelt's 1st U.S. Volunteer Cavalry had to leave most of its horses behind), the 17,000 troops of the Army's V Corps under the command of Major General William R. Shafter arrived east of Santiago during the second week of June. After a harrowing two-day disembarkation at Siboney and Daiquirí, eased only by the absence of Spanish resistance, Shafter began the march to Santiago. Although the Army undertook this operation to help the Navy defeat the Spanish fleet at Santiago, cooperation between the two services ended once the Army was ashore.

While Sampson wanted V Corps to use the coastal road to approach the shore fortifications around Santiago Bay, Shafter instead insisted upon an inland approach from the northeast of Santiago. From Siboney and Daiquirí, Shafter's force, comprising mostly regulars and the Rough Riders (Roosevelt's cavalry), made their way on foot over unfamiliar roads through rocky terrain and dense undergrowth. At Las Guàsimas, Major General Joseph Wheeler—a Confederate veteran of the Civil War brought out of retirement in a show of regional solidarity—and his advance force of 1,000 made first contact with the Spanish. After a brief fight, the 1,500 Spanish evacuated the small town. On July 1, as the Americans approached the San Juan Heights around Santiago, Shafter divided his force, sending Brigadier General Henry Lawton and more than 6,000 troops to prevent the Spanish garrison at nearby El Caney from harassing the American rear. The remainder of the American force advanced on Spanish positions on the Heights. The intent was to coordinate the attacks, with Lawton's attack on El Caney to take only two hours so that he could then support the assault on the Heights. Instead, the Battle of El Caney lasted nearly twelve hours.

Despite the absence of Lawton's 6,000 men, Shafter proceeded with his plan. With more than 8,000 men, including the all-black 9th and 10th Cavalry (the Buffalo Soldiers) and Roosevelt's Rough Riders, Brigadier General Jacob F. Kent's division attacked on the left of the Heights while Wheeler's dismounted cavalry assaulted the right. The attack began at dawn on July 1, going badly from the start. A Signal Corps balloon tethered among advance units alerted the 500 Spanish on the Heights to the American position, while the black powder from their old Springfields provided clear targets for Spanish riflemen. After a morning's fighting marked by heat and a short water supply, Wheeler's force made it to the top of Kettle Hill, forcing the Spanish defenders to retreat. Seeing Kent's assault on San Juan Hill foundering, Roosevelt and the Rough Riders charged, on foot, up San Juan Hill alongside the Buffalo Soldiers. The Spanish retreated to Santiago, but not without exacting 205 American killed and 1,180 wounded. Spanish casualties were 215 killed and 376 wounded.

THEODORE ROOSEVELT REPORTS FROM SANTIAGO DE CUBA

In the following report to Brigadier General Leonard Wood, Lieutenant Colonel Theodore Roosevelt describes the actions of the Rough Riders at the Battles of El Poso, Kettle Hill, San Juan Hill, and Santiago de Cuba. Roosevelt not only details combat action, but notes the severe logistical problems that plagued American forces in Cuba as well as the suffering of the sick and wounded due to lack of medical supplies and exposure. He also mentions the all-black 9th Infantry at San Juan Hill as well as the death of his friend, Captain William Owen ("Bucky") O'Neill. O'Neill had been a judge, sheriff, and mayor in Yavapai County, Arizona, and had settled into retirement when the call for volunteers went out for the 1st U.S. Volunteer Cavalry. On July 1, 1898, O'Neill had just boasted that no Spanish bullet could kill him when he was struck in the mouth moments later by a Spanish bullet. He died instantly.

Camp Hamilton, near Santiago de Cuba
July 20, 1898
Brig. General Leonard Wood
Commanding Second Brigade, Cavalry Division

Sir,

In obedience to your directions, I herewith report on the operations of my regiment from the first to the 17th instant, inclusive... .

On the morning of the first my regiment was formed at the head of the Second Brigade, by the El Poso sugar mill. When the batteries opened the Spaniards replied to us with shrapnel, which killed and wounded several of the men of my regiment. We then marched toward the right and my regiment crossed the ford before the balloon came down there and attracted the fire of the enemy, so that at that point we lost no one. My orders had been to march forward until I joined Gen. Lawton's left wing, but after going about three quarters of a mile I was halted and told to remain in reserve near the creek by a deep lane. The bullets dropped thick among us for the next hour while we lay there and many of my men were killed or wounded; among the former was Captain O'Neill, whose loss was a very heavy blow to the regiment, for he was a singularly gallant and efficient officer. Acting Lieutenant Haskell was also shot at this time. He showed the utmost courage and had been of great use during the fighting and marching. It seems to me some action should be taken about him.

You then sent me word to move forward in support of the regular cavalry, and I advanced the regiment in column of companies, each company deployed as skirmishers. We moved through several skirmish lines of the regiments ahead of us, as it seemed to me that our only chance was in rushing the entrenchments in front instead of firing at them from a distance. Accordingly we charged the blockhouse and entrenchments on the hill [Kettle Hill] to our right against heavy fire. It was taken in good style, the men of my regiment thus being the first to capture any fortified position and to break through the Spanish lines. . . . At the last wire fence up this hill I was obliged to abandon my force and after that went on foot. After capturing this hill we first of all directed a heavy fire upon the San Juan hill to our left, which was at the time being assailed by the regular infantry and cavalry, supported by Capt. Parker's Gatling guns. By the time San Juan was taken a large force had assembled on the hill we had previously captured, consisting not only of my own regiment but of the 9th and of portions of other cavalry regiments. . . . The Spaniards attempted a counter attack that afternoon but were easily driven back, and then and until dark we remained under a heavy fire from their rifles and great guns, lying flat on our faces on the gentle slope just behind the crest. Capt. Parker's Gatling battery was run up to the right of my regiment and did most excellent and gallant service.

In order to charge, the men had, of course, been obliged to throw away their packs, and we had nothing to sleep in and nothing to eat. We were lucky enough, however, to find in the last blockhouse captured its Spanish dinners still cooking, which we ate with relish. They consisted chiefly of rice and peas, with a big pot containing a stew of fresh meat, probably for the officers. We also distributed the captured Spanish blankets as far they would go among our men, and gathered a good deal of the Mauser ammunition for use in the Colt rapid fire guns which were being brought up. That night we dug entrenchments across our front. At three o'clock in the morning the Spaniards made another attack upon us, which was easily repelled, and at four they opened the day with a heavy rifle and shrapnel fire. All day long we lay under this, replying whenever we got the chance. In the evening, at about eight o'clock, the Spaniards fired three guns and then opened a very heavy rifle fire, their skirmishers coming well forward. I got all my men down into the trenches, as did the other commands near me, and we opened a heavy return fire. The Spanish advance was at once stopped and after an hour their fire died away. This night we completed most of our trenches and began to build bomb-proofs. The protection aforded [sic] to our men was good and next morning I had but one man wounded from the rifle and shell fire until twelve o'clock, when the truce came... .

The Spanish guerillas were very active, especially in our rear, where they seemed by preference to attack the wounded men who were being carried on litters, the doctors and medical attendants with Red Cross bandages on the arms, and the burial parties. I organized a detail of sharpshooters and sent them out after these guerillas, of whom they killed thirteen. Two of the men thus killed were shot several hours after the truce had been in operations, because in spite of this fact they kept firing upon our men as they went to draw water. They were stationed in trees and owing to the density of the foliage and to the use of smokeless powder rifles it was an exceedingly difficult matter to locate them.

For the next seven days, until the 10th, we lay in our lines while the truce continued. We had continually to work at additional bomb-proofs and at the trenches, and as we had no proper supply of food and utterly inadequate medical facilities the men suffered a great deal. The officers clubbed together to purchase beans, tomatoes, and sugar for the men, so that they might have some relief from the bacon and hardtack. With a great deal of difficulty we got them coffee. As for the sick and wounded they suffered so in the hospitals when sent to the rear from lack of food and attention that we found it less to keep them at the front and give them such care as our own doctors could... .

On the 11th we were moved 3/4 of a mile to the right, the truce again being on. Nothing happed here, except that we continued to watch and do our best to get the men, especially the sick, properly fed, and having no transportation and being unable to get supplied through the regular channels we used anything we could find—captured Spanish cavalry horses, abandoned mules, which had been shot, but which our men took and cured. By these means and by the exertions of the officers we were able from time to time to get supplies of beans, sugar, tomatoes, and even oatmeal, while from the Red Cross people we got one invaluable load of rice, cornmeal, &c. All of this was of the utmost consequence, not only for the sick but for the well, as the lack of proper food was telling terribly on the troops. It was utterly impossible to get them clothes and shoes, those they had were in many cases literally dropping to pieces.

On the 17th the city surrendered. On the 18th we shifted camp there, the best camp we have had, but the march hither under the noonday sun told very heavily on our men weakened by under-feeding and overwork, and next morning 123 cases were reported to the doctors, and I now have half of the six hundred men with which I landed four weeks ago fit for duty, and these are not fit to do anything like the work they could do then. As we had but one wagon, the change necessitated leaving much of the stuff behind, with a night of discomfort, with scanty shelter and with scanty food, for most of the officers and many of the men... . Yesterday, I sent in a detail of six officers and men to see if they could not purchase or make arrangements for a supply of proper food and proper clothing for the men, even if we have to pay for it out of our own pockets. Our suffering had been due primarily to lack of transportation and of proper food or sufficient clothing and of medical supplies... .

Very Respectfully,
Theodore Roosevelt

Source: National Archives.

With Santiago now vulnerable from the northeast, the Spanish began to run out of options. Not knowing that the American force was decimated by disease, exhaustion, and limited supplies, the Spanish withdrew to a strong defensive line around Santiago. Conditions in Santiago deteriorated as well, as food and ammunition both ran dangerously low. Cevera was ordered to take the fleet out of the bay and make a run for safety, but the U.S. fleet picked off the Spanish ships as they attempted to escape. In less than two hours, the American fleet of six ships ran two Spanish ships aground, sank two, and severely damaged three more, all at the cost of—like Dewey's victory—1 sailor to the loss of 300 Spanish killed. Despite the destruction of the Spanish fleet at the Battle of Santiago Bay, Shafter could not advance against the strong defenses surrounding the city. General Miles arrived with reinforcements, however, which convinced the Spanish to surrender on July 16 on the condition that they be transported back to Spain.

On July 21, Miles sailed with a force from Guantànamo to Ponce, Puerto Rico, planning to capture the island. Disease had so weakened V Corps that Miles could take only 3,000 troops, hardly an adequate force with which to challenge the 8,000 Spanish troops garrisoned at San Juan. When 10,000 reinforcements arrived in early

August, Miles divided his force into four columns and advanced toward San Juan. Meeting little resistance, Miles reached San Juan just as word arrived that an armistice had been agreed to on August 12.

In the Philippines, American forces faced a complicated political situation. By July, 15,000 American troops under Major General Wesley Merritt arrived near Manila, convincing the Spanish commander there that resistance was futile. Filipino rebel leader Emilio Aguinaldo had positioned his 10,000 insurgents around Manila, keeping the Spanish bottled up in the city by land while Dewey's fleet prevented escape by sea. Their actions were inspired in part by a vague promise from Dewey of Filipino independence after the Spanish were defeated.

Despite Aguinaldo's cooperation with Dewey, the McKinley administration decided against giving the Filipinos their independence and instead chose to keep the islands. Strategically, the United States had little choice if it wanted influence in Asia and the western Pacific. After Aguinaldo learned there would be no independence, he took action. In August, he established a revolutionary government, with him as president. Relations between Aguinaldo and the American military command began to break down, leaving doubt about how the Filipino insurgents would react when the Army commenced its attack on Manila.

As Merritt positioned his forces around Manila and talks began with Aguinaldo to convince him to keep his forces out of the ensuing fight, the Spanish wanted to surrender but were under strict orders from Madrid to at least make a show of resistance before capitulating. In order to preserve some modicum of Spanish honor, Merritt agreed to what amounted to a brief staged battle, after which the Spanish would lay down their arms and surrender Manila. Aguinaldo reluctantly agreed to remain on the sidelines during what was essentially a demonstration. On August 13, the day after the armistice, Merritt began the land Battle of Manila. For a short time it seemed that the confrontation might become a real battle because some of Aguinaldo's men joined in what they thought was an actual fight. Order was gradually restored, and after a few hours fighting, during which several American soldiers were killed because of the confusion caused by the Filipinos, the Spanish surrendered.

The Treaty of Paris in December 1898 formally ended the war between Spain and the United States. Cuba gained its independence, while Spain handed over Puerto Rico and Guam to the United States. As for the Philippines, the United States paid $20 million to Spain for the islands. In just the span of a few weeks, the United States had acquired an empire.

War with Spain cost 400 American combat deaths and more than 2,000 dead from disease. In Cuba, typhoid, yellow fever, and malaria so decimated American troops in Santiago that officers sent a joint letter to Shafter recommending that the Army be withdrawn from Cuba immediately. Unfortunately, the press published the letter before Shafter saw it, creating an embarrassment for the Army and popular outrage. Evacuation of American forces began sooner than originally planned. A sick camp established at Montauk Point on Long Island held the troops from Cuba under quarantine, but under appalling conditions. For the Army Medical Corps, tropical disease became a topic of study that ultimately resulted in effective preventive measures for yellow fever and malaria.

◆ INSURRECTIONS AND REBELLIONS

[After the Spanish-American War, the United States reluctantly accepted a role on the world stage, a role that obligated the military to undertake more duties outside the territorial United States. Imperialism brought with it a more demanding need to protect American citizens and property abroad, greater roles in maintaining order and promoting nation building in the new American possessions, and occasional situations where it was necessary to cooperate at unprecedented levels with other foreign powers in times of crisis.]

[Following the end of the war with Spain, the Philippine Insurrection placed the U.S. Army in an extremely delicate situation. Aguinaldo's rebel forces remained intact and vowed to resist American occupation. To maintain order, the Army had to either negotiate a settlement with Aguinaldo or force an end to rebel resistance. Remote islands peopled by other groups who did not see eye to eye with Aguinaldo further complicated the political and military situation in the Philippines. During the two years of open insurrection, the Army had to maintain in the Philippines a force that was many times the size of the one that had defeated the Spanish at Manila. Maintaining a logistical line not only from the United States to the Pacific, but also among the major islands in the Philippines taxed American resourcefulness. Moreover, the brutal nature of the insurrection, combined with multiple atrocities committed by both sides, further complicated the challenge.]

Fighting began after Aguinaldo established the new Republic of the Philippines. In February 1899, insurgent and American patrols clashed; then violence broke out in Manila. Major General Elwell S. Otis, Merritt's replacement, had only 12,000 troops to defend Manila against 40,000 rebel insurgents under Aguinaldo. As Aguinaldo's forces withdrew from around Manila, the conflict quickly deteriorated into a guerrilla war fought in the thick jungles of Luzon and surrounding islands where the insurgents had a clear advantage. To make matters worse for the Americans, the Moro peoples of the southern Philippines also violently resisted American rule. The Army was ill-prepared and ill-suited for countering such an insurgency.

[New American regular and volunteer regiments arrived as old ones were sent back to the United States for postwar demobilization. Within a short time, Otis had an entirely new and mostly inexperienced army under his command. Otis focused on gaining control over major population centers and logistical routes, and then establishing stable government in those areas. The Army built schools, hospitals, and other public works projects. The Army was fighting and nation building at the same time. During 1899, Otis made great progress against Aguinaldo, using columns under General Lawton to control the Santa Cruz region and under Major General Arthur MacArthur to suppress insurgent activity in the San Fernando region.]

After these areas were secure, Otis went after Aguinaldo who had holed up in the northern mountains of Luzon. A three-column approach ultimately defeated the bulk of the rebel forces, but Aguinaldo escaped. Boldly posing as a captured American soldier, Brigadier General Frederick Funston finally captured Aguinaldo in March 1901. With the rebel leader's capture, organized resistance in Luzon largely ended. Nonetheless, MacArthur, who replaced Otis in 1900, had to continue operations in order to put down isolated pockets of resistance. In these small, hard-fought engagements, the Army incurred more casualties than it had during the open insurrection.

In Samar, the Moro peoples continued their resistance. If the war in Luzon had been bitterly fought, the war against the Moro was even more so. Employing tactics reminiscent of the colonial wars, including the destruction of entire villages and ambushes, the United States finally brought Moro resistance to an end. It was in this campaign that Captain John J. ("Black Jack") Pershing, who as a white officer fought alongside the all-black 10th Cavalry at San Juan Hill, gained a reputation not only for his fighting skill, but his ideas on pacification. Even the Army grew uncertain about the morality of its campaign in Samar, court-martialing Brigadier General Jacob Smith for the excessively brutal tactics used to overcome the Moro.

More than 125,000 American troops were involved in the Philippine Insurrection, and 4,500 of them died. Estimates for Filipino losses from combat, starvation, and disease range from 200,000 to as high as 600,000. The war became increasingly unpopular in the United States, creating a strong and effective antiwar and anti-imperialist movement. Few anticipated the intensity and cost that keeping the Philippines would entail.

Meanwhile, the Boxer Rebellion erupted in China in 1900, threatening the lives and property of foreigners across China and in particular the capital city of Peking. The "Boxers," as they were called by Westerners, resented foreign influence in China, especially that of Christian missionaries. With the indirect approval of China's Dowager Empress, the Boxers attacked mission outposts in the countryside, killing missionaries and several of the Chinese converts. They then besieged the Diplomatic Quarter of the Imperial City, forcing the legation staffs and their military guards to band together to defend themselves from certain slaughter if the Boxers broke through their defenses. Small units of American, British, and Japanese troops tried to reach the city, but all failed.

As the besieged legations held on, an international expedition was formed comprising 19,000 British, French, Japanese, Russian, German, Austrian, Italian, and American troops—including the 9th Infantry, 14th Infantry, and 6th Cavalry from the Philippines—to relieve the legations in Peking. Disembarking at Tientsin in August, the relief force fought its way over the seventy miles to Peking. There, in a series of poorly coordinated and costly attacks, it finally reached the Diplomatic Quarter on August 15. The Boxer Rebellion broke apart into scattered pockets of resistance that were eventually put down by foreign troops. Lacking a security contingent, American forces withdrew from Peking as quickly as possible. Two hundred American troops were killed or wounded in the operation in which, for the first time since the American War for Independence, the United States had militarily allied with foreign forces.

◆ **CONCLUSION**

In 1907, a modern American battleship fleet left for a world tour. Passing in review off Long Island before a very proud President Theodore Roosevelt, the fleet, painted a brilliant white with pennants fluttering in the breeze, must have been a spectacular sight. The Great White Fleet, as it was called, was a symbol of American power in the modern industrialized world and a clear warning that the United States was going to be a significant player in world affairs. The U.S. Army and Navy had struggled through a tumultuous transformation since the Civil War. Both had adopted new technology and new ideas, both had survived serious tests of their abilities, and both emerged modernized. Moreover, a new spirit of professionalism now pervaded both services. The foundation for American military power in the twentieth century was firmly laid.

Further Reading

Ambrose, Stephen E. *Upton and the Army*. Baton Rouge: Louisiana State University Press, 1964.

Bradford, James C., ed. *Crucible of Empire: The Spanish-American War and Its Aftermath*. Annapolis: Naval Institute Press, 1993.

Coffman, Edward M. *The Old Army: A Portrait of the American Army in Peacetime, 1784–1898*. New York: Oxford University Press, 1988.

Connell, Evan S. *Son of the Morning Star*. New York: New Point Press, 1984.

Cooper, Jerry M. *The Rise of the National Guard: The Evolution of the American Militia, 1865–1920*. Lincoln, Nebraska: Bison Books, 2002.

Dobak, William, and Thomas D. Phillips. *The Black Regular, 1866–1898*. Norman, Oklahoma: University of Oklahoma Press, 2001.

Gates, John M. *Schoolbooks and Krags: The United States Army in the Philippines, 1898–1902*. Westport, Connecticut: Greenwood Press, 1973.

Hampton, H. Duane. *How the U.S. Cavalry Saved Our National Parks*. Bloomington: Indiana University Press, 1971.

Kristin L. Hoganson. *Fighting for American Manhood: How Gender Politics Provoked the Spanish-American and Philippine-American Wars*. Yale University Press, 1998.

Leeke, Jim. *Manila and Santiago: The New Steel Navy in the Spanish-American War*. Naval Institute Press, 2009.

Linn, Brian. *The Philippine War, 1899–1902*. Lawrence: University of Kansas Press, 2000.

Marshall, S. L. A. *Crimsoned Prairie: The Wars between the United States and the Plains Indians*. New York: Scribner's, 1972.

Musicant, Ivan. *Empire by Default: The Spanish-American War and the Dawn of the American Century*. New York: Henry Holt, 1998.

Nenninger, Timothy K. *The Leavenworth Schools and the Old Army: Education, Professionalism, and the Officer Corps, 1881–1918*. Westport, Connecticut: Greenwood Press, 1978.

O'Connell, Robert L. *Sacred Vessels: The Cult of the Battleship and the Rise of the U.S. Navy*. Boulder, Colorado: Westview Press, 1991.

Preston, Diana. *The Boxer Rebellion: The Dramatic Story of China's War on Foreigners that Shook the World in 1900*. New York: Walker and Company, 2000.

Reardon, Carol. *Soldiers and Scholars: The U.S. Army and the Uses of Military History*. Lawrence: University Press of Kansas, 1990.

Reckner, James R. *Teddy Roosevelt's Great White Fleet*. Annapolis: Bluejacket Books, 1988.

Seager, Robert. *Alfred Thayer Mahan*. Annapolis: Naval Institute Press, 1977.

Trask, David F. *The War with Spain in 1898*. Lincoln: University of Nebraska Press, 1996.

Utley, Robert M. *Frontier Regulars: The United States Army and the Indian, 1866–1891*. New York: Macmillan, 1973.

mysearch**lab** Connections: Sources Online • • • • • • • • • • • •

READ AND REVIEW

Review this chapter by using the study aids and these related documents available on MySearchLab.

Study Plan

Chapter Test

Essay Test

Documents

Little Bighorn Recollection by Cheyenne Warrior Two Moons (1876)

This document tells the story of the Little Bighorn from the "other" side.

Commodore Schley's Report on Naval Battle of Santiago (1898)

Commodore Schley's report details the American navy's rout of the Spanish fleet off Cuba's Santiago Bay.

USS *Olympia*'s Report of Battle of Manila Bay (1898)

This document gives Admiral Dewey's report on the destruction of the Spanish fleet at Manila Bay in the Philippines.

RESEARCH AND EXPLORE

Explore the following review questions using the research tools available on www.mysearchlab.com.

1. What challenges confronted the Army following the Civil War?
2. What is the significance of the Spanish-American War?
3. How did Alfred Thayer Mahan influence the Navy's development?
4. Why is Emory Upton important?

"Over There"

◆ INTRODUCTION

The Great War posed enormous challenges for all the armies that fought in it, and for the governments and societies that raised and fielded them. American involvement in the war, while belated, brought the United States firmly back into involvement with the affairs of Europe—a process that has not yet ended almost a century later. The American military, and especially the U.S. Army, was afforded a brutal introduction to the realities of modern industrial warfare while the administration of President Woodrow Wilson assumed a leading role in the attempt to forge a postwar settlement, although the opportunity was very largely squandered.

◆ PROVING GROUND: THE PUNITIVE EXPEDITION

In 1914, Americans were concerned as much with the state of relations with Mexico as with those between the European great powers, and war with the former seemed more likely. The Mexican revolution of 1911 degenerated first into reaction and then into civil war; the Wilson administration sought to influence the course and nature of events in Mexico not least because it feared intervention by other powers—Germany or even Japan—taking advantage of Mexico's troubles. The earlier, relatively small-scale mobilization of forces in 1911 and 1913 had resulted in generally fruitless attempts to confine the conflict to the Mexican side of the border. In April 1914 Wilson intervened more directly, sending a force of Marines to the coastal city of Vera Cruz, which was bombarded and occupied till the end of the year. Mexican civilian casualties were extensive, while the U.S. force lost 19 killed and 47 wounded. The death toll in the city served merely to inflame anti-American feeling in the country, although the American presence enabled the Wilson administration to arm and equip the constitutionalist faction within the country that then went on to defeat a number of its rivals.

The 1916 Punitive Expedition was prompted by an incursion into New Mexico by the forces of Francisco ("Pancho") Villa that included a raid on the town of Columbus in March, resulting in fifteen deaths among its citizenry and local soldiers. Villa was a frustrated presidential rival, and his force numbered little more than 500. The response was disproportionate: a "punitive" force of some 12,000 equipped with reconnaissance aircraft and motorized transport, commanded by Brigadier General John J. ("Black Jack") Pershing, that penetrated over 400 miles into Mexico. Mexican nationalism was galvanized by the American intervention, and although there were few real engagements (the most notable being at El Carrizal, which was a technical victory for the Mexicans), the expedition found itself fighting both Villa's troops, which grew rapidly in number, and units of the Mexican federal army dispatched by the interim president, Venustiano Carranza. The American incursion, and the local response to it, also generated a flow of refugees—Americans resident in Mexico—back across the border into the southern United States.

To enable the use of regular units and maintain border protection against bandits and armed bands, the government called up and federalized the National Guard in Texas, Arizona, and New Mexico in May and, when this proved inadequate to the task, called up guardsmen nationally in mid-June. The mechanism used to accomplish this, the newly legislated National Defense Act of 1916, had greatly increased federal powers over the National Guard but had done little to improve its efficiency or effectiveness. Many National Guard soldiers declined call-up, because they were either unwilling to accept duty under federal control in circumstances short of war or disliked the tedious and unromantic tasks they were allocated on the American side of the border. Of around 95,000 men on the National Guard's muster rolls, half failed to report and another 24,000 failed the medical exam.

Recruiting to make good the shortfall was disappointing, a reflection, in part, of disenchantment with the tasks allocated to the men. The shortcomings in the mobilization of the National Guard, which to some extent reflected the old culture of the National Guard that had been exposed during the mobilization for the Spanish-American War in 1898, confirmed for many regular officers that the National Guard was ill-suited to the role of a reserve able to be utilized effectively in a national emergency.

In January 1917, Washington ordered the withdrawal of Pershing's force. Following the promulgation of a new constitution and the election of Carranza as president in March, the U.S. government extended official recognition to Mexico; the tensions that had characterized American-Mexican relations began to recede. Increasingly strained relations with Germany had by now taken their place.

◆ "OVER THERE"

Although the Punitive Expedition had made early use of emergent military technologies such as aircraft, and had demonstrated some benefits of the introduction of motorization, the U.S. Army in 1917 was not a modern army. The benefits of recent field service in Mexico were undoubted, but should not be overstated. Pershing confirmed the high estimation in which he was held through the skillful discharge of a difficult command hedged by complex political influences and pressures, but these were a mild foretaste of the situations he would encounter in Europe.

Isolationist sentiment and a sense that the squabbles of the Old World had nothing to do with the New World were quickly replaced in significant quarters by a belief in the desirability of an Allied victory. Economic issues were important: Supplying the industrial war needs of the Allies was enormously profitable for the United States, and the transfer of capital and assets that took place as a result marked the beginning of Western Europe's financial net indebtedness to the United States that was to accelerate even more markedly in the next world war. The effect of German submarine warfare in the Atlantic on American opinion is well known—especially the furor over the sinking of the passenger liner *Lusitania* in May 1915—but the successful and shrewd British-organized propaganda that depicted German atrocities during the advance into Belgium in the war's opening weeks also turned public opinion in many quarters against Germany.

German naval activity and the threat it posed to freedom of navigation on the high seas persuaded the Wilson administration to scrap existing plans for modernizing, but not enlarging, the U.S. Navy in favor of a new fleet expansion program that would see the creation of a navy to rival the Royal Navy—a navy "second to none," in the slogan of the day. Enabled by the Naval Act of 1916, the program emphasized capital ships and surface warfare fashioned to meet a Japanese threat in the Pacific and to defend the waters of the Western Hemisphere; the war at sea that was actually being fought as

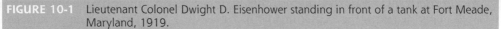

FIGURE 10-1   Lieutenant Colonel Dwight D. Eisenhower standing in front of a tank at Fort Meade, Maryland, 1919.

Source: National Archives and Records Administration.

part of the war in Europe hinted at the decline of the battleship and the need to counter the threat posed by the submarine.

Germany's renewal of unrestricted submarine warfare led directly to American entry into the war in April 1917, and it was a threat with which the Navy initially was ill-equipped to deal. Naval technologies had also undergone a revolution. Oil replaced coal, naval gunnery had built on prewar advances, and there were further developments in areas such as communications at sea, most of which were only partly absorbed or poorly understood by the Navy in April 1917.

The U.S. Army in 1914 was tiny by comparison with its European counterparts. Like the British, but unlike the major European powers, a true general staff organization was a recent phenomenon—created in the Root reforms of 1903 in response to shortcomings revealed in the Spanish-American War. Ranking seventeenth in the world and with a strength of 135,000, the U.S. Army lacked modern weaponry—tanks, aircraft, chemical weapons, heavy artillery—and modern warfighting experience, the Punitive Expedition notwithstanding. The armies of Europe did not rate it highly, if at all.

By the time the United States entered the war, the strategic direction of the Allied war effort had been well and truly decided, and the United States exercised little influence over it (a fact that applied equally to the smaller belligerent powers). The decisive theater for the western Allies (Britain and France, since the Russians were in the process of withdrawing from the war by the middle months of 1917) was the Western Front in France and Belgium, and it was there that the main effort against the main enemy army would continue to be made. Heavily reliant upon the Allies for military equipment, the American Expeditionary Force had little choice about conforming to the broad thrust of Allied strategy.

The Joint Army-Navy Board that had emerged from the 1903 reforms had given the United States the beginnings of national security policy machinery charged with planning for the defense of the United States and the Western Hemisphere, but this had little to do with the conduct of the war in Europe. Herein also lay the early development of the so-called Color plans—contingency planning for war with Germany, with Japan, and even with Britain. Plan ORANGE, for the conduct of war with Japan in the Pacific, laid the basis for the U.S. Navy's operations in the Pacific War in the *next* generation, but had little impact on the conduct of the war about to be fought.

The fighting in 1916 had been enormously costly for the British and French, and the campaigns of 1917 were as bad, if not worse. From the perspective of the Western Allies the need was for immediate reinforcement of their own, sorely debilitated ranks; London and Paris expressed a preference for American units that could be incorporated, and subsumed, into their own armies as quickly as possible. This was generally unacceptable to American opinion and policy makers, for a number of reasons. Having steered a political course that sought to avoid commitment to the war, President Wilson now needed to galvanize American opinion in support of involvement, and this was much easier to do if the American military effort was clearly identifiable. Irish-American opinion was a factor here, given the suppression of the "Easter Rising" in Dublin in 1916 and the ensuing Anglo-Irish War between British forces and the armed wing of Irish Nationalism. Professional military opinion within the United States equally would not accept the implicit slur on its capabilities and standing implied by subordination to the militaries of other nations, especially ones whose achievements to date left room for doubt. As Commander-in-Chief of the American Expeditionary Force, Pershing determined that American arms should play a decisive part in securing the defeat of Germany. Wilson's enunciation of the Fourteen Points as the basis of American war aims likewise implied minimal alignment with the war aims of the Allies, also reflected in the fact that the United States entered the war not as an ally but rather as an associated power.

The recruitment, deployment, and maintenance of the American Expeditionary Force represented the largest military challenge in American history to that time, and the most complex since the Civil War. Pershing arrived in France with a small staff in late May 1917 and concluded that an American army of at least 1 million men should be in the field within 12 months, with an ultimate goal of deploying a force of up to 3 million men in Europe. Three key issues confronted the Army and government in achieving these aims: manpower, force structure, and training, to which could be added equipment, inter-Allied relations, and the selection of an appropriate area of operations. All proved taxing.

European military systems were based on a conscript system, with annual intakes serving lengthy periods of reserve obligation after their conscript service ended. It was this system that had enabled the French, Germans, Russians, and Austro-Hungarians to field such large armies so quickly in the war's opening months. Britain had long relied on an army based on long-service regular enlistments, while the constituent parts of the Empire had no standing forces worth speaking of before the war's outbreak. Such systems, and the rejection of conscription as "un-British," could not be sustained in the face of the demands of modern industrial warfare waged by mass armies and replete with mass casualties. By 1916, Britain and the Dominions were forced to embrace conscription, however reluctantly, with all its attendant changes and implications.]

[In the United States, talk of conscription brought memories of the antidraft riots during the Civil War. Secretary of War Newton D. Baker implemented a selective service scheme as the basis for American manpower policy, reflected in the Selective Service Act of May 1917. With the decision to conscript in this manner, the Army became a truly national army for the first time, with over 70 percent of its troops drafted, a fact that in turn altered the nature of the Army as an institution. Reflecting the political difficulties that accompanied the decision for war, the Wilson administration placed much of the responsibility for overseeing the draft in civilian rather than military hands and granted generous exemptions.]

[Manpower drives force structure, and initially Army authorities did not envisage raising the mass army that would ultimately take the field by late 1918. Tasked with estimating the resources needed to ship 500,000 troops across the Atlantic, the War College Division of the General Staff concluded in March 1917 that the war would need to continue into 1919 to move beyond naval and economic participation and bring to bear an organized and trained ground force in Europe. The logistical and organizational problems of building such an army would be overcome later rather than sooner, so the thinking went. Pershing's headquarters moved to France in June 1917, and from there he planned for an American Expeditionary Force of 30 divisions, numbering around 1.1 million men, for use in a major offensive early in 1919 aimed at breaking German resistance and ending the war on Allied terms. /

The economic mobilization of the United States in support of such an ambitious and complex undertaking involved creating a partnership between government and business during a period when Progressive-Era government regulation of business was just beginning to take hold. During the war, American industry largely regulated itself within parameters set by the administration and by Congress, the whole being driven by the enormous and growing demand for material emanating from federal government agencies. All of this was overseen by the War Industries Board, itself answerable to Wilson, and various other, mostly competing, agencies. The war provided business and industry with numerous opportunities, both for profit and the enhancement of political and administrative muscle within the private sector. Big business probably economically benefited from the war more than any other segment of American society.

These benefits flowed not only from supplying and underwriting American mobilization but also through the growing economic support of an increasingly financially embattled alliance, principally Britain and France. To take but one example, the war made J. P. Morgan and Company the world's biggest buyer of goods, one whose purchases for the Allied powers between January 1915 and April 1917 were valued at $3.16 billion in a series of transactions that further involved almost 20,000 other firms in subcontracting roles. Such strong growth *before* the entry of the United States into the war, however, meant that in key areas of the economy there was little room for immediate growth after April 1917; this, in turn, produced distortions in the American economy, at least while the war lasted.

In strategic terms, 1917 was another desperate year for the Allies, with little sign by year's end that the United States was in much of a position to make a difference—the American Expeditionary Force still numbered fewer than 200,000 men in December

1917. The great German offensive of March–April 1918, part of Germany's last strategic gamble to win the war before the American Expeditionary Force could get fully mobilized, was defeated by the weary French and British Empire armies, as well as through strategic miscalculation and overreach on the part of the German High Command.

The relative failure of American mobilization in 1917 prompted changes to both economic and industrial regulation and the capacity of the War Department to deal coherently with business, as well as to the organization of the Army and the system of draft registration and induction. Many of these problems mirrored those in Britain and elsewhere earlier in the war, while the creation of a mass army from scratch in a short space of time taxed every combatant nation that attempted it.

The Allied manpower situation had been severe at the end of 1917, and following the defeat of the German offensives it was dire. The U.S. Army had generated large numbers of men in uniform but still exercised little real combat power or offensive capability. Its units and formations were much larger than those of their Allied counterparts because of the organizational assumptions under which the Americans operated—battalions included 1,000 men, and divisions numbered over 26,000. The British could transport U.S. soldiers across the Atlantic while the French could equip them; and under extreme military, political, and social pressures after nearly four years of war, they proposed incorporating American units into British and French divisions, in the interests of economy, efficiency, and suspicion of American capabilities. An independent U.S. Army, however, was central to Wilson's desire to dictate the ensuing peace in terms of the Fourteen Points and to remake the old world order.

The real architect of the independent American military force and the dogged defender of American military reputation was the Commander-in-Chief of the American Expeditionary Force, Pershing. Field Marshal Sir Douglas Haig, commanding the British armies in France, noted Pershing's obstinacy on this point in May 1918, further observing that Pershing wanted an independent command though he had no army, nor even a corps, at the time to command. Still, Pershing had the ability to play the role of courtier with Allied commanders and politicians while commanding an army at the same time. Arguably, Pershing was the only American general officer who could command the American Expeditionary Force. Although he did not fully appreciate the tactical situation on the Western Front, few officers in any of the fighting armies did. He had a strong personality, perhaps strengthened by the death of his family in the Presidio fire, and he could be inflexible, impatient, and even ruthless toward his subordinate officers and staff.

Pershing's contemporaries in the Allied high command criticized him because to them he seemed single-minded in his pursuit of American goals at the expense of Allied objectives. Pershing, in some ways, was a flawed commander. His stubborn self-righteousness, his unwillingness to correct initial misconceptions such as those that marred the doctrine and training of the American Expeditionary Force, and his stormy relationship with Allied military and civilian leaders hurt the military and political effectiveness of his army.

American commitment to an independent American army in France often meant relearning the lessons already paid for in Allied blood. Pershing argued that the American Expeditionary Force should occupy a section of the front to the south of the French, positioned between the Argonne Forest and the Vosges Mountains and with the aim of dislodging the Germans around Metz and potentially threatening industrial centers in the Saar valley, without which Germany could not continue the war. This was indeed the eventual area of operations for the American Expeditionary Force, but with it came an implicit assumption (in Pershing's case, explicitly expressed) that operations in this sector would involve "open warfare" rather than the relentless attritional grind of the trenches associated with the warfare of previous years.⌐

Pershing held the Allied armies in low regard, believing that the American Expeditionary Force had little of value to learn from them; he was altogether wrong. He insisted on high standards of drill, discipline, and marksmanship among American units, which was fine as far as it went, but he missed the point about the value of massed and coordinated fire against area targets rather than the traditional aimed fire against point targets emphasized in American training doctrine. His invocation of the importance of skill with the bayonet was irrelevant and straight out of 1914. Nor did senior American officers always appreciate or understand the need for careful preparation and the evolution of battle techniques within the British and French armies. Pershing dismissed the careful approach to "bite and hold" limited-objective offensives that had evolved from bitter experience in the British sector, and he advocated a return to the concept of unlimited offensives—an approach that had died in the other armies, along with many of its proponents, in the war's early years.⌐

FIGURE 10-2   General John J. Pershing, General Headquarters, Chaumont, France, October 19, 1918.

Source: National Archives and Records Administration.

As part of the argument within the Allied high command over the utilization of American troops in combat, and their preparation for it, Pershing agreed in early 1918 that six American divisions would be brought to France on British shipping to train with the British and French armies while their equipment caught up with them, after which they would return to the American Expeditionary Force in the summer. Pershing was thus able to concentrate greater numbers of American soldiers in France more quickly than the American shipping schedules would allow, while the divisions grouped under the American II Corps headquarters were exposed to tactical methods and thinking in advance of anything then being taught in the American Expeditionary Force's schools of instruction.

Still, Pershing remained highly suspicious of Allied intentions toward American units under their temporary command. He refused permission, for example, for the participation of a number of infantry companies in an attack at Hamel by the Australians, with whom they had been training, on July 4, 1918 (some of the Americans went in anyway). His refusal undoubtedly reflected the renewed pressure for incorporation of American troops into Allied formations during May and June, and also reflected both British and French desperation over manpower and the general state of inter-allied relations at the most senior levels of the Allied high command. Pershing engaged in a great deal of "horse trading" with the French, offering short-term reinforcement in exchange for their support in forcing changes to British shipping schedules; doing so enabled him to concentrate greater numbers of units and formations in France, where he might finally begin to form an American field army more quickly.

Rapid expansion of this kind brought with it additional problems, ones that the British armies, again, had faced in the first half of the war. As Haig had pointed out, large armies consume skilled manpower at an exponential rate, one that the tiny prewar American military was entirely ill equipped to meet. The obvious solution to this was training. The American Expeditionary Force, like its Allied counterparts, created an elaborate system of schools and courses to train officers, in particular, for both tactical command and higher staff functions. The existing core of prewar regular officers proved to be invaluable, especially those who had received higher-level schooling at the Command and General Staff College and the Army War College; but as the British had also found, there were never enough of these educated officers to go around, and they were generally overrepresented at the senior levels of the American Expeditionary Force. By the end of the war, over 80 percent of chiefs of staff at the army, corps, and division levels were Staff College graduates. Attendance at courses of instruction in France took officers away from their units and formations while they trained, however, and the standard remained uneven in any case. As late as August 1918, senior American staff officers, after reviewing divisions at the front, noted the absence of uniform organization and function among division staffs.

Three elements of the American Expeditionary Force posed additional problems for the high command: the National Guard, the U.S. Marines, and African-American soldiers. Regular-militia relations presented all the old problems anew, ones to which Pershing was keenly attuned. Some regular Army officers hoped that the war would result in termination of the militia movement once and for all. Neither the Guard nor the War Department was prepared for a remobilization of state forces so soon after the Punitive Expedition. The necessary reorganization of Guard units and formations to conform to that being applied in the American Expeditionary Force led to the merger, disbandment, or conversion of units, with concomitant reduction of responsibilities or loss of command among many citizen officers, all without much regard by regular Army officers toward their Guard brethren.

Unhappiness at their changed circumstances was understandable but also reflected the age-old problem of the provincial nature of the National Guard. Some 12 percent of the wartime army had enlisted as guardsmen, and they made up nearly a fifth of the American Expeditionary Force; but their distinctive identities were largely destroyed by and through wartime service, and they never again dominated the army structure. But the National Guard, or at least its political backers, did not go quietly; to rebut criticism of the firing of senior Guard officers from commands in France, Pershing had dossiers compiled to show that relief from command was invariably for cause, and favored neither Guard nor regular officers over the other.

The Marines, as usual, provided magnificent combat soldiers, perhaps at times given to excesses of martial ardor such as at the Battle of Belleau Wood. Two Marine regiments formed a brigade of the 2nd Infantry Division, but the Marine Corps' desire to form a separate Marine division was frustrated by Pershing for institutional and political reasons. It may have been some comfort to the Marines to know that the 4th Brigade represented the single largest accrual of combat power in the history of the Corps to that point. The overall strength of the Corps grew from around 10,000 to more than 75,000 during the war.

The experiences of African-American soldiers in a persistently "Jim Crow" military were of a different order entirely. This, of course, reflected much peacetime and civilian practice in the United States, although it puzzled many European observers. Both the French and British armies made widespread use of nonwhite colonial soldiers in combat formations. While racism was institutionalized in both of those armies and the broader societies they represented, British attitudes toward Indian soldiers, for example, conveyed a healthy level of respect and were almost never characterized by the viciousness apparent in race relations within the United States. Indeed, African-American soldiers were not the only ones who discovered that there was a much less vicious racial environment in Europe than in the United States. Many American jazz musicians, who pursued highly successful careers in Europe from the 1920s to the 1960s, encountered similar experiences.

The Army made a conscious decision to utilize the majority of black soldiers in noncombatant supporting roles, often as little more than laborers. Attempts at more-or-less complete segregation failed, since black as well as white soldiers found themselves in proximity to each other on troop ships, in training camps, and in French urban centers when on leave. Many white soldiers resented this, while many black soldiers objected to the demeaning status often accorded them. They also objected strenuously, if ineffectively, to the way in which the disciplinary system protected white soldiers who attacked and abused them. The relative social freedom that black soldiers enjoyed while on leave in France infuriated many Southern whites, as did their open interaction with French women.

More than 200,000 African-American soldiers served in Europe as part of the American Expeditionary Force. Only two groups, in the main, had the opportunity to see combat. In a rehearsal of similar problems and outcomes in the Mediterranean theater in the next world war, the Army formed the 92nd Division for active duty, but its men were poorly trained, its officers were divided along racial lines, and its performance at the front was poor. Four regiments formed from existing National Guard divisions—the 369th, 370th, 371st, and 372nd—fought with French formations, including a Moroccan division. Largely officered by African-Americans, these units distinguished themselves repeatedly, with many members receiving French gallantry decorations. The contrast provided by the 92nd Division once again demonstrated that bad leadership and inadequate training produces undermotivated and ill-prepared soldiers; it was the 92nd Division that the interwar army remembered, not the regiments in French service. The 92nd Division was raised through a racialist process, and its performance reflected the racist context in which it operated.

Although the March 1918 offensive is the best known, the Germans mounted a succession of increasingly weak and unsuccessful assaults between March and July. These were defeated by the combined efforts of the British and French armies with minimal assistance from the American Expeditionary Force, although in May the American 1st Division captured positions around Cantigny while fighting in the French sector of the front, at a cost of 1,067 casualties. Although ultimately failures, several of the German post-March offensives placed the Allied armies under severe pressure. For a week in May–June, the German assault pushed the outnumbered French and British divisions back across the Marne to again threaten Paris. The American 2nd Division, which included the Marine regiments, and the 3rd Division were temporarily placed under French command to defend the crossings at Château-Thierry.

The advent of the oversized American division made a considerable difference to a faltering and demoralized French defense. It was during this consolidation of the defensive positions that a Marine famously responded to a French order to withdraw with "Retreat, hell. We just got here." Going over to the attack, the Marine brigade assaulted and took Belleau Wood at a cost of 1,087 casualties and then beat back German counterattacks for a further 20 days through most of June, while suffering a total of 5,200 casualties, including 750 killed. These casualties amounted to more than half the brigade's strength.

The Marines received the bulk of the publicity because of an American Expeditionary Force policy that prohibited press mention of specific units or branches of the Army, despite the fact that the other brigade in the 2nd Division, the Army's 3rd Brigade, suffered 3,200 casualties of its own in the fighting in this sector. Heavy casualties in such grueling fights for otherwise unimportant positions were inevitable (and incurred by all combatant armies), but it is equally clear that senior officers in the 2nd Division paid less attention to careful artillery preparation than their experience on the Western Front warranted and perhaps placed too great a reliance on "vigor" and a willingness to keep going forward when heavy and sustained casualties suggested otherwise.

The period from late July 1918 to the end of the war in November is called the Hundred Days Offensive, during which the Allied armies mounted a series of offensives that broke through successive German defensive lines, pushed German formations back into a rolling series of retreats, and culminated in the defeat of the German Army in the field to the extent that Germany agreed to an armistice in November. It was during this final phase of the war that the American Expeditionary Force began

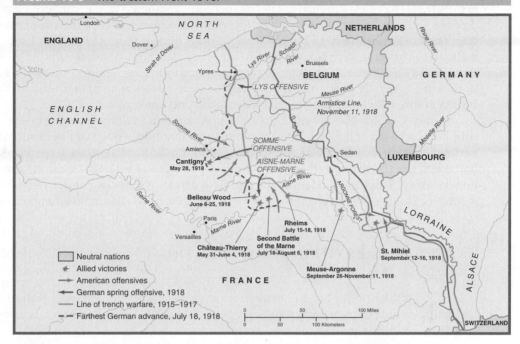

FIGURE 10-3 The Western Front 1918.

to come into its own, certainly as an independent and increasingly powerful military presence on the front lines. American divisions took a leading part in the French offensive along the Aisne and Marne rivers in late July, negating earlier German gains in ground. French tanks in significant numbers assisted the American assaults toward Soissons, which were otherwise characterized by lack of artillery preparation, breakdowns in communications, and tactical ineptness. The French, however, took notice of their American brothers in arms, noting that their courage often bordered on recklessness. This remained a valid criticism to the war's end.

The American 1st Army, comprising 5 French and 15 American divisions, was activated on August 10, in an unambiguous communication of Pershing's long-held resolve to maintain American independence in the field. He was less successful, however, in persuading the British and French to accept his strategic conception for its use. The St. Mihiel Offensive was intended originally to reduce the salient in that area and drive toward German positions around Metz; these objectives were reduced when the Supreme Commander, Marshal Ferdinand Foch, accepted Haig's plan for an envelopment of the German Army that required U.S. forces to drive north through the Meuse-Argonne region and cut German communications around Sedan. The resulting offensive eliminated the salient at a cost of 7,000 U.S. casualties, inflicting some 17,000 on the Germans (most of them prisoners) while again exposing shortcomings in command, staff work, and appreciation of what was actually possible in an offensive, even in the latter days of the war.

Over a million American troops, most of whom lacked combat experience, fought in the Meuse-Argonne Offensive. This inexperience combined with a stubborn German defense to cause severe casualties. The offensive demonstrated both the strengths and weaknesses of the American Expeditionary Force. Few of the divisions that took part in the initial assaults were combat experienced; in at least one division—the 79th—half the enlisted men had been in uniform for less than six months. Senior commanders and staffs were generally good, but there remained weaknesses in command and administration at lower levels, compounded by disparities in training.

By mid-October the defensive lines of the *Krimhilde Stellung* had been taken, and with the activation of the U.S. 2nd Army, Pershing relinquished the cumbersome "dual hatting" system that had seen him commanding both the American Expeditionary Force and the field army rather than fulfilling his duties as head of a national expeditionary army. The commanders of the two field armies, Generals Hunter Liggett and Robert L. Bullard, were able and experienced officers of considerable attainment.

CAPTAIN HARRY TRUMAN WRITES HOME TO BESS, 1918

Harry Truman began his military service as a private in the Missouri National Guard and retired over thirty years later as a colonel in the Army Officers Reserve Corps. As a 33-year-old captain, Truman commanded Battery D of the 129th Field Artillery and saw intense action in just a few months in France. In the letter below to his wife Bess, Truman writes about the 100-mile march from the Vosges Mountains to the Argonne Forest through rain and mud and occasional shelling from German lines.

Somewhere in Parle Vous
September 1, 1918

Dear Bess:

I am the most pleased person in the world this morning. I got two letters from you and have accomplished my greatest wish. Have fired 500 rounds at the Germans at my command, been shelled, didn't run away, thank the Lord, and never lost a man. Probably shouldn't have told you but you'll not worry any more if you know I'm in it than if you think I am. Have had the most strenuous week of my life, am very tired but otherwise absolutely in good condition physically, mentally, and morally.

It has been about two weeks since I've written you because I haven't had the chance. They shipped me from school to the front *in charge of Battery D* and the Irish seem to be pleased over it. We went into position right away and fired 500 rounds at them in 36 minutes. Two of my guns got stuck in the mud; it was dark and raining and before I could get away [?] came the reply. I sent two of the pieces to safety and the horses on the other two broke away and ran every which direction but my Irishmen stayed with me, except a few drivers who were badly scared and my first sergeant. We covered up the two guns I had stuck with [?] and things, and one of my lieutenants, [?] is his name and myself then collected up all the horses we could and got the men together, caught up with the other two pieces, and went to safety. I slept for 24 hours afterwards and am now back of the lines awaiting another chance. I went back the next night and got my guns. Every man wanted to go along but I took only the two sections who belonged to the guns.

My greatest satisfaction is that my legs didn't succeed in carrying me away although they were very anxious to do it. Both of my lieutenants are all [?]. One of them, Jordan by name, came back with the horses off the other two pieces to pull me out and I had to order him off the hill. Four horses were killed; two of them outright and two had to be shot afterwards.

I am in a most beautiful country and it seems like a shame that we must spread shells over it but as the French say, Boche are hogs and should be killed. Please don't worry about me because no German shell is made that can hit me. One exploded in 15 feet of me and I didn't get a scratch, so you can see I have them beaten there.

. . . . I am so sleepy I can't hardly hold my eyes open but will write again as soon as I can . . . .

Yours Always, Harry

Source: National Archives and Records Administration.

The hard slogging and heavy casualties in the first phase of the offensive earned criticism and snide remarks from some of the Allied high command, but the very real difficulties experienced by American formations reflected both weaknesses specific to the American Expeditionary Force and the difficulties of coming to terms with the tactical and operational challenges of the Western Front. In the war's last days, the 1st Army reached positions around Sedan while the 2nd Army launched assaults toward Metz, as Pershing had originally intended. Hammered from three directions by Allied armies, and with manpower losses long past the critical point, the German government sued for an armistice, which came into effect on November 11. This final phase of the war cost the American Expeditionary Force more than 26,000 dead and close to 100,000 wounded.

◆ THE NAVY IN THE GREAT WAR

The war at sea tends not to receive the attention often lavished on the Western Front, but the control of sea lines of communications and the neutralizing of the German fleet by the Royal Navy were critical to the Allies' capacity to fight and win the war. The ability of the American Expeditionary Force to take the field at all was dependent on sea transportation, and the greatest threat to this was posed by the successive German submarine offensives blockading Britain and attempting to cut the sea links across the Atlantic. Although the threat posed by the submarine, both potential and actual, should have been clear following German successes in 1915, the "battleship mentality" was still predominant within the senior ranks of the U.S. Navy when the nation went to war in 1917.

Senior American naval opinion was by no means entirely backward looking. In particular, while on a special mission to the Admiralty in London in March 1917, Admiral William S. Sims, serving as president of the Naval War College at the time, argued hard and effectively in support of those British naval officers who advocated a convoy system as the key to defeating the submarine menace. Experimental convoying in May 1917 proved the point, and thereafter the U.S. Navy and merchant fleet contributions to the convoy system and the antisubmarine campaign were fundamental to Allied success in this dimension of the war. The American industrial effort provided dramatically more numbers of merchant vessels and escort ships, and American ships played an important part in laying the mine barrage in the North Sea between Scotland and Norway to restrict German submarines' freedom of movement. The U.S. Navy increased to an unprecedented size of almost half a million men and over 2,000 ships, ranging from simple transports to battleships.

As Commander of U.S. Naval Forces Operating in European Waters, Sims had his headquarters in London, with a large staff and constant interaction with his British counterparts. This was not how the U.S. Navy had initially conceived of its role in the war, planning instead to safeguard the coastal waters of the Western Hemisphere, but it reflected the reality of the naval war in the latter years of the conflict and the pressing needs of the Allied war effort. Aircraft were also pressed into embryonic service in the antisubmarine campaign. The U.S. Navy's principal role—safeguarding convoys— was not the glamorous "big ship" mission envisaged by many before the war, but it was a vital contribution to winning of the war at sea.

◆ THE AMERICAN AIR WAR

If the war at sea failed in large part to realize the aspirations of that generation of naval officers, the same could not be said of the war in the air. In common with other Western militaries, American forces had begun to develop military aviation capabilities before 1914, but these were still nascent when the United States entered the war three years later. Young Americans keen to fly impatiently volunteered for service with the Royal Flying Corps and the French aerial service (in the latter case forming the Lafayette Escadrille) before the United States entered the war, and subsequently provided a small core of combat-experienced aircrew to the American Expeditionary Force's Air Service. Like its British counterpart, this service quickly became the plaything of ambitious and powerful personalities, including Colonel Billy Mitchell, relatively young and junior in rank due to the lack of a prewar senior officer corps interested in what many before the war derided as a "pastime" with little serious military application.

Like much of the rest of the American Expeditionary Force, the Air Service only really made an impression at the front from the middle of 1918, and while its wartime expansion was both rapid and exponential, its roles and missions emphasized reconnaissance and countering the threat posed by German fighters rather than offensive action through aerial bombardment. In this, the visionaries in its ranks shared many of the frustrations of their wartime comrades in the British Royal Air Force, which, thanks to the efforts of General Hugh Trenchard, had become an independent service in the British military. Still, the American flyers provided good propaganda for the folks at home. Aces—like race-car driver Eddie Rickenbacker, who shot down twenty-six German planes—became celebrities.

◆ IMPACT OF AMERICAN INVOLVEMENT IN THE GREAT WAR

In intervening in the first world war, the United States had mounted a massive effort in its own terms, but one that impressed its war-weary and sorely damaged allies much less than it did many Americans. From their perspective, the Americans entered late and did relatively little, which was both fair and wrong in roughly equal measures. The 60,000 combat deaths suffered by American forces paled beside those incurred by the French, Russians, or British; and the United States had known neither enemy occupation nor the devastation of countryside and infrastructure fought over repeatedly; neither aerial bombardment nor the bitter aftermath of defeat, collapse, and revolution. American intervention in the affairs of the "Old World" in 1917–1919, and the beginnings of the shift in economic, military, and diplomatic power that this presaged, did not necessarily become evident to, or impress, the other victorious powers who met at Versailles in 1919 to divide the spoils.

U.S. forces took part in the occupation of the Rhineland in western Germany alongside the French and British, reaching a high of 262,000 troops in February 1919. When it became clear that there would be no civil disturbances in the occupied areas and that the German government would, however reluctantly, sign the Treaty of Versailles, the demobilization of the American Expeditionary Force in Germany began in earnest; by November 1919, there were only 15,000 American soldiers left in Germany, and all remaining U.S. troops had departed the occupied zone by January 1923, their responsibilities assumed by the French. Those not tasked with occupation duties looked forward to speedy repatriation and demobilization in the United States, and like the soldiers of every army that had traveled from outside Europe, were frustrated by the shortage of shipping and conflicting priorities for its use.

Pershing initially insisted on maintaining wartime standards and requirements and the substitution of drill for purposeful military activity; this not only made him deeply unpopular, but badly affected morale in a climate where soldiers in some armies were staging protests and even mutinies in response to the apparent dilatoriness and lack of concern for their welfare exhibited by the high command. Pershing soon relented and introduced sports and educational programs, in line with the British and Empire armies also waiting homeward shipment. The majority of American soldiers did not leave Europe until the spring of 1919. Once the repatriation process got under way, however, the shipment of men accelerated rapidly; the last combat division sailed from France for the United States in August of that year, although the last Americans did not depart until the beginning of 1920.

The "war to end all wars" was, of course, nothing of the sort. Wars never end tidily. Even before the armistice, the Allies—the United States included—found themselves being dragged into Russian affairs following the October revolution that brought the Bolsheviks to power, initially at least in the major urban centers. Opposition to Communist rule by a loose and often conflicting coalition of non-Communist, nationalist, and monarchist elements grouped under the label of "White Russians" dragged the country into a horrendous civil war that lasted until the early 1920s.

American forces were committed in two distinct theaters and for two distinct reasons. The 339th Infantry regiment and supporting units, about 5,000 men in total, were deployed to North Russia as part of an allied expeditionary force initially designed to prevent the vast stockpiles of military supplies stored there to support the old tsarist army from falling into German hands. Inevitably, the American contingent, under British command, became drawn into the murky processes of the civil war in support of the Whites; the American units saw considerable, if sporadic, action against Soviet forces in the area, as their casualties of 139 killed and 266 wounded attested. They also suffered from poor morale and discipline problems after the armistice came into effect, because they were not withdrawn from Russia until the summer of 1919 and had to endure the harsh Russian winter while waiting to be relieved.

Another 9,000 men of the 27th and 31st Infantry Regiments and supporting units were committed to Siberia at the same time, initially in what could be described as the first occasion on which the United States used military force in support of purely diplomatic ends. In addition to assisting the Czech Legion, whose efforts to get eastward to a warm-water port and take ships to Europe to fight the Germans and Austro-Hungarians had captured popular imagination in the United States, the American role in the intervention in Siberia also was intended to deter Japanese expansionist tendencies in the region. Inevitably, again, the intervention force became involved in the civil war in aid of the White armies, although it saw much less combat than did outside forces elsewhere in Russian territory. The Americans there suffered 35 killed and just 52 wounded. They were withdrawn in early 1920 after the Whites in the area collapsed, leaving the Japanese to meddle in Russian affairs for several more years until they, too, withdrew following the Red victory in the Russian civil war.

◆ CONCLUSION

American involvement in the Great War was far more important to and for Americans than it was for anyone else; but this is true largely because the war ended when it did, in November 1918. Had the war gone on into 1919, as some senior Allied figures at the time certainly believed likely, then the weight of American numbers and the sharp increase in American combat capability that was the inevitable fruit of broader experience would have proven irresistible, coupled of course with the rapid decline in German manpower stocks and military effectiveness that would have benefited Allied arms generally. Pershing, in fact, lamented that the war ended in 1918, because in his estimation the American Expeditionary Force was just approaching maturity as an effective fighting force when the armistice suddenly ended the fighting.

Pershing was unmistakably the creator of the American Expeditionary Force, and it bore his stamp, for both good and ill. The experience of the American Expeditionary Force, and the disastrous military and exceedingly slow industrial mobilization, greatly affected American military and mobilization plans in World War II. The Great War experience of the Army and the Navy would have implications for the peacetime development of American arms in the war's aftermath and through the long, and sometimes bitter, years of the peace. Their fullest fruit, as in other armies, would not be harvested until the next world war.

Further Reading

Beaver, Daniel R. *Newton D. Baker and the American War Effort, 1917–1919*. Lincoln: University of Nebraska Press, 1967.

Coffman, Edward M. *The Hilt of the Sword: The Career of Peyton C. March*. Madison: University of Wisconsin Press, 1966.

Coffman, Edward M. *The War to End All Wars: The American Military Experience in World War I*. Madison: University of Wisconsin Press, 1968.

DeWeerd, Harvey A. *President Wilson Fights His War: World War I and the American Intervention*. New York: Macmillan, 1968.

Fleming, Thomas J. *Illusion of Victory: Americans in World War I*. New York: Basic Books, 2004.

Freidel, Frank. *Over There: The Story of America's First Great Overseas Crusade*. Rev. ed. New York: McGraw-Hill, 1990.

Grotelueschen, Mark E., *The AEF Way of War: The American Army and Combat in World War I*. New York: Cambridge University Press, 2007.

Halpern, Paul G. *A Naval History of World War I*. Annapolis: Naval Institute Press, 1994.

Keene, Jennifer. *Doughboys, the Great War, and the Remaking of America*. Baltimore: Johns Hopkins University Press, 2001.

Kennedy, David M. *Over Here: The First World War and American Society*. New York: Oxford University Press, 1980.

Koistinen, Paul A. C. *Mobilizing for Modern War: The Political Economy of American Warfare 1865–1919*. Lawrence: University Press of Kansas, 1997.

Millett, Allan R. *The General: Robert L. Bullard and Officership in the United States Army, 1881–1925*. Westport, Connecticut: Greenwood Press, 1975.

Pershing, John J. *My Experiences in the World War*. London: Hodder & Stoughton, 1931.

Sheffield, Gary. *Forgotten Victory: The First World War: Myths and Realities*. London: Headline, 2001.

Smythe, Donald. *Pershing: General of the Armies*. Bloomington: Indiana University Press, 1986.

Strachan, Hew. *The First World War: Volume 1: To Arms*. New York: Oxford University Press, 2001.

Trask, David F. *The American Expeditionary Force and Coalition Warmaking, 1917–1918*. Lawrence: University Press of Kansas, 1993.

Vandiver, Frank E. *Black Jack: The Life and Times of John J. Pershing*. College Station: Texas A&M University Press, 1977.

Yockelson, Mitchell A. *Borrowed Soldiers: Americans under British Command, 1918*. Norman: University Press of Oklahoma, 2008.

Zieger, Robert H. *America's Great War: World War I and the American Experience*. Lanham, Maryland: Rowman and Littlefield, 2000.

mysearchlab Connections: Sources Online • • • • • • • • • •

READ AND REVIEW

Review this chapter by using the study aids and these related documents available on MySearchLab.

Study Plan

Chapter Test

Essay Test

Documents

Eugene Kennedy, A "Doughboy" Describes the Fighting Front (1918)

This letter, typical of thousands sent home by American soldiers in France during the Great War, tries to explain the combat experience to loved ones at home.

Woodrow Wilson, The Fourteen Points (1918)

In this document, President Wilson explains American objectives in the Great War. These became the basis for the armistice concluded on November 11, 1918.

Reverend F. J. Grimke, Address to African-American Soldiers Returning from War (1919)

This document highlights the disconnect that many African-American veterans felt after fighting in a war to "save the world for democracy" only to return home as second-class citizens in a nation plagued by racism.

RESEARCH AND EXPLORE

Explore the following review questions using the research tools available on www.mysearchlab.com.

1. What were the realities of warfare as encountered by U.S. soldiers on the Western Front?
2. What impacts did the war have on the United States at home and abroad?
3. How did issues of race influence the war experience?

The Interwar Years

1938	Naval Act of 1938
	RAINBOW plans
1939	Germany seizes Czechoslovakia
	Germany invades Poland

◆ INTRODUCTION

The Great War forced a reluctant United States to reconsider its diplomatic and military traditions. The world had changed, dramatically. Disgusted and ashamed of the death and destruction of four years of total industrialized warfare, the great powers sought ways to prevent such a war from happening again. Even though the Senate had rejected President Woodrow Wilson's League of Nations, the United States was far from isolationist following the war. Instead of being bound by treaty to a collective security arrangement that might not be in its best interests, the United States chose to maintain the option of unilateral action while using multilateral approaches to security concerns when necessary. Following this trend, the United States would be a leader in the disarmament movement of the 1920s but would also slowly increase its own military capabilities to unprecedented levels.

The war in Europe stretched American military and industrial mobilization to its organizational limits, with less-than-spectacular results. During the 1920s and 1930s, the United States would develop new strategies to improve both systems in case of another conflict. Despite having fought a war for the first time on European soil, the United States continued to see the Atlantic and Pacific Oceans as its great security moat and thus continued to invest heavily in capital ships. The advent of airplane technology, however, forced the United States to incorporate this power of seemingly unlimited potential into its arsenal and develop doctrine regarding its use in war.

◆ POSTWAR DUTIES

The sudden end to the war in November 1918 sped up plans for demobilizing the massive force that the United States had built essentially from scratch in 1917. The problem with demobilizing such a large force was finding a rate of discharging servicemen that brought the boys home as soon as practicable but did not do undue harm to the American economy or endanger postwar occupation responsibilities. Limited troop transport was also a problem. War industries also demobilized and returned to peacetime production. Because industrial mobilization had been so slow and somewhat disorganized, war industries had just approached peak production levels when the war abruptly ended. Thus, huge surpluses of equipment, weapons, ammunition, and other war material existed at the end of the war. The War Department decided to maintain a large amount of this equipment for future use. An unintended consequence of maintaining this circa-1918 equipment, however, was that throughout the 1920s and 1930s, the military was slow to procure new modern equipment.

With its demobilized force, the Army still had duties to perform. It continued to patrol the Mexican border and help quell domestic disturbances. In addition to assisting local law enforcement to restore order in some of the violent race riots during the 1920s, the Army dispersed the famous Bonus Army in Washington in July 1932. Demanding their bonus payment early for serving in the Great War because of the Great Depression, veterans descended upon Washington, setting up a shantytown outside the city. Fearing riotous violence instigated by suspected socialists and Bolsheviks among the group, President Hoover ordered Army Chief of Staff General Douglas MacArthur to break up the Bonus Army. MacArthur himself commanded the force of 600 cavalry and infantry, which included Majors Dwight Eisenhower and George Patton, as it moved the veterans from their camp. Much of the shantytown burned to the ground, and several shoving matches between the regulars and the veterans broke out. It was a controversial event from which the Army, and MacArthur in particular, took some time to recover.

The Army also coordinated the Civilian Conservation Corps (CCC), one of President Franklin Roosevelt's New Deal programs to ease the effects of the Great Depression. In 1933, the Army mobilized over 300,000 young men at more than 1,000 camps across the United States to put them to work on projects that ranged from building roads to mending fences. Although the program did not significantly affect the economic crisis, it did pay thousands of unemployed young men a subsistence wage, complete beneficial public works projects, and give the American people a sense that the federal government was at least trying to alleviate the effects of the Great Depression. Moreover, thousands of regular and reserve officers gained valuable command experience while running camps and overseeing CCC projects.

◆ THE ARMY OF THE UNITED STATES

The American experience in the Great War convinced many in military and political circles that the American military establishment needed a major overhaul. The expansible army concept, dating back to the early nineteenth century, had not worked well in the massive mobilization effort required in 1917. Industrialized warfare required new and improved military organization. In 1920, Congress passed a new national defense act that radically altered the organizational structure of the Army and provided for a better-trained and better-prepared military force should war again threaten the United States.

The National Defense Act of 1920 created what it called the Army of the United States, which included a regular army of professionals, a civilian-based National Guard, and civilian reserves of both officers and enlisted men. The new Army had an authorized strength of over 17,000 officers and 280,000 enlisted personnel—although throughout the 1920s and into the early 1930s, lack of a real security threat and then the Great Depression kept the Army at well below authorized strength. Included in the Army were new air, chemical warfare, and financial branches.

The Army would be administered through a general staff system much like the one that Pershing had used in commanding the American Expeditionary Force in France. The War Department would be responsible for mobilization and war planning, dividing the responsibilities between the Chief of Staff and the Secretary of War's office. In 1921, Pershing became Chief of Staff and reorganized the General Staff into specific divisions: G-1 was for personnel; G-2 handled intelligence; G-3 was responsible for training troops and conducting operations; and G-4 orchestrated logistics and supply. Pershing also added a War Plans Division to carry out planning functions mandated by the National Defense Act.

The new Army would be spread across nine commands, or corps, each with one regular, two National Guard, and three reserve divisions. In addition, the Army manned military departments created in Panama, Hawaii, and the Philippines. Because the Army was under strength, many tactical units remained skeletal or simply existed on paper. With new mobilization plans, however, National Guard and Reserve units could quickly fill out the Army to more than 2 million men in a matter of just a few months.

The new National Guard became a key component of the Army of the United States, one that both addressed defense needs and satisfied concerns among states that their right to maintain a militia had not been eroded by the 1917 mobilization of state guard units. The National Defense Act authorized a National Guard of over 400,000 troops, but throughout the 1920s the National Guard normally maintained only about 180,000. The huge surplus of material after the war made equipping Guard units quite easy. Regular Army officers trained Guard units, including 48 times a year at their respective armories and for 2 weeks each year in the field.

The National Guard and regular Army were augmented by the Reserves, also created by the National Defense Act. The Enlisted Reserve Corps did not experience the postwar prestige that came with Guard service, but nonetheless provided continued training and readiness to thousands of men, mostly veterans of the Great War who already had military training and experience. More successful was the Officers' Reserve Corps, made up of veteran officers as well as a steady stream of newly commissioned officers. Such a large pool of trained officers made mobilization for World War II much more effective and efficient.

The Reserve Officer Training Corps (ROTC) and the Citizens' Military Training Camp program (CMTC) became the principal training ground for commissioning new officers. The National Defense Act increased the number of ROTC programs at colleges and universities across the United States. Over 325 schools had ROTC programs by 1928, commissioning over 6,000 new second lieutenants annually. The CMTC worked through summer training camps rather than colleges and universities. Completing a 4-week summer training camp each year for 4 years qualified one for commissioning in the Reserves. Over 30,000 participated in this alternative commissioning program. Both the ROTC and CMTC greatly helped the Army maintain its officer needs for the Reserves and the National Guard, as well as for the regular Army itself.

Professional military education in the Army was reinvigorated to levels not seen since the 1880s. In addition to officer training programs at West Point and in ROTC programs across the United States, over thirty Army schools provided specialized training for most branches of the Army. Primarily directed toward officers, these schools educated not only regular officers, but officers from the Reserves and Guard components as well. Like the professional military education schools in Great Britain and Germany, the U.S. Army Command and General Staff College, the Army War College, and the Army Industrial College provided advanced education and training to more senior officers. The purpose of these schools was to produce competent officers who could command at various levels during a war rather than to allow for in-depth study of war theory. Although no revolutionary thought or great military theorist emerged from these schools, the great importance placed upon military education is significant.

Perhaps the greatest weakness of the Army of the United States was its lack of interest in armor during the 1920s. Despite the impact of new tank technology in the Great War, Army strategists saw little use for the vehicles beyond infantry support. As a consequence, the infantry absorbed the Tank Corps after the war. Little valuable research and development funds went toward tank warfare. Only one experimental tank brigade existed during the 1930s, and as World War II approached, the Army had only four mechanized units.

Great Britain and Germany, on the other hand, recognized the tank's strategic and tactical potential in combat operations. Convinced that armor could operate as mechanized units on a battlefield and break through enemy lines, British military leaders gave armor a role independent of infantry support. Germany pioneered tank tactics by concentrating fast but large armor units to achieve a sort of "shock and awe" impact on the enemy; ideas and techniques developed in concert with the Red Army in the 1920s during the so-called "Black Reichswehr" period. The British, Germans, and Soviets developed new, faster, and more lethal tanks and other armored vehicles during the 1920s and 1930s, while the United States did comparatively little. Equally, the financial strictures of the 1930s imposed serious interruptions on developments in all Western armies, while political interference in the Soviet Union largely killed innovation there in the same period.

◆ DOCTRINE FOR AIRPOWER

The rapid advancement of aviation technology during and after the Great War challenged airpower advocates and detractors alike. The Army's traditional role as land force and the Navy's time-honored function as ocean fleet did not allow for the easy integration of aircraft into their strategic or operational thinking. Airpower enthusiasts went so far as to suggest that armies would be obsolete, as aircraft alone could bring an industrialized nation-state to its knees through strategic bombing. The main disagreements centered on exactly how airpower should be used.

Among these enthusiasts were British General Sir Hugh Trenchard, Italian Air Chief Guilio Douhet, and American Brigadier General Billy Mitchell. Trenchard had been instrumental in making the Royal Air Force an independent service during the war. Douhet wrote extensively on the use of airpower and theorized that bombers targeting civilian populations, rather than only industrial targets, could force such political chaos in a country as to make its government to come to terms. Wars would be shorter and less destructive, which was precisely the remedy that war-weary people sought after the seemingly endless slaughter of the Great War.

General Mitchell enthusiastically shared these ideas. The Army and Navy, however, promoted a more conservative doctrine that aircraft could be useful in supporting air and naval operations through missions involving pursuit of enemy aircraft, bombardment of enemy positions, attack on enemy forces in battle, observation of enemy troop movements, and artillery support. There was no concept of joint Army and Navy air operations and only minimal thought given to how airpower could be used to repel a sea-borne invasion of the United States. Mitchell, on the other hand, radically suggested that airpower alone could not only defend the United States, but win future wars in which land and sea forces would be obsolete.

Like Trenchard, Mitchell wanted an independent air force that would train, maintain, and operate all American military air assets. To gain support for his radical ideas, Mitchell boldly dared the Navy to allow aircraft to attack a battleship. Mitchell hoped to prove once and for all that battleships were no longer invulnerable in the age of air. The Navy eagerly accepted, hoping the tiresome Mitchell would make himself look the fool.

Off the Virginia Capes in 1921, Mitchell got his chance. Using a stationary, unmanned German battleship, the *Ostfriesland*, as his target, Mitchell organized a squadron of Army bombers from Langley Field to "attack" the battleship. The Navy had set strict rules to guide the experiment. Only one bomb could be dropped at a time. After each bomb, investigators would board the ship to examine the damage, if any. Mitchell probably never had any intention of following these rules. Dropping over sixty 2,000-pound bombs at the anchored vessel, the Army bombers scored 16 direct hits, none of which were closely observed by the Navy board of investigators according to the predetermined rules. Mitchell sank the battleship, but he and the Navy disagreed on the meaning of the result. Mitchell claimed his point proven—battleships were vulnerable to air attack. The Navy rightly claimed that Mitchell's test had been in a controlled environment. The weather was perfect, the ship at anchor, and no antiaircraft fire dissuaded the attacking bombers. For the Navy, Mitchell had just proven how difficult it would be for aircraft to successfully attack a battleship, much less a fleet of battleships.

Mitchell was a maverick who enjoyed talking to the press. When the War Department and Navy Department would not yield to what seemed to him overwhelming evidence of air superiority, he went to the public to plead his case. In an attempt to at least quiet the outspoken aviator, the War Department transferred Mitchell to San Antonio, Texas, in 1925, demoting him to colonel. He had already approached the fine line of insubordination, but in September 1925 he crossed it for good. On the morning of September 3, the Navy airship *Shenandoah* crashed during a storm in Ohio, adding to a string of recent air accidents. Fourteen crewmen were killed. Outraged at what he considered needless loss of life, Mitchell spoke to the press, going so far as to claim the Army and Navy were incompetent, even criminally negligent. The Army charged Mitchell with insubordination. His court-martial was a public sensation. Convicted, Mitchell resigned his commission in the hope of being able to promote airpower unhindered by a military chain of command.

Mitchell's was not a voice in the wilderness, just too radical a voice. Many in the Army and Navy, and in Congress, recognized the importance of airpower to future conflicts. Still, Congress and a special investigating board appointed by President Calvin Coolidge rejected the idea of an independent air force. Whatever air development would come would be done under the current military structure.

FIGURE 11-1   Bombing the Ostfriesland, July 21, 1921.

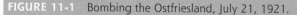

Source: Library of Congress Print and Reproductions Division [LC-USZ62-9112]

COLONEL BILLY MITCHELL'S STATEMENT TO THE PRESS, SEPTEMBER 1925

Following the *Shenandoah* disaster, Mitchell gave the press a prepared statement of over 6,000 words, blasting the Army and Navy, indeed the U.S. government, for what he considered the inexcusable state of American military aviation. Mitchell fervently believed in what he was saying, but for the Army such accusations crossed the line of acceptable conduct for a senior officer. Mitchell wanted a chance to air his grievances in public, and he was about to get that opportunity. This statement directly led to his court-martial. Here are the opening and closing excerpts from his statement.

> I have been asked from all parts of the country to give my opinion about the reasons for the frightful aeronautical accidents and loss of life, equipment and treasure that has occurred during the last few days. This statement therefore is given out publicly by me after mature deliberation and

after sufficient time has elapsed since the terrible accident to our naval aircraft, to find out something about what happened.

About what happened, my opinion is as follows: These accidents are the direct result of the incompetency, criminal negligence and almost treasonable administration of the national defense by the Navy and War Departments. In their attempts to keep down the development of aviation into an independent department, separate from the Army and Navy and handled by aeronautical experts, and to maintain the existing systems, they have gone to the utmost lengths to carry their point. All aviation policies, schemes and systems are dictated by the non-flying officers of the Army and Navy, who know practically nothing about it. The lives of airmen are being used merely as pawns in their hands.

The great Congress of the United States, that makes laws for the organization and use of our air, land, and water forces, is treated by these two departments as if it were an organization created for their benefit, to which evidence of any kind, whether true or not, can be given without restraint. Officers and agents sent by the War and Navy Departments to Congress have almost always given incomplete, miserable or false information about aeronautics, which either they knew to be false when given or was the result of such gross ignorance of the question that they should not be allowed to appear before a legislative body... .

This condition must be remedied. It is not in the field of partisan politics, it concerns us all. The American people must know the facts and with their unfailing common sense and ability, they will surely remedy it.

As far as I am personally concerned, I am looking for no advancement in any service. I have had the finest career that any man could have in the armed service of our United States. I have had the great pleasure of serving in all our campaigns from the Spanish War to the present and of commanding the greatest air forces ever brought together on the planet. I owe the government everything—the government owes me nothing. As a patriotic American citizen, I can stand by no longer and see these disgusting performances by the navy and War Departments, at the expense of the lives of our people and the delusion of the American public.

The bodies of my former companions of the air molder under the soil in America and Asia, Europe and Africa—many, yes, a great many, sent there directly by official stupidity. We all make mistakes, but the criminal mistakes made by armies and navies, whenever they have been allowed to handle aeronautics, show their incompetence. We would not be keeping our trust with our departed comrades were we longer to conceal these facts.

This, then, is what I have to say on this subject and I hope that every American will hear it.

Source: "Col. Mitchell's Statements on Govt. Aviation," *Aviation* 11 (September 14, 1925): 318–320.

Unconnected to Mitchell's pleas for an independent air arm, Congress created the Army Air Corps in 1926, with an authorized strength of over 17,000 officers and men and 1,800 aircraft. Congress also instituted a five-year expansion and modernization program for the Air Corps. This program paid solid dividends, for throughout the 1930s, Army aircraft improved in both type and efficiency; and by the beginning of World War II, the United States indeed had one of the best air forces in the world. Moreover, by creating an Army Air Corps, Congress had removed the stigma of air service in the Army and helped establish a culture open to sound strategic and tactical ideas. By the late 1930s, the Army Air Corps Tactical School thrived at Maxwell Field in Alabama, training a generation of tactical and strategic air thinkers that would have much success in World War II and beyond. It is intriguing that the Army ultimately advocated airpower but did not exercise similar enthusiasm for armor.

Naval aviation did not experience the Army's internal and public travails in seeking a mission for airpower. The Naval Air Service had been created in 1917 and understandably blossomed during the war to over 50,000 officers and men with over 2,000 land- and sea-based aircraft. After the war, the Navy issued a doctrinal statement that called for a naval air service capable of accompanying and protecting the fleet wherever it might be in the world.

Mitchell's highly publicized sinking of the *Ostfriesland* inspired and even converted some senior naval officers, such as Admirals William Fullam and William S. Sims, to the notion that naval airpower had a role in fleet operations. Sims had already studied what might happen if two fleets of equal strength in capital ships faced each other with one side having more aircraft carriers than the other. He concluded that the superiority lay with the fleet that had more aircraft carriers. Air superiority at sea would expose the enemy's fleet to massive air assault and battleship bombardment, the combination of which would be decisive. At a public demonstration of military aircraft in San Diego, Fullam noted how easily ships in San Diego Bay could have been destroyed. With the strong support of the Navy's Chief of Aeronautics, Rear Admiral William A. Moffett, the Navy built its first carrier, the *Langley*, from a converted collier. The carriers *Lexington* and *Saratoga* were both converted heavy cruisers.

The Navy wholeheartedly embraced airpower as a complement to fleet operations. Congress increased budgets for naval aviation, adding more planes to the fleet. New carriers were built. At the Naval Academy at Annapolis, students received aeronautical instruction, including flight and navigation training, and air service billets grew to equal the importance of sea duty. Naval aviators even became celebrities. It had been a Navy pilot—Lieutenant Commander A. C. Read, flying a Curtis airplane—who made the first transatlantic flight (Newfoundland to the Azores to Portugal) in 1919. The polar explorer Commander Richard E. Byrd flew over the North Pole in 1926 and over the South Pole in 1928. Navy flyers routinely won the air races and competitions that were so popular in the 1920s.

◆ FIRST LINE OF DEFENSE: THE FLEET

The Navy remained the first line of defense for American security. The notion of a navy second to none, heralded by the Navy Act of 1916, remained in place after the war. The Naval Act of 1919 was intended to continue the building program of the

FIGURE 11-2   Shacks put up by the Bonus Army on the Anacostia flats, Washington, DC, burning after the battle with the military, 1932.

Source: National Archives and Records Administration

prewar 1916 act. But in the postwar disarmament environment, both the United States and Great Britain, the world's leading naval power, considered the financial cost of expanding their navies, and agreed in principle to some sort of naval limitation to avoid setting off another arms race. Moreover, some naval strategists began to question the Mahanian focus on the battleship fleet as the primary means of naval maneuver. The devastating use of submarines by Germany and the advent of military aviation during the war could indeed ultimately make battleships obsolete. As had been the case in the past, however, overcoming traditional doctrine with new technology proved extremely difficult. Placing all the naval eggs into the battleship basket in the strategic and technological environment of the 1920s could prove to be shortsighted policy.

With the American and British fleets still building new ships, and Japan solidifying its position as a naval power in the western Pacific, representatives from the United States, Great Britain, Japan, France, Italy, China, Belgium, the Netherlands, and Portugal met in Washington in late 1921 to discuss the concept of limiting naval arms and maintaining the balance of power in Asia and the Pacific. It is worth noting that the idea of scrapping American battleships already under construction and limiting future building came from the State Department, not the Navy Department. Nonetheless, the idea of arms reduction struck a popular chord in the postwar world.

Three agreements came from the Washington Naval Conference of 1921–1922. First, Great Britain, the United States, Japan, France, and Italy agreed to a naval limitation treaty based upon a ratio of 5:5:3:1.7:1.7, respectively, for battleships and, interestingly, aircraft carriers. The so-called Five-Power Treaty also called for a ten-year moratorium on building battleships and cruisers. The agreement recognized that Great Britain and the United States had larger geographic and economic security interests and that Japan had significant regional security interests, though Japan protested its second-rate status in the agreement. Great Britain, the United States, France, and Japan also signed the Four-Power Treaty that called for a conference of the signatories to settle any disputes over possessions in the Far East. Finally, the Nine-Power Treaty obligated each signatory to respect the Open Door policy in China in what turned out to be a vain attempt to recognize the territorial integrity and sovereignty of China.

The U.S. Navy came out of the Washington Naval Conference in ship shape, considering that the British navy was aging and the Japanese fleet was still small in comparison. American battleships were newer, and the ones chosen for scrapping probably would not have been completed anyway because of congressional funding cuts. The whole point of the accord was to prevent the United States, Great Britain, and Japan from having the overall naval strength to conduct offensive operations in the Pacific, so long as the treaty was followed and in place. The Washington Naval Conference had a Wilsonian aspect, as the United States used a multilateral agreement in an attempt to collectively prevent another world war—or at least a war in the Pacific, a prospect that many post-Great War strategists feared.

The U.S. Navy in the 1920s, then, was built around the Five-Power Treaty and in fact was under the strength allowed in the agreement by as much as 35 percent. The money saved from the treaty limitations, however, allowed the Navy to greatly improve the quality of its fleet at the expense of quantity. In 1933, the Navy boasted only 100 modern ships and submarines, manned by 90,000 officers and men.

A 1927 conference at Geneva to further limit cruisers and place limitations on destroyers and submarines came and went without agreement. In 1930, however, such limitations were agreed upon at the London Naval Conference. In addition to placing new limitations on cruisers, destroyers, and submarines, the agreement reached in London extended the ten-year capital shipbuilding moratorium to 1936. The great flaw of the London Naval Conference was that in the final agreement, the powers left themselves a dilemma that could result in a new naval arms race. If any one of the signatories believed its security under threat from another nation, it could suspend its part of the agreement and add more ships. But if any one of the signatories pulled out or broke the agreement and built more ships or increased tonnage, the rest of the signatories could do likewise. If one country suspended or broke the agreement, then the whole thing was off.

All of the signatories assuredly violated the spirit of the naval accords, but Japan openly broke the treaties in the early 1930s when it began expanding its sphere of influence in Asia and the Pacific. After 1933, the Washington and London agreements were indeed finished. President Franklin Roosevelt, who had served as Assistant Secretary of the Navy during the Great War, began building a stronger navy as soon as he took office in 1933. As part of the National Industrial Recovery Act of 1933, Roosevelt ordered over $200 million spent on building 32 ships through 1936. In 1934, Congress passed the Vinson-Trammel Act, which authorized the replacement of outdated ships, including 1 carrier, 2 cruisers, 14 destroyers, and 6 submarines in 1935 alone, followed by similar replacements through 1942. It is important to understand, however, that these increases in naval shipbuilding would only bring the U.S. Navy up to its treaty limits, even though the treaties had largely ceased to exist. And with the lead time required to build a capital ship, few of these vessels would actually join the fleet before the 1940s.

◆ THE MARINE CORPS AND THE DEVELOPMENT OF AMPHIBIOUS WARFARE

Despite its expansive role in France as part of the American Expeditionary Force during the Great War, the Marine Corps radically demobilized after the conflict and continued to fine-tune its mission. Between intervention operations and occupation duties in Nicaragua, Hispaniola, and China and developing an amphibious warfare and base seizure doctrine, the effective but still small Marine Corps was quite busy during the 1920s and 1930s.

In 1926, the Marines landed in Nicaragua to end political chaos there and did not withdraw until 1933. Disputes between the Nicaraguan Liberal and Conservative politicos over election results in 1924 and 1925 erupted in violence that approached civil war. Throughout 1926, the American legation in Nicaragua used Marine shore parties to protect American lives and property. By late 1926, however, Liberal forces had killed an American citizen and sacked some American-owned warehouses. The Coolidge administration supported the Conservative government that had been elected previously, and in early 1927 the president ordered a major intervention into Nicaragua. By February, the 5th Marine Regiment was on shore, supported by a six-plane observation squadron. With one battalion defending Managua against Liberal forces, smaller units occupied strategic towns along the railroad from Managua to the coast.

Coolidge sent former Secretary of War Henry Stimson to work out an agreement between the Conservatives and Liberals. With Marine units strategically placed to prevent the two armies from taking advantage of the temporary cease-fire, Stimson brought the two parties together in the so-called Peace of Tipitapa. New elections would be held in 1928, and both armies would disband and be replaced by a new national Nicaraguan army. The 11th Marine Regiment arrived to help implement the peace accord.

Some Liberal bands held out, including one led by Augusto Cesar Sandino, who had refused to sign the Peace of Tipitapa. The Marines were caught in an impossible situation. They had to simultaneously disarm rebel bands, build a new Nicaraguan army, and pacify large regions of the countryside. Sandino presented the most troubling problem. Marine Brigadier General Logan Feland sent a force of over 200 Marines deep into territory controlled by Sandino to bring him in, by force if necessary. Sandino, however, hit first in an attempt to surprise the Marines and their Nicaraguan *Guardia* allies. Fighting in the predawn darkness, the Marines recovered quickly and repulsed several assaults by Sandino's force of over 600 men. With daylight came help from above, as the Marine observation planes strafed and even dive-bombed Sandino's positions. This may have been the first use of dive-bombing techniques in military aviation history. Sandino lost heavily, with perhaps as many as 100 killed to the Marines' 1. This incident led to almost five years of war with the so-called *Sandinistas;* it ended finally with the establishment of the Somoza dictatorship in 1933, which remained in power until the late 1970s.

Marines garrisoned Shanghai and Tientsin in 1927 to protect American lives and property amidst the Chinese civil war and the threat of foreign intervention from Great Britain and Japan. Marine units found themselves caught in a complicated situation between rival warlords and Chinese nationalist forces, not to mention foreign maneuverings, in China. General Smedley Butler returned from a turbulent two-year leave, serving as director of public safety for the city of Philadelphia, to command the 3rd Brigade in China. While the bulk of the Marine force was withdrawn by 1930, the 4th Marine Regiment stayed on station in China under these conditions until the outbreak of World War II.

Occupation duty for the Marines also included extended stints on Hispaniola in the Caribbean. All told, the Marines lost fewer than 100 officers and men from combat action while fulfilling these often thankless duties in the Caribbean, Latin America, and China. Trying to make the most of this difficult duty, the Marines gained valuable experience that would serve them well in the Pacific during World War II. Many Marine officers, such as Captain Lewis ("Chesty") Puller, learned a great deal about small-unit action, guerrilla warfare, and pacification. In 1925 the Marine Corps even published a pacification guide, the *Small Wars Manual*, based mostly upon the writings of Majors Samuel M. Harrington and Harold H. Utley. Occupation and intervention duty, however, convinced many in the State Department and Congress that these duties were the Marine Corps' principal function. As unpopular as pacification became by the 1930s, the Marine Corps needed to distance itself from these missions and refocus on creating an effective advance base force for the Navy.

Wanting to narrowly define its unique mission beyond being an imperial constabulary, the Marine Corps boldly took the position that assault from the sea against fortified positions was possible, if not necessary, especially in a war in the Pacific. Holding and maintaining advance bases for the Navy would be paramount, and only the Marines could do it. Under the direction of Commandant John A. Lejune, the Marines studied amphibious assault, learning from experience and the disastrous British campaign against the Turks at Gallipoli during the Great War. Important doctrinal concepts were worked through by Major Earl H. Ellis, especially in his 1921 paper "Advanced Base Operations in Micronesia," which was to prove prophetic of the course of operations in the Pacific in 1943–44.

This study assumed that with the support of naval gunfire and air strikes against enemy positions, waves of Marines with heavy equipment, such as tanks and artillery, could sweep ashore from landing craft. Landing exercises in the mid-1920s proved problematic since neither the Marines nor the Navy had landing craft or transport to carry the tanks, artillery, and other necessary equipment to successfully assault a beach from the sea. With little funding to put into research and development of landing craft, yet tasked with developing the tactical means to carry out amphibious assaults, the Marines instead spent much of the pre-World War II years developing the theoretical concepts of amphibious assault.

This effort paid off in the early 1930s with the publication of *Tentative Manual for Landing Operations* and the establishment of a Fleet Marine Force within the Pacific Fleet. The *Manual* outlined a doctrine for amphibious assault, including pre-landing bombardment, air support, ship-to-shore communications, and the continual flow of supplies and reinforcements during the landing. By creating a Fleet Marine Force, the Navy and Marines committed themselves to developing landing craft and other support equipment for amphibious operations. It was through this effort that the landing craft familiar in World War II were first developed. The Fleet Marine Force would require a minimum of 25,000 Marines in wartime. In the mid-1930s, the entire Marine Corps numbered just over 16,000 officers and men, making landing exercises recreating wartime conditions all but impossible. Still, when World War II began, the Marine Corps had in place a doctrine to guide island assaults in the Pacific. Amphibious assault had been the butt of many a joke among the Army, which ironically found itself indebted to the Marine Corps as it conducted major amphibious assaults in both the European and Pacific theaters during World War II.

◆ WAR PLANNING

During the interwar years, perhaps the most critical function undertaken by the American military was updating mobilization and war plans. The military and industrial mobilization for both the War with Spain and the Great War had been nothing short of shameful. The color-coded war plans that had been around since the early 1900s were in much need of updating. The advent of militarism in Nazi Germany and Imperial Japan in the 1930s created even more impetus for improving mobilization and war plans.

Creating a mobilization plan that coordinates industrial capacity and manpower needs with security requirements is extremely difficult, particularly when war might suddenly befall a nation rather than allow for a gradual buildup. To overcome this difficulty, the Army-Navy Munitions Board tried to coordinate procurement and supply between the two services. The Army Industrial College studied logistics and industrial mobilization. In addition, the National Defense Act of 1920 made the War Department responsible for mobilization and created a special assistant secretary position in the War Department to carry out this function. Industry representatives and even Bernard Baruch, who had chaired the War Industries Board during the last year of the Great War, assisted the War Department by providing data, ideas on how to transform peacetime production to wartime production, and information on manpower needs that the War Department would have to balance against military manpower needs.

In 1930, the War Department created an Industrial Mobilization Plan to ensure that no disconnect existed between putting the nation's industrial might on a wartime footing and the requirements of the military as it first ensured the security of the United States and then conducted offensive campaigns to defeat the enemy. The first plan found few supporters in Congress, which thought the plan too decentralized and too advantageous to industry considering the economic crisis racking the country at the time. A revision of the Industrial Mobilization Plan greatly increased centralized planning, gave the War Department authority to put price and wage controls in place, and almost gave the military complete control over the American economy during a war. Although the Industrial Mobilization Plan was much needed, its timing could not have been worse. Aside from the Great Depression, the Senate investigation of profiteering by munitions manufacturers during the Great War made suspect any union between the War Department and American industry, war or no war. The War Department and Congress remained more or less at an impasse until the late 1930s, when the threat of another major war became much more real.

Bringing together American industrial potential with its military might in a cohesive plan continued to elude planners. The 1937 Protective Mobilization Plan, the brainchild of Secretary of War Harry Woodring and Army Chief of Staff Malin Craig, made the most progress toward this end. In addition to organizing American industry for war production, the plan realized the interdependence of the military and the American economy during wartime. Militarily, it used the National Guard and the Navy to provide a first line of defense while the Army mobilized to meet wartime needs. This plan included specific details on training camps for individuals and units to avoid repeating the serious shortcomings of the 1917 mobilization. The plan assumed a mobilization similar in size to that of 1917; in fact, the mobilization that began in 1939 was ultimately over twice that size. The plan also assumed that the United States would be at war almost overnight, rather than envisioning the gradual, escalating crisis the United States faced from 1939 to the Japanese attack on Pearl Harbor in December 1941.

The military needed new equipment. The stockpiles left over from the Great War had long been exhausted and worn out. The economic crisis did not help matters, as the federal government had a difficult time finding the money to update weapons, equipment, and facilities. The Army needed modern artillery, mechanized vehicles, antiaircraft weapons, and updated infantry arms. The other problem the Army faced was that it could not predict to Congress what type of future war the United States might face. Another war in Europe would require different force structure and equipment than would a war in the Western Hemisphere—say, against Mexico, or an attack on the Panama Canal. Thus, the Army's safest, though not most effective, policy became to spread funding thinly across several types of units and to opt for increased and better-trained manpower rather than modernization.

A few bright spots surfaced, however, including replacing the 1903 Springfield rifle with the M-1 Garand semiautomatic rifle and adopting modern mortars and howitzers for infantry and artillery use. The horse was finally phased out as a means of transportation, being completely replaced by motorized transport. Smaller, more mobile divisions took the place of the large, cumbersome division model established in 1917. By the mid-1930s, manpower needs were also at least partially addressed, as the Army increased in size to 165,000 enlisted men.

The Air Corps found growth during the mid-1930s as well. In 1931, both the Army and Navy concurred that the Air Corps should be the lead in repelling a sea-borne invasion of the American coast. Long-range patrolling from Hawaii and the Philippines, as well as the Panama Canal Zone, was added to the growing list of Air Corps responsibilities. Mitchell's disciples tactfully argued for an expanded bombing mission for the Air Corps. By 1934, the Air Corps boasted 11 attack squadrons, 20 observation squadrons, 17 attack squadrons, and 27 bomber squadrons. The new emphasis on pursuit and bombing gave rise to new strategic and tactical doctrine, including daylight precision bombing of industrial targets and formation flying of bombers for self-defense against enemy interceptors, which arguably would allow bombers to penetrate deep into enemy territory. New aircraft that utilized mono-wing, closed-canopy designs with more powerful engines made these missions possible. By the eve of World War II, tactical air support for ground operations and strategic bombing, à la Mitchell, had become firmly entrenched in Air Corps doctrine.

The Navy enjoyed some expansion after the collapse of the limitation agreements and increased Japanese naval building. The Naval Act of 1938 authorized a $1.1 billion 10-year building program that would place the Navy at 20 percent over the old tonnage limits and double the size of naval aviation to over 3,000 aircraft. By comparison, in 1939, the Navy had 15 battleships to Japan's 10, five carriers to Japan's six, 36 cruisers to Japan's 37, 104 destroyers to Japan's 122, and 56 submarines to Japan's 62. Japan had 500 carrier-borne aircraft, while the United States maintained over 800. Still, the Navy, especially in the Pacific, was woefully short on adequate forward bases, a problem that was not addressed until war broke out in the Pacific in 1941. Beyond the Western Hemisphere, the fleet would be hamstrung by a tenuous logistical line back to the United States. Manpower also lagged, as the Navy was at only 80 percent strength in 1939 with 125,000 officers and men. While strides had been made to improve naval readiness, the Navy, along with its Marines, remained underprepared for major conflict.

War planning during the 1920s and 1930s focused on possible conflict with Great Britain, which was unlikely, and with the Empire of Japan, which was more likely. War Plan ORANGE supposed a Pacific war against Japan. First proposed in 1903, the joint Army-Navy plan assumed that the conflict would be a naval war in which Japan would quickly overrun American possessions in the Pacific, including Guam and the Philippines. Once fully mobilized, American naval forces and airpower would then retake these possessions and others necessary for basing to finally blockade the Japanese home islands. Exhibiting the influence of Mahan, the plan called for a climactic, decisive fleet action to decide who ruled the waves in the Pacific.

War Plan ORANGE had many defects, but chief among them was advance basing. Securing advance bases in forward areas was a problem, because until the 1930s the Navy and the Marine Corps had little means of doing so. The handful of American possessions in the western Pacific offered basing alternatives, but the Army and Navy could not decide where to establish their primary base. Manila and Guam were the principal candidates. Because the Army and Navy were unable to decide before 1922, the Five-Power Treaty made the decision for them, as the agreement included a provision prohibiting the construction of new bases. Pearl Harbor in Hawaii already existed, and though not yet developed enough to base the Pacific Fleet, it was as far west as the United States could get under the agreements. The Navy argued that it could maintain a supply line from Pearl Harbor to keep the hungry Pacific Fleet operating. Disagreement arose regarding whether to defend Manila. The Army, quite naturally, wanted to hold it until reinforced. The Navy debated whether reinforcements could even get to the Philippines in time to save the Army garrison.

Even Pearl Harbor was not invulnerable to attack. As early as 1919, Admiral William B. Fletcher warned that aircraft from a carrier fleet could easily surprise military bases in Hawaii and probably destroy them before any effective defense could be mounted. In 1921, Major General Charles T. Menoher authored a report claiming that Pearl Harbor and other military installations on the island of Oahu were defenseless unless the United States had air superiority, which in 1921 it did not. During the 1930s, in accordance with War Plan ORANGE revisions and in response to Japanese aggression in China, the Navy deployed the bulk of its fleet to the Pacific, including the new carriers *Lexington* and *Saratoga*.

By 1938, it was apparent that the United States might face a simultaneous two-ocean war. The color-coded war plans designed to fight a single enemy would not suffice if the United States had to fight Germany and Japan at the same time. To plan for this worst-case scenario, the War Department ordered a review of all war plans. The recommendations became known as the RAINBOW war plans. Five scenarios were studied. RAINBOW 1 called for the defense of the entire Western Hemisphere, not just the United States and its own possessions, as had been policy in the past. RAINBOW 2 and RAINBOW 3 supposed that the United States would fight in the Pacific against Japan, basically following war plan ORANGE while its allies, France and Great Britain, fought Germany in Europe. RAINBOW 4 envisioned an Atlantic war fought by the United States without allies. RAINBOW 5 assumed an alliance with France and Great Britain and recommended giving primacy to the Atlantic theater while holding in the Pacific. Assuming the loss of Guam and the Philippines, RAINBOW 5 proposed to defend the Panama Canal Zone, the Atlantic coast, and shipping lanes across the Atlantic as well as conducting land operations in Europe, perhaps even Africa, all while fighting a defensive war in the Pacific. In essence, RAINBOW 5 was a defeat-Germany-first strategy, and it was this plan that ultimately provided the basis for war planning during World War II.

◆ **CONCLUSION**

In August 1928, Secretary of State Frank Kellogg and French Premier Aristide Briand signed a remarkable agreement called the International Treaty for the Renunciation of War. More commonly known as the Kellogg-Briand Pact, the agreement stated that signatories to the treaty would renounce war as a means of achieving national policy objectives. In all, more than sixty countries signed the agreement, including Germany, Japan, and Italy. The only exception for war was self-defense, which was vaguely defined in the treaty. Such a concept, to outlaw war, was certainly understandable in the post-Great War world. It was, however, naïve and idealistic in the worst Wilsonian tradition.

In the 1930s, the world again seemed to tumble without reason toward conflict. The events are well known. Germany rejected the Treaty of Versailles, rearmed, and then undertook an escalating policy of aggression in Europe. Japan disavowed the League of Nations and undertook an overtly aggressive policy of expansion in Asia. Even Italy, a weak and ill-governed state, became enamored with the expansionist urge in its conquest of Ethiopia. Even more troubling was that these states denounced democracy and liberal capitalism for political theories that espoused National Socialism and militaristic nationalism. These nations chose their paths for numerous reasons, including the Treaty of Versailles, the Great Depression, and what they perceived as real threats to their national interests and security. The United States responded with a series of neutrality acts passed by Congress that were designed to prevent the nation from being sucked into war, as it had been in 1917—at least in American political memory.

The United States also responded with better military preparedness than it had during the Great War. As the prospect of war loomed ever greater in the late 1930s, the American military was better prepared for conflict than ever before. Although not perfect by any means, the Army and Navy, as well as American political leaders, had learned valuable lessons from mistakes in the Great War. These mistakes would at the very least be minimized as the United States prepared to enter the greatest, costliest, and perhaps most tragic conflict in human history. Still, as the United States entered World War II, it did so with a military culture built around loyalty and toeing the party line. During the interwar period, the American military had not tolerated mavericks or independent thinkers very well. This rigid attitude toward new and different ideas would have to become more flexible and accommodating in order for the United States to successfully fight the next world war.

Further Reading

Bartlett, Merrill L. *Lejune: A Marine's Life, 1867–1942*. Columbia: University of South Carolina Press, 1991.

Biddle, Wayne. *Barons of the Sky: From Early Flight to Strategic Warfare*. New York: Simon & Schuster, 1991.

Buckley, Thomas H. *The United States and the Washington Conference, 1921–1922*. Knoxville: University of Tennessee Press, 1970.

Hurley, Alfred F. *Billy Mitchell: Crusader for Air Power*. Rev. ed. Bloomington: Indiana University Press, 1975.

Kaufman, Robert G. *Arms Control during the Pre-Nuclear Era: The United States and Naval Limitation between the Two World Wars*. New York: Columbia University Press, 1990.

Melhorn, Charles M. *Two-Block Fox: The Rise of the Aircraft Carrier, 1911–1929*. Annapolis: Naval Institute Press, 1974.

Miller, Edward S. *War Plan Orange: The U.S. Strategy to Defeat Japan, 1897–1945*. Annapolis: Naval Institute Press, 1997.

Murray, Williamson, and Allan R. Millett. *Military Innovation in the Inter-War Period*. Cambridge: Cambridge University Press, 1996.

Musicant, Ivan. *The Banana Wars: A History of United States Military Intervention in Latin America from the Spanish-American War to the Invasion of Panama*. New York: Macmillan, 1990.

Trimble, William F. *Admiral William Moffett: Architect of Naval Aviation*. Washington, D.C.: Smithsonian Institution Press, 1994.

Ulbrich, David J. *Preparing for Victory: Thomas Holcomb and the Making of the Modern Marine Corps, 1936–43*. Annapolis: Naval Institute Press, 2011.

mysearchlab Connections: Sources Online • • • • • • • • •

READ AND REVIEW

Review this chapter by using the study aids and these related documents available on MySearchLab.

Study Plan

Chapter Test

Essay Test

Documents

USMC Small Wars Manual (1940)

Based upon experience in the Caribbean and Central America, the Marines' Small Wars Manual of 1940 was influential in the creation of the new counterinsurgency manual (FM 3-24) published in 2006 as a result of the wars in Iraq and Afghanistan.

Washington Naval Treaty (1922)

This treaty among the United States, Great Britain, France, Italy, and Japan limited naval assets and hoped to prevent war in the Pacific.

Veterans' March to Washington (1932)

This broadside announces the Bonus Army gathering in Washington, D.C., calling the "rank and file" of veterans of the Great War, regardless of race, to demand early payment of their "bonus."

RESEARCH AND EXPLORE

Explore the following review questions using the research tools available on www.mysearchlab.com.

1. What impact did the Great War have on the U.S. military?
2. How did Americans perceive the emerging strategic threats of the 1930s?
3. What were the major limiting factors on greater U.S. preparedness before 1941?

A Second Great War

1944	Invasion of New Guinea
	Invasion of Saipan
	Operation OVERLORD—Invasion of Normandy
	Marianas "Turkey Shoot"
	Invasion of Guam
	Liberation of Paris
	Operation MARKET GARDEN—Airborne assault on Holland
	Battle of Leyte Gulf
	Battle of the Bulge
1945	Allied bombing of Dresden
	Invasion of Iwo Jima
	Invasion of Okinawa
	Liberation of Philippines
	Germany surrenders
	Atomic bombs dropped on Hiroshima and Nagasaki
	Japan surrenders

◆ INTRODUCTION

With the Spanish-American War, the United States began to emerge as a world power. Yet, even after the Great War, American military power was potential rather than realized. By 1945, however, the United States had emerged as the leader of the non-Communist world and faced only one rival, the Soviet Union, in the competition for world dominance.

World War II was the greatest war in human history. Fought on a truly global scale, it involved the creation of a great coalition to defeat and destroy powerful opponents, some of whom personified evil in its purest form. The physical destruction was exceeded only by the human toll. Unlike the Great War of 1914–1918, in which the majority of casualties were sustained by the armed forces of the various combatant nations, in World War II civilian deaths eclipsed military ones, with millions of civilians killed as a result of purposeful attempts to wipe out whole races or classes of people. Nonetheless, World War II is remembered, at least in part, as the "good war."

World War I had not resolved the "German problem" in central Europe, but had merely checked German power while creating the basis for powerful new grievances among the German people. The Russian revolution and the triumph of Bolshevism, the growth and success of Italian Fascism in the 1920s, and the aggressive expansionist policies pursued by the Japanese from 1931, initially against China, were all legacies of the Great War; all of these contributed to the outbreak of a new world war in 1939, and helped to determine the course and, to some extent, the outcome of that war.

◆ PREPARING FOR WAR

To a degree, the United States contributed to the deteriorating international situation that developed during the interwar period. Congressional rejection of the League of Nations and a strong resurgence of the isolationist strand in American popular attitudes made it difficult for the Roosevelt administration to support Britain and the first anti-Axis coalition between 1939–1941. Moreover, the likely German dominance of the European continent further increased American reluctance to get involved in events there. Passage of the Neutrality Acts in the late 1930s severely restricted American support to all of the belligerents, regardless of whether they were democracies or dictatorships. The United States seemed committed to preventing the mistakes that led it into World War I.

After the German invasion of Poland in September 1939, American policy continued to focus on the defense of the Western Hemisphere—essentially the continental United States and the seaward approaches from the Pacific and Atlantic oceans and the Caribbean. Not until the middle of 1940—with the French surrender, Germany triumphant, the Soviet Union neutralized through a nonaggression pact signed with Germany, and Britain and its empire left alone to face the Axis—was there significant change in American policy. Even then, however, the Roosevelt administration was constrained by isolationist sentiment among the public and in Congress; in the second half of that year, however, its policy began to tip decisively toward aiding Britain in its struggle for national survival. Assistance arrived via a "bases for destroyers" agreement through which the United States transferred fifty elderly destroyers to the British in exchange for basing rights in British territory in the Western Hemisphere.

Roosevelt also moved to improve military preparedness. The fleet doubled in size, including authorization for 11 additional aircraft carriers, and the Army Air Corps began a major expansion to nearly 8,000 combat aircraft of all types. Neither of these developments made an immediate impact, and most of the new warships only came on line in 1943, but these moves laid the foundation of a readiness program that stood the armed forces in good stead once the United States actually entered the war.

The Army underwent the biggest changes. In June 1940, the National Guard was federalized, while the passage of the Selective Service and Training Act in September brought more than half a million draftees into the ranks. In the short term, rapid expansion actually reduced the Army's capabilities because large numbers of soldiers and officers were diverted to training and administrative duties. Despite the growing pains, by mid-1941 the Army could field 1.2 million men. In September, the Army put the finishing touches to its Victory Program plan for the expansion and organization of the ground forces: a ground army of 213 divisions and an air corps (soon to be re-designated the U.S. Army Air Forces) of 195 air groups. Almost half the Army was tested in a major exercise in Louisiana in the same month, with rising officers such as George Patton, Dwight Eisenhower, Walter Krueger, and Mark Clark playing key roles in planning and executing the exercises.

Lend-Lease was the final major development in American policy before the United States formally entered the war. Announced in March 1941, the program supported the British war effort by giving London wide-ranging access to American war industry without requiring Great Britain to pay from its rapidly diminishing stock of dollars. Although there were repayment provisions in the legislation, and while Lend-Lease was absolutely vital for Great Britain's war effort, the program ultimately beggared the British economy. In May, its provisions were extended to the Nationalist Chinese and subsequently to the Soviets, the Free French, and a range of other Allied combatants.

By late 1941, the United States had made considerable advances in preparing for war; even so, it was not at all clear on what basis the country would enter the conflict. Roosevelt faced complex strategic choices. There was growing concern about Japanese intentions in the Far East, despite the adoption of a "Germany First" strategy that assumed a German victory over Britain would pose greater challenges for the United States than would short-term Japanese gains in the Pacific. The surprise Japanese attack on Pearl Harbor on the morning of December 7, 1941, was not the immediate answer to Roosevelt's strategic dilemma; although it pitched the country into the war, it mobilized outraged American opinion against Japan, not Germany. Roosevelt swiftly declared war on Japan on December 8. Within two days, Hitler answered with an act of extraordinary strategic folly, declaring war on the United States in an entirely needless and unprovoked manner that now allowed American resources to be pitched into the conflict alongside the British and Soviets.

The most significant strategic decision concerned the priority that the United States would give to the various combat theaters. American planners recognized that if the Germans defeated Britain, the emerging Allied cause might not prevail; but if Britain could be sustained, they were unlikely to lose however difficult the fight. British and American planners had worked out the elements of the Germany First strategy in the first months of 1941, while the United States was still out of the war. This approach was further reflected in the final RAINBOW plan. The Washington Conference, which convened shortly after Pearl Harbor in December 1941–January 1942, confirmed these decisions and laid out the essentials of Anglo-American strategy for the rest of the war.

The American war was fought in three main theaters: North Africa and the Mediterranean, the Pacific, and, after June, 1944, Northwest Europe. The wars against Germany and Japan were not coordinated efforts in any but the most general sense and competed for priority at different stages of the war, especially for essential equipment like airplanes and landing craft.

◆ THE WAR IN THE PACIFIC

Relations between the United States and Japan had deteriorated steadily after the mid-1930s, largely over Japanese actions in China and the retaliatory sanctions imposed by the United States on oil imported into Japan. The Japanese advance into Southeast Asia at the end of 1941 was driven by a need to secure resources, specifically strategic materials like oil, rubber, and tin to fuel Japanese industry and maintain the armed forces. Dutch and British colonies of the East Indies (now Indonesia) and Malaya (now Malaysia) had the richest supply of these resources in the Pacific, and the attacks upon the American Pacific Fleet at Pearl Harbor and American and Filipino forces in the Philippines were intended to preempt American ability to interfere in Japanese ambitions.

Each attack was only partially successful. The American Pacific Fleet was badly damaged by the Japanese, but the vital aircraft carriers were at sea and untouched, and thus still a serious threat to Japan's plans. Although American and Filipino forces held out on Corregidor for six months—far longer than the Japanese anticipated—the conquest of the rest of Southeast Asia was completed in just three months, well in advance of Japanese planning assumptions. The force deployed by the Japanese was far smaller than those it faced, a testimony to the advantage of surprise, enhanced combat capability derived from the war in China, and the arrogance and overconfidence of the British and Americans.

The early months of the Pacific War were a disaster for the Allies everywhere. Japan occupied Southeast Asia, overran Burma, threatened the British position in India, appeared to have isolated Australia and allied positions in the South Pacific, and continued to wage a savage war in China. For the time being, therefore, the Japanese enjoyed the strategic initiative, but their advantages in the longer term were more apparent than real. Japanese industrial capacity could not hope to match that of the United States, and in shipping and aviation alone American building programs dwarfed Japan's, readily replacing the losses sustained in the first months of the war and then overwhelming the Japanese forces with material. Throughout the war, Japan maintained large forces in China, Manchuria and Korea, and the Japanese home islands, and as the American submarine campaign gained in intensity and paralyzed and then gradually destroyed the Japanese merchant marine capability, the forces scattered throughout Asia and the Pacific were increasingly isolated and rendered strategically immobile.

Rivalry within the Japanese high command produced failures of coordination between the army and navy, while Japanese strategy always operated from flawed assumptions and unrealistic expectations. Their advantages were further negated by the American ability to decipher and analyze key communications codes and effectively utilize the resulting intelligence. Some of these factors were evident by mid-1942. The failure to sink the American carriers at Pearl Harbor enabled the United States to stage the dramatic, if strategically irrelevant, air raid on Tokyo by carrier-based B-25 bombers in April (the "Doolittle raid"), while the involvement of two American carriers in the Battle of the Coral Sea in May prevented Japanese attempts to cut sea lines of communication with Australia. The more decisive Battle of Midway in June, prompted by intelligence intercepts, resulted in heavy losses to the Japanese of planes and aircrew as well as a carrier—losses that they were increasingly unable to replace.

The war in the Pacific remained overwhelmingly an American war, despite the presence and roles of other principal allies such as the British, Chinese, and Australians. The United States enjoyed little real influence with the Chinese despite heavily underwriting aspects of the war effort, and the Chinese military and political levels were corrupt and often incompetent, although there were exceptions. The British dominated Southeast Asia Command and the conduct of the war in Burma as well as the defense of India. Only in the Southwest Pacific, under General Douglas MacArthur, and in the Pacific Ocean area, under Admiral Chester Nimitz, did significant non-American forces from Australia and New Zealand make effective contributions to the anti-Japanese struggle. Even then, the command arrangements remained essentially American, and the strategy for the war was determined in Washington and London through the Combined Chiefs of Staff.

MacArthur's theater was dominated by the U.S. Army and involved a series of advances and amphibious assaults northward through Papua New Guinea to the Philippines, utilizing American airpower and American and Australian ground forces. The Pacific theater was dominated by the Navy and the Marines, and in conformity

FIGURE 12-1   World War II in the Pacific.

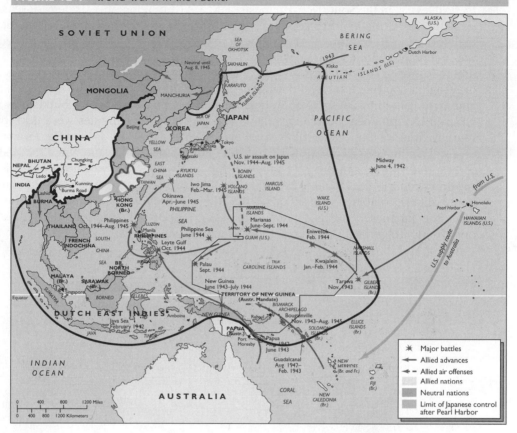

with the prewar ORANGE plans for war with Japan, it saw American forces advance westward across the Pacific in a series of surface battles and amphibious advances dominated by carrier aviation. Both were supported by the offensive anti-shipping campaign successfully waged by American submarines operating from bases across the Pacific.

The weakness in the Japanese position was demonstrated in the second half of 1942 and early 1943 in the simultaneous campaigns in the Solomons and Papua. The terrain in Papua dictated a grim, low-level infantry war, with the Japanese suffering 90 percent losses by the time the Australians retook Papua at the beginning of 1943. Although it involved sustained ground combat as well, the fighting in the Solomons was dominated by air and naval engagements; and in this area American forces gradually exerted dominance over the previously unstoppable Japanese, who suffered heavy losses in aircraft, aircrew, and surface ships. The key Japanese weakness, however, was logistic: They were unable to mount and sustain two campaigns in the South Pacific simultaneously, while the severe losses suffered through defeat in detail in these campaigns further reduced their combat power and effectiveness.

American forces refined and developed their thinking at both the strategic and tactical levels. In the Southwest Pacific area, MacArthur adopted a strategy of selected advances, isolating and bypassing the large Japanese forces based at Rabaul, clearing New Guinea, and forcing the Japanese to adopt a new defensive line centered on the Philippines and the Marianas in the central Pacific. The Marines and naval forces under Nimitz gradually mastered the techniques of large-scale amphibious assault, drawing on doctrine fashioned during the interwar period and refining it through trial and error. Casualties in early operations such as Tarawa were heavy, but as new and specialized equipment became available and tactics and techniques were developed to utilize it more effectively, the balance again swung decisively against the Japanese.

MacArthur's objective now became the Philippines, while the Navy focused on seizing the Marianas in order to establish forward bases from which to mount long-range bombing of the Japanese home islands. This two-prong approach to the Japanese home islands, combined with actions in the Aleutian Islands, China, and Burma, would force the Japanese to spread their forces even more thinly and give the Allies the opportunity to gradually tighten a noose around Japan.

FIGURE 12-2 Marine aiming at a Japanese sniper on Okinawa, June 22, 1945.

Source: National Archives and Records Administration.

In contrast with interwar planning and war gaming, the United States thus mounted a dual drive on Japan that culminated in 1944 in a series of stunning advances and crippling defeats for the Japanese. As well as deploying vast air, naval, and ground forces, the United States had created a robust logistic system that enabled it to mount more or less continuous operations, denying the enemy any respite. The Japanese were caught in an increasingly vicious spiral, losing experienced personnel (especially pilots) and equipment that they could not replace, and were forced to field inadequately trained and inexperienced men who then suffered even heavier losses.

During the Battle of the Philippine Sea in June 1944, Nimitz's forces inflicted further devastating losses, affecting Japan's ability to wage aero-naval warfare. In the Great Marianas Turkey Shoot, as it was quickly dubbed, Japanese losses included 3 aircraft carriers and 480 aircraft, against American losses of just 130 aircraft and only 76 aircrew. The Japanese defensive position was coming unhinged, and the further American victory at the Battle of Leyte Gulf in October, the only battleship-type fleet engagement of the Pacific War, ensured the success of MacArthur's landings in the central Philippines. The battle also saw the final destruction of what was left of the Imperial Japanese Navy, ensuring as well that those Japanese ground forces still deployed throughout the Pacific were now effectively isolated from reinforcement and further assistance.

Increasingly desperate, the Japanese introduced tactical changes in an attempt to counter the overwhelming superiority now enjoyed by American forces. On the ground, defending forces henceforth allowed the Americans to land, then fought them to the death from well-constructed and positioned defenses—bunkers and natural cave systems. The Japanese were all but annihilated in such battles, but American casualties increased sharply as well. First encountered at Peleliu in September 1944, these tactics were to culminate in the costly and horrendous fighting for Iwo Jima (February–March 1945) and Okinawa (April–June 1945) as the Allies drew ever closer to the sacred soil of Japan itself. In the air, and to some extent at sea, the enemy introduced kamikaze units dedicated to inflicting losses through suicidal attacks, especially against American ships. Making their first appearance in October 1944, the kamikaze were a further measure of the degradation in quality of the Japanese forces. Pilots now lacked the training and experience to enable them to meet their American counterparts in aerial combat and could inflict losses only through their own intentional deaths.

American advances and capture of territory in the western Pacific provided bases for the Army Air Force to begin the devastation of the Japanese homeland, through both day and night bombing campaigns. The raids on Tokyo in March killed 84,000 people and left large parts of the capital destroyed through the use of incendiary munitions, and by June most of Japan's major urban centers were destroyed; 900,000 civilians were killed and as much as 80 percent of the infrastructure was wiped out. The Japanese government, however, continued to believe that a defense of the home islands against amphibious assault was both sustainable and capable of bringing victory—or, if not, of ensuring the destruction of Japan and thus avoiding the disgrace of defeat and surrender. American casualties incurred on Okinawa, where roughly 12,000 had been killed and well over 30,000 wounded, together with the knowledge that sizeable forces in southern Japan were planning for a determined last stand—with the implications this carried for the civilian population as well—helped persuade

President Truman and his advisors to use the atomic bomb as a means of forcing the enemy's surrender. The bombing of Hiroshima on August 6 and Nagasaki on August 9 prompted the Japanese emperor on August 10 to order the government and armed forces to surrender.

◆ MEDITERRANEAN THEATER AND THE RISE OF AMERICAN LEADERSHIP

The war in the Mediterranean was the longest single continuous campaign of the war, beginning in 1940 following Italy's declaration of war in June and ending only with the surrender of German and remnant Fascist forces in northern Italy in May 1945. As in the Pacific and Southeast Asia, fighting in the Mediterranean had a colonial warfare dimension, since Italy, Great Britain, and France all held colonies and/or protectorates in North Africa and the Middle East. This complicated matters for American leaders, who did not share the sense of priority accorded the theater by their British ally in particular. Roosevelt and Churchill had agreed to place the untried but highly respected General Dwight Eisenhower in overall command of Allied forces in North Africa. Eisenhower would later be named Supreme Allied Commander of Allied Expeditionary Forces in Europe.

By the time American forces came into action in North Africa in November 1942, the seesaw of advantage in the North African campaign had resolved itself largely in favor of the Allies, although there was still plenty of hard fighting to be done before North Africa was finally cleared of German and Italian forces. The great virtue of American involvement in this phase was the opportunity it provided to "blood" units and formations; expose weaknesses in equipment, doctrine, and training; and weed out incompetent combat leaders, especially more senior ones, who were inadequate to the stresses and challenges of modern industrial warfare.

The first taste of the war in Europe for the United States came as part of an Anglo-American invasion of Morocco against the Vichy French, called Operation TORCH, which opened a second front to the rear of the retreating Axis forces being driven across North Africa by the British 8th Army, based in Egypt. The political situation in the French colonies was very complex, and the Allies received assistance from supporters of the Free French while nonetheless negotiating an end to the fighting with Vichy authorities. The Germans immediately occupied the southern, Vichy-controlled part of France in response and stalled the American attempt to move rapidly into Tunisia.

The early encounters with the German Wehrmacht—the best-known action being at Kasserine Pass—saw inexperienced and outclassed American units bested and quickly disheartened by better-trained, better-led, and better-equipped German opponents. At this early stage of the American war, the difference between amateurs and deeply seasoned professionals was readily apparent. There were some high-level firings, including the commander of the American II Corps General Lloyd Fredendhall, to make room for a new wave of younger, tougher, and better-prepared leaders, including General George S. Patton and his new deputy corps commander, General Omar Bradley.

American dominance of the Anglo-American alliance was less obvious at this stage, with the more experienced British winning many of the early arguments on [the Combined Chiefs of Staff over strategy and future direction of the Allied war effort. A good example of this situation was the continuation and expansion of the war in the Mediterranean, decided at a[conference in Casablanca in January 1943. At the conference, the allies approved an invasion of Sicily with the aim of knocking Italy out of the war.] (Here Churchill famously, and mistakenly, claimed that Italy constituted the "soft underbelly of Europe.") This plan in turn was later extended to include an invasion of mainland Italy itself. The argument was partly about reasserting British and, to a lesser extent, French supremacy in the Mediterranean and safeguarding strategic routes to India through the Suez Canal.]But, it also reflected British hesitancy over American advocacy of a[cross-channel invasion of France in 1943, which the British judged (probably correctly) to be premature.] The surrender of a quarter of a million German and Axis troops in Tunisia in May 1943 meant that resources deployed in North Africa had to be used somewhere, and a further campaign in the Mediterranean seemed the most attractive of the limited options available.]

[The Sicilian campaign fought in July–August 1943 returned mixed results, as America's early wartime campaigns tended to do. The enormous number of prisoners taken in Tunisia was not replicated in Sicily, with the modest force of German defenders eventually passing easily across the Straits of Messina to mainland Italy after a vigorous and protracted defense of the island. While Operation HUSKY also proved to be a useful test for training, equipment, and doctrine, the test results were by no means encouraging, and the initial landings were marked by confusion and muddle. The least impressive aspect of the campaign, however, was at the highest levels of command and strategic direction. The commanders of the American 7th and British 8th Armies—Patton and General Bernard Law Montgomery, respectively—did not care for each other, disagreeing on the best way to quickly roll up the enemy, and offering little active support to each other. Their superiors, Eisenhower and General Sir Harold Alexander, allowed them to get away with it, reflecting the still nascent nature of inter-Allied relations at this stage, even at senior levels and between individuals who got along well personally.]

[The Sicilian campaign was followed by the invasion of mainland Italy, again because the forces were in place and there was not a convincing alternative. Moreover, the Allies misread the intensely complex internal political situation. Mussolini was removed from power as a consequence of the invasion of Sicily, but this simply prompted the Germans to move forces rapidly southward to counteract or neutralize defeatism in the Italian armed forces and deny the Allies any easy victories. The Italian surrender in September thus represented no advantage at all to the Allies while removing a number of constraints on the Germans. The Italian terrain proved a gift for the defenders, who demonstrated all their usual tenacity, defensive, and engineering skill to strongly contest every mile of the Allies' northward advance. By the winter of 1943, the Allied armies were stuck in front of the enemy's Gustav Line defenses, 100 miles from Rome, and faced strong natural defenses with which to contend, such as the Rapido River and the heights of Monte Cassino.]

Until its last days, the campaign in Italy offered the Allies a series of bloody frustrations. The attempted amphibious landing at Anzio in January 1944 nearly proved a disaster. Rather than circumventing the German defenses and taking the pressure off the Allied advance, the landing forced the commander of the American 5th Army, General Mark Clark, to renew the offensive to save the beachhead. Repeated attempts to take the German defenses at the foot of Monte Cassino prompted the decision to level the monastery on its heights with heavy bombing; the Germans at first had respected the monastery's neutrality as a religious house, but then moved into the ruins and created formidable defenses that had to be captured, laboriously and bloodily, by Allied infantrymen.

Rome finally fell on June 4, 1944, after being declared an open city and with a calculated political gesture on Clark's part that was designed both to snub the British and gain the publicity in advance of the D-Day landings in Normandy two days later. Many of the soldiers who fought there believed that Italy was a forgotten or neglected theater after the main focus switched to Northwest Europe, and there were certainly grounds for thinking this. Following the capture of Rome, the Germans reestablished their defenses, formidable as always, along the Gothic Line. The American high command, increasingly dubious about the worth of the Italian campaign at all, began to shut down its commitment there.

Seeking at last to open a second front through an invasion of southern France, Operation ANVIL/DRAGOON withdrew six American and French divisions from the Italian campaign to be fed into a new advance through the Rhone Valley. There, they were intended to link up with the armies moving eastward across northern France toward Germany. By September, the Gothic Line had been breached in places; but attention had now moved decisively from the Italian fighting, rendered truly a sideshow, especially from the American point of view. The campaign petered out in the final days of the war and amidst further political complexity, this time represented by surrender negotiations with rogue elements in the German command and uneasy standoffs with Tito's Yugoslavian communist partisan forces moving into northern Adriatic Italy and bumping against Allied units. The American 5th Army suffered nearly 200,000 casualties in the course of the campaign. Its contribution to final Allied victory against Germany remains controversial.

◆ NORTHWEST EUROPE (1944–1945)

The American high command had wanted to launch an invasion of Northwest Europe and take the fight to the Nazis in 1942, within months of entering the war. The real war dictated otherwise, a conclusion reinforced by the disastrous British/Canadian amphibious raid at Dieppe that same year. The second-front debate percolated along as part of the Anglo-American strategic dialogue thereafter, with the addition of regular demands from the Soviets to help relieve pressure on the Eastern Front in some of the direst periods of the war in the East. As suggested already, the Americans increasingly regarded British enthusiasm for extending the Mediterranean campaign as a means of avoiding the hard fighting that an invasion of France would entail, while the British feared the consequences of an abortive invasion on a multidivisional scale before the training, technology, and doctrine were sufficiently developed to deal with the increasingly daunting German defenses in France.

FIGURE 12-3   World War II in Europe.

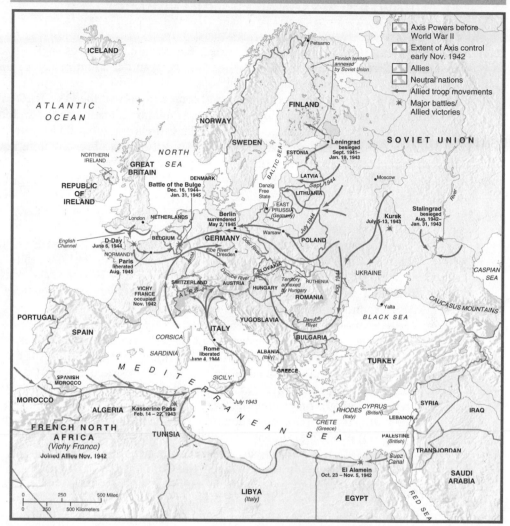

[The period in which Operation OVERLORD developed emphasized the shift in the balance in the Western alliance between the British and the Americans to the latter's advantage. Resources, including divisions and equipment such as landing craft, ships, and aircraft, were earmarked for Normandy at the expense of both the Mediterranean campaign and the Pacific, while after D-Day the American high command strongly argued for the "second front to the second front" through southern France to assist the main advance and the breakout of Allied forces. The delay in launching the invasion also enabled the Allies to marshal the enormous logistic effort needed to help its success, as well as giving them time to solve the problems presented by so vast an undertaking and to deceive the Germans as to their intentions.]

EISENHOWER'S PERSONAL MEMORANDUM OF JUNE 3, 1944

As Supreme Allied Commander of Allied Expeditionary Forces in Europe, Eisenhower had full responsibility for the planning and conduct of Operation OVERLORD, the most ambitious amphibious invasion in history to that point. On June 3, Eisenhower outlined his concerns and confidence about the OVERLORD plan. Eisenhower's difficult task included not only military planning and coordination but also navigating the delicate waters of the various and often divisive political interests of Great Britain, the United States, and the Free French. Note how this memorandum addresses both military and political matters.

3 June 1944
Memorandum

1. Subjects:
    a. Proper coordination with the French
    b. Weather
    c. Beach and undersea obstacles
    d. Future success of the air in breaking up effectiveness of hostile ground units
    e. Future organization
2. The matter of coordination with the French has been highly complicated because of lack of crystallization in ideas involving both the political and military fields. Specifically, the president desires that co-ordination be effected with the French on the basis of dealing with any group or groups that can effectively fight the Germans. His Directive apparently recognizes the influence of the National Committee of Liberation in France but he is unwilling to promise an exclusive dealing with the group since that, he apparently believes, would be tantamount to recognizing the Committee as a provisional government of France, set up from the outside.

    We have our direct means of communication with the Resistance Groups of France but all our information leads us to believe that the only authority these Resistance Groups desire to recognize is that of DeGaulle and his Committee. However, since DeGaulle is apparently willing to cooperate only on the basis of our dealing with him exclusively, the whole thing falls into a rather sorry mess. DeGaulle is, of course, now controlling the only French military forces that can take part in this operation. Consequently, from the purely military viewpoint we must, at least until the time that other French forces might conceivably be organized completely independent of his military and political matters go hand in hand and will not cooperate militarily unless political recognition of some kind is accorded him. We do not seem to be able, in advance of D-day, to straighten the matter at all. I have just learned that DeGaulle has failed to accept the Prime Minister's invitation to come to England, saying that he would make his decision this afternoon.

The rapid sorting out of all the conflicting ideas is quite necessary if we are to secure the maximum help from the French both inside and outside the country.

3. The weather in this country is practically unpredictable. For some days our experts have been meeting almost hourly and I have been holding Commander-in-Chief meetings once or twice a day to consider the reports and tentative predictions. While at this moment, the morning of June 3rd, it appears that the weather will not be so bad as to preclude landings and will possibly even permit reasonably effective gunfire support from the Navy, the picture from the air viewpoint is not so good.

Probably no one that does not have to bear the specific and direct responsibility of making the final decision as to what to do, can understand the intensity of these burdens. The Supreme Commander, much more than any of his subordinates, is kept informed of the political issues involved, particularly the anticipated effect of delay upon the Russians. He likewise is in close touch with all the advice from his military subordinates and must face the issue even when technical advice as to weather is not unanimous from the several experts. Success or failure might easily hinge upon the effectiveness, for example, of airborne operations. If the weather is suitable for everything else, but unsuitable for airborne operations, the question becomes whether to risk the airborne movement anyway or to defer the whole affair in the hopes of getting weather that is a bit better. My tentative thought is that the desirability for getting started on the next favorable tide is so great and the uncertainty of the weather is such that we could never anticipate really perfect weather coincident with proper tidal conditions, that we must go unless there is a real and very serious deterioration in the weather.

4. Since last February the enemy has been consistently busy in placing obstacles of various types on all European beaches suitable for landing operations. Most of these are also mined. Under ordinary circumstances of land attack these would not be particularly serious but because they must be handled quickly and effectively before the major portion of our troops can begin unloading, they present a hazard that is a very considerable one. It is because of their existence that we must land earlier on the tide than we had originally intended. This gives us a chance to go after them while they are still on dry land because if their bases were under water they would be practically impossible to handle. If our gun support of the operation and the DD tanks during this period are both highly effective, we should be all right.

The under-water obstacles, that is, the sea mines, force us to sweep every foot of water over which we operate and this adds immeasurably to the difficulties in restricted waters in which we are operating. The combination of under-sea and beach obstacles is serious but we believe we have it whipped.

5. Because the enemy in great strength is occupying a country that is interlaced with [a] fine communication system, our attack can be looked upon as reasonable only if our tremendous air force is able to impede his concentrations against us and to help destroy the effectiveness of any of his counter attacks. Weather again comes into this problem, because it is my own belief that with reasonably good weather during the first two or three weeks of the operation, our air superiority and domination will see us through to success.

6. Lately we have been studying earnestly the question of future organization, assuming that we have established a beachhead so firmly that we no longer fear being kicked into the sea. All British land forces will quickly be in and I personally doubt that the British will be able to maintain more than fifteen or sixteen Divisions in active warfare in this theater. This means that the bulk of the land forces must come from the United States. Logically, also, there should come about eventually the desirability of undertaking offensive operations in fairly distinct zones of advance, with each of the ground groupments supported by its own distinct air force at least so far as fighter and fighter bombers are concerned. When this comes about every factor of simplicity in organization, national pride, efficiency in administration, etc., indicates the further desirability of having two principal ground commanders, one operating to the Northeast, one to the East. (I believe, however, that the British formation will probably have to be reinforced by an American Army or at least a Corps.) Pending this particular development it will still be necessary to begin the establishment in Europe of an American Army Group Headquarters. I plan to have Bradley command this new headquarters during the transition period, that is, until we are completely established and ready to undertake operations in distinct zones of advance. He will operate during the transition period under Montgomery. Finally, Bradley and Montgomery will report directly to me.

At that time a certain portion of the so-called "tactical" air force, that is, medium bombers and possibly some of the long range fighters, will remain under the C-in-C A.E.F. This portion of the tactical air force will be available to assist either Army Group.

I have already issued a tentative directive to plan for future organization of the ground and air forces along the lines indicated in this paragraph.

Source: Dwight D. Eisenhower Library and Museum.

The initial landings on June 6 were a success, although for the Americans landing at Omaha Beach a very costly one. Thereafter, things developed less smoothly. The original intention was to take the city of Caen, with its transportation hub, and break out into the open country beyond, but the British moved cautiously and the opportunity was lost. Instead of an early campaign of rapid movement, the Normandy fighting quickly degenerated into a brutal contest for small gains in ground through the difficult *bocage* country, small fields lined with thickly wooded hedgerows, that provided ideal defensive terrain for the Germans, who exploited it effortlessly. Within weeks, the Allies had landed more than a million men in northwestern France and the invasion was an accomplished fact. Nonetheless, it took a further assault, called Operation COBRA, by Bradley's 12th Army Group at the end of July to crack open the weakening German defenses and begin a rapid and unstoppable advance, by Patton's 3rd Army, across France toward Paris and beyond. Tactical airpower and heavy "strategic" bombers, deployed in a tactical role, were central to American success.

Strategic bombing had in fact been the major effort against German-occupied Europe since the beginning of the war. The British had launched bombing raids on targets in Germany and Western Europe because air assault was the only means of attacking the enemy after Germany had conquered Europe, but the early results were limited

FIGURE 12-4   American assault troops of the 16th Infantry Regiment, injured while storming Omaha Beach, wait by the Chalk Cliffs for evacuation to a field hospital for further medical treatment. Collville-sur-Mer, Normandy, France, June 6, 1944.

Source: National Archives and Records Administration.

and expensive in aircraft and aircrew losses. The technology of the time was unable to meet the expectations of airpower's decisive potential as identified by interwar theorists and enthusiasts. These losses dictated one of the fundamental characteristics of the bombing offensive waged by the Royal Air Force's Bomber Command—night bombing of area targets, that is, cities. The losses and damage inflicted on Germany's cities and on German civilians led, in turn, to the development of an increasingly sophisticated air defense system, with advances on one side being matched by technological, tactical, and doctrinal developments on the other.

The U.S. Army Air Forces believed in precision daytime bombing on industrial and military targets rather than on civilians in cities. They suffered the same initial loss rates as the Royal Air Force had before it switched to night bombing. In January 1943, Roosevelt, Churchill, and the Combined Chiefs of Staff initiated a Combined Bombing Offensive, designated Operation POINTBLANK, in which the British would bomb at night and the Americans by day with the idea, among others, that such round-the-clock bombing would place the German air defenses and economy under a strain too great to bear.

The Americans also opted to concentrate on the German aircraft industry and the Luftwaffe's airfields in an attempt to further damage their capacity to counter the bomber streams. This had only limited effect, however, and losses continued to be heavy primarily because the bombers attacking beyond the limits of fighter aircraft range were unescorted for the most dangerous part of the raid and were shot down in considerable numbers as a result. German day and night fighter pilots became increasingly skilled in air defense tasks, and new planes, equipment, and techniques were quickly adopted in order to maintain the advantage. Life expectancy among Allied bomber crews resembled that of infantry subalterns on the Western Front in 1916–1917.

The critical factor that turned the tide for the Allies was the development and deployment in increasingly large numbers of fighter aircraft with the range necessary to protect the bombers to the target and back again. New types, modifications of existing types, and the addition of external fuel tanks all played a part in this. Another factor was the creation of the 15th Air Force, based in Italy, to complement the 8th Air Force operating from Britain. The Germans now had to deal with two bomber streams and thus divide their defenses. Although in 1944 Germany produced more aircraft than previously because of changes to the organization of labor within aircraft factories, the enemy lacked sufficient numbers of skilled pilots to man all the aircraft actually available, while increasing pressure on the air defenses produced an upswing in losses that were now almost impossible to recoup.

In advance of D-Day, Allied bomber forces were assigned numerous targets across France in addition to specific targets just behind the intended invasion area in order to deceive the Germans and interfere with their ability to move reinforcements easily. The attendant "transportation plan" was important in degrading Germany's ability to successfully counter the Normandy invasion. By early 1945, Allied bomber forces were actually running out of worthwhile targets to attack.

The rapid advance of the French and American divisions that landed in southern France in August 1944 meant that the Allies quickly formed a continuous front by September, cutting off German forces remaining in southern and western France. Success now hobbled operations, with the logistic system, awesome though it was, unable to sustain multiple armies advancing on multiple fronts simultaneously. The Germans rationalized their forces and defenses along the Franco-German border region (the so-called Siegfried Line), while the Allies were further diverted by Montgomery's quixotic and unsuccessful Operation MARKET GARDEN into Holland to seize crossing points over the Rhine at Arnhem. Faced with manpower difficulties as well as supply problems, Eisenhower gave priority to Montgomery's 21st British Army Group, reinforced it with several American units, and placed operational restrictions on remaining American forces occupied in taking the Siegfried Line to get across the Rhine. The debate at the highest levels over a broad front or narrow front advance was thus resolved more or less in favor of the latter. In doing so Eisenhower was being a good ally, but not necessarily a good strategist.

The fighting in the autumn mud and wet cold was grueling, bitter, and costly as the Germans found new reserves of determination in seeking to deny Allied entry into Germany. Guilty perhaps of an understandable belief in inevitable victory, the Allies failed to see the preparations for a major new offensive in the rugged Ardennes against thinly spread American forces. In what is popularly known as the Battle of the Bulge, the revitalized German forces advanced fifty miles in short order, capturing large numbers of prisoners, a group of whom were murdered at Malmedy.

Although initially successful, the Germans could not in fact sustain their momentum. When the weather cleared and Allied tactical airpower could again be deployed against Germans, the offensive was defeated. American and British armor also played pivotal roles in repulsing the German advance. American losses were heavy, on the order of 100,000 men, while German losses amounted to over 120,000. But the most important consequence was the loss of armor and other heavy equipment that the German war industry could not replace, a weakness that eliminated Germany's ability to mount large-scale sustained operations against the Allied advance.

As German capacity to resist diminished, Allied offensive capacity increased, with simultaneous offensives launched on both the Eastern and Western Fronts in January 1945. Once the German fronts began to crack, the torrent proved unstoppable; and although resistance continued to the bitter end, the end itself was inevitable. Hitler committed suicide at the end of April, with the Soviets already in the streets of central Berlin and American forces invading Austria and Czechoslovakia. The remaining German authorities surrendered their devastated country on May 7.

◆ WOMEN AND MINORITIES IN THE WAR EFFORT

Great wars often produce short-term social changes with long-term implications. World War II provides an excellent example of this process at work, not just in the United States but among many of the other combatant nations as well. This proved especially true in the case of various minorities in the American population in terms of employment, social position, and economic advantage. It also proved true across the population as a whole, of course, with higher wages and increased employment in war industries counteracting the lingering effects of the Depression, but women and minorities also benefited.

Change and opportunity were reflected in two major areas: the civilian economy and the ranks of the armed forces. The expansion in industry and the military quickly soaked up the 7 million unemployed, who in turn were joined by millions more outside the formal workforce. The demands for labor provoked internal migration on a large scale, with black and white Americans moving from the rural south and other agricultural areas to the hubs of manufacturing industry in the Northeast and Midwest. The industrial workforce grew by 10 million workers in the course of the war, while wages increased by 68 percent. The Great Depression of the 1930s essentially vanished. The basis of postwar prosperity thus was laid in wartime prosperity.

The armed forces remained racially segregated throughout the war, but opportunities were still available to women and minorities in a manner and on a scale not previously experienced. Women's auxiliary services had been created during World War I, and were reformed in World War II to utilize skilled female personnel and to free men for the fighting forces, from which women remained barred. Women served overseas in significant numbers, and not only in the nursing services: 333,000 women, out of a total of 16 million, served in uniform across the war, and in late 1945 there were still 266,000 in service. Women were not included in the draft.

The draft was, however, extended to include African-Americans and other racial minorities. Provisions within the Selective Service and Training Act forbade discrimination on racial grounds, but many inside and outside the armed forces resisted attempts to dilute segregation within the military. New black units were created within the Army and the Army Air Forces, with mainly white officers and black enlisted men, just as had been the case in the interwar period. Four fighter squadrons and a bomber group were raised and trained separately, at heavy expense, at Tuskegee, Alabama. The fighter squadrons served with great distinction in the Mediterranean theater, but the bomber group never reached operational status.

Three black Army divisions were also created to absorb the increased number of black infantry, artillery, and tank units: the 2nd Cavalry and the 92nd and 93rd Infantry. The 92nd eventually saw service in Italy, and the 93rd in the Pacific on Bougainville. Some units fought with distinction, others less so—just like the plurality of white units across the army. Soldiers in the combat units were sometimes discriminated against by their own (white) senior command. There was an unofficial policy in the 92nd Division, for example, that no black soldier was to be awarded the Medal of Honor, despite the fact that a number were recommended. Some of these were finally awarded as late as the 1990s. Contemporary racism defined the black experience in World War II as it had in World War I.

Most African-Americans served in quartermaster units within the Services of Supply and in transportation units in Europe and the Pacific. The most famous of these units was the Red Ball Express in Europe, and many of those deployed overseas to Britain or elsewhere in Europe found a refreshing absence of discrimination among the local civilian population, in marked contrast to what they knew back in the United States or within the ranks of the American military.

Two other groups also distinguished themselves in armed service. Navajo soldiers, made famous as the Wind Talkers, were utilized in the Pacific as signalers because their language defied Japanese attempts to interpret it. Japanese-Americans, whether Issei or Nissei, fought in Italy where their 442nd Regiment became the most decorated unit in the U.S. Army. Many of these soldiers left families behind in internment camps in the western United States (not including Hawaii) when Japanese-Americans were forcibly interned after Pearl Harbor.

◆ THE BOMB

The decision to end the Pacific War by dropping atomic bombs on the Japanese cities of Hiroshima and Nagasaki remains one of the most controversial episodes of the war. The event had profound implications for the future of warfare and the use of force in the postwar world. Much about the decision and the reasoning behind it is contested. The Manhattan Project, which secretly built the atomic bombs, represented an unprecedented level of federal support for scientific research, but this did not overshadow the incredible destructive power of these new weapons.

There were serious concerns at the highest political and military levels about the likely cost of actually invading the Japanese home islands in late 1945 and early 1946, as the United States planned to do. Large divisions of regular forces heavily defended the southern part of Japan. Moreover, the Japanese government had made extensive preparations, including massed suicide attacks and the utilization of the civilian population, to repulse an Allied invasion. There can be little doubt that a full-scale assault would have been horribly expensive not merely in American and Allied casualties, but in Japanese ones as well.

Geopolitical considerations also played a part, as Soviet intentions in Manchuria had to be checked. Although the bombs were not dropped simply to send a signal to the Soviets, it is still reasonable to suggest that this was a factor in the decision to utilize these weapons. Nor was the use of the bomb racially motivated, as is sometimes alleged. Many of the scientists who worked on the Manhattan Project were Jewish, and others were refugees from Nazi Germany. Indeed, the bomb was built with its possible use against Germany in mind. The fact is that the successful testing of the device did not occur until July—after Germany's surrender. There were a variety of reasons for using the atomic bomb, and in 1945 scientists and political and military leaders had a less-than-full appreciation of the effects of the weapon, as well as of the moral and other implications of its use.

◆ CONCLUSION

World War II was the greatest and most destructive conflict in history, and one that helped to cement the United States' rise to global dominance. The Allies could not have won the war without the involvement of the United States, and with American involvement they ultimately could not lose it, either. It is important to understand, however, that especially in Europe allied forces played a major role in enemy defeat; the Soviets had many more divisions in the field, fought the majority of the German forces deployed on the continent, and tore the heart out of the German war effort in a series of extensive and very costly offensives. Britain provided significant forces but, more importantly, was the major staging area for the allied return to Western Europe. The United States was much more the driver of the war against Japan, but even here the allied efforts by Australia and China need to be considered.

By taking a leading part in the occupation of Germany and the overwhelming lead in the occupation of Japan, the United States remade those societies along liberal-democratic and capitalist lines, and helped both to create the economic miracles in those countries and to reshape them as participatory democracies and significant allies in the ensuing Cold War with the Soviet Bloc. The seeds of success in the Cold War, ultimately, were sown through the generosity of the Marshall Plan for the reconstruction of defeated enemies and the farsighted decisions by the Truman administration not to repeat the failures that occurred after 1919 and to remain engaged with the rest of the world.

For the American military, World War II was a triumph of mobilization, procurement, leadership, and combat capability. Over 16 million Americans had been equipped, trained, and deployed to fight this war. Over 291,000 of them died in battle, with another 113,000 dead from other causes. Over 670,000 had been wounded. Victory over Germany and Japan, however, did not guarantee a lasting peace. A new and different conflict was brewing even as World War II was still being fought.

Further Reading

Ambrose, Stephen E. *Band of Brothers: E Company, 506th Regiment, 101st Airborne from Normandy to Hitler's Eagle's Nest*. New York: Simon & Schuster, 1992.

Ambrose, Stephen E. *D-Day June 6, 1944: The Climactic Battle of World War II*. New York: Simon & Schuster, 1994.

Atkinson, Rick. *An Army at Dawn: The War in North Africa, 1942–1943*. New York: Henry Holt, 2002.

Castello, John. *The Pacific War, 1941–1945*. New York: William Morrow, 1981.

Chappell, John D. *Before the Bomb: How Americans Approached the Pacific War*. Lexington: University Press of Kentucky, 1996.

Crane, Conrad C. *Bombs, Cities, and Civilians: American Airpower Strategy in World War II*. Lawrence: University Press of Kansas, 1993.

D'Este, Carlo. *Eisenhower: A Soldier's Life*. New York: Owl Books, 2002.

Doubler, Michael D. *Closing with the Enemy: How GIs Fought the War in Europe, 1944–1945*. Lawrence: University Press of Kansas, 1994.

Hasegawa, Tsuyoshi. *Racing the Enemy: Stalin, Truman, and the Surrender of Japan*. Cambridge: Harvard University Press, 2005.

James, D. Clayton. *A Time for Giants: The Politics of the American High Command in World War II*. New York: Franklin Watts, 1987.

Klinkowitz, Jerome. *Pacific Skies: American Flyers in World War II*. Jackson: University Press of Mississippi, 2004.

Koistinen, Paul A. C. *Arsenal of World War II: The Political Economy of American Warfare 1940–1945*. Lawrence: University Press of Kansas, 2004.

Larrabee, Eric. *Commander in Chief Franklin Delano Roosevelt, His Lieutenants and their War*. New York: Harper and Row, 1987.

Leary, William M. *We Shall Return: MacArthur's Commanders and the Defeat of Japan, 1942–1945*. Lexington: University Press of Kentucky, 2004.

Linderman, Gerald F. *The World within War: America's Combat Experience in World War II*. New York: Free Press, 1997.

Mansoor, Peter R. *The GI Offensive in Europe: The Triumph of American Infantry Divisions, 1941–1945*. Lawrence: University Press of Kansas, 1999.

Murray, Williamson, and Allan R. Millett, eds. *A War to be Won: Fighting the Second World War*. Cambridge: Harvard University Press, 2001.

O'Neill, William L. *A Democracy at War: America's Fight at Home and Abroad in World War II*. Cambridge: Harvard University Press, 1993.

Overy, Richard J. *The Air War, 1939–1945*. Dulles, Virginia: Potomac Books, 1995.

Overy, Richard J. *Why the Allies Won.* New York: Norton, 1997.

Rhodes, Richard. *The Making of the Atomic Bomb.* New York: Simon & Schuster, 1988.

Schaffer, Ronald. *Wings of Judgment: American Bombing in World War II*. New York: Oxford University Press, 1985.

Schrijvers, Peter. *The G.I. War against Japan: American Soldiers in the Pacific and Asia during World War II*. New York: New York University Press, 2005.

Sherry, Michael S. *The Rise of American Air Power: The Creation of Armageddon*. New Haven: Yale University Press, 1987.

Spector, Ronald H. *Eagle against the Sun: The American War with Japan*. New York: Random House, 1985.

Syrett, David. *The Defeat of the German U-Boats: The Battle of the Atlantic*. Columbia: University of South Carolina Press, 1994.

Weigley, Russell F. *Eisenhower's Lieutenants: The Campaigns of France and Germany, 1944–1945*. Bloomington: Indiana University Press, 1981.

Weinberg, Gerhard L. *A World at Arms: A Global History of World War II*. Cambridge: Cambridge University Press, 1994.

mysearchlab Connections: Sources Online

READ AND REVIEW

Review this chapter by using the study aids and these related documents available on MySearchLab.

Study Plan

Chapter Test

Essay Test

Documents

Franklin D. Roosevelt, The Four Freedoms (1941)

President Roosevelt's State of the Union message of January 6th was designed to remind Americans of the values we hold most dear and what our responsibility might be to preserve those ideals.

Jim Crow in the Army Camps (1940) and Jim Crow Army (1941)

These documents highlight the racism and segregation experienced by African-American soldiers throughout World War II, which in part led to the integration of the Armed Forces by President Harry Truman's Executive Order 9981 following the war in 1948.

Barbara Woodall and Charles Taylor, Letters to and from the Front (1941–1944)
These letters typify the wartime experience of both the soldier on the frontline and the spouse coping at home.

RESEARCH AND EXPLORE

Explore the following review questions using the research tools available on www. mysearchlab.com.

1. What was the significance of U.S. involvement in World War II?
2. What was the war's impact at home on minorities and women?
3. How did the U.S. military fight the war? What common themes emerge in consideration of an "American way of war"?

Postwar Reform and New Military Challenges

1951	Truman relieves MacArthur
	Peace Talks begin
1952	Eisenhower elected President
1953	Armistice ends fighting in Korea

◆ INTRODUCTION

World War II had been a stunning success of not only American combat arms but also centralized, federally controlled industrial mobilization. In the traditional postwar rush to demobilize, however, the United States faced a new and different enemy: the Soviet Union and Soviet Communism. The total defeat of German fascism and Japanese militarism had not left the world in complete peace. Instead, the United States and its allies in the West and the Soviet Union, its Eastern Bloc satellite states, and later China entered into a new type of conflict that became known as the Cold War. Misunderstandings of the other's security needs, mutual suspicion of each other's political and economic philosophies, and in some ways just old-fashioned realpolitik set the stage for a war that would ultimately be fought regionally, on a variety of levels, under the near-constant threat of nuclear holocaust.

Facing what it considered a threat to American liberty and the free world, the United States had to reorganize its military establishment, create a cohesive grand strategy to fight this war, and convince the American people to finally and fully accept a huge defense organization of unprecedented cost and size. Strategic concepts, such as containment, brought together diplomatic, economic, political, and military strategies to form a multifaceted approach to war on a scale that would surpass that of World War II. The Korean Peninsula provided the first geographic place to fully test this new approach. The United States had broken its tradition of oceanic security and minimal peacetime forces for good.

◆ DEFENSE REORGANIZATION AND CREATION OF AN INDEPENDENT AIR FORCE

During World War II, bureaucratic tangles, interservice squabbles, and budget worries prompted then Army of Chief of Staff General George C. Marshall to lay the foundation for postwar defense reorganization and unification. Wartime demands naturally required that serious attention to reform be delayed until the war ended, but after Japan surrendered, the Army and Navy quickly began arguing over the best way to unify command and administration of the defense establishment. In a tense debate that the press dubbed "The Battle of the Potomac," the Army enthusiastically supported an independent Air Force and also pressed for the creation of a single cabinet-level office to oversee all three services. In contrast, the Navy opposed both the creation of an Air Force and merging the services under a single secretary, preferring a looser arrangement that provided only for coordination of the services. The dispute continued until interservice negotiations and congressional hearings ended in passage of the National Security Act of 1947.

Enacted in July, the National Security Act redrew and modernized the national defense organization, creating the bodies that are currently responsible for formulating

American foreign policy. The most important of these advisory groups was the National Security Council, comprising, at minimum, the president and vice president, and the Secretaries of State and Defense. In addition, the act created the successor to the World War II Office of Strategic Services, the Central Intelligence Agency, the most important civilian intelligence-gathering institution. The Central Intelligence Agency's director also sat on the National Security Council.

Changes to the military establishment included an independent Air Force and a Joint Chiefs of Staff responsible for providing military counsel to the president. Joint Chiefs of Staff members were the newly created Chiefs of the Army and Air Force Staffs and the Chief of Naval Operations. However, Congress provided for coordination and supervision, rather than unification, of the defense establishment. A new Department of Defense replaced the old War Department, and new Departments of the Army, Navy, and, most controversially, Air Force now existed as part of the Department of Defense. Although the legislation replaced the Secretary of War and the Secretary of the Navy with a single Secretary of Defense, that office was given little power. Given the weak authority of the office and the demands on the military created by the postwar shifts in the balance of power, the first Secretary of Defense James Forrestal (previously Secretary of the Navy) faced an unusually difficult task. Interservice competition and disagreement reemerged with new vigor as each service scrambled to protect its interests.

Because military aviation is inherently expensive, the rivalry between naval aviators and the Air Force was especially malicious, with the Navy contending that the Air Force was maneuvering to eliminate naval air altogether. The Navy also defended its organic air arm with the argument that naval air power was uniquely suited to a tactical mission, a defense need that the Air Force ignored by focusing on strategic bombing. Naval aviators were not willing, however, to give up strategic air capabilities. Advocates for the Air Force accused the Navy of using the tactical air argument as a ruse to create a second air force. The Navy was also on the defensive against the Army's claim over control of all ground forces, a move the Navy considered a direct threat to the Marine Corps. Trying for compromise, Forrestal suggested that each service receive an equal portion of the defense budget. Dissatisfied with one-third of a much-reduced defense appropriation, the services took their disputes into the public arena.

Disappointed with Forrestal's inability to resolve the feud, President Truman replaced him with Louis A. Johnson. Truman thought that Johnson's tireless, no-nonsense style and widely recognized talent for administration was what a Secretary of Defense needed to get the job done. Moreover, Johnson's background as a World War I infantry officer, National Commander of the American Legion, and Assistant Secretary of War under Roosevelt gave him the experience needed to gain the respect of the service chiefs. Indeed, the Army and Air Force were pleased with Johnson's appointment, partly because he was well known for his pro–Air Force opinions. As one might expect, however, the Navy was apprehensive over the new secretary's influence on its future.

Johnson was sworn in on March 28, 1949, and immediately began pushing for defense unification. Within two weeks he announced that all public statements by active or retired personnel had to be approved by the Office of the Secretary of

Defense. Naval officers were irate because they believed Johnson was purposely preventing them from openly pressing the Navy's case. The secretary further angered the Navy by approving the Air Force's purchase of thirty-six B-36 bombers in place of fighters and medium-range bombers. The Navy brass now considered Johnson their archenemy.

◆ REVOLT OF THE ADMIRALS

Less than a month after taking office, Johnson sparked the Revolt of the Admirals by canceling construction of the *United States*, the Navy's 1,090-foot-long, 65,000-ton supercarrier, designed to provide naval aviation with a strategic bombing role. Not only would strategic bombing ensure the Navy's relevance, but it also would ensure that the sea services were given a substantial share of the defense budget. Senior naval officers had pinned the Navy's future on the *United States*; the keel had been laid just days before Johnson stopped the program. Although Johnson discussed the ship's future with the service chiefs and with the chairmen of the House and Senate Armed Services Committees, he did not talk over the matter with the service secretaries.

The cancellation order was delivered to Navy Secretary John L. Sullivan and the press at the same time on the morning of April 23, 1949. Sullivan immediately resigned; his letter of resignation lambasted Johnson for not consulting with the Navy on an issue considered vital to its future. Johnson was unruffled, however, because he had taken a big step toward his twin goals of cutting the defense budget and unifying the defense establishment. Moreover, it gave him an opportunity to demonstrate that he was in charge.

Naval officers, especially within aviation, were determined to fight for their service's future and made sure that an anonymous document (actually prepared by Cedrick R. Worth, a special assistant to the Undersecretary of the Navy) made its way to the House Armed Services Committee. The document implicated Johnson and the Secretary of the Air Force in falsifying information on the B-36 so that the program could continue to the benefit of the airplane's manufacturer. The committee called for an investigation and scheduled hearings for August and October. A long list of witnesses, including Worth, discredited the Navy's charges and reinforced public and congressional support for unification and the Air Force.

Furthermore, amendments to the National Security Act gave the Secretary of Defense greater authority over the services, easing his efforts to enforce economy, especially across-the-board cuts in Navy programs. This new threat prompted the Navy to continue its fight. In early September, Captain John G. Crommelin, a naval aviator serving as a staff officer to the Joint Chiefs, publicly charged that Johnson and the Joint Chiefs of Staff wanted to destroy the Navy. Francis Matthews, the new Secretary of the Navy, reassured Johnson and the Chief of Naval Operations. He also convinced Carl Vinson, the Chairman of the Senate Armed Services Committee, to postpone further hearings. However, Admiral Arthur W. Radford intervened to change Vinson's mind.

During the first days of the October hearings, several influential Navy officers—including Admirals Radford, William F. Halsey, Ernest J. King, and Captain Arleigh A. Burke—presented the Navy's case against the Air Force and Secretary Johnson. Secretary Stuart Symington followed to deliver the Air Force's presentation. His evidence was enough to defeat the Navy, but Army General Omar N. Bradley, recently appointed Chairman of the Joint Chiefs of Staff, gave the Navy a fierce tongue-lashing for its stubborn and short-sighted opposition to unification. Worse, Bradley accused the Navy of rejecting civilian control of the military. The Navy's gamble had failed. Unification proceeded and the Air Force retained control of the strategic air mission. In addition, all the officers involved in the revolt—except for Arleigh Burke, who was promoted to admiral—were punished. Although interservice rivalries continued, the Navy's fortunes soon revived as it became clear that sea power remained vital to national defense.

◆ INTEGRATION OF THE ARMED FORCES

Postwar reform of the military included the integration of African Americans into the armed forces. Although blacks had served in every American war, they had never been treated as equal to white soldiers. Furthermore, although African Americans wore their uniforms proudly and expected that their efforts would earn social and legal equality for blacks in the United States, neither their service nor its relationship to the full rights of citizenship was officially recognized. After World War II, African Americans were especially determined that their service and their citizenship be acknowledged, and so they threatened to boycott the armed forces. If blacks had imposed the ban, it would have seriously imperiled military manpower.

Already sympathetic to black civil rights, President Truman was also concerned about military preparedness. In addition, African Americans traditionally supported the Democratic Party, and Truman did not wish to alienate an important group of voters during a campaign. On July 26, 1948, Truman issued Executive Order 9981 declaring "that there shall be equality of treatment and opportunity in the armed forces without regard to race, color, religion, or national origin." However, he failed to define the deadline for instituting the new policy. As a result, integration did not fully occur until the Korean War.

The Navy and Air Force were generally cooperative. During World War II, the Navy had begun integration and proposed to continue that policy. The Air Force had planned to begin integrating, but suggested to Truman that perhaps it could use merit to determine which blacks could serve in white units. Dissatisfied with such a limited approach, Truman made it clear that integration was going to happen and that the services needed to move quickly. By the summer of 1949, the Secretary of Defense had approved both the Air Force and Navy desegregation plans, but the Army was dragging its boots. Army officials simply did not wish to integrate the service and looked for ways to subvert the president's order.

EXECUTIVE ORDER 9981

In July 1948, President Truman issued Executive Order 9981 directing the Armed Services of the United States to begin desegregating. It was a politically risky and socially controversial move. Truman knew it had to be done, however, regardless of how unready American society was to accept it and how resistant the military would be to this unprecedented interference into its own affairs.

WHEREAS it is essential that there be maintained in the armed services of the United States the highest standards of democracy, with equality of treatment and opportunity for all those who serve in our country's defense:

NOW THEREFORE, by virtue of the authority vested in me as President of the United States, by the Constitution and the statues of the United States, and as Commander in Chief of the armed services, it is hereby ordered as follows:

1. It is thereby declared to be the policy of the President that there shall be equality of treatment and opportunity for all persons in the armed services without regard to race, color, religion, or national origin. The policy shall be put into effect as rapidly as possible, having due regard to the time required to effectuate any necessary changes without impairing efficiency or morale.

2. There shall be created in the National Military Establishment an advisory committee to be known as the President's Committee on Equality of Treatment and Opportunity in the Armed Services, which shall be composed of seven members to be designated by the President.

3. The committee is authorized on behalf of the President to examine into the rules, procedures, and practices of the Armed Services in order to determine in what respect such rules, procedures, and practices may be altered or improved with a view to carrying out the policy of this order. The Committee shall confer and advise the Secretary of Defense, the Secretary of the Army, the Secretary of the Navy, and the Secretary of the Air Force, and shall make such recommendations to the President and to said Secretaries as in judgment of the Committee will effectuate the policy hereof.

4. All executive departments and agencies of the Federal Government are authorized and directed to cooperate with the Committee in its work, and to furnish the Committee such information or the services of such persons as the Committee may require in the performance of its duties.

5. When requested by the Committee to do so, persons in the armed services or in any of the executive departments and agencies of the Federal Government shall testify before the Committee and shall make available for use of the Committee such documents and other information as the Committee may require.

6. The Committee shall continue to exist until such time as the President shall terminate its existence by Executive order.

Harry Truman
The White House
July 26, 1948

Source: Harry S. Truman Library and Museum.

When the order was first announced, Army officers noted that it did not specifically require integration of the Army. On July 27, Army Chief of Staff General Bradley declared that the Army would not integrate until society fully accepted the equality of African Americans. Although the Secretary of the Army agreed that the service had to integrate, he did not think it had to take place immediately. He also argued that the Army was not the place to conduct social experiments. Each proposal the Army submitted included provisions for segregated units with 10 percent enlistment quotas for blacks. Finally, in December 1949, the Army agreed to integrate its units; but the service refused to abolish the quota until February 1950, when Truman consented to letting the Army reestablish the quota if too many African Americans enlisted. Clearly, the Army did not intend to integrate.

Combat losses in Korea, combined with a breakdown in discipline under fire of the all-black 24th Infantry Regiment, forced the Army to disperse African American soldiers throughout the service. Nevertheless, by the end of the war the Army could claim that 95 percent of its black members were serving in integrated units.

In 1948, Truman also signed the Women in Military Service Act, which for the first time permitted women permanent status in the U.S. armed forces. Although historically women were heavily recruited for wartime service, they had not been allowed to remain in uniform after a war ended. The new law restricted the number of women in the services to no more than two percent of authorized manpower. There were also limits on promotions for women, and women were specifically prohibited from combat. Furthermore, women could be discharged without cause at any time. Married women and women with children could not serve. While the restrictions eased somewhat over the following decades, real changes did not occur until the U.S. introduced the All-Volunteer Force in 1973.

◆ CONTAINMENT AND THE MILITARY

World War II ended with a bipolar power structure characterized by an ideological contest between the Communist Soviet Union and the capitalist and democratic United States. Initially, the atomic bomb made the United States the undisputed global military superpower. With the bomb, the American military could reduce its conventional forces. Thus, American industry reverted to the production of consumer goods, the armed forces quickly demobilized, and the defense budget shrank. World events, however, forced American foreign policy to become increasingly dependent upon military indemnification.

Allied cohesion, strained during the last months of the war, began to crumble soon after Japan's surrender when the Soviet Union strongly objected to the terms of a series of peace treaties with the former Axis states. On February 22, 1946, an American diplomat to the Soviet Union, George F. Kennan, wrote the Long Telegram. In the telegram, Kennan captured the deepening American-Soviet estrangement when he declared that due to the Soviet fear of capitalist encirclement, Stalin zealously believed the two countries could never reach a permanent *modus vivendi*. Relations worsened over the next several months, when the Truman administration refused a reconstruction loan to the Soviet Union because of disagreements about the future of Eastern

Europe. Also, in June 1946 the Soviets rejected a proposal for an International Atomic Development Authority, which would admittedly give the United States *de facto* control over atomic research worldwide. By September, presidential advisor Clark Clifford was secretly counseling Truman to prepare for a total "war on all fronts" against Soviet aggression.

Ultimately, the development of America's containment policy made 1947 the pivotal year for postwar American–Soviet relations. Economically devastated, Great Britain announced its withdrawal from commitments in Turkey and Greece despite Western assumptions of Soviet interference in the region. Determined to defend the Free World and fearful that Great Britain's pullout might mean conceding Middle Eastern resources to the Soviets, the president proclaimed what came to be known as the Truman Doctrine. In an address to Congress in March, Truman declared that the United States would "support free peoples who are resisting attempted subjugation by armed minorities or by outside pressures" and urged Congress to provide millions of dollars in economic and military aid, including military advisors, to preserve Turkish and Greek sovereignty. Indeed, American assistance was largely military, particularly in Greece.

In July 1947, Kennan anonymously published an article in the journal *Foreign Affairs*. The article, titled "The Sources of Soviet Conduct," expanded upon his earlier analysis. Now Kennan urged the United States to develop a coherent foreign policy, centered on using every method short of war to obstruct Soviet expansion. In June, Secretary of State George C. Marshall had introduced the European Recovery Program, known as the Marshall Plan, to jump-start Europe's postwar economic recovery with $16 billion in aid. While the administration genuinely wanted to improve living conditions for people on the devastated continent, it also wanted to prevent the spread of Communism by helping to establish strong and stable European economies through the Marshall Plan. Moreover, the policy also promised to promote American economic health through multilateral trade. As with the Truman Doctrine, however, Marshall Plan funds largely went to military aid. In 1951, Congress merged the Plan with the Military Defense Aid Program; a year later, the program became the Mutual Security Administration and continued to provide European nations money for their armed forces.

While underwriting economic recovery in Europe, the Marshall Plan also increased tensions between East and West, particularly on the issue of German reunification. Economic conditions in occupied Germany were so bad that the currency of choice was American cigarettes rather than the hyperinflated reichsmark.

During the summer of 1948, the United States, Great Britain, and France joined their occupation zones in an effort to save the German economy; the joined zones quickly became the West German Republic, and the constitutional process to set up self-government in the region was soon under way.

With a self-governing West Germany looming, the Joint Chiefs of Staff began pressing Truman to form a Western Europe–based military alliance that could include German troops. The Senate also passed the Vandenberg Resolution, which urged American cooperation with regional collective security agreements, such as the Brussels Treaty, and claimed, under Article 51 of the United Nations Charter, the right to unilateral or multilateral self-defense. To the Soviet Union, the imminent military alliance between Western Europe and the United States was certainly contrary to its security interests.

Feeling increasingly threatened and isolated, the Soviets attempted to divide the nascent alliance by blockading all surface routes into West Berlin. They also impaired city services by reducing the amount of electricity received by the western part of the city and by freezing West Berliners' accounts in the central bank, which was located in the Soviet zone. If the Soviet Union successfully usurped West Berlin, American credibility in Germany, if not the world, would dissolve. Because Soviet forces in Germany outnumbered Allied forces three to one, the confrontation had to be resolved peacefully.

Truman ordered what became known as the Berlin Airlift to supply the beleaguered city; he also ordered an embargo on vital industrial supplies needed in East Berlin. Between June 1948 and May 1949, military planes arrived daily, every three minutes, delivering a total 0.5 ton of goods per resident. Over the course of 15 months, the airlift delivered over 2.3 million tons of supplies on over 275,000 flights into West Berlin. Sixty pilots and airmen were killed in plane crashes during the operation. The Soviets could do little but watch. Truman gave the impression that the United States was willing to use atomic weapons against the Soviet Union if it interfered with the operation or threatened West Germany.

Stalin's ploy had failed. Instead of starving West Berlin and forcing the American hand, it instead nurtured the alliance between the United States and Western Europe.

FIGURE 13-1   Truman photographed with women of the Armed Forces, October 31, 1951.

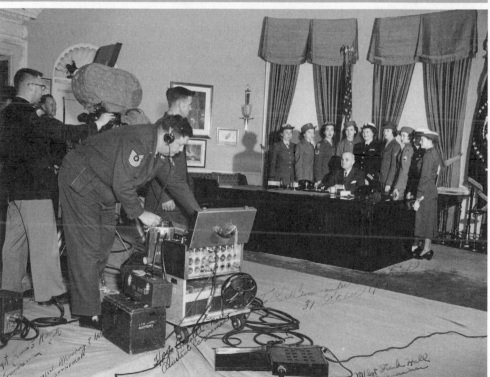

Source: Harry S. Truman Library.

Despite the traditional American fear of involvement in foreign wars and entangling alliances, on July 21, 1949, the Senate approved American membership in the new North Atlantic Treaty Organization, or NATO. Originally comprising the United States, Great Britain, Canada, France, Italy, Norway, Iceland, Portugal, Belgium, Denmark, Luxembourg, and the Netherlands, NATO was a permanent military alliance that defined "an armed attack against one or more" of the members as "an attack against them all" and promised aid, including military action, to the threatened alliance member.

The concern voiced by the Senate over membership in NATO was deep-seated and sincere. Indeed, NATO represented the nation's first formal military alliance with Europe since the American Revolution, as well as its first official peacetime military partnership. Nonetheless, American membership was crucial for NATO's deterrent effect against Soviet aggression in Western Europe because the United States still held a monopoly on atomic weapons. Thus, NATO served as a warning to the Soviet Union that if it stepped too far out of bounds it would be subject to an atomic response.

Still, the true purpose of NATO was to prevent nuclear war. The Mutual Defense Assistance Bill, a $1.5 billion military aid package intended to modernize and enlarge European armed forces, accompanied Senate approval of the NATO alliance. Truman also hoped that NATO would serve as a conduit for reintegration of the new Federal Republic of Germany (West Germany), in part because NATO needed West German manpower, resources, and basing sites. Interest in West German membership in NATO increased when the Soviet Union exploded an atomic device in September 1949, thus ending the American atomic monopoly. Creation of the Communist German Democratic Republic of East Germany a month later further increased support for West German NATO membership. West German manpower was now vital to balancing the Communist threat to Western Europe. Unfortunately for the German people, it looked like the next war would also be fought primarily in Germany.

Communism seemed also to be making gains in Asia, where the Chinese Communist Party of Mao Tse-Tung defeated Chinese Nationalist forces under Chiang Kai-shek in 1949, pushing what remained of the non-Communist army off mainland China onto the island of Taiwan. In light of Communist successes, Truman ordered a reassessment of American foreign and defense policy. The National Security Council's Policy Planning Staff prepared National Security Council Study 68, better known as NSC-68, which argued that the Soviet Union was aggressively expansionist and that its primary target was the United States.

According to NSC-68, conflict was inherent in the ideological disagreement between the Free World and Communism; thus, the United States should adopt a "bold and massive program" of defense buildup in support of a dynamic global containment policy aimed at destroying the Soviet Union. The study also argued that the United States had to build more atomic weapons and hurry the development of the hydrogen bomb. Containment had lost its essentially defensive character. The NSC-68 conclusions provided the foundation for unprecedented peacetime defense expenditures and military buildup, and the development of what President Dwight D. Eisenhower would later call the military-industrial complex.

Although American military planning remained focused on a European-based war against the Red Army, the United States soon found itself fighting in Asia instead.

However, the Asian war served as the immediate justification for implementing the recommendations in NSC-68 and brought to the fore concepts of limited war in the nuclear world.

◆ THE KOREAN WAR

As Japan collapsed under the horrific weight of the atomic bomb, the Soviet Union declared war against what remained of the Japanese Empire on August 8, 1945. Within two days, Soviet troops had moved into the far northeastern regions of the Korean Peninsula. On August 15, President Truman and Soviet Premier Stalin approved the division of Korea at the 38th parallel, with the Soviet Union to occupy the industrial north and the United States to garrison the agricultural south. The dividing line had been chosen primarily because the Soviet Union agreed not to move south of that parallel.

Despite wartime agreements that Korea would be unified as a free and independent state, reunification discussions between the Soviets and Americans quickly broke down. Frustrated at the lack of progress, the United States referred Korean reunification to the United Nations General Assembly, which in turn called for nationwide elections. In the meantime, as was happening in Europe, the occupation governments in both North and South Korea did their best to create Korean political institutions reflecting the ideologies of their occupiers. Although the Soviets refused to hold elections in the North, United Nations elections took place in the South in May 1948.

Syngman Rhee was elected president of the Republic of Korea (South Korea). The elderly Rhee was a staunch nationalist who had been educated in the United States and had lived there for much of his long exile from his home country. Although Rhee's authoritarian character disqualified him as a republican, the Cold War meant that his reliably anti-Communist sentiment outweighed other considerations. Kim Il Sung, backed by the Soviet Union, became prime minister of the Democratic People's Republic of Korea (North Korea) in September.

In December, the United States agreed to continue economic and military aid to South Korea. When World War II ended, the U.S. Army occupation government in Korea began training a South Korean military. Rhee's open intent to reunite the peninsula, however, prompted the United States to limit South Korean armaments to light artillery and a few small aircraft, all of which were worn and outdated World War II designs. In contrast, the Soviet Union equipped the North Korean Army with heavy artillery and tanks. Also, many of the North's soldiers had been trained in the Soviet Union. However, at the urging of the United Nations, Red Army troops withdrew from North Korea in late 1948, and the United States pulled its occupation forces out of South Korea the following summer. Several hundred Soviet and American military advisors remained to continue training programs.

Although the United States continued to assure South Korea that it had American support, the Truman administration's actions suggested to the world that South Korea would have to take care of itself. Preoccupied with securing Western Europe against Communist expansion, American policy makers were reluctant to expand commitments in Asia. Military leaders also considered events in Asia secondary to what was happening in Europe. The postwar U.S. Army had been reduced to approximately

591,000 men, organized into 10 undermanned and poorly equipped divisions. About one-third of Army manpower was on occupation duty around the world, with the largest number, roughly 108,500, in the Far East.

The United States sent mixed signals to the Soviet Union regarding its policy in Korea. Speaking before the National Press Club in January 1950, Secretary of State Dean Acheson implied that the United States did not consider Korea a vital national security interest. Defining the American defense perimeter in Asia, Acheson included the Aleutian Islands, Japan, the Ryukyu Islands, and the Philippines, but not Taiwan or Korea. He also declared that if nations were attacked they must rely upon their own resources until the United Nations could assist them. His speech may have been intended as a message to Communist China that the United States wanted to avoid a conflict over Taiwan, but Kim Il Sung also was listening. Also, General Douglas MacArthur, the American military governor of occupied Japan and Commander-in-Chief, Far East Command, publicly declared his opposition to a general Asian war.

For some time, Kim had been pressing Stalin to support a North Korean attempt to forcibly reunite the peninsula. Kim had interpreted Acheson's speech as an indication that North Korea could attack the south without fear of American intervention, and he again approached Stalin for support. Finally, after exploding its own atomic weapon and having completed an alliance with Mao's China, the Soviet Union was willing to give Kim the go-ahead. Stalin was not particularly interested in a reunited Korea; rather, he saw a Korean war as an opportunity to weaken China by forcing it into a war with the United States. A weakened China would have to take a subservient position to Soviet strategy. Kim also consulted with Mao, but Mao was not kept apprised of North Korean plans. When war came, China was caught by surprise.

◆ PHASE I: THE UNITED NATIONS DEFENSIVE (JUNE 27–SEPTEMBER 15, 1950)

With Stalin's blessing and Soviet military advisors' assistance, North Korea invaded South Korea in the early hours of June 25, 1950. At Truman's request, the United Nations Security Council quickly condemned Kim's action and called for the immediate withdrawal of North Korean forces. Kim refused, and on June 27 the Security Council passed a second resolution asking member states to provide military assistance to South Korea. Seoul, the South Korean capital, fell to North Korean troops the following day.

Despite the American military's lack of readiness, the United States had to act quickly or risk losing credibility with its allies. Ammunition and other equipment was immediately shipped to help shore up South Korean resistance, and on June 26, Truman authorized American air and naval attacks against the invading forces. Two days later, Far East Air Forces (FEAF) began attacking military targets between Seoul and the 38th parallel. The next day, the 3rd Bombardment Group made the first American air raid on North Korea, bombing the airfield at Pyongyang. The FEAF Bomber Command followed this raid with sporadic B-29 missions against North Korean targets through July. Then, in August, B-29s made concerted and continuous attacks on North Korean marshaling yards, railroad bridges, and supply dumps. These raids made it difficult for the enemy to supply, reinforce, and move its front-line troops. On June 30, Truman gave MacArthur the authority to take whatever military action was needed to repel the invasion.

The United States was confident that it would easily turn back the North Korean invasion force. When a task force of 400 infantrymen, a large majority of whom were untried in combat, failed to block the road to Pusan, American certainty faltered. Task Force Smith—named for its commander, Colonel Charles B. Smith—held as long as it could, but the men were soon literally running for their lives. MacArthur claimed that Smith and his men had traded space for much-needed time, but in reality Task Force Smith had been an arrogant tactical disaster that had no effect on the military situation.

On July 7, the United Nations Security Council recommended formation of a single command over the international forces that would be fighting in Korea. Because the United States would clearly be the dominant member, the Security Council asked for an American commander. MacArthur became Commander-in-Chief, United Nations Command, and the U.S. Eighth Army Commander, Lieutenant General Walton H. Walker, took command of all United Nations ground forces.

Walker's forces, all under strength and missing entire elements, included the 7th, 24th, and 25th Infantry Divisions, the 1st Cavalry Division, and the 29th Regiment. The unpreparedness of Walker's troops dictated his strategy. Throughout the rest of July and the first few days of August, the Eighth Army fought a defensive war, delaying the North Korean advance as much as possible while waiting for reinforcements. During

FIGURE 13-2   Marines moving toward Vijongbu, Korea, October 2, 1950.

Source: Harry S. Truman Library.

brutal fighting, the North Koreans steadily drove the Americans and South Koreans southward. Casualties mounted and the numbers of missing multiplied. During the Battle of Taejon, the 24th Infantry Division's commander, General William F. Dean, became separated from his men and was later taken prisoner by the North Koreans. He remained a prisoner of war until September 1953.

By August 4, Walker's forces had been pushed into a small beachhead around the southern port of Pusan. Determined to hold, Walker established a defense in depth, stretching through the hills north of Pusan and west along the Naktong River. The Sea of Japan was at his back. In their static position, Walker's units could better support each other and more easily move reinforcements to threatened sectors. For the next six weeks, Walker's force held the Pusan Perimeter against intense North Korean attacks, while supplies and additional troops arrived in preparation for a breakout. As United Nations forces gained strength, the North Korean Army, unable to replace personnel or destroyed equipment, weakened. Its logistical line was stretched to the breaking point as American air strikes further hampered resupply.

◆ PHASE II: THE UNITED NATIONS OFFENSIVE (SEPTEMBER 15–NOVEMBER 2, 1950)

As Eighth Army defended the Pusan Perimeter, MacArthur planned a risky amphibious assault at Inchon, a port city on the western coast, just south of Seoul. Dubbed Operation CHROMITE, the landing was intended to relieve the pressure against Pusan by completely severing the North Korean supply line, recapturing the South Korean capital, and then blocking the Communist retreat. MacArthur gave his favorite subordinate, Major General Edward M. Almond, command of the reactivated X Army Corps, now comprising the 1st Marine Division and the Army's 7th Infantry Division, along with a South Korean Marine Regiment and several thousand South Korean soldiers.

A nine-nation naval task force supported the landing. Naval guns bombarded Communist-held coastal defenses in coordination with carrier-based air attacks. Underwater demolition teams cleared mines and other obstacles to the landing, and ships and amphibious assault craft ferried the Marines to their landing points. On September 15, two Marine regiments secured Wolmi Island just outside the causeway into Inchon. Later that afternoon, two more Marine regiments landed at Red Beach and Blue Beach, where they had to scale high seawalls. Protected from enemy air attack by air superiority and encountering only scattered enemy resistance, the Marines had surrounded Inchon by the following morning. Four days after the landing, the 1st Marine Division was advancing toward Seoul while the 7th Division moved to block Communist troops retreating from Pusan. On September 29, Seoul was liberated for the first time in the war.

Eighth Army broke out of the Pusan Perimeter on September 19 and began pushing north, battling North Korean forces en route. A week later, Eighth Army linked with the southern elements of X Army. In October, United Nations forces began advancing north toward the Yalu River, at the northern border between North Korea and China. Eighth Army followed a western route up the peninsula, while X Corps was taken by sea to the port of Wonsan, on the eastern coast of North Korea. South Korean units led the advance through much of the Wonsan Campaign, seizing the North Korean capital, Pyongyang, on October 19 before American forces reached the city.

With a promise of "home by Christmas" and hoping to avoid the severe conditions of the Korean winter, MacArthur ordered his commanders to press north as quickly as possible. Eighth Army advanced in two columns, while Almond moved northward and slightly inland from Wonsan. It looked as if the war would soon be over, with the Korean Peninsula reunited under a non-Communist government.

◆ PHASE III: THE COMMUNIST CHINESE FORCES (CCF) INTERVENTION (NOVEMBER 3–JANUARY 24, 1951)

With United Nations forces at or at least very near the Chinese border with North Korea, Chinese Communist Army units entered North Korea in mid-October; but the level of Chinese involvement was at first uncertain. Late in October, one of X Corps' South Korean elements advancing toward the Changjin (Chosin) Reservoir encountered a Chinese force. The battle lasted several days, under brutal conditions, until the 7th Marine Regiment broke the Chinese line near the reservoir. On November 6, the Chinese broke contact. During the same period, near the Chongchon River in the west, Chinese forces pushed Eighth Army back under severe attack. Russian-designed MIG-15 fighter jets had also entered the air war.

During the next few weeks, MacArthur tried to assess the strength of Chinese forces in Korea. Despite rising estimates, he was convinced that the Chinese were too weak to mount a major offensive and that United Nations forces should continue the push north. Eighth Army recovered and continued its two-prong advance, while X Corps turned slightly northwest toward Walker's command. Walker launched the United Nations counteroffensive on November 24. During the following night, the Republic of Korea II Corps took the brunt of a strong counterattack by China's XIII Army Group. On November 27, X Army's 1st Marine Division and elements of the Army 7th Division were attacked by China's IX Army Group near the Changjin Reservoir. Declaring that the conflict was now "an entirely new war," MacArthur ordered Walker to retreat along whatever escape route possible and instructed Almond to withdraw to the eastern port of Hungnam for evacuation south.

Hoping to check the attack, Walker moved his reserves forward, but they could not stop the Chinese. Walker withdrew south across the Chongchon River, where the American 2nd Division fought a ferocious delaying action at Kunu-ri. Through the last few days of November, the division suffered nearly 5,000 casualties while screening the rest of the Army's initial retreat toward Seoul. Under pressure of the Chinese advance, Eighth Army's withdrawal turned into a headlong flight to safety as officers lost control and units disintegrated. Desperate to lighten their loads, soldiers discarded weapons and equipment as they fled. By mid-December, the longest retreat in American military history was over.

Walker regrouped his force, forming a defensive line around the South Korean capital. On Christmas Eve, Walker died when his jeep collided with a truck. Two days later, General Matthew B. Ridgway took command of Eighth Army and immediately began reorganizing his shaken and disheartened force. Having commanded the 82nd Airborne Division in World War II, Ridgway was an experienced combat leader who understood that soldiers were intolerant of "tall talk" and hyperbole, and he made a point of addressing them straightforwardly and respectfully. He also firmly believed in the resilience and ability of American fighting men. The soldier's characteristic initial skepticism of officers quickly gave way to trust and respect for the new commander.

MacArthur had limited expectations of what Ridgway could do with the demoralized troops, asking only that he hold Seoul as long as possible. On January 4, 1951, Eighth Army evacuated the capital only slightly ahead of attacking Chinese troops, destroying bridges across the Han River as it retreated. Ten days later, Ridgway established a defensive line just below the 38th parallel. When the Chinese broke off their offensive, Ridgway began to think that the Communist armies could be defeated with current force strength. Taking advantage of the enemy's inability to supply extended offensives, Ridgway decided to fight a war of maneuver. When the Communists attacked, Ridgway ordered delaying actions, and when the weakened enemy pulled back, he attacked.

While Eighth Army was retreating southward, soldiers and Marines fought for their survival at the Changjin Reservoir. To the east of the reservoir, a 3,000-man task force under Lieutenant Colonel Don C. Faith Jr. was approaching the Yalu River when it was attacked by a much larger Chinese force. Between November 17 and December 1, Task Force Faith fought a retrograde action toward American lines at Hagaru-ri, west of the reservoir. Unable to drive vehicles across the frozen reservoir, Task Force Faith made its way along a road that was constantly under attack, its progress further checked by enemy-constructed roadblocks. Winter gear had not reached the combat troops, so the men wore only summer uniforms as protection against temperatures that fell past 30 degrees below zero. Despite airdrops, food and ammunition were in short supply. Task Force Faith was decimated; fewer than 400 men survived the ordeal. Faith died during the battle from wounds received while leading an attack against a roadblock.

To the west of Changjin, the 1st Marine Division was spread out along a road leading from the coast to the reservoir, a deployment that allowed the enemy to isolate and surround individual formations. Led by Lieutenant General O. P. Smith, the Marines and soldiers who had reached Hagaru-ri started back toward the port of Hungnam. Unwilling to convey a sense of defeat to his men and at the same time accurately describing the situation, Smith responded to a question about the withdrawal: "Retreat hell! We're attacking in a different direction!" Indeed, over the next two weeks Smith's men, with the help of air support, fought their way through frigid temperatures and enemy attacks to the coast, where they were evacuated by sea to South Korea. During their retreat, the Marines crippled many of the attacking enemy formations.

When 1951 began, MacArthur had predicted that without massive reinforcement, or direct attacks against mainland China, United Nations forces would likely be pushed out of Korea. However, when Army Chief of Staff General J. Lawton Collins visited South Korea in mid-January, the new situation convinced him the fight was still on. Before leaving, Collins announced, "We are going to stay and fight."

◆ PHASE IV: FIRST UNITED NATIONS COUNTEROFFENSIVE (JANUARY 25–APRIL 21, 1951) AND CHINESE SPRING OFFENSIVE (APRIL 22–JULY 8, 1951)

Operation THUNDERBOLT began on January 25. Aided by air support, elements of Eighth Army pushed north on either side of the Han River, retaking Inchon, Kimpo airfield, and Suwon before establishing a defensive line a few miles south of the capital in early February. For three days, beginning on February 13, United Nations forces and the Chinese battled for Chipyong-ni, a crossroads southeast of Seoul near the Han River. The fighting was close range and bloody, resulting in the first tactical defeat for the Chinese since intervening.

A few days after Chipyong-ni, Ridgway launched an offensive, Operation KILLER, aimed at forcing the Chinese back north of the Han River. By the beginning

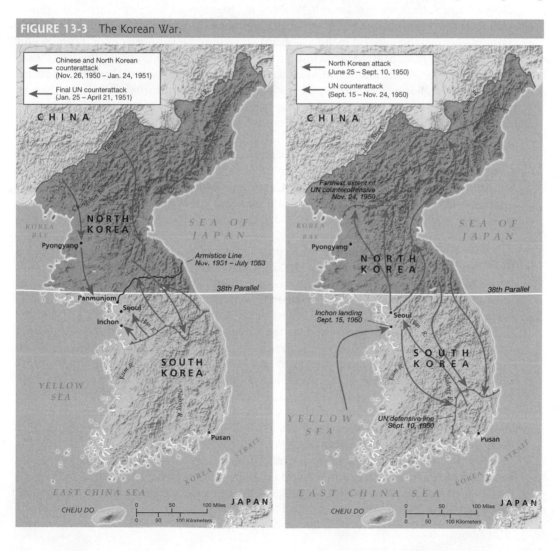

FIGURE 13-3   The Korean War.

of March, the CCF had abandoned its positions south of the river. Operation RIPPER, a general offensive to recapture Seoul, followed KILLER. When the United Nations counteroffensive ended, Eighth Army had regained control of the capital and established a defensive line slightly north of the 38th parallel.

Having regained control of South Korea, the Truman administration decided to pursue a negotiated end to the war. The objective had changed from preserving a South Korean state to unifying the Korean Peninsula and then back to preserving a South Korean state. These changing war aims were a classic case of military success on the battlefield driving the political objectives of the war, rather than the other way around.

Before the president could make an offer, however, MacArthur announced that he was prepared to negotiate an armistice. Worse, he threatened to attack China if the Communists refused peace talks. MacArthur then began to lobby a friend, Republican Congressman Joseph W. Martin, to support his position. Throughout the war, the relationship between MacArthur and Washington had been strained, largely because the general inclined toward stretching his authority. For Truman and the Joint Chiefs of Staff, MacArthur's threat to expand the war was the last straw. Moreover, MacArthur's letter to Martin, who led the opposition to Truman's policies in the House of Representatives, clearly challenged the authority of the president as commander-in-chief. In fact, MacArthur believed that as theater commander he was entitled to act on his own, without consulting even the president. In order to preserve civilian control of the Army, Truman relieved MacArthur, naming Ridgway as his successor. Lieutenant General James A. Van Fleet took over Eighth Army. Although Truman's action caused him serious political trouble, it resulted in better relations between Washington and the Far East Command. MacArthur returned to the United States, exalted by many—including Congress—as a great American hero rather than as an overeager military commander who had caused a serious crisis in American civil-military relations.

MacArthur enjoyed widespread respect and popularity, and public reaction to his relief was immediate and intense. Truman received thousands of letters criticizing him for firing MacArthur. Letter writers called Truman's actions atrocious. Youngsters responded equally strongly, with one young writer contending that the president was "every dumb thing I can think of." The Senate Armed Forces and Foreign Relations Committees began hearings into Truman's decision on May 3, 1951. Lasting seven weeks, the hearings gave MacArthur the chance to declare publicly his belief that the United States had to commit to the destruction of communism through military action. The military implications of his suggested policies made many Americans question their initial disapproval of his dismissal. In addition, the hearings allowed the Joint Chiefs of Staff an open forum in which to expose the flaws in MacArthur's proposals and to explain the risk he posed to civilian control of the military. Disillusioned with a man they had revered, Americans soon lost interest in the hearings.

Shortly after Van Fleet took command, Chinese and North Korean forces launched a spring offensive. Ordered to retake Seoul, the Communist armies pushed the United Nations troops southward several miles from the capital before Van Fleet's force stopped their advance. Enemy units had to withdraw and regroup because they ran out of supplies. In mid-May, the Chinese and North Koreans renewed their offensive, this time directing pressure against weak points in the eastern part of the defensive line. Despite forcing a breach, the enemy could not make headway against Eighth Army's determined defense. Pulling back, the Communists established their own defensive line opposite Eighth Army, just north of the parallel.

The stalemate also presented an opportunity for ending the war. Toward the end of June, the Soviets and Chinese proposed negotiating an armistice. Although the South and North Korean governments wanted to continue fighting until reunification, their patrons were not willing to risk domestic and international political costs for what had become a strategically questionable war. Negotiations began on July 10 in Kaesong, in far western North Korea just north of the 38th parallel. Vice Admiral C. Turner Joy led negotiations for the United Nations command opposite Lieutenant General Nam Il, Chief of Staff of the North Korean People's Army. They quickly agreed that combat would continue until they agreed upon armistice terms. From then on, the conflict became a war of fighting while negotiating. The war turned into an intense clash of patrols and small but bloody battles in which places like Pork Chop Hill and Bloody Ridge repeatedly changed hands. The closing phase of the Korean War lasted two years, forcing combat soldiers to endure two more frigid Korean winters and two more sweltering Korean summers as peace talks dragged on.

◆ **PHASE V: FIGHTING WHILE NEGOTIATING (JULY 9, 1951–JULY 27, 1953)**

Eastern portions of the defensive line had United Nations forces positioned north of the 38th parallel. Beginning at Seoul, the western section of the line lay below the parallel. Joy contended that the current position was geographically more secure and thus easier to defend. Communist negotiators, however, insisted that the division between North and South must revert to the prewar border. When Joy would not concede, the Communists broke off negotiations on August 23. Hoping that military pressure would bring them back to the negotiating table, Ridgway launched a new offensive to extend United Nations–controlled territory.

Van Fleet ordered X Corps to advance the eastern position a minimum of five miles north. In mid-August, elements of Almond's corps began an attack against a group of three hills and the ridges that connected them, in an area that American soldiers nicknamed "The Punchbowl." Beginning in mid-August, the 2nd Infantry Division battled heavily entrenched North Korean troops for control of a strategically unimportant ridge. Known as Bloody Ridge, the territory changed hands several times over the course of the battle, each time taking a heavy toll on both forces. In close combat, American infantrymen cleared the Communist defenders from their entrenchments, finally pushing them from the ridge in early September. The western portion of the line was also advanced several miles, largely to increase the security of the South Korean capital and its rail lines.

Negotiations began again at the end of October, when the Communists ceased insisting on the original demarcation line as the postwar border. Instead, the delegates agreed that the border would be the current line of contact if the war ended within a month. Peace talks quickly came to another halt over disagreements about conditions for exchanging prisoners of war. By that time, the opposing forces had fully dug in, creating conditions reminiscent of the Great War in terms of the living conditions and recurrent battles over small portions of territory. Arbitrators continued to assume that their forces' present positions would determine the postwar division of Korea.

Van Fleet redeployed his forces to strengthen strategically important sections of the line, such as the region around Seoul. He also rotated battle-weary units out of the line, relieving them with National Guard units from the 40th and 45th Infantry Divisions. Concurrently, air and naval pressure against the North intensified, particularly around Pyongyang. Although fighting continued, the summer and early fall of 1952 were comparatively quiet. In October, however, combat briefly intensified as each side hoped to expand its territorial control before the war ended. Eastern units again experienced the heaviest fighting. Communist forces were keen to take White Horse Hill because it would allow them to control the road to the important city of Chorwon. The South Korean division defending White Horse held its ground over several days against strong Chinese attacks. Similar contests in October and November also did little to improve either side's position. Unable to exert effective pressure against the enemy on the ground, the United Nations command further expanded the air war against North Korea.

Lieutenant General Maxwell D. Taylor became Eighth Army commander in February 1953 when Van Fleet retired from the Army. Despite a large exchange of sick and wounded prisoners of war in April, armistice negotiations continued to creep along, stymied by disagreement over repatriation of prisoners. Although less frequent and generally not as intense, fighting continued. The contest for Pork Chop Hill was typical of the combat during the last months of the war. On the night of March 23, the Chinese attacked and won control of the hill from the American defenders. The next morning, the Americans returned with reinforcements and reclaimed Pork Chop. In a bloody attack on April 16, the Chinese again took the hill. Both sides then bombarded it with artillery and brought in reinforcements. Before dawn the next morning, American troops attacked Chinese positions. After a day of close combat, including bayonet attacks, the Communists were driven off. On the morning of April 18, however, the Chinese attacked again but were finally forced off Pork Chop. Over the next several weeks, both sides punished the hill with artillery; and on July 6, the Chinese infantry again attacked. For the next five days, each side brought in reinforcements; the Americans ultimately committed five battalions to the fight. Expecting an armistice at any moment and unwilling to commit more troops to the contest, Taylor abandoned the hill to the Chinese.

Disagreement between the negotiators was not the only reason reaching a peace agreement was difficult. Rhee was unhappy about ending the war without the Korean Peninsula being reunited under his authority. In the middle of June, negotiations were thwarted again when Rhee freed nearly 30,000 North Korean prisoners who did not want to return north. Although he claimed that the prisoners had escaped, his actions nearly derailed the peace talks altogether. Also as a result of Rhee's actions, the Chinese began their attacks against Pork Chop Hill as well as other points. United Nations forces lost control of the area around Pork Chop and almost lost several miles of territory along the western section of the front.

The last combat action of the Korean War took place on July 26, 1953. On the following morning, July 27, negotiators signed an armistice. Although Stalin had died in March and new Soviet leadership had somewhat softened Cold War divisions, the Soviet dictator's passing probably did not affect the eventual armistice. Although North Korea gained some territory that it had not controlled in November 1951, it lost nearly 1,500 square miles overall. Delegates also agreed to a demilitarized zone extending two kilometers on either side of the line of demarcation to serve as a buffer against attack by either nation against its neighbor. The Korean War had cost over 37,000 Americans killed and more than 100,000 wounded. South Korea lost over 250,000 killed, over 400,000 wounded, and at least 1 million civilians killed. Together, some 1.3 million Chinese and North Korean troops died in the conflict. Because no peace treaty formally ended the war, the United States continues to maintain over 30,000 troops along the Demilitarized Zone between North and South Korea, which is arguably one of the most dangerous places in the world.

◆ **CONCLUSION**

Although it lasted little more than three years, the Korean War profoundly affected American strategic thinking. The Korean War changed the way American policy makers approached the Cold War world. American containment policy originally formed around providing economic aid to countries threatened by Communism, but substantial military underwriting was now required to support allies and threatened nations alike. The Korean War had made military force a permanent part of American containment policy, leading to the first large standing Army in American history. Moreover, although foreign and military policy and planning remained focused on the Soviet threat to Western Europe, the Korean War irreversibly involved the United States in Asian affairs. American policy makers' understanding of the threat posed by the Communist forces in Vietnam, and the decision to involve U.S. combat troops in that war were heavily influenced by the Korean War. The continued presence of the United States' Eight Army in South Korea testifies to the significance of the Korean War for American military policy.

Further Reading •

Acheson, Dean. *Present at the Creation: My Years in the State Department.* New York: Norton, 1969.

Appleman, Roy. *Disaster in Korea: The Chinese Confront MacArthur.* College Station: Texas A&M University Press, 1989.

Appleman, Roy. *East of Chosin.* College Station: Texas A&M University Press, 1987.

Appleman, Roy. *Ridgway Duels for Korea.* College Station: Texas A&M University Press, 1990.

Barlow, Jeffrey. *Revolt of the Admirals: The Fight for Naval Aviation, 1945–1950.* Dulles, VA: Potomac Books, 1998.

Blair, Clay. *The Forgotten War: America in Korea, 1950–1953.* New York: Times Books, 1987.

Brands, H. W. *The Devil We Knew: Americans and the Cold War.* New York: Oxford University Press, 1993.

Collins, Lawton J. *War in Peacetime: The History and Lessons of Korea.* Boston: Houghton Mifflin, 1969.

Cumings, Bruce. *The Origins of the Korean War. Vol II. The Roaring of the Cataract, 1947– 1950.* Princeton: Princeton University Press, 1990.

Halberstam, David. *The Coldest Winter: America and the Korean War.* New York: Hyperion Books, 2008.

Hastings, Max. *The Korean War.* New York: Simon & Schuster, 1987.

Holm, Jeanne. *Women in the Military: An Unfinished Revolution.* New York: Presidio Press, 1992.

Ireland, Timothy P. *Creating the Entangling Alliance: The Origins of the North Atlantic Treaty Organization.* New York: Greenwood Press, 1981.

Kaufman, Burton I. *The Korean War: Challenges in Crisis, Credibility, and Command.* 2nd ed. New York: McGraw-Hill, 1997.

Lurie, Jonathan. *Military Justice in America: The U.S. Court of Appeals for the Armed Forces, 1775–1980.* Lawrence: University Press of Kansas, 2001.

MacGregor, Morris J., Jr. *Integration of the Armed Services, 1940–1965.* Washington, D.C.: U.S. Army Center for Military History, 1981.

Pearlman, Michael D. *Truman and MacArthur: Policy, Politics and the Hunger for Honor and Renown.* Bloomington: Indiana University Press, 2008.

Rees, David. *Korea: The Limited War.* New York: St. Martin's Press, 1964.

Stueck, William. *The Korean War: An International History.* Princeton: Princeton University Press, 1995.

Witt, Linda, et al. *"A Defense Weapon Known to Be of Value": Servicewomen of the Korean War Era.* Lebanon, New Hampshire: University Press of New England, 2005.

PEARSON mysearchlab Connections: Sources Online • • • • • • • • • • •

READ AND REVIEW

Review this chapter by using the study aids and these related documents available on MySearchLab.

Study Plan

Chapter Test

Essay Test

Documents

A Report to the National Security Council—NSC-68 (1950)

NSC-68 was the first broadly conceived national security strategy in American history and served as the cornerstone of American Cold War strategy to defeat the Soviet Union without resorting to nuclear war.

Women's Armed Services Integration Act (1948)

In this document, Congress declared that women should have greater opportunity, short of combat, to serve in the American military beyond brief periods of service during wartime.

Order Relieving MacArthur (1951)

In response to General MacArthur's repeated insubordinate behavior toward the President, President Truman, as commander-in-chief, relieved General MacArthur as the supreme American commander in the Korean War.

RESEARCH AND EXPLORE

Explore the following review questions using the research tools available on www. mysearchlab.com.

1. Explain the reasons for the "revolt of the Admirals."
2. Why is Executive Order 9981 important?
3. What is the significance of the Korean War?

Challenges of the Cold War

◆ CHRONOLOGY

◆ INTRODUCTION

The Korean War had shown how difficult it could be to achieve limited objectives in the fight against Communism without the use of nuclear weapons, without a congressional declaration of war, and without full mobilization. It had also once again exposed the delicate balance between military command in the field and civilian control of policy objectives, as well as the difficulties of matching military objectives with war aims. NSC-68 had been put to the test, but the new Eisenhower administration wanted to make significant economic, political, and strategic changes to containment doctrine. The Kennedy administration would also alter containment to meet changing strategic conditions. Still, an arms race, nuclear and conventional, intensified over the course of the 1950s and early 1960s, as did interservice rivalry and competition over limited budget resources. The Cold War entered its most dangerous period, challenging the traditional American way of war.

◆ STRATEGIC CONTOURS

President Eisenhower had ended the stalemate in Korea and preserved the independence, though tenuous, of the South Korean republic by the armistice agreement of July 1953. He had rejected General Douglas MacArthur's recommendation to use tactical nuclear weapons in North Korea as well as Secretary of State John Foster Dulles' suggestion that the war be widened to include attacks in Manchuria and a naval blockade of the Chinese coast. Far from being squeamish about the use of nuclear weapons, Eisenhower instead saw little strategic value in their use in the Korean situation. Likewise, widening the war risked alienating European allies, not to mention starting another world war. The strategic objectives in Korea did not warrant either course of action. The Soviets, Chinese, and North Koreans also understood the concept of limited war for limited objectives. Yet, nuclear weapons had proven useful without actually being used. Though the American nuclear arsenal far outmatched and outnumbered the Soviet one, the mere existence of such power had served as a deterrent against expanding the Korean War and had made leaders on both sides think twice about objectives and capabilities to attain those objectives.

Perhaps the biggest problem facing national security policy makers in the 1950s involved the question of exactly how to use nuclear weapons to achieve policy objectives. Nuclear weapons rapidly reached such destructive levels that "winning" a nuclear war had become a questionable concept. Even the tactical use of nuclear weapons came under military, diplomatic, moral, and ecological scrutiny. The very idea that the most powerful weapon ever developed by man potentially could be of no use seemed unfathomable. In this paradoxical paradigm, American and Soviet leaders struggled to find a strategic use for nuclear weapons.

The United States decided to maintain a large nuclear arsenal as a deterrent to Soviet aggression. By 1954, the United States had embarked on a massive expansion of its nuclear arsenal. Advances in the Soviet arsenal now required that the United States maintain the nuclear capacity to survive a first strike by the Soviet Union and deliver a retaliatory strike to "win" a nuclear exchange. To achieve strategic superiority, the Truman and Eisenhower administrations poured money into the development of new nuclear weapons and better means to deliver them. Massive defense budgets, anticipated in NSC-68, in turn caused intense competition among the services, especially the new Air Force, for budget resources. The Air Force reaped the benefits, having the best means to deliver nuclear weapons. Beginning with B-47A Stratojets, then the B-52 intercontinental bomber, the Air Force's Strategic Air Command (SAC) maintained around-the-clock air delivery capability, which it maintained through the end of the Cold War.

Ground forces also benefited, though not without going through some rough budgetary and doctrinal adjustments. Despite the limited nature of the Korean War, the guerrilla nature of the French Indochina conflict, and increasing small wars of national liberation around the globe, the U.S. Army continued to focus on the concept of general war with the Soviet Union in Europe. As is so often the case in American military history, the United States rarely fights the war it had been preparing to fight.

◆ NATO AND PREPARING FOR WAR IN EUROPE

The United States and its European allies in NATO differed on their concept of war in Western Europe. American war planners considered the potential size of a mobilized Soviet army, Soviet nuclear capability, American nuclear availability, and nonnuclear defense in planning for a Soviet invasion of Western Europe. NATO's original purpose of deterrence through collective security eroded as it became more apparent that Western Europe, primarily Germany, would be a nuclear rather than a conventional battleground. The United States had hoped NATO countries could provide a temporary nonnuclear defense of Europe before American nuclear capability would have to be used to stave off a Soviet invasion. Even as late as 1954, American military planners projected that only about 8 percent of the American nuclear arsenal could be used in Europe. The remainder had to be held in reserve for a direct attack on the Soviet Union and China. American tactical nuclear weapons had developed well beyond similar Soviet capabilities, so planners assumed that nuclear weapons would be used on Soviet military assets rather than cities.

Europeans, understandably, did not relish the destructive horror of another nonnuclear conventional conflict in Europe, nor did the certain horror of a nuclear exchange in central Europe appeal either. While the United States pressured NATO countries to build up conventional forces, Europe worried about the growing American reliance upon nuclear weapons in Europe. As the nuclear option became more apparent, many NATO countries saw little point in spending scarce resources on conventional forces that were rapidly becoming obsolete. By 1955, with a rearming Germany now a member of NATO and American nuclear capability increasing, American planners thought that NATO's conventional forces could stall a Soviet attack, forcing Soviet divisions to concentrate their mass to break the NATO defensive line. This concentration of Soviet forces would in turn allow American tactical nuclear weapons to pulverize Soviet forces. Assuming that Soviet nuclear capability was far behind that of the United States, American planners did not fear a similar Soviet strike upon bunched NATO forces.

In response to Germany's entry into NATO, the Soviet Union formed the Warsaw Pact, organizing its Eastern European satellites into a military alliance to stand toe-to-toe against the United States and NATO. NATO had been, and remained a voluntary association, which made broad acceptance of American strategic concepts consistently problematic. The new Warsaw Pact, on the other hand, answered directly and instantly to the strategic whims of the Soviet Union. Lines of communication and chains of command in NATO could be convoluted and cumbersome, while Warsaw Pact nations had a single chain of command that both originated and ended in Moscow.

◆ **EISENHOWER'S NEW LOOK**

War in Korea, commitments in Europe, the defense buildup in the United States, and investment in new military technologies placed an incredible strain on the American federal budget and economy. When Dwight Eisenhower took up residence in the White House in 1953, he brought with him decades of military and diplomatic experience, and a concern that the Cold War might not only make the American economy dependent upon defense spending, it could indeed break it. With the advent of the hydrogen bomb and the means to deliver this most destructive of weapons, using military force to achieve victory in the Cold War seemed less likely. Instead, decades of spending, buildups, and asymmetrical conflicts appeared the more likely course of this new type of conflict. Even though planners continued to focus on a climactic battle in Europe and the buildup of nuclear and conventional forces, Eisenhower demanded that defense expenditures be brought down to levels that would not overburden the American economy, but did little to address the need for conventional responses to nonnuclear conflict.

Projections by the United States held that the Soviets might have a hydrogen bomb by 1957. Once they got it, the Joint Chiefs of Staff argued, a nuclear exchange would be more certain than ever before. Admiral Arthur Radford, Chairman of the Joint Chiefs of Staff, even proposed a preventive war against the Soviet Union, thereby using the American nuclear advantage rather than waiting until the Soviets achieved parity. He worried about the possibility of a nuclear war or a lengthy stalemate that would drain American economic resources. Although Eisenhower wisely dismissed Radford's preemptive war, he wanted a way to cut costs while maintaining a strong military deterrent to prevent a Soviet attack.

Cutting costs became a critical part of any new defense strategy. With increased defense budgets and massive spending in the Korean War, inflation had wracked the American economy. While strategic planners doubted that the Soviet Union could defeat the United States militarily, a lengthy military buildup could give the Soviet Union the advantage economically. At some point, the American economy could collapse under the protracted strain of the Cold War. To avoid such a scenario, the United States had to cut military spending, yet stay stronger than its adversary for the long haul—perhaps for decades.

In early 1953, the Joint Chiefs of Staff gave Eisenhower a means to cut costs and maintain the strategic initiative. Reasoning that nuclear weapons were much cheaper to build and maintain than conventional forces, the Joint Chiefs argued that the only way to cut costs was to cut conventional forces. This approach could work only if nuclear weapons were deployed and used without restraint. The deterrent effect could be maintained only if the Soviet Union believed that any aggression on its part would result in massive American nuclear retaliation. Cheaper but more nuclear weapons equaled a change in the strategic landscape. The United States had to be willing to use its nuclear arsenal. The question was, and still remains, does the United States have the will to use nuclear weapons?

Eisenhower brought these concepts together in NSC 162/2 in October 1953. This guideline for the use of military force to achieve national strategic objectives radically altered how nuclear weapons might be used. NSC 162/2 allowed for the use of nuclear devices whenever military strategy dictated it. In the future, according to the document, in limited regional wars, such as in Korea, the United States would have a clear nuclear option. Now the United States could use nuclear weapons in limited war, general war, or whatever situation it saw fit. Such a policy for using nuclear weapons allowed for both a reduction in conventional forces and a strong deterrent against the Soviet Union, which now had to consider that the United States would use nuclear weapons in a variety of situations. In NSC 162/2 the United States had a deterrent policy for both general and limited war, and the country could save money by cutting conventional forces.

Project Solarium, an intensive study of American strategic alternatives, helped Eisenhower pull together these new strategic concepts. The alternatives under consideration included continuing the containment policy developed under the Truman administration, adding massive retaliation to containment doctrine, and focusing on regional military, diplomatic, and economic success to discourage the Soviet Union and its Communist allies. Using the Joint Chiefs' move toward a more nuclear and less conventional force, the new nuclear guidelines in NSC 162/2, and Solarium's massive retaliation alternative, Eisenhower formulated a new strategic framework to fight the Cold War. His framework became known as the New Look.

Secretary of State John Foster Dulles made the New Look public in January 1954. In a speech to the Council on Foreign Relations, Dulles warned of the increasing economic burden caused by the Cold War rivalry with the Soviet Union and announced that the United States must seek strength and deterrence at a cost that the American economy could safely absorb. By increased reliance upon airborne nuclear weapons, the United States could and would respond to crisis with massive force when, where, and by whatever means it chose. Massive retaliation became part of the New Look. The great dilemma that the nuclear New Look created, however, was that by relying on such a destructive force for all contingencies, the actual deployment of nuclear weapons might become obsolete because the destruction caused would likely far outweigh the objectives gained. But in 1954, such a strategy could work because the Soviets' ability to retaliate with nuclear weapons was weak. If the New Look and massive retaliation could deter the Soviets, American planners reasoned, the Soviets would resort to political and economic strategies to subvert American influence. To counter such strategies, the United States had to maintain a strong economy; thus the New Look served both ends.

Eisenhower began cutting. The Army went from 20 combat divisions in 1954 to 15 in 1957. With over 40 percent of its force deployed in Europe and other overseas posts, the Army had little capacity for a major conventional war outside the European continent. The New Look reduced the Navy's 765,000 sailors and 1,126 combat ships to 650,000 men and 1,030 combat ships. The Marine Corps' three divisions operated at reduced strength, going from 244,000 men to 190,000 men. As the principal delivery arm for the American nuclear arsenal, the Air Force avoided drastic cuts and even gained continental defense wings. However, the service lost several transport and troop carrier wings. During fiscal year 1957, the Air Force turned to an all-jet bomber force for Strategic Air Command (SAC) as the new B-52 bomber filled out all SAC wings.

The New Look intensified interservice rivalry. All services invested in ballistic missile research, resulting in duplicated effort and capability. Intermediate-range ballistic missiles (IRBMs) such as the Air Force's Thor missile, the Navy's Polaris nuclear submarine program, and the Army's Jupiter missile system each gave the United States missile delivery capacity in Europe and Alaska. Polaris went further, allowing for a mobile retaliatory strike force via nuclear-powered submarines.

The 1957 launch of the Soviet Sputnik satellite by an R-7 rocket, however, brought intercontinental ballistic missiles (ICBMs) to the forefront. If the Soviets could place a small satellite in space, they certainly could deliver a nuclear warhead by rocket to a target in the United States. The American Atlas, Vanguard, and Titan ICBM programs had apparently fallen behind Soviet capabilities. While the United States countered Sputnik in 1958 with a modified Jupiter IRBM, the Soviet Sputnik launch spurred the services into action, each promoting its own ICBM program as the answer to stay ahead of the Soviets. Even the Air Force admitted that ICBMs could eventually make SAC obsolete. A B-52 could be shot down; an Atlas ICBM could not, and the Atlas could potentially deliver a much larger warhead than could a single B-52.

Aside from several private and public investigations into why the United States was behind the Soviets, and threatened by a supposed missile gap, Sputnik resulted in two important long-term developments for the United States. First, Congress passed the National Defense Education Act, which provided funds for university graduate programs in the sciences and engineering, and revised public school curriculums to offer more science courses at the elementary and secondary levels. Second, Congress passed the Defense Reorganization Act of 1958. To overcome duplication of effort and expense, and to minimize competition among the services, the Defense Reorganization Act gave the Secretary of Defense new and extraordinary powers. The secretary now had the power to assign new weapons systems to an individual service, alter service functions and capabilities, and exercise direct command via the Joint Chiefs of Staff over interservice commands. The latter command function added a new and controversial layer of civilian control over the military.

Congressional hearings and Eisenhower's own investigation, the Gaither Committee, still expressed alarm in response to Sputnik. Various findings urged Eisenhower to increase second-strike capability, to invest more in missile technology, and to address the strategic dilemma posed by limited war under the New Look. The Gaither Committee recommended massive increases in an accelerated ICBM program, warning that the United States might not close the missile gap until 1960 or 1961. Later studies of Soviet capabilities clearly showed that there was indeed no missile gap. Eisenhower did not overreact. He understood the incredible difficulties in building a viable ICBM platform and knew that Soviet ICBM capabilities were certainly exaggerated. He instead followed up on commitments to place IRBMs in Europe and Turkey, knowing that the Soviet Union would still not risk war even with ICBM capability because of the massive first- and second-strike delivery capacity of the United States.

◆ THE RISE OF CIVILIAN STRATEGISTS

Sputnik also accelerated critiques of the New Look among academics and other think-tank strategists. The Army hired civilian strategists to argue its case for a nonnuclear alternative to the New Look. The United States, the Army argued, must have an option other than nuclear weapons. Henry Kissinger, a Harvard professor, supported the return of a conventional alternative. Herman Kahn, of the Air Force's RAND think tank, argued that in the Cold War controlled conflict escalation could achieve political objectives. With only a nuclear option, controlled escalation might not be possible. A nonnuclear alternative had to exist in order to respond to a nonnuclear threat by the Soviets. Credible response did not have to be massive, but it certainly had to be appropriate. In 1959, retiring Army Chief of Staff Maxwell Taylor wrote a scathing critique of the Eisenhower New Look in a book called *The Uncertain Trumpet*. He was one of the leading proponents of a new strategic concept, called Flexible Response, that would replace the New Look in the Kennedy administration.

Other critics of the New Look included Robert Osgood, who focused attention on the necessity for conventional warfare capability, and Bernard Brodie, who argued that the United States, like all military powers, was bound by its past. That very past restricted fresh strategic thinking in the missile age. Brodie offered the most in-depth critique of the strategic dilemmas presented by the New Look. Deterrence as a strategy ran counter to the use of the offensive in Western warfare. The offensive in the nuclear age, however, meant a preemptive strike to destroy the enemy's second-strike capability. Deterrence, according to Brodie, was basically preventive war in disguise. He rejected the use of tactical nuclear weapons in limited war situations, noting that containing limited wars in the hope of preventing an all-out war would be very difficult if nuclear weapons were used on the regional level. The nuclear age, Brodie argued, had made limited war so vastly different from what it was in the past that fighting limited wars would require a revolution in strategic thought.

Whatever strategists thought about the New Look, few disagreed with the need for a coherent continental defense system to protect the United States from a Pearl Harbor–like attack by the Soviet Union. Working with Canada, the United States established an early warning radar system, called Distant Early Warning (DEW), across subarctic Canada and Alaska in 1957. The Continental Air Defense Command coordinated air interceptors and ground antiaircraft defense networks. The new Nike Ajax antiaircraft missile provided accurate long-range defense capability with batteries strategically located around the United States.

◆ SIOPs

Eisenhower also saw the need to overcome the growing rivalry between the services in nuclear attack targeting. Each service had its own strategic and tactical plans for a nuclear attack, both first-strike and retaliatory. As a result, each service planned to act against the same nuclear targets in the Soviet Union, China, North Korea, and in other Communist states. Eisenhower wanted to eliminate waste as well as potential command problems that would arise during a nuclear attack. The president knew from personal experience that the lack of a unified attack plan could cause chaos, which could be fatal for the United States in an all-out nuclear strike.

In 1957, Eisenhower ordered the Joint Chiefs and the Secretary of Defense to begin work on a single integrated operational plan (SIOP) for a nuclear attack, to be put in place by 1962. SIOP-62 was—and remains—one of the most secret of American war plans. When presented with an early draft of SIOP-62, Eisenhower claimed that it "frightened the devil out of me."

SIOP-62 provided for a preemptive attack if early warning detected an imminent Soviet nuclear assault on the United States. Plans called for the delivery of over 3,200 nuclear devices on over 1,000 targets in the Soviet Union, China, and Communist satellite states in Eastern Europe and Asia. Such an attack, the plan predicted, would destroy over 150 cities and kill hundreds of millions of people around the world. Even the retaliatory option in SIOP-62 included over 1,700 nuclear bombs delivered on over 700 targets. This was a plan to win a nuclear war.

SIOP-62 combined the nuclear capabilities of the Army, Navy, and Air Force for the first time in a cohesive attack plan. Polaris submarines, Strategic Air Command, ICBMs—all would be unleashed on the Soviet Union in a coordinated, devastating assault. The first drafts of the plan alarmed military leaders. Overkill seemed to be the most common complaint. How many 80-kiloton devices did it take to destroy a target? The target list did not discriminate between Communist countries at war with the United States and those that were not. Would the United States still attack them all?

Kennedy tried to make SIOP fit his Flexible Response strategy by allowing the military to pick and choose targets instead of hitting them all, as SIOP-62 dictated. SIOP-63 gave more discretion, including options to strike only military targets, but still maintained the capacity for complete destruction of the Soviet Union and China.

FIGURE 14-1   USS *Nautilus* (SS-571), the Navy's first atomic powered submarine, on its initial sea trials, January 20, 1955

Source: National Archives and Records Administration.

◆ REGIONAL CHALLENGES

The New Look strategy, with its preoccupation with massive retaliation as a deterrent, could not influence events in several regional Cold War crises. Indochina, Quemoy and Matsu, the Middle East, and Cuba are a few of the places that became hotly contested Cold War arenas. The loss of a U-2 spy plane over the Soviet Union in 1960 only intensified the warming of the Cold War. The United States used a variety of tools to approach these crises in order to achieve political objectives without risking broader conflict. Far from being representative of the New Look, these regional conflicts instead reflected the increasing diversity of Cold War strategy.

INDOCHINA

The United States had supplied military aid to France in its fight to maintain the pre-World War II colony of Indochina (Vietnam, Laos, and Cambodia) since 1950. The United States supported Viet Minh leader Ho Chi Minh's efforts to fight Japanese occupiers in the region during the war. Despite this close association, Ho's Communist connections and America's diplomatic maneuvers to keep France on board with NATO military commitments in Western Europe dictated severing the tie with what was now an insurgency against French rule.

The Communist takeover of China in 1947 dramatically changed the French war against Ho's insurgents. With supplies freely flowing across the Chinese border, Ho's guerrillas became a real army. To counter the growth of Ho's forces, the United States supplied the French with excess war material from its own war in Korea. French reverses, however, negated much of this American aid. Before 1951, French commanders relied on static garrisons, which the Viet Minh overran. Attempts to draw the new Viet Minh army into a set-piece climactic battle never materialized. In 1951, the French tried a new strategy. Using mobile forces and massive firepower, the French scored early successes; but the Viet Minh proved adaptable and adjusted to the new French strategy.

As the Communist nature of Ho's movement became more apparent and the Cold War intensified, the United States came to see Indochina as a critical Cold War battlefield to preserve the region against further Communist aggression. North Korea was already under Communist control, and the threat to South Korea remained. The Domino Theory held that if one country fell in Southeast Asia, then others could soon follow. The momentum of Communist expansion could then be too great to stop. Furthermore, the region's abundance of rubber, tungsten, and rice made Southeast Asia strategically important.

By 1953, French support for the war in Indochina had evaporated. High casualties, especially among the officer corps, and no sign of progress toward defeating the Viet Minh and establishing semi-independent states under a French union made the war unpopular. Still, the Eisenhower administration increased military aid and called for the French to replace unimaginative commanders with more dynamic generals. One of the new French commanders, General Henri Navarre, hoped to force the Viet Minh army into a decisive battle. To do this, he boldly established a base of operations deep inside Viet Minh–held territory in a valley called Dien Bien Phu. At first,

Navarre wanted to conduct aggressive operations from Dien Bien Phu against Viet Minh supply lines along the Laotian border. The rough mountainous terrain, however, convinced Navarre instead to use the large base he had established on the valley floor as bait to entice the Viet Minh into a mass assault. With the Viet Minh concentrated in a small area, Navarre reasoned, he could annihilate them with air strikes and artillery positioned around Dien Bien Phu.

As the diplomatic landscape evolved in early 1954, the Viet Minh found themselves in a position to force the French out of Vietnam for good. Talks at Berlin and Geneva would favor the Viet Minh if they could defeat the French at Dien Bien Phu. Well-supported by the Soviet Union and China, the Viet Minh assaulted the French outpost. With this, the Viet Minh should have fallen into Navarre's trap, but the French failed to stop the incredible buildup of Viet Minh artillery and antiaircraft guns in the hills surrounding the outpost.

As the Viet Minh overran the surrounding artillery positions, the French government begged the United States to intervene militarily to save Dien Bien Phu. The French asked for bombing, ground troops, even nuclear weapons; but Eisenhower rejected French requests for help. Dien Bien Phu is close to the Chinese border, and the president feared that American intervention there might trigger a wider war, as had occurred in 1951 when American forces approached the Chinese border in North Korea. Moreover, Eisenhower wanted congressional approval before placing American forces in harm's way. Such authorization would take time, which the French did not have. The risk of uncontrolled escalation and the fact that the region simply was not strategically important enough to warrant direct American military intervention convinced Eisenhower to let Dien Bien Phu fall, which it did on May 7, 1954. Exhausted, the French stopped military operations in Indochina and sought a settlement at ongoing peace talks in Geneva.

The United States also wanted an end to the war, and hoped that the Geneva settlement would open the door to political and economic ways to halt Communist expansion in Southeast Asia. The agreement promised Vietnam-wide elections in 1956, but they did not take place. This set the stage for the United States to take over France's colonial aspirations in the region in pursuit of its own anti-Communist objectives. At Geneva, the Soviet Union pressured the Viet Minh to accept the agreement because it also feared that the conflict would broaden into a general war. Perhaps the threat of massive retaliation had influenced the end of the French-Indochina War after all.

Militarily, French withdrawal from Indochina gave birth to a new regional collective security arrangement among Southeast Asian nations and the United States. The Southeast Asia Treaty Organization (SEATO) included the Philippines, Australia, New Zealand, France, and Great Britain, in addition to the United States. SEATO obligated signatories to guarantee the security of Pakistan, Malaya, and Thailand as well as two new states neutralized by the Geneva agreement, Laos and Cambodia. Like NATO, SEATO relied on a regional conventional deterrent backed up by the New Look of the United States.

The French Indochina War exemplifies the limited regional conflicts that began to characterize the Cold War. Regional revolutionary wars went beyond military means to include social and psychological resistance, ideas that rallied populations to such effective levels that popular guerrilla armies successfully challenged conventional forces.

Occurring just as the New Look was formalized, the war in Indochina should have signaled military strategists that regional limited wars required conventional responses. Still, the United States had restrained its military response at Dien Bien Phu and had reached an agreement that, although it did not resolve the issue of Vietnamese independence and unification, it at least provided the conditions for a possible peaceful resolution in the future. Unfortunately, this was not to be.

◆ QUEMOY AND MATSU

Fresh out of the Korean War, the United States again came close to open war with China in 1954 and again in 1958 over the contested islands of Quemoy and Matsu. Claimed by Taiwan, the tiny offshore islands had strategic value in blocking an amphibious invasion of Taiwan from mainland China. China shelled the islands briefly in 1954, prompting Eisenhower to invoke the New Look by threatening the use of nuclear weapons against China and petitioning Congress to authorize the president to defend Taiwan if China moved to take the islands. While the United States was obligated by treaty to defend Taiwan (the treaty also gave the United States the power to veto any attack planned by Taiwan against China), the Sino-Soviet agreements could easily be activated if the United States got into another war with China. Under these agreements, the Soviet Union could use such a scenario to start a war in Europe. Quemoy and Matsu were much less strategically important than Europe. Eisenhower, his nuclear threat aside, hardly saw the value in going to war over the two islands—especially after recently getting out of Korea and refusing to aid the French at Dien Bien Phu.

The Chinese shelled the islands again in 1958, this time in response to Taiwan's move of nearly a quarter of its army to the islands. American military planners advised that the islands could not repel a Chinese invasion unless bases along coastal China were first destroyed in a nuclear attack. Taiwan had tried to back the United States into a strategic corner by risking so much of its army. Although America had not acted in 1954, Taiwan gambled that the United States would, nevertheless, take the threat to the islands seriously and come to Taiwan's aid. The gambit nearly worked. Eisenhower ordered the Navy to escort Taiwanese supply ships to the islands, and allowed Taiwanese Air Force jets to be armed with American missiles. An Army-Marine joint strike force of several thousand men joined the Taiwanese Army on the islands. Fearing nuclear war over two small islands, the Soviets pressured the Chinese to back down, which they did.

Quemoy and Matsu demonstrated how close to the brink of nuclear war the nuclear powers seemed willing to go. Of course, as with the New Look, such brinkmanship depended on the certainty that saner heads would prevail and one side would back down.

◆ THE MIDDLE EAST

Postwar nationalism and conflict between Arabs and the new Israeli state, combined with increased oil production in the area, made the Middle East a tensely contested region in the early Cold War. Soviet interest in Iranian oil production gave the United States due cause for concern. Eisenhower worried that Soviet expansion via Iran might jeopardize the entire Middle East and Western dependence upon the region's oil. Eisenhower approved a CIA-sponsored coup, organized and carried out by Kermit Roosevelt, to overthrow Iranian leader Mohammed Mossadeq in 1953 to prevent the spread of Soviet influence in Iran. The new government, under the Shah of Iran and supported by $45 million in American aid, had severe economic problems to overcome. Eisenhower sent Herbert Hoover, Jr., son of the president, to negotiate a new oil deal with the Shah's government. In the end, the agreement gave the major American oil companies a virtual monopoly on Iranian oil production and distribution. National security interests in the Cold War apparently overrode American antitrust traditions.

In 1955, the Baghdad Pact (Turkey, Iran, Iraq, Pakistan, and Great Britain) provided a tenuous American-supported collective security system in the region. The United States did not directly participate in the alliance for fear of upsetting the already delicate relationship among Middle Eastern nations and America. With NATO in place in Western Europe and SEATO in Southeast Asia, the Baghdad Pact group provided yet another collective security alliance on the periphery of Communist China and the Soviet Union. Containment had indeed taken many forms.

The Suez Crisis of 1956 was resolved without American military interference, but just barely. Egyptian President Abdel Nasser ordered the nationalization of the Suez Canal in July 1956, prompting angry protests from Great Britain and France. Nasser took this drastic step in retaliation against the United States for pulling financial support for the massive Aswan Dam project. Eisenhower decided to withdraw support in response to Nasser's attempt to attract Soviet interest in the project. Egypt planned to use toll proceeds from the canal to finance the dam, but Great Britain and France opposed this plan. The West likened Nasser to Hitler and brought up the haunting specter of Munich as justification for standing firm against Nasser's brazen act.

Eisenhower ruled out military action consistently throughout the crisis. Fearing the effect of the use of military force on world opinion, not to mention his own reelection bid in the 1956 presidential campaign, Eisenhower sought a peaceful solution to the crisis. For Nasser, Egyptian nationalism was at stake. For Great Britain and France, their role as imperialist leaders in the region had been jeopardized, as had the stock certificates of stockholders in the Suez Canal Company. Despite the best efforts of Eisenhower and Secretary of State Dulles, armed conflict erupted when the British bombed Egyptian bases, and the Israelis, under secret agreement with the British and French, attacked the Sinai and the Gaza Strip in October.

Furious, Eisenhower worried that the Suez conflict could expand into a world war. On November 5, the Soviet Union warned that it would launch missiles against French and British cities unless they immediately stopped their attack on Egypt. With American forces around the world on full alert, Eisenhower feared the worst. Then the Soviets suggested a joint American-Soviet military intervention to end the fighting. Although not a sincere proposal, it nevertheless made great Communist propaganda, allowing the Soviets to make themselves look like peacemakers. As suddenly as the crisis began, it ended. Bombarded with negative domestic and worldwide public opinion, the British and the French decided to obey the United Nations resolution calling for immediate cessation of hostilities. Cessation of hostilities made the Soviet Union look like the savior of Egypt, if not the Middle East. But, to prevent the expansion of Soviet influence in the region, the United States now had to fill the void left by Great

Britain and France. As a result of Eisenhower's refusal to use military force in this situation, however, there had not been a broader war.

One major result of the Suez crisis was the Eisenhower Doctrine. In January 1957, Congress authorized the president to defend any Middle Eastern nation attacked by a Communist state and provided $200 million in economic and military aid to Middle Eastern nations. Initiating the Eisenhower Doctrine, however, depended on a nation in the region requesting such aid. Countries like Egypt and Syria would probably not ask for American help. In many areas of the Middle East, Arab nationalism threatened stability much more than did the expansion of Communism.

The Eisenhower Doctrine was put to the test in 1958. Egyptian-backed rebels began attacks in Lebanon and also assassinated the King of Iraq. Jordan and Lebanon asked for American assistance. Units of the American Sixth Fleet, the Marines, and the Army moved into Beirut without firing a shot. British airborne forces landed in Jordan, supplied by the U.S. Air Force. American forces in Turkey stood ready to move into both Lebanon and Jordan. Bolstered by American and British forces, the Lebanese and Jordanian governments restored order, allowing American and British forces to leave, promptly, after only two months. Eisenhower had again avoided massive military action in the confused world of nationalism and the Cold War. The New Look seemed to be evolving into something different.

◆ U-2 SHOOTDOWN

American U-2 spy planes had flown intermittent high-altitude missions over the Soviet Union since 1952. Each flight was operated by the CIA instead of the Air Force. Knowing that Soviet air defense systems could detect the planes but not shoot them down, Eisenhower approved the flights. With effective spy satellites still years away, the U-2 provided the only means to photograph Soviet capabilities and movements. Even with this supersonic aircraft and the poor state of Soviet air defense capabilities, the infrequency of flights made it difficult to accurately assess what the Soviet Union was doing inside its borders. The U-2 could, however, accurately photograph not only Soviet bombers sitting in the open on Soviet airfields, but open Soviet missile silos. Though imperfect, U-2 missions provided the first real independent assessment of Soviet air and ground forces.

The Soviets desperately wanted to stop U-2 flights, but until 1960 their air defense network did not have an antiaircraft missile capable of reaching the high-altitude flights. Just two weeks before the Paris summit between the United States and the Soviet Union aimed at rapprochement was scheduled to begin, the Soviets got their wish. On May 1, 1960, a Soviet antiaircraft missile shot down a U-2, piloted by Francis Gary Powers. For the United States, the timing could not have been worse.

Assuming Powers was dead, the Eisenhower administration at first denied any wrongdoing, claiming the flight had been a weather reconnaissance mission that had strayed into Soviet airspace. A few days later, the Soviet Union announced to a stunned United States that Powers was alive and had admitted the true nature of his flight mission. The Soviets tried Powers for espionage and sentenced him to ten years in prison. He was exchanged, however, in 1962 for a Soviet operative held in the United States. Embarrassed, the Eisenhower administration had to backtrack and admit the true nature of the U-2 program. Eisenhower, to his credit, took full responsibility. In

Paris, Khrushchev grandstanded in protest of the U-2 spy missions and walked out of the summit before substantive talks got under way. Although Eisenhower stopped U-2 missions over the Soviet Union, the United States continued flyovers of other Communist states. By the early 1960s, satellites had advanced enough to provide useful data. Moreover, they could not be shot down.

EISENHOWER RESPONDS TO U-2 SHOOTDOWN

President Eisenhower issued the following statement in an attempt to regain control of the public relations disaster that began with the State Department's explanation of the U-2 shootdown. It is classic Eisenhower-speak. Note what he says—and what he does not say. He can appear to explain the situation but at the same time say absolutely nothing of substance. Note also how Eisenhower must explain to the press, and the American people, the purpose of intelligence gathering and its critical role in protecting the security of the United States. His approach is as if he were lecturing a class.

News Conference Statement by the President, May 11, 1960

I have made some notes from which I want to talk to you about this U-2 incident.

A full statement about this matter has been made by the State Department, and there have been several statesmanlike remarks by leaders of both parties.

For my part, I supplement what the Secretary of State has had to say with the following four main points. After that I shall have nothing further to say—for the simple reason that I can think of nothing to add that might be useful at this time.

First point is this: the need for intelligence-gathering activities.

No one wants another Pearl Harbor. This means that we must have knowledge of military forces and preparations around the world, especially those capable of massive surprise attack.

Secrecy in the Soviet Union makes this essential. In most of the world no large-scale attack could be prepared in secret. But in the Soviet Union there is a fetish of secrecy and concealment. This is a major cause of international tension and uneasiness today. Our deterrent must never be placed in jeopardy. The safety of the whole free world demands this.

As the Secretary of State pointed out in his recent statement, ever since the beginning of my administration I have issued directives to gather, in every feasible way, the information required to protect the United States and the free world against surprise attack and to enable them to make effective preparations for defense.

My second point: the nature of intelligence-gathering activities.

These have a special and secret character. They are, so to speak, "below the surface" activities.

They are secret because they must circumvent measures designed by other countries to protect secrecy of military preparations.

They are divorced from the regular, visible agencies of government, which stay clear of operations involvement in specific detailed activities.

These elements operate under broad directives to seek and gather intelligence short of the use of force, with operations supervised by responsible officials within this area of secret activities.

We do not use our Army, Navy, or Air Force for this purpose, first, to avoid any possibility of the use of force in connection with these activities and, second, because our military forces, for obvious reasons, cannot be given latitude under broad directives but must be kept under strict control in every detail.

The activities have their own rules and methods of concealment, which seek to mislead and obscure—just as in the Soviet allegations there are many discrepancies. For example, there is some reason to believe that the plane in question was not shot down at high altitude. The normal agencies of our Government are unaware of these specific activities or of the special efforts to conceal them.

Third point: How should we view all of this activity?

It is a distasteful but vital necessity.

We prefer and work for a different kind of world—and a different way of obtaining the information essential to confidence and effective deterrence. Open societies, in the day of present weapons, are the only answer.

This was the reason for my open skies proposal in 1955, which I was ready to instantly put into effect, to permit aerial observation over the United States and the Soviet Union which would assure that no surprise attack was being prepared against anyone. I shall bring up the open-skies proposal again in Paris, since it is a means of ending concealment and suspicion.

My final point is that we must not be distracted from the real issues of the day by what is an incident or a symptom of the world situation today.

This incident has been given great propaganda exploitation. The emphasis given to a flight of an unarmed, nonmilitary place [sic] can only reflect a fetish of secrecy.

The real issues are the ones we will be working on at the summit—disarmament, search for solutions affecting German and Berlin, and the whole range of East-West relations, including the reduction of secrecy and suspicion.

Frankly, I am hopeful that we may make progress on these great issues. This is what we mean when we speak of "working for peace."

And, as I remind you, I will have nothing further to say about this matter.

Source: Dwight D. Eisenhower Library and Museum.

◆ KENNEDY AND THE COLD WAR

The nonexistent missile gap became the chief issue of the 1960 presidential election. Having been chided for being weak on Communism in 1952, largely because of Truman's conduct of the Korean War, the Democrats now took the offensive against the Republicans on military preparedness. Eisenhower's loss of Cuba to rebel leader Fidel Castro, the growing debacle in Indochina, the Soviet shootdown of an American U-2 spy plane, and other humiliations pointed to what critics claimed was the inherent weakness of the New Look. The all-or-nothing option could not operate in a Cold War that now demanded limited war approaches to regional nationalist conflict. Kennedy's victory over Eisenhower's vice president, Richard Nixon, in 1960, brought a new national security strategy and policy-making style to the White House. Gone were Eisenhower's weekly National Security Council meetings and formalized decision-making process via a military-style staff system. Instead, Kennedy relied heavily on advisors, systems analysis, and informal decision making. Having been elected on a campaign highlighting the crisis of Communist expansion in the world, Kennedy could not divorce his rhetoric from geopolitical realities of the new so-called third force player—nations or groups of nations that exercised influence exceeding their economic and military strength—in the Cold War.

◆ BUILDING A FLEXIBLE RESPONSE

To better prepare the United States to deal with this new phase of the Cold War, Kennedy appointed the dynamic former chief of Ford Motor Company, Robert S. McNamara, to head the Defense Department. McNamara brought to the huge bureaucratic defense establishment a slashing style, built upon maximum business efficiency, called the planning-programming-budgeting system. McNamara disagreed with Eisenhower's overreliance on nuclear retaliation. In order to replace the New Look with Flexible Response, the Department of Defense had to prepare the armed services to appropriately respond to the range of threats that now characterized the Cold War. To do this, the services had to be streamlined, reequipped, and properly trained, all at the lowest possible financial cost. Such a task was most fitting for a businessman like McNamara. Centralization, cost cutting, and long-range planning became the principal means of McNamara's Department of Defense to achieve Flexible Response.

McNamara continued to gradually replace fixed-wing bombers with missiles as the primary means to deliver large nuclear warheads, but he also dramatically increased the armed services' conventional capability to respond to regional crises, such as Cuba and Vietnam. To maintain American nuclear superiority and retaliatory capability, McNamara increased the number of ICBM silo sites and nuclear submarines with Polaris missiles. Through modest budget increases, McNamara increased the size of Army, Navy, Marine, and Air Force conventional forces and added new specialized units and equipment.

In the Army, for example, Kennedy's pet project for an elite guerrilla-style unit and the use of helicopters for ground combat support became reality. Army Special Forces already existed, but under McNamara and Kennedy the elite force became experts in small-unit guerrilla tactics and nation-building strategies, which, when combined, came to be known as counterinsurgency. Army Special Forces, also then known as the Green Berets, became the elite force of the American military, and soon each service enhanced their rough equivalents. New equipment also changed the battlefield. For example, the Army and Marines had used helicopters during and since the Korean War mainly for reconnaissance and medical evacuation, but now both services gave rotary aircraft a central combat role. Air assault and air mobility, based on the French model, seemed perfectly suited for small, regional conflicts in difficult terrain, such as that in Vietnam. McNamara's Army–Air Force Strike Command gave joint capability to new concepts of air mobility on the battlefield.

Through McNamara's micromanagement of the Department of Defense, Kennedy gained a military force that could maintain massive retaliatory capability yet conventionally respond to lesser crises with a variety of tools, including use of force, nation building, and military advising. While the services experienced growing pains under McNamara's program, they were arguably better organized, equipped, and prepared to meet the new challenges of the Cold War. Crises in Berlin, Cuba, and Vietnam made mixed use of this new Flexible Response.

◆ THE BERLIN CRISIS

The trickle of East Germans sneaking through the West Berlin gap into West Germany was reaching flood stage by early 1961. Khrushchev threatened to close the border completely, with military force if necessary. Kennedy and Khrushchev met in June 1961 in Vienna to discuss the crisis. The Soviets wanted a treaty restoring Berlin to their control, while the Western powers wanted to maintain the four-power status of the divided city. Khrushchev issued an ultimatum to a berated Kennedy, demanding a settlement by December or he would seal off the city from the west, an act that would surely provoke a war in Europe. Failing to understand the growing split between the Soviet Union and China, and still clinging to his missile gap campaign rhetoric, Kennedy lost the initiative in the Berlin crisis and left himself with few diplomatic and military options.

A speech by Kennedy in July implied that the United States might take no action if West Berlin was not attacked or disturbed by Soviet attempts to stop the flood of refugees into West Germany through Berlin. On August 13, 1961, East German laborers began constructing the Berlin Wall, arguably the most potent symbol of the Cold War. It gave Kennedy a way out of the crisis. Khrushchev stopped threatening West Berlin. With the wall up, only a few brave East Germans dared attempt to escape to the west side of the city.

Kennedy ordered an attack plan drawn up in case of a Soviet move against Berlin. A small attack force of low-flying bombers could get past the weak Soviet early warning detection system and knock out Soviet ICBM silos in the western part of the country before the Soviets could get a missile off the ground. Unlike SIOP and its hundreds of targets, striking a mere forty-two targets could so weaken the Soviets that they would not be able to continue offensive operations against Berlin and West Germany. In November, Khrushchev withdrew his ultimatum for a December settlement. He had achieved his objective. The Berlin Wall plugged the hole in the dike meant to keep East Germans on the Soviet side of the Iron Curtain. The Soviet Union had displayed the ability for achieving limited objectives through means that limited American retaliatory action.

FIGURE 14-2   American tanks and troops at Checkpoint Charlie, a crossing point in the Berlin Wall between the American and Soviet sectors of the city at the junction of Friedrichstrasse, Zimmerstrasse, and Mauerstrasse, February 1961.

Source: Express Newspapers/Stringer/Hulton Archive/Getty Images.

◆ MISSILES IN CUBA

Kennedy took a black eye in the Berlin Crisis that added to the one he received earlier in the failed Bay of Pigs invasion aimed at overthrowing the Soviet allied Cuban leader Fidel Castro. In response to American deployment of nuclear missiles in Turkey and Europe, Khrushchev boldly decided to deploy similar weapons in Cuba in 1962. The Soviet operation to deploy the missiles to Cuba, Operation ANADYR, was secret and risky. Khrushchev feared American naval interference if American spy satellites recognized missile parts on the decks of Soviet freighters headed to Cuba, so he ordered the parts hidden underneath tractors and other agricultural machinery. Soviet naval captains had orders to scuttle their vessels if American naval forces threatened to board them.

Word of the deployment leaked; and before long, American U-2 overflights had detailed photographs showing construction of missile launch platforms as well as the missiles themselves. In October 1962, Kennedy ordered plans for an invasion of Cuba—not by CIA-supported rebels, but by U.S. armed forces. The Joint Chiefs and Secretary of State Dean Acheson supported immediate military action to destroy the missiles already being assembled in Cuba. As an alternative plan, Kennedy also discussed a naval blockade of Cuba to stop further delivery of Soviet missiles and equipment. The president's brother, Attorney General Robert Kennedy, and Secretary of

Defense McNamara argued in favor of the blockade. On October 22, a Soviet anti-aircraft missile shot down a U-2 spy plane over Cuba, killing its pilot. Castro cabled Khrushchev, demanding an immediate nuclear assault on the United States. Soviet commanders in Cuba had at their disposal tactical nuclear weapons for battlefield use that were ready to fire. Kennedy placed the U.S. military around the world on highest alert. That evening, Kennedy made a dramatic television address to the world announcing the blockade or "quarantine," as he called it, of Cuba.

To describe the situation as tense does not begin to appreciate conditions in October 1962. Nonetheless, the crisis was resolved. Using diplomacy while threatening use of force, Kennedy managed to broker a deal in which the United States agreed to withdraw American missiles from Turkey—they were supposed to have been withdrawn a year earlier, but had not been. Further, Kennedy promised not to invade Cuba in exchange for the Soviets' agreement to withdraw their missiles from Cuba. This offer also gave Khrushchev a face-saving way out. Kennedy's willingness to risk global nuclear war over Cuba surprised Khrushchev, who thought Cuba not worth such a price. Kennedy had maintained tight control of American commanders around Cuba in order to minimize the potential for an accidental attack. An unintended consequence of this control was the establishment of a tradition of executive interference with local commanders, bypassing the regular chain of command.

The crisis represented a point of maximum danger in the Cold War, but it also highlighted the difficulties in the evolution of Flexible Response from the old New Look. For many Americans, if not for people around the world, the resolution of the Cuban missile crisis made it appear that Kennedy had saved humanity from nuclear holocaust and resurrected his prestige.

◆ CONCLUSION

By the end of 1963, Kennedy was dead, and his vice-president, Lyndon Baines Johnson, was president. Kennedy had already placed over 15,000 military advisors, including hundreds of Green Berets, in South Vietnam to help train and equip South Vietnamese military forces to fight the North Vietnamese–supported insurgency there. Cuba remained a thorn in the side of the United States, as Castro survived CIA attempts on his life. NATO's stability was uncertain. France threatened to withdraw, and there were continuing disagreements over nuclear versus conventional strategies and obligations. China was moving out from under the shadow of the Soviet Union to act as a Communist power in its own right. Thus, despite a nuclear test ban treaty signed by the United States and the Soviet Union in 1963, the Chinese successfully tested a nuclear bomb in 1964. Clearly, the Cold War was in full swing.

The American military had grown—dramatically—in size, capability, and purpose since the Korean War. Eisenhower had made the United States the strongest nuclear power on the planet. Kennedy then balanced nuclear power with nonnuclear capabilities. McNamara's management style eliminated waste and created financial balance between weapons programs and manpower. Military leaders debated the merits of nuclear force and limited conventional response. Nation building and counterinsurgency were just two of the many new strategies and policies added to the American military's arsenal of unconventional capabilities. While the threat of nuclear war did not disappear, the United States found itself fighting small wars in far-off places. After spending more than a decade preparing to fight nuclear and conventional war in Europe, ironically the United States became embroiled in a lengthy unconventional conflict in Southeast Asia that would shake the military, indeed the nation, to its very core. Even at home, the National Guard and the regular Army were used to quell domestic disturbances with greater and alarming frequency, a trend that continued into the early 1970s.

Further Reading

Allison, Graham T., and Philip Zelikow. *Essence of Decision: Explaining the Cuban Missile Crisis*. 2nd ed. New York: Addison Wesley, 1999.

Ashton, Nigel John. *Eisenhower, Macmillan, and the Problem of Nasser: Anglo-American Relations and Arab Nationalism, 1955–1959*. London: Macmillan, 1996.

Bacevich, A. C. *The Pentomic Era: The U.S. Army between Korea and Vietnam*. Washington, D.C.: National Defense University Press, 1986.

Beschloss, Michael. *Mayday: Eisenhower, Khrushchev, and the U-2 Affair*. New York: Harper, 1986.

Divine, Robert A. *Eisenhower and the Cold War*. New York: Oxford University Press, 1981.

Duiker, William J. *U.S. Containment Policy and the Conflict in Indochina*. Stanford, California: Stanford University Press, 1994.

Fall, Bernard. *Hell in a Very Small Place: The Siege of Dien Bien Phu*. London: Macmillan, 1967.

Feaver, Peter. *Guarding the Guardians: Civilian Control over Nuclear Weapons in the United States*. Ithaca: Cornell University Press, 1992.

Freedman, Lawrence. *The Evolution of Nuclear Strategy*. London: Macmillan, 1989.

Friedman, Norman. *The Fifty-Year War: Conflict and Strategy in the Cold War*. Annapolis: Naval Institute Press, 2000.

Furensko, Aleksandr, and Timothy Naftali. *"One Hell of a Gamble": The Secret History of the Cuban Missile Crisis*. New York: Norton, 1997.

Gaddis, John Lewis. *Strategies of Containment: A Critical Appraisal of Postwar American National Security Policy*. New York: Oxford University Press, 1982.

Gaddis, John Lewis. *We Now Know: Rethinking Cold War History*. Oxford, England: Clarendon Press, 1997.

Gelb, Norman. *The Berlin Wall: Kennedy, Khrushchev, and a Showdown in the Heart of Europe*. New York: Times Books, 1987.

Kaplan, Fred. *The Wizards of Armageddon*. Stanford, California: Stanford University Press, 1991.

Levering, Ralph B. *The Cold War: A Post-Cold War History*. Arlington Heights, Illinois: Harlan Davidson, 1994.

Miller, David. *The Cold War: A Military History*. New York: St. Martin's Press, 1998.

Munton, Don, and David A. Welch. *The Cuban Missile Crisis: A Concise History*. New York: Oxford University Press, USA, 2011.

Nichols, David A. *Eisenhower 1956: The President's Year of Crisis—Suez and the Brink of War*. New York: Simon & Schuster, 2011.

Roman, Peter J. *Eisenhower and the Missile Gap*. Ithaca: Cornell University Press, 1995.

Steiner, Barry H. *Bernard Brodie and the Foundations of American Nuclear Strategy*. Lawrence: University Press of Kansas, 1991.

Westad, Odd Arne. *The Global Cold War: Third World Interventions and the Making of Our Times*. Cambridge: Cambridge University Press, 2007.

Windrow, Martin. *The Last Valley: Dien Bien Phu and the French Defeat in Vietnam.* Cambridge, Massachusetts: Da Capo Press, 2004.

mysearchlab Connections: Sources Online • • • • • • • • • •

READ AND REVIEW

Review this chapter by using the study aids and these related documents available on MySearchLab.

Study Plan

Chapter Test

Essay Test

Documents

Summary of Executive Committee Meeting on Cuban Missile Crisis (1962)

This document relates the intense debate over what to do about Soviet missiles in Cuba and avoiding all-out nuclear war with the Soviet Union.

Memo to Secretary of State John Foster Dulles from President Dwight D. Eisenhower Regarding Ceasefire during Suez Crisis (1956)

In this document, President Eisenhower discusses American strategy regarding the Suez Crisis in light of the broader Cold War with the Soviet Union.

Dwight Eisenhower Articulates Domino Theory (1954)

In this document, President Eisenhower explains his concern about the spread of communism in Asia.

John F. Kennedy on the Berlin Crisis (1961)

In this document, President Kennedy expresses his concerns over the Soviet move to build a wall dividing East and West Berlin, a wall that came to symbolize the Cold War perhaps more than any other edifice until joyous protesters dismantled it in 1989.

RESEARCH AND EXPLORE

Explore the following review questions using the research tools available on www. mysearchlab.com.

1. What are the differences between the New Look and Flexible Response?
2. Why is the Cuban missile crisis important?
3. Explain the significance of Dien Bien Phu.
4. How did the Suez crisis affect American policy in the Middle East?

CHAPTER 15

Vietnam

◆ CHRONOLOGY

1946	Ho Chi Minh declares independence for Vietnam
	French Indochina War begins
1950	United States begins military assistance to France in Indochina
1954	Siege of Dien Bien Phu
	Geneva Accords
1955	American military advisors begin training South Vietnamese army
1959	North Vietnam decides to fight insurgency war in South Vietnam
1962	Military Assistance Command Vietnam established
1963	Diem murdered in coup
	Battle of Ap Bac
1964	Tonkin Gulf Incident and Congressional Resolution
1965	Operation ROLLING THUNDER begins
	Battle of Ia Drang
	Johnson "Americanizes" the war
	American troop strength at nearly 200,000
1966	American troop strength at nearly 400,000
1967	Operation CEDAR FALLS
	American troop strength at nearly 500,000

1968	Tet Offensive
	My Lai Massacre
	ROLLING THUNDER ends
	Tentative peace negotiations begin
	American troop strength at nearly 535,000
1969	Vietnamization and American troop withdrawal begins
	American troop strength falls to 475,000
1970	Peace talks begin in Paris
	Cambodia invasion
	Students killed at Kent State University
	American troop strength falls to 334,000
1971	Operation LAM SON 719
	Lieutenant William Calley convicted in My Lai killings
	American troop strength falls to 140,000
1972	Easter Offensive
	Linebacker bombing campaigns
1973	Cease-fire agreement signed in Paris by the United States and North Vietnam
	Last American combat and support forces withdraw
1975	North Vietnam conquers South Vietnam
1995	The United States extends formal diplomatic recognition to Vietnam

◆ INTRODUCTION

Vietnam was America's longest war, its most socially divisive since the Civil War, and the most misunderstood conflict of modern times. It continues to cast a shadow over American public life and popular culture, reflecting its role as the defining event for the "baby boom" generation that came of age during the 1960s and 1970s. The conduct of the war at the highest levels was characterized by hubris and marked a culminating point in American Cold War policy and international behavior, while defeat in 1975 prompted serious introspection within the armed forces and, ironically, led to a far-reaching renaissance in American military power.

More has been written on American involvement in Vietnam than on any American conflict other than the Civil War. This output reflects the size of the group affected by the war (some 2.5 million Americans served in Southeast Asia), and it indicates that Americans tend to determine the importance of a conflict in terms of its domestic rather than its international impact.

◆ EARLY AMERICAN INVOLVEMENT

The United States became involved in Vietnam by way of broader Cold War concerns mostly relating to Western Europe. Like Korea before them, the French colonial territories of Indochina were of little interest or importance to the United States. French attempts to reimpose colonial rule after World War II were doomed to failure, but it was American concern that France make a credible military and political contribution to the NATO alliance in Europe that led to massive underwriting of the French military effort against North Vietnamese leader Ho Chi Minh.

The French defeat at Dien Bien Phu in May 1954 effectively ended the fighting in Indochina, leaving Communist forces in nominal control of the north, while French forces tenuously held the south. Among the topics discussed at the Geneva Conference that spring was a satisfactory settlement for Indochina. The result, however, was far from satisfactory for either side, as Vietnam was divided into north and south. The French withdrawal from the region compelled the United States to fill the subsequent power vacuum in the south in order to deny the newly created entity, the Republic of Vietnam, to the Communists in the north. Ho Chi Minh and the Communists represented the nationalist aspirations of a large proportion of the Vietnamese people, and the search for credible alternatives and a legitimate client state in the south was to be an enduring problem for American policy thereafter.

Direct involvement in Vietnam was a gradual process, beginning in earnest during the Eisenhower administration. The United States and its allies increasingly backed Ngo Dinh Diem, an authoritarian Catholic in a country overwhelmingly Buddhist. Diem's government had enjoyed considerable success in the second half of the 1950s in defeating internal threats to stability from both Communist and non-Communist sources. The methods employed were heavy-handed, and pressure placed on the Communist networks in the south led Hanoi to restart the revolutionary struggle to unite the country under Communist rule in 1958–1959. At several points between then and American commitment of combat forces in 1965, the United States was faced with the choice to reinforce Diem, and equally ineffective leaders, or to withdraw support. Each time, the United States appears to have done just enough to stave off imminent disaster without arriving at a clearly thought-out strategy for a permanent and successful solution. The image of a quagmire, frequently invoked in accounts of the war, owes something to this haphazard process.

The American military that fought the war initially entered the conflict at the peak of effectiveness, self-confidence, and apparent technological superiority. It was a military fashioned to face off against Soviet forces on the plains of Central Europe, however, and despite the creation of Special Forces capabilities (notably the "Green Berets") and some enthusiasm within the Kennedy administration for what has been termed "the cult of counterinsurgency," it was not shaped especially well for the challenges posed by revolutionary guerrilla war in mainland Southeast Asia.

Fashioned in the experiences of the Second World War, the American military increasingly emphasized the roles of firepower, mass, and technology as solutions to the problems posed on the battlefield. There was a strong belief in the efficacy of airpower throughout the American military, but particularly within the U.S. Air Force. Consistent with its general doctrine, the Air Force proposed a campaign of strategic nonnuclear bombing on major industrial and military targets in North Vietnam. The Army organizationally and doctrinally exploited the potential arising from the helicopter, using it on the battlefield in tactical situations through the creation and evolution of air mobility and the conversion of the Army's 1st Cavalry Division to an airmobile role.

The American war can be divided into four broad phases. From the mid-1950s until the end of the American commitment, a substantial training and advisory effort was mounted to create, develop, and sustain the Republic of Vietnam Armed Forces, especially the Army of the Republic of Vietnam (ARVN). Until the deployment of large numbers of American combat troops and the decision to Americanize the war in 1965, the advisory war represented the major American effort in the country. Between 1965 and 1969, American combat units fought the "big unit" war so familiar to movie audiences and associated ineluctably with General William C. Westmoreland, the commander of the American Military Assistance Command Vietnam (MACV). The third phase, between 1969 and 1972, followed the election of President Richard Nixon. Nixon had campaigned on a promise to end the war (or, at least, American involvement in it), and this third period saw the Vietnamization of the conflict with the United States turning over responsibility for much of the war's conduct to the ARVN. American troop levels dropped significantly, and Westmoreland's successor, General Creighton W. Abrams, placed a renewed emphasis on pacification.

To most intents and purposes, American forces had been withdrawn from major ground combat by 1972. The final phase, from American withdrawal until the fall of Saigon in 1975, saw the South Vietnamese solely responsible for their own defense with only nominal financial and material support from the United States. Increasingly embattled by a resurgent enemy no longer wary of American airpower and ultimately betrayed and abandoned by their American patrons, the corrupt South Vietnamese government and its rapidly decaying military forces had little chance against the North's well-supplied and well-trained conventional forces.

◆ THE ADVISORS' WAR

The advisors' war is the aspect of American involvement least known or understood. Military advising was the part of the American effort that brought American personnel into the closest and most sustained contact with their South Vietnamese counterparts. At some times and places, American advisors were brought closest to the pacification and counterinsurgency tasks that were central to the guerrilla struggle in the villages.

Especially in the southern Mekong River delta and in the central highlands working with the Montagnards, American military advisors often found themselves largely outside the formal American military structure and relatively isolated from other Americans. Those advisors who worked within the Vietnamese military were often prized by their Vietnamese charges for the access to American fire support that they could seemingly instantly provide. In keeping with the Korean War experience, the Vietnamese military was fashioned in an American image, designed initially to counter or repel a conventional military invasion of the south along the lines the North Koreans had attempted in 1950. This was not the nature of the threat they faced, however, and the ARVN was ultimately ill-suited to waging a "hearts and minds" campaign in the countryside.

Diem's ouster and murder in late 1963 ushered in a period of chronic political instability and revolving-door governments installed and removed by coup and countercoup. American attempts to sustain a viable non-Communist South Vietnam were unraveling; this was especially apparent to the advisors on the ground, some of whom became staunch critics of the way in which the advisory effort was conducted and of the unrelenting and increasingly unrealistic optimism with which higher authority presented it. By 1963 there were 16,000 American military personnel in Vietnam, and while they enjoyed success in some areas—especially in arming and training the hill tribes—their efforts elsewhere appeared futile. For example, in the Battle of Ap Bac, in January 1963, a large ARVN force supported by armored personnel carriers attempted to assault a well-entrenched enemy position. Casualties among the attacking force were heavy, numbers of armored vehicles and American helicopters were destroyed or damaged, and the attack was generally regarded as a failure—and a controversial one at that.

President Lyndon Johnson faced difficult decisions in the course of 1964, a presidential election year. Johnson himself, though generally remembered as a war president, was in fact focused on domestic issues arising from his Great Society program, but his presidency was increasingly overshadowed by the war in Southeast Asia. It is sometimes suggested that the Johnson administration always did enough not to lose the war, yet never enough to win it outright; this misunderstands the real nature of the struggle in South Vietnam, which in the end could be won only by the South Vietnamese themselves, and the range of domestic constraints under which Johnson labored.

The approach of the Kennedy administration—advisors, training, and material assistance—had not produced the desired results, and in late 1964 Johnson decided to take the war to North Vietnam in an attempt to break enemy resolve through a campaign of strategic bombardment. In August, Congress overwhelmingly passed the Tonkin Gulf Resolution, which authorized Johnson to take whatever measures he saw fit to defend Americans and American interests in Vietnam and to uphold American obligations to the Southeast Asia Treaty Organization. The spur for this move was provided by supposed attacks against American destroyers operating off the coast of North Vietnam. Recent evidence challenging whether the attacks were real or a misreading of events by the American ships involved remains highly contentious.

◆ AMERICANIZING THE WAR

Operation ROLLING THUNDER was approved in February 1965 but went much less far in its scope and intensity than bombing advocates within the military and the administration wanted. Essentially a campaign of graduated escalation, it was intended to increase pressure on Hanoi and send a signal to the enemy that continued support for the war in the south would have serious consequences within the north. This assumed that the Communists were susceptible to such argument and vulnerable to such pressure. Neither was the case. For the Communists, this was a war of national unification and independence, war aims that were not susceptible to negotiation. For the United States, limited war theory guided the American approach to Vietnam, hoping to achieve political objectives through the use of graduated military force while keeping the conflict contained in Vietnam.

Washington fundamentally misunderstood its enemy and the nature of the war the United States was embarking upon. Not only was the immediate response to the bombing a heightened North Vietnamese operational tempo in the south, with attacks upon American facilities and the bases from which some of the bombing missions were being launched, but in time, and with Chinese and Soviet assistance, the airspace over North Vietnam became one of the most intense air defense environments in the world. American losses steadily mounted.

During the Great War for Empire, British General James Wolfe maintained that war is an option of difficulties—an apt appraisal of the options Johnson faced in Vietnam just over two hundred years later. Johnson did not want the war, and his senior advisors do not appear to have believed, in private, that it could be won. Enemy

FIGURE 15-1   During the Pink Rose test program, target areas near Tay Ninh and An Loc, Vietnam, were sprayed with defoliation agents twice and with a drying agent once. Ten flights of three B-52s each dropped 42 M-35 incendiary cluster bombs, per aircraft, into the target areas, setting fires that burned the heavy growth as well as enemy fortifications hidden there. Sweeping over the tree-tops, this C-123 Ranch Hand aircraft sprays defoliant over the target areas.

Source: National Archives and Records Administration.

activity increased in intensity and effectiveness, and American officials in Saigon grew pessimistic about the ARVN's combat performance as well as South Vietnam's future. At the same time, Johnson did not wish to strengthen opposition in the United States by being seen to have "lost" Vietnam in the manner that Truman was alleged to have "lost" China in 1949. Withdrawal, therefore, was not an option.

In Saigon, Westmoreland enthusiastically advocated committing American ground combat troops to the fight, and between April and July, Johnson approved force requests that amounted to nearly 200,000 American troops, with additional forces offered from South Korea, Thailand, Australia, New Zealand, and the Philippines in response to strong pressure from Washington. The "American" war had begun in earnest.

Considerable divisions existed within the American command authority over the war and its conduct, and this did little to assist in the formulation of coherent and effective strategy. The most important of these differences centered on the Secretary of Defense, Robert S. McNamara. Brought in by Kennedy from the Ford Motor Company to rein in the defense budget and make the Pentagon more efficient and responsive, McNamara surrounded himself with "whiz kids," bright young technocrats schooled in systems analysis and with neither military experience nor respect for those who had it. McNamara himself treated the Joint Chiefs of Staff with thinly veiled contempt, while the vociferous demands for quantification of results helped to drive the "body count" culture that emerged as a result of the 1965 Battle of Ia Drang, in which American forces first squared off against the North Vietnamese Army. The Chief of Staff of the Army, General Harold K. Johnson, agonized over whether to resign in protest at the misconduct of the war and subsequently regretted that he had not done so.

With heavy losses through combat and even heavier ones through desertion, the ARVN was incapable at this stage of holding its own against the Viet Cong and the North Vietnamese Army. Consequently, Westmoreland's decision to fight the war with American Army and Marine units was probably justified, for a time. In 1965–1966 the big-unit war, pursuing an aggressive and capable enemy across the length and breadth of the country, staved off collapse and bought time to rebuild South Vietnamese capabilities. Too little advantage was taken of this opportunity, however; the attitude seemed frequently to be that the South Vietnamese were simply in the way. Nor did the big-unit approach have much to offer the process of pacification, which many Americans regarded as a "second order" task fit only for the ARVN while the Americans fought the "real" war.

But it was expensive in casualties, and American combat units suffered heavy losses while undoubtedly inflicting them as well. This strategy of attrition was really no strategy at all and misunderstood the nature of revolutionary war and the problems it posed. Military force was only one part of the security equation, but in this phase of the war it received the greatest emphasis from Westmoreland and his superiors, perhaps because it was the one aspect of the war that they felt they understood and could deal with.

There were, in fact, four different ground wars in Vietnam at any one time, and where a soldier operated largely determined the nature of his operational experience. The most intense combat environment was in the northern provinces adjoining the 17th parallel, where the Marine Corps and the best of the ARVN formations, such as the airborne, were deployed. The mountains and thick jungles of the interior also saw sustained heavy combat, where much of the fighting was done by the Montagnards, tribesmen whom the South Vietnamese regarded as inferiors. The more heavily populated central and southern regions brought combat units into close contact with villagers, many of whom were wounded or killed by American firepower and a willingness of the Viet Cong to use civilians to shield their own fighting units. Finally, the Mekong River Delta in the south came closest to the classic image of a war fought by black-pajama-clad Viet Cong. Much of the fighting in this area was done by the ARVN, accompanied by American advisors. Generally, the Americans stayed out of the cities, such as Saigon and Hue, leaving security there to the South Vietnamese—although there were exceptions to this, such as during the Tet Offensive in 1968 and the fighting for Hue.

Hanoi matched the American force buildup in the south, despite suffering heavy casualties at the hands of American firepower. Regular North Vietnamese units and formations were deployed in increasing numbers, in part to replace casualties among the Viet Cong and match the combat capabilities of American units. The slogan adopted by many soldiers of the North Vietnamese Army—"born in the north to die in the south"—acquired a grim certainty in this period of the war.

The Viet Cong and North Vietnamese Army made extensive use of rocket and mortar attacks (especially on the large, vulnerable American base areas located across South Vietnam), mines, snipers, ambushes, and bunker systems, but were also quite prepared to engage in set-piece conventional actions, especially in the northern provinces. Tactically, enemy units often attempted to close with and "hug" opposing units in order to negate American advantages in fire support, especially from helicopters and other aerial platforms. Using heavier, crew-served automatic weapons, they inflicted significant casualties upon American helicopter units and their crews. Regular northern units and provincial Viet Cong formations, in particular, were not an enemy to be taken lightly.

Although the ARVN was created in imitation of its American patron, it had some important differences and limitations. Corruption, political patronage, and incompetence were real problems right up to the fall of Saigon in 1975. There were, however, a growing number of honest and competent officers in senior command positions, especially after 1968, to whom Americans generally paid less attention. Indeed, there were also many courageous and tenacious ordinary soldiers and junior officers for whom the war never ended and who did not enjoy the luxury of a twelve-month tour of duty, whose performance also went unnoted.

FIGURE 15-2 A machine gunner and a rifleman from the 5th Marine Regiment fire at the enemy near the Demilitarized Zone in Vietnam, May 23, 1967.

Source: National Archives and Records Administration.

FIGURE 15-3 The War in Vietnam.

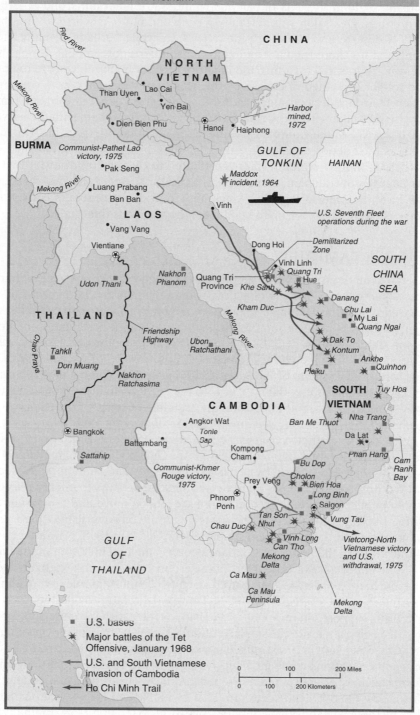

At its height, the ARVN numbered more than half a million men, with perhaps as many again in a variety of part-time militias, irregular units, and other paramilitary formations. Desertion was certainly a problem, but it is worth noting that very few ARVN deserters went over to the other side, while perhaps as many as 90,000 Viet Cong and northern regulars rallied to the southern government during the course of the war. Associated with this, the majority of ARVN divisions were regionally based, and soldiers operated in the same provinces from which they were conscripted and in which their families continued to reside. Aside from concern for their families generally, many soldiers from the villages felt an obligation to help with the harvest and similar tasks. When the Communists launched their final offensive in 1975, many ARVN soldiers took action to safeguard their families, in some cases attaching them to units as these withdrew, which further contributed to the general disorder that was part of the enemy's overall plan. Generally, as a result of all this, the ARVN suffered from a low level of strategic mobility, which limited its effectiveness in conventional operations when these again came to dominate the war in its final stages.

◆ THE AIR CAMPAIGN

The air campaign over North Vietnam occasioned great controversy within the United States and beyond. Using global propaganda, the North Vietnamese and others skillfully exploited the campaign to put pressure on Washington to cease the bombing—a sign, perhaps, that it was more effective than apologists for Hanoi sometimes cared to admit. Operation ROLLING THUNDER remains controversial for several reasons. Critics of the way the war was conducted point to the "coercive" use of airpower in this way as an example of the Johnson administration compelling the armed forces to observe limitations that did not apply to the enemy—fighting with one hand tied, as it were. The strategic thinking behind the "sending of signals" and the process of bombing halts followed by renewed intensification of the campaign was in any case flawed.

Even with restrictive rules of engagement and serious attempts to limit damage and civilian casualties, the technology of the time could not eliminate collateral damage. This was seized upon by America's critics at home and abroad, aided and abetted by those—such as Jane Fonda—who lent themselves to enemy purposes through highly publicized visits to Hanoi, where they made naïve and ill-considered criticisms of the bombing in particular and more generally of American objectives in the war. Johnson ended the bombings completely in October 1968, following his decision to withdraw from the 1968 presidential election campaign in March of that year.

The importance of helicopters in the ground war in South Vietnam has been noted already, but fixed-wing aircraft played an equally important role in providing air support to American and allied ground forces. Transport aircraft provided an extensive network of logistic support and resupply flights that, together with the close air support provided by attack aircraft, made the skies over South Vietnam some of the busiest in the world.

Close air support missions dropped huge quantities of explosives and napalm on enemy positions while an extensive program of aerial defoliation, using chemical agents such as Agent Orange, stripped vast acreages of the rural countryside to deny the enemy the overhead cover provided by jungle and forest. In a further demonstration of their versatility as a bomber platform, B-52 bombers originally designed to carry nuclear weapons into the heart of the Soviet Union were used in Arc Light missions, dropping large tonnages of high explosive from great and undetectable heights upon otherwise inaccessible enemy positions along the Ho Chi Minh Trail, for example, and causing heavy damage and considerable effect on enemy morale.

◆ **NAVAL OPERATIONS**

Winding from the North Vietnamese border with Laos southward through Cambodia and then into South Vietnam at various points, the Ho Chi Minh Trail itself was the result of another success against the enemy's war effort, this time at sea. The maritime war had several components: blue water; brown water; harbor and port defense, especially in the waters around the port of Saigon; and naval activities ashore.

Operation SEA DRAGON, commenced in October 1966, involved offensive operations against shore targets in North Vietnam designed to complement ROLLING THUNDER. Operation MARKET TIME, directed against sea-borne infiltration of supplies and personnel southward along the coast, proved so successful in stemming the flow of logistic support from the north by 1967 that it led the Communists to find other, safer means of resupplying the south along the Ho Chi Minh Trail and through the supposedly neutral Cambodian port of Sihanoukville.

The brown-water riverine war, encompassed by Operation GAME WARDEN, utilized vessels of the U.S. Navy, the South Vietnamese Navy, and the U.S. Coast Guard against Viet Cong movement along South Vietnam's internal waterways, assisted by the Coastal Groups, South Vietnamese paramilitaries more commonly known as the "junk force." The riverine war was dangerous and intense, and enemy contact and casualties were frequent.

The air and naval wars were always an adjunct to that fought on the ground. In 1967, the size of the forces on each side continued to grow, the intensity of the fighting was maintained, and the enemy usually retained the tactical initiative. American forces grew that year from 385,000 to 486,000, though the number of allied maneuver battalions only increased from 256 to 278. Despite the emphasis on large-scale search and destroy operations, the Viet Cong and North Vietnamese usually evaded American and ARVN forces when they wished, initiating contact up to company level (and sometimes higher) and frustrating Westmoreland's grand designs. The fighting in the five northern provinces of I Corps was especially fierce, but throughout the country the casualty rate for American forces more than doubled over that suffered in 1966: over 9,000 combat deaths and over 60,000 wounded. Enemy battle deaths were estimated to have reached nearly 90,000 for the year.

◆ **TET**

Westmoreland's optimistic reporting on the situation on the ground, together with the ferocity of the combat and the heavy losses imposed on the enemy, made the impact of the Tet Offensive at the end of January 1968 all the more powerful. Distracting attention through sustained operations along South Vietnam's borders and against the Marine outpost at Khe Sanh, the enemy moved sizeable forces against the cities and major urban centers throughout South Vietnam. Tet, the festival of the lunar new year, is the most important holiday in the Vietnamese calendar and had routinely been marked by brief holiday truces between the combatants; in the lead-up to the offensive, much of the ARVN was on leave. Although Westmoreland remained distracted by the fighting at Khe Sanh and further inland and by the battering the enemy had taken in 1967, he was persuaded to station additional American battalions in the vicinity of Saigon just before the offensive was launched, greatly enhancing MACV's capacity to respond quickly to the assaults on the capital. The Tet Offensive was intended to provide the final stage in protracted revolutionary warfare along the Maoist model—the nationwide popular uprising that would sweep away the Americans and their "puppets" in Saigon.

In an attack launched on the night of January 29–30, the Viet Cong hit 36 of the 44 provincial capitals, 5 out of 6 autonomous cities, 64 district capitals, and numerous South Vietnamese and American bases and military facilities, including 23 airfields. From the American perspective, the greatest shock involved the breaching of the compound wall at the American Embassy in Saigon by a small detachment of Viet Cong sappers, most of whom were killed in the ensuing firefight with American military police units. Television images of this tiny aspect of the great offensive that was unfolding, played repeatedly on news broadcasts in the United States, fatally undermined Westmoreland's confident assertion at the end of the previous year that there was "light at the end of the tunnel" in Vietnam.

The most significant aspects of the Tet Offensive were, in fact, the things that did not happen: there was no mass uprising in support of the Viet Cong, the ARVN did not desert, the National Police did not collapse, and the Saigon government did not lose its nerve or its capacity to respond. Soldiers and police fought fiercely and well, and in many instances they ejected or exterminated the attackers in short order. Saigon was largely cleared of the enemy within a week of the offensive's launch. Intense fighting led to widespread destruction and considerable numbers of civilian casualties. The old imperial capital of Hue, in the north, was largely destroyed and thousands of its citizens killed or rendered homeless. At least 3,000 "enemies of the people" were rounded up in the city by the Viet Cong, murdered, and then buried in mass graves. Intense fighting continued before petering out in late February.

A MEDAL OF HONOR AT HUE

In all wars, soldiers commit extreme acts of heroism under the most difficult combat conditions. Vietnam, of course, was no different. Following is one of several eyewitness statements attesting to the bravery under fire of Staff Sergeant Joe Hooper of Company D, Second Battalion, 501st Infantry, 101st Airborne Division during the Battle of Hue on February 21, 1968. Sergeant Hooper was subsequently awarded the Medal of Honor, the highest award for bravery under fire given by the United States, for his actions that day.

Eyewitness Statement of 2nd Lieutenant Lee Grimsley, Company D, Second Battalion, 501st Infantry, 101st Airborne Division, March 12, 1968

On 21 February 1968, the Delta Raiders were involved in a joint assault on a North Vietnamese regimental base area a few miles west of Hue. Company D had the mission of assaulting a dense woodline within which the enemy had built strong bunkers interlinked by trenches. My platoon was on the left of the company as it advanced, and as we approached a river close in front of the enemy lines we were taken under intense fire from the enemy. Many of the men sought cover, but Sgt. Hooper rallied several men and attacked across the river directly into the enemy fire. These men cleared several bunkers on the opposite shore and inspired the rest of the company to continue the advance. From here Sgt. Hooper moved out among the thick bamboo aiding wounded and evacuating them. In so doing he was wounded himself by the many grenades which were falling in the area. Yet he refused evacuation and treatment and returned to the woodline where he single-handedly attacked and wiped out a triple-bunker complex which had been firing rockets into our lines. He then returned and brought forward a number of men who had gotten no further than the river bank. He led them in a sweep and overran several more bunkers. Sgt. Hooper personally knocked out three houses and a shrine with LAWs [M-72 Light Anti-Tank Weapon]; each building had been the source of concentrated fire on our men. At one point Sgt. Hooper killed a North Vietnamese officer with his bayonet. Coming back to bring his men forward again I saw that his wounds had been compounded and urged him to move to the rear. But he desisted. Instead he moved out alone against a building which was issuing heavy fire at our men and eliminated it with hand grenades and rifle fire. As the line advanced, Sgt. Hooper moved out ahead and dashed down a trenchline running in front of four bunkers, tossing grenades into them as he went by, thus killing all these defenders except two whom he captured when they staggered out of their bunker. After clearing these bunkers Sgt. Hooper moved up to another one, one of the very last to hold out, and started firing into a machine gun bunker just a short distance away. However he apparently learned that the bunker he was firing from was still occupied as he shortly threw a white phosphorous grenade into and then continued to fire into the machine gun bunker and the bunker adjacent it. His rifle fire effectively cleared both bunkers. Sgt. Hooper spent the rest of the day caring for the wounded and making sure they were well taken care of. Yet he still refused to be evacuated while he organized his men and prepared them for the next day's fighting. Only the next morning did he allow himself to be evacuated.

It is difficult to adequately praise Sgt. Hooper for his action on this day. He destroyed more enemy positions and killed more enemy soldiers by himself than some companies claimed at the end of the day. And it is certain that without his inspiration and amazing courage the platoon and

> company's success would have been a great deal less than they were and
> possibly might have been no success at all.
>
> Lee Grimsley
> 2Lt. Infantry
> Platoon Leader
>
> *Source:* National Archives and Records Administration.

The two most significant and long-term outcomes of Tet were the fatal under-mining of American resolve and the near destruction of the Viet Cong. Because the American and South Vietnamese military response to the Tet Offensive nearly destroyed the Viet Cong, after mid-1968 the proportion of North Vietnamese regulars in South Vietnam increased dramatically and continued to do so for the remainder of the war. In late 1965, they had made up 25 percent of the enemy force in-country; by June 1968 this had grown to 55 percent, and to 70 percent overall if northerners drafted into Viet Cong units are included. It has been suggested subsequently that the destruction of the indigenous southern movement in 1968 enabled Hanoi to tighten its control over the revolutionary movement in the south.

Predictably, Westmoreland responded to the Tet Offensive by demanding an additional 205,000 American troops. Johnson had little choice but to deny the request. Under intense political pressure at home and himself realizing the futility of the war in Southeast Asia, Johnson shocked the nation in a speech on March 31, 1968, by first opening the door for negotiations with North Vietnam and then announcing he would not run for reelection. By mid-year Westmoreland had returned to the United States to take up the post of Chief of Staff of the Army, replaced in Vietnam by General Creighton W. Abrams. President Johnson, facing certain defeat if he ran, declined to be considered for the Democratic Party nomination for another term as president.

Americans killed in action exceeded 500 per week in February and March 1968, and although enemy losses were staggering—over 45,000 in the first three weeks of February alone—support for the war in the United States declined still further and never recovered. Tet had been a military defeat but a political victory for North Vietnam and became the turning point in the American war.

◆ VIETNAMIZATION

Richard Nixon came to the presidency in 1969 with the intention of withdrawing from Vietnam, but of doing so "honorably." This was much easier said than done. In fact, roughly as many Americans were killed in Vietnam under Nixon's adminis-tration as had been under Johnson's. On several occasions Nixon appeared to widen the war, dangerously in the view of his detractors, as he sought a means to get out of Vietnam while leaving the South Vietnamese with a reasonable chance of holding the Communists at bay.

Abrams paid much more attention to training and equipping the ARVN, building up the regional and popular force militias in the villages, and doing general pacification tasks aimed at strengthening the authority and legitimacy of the government in Saigon at the expense of the Viet Cong and the National Liberation Front. Considerable advances were made in these areas, and it has been argued that a greater emphasis on them earlier in the American war would have produced stronger long-term results. While this may be true, it overlooks two things: the greatly weakened state of the Viet Cong after 1968, which made it easier to counter them in the countryside than had been the case in 1966–1967, and the implacable resolve in Hanoi to win the war and unify the country.

Often intense fighting continued while the ARVN was modernized, and greatly increased resources were poured into pacification. At the same time, the Nixon administration intensified the peace talks with the Communists in Paris that Johnson had initiated in mid-1968; President Nixon also announced a timetable for gradual troop withdrawals in June 1969.

In an effort to restrict the enemy's capacity to operate effectively within South Vietnam, Nixon authorized moves to interrupt the Communist resupply system running through "neutral" Cambodia, with heavy air attacks against the sanctuaries and base areas commencing in March 1969. Following a coup against Prince Norodom Sihanouk by pro-American elements in the Cambodian armed forces, a joint American-ARVN force of 20,000 troops launched ground and air assaults against the enemy base areas across the Cambodian border in May 1970. Militarily, this inflicted considerable losses, but in the United States the Cambodian incursion reinvigorated the antiwar movement and added to the domestic political problems of the Nixon administration.

Domestic opposition to the war flared as Nixon ordered the FBI to increase surveillance on antiwar groups in the United States, and National Guard troops shot and killed four students on the campus of Kent State University in Ohio during an antiwar demonstration. Press reports and congressional investigations revealing the brutal murder of Vietnamese civilians at My Lai by troops in the Americal Division back in March 1968 only added to the American public's disenchantment with the war. Even Vietnam veterans began protesting the war through groups such as Vietnam Veterans Against the War, and the so-called Winter Soldier hearings made public alleged atrocities committed by American forces in Vietnam.

◆ ANTIWAR ACTIVISM

The American commitment to Vietnam was always controversial, though in its early stages opposition was largely confined to political groupings on the Left and traditional peace activists such as the Quakers. Support for military regimes in the Republic of Vietnam became increasingly difficult to sell to the American public as the casualty rates rose, U.S. servicemen came home to local cemeteries all over the country, and the aims, purpose, and outcomes of the war remained unclear, at best. President Johnson inherited a war and a commitment not of his making and decidedly opposed to his own inclination to build the "Great Society" at home; but it was on his watch that the war was inexorably lost, at least in American living rooms and on American campuses.

Loss of confidence in American purpose in Vietnam transcended social class and political affiliation. Antiwar sentiment can be divided roughly into two parts: the active antiwar movement that was the visible face of the era on campuses, on the streets, and outside draft offices, and the growing disenchantment felt by many respectable Americans who abhorred the more violent activities of the first group while nonetheless withdrawing their support for the prosecution of the war. Demonstrations against official policy grew from the major peace marches in 1965 to the large-scale mobilization of protestors outside the Pentagon in October 1967 and culminated in the use of troops during the protests at Kent State and elsewhere in March 1970 that resulted in the shooting deaths of four students by the Ohio National Guard.

Dissent was widespread, sometimes intense, and was fueled by widespread media coverage, though certainly not caused by it. Popular culture reflected this, though one should beware of assuming that antiwar sentiment was all-pervasive. The political environment under Nixon became increasingly volatile—something that the President encouraged by his policies and behavior—but the sentiment in the country was increasingly one of profound weariness with a war that was clearly lost. The divisions produced within the country as a result of the war remain with Americans still, as the public debate over recent conflicts since 9/11 suggests.

◆ PEACE WITH HONOR

The United States was caught between conflicting pressures to end its part in the war, reassure its allies in Southeast Asia and the Pacific, and create a viable South Vietnam that could survive after the withdrawal of American ground troops. The results remained mixed. A measure of political stability had been created with the reelection of Nguyen Van Thieu to the presidency in 1971, but the poor performance of the ARVN during Operation LAM SON 719 in Laos the same year suggested that it was incapable of defeating the Communists on its own. On the other hand, when the North Vietnamese launched a major, countrywide offensive at Easter in 1972, the ARVN performed credibly, especially at places such as An Loc. The key, however, was the stiffening of American advisors and the close air support they controlled—factors that would soon be removed.

Nixon authorized further heavy bombing against targets in North Vietnam; Operation LINEBACKER effectively targeted communications and transportation infrastructure and heavily damaged the economy. North Vietnamese willingness to conclude an agreement, albeit one that favored their position within the south, was encouraged through further air attacks at Christmas in 1972 through Operation LINEBACKER II, which finally brought about the signing of the Paris Peace Accords in January 1973. South Vietnam was promised immediate American military support in the face of any further northern aggression, and substantial continuing military aid.

While giving the United States a way out of the war, the Paris agreements ironically brought no peace to Vietnam and left substantial Communist forces in place in the south, from where they were able to undermine attempts by Thieu's government to maintain its authority and legitimacy. Nixon's domestic political troubles arising from the Watergate scandal and his ensuing resignation, together with passage of the War Powers Resolution in 1974 that significantly limited a president's ability to use military force, robbed South Vietnam of any remaining hope of survival in the face of mounting northern military activity.

What was originally planned as a limited offensive in April 1975 quickly gained momentum in the face of command confusion in Saigon, rapid local successes on the part of the enemy, and disintegration in the ARVN. While some units fought to the last—such as the 18th Division at Xuan Loc that barred the road to Saigon for almost two weeks—the collapse was generally rapid. On April 30, having replaced Thieu in the hopes of furthering some form of negotiations, President Duong Van Minh surrendered his country. The Vietnam War was finally over.

◆ THE AMERICAN EXPERIENCE IN VIETNAM

Vietnam was the last American war to be fought by an army heavily manned by conscripts, giving way to the all-volunteer military after 1974 that was very much part of the reaction to that war and its costs. The burden of service was not equally or equitably shared, however. The average age of soldiers in Vietnam was 19 (compared to 26 in World War II). Ethnic minorities and the economically disadvantaged were overrepresented in the ranks because of the draft and misguided programs such as Project 100,000, and they were subsequently overrepresented among the casualties. The sons of the middle class and opinion-forming elites had numerous options to avoid service in Vietnam, and many took them. College deferments, leaving for Canada, or loitering in the National Guard were alternatives to active duty.

Although they represented 12 percent of the American population, African Americans made up 31 percent of the rank and file in infantry battalions in 1965. Their casualty rates for the war as a whole reflected their proportion in the population at large, 12 percent; but, especially early in the war, the casualty rate was disproportionate: 24 percent in 1965, 19 percent in 1966, and 13 percent in 1968. Class, education, and region were also factors in determining who served, and who did not. Southerners were overrepresented, with 28 percent of soldiers originating there, while those from low-income backgrounds were twice as likely to serve in the military and to see combat as were those from families with higher incomes.

The twin issues of discipline within the ranks and of atrocities committed by American military personnel also loom large in popular memory and understanding of Vietnam. Morale unquestionably suffered the longer the war lasted, and there were serious problems with drug abuse; racial conflict; the murder, or fragging, of officers and noncommissioned officers (NCOs); desertion; and general indiscipline as the United States drew down its forces in Vietnam and turned the war over to the Vietnamese. These problems were not confined to the forces serving in Southeast Asia, but also infected American forces in the United States and in Europe.

The war's effect on the American military as an institution was corrosive over time, and required considerable corrective action after the withdrawal from Vietnam before being restored to a semblance of organizational health. One clear sign of this decline in standards was the perpetration of atrocities against the civilian population, most notoriously represented by the murder of at least 122 and perhaps as many as 400 Vietnamese civilians in the hamlet of My Lai in March 1968. My Lai was neither an isolated incident nor representative of the behavior of the majority of soldiers who served in Vietnam; but it is probably fair to say that the only junior officer convicted in the atrocity, Lieutenant William Calley, would not have qualified for an officer's commission at all if the quality of manpower had not been so degraded by the draft, lower recruitment standards, and deferments. There were also clear failures in command and oversight along the chain of command, but those responsible were not held accountable. For the American public, the wanton killing of civilians by American boys and the Army's attempt to cover up the incident equally eroded the military's traditional position of high esteem among Americans.

The other issue that continues to resonate in American life is that surrounding military personnel listed as missing in action, or MIA. It is impossible to determine exactly how many Americans the North Vietnamese took prisoner, but the great majority of them were aircrew shot down inside North Vietnam. Between February and April 1973, a total of 566 Americans were released and repatriated; this left a further 2,483 who were officially unaccounted for. This number has gradually diminished over time to around 1,200, and it seems highly unlikely that any American captives are still alive and held inside Vietnam, Laos, or Cambodia. The lack of cooperation by Hanoi after the war and into the mid-1990s in determining the fate of those missing fueled the conspiracy industry that surrounds the issue, which did little to help the families of MIAs. The treatment of those detained was barbarous, including the widespread and sustained use of torture and attempted exploitation for propaganda purposes.

Since establishing formal diplomatic relations with Vietnam in 1995, both the United States and Vietnam have worked together to recover remains of American soldiers. Through DNA testing, this process has resulted in the positive identification of many missing servicemen. In fact, the remains in the Tomb of the Unknown Soldier for Vietnam at Arlington National Cemetery were identified through DNA technology.

◆ CONCLUSION

Vietnam was America's longest war and its most divisive since the Civil War. The cost in blood alone was considerable: 58,000 dead and around 300,000 wounded, with countless other lives blighted by the war and its aftermath. Enemy casualties were higher: at least 660,000 combat deaths, with another 60,000 or more killed inside North Vietnam by the bombing. South Vietnamese casualties were also higher than those of the United States: at least 250,000 killed and more than half a million wounded; the loss of the war, and of the country; and reeducation camps for some, and a diaspora to countries around the world for others.

The war made the United States unsure of itself, strained relations with European allies, put the American military into turmoil, and left the American people disgusted and then increasingly apathetic to America's role in the Cold War world. It took an immense effort for the American military to recover from this war—and for the American people to regain their confidence in America's military institutions.

Further Reading •

Andrade, Dale. *Trial by Fire: The 1972 Easter Offensive, America's Last Vietnam Battle*. New York: Hippocrene Books, 1994.

Berman, Larry. *Planning a Tragedy: The Americanization of the War in Vietnam*. New York: Norton, 1982.

Davidson, Phillip B. *Vietnam at War: The History, 1946–1975*. New York: Oxford University Press, 1988.

Heineman, Kenneth J. *Campus Wars: The Peace Movement at American State Universities in the Vietnam Era*. New York: New York University Press, 1993.

Herring, George C. *America's Longest War: The United States and Vietnam 1950–1975*. 4th ed. New York: McGraw-Hill, 2002.

Hess, Gary R. *Vietnam and the United States: Origins and Legacy of War*. Rev. ed. New York: Twayne Publishers, 1998.

Karnow, Stanley. *Vietnam: A History*. New York: Vintage Books, 1983.

Krepinevich, Andrew F., Jr. *The Army and Vietnam*. Baltimore: Johns Hopkins University Press, 1986.

Levy, David W. *The Debate over Vietnam*. Baltimore: Johns Hopkins University Press, 1991.

Lewy, Guenter. *America in Vietnam*. New York: Oxford University Press, 1978.

Macdonald, Peter. *Giap: The Victor in Vietnam*. New York: Norton, 1993.

McMaster, H. R. *Dereliction of Duty: Lyndon Johnson, Robert McNamara, The Joint Chiefs of Staff, and the Lies that Led to Vietnam*. New York: Harper Collins, 1997.

Milam, Ron. *Not a Gentleman's War: An Inside View of Junior Officers in the Vietnam War*. Chapel Hill: University of North Carolina Press, 2009.

Moore, Harold G., and Joseph G. Galloway. *We Were Soldiers Once … and Young: Ia Drang— The Battle that Changed the War in Vietnam*. New York: Random House, 1992.

Murphy, Edward F. *Semper Fi—Vietnam: From Da Nang to the DMZ, Marine Corps Campaigns, 1965–1975*. Novato, California: Presidio Press, 1997.

Schreadley, R. L. *From the Rivers to the Sea: The U.S. Navy in Vietnam*. Annapolis: Naval Institute Press, 1992.

Sorley, Lewis. *A Better War: The Unexamined Victories and Final Tragedy of America's Last Years in Vietnam*. New York: Harcourt, 1999.

Spector, Ronald H. *After Tet: The Bloodiest Year in Vietnam*. New York: Free Press, 1993.

Westmoreland, William C. *A Soldier Reports*. New York: Doubleday, 1976.

mysearchlab Connections: Sources Online • • • • • • • • • • •

READ AND REVIEW

Review this chapter by using the study aids and these related documents available on MySearchLab.

Study Plan

Chapter Test

Essay Test

Documents

Policy Statement on American Objectives in Southeast Asia (1952)

In this document, the Truman administration's National Security Council outlines what it hopes to achieve through containing communism in Southeast Asia, and specifically how and why the United States will continue to support the French in its war against communist forces in Indochina.

Martin Luther King, Jr., Conscience and the Vietnam War (1967)

In this speech, King explains for the first time his opposition to the American war in Vietnam, including citing the disproportionate service of African Americans.

Letter from President Nixon to President Nguyen Van Thieu (1973)

On January 27, 1973, a truce was signed. In return for all American prisoners of war, the United States agreed to remove its troops from South Vietnam within sixty days. The clauses allowed for the North Vietnamese to keep their troops in the South, guaranteeing the area's future control by the North. This document is a letter from President Nixon to South Vietnamese President Nguyen Van Thieu before the signing of this truce.

RESEARCH AND EXPLORE

Explore the following review questions using the research tools available on www. mysearchlab.com.

1. What was the intention behind U.S. involvement in Vietnam?
2. Why did Americans increasingly turn against the war?
3. What were the war's long-term consequences for the U.S. military?

Military Challenges in a Changing World

◆ **INTRODUCTION**

Rebuilding the post-Vietnam American military while still fighting a Cold War against the Soviet Union in a geopolitical environment that saw an increasing number of conflicts across the developing world was indeed a great challenge for the United States. Force structure, procurement, and doctrine would have to adapt to this changing world throughout the 1970s, 1980s, and well into the 1990s. From the low point of the immediate post-Vietnam years, the American military would see the fulfillment of its rebuilding in the triumph of American combat arms in the Gulf War of 1991. With the end of the Cold War, however, and a tendency to use military force in situations that were peripheral to American interests, the American military continued to be challenged.

◆ TOWARD A NEW MILITARY

Regardless whether they opposed or supported the war, Americans found little that was honorable in the nation's Vietnam experience. The public not only faulted civilian and military policy makers, but it also criticized the soldiers who fought in Southeast Asia. Atrocities, such as those committed by American troops at My Lai, convinced some of the war's opponents that American soldiers were "baby killers," while supporters of the war often tried to blame the American failure on the indiscipline of drug-addicted, "fragging," and mutinous enlisted men. Indeed, during the immediate post-Vietnam years military morale reached its lowest levels since perhaps the early years of the American Revolution, and popular support of the defense establishment was at a twentieth-century nadir. As a result, the Pentagon had to accept the end of the draft, alter enlisted personnel policies, and learn to fight with a leaner, all-volunteer force.

After World War II, Americans temporarily disregarded their traditional dislike of involuntary military service and supported a large standing army manned by conscripts. By the 1960s, however, glaring social inequalities and questions concerning American involvement in Vietnam combined with draft boards dominated by white elites to make selective service more difficult to accept. In 1967, President Lyndon B. Johnson attempted to placate antidraft protesters by making small changes in draft legislation, but his failure to reform conscription only sparked increased dissent. During the 1968 presidential campaign, Republican candidate Richard M. Nixon argued in favor of a smaller all-volunteer military, but he also signaled his reluctance to make drastic changes as he cautioned against ending selective service until American military involvement in Vietnam had ended.

After he was elected president, Nixon tried, as Johnson had, to mollify antidraft protesters with small gestures such as ordering a study of terminating the draft. Ultimately, however, increased agitation prodded Nixon to reform local draft boards by increasing minority membership and excluding service personnel and anyone younger than thirty years of age from board membership. Shortly thereafter, Nixon tried to make the draft seem fairer by instituting a draft lottery and dismissing the increasingly unpopular Selective Service chief, General Lewis B. Hershey. Yet, nothing the president did appeased opponents of the draft until American forces began leaving Vietnam and draft calls became smaller. From then on, antidraft agitation declined. Although some lawmakers worried that protesters would renew their outcry when Congress extended the draft in 1971, restricting reauthorization to only two years and including a pay raise for enlisted service members diluted antidraft sentiment. More importantly, no draftees were sent to Vietnam after mid-1972.

Military leaders were intensely skeptical of an all-volunteer force. Global military commitments required large armed forces, and motivation for volunteerism was not what military or political leaders expected. Hoping to avoid being assigned to combat units, substantial numbers of draft-eligible men volunteered to serve in the armed forces. By the early 1970s, over 50 percent of volunteers admitted that they enlisted because they expected to be drafted and believed that enlisting would allow them to choose a noncombat specialty. The Army argued that ending conscription would endanger national defense because the military would have to lower intelligence standards for recruits to meet manpower requirements. Some military leaders also opposed an all-volunteer force for fear that the aggressive recruiting campaigns required for volunteerism would cheapen the image of the armed services.

Nevertheless, in 1969 the Army studied whether an all-volunteer force could work. The study, Project Volunteer in Defense of the Nation, or PROVIDE, concluded that although an all-volunteer force was possible, it would increase military costs because volunteers would expect higher pay and better benefits than conscripts had received in the past. Also, the report suggested that the Army would have to recruit more women if it wanted to meet manpower needs.

The White House and the Department of Defense also conducted their own separate studies. In March 1969, Nixon appointed the Commission on an All-Volunteer Armed Force, known as the Gates Commission after its chairman, former Secretary of Defense Thomas M. Gates. The Department of Defense study group, Project Volunteer, convened in April of the same year, also with the goal of deciding how the services could best develop an all-volunteer force. Both the Department of Defense study, which was heavily influenced by PROVIDE, and the Gates Commission report agreed that an all-volunteer force was feasible.

Nevertheless, there were important differences between the reports regarding how to implement an all-volunteer force. The Gates Commission concluded that simply increasing enlisted pay was sufficient to spur enlistments, while Project Volunteer argued that although better pay was important, a successful all-volunteer force also required better working and living conditions for enlisted service members as well as an intensified recruitment effort for both enlisted members and officers.

Secretary of Defense Melvin Laird presented the Department of Defense recommendations to Nixon in March 1970. Draft authorization was due to end in 1971, but Laird recommended that draft authority continue and draft calls be decreased, in tandem with the reduction of the American presence in Vietnam, until there was a "zero draft." Temporarily retaining the draft offered insurance against the military's probable failure to recruit sufficient manpower in the near term. Laird also proposed a 20 percent pay increase for junior enlisted personnel, more and better on-base housing, improved housing allowances for personnel who lived off base, and making junior enlisted service members eligible for on-base housing. Moreover, Laird recommended that the military provide health care for service members' families and that the government pay moving expenses for families of married service personnel who were transferred to new duty stations. Laird further urged improved educational and training programs, and an increase in civilian hiring to reduce the amount of support duty that enlisted members had to perform. In addition to these quality-of-life improvements, Laird wanted to expand each service's recruiting program. Nixon accepted these proposals and asked Congress to add $2 billion to the 1972 budget to fund them.

Unfortunately for the military, the Army and Department of Defense studies were classified, leading the public to assume that the Gates Commission had implemented the changes against the opposition of military decision makers. Even the *Army Times* inaccurately reported that the Pentagon resisted not only the all-volunteer force but also improvements for service life. While it is true that the armed forces preferred the guaranteed manpower provided through selective service, the American military recognized the inevitability of an all-volunteer force and began planning for the end of conscription.

Making the most of the draft's two-year extension, the Army began experiment-ing with the best way to implement the proposed changes. Under a program dubbed Project VOLAR, experiments were conducted at four stateside Army posts: Fort Benning, Fort Bragg, Fort Carson, and Fort Ord. To encourage recruits to choose combat service, the Army began offering proficiency pay for enlisted personnel who met specified performance standards. The Navy, Marines, and Air Force instituted enlistment bonuses for recruits who chose a combat specialty. Each service also added recruiters and increased budgets for recruitment advertising. Cost-free changes intended to improve daily life were also introduced, including the elimination of daily reveille, loosened travel restrictions, and better communications between enlisted per-sonnel and their superiors.

◆ REFORMING TRAINING, RETHINKING DOCTRINE

Soldiers sent to Southeast Asia had been trained in a World War II era–designed system that provided rapid basic training before men were shipped out as individual replacements to manpower-hungry units. Conceived in expectation of mass mobiliza-tion and large numbers of draftees, the training plan met the manpower needs of a military fighting a worldwide war. The armed forces, particularly the Army, concluded that an outdated training scheme had contributed to the breakdown of unit cohesion and discipline in Vietnam. Ending the draft meant that the military could no longer plan around a large, quickly mobilized manpower pool. In addition, the United States was convinced that it was at a technological and manpower disadvantage to the Warsaw Pact. A better-trained, more professional military would help reduce that handicap.

In the past, a small professional military quickly trained conscripts in the basics of soldiering, following a prescribed syllabus through all levels of training. Completing an exercise or spending the required amount of time on any given subject, rather than going through an assessment of performance, determined when a service member or a unit had completed training. To help offset reduced manpower, the armed forces intensified training based on assessment of performance. In the Army, for example, training was taken over by the new Training and Doctrine Command. At each level of training, soldiers and their units were assessed according to performance rather than task completion.

Withdrawing from Vietnam also prompted doctrinal changes. For example, for more than a decade the Army had directed its resources toward the counterinsurgency effort in Southeast Asia. As a result, it was both doctrinally and technologically out-paced by potential enemies who had maintained conventional forces. Determined to catch up, the U.S. military focused its intellectual energy on restructuring and modern-izing its forces. To do so required the military to predict future conflict in order to be prepared for such conflicts.

Planners identified two likely scenarios for future conflict—a "small" war in a developing nation fought by light infantry, and a conventional war in Western Europe employing mechanized forces. The Nixon Doctrine also influenced the way the mili-tary prepared for the future. In July 1969, President Nixon told reporters while visiting Guam that unless Asian nations were being threatened with nuclear attack, the United States expected their governments to handle conflicts without American assistance.

Over time, Nixon's statement was refined and eventually interpreted as an indication that the American military should be prepared to fight one-and-a-half wars. That is, the United States should plan for being able to simultaneously fight a small war and a large conventional war. Although the first scenario seemed most likely, the eighteen-day Arab-Israeli War fought in October 1973 brought home to the Army that a mechanized war could potentially be the most difficult conflict to fight.

Doctrinal changes were also influenced by new technology, which had become much more deadly than it had been ten years earlier, allowing a combatant to employ the new weapons with lethal effectiveness against a larger enemy. Israel's destruction of Egyptian and Syrian tank forces with a light, infantry-borne antitank weapon, the M72 LAAW (or LAW), for example, demonstrated not only the power of new military hardware but also the vulnerability of armor fighting without support from other combat arms. Clearly, a well-trained, well-equipped smaller enemy posed a serious threat to even the largest, most modern armed force. How much greater a danger, then, was the Soviet Union? While the American military had been fighting a counterinsurgency war, the Soviet Union had modernized and restructured its forces. After a decade of relative neglect, conventional warfare once again became the Army's doctrine *du jour*.

Planning for conventional war, however, did not mean a return to pre-Vietnam era ideas. In the past, the United States had been almost proudly ill-prepared for war, typically making a poor early showing while mobilizing and training its fighting force. Powerful new weapons now made fighting while preparing too perilous, and the end of conscription made it virtually impossible. The modern battlefield demanded that the United States win its first battle or risk losing the initiative. Improved technology required a better-educated, more intensively trained soldier, while the end of the draft meant that the country had to fight with a leaner force.

General William E. DuPuy, commander of the new Army Training and Doctrine Command, took the lead in articulating an updated doctrine. Called AirLand Battle, this post-Vietnam doctrine was not actually new. At its core, AirLand Battle emphasized the long-standing basic elements of tactics and strategy. However, improvements in technology and air warfare techniques made it clear that airpower was essential to successful ground warfare, and the new doctrine recognized airpower's vital role. In DuPuy's iteration, AirLand Battle relied on the primacy of the defensive. By 1977, DuPuy's successor, General Donn A. Starry, revised Army doctrine to focus on the offensive and the indirect approach.

By 1982, the lessons of the Arab-Israeli War were fully absorbed, and AirLand Battle was again revised this time emphasizing winning the first battle against a larger enemy. Moreover, in part because of American technological capability, armor began to contest the infantry's status as "queen of battle." Yet, neither arm could fight effectively without the other, thus the symbiotic relationship between infantry and armor prevented the tank from making the infantryman obsolete. Indeed, superior technology was essential to a leaner, more lethal all-volunteer force. As a result, the military introduced a number of new or upgraded weapons systems, including the Army's M-1 Abrams tank and M-2 Bradley infantry fighting vehicle; the Air Force's F-15E dual-role fighter and B-1B multimission bomber; and the Navy's nuclear-powered aircraft carriers and more-advanced carrier-based aircraft such as the F/A-18 and the S-3, a submarine hunter.

Just as a smaller military encouraged increased interest in technology, it also spurred movement toward reducing the "tooth to tail" ratio. Divisions were reduced to two active brigades, and when needed, a reserve brigade would bring the division to full strength. In addition, the Army began to redesign its organization around the light infantry division. Initially, the restructuring emphasized the use of technology, such as a light armored vehicle. Because of reduced manpower, however, light infantry divisions ultimately became smaller, more easily transported units. A smaller, less cumbersome division meant that the United States could more rapidly deploy to trouble spots around the globe, thus alleviating an increasing concern after the Iranian hostage crisis and the Soviet invasion of Afghanistan.

Adoption of light infantry divisions prompted sometimes intense debate between critics, who feared that lighter divisions could not stand up to potential threats, and proponents, who argued that the deployability of a light division offset its lack of armor. Opponents also worried because when first introduced, light infantry divisions trained only for low-intensity conflict. In addition, there were complaints that the United States was fielding a "hollow" force. Nevertheless, the emphasis on lighter and more rapidly deployable divisions continued.

◆ COLD WAR AND THE MILITARY

Under President Jimmy Carter, a graduate of the Naval Academy, the American military suffered fairly significant budget cuts. The inflation-ridden economy of the 1970s made such measures unavoidable. The Carter administration also had a noninterventionist approach to conflict occurring in the developing world and had tried to reduce nuclear armaments in intensive talks—such as the SALT II negotiations—with the Soviet Union. Carter cut the B-1 bomber program, as well as naval shipbuilding, and reduced budgets for the general post-Vietnam rebuilding programs.

While making these cuts, the Carter administration also realized that American nuclear power, particularly the capacity for a gradually escalating nuclear conflict, had fallen far behind that of the Soviets. The United States needed more-versatile means to deliver nuclear warheads. Carter's Presidential Directive 59 of 1979 called for more multipurpose nuclear capability to allow for a more flexible nuclear response. The Air Force's MX intercontinental ballistic missile and the Navy's Trident missile provided some flexibility while platforms for nuclear missiles, such as the Navy's Ohio class submarine and the Air Force's cruise-missile-capable B-52s, offered more-versatile means of delivery.

Carter came into office hoping that a foreign policy focused on human rights and peaceful initiatives would give the United States a moral edge in the Cold War, especially when the conflict between the United States and the Soviet Union involved the developing world. Such an approach, however, proved a disappointment because the developing world seemed to be exploding with ethnocentric nationalism and religious extremism. Soviet aggression in Afghanistan, while only indirectly Cold War–related, also convinced the Carter administration to reconsider its foreign policy. By 1979, Carter embraced a more aggressive approach to world affairs; by 1980, the United States, under Carter's guidance, became the policeman of the Persian Gulf. This change in foreign policy, in turn, meant a more ambitious defense policy. As Carter left office in 1981, defense budgets were already on the rise to meet the changing geostrategic world.

When Ronald Reagan became president in 1981, American foreign policy took an even more dramatic turn. Convinced that communism was an inherently expansionist ideology that could be defeated only by strength, Reagan's primary foreign policy goal was to prevent the Soviet Union from further spreading its influence, especially in the Middle East and Central America. Reagan took a hard-line approach toward the Soviet Union, using extremely aggressive rhetoric while pushing a massive military buildup through Congress. Reagan argued that this more aggressive stance would achieve "peace through strength."

During the Reagan presidency, the military budget increased by an average of 8 percent per year. Increased defense spending was part of a multipronged strategy aimed at forcing the Soviet Union to bankrupt itself by trying to keep pace with the American military buildup. Bigger defense budgets meant that service members received pay raises that brought them nearer parity to their civilian peers, and allowed the Pentagon to press ahead with its modernization plans. In addition, Reagan's unabashed patriotism helped renew pride in military service. Moreover, increased defense budgets meant new procurement, which reinvigorated the American defense industry.

One of Reagan's most controversial moves was his proposal for a space-based missile defense system he called the Strategic Defense Initiative, which opponents to the system nicknamed "Star Wars." In theory, armed satellites orbiting the globe would destroy nuclear missiles fired at the United States before the weapons entered the earth's atmosphere. Rather than counter these American defense budgetary increases and technological developments with its own buildup, the Soviet Union pursued arms reduction negotiations. This was especially true after Mikhail Gorbachev became General Secretary in 1985. In 1988, the United States and the Soviet Union completed the Intermediate Nuclear Forces Treaty, the first nuclear arms treaty that actually eliminated such weapons rather than setting limits on their numbers.

Still, the developing world continued to edge toward the forefront of this second Cold War. Under the Reagan Doctrine, the administration also provided support to anti-Communist groups around the world, including the mujahidin fighting against the Soviet invasion of Afghanistan and the Contra rebels in Nicaragua. The Reagan administration's support of the Contras precipitated the most damaging scandal of the Reagan presidency, the Iran-Contra Affair, during which Marine Lieutenant Colonel Oliver North and National Security Advisor Robert McFarlane orchestrated secret arms sales to Iran, channeling the proceeds to the Contra rebels in Nicaragua. In most instances support did not include the commitment of American troops, but in some cases, Reagan did not hesitate to use military force, even though the objectives were not always primary to American interests.

◆ DESERT ONE, LEBANON, GRENADA, AND DEFENSE REORGANIZATION

The seizure of fifty-two American hostages from the U.S. Embassy in Tehran by Islamist militants in November 1979 provided the final chapter of the Carter presidency and the backdrop to the 1980 presidential election. The failure of the attempt to rescue these hostages in an overly elaborate and ambitious operation dubbed Desert

One (officially as Eagle Claw) was to contribute to Carter's defeat by Reagan and led to some necessary and overdue reforms in the way the United States organizes and mounts joint operations. Failure is explained by inadequate preparations and too many things going wrong, taking contingent assumptions with them; the operation resulted in eight dead and four wounded, the loss of a number of aircraft, and the further public humiliation of American policy and purpose in a highly unstable and volatile context. An internal investigation noted failures in command and control and planning, but most importantly the inability of the U.S. services to operate effectively in a joint environment. It is sometimes suggested that the impetus to the Goldwater-Nicholls Act of 1986 and other pressures towards "jointness" and interoperability came from the specter of burning aircraft and frustrated intent in the sands near Tabas in Iran.

As part of a multinational force, Reagan ordered the Marines to Beirut in August 1982 to help enforce a United Nations–brokered agreement ending the Israeli retaliatory invasion of Lebanon. Despite a fairly peaceful beginning to the operation, the assassination of the newly elected Lebanese president caused Israel to deploy troops throughout West Beirut in mid-September. In just a few days, approximately 800 Palestinian noncombatants living in refugee camps in Beirut were slaughtered. Appalled, Reagan announced he was sending in more Marines, and by year's end over 1,800 had been deployed. While the Marines were primarily intended to aid the Lebanese government in regaining its authority, their presence also exerted pressure on Lebanese officials to accept Israel's terms for withdrawal. In essence, the Marines had been placed in a dangerous political situation that their presence only exacerbated.

The Marines established a protective perimeter around Beirut International Airport and by February 1983 were frequently the focus of Israeli and Palestinian military pressure. Early that month, Reagan refused to set a time limit for the Marine presence in Beirut. Despite an agreement to end the war, signed by Lebanon and Israel in May, by late August the Marine perimeter was frequently under fire from various factions. On the 29th, two marines were killed and 14 wounded during a mortar and rocket attack. Violence escalated as the Navy bombarded terrorist targets in Beirut from ships in the Mediterranean. More Marines died in skirmishes with Lebanese militias. In mid-September, the battleship *New Jersey* joined the ships off Lebanon.

At that point, Congress stepped in and placed an eighteen-month deadline for the withdrawal of the Marines. Because the Marines were now openly supporting the Christian-dominated government, they were more frequently subject to attack by hostile Palestinian militias. Finally, in October 1983, two truck bombs destroyed the Marine barracks at the airport, killing 241 people, including 220 Marines. Failures in security, joint communication, and intelligence had left the Marine barracks open to such a devastating attack. Despite congressional pressure for an immediate withdrawal, Reagan tried to maintain a military presence in Beirut. The increasing violence finally forced Reagan to order the Marines to leave Lebanon for good in early 1984. Their presence had been virtually ineffective in maintaining order and had arguably made the situation worse. Moreover, the lack of centralized command for the operation resulted in a lack of strategic cohesion and purpose. Arguably, the intervention in Lebanon was doomed to disaster from the start.

The disaster in Lebanon and other uncertain diplomatic and military steps in the Middle East frustrated the Reagan administration and the military. An operationally ugly but nonetheless successful assault on the tiny Caribbean island of Grenada, however, eased the pain somewhat. The government of Grenada had been overthrown, and its leader killed by socialist revolutionaries supported by Cuba on October 19, 1983, endangering American students attending the island's medical school. Shocked at this violence in the Caribbean and needing a foreign policy success, Reagan ordered an assault on Grenada to rescue the American students and end Cuban influence on the island. In Operation URGENT FURY, each service insisted on playing a role, which resulted in an operational plan more focused on service participation than on effectively achieving mission objectives. With little time for planning a rather complicated joint operation, there was plenty that could go wrong—and plenty did.

The operation began on October 25 and ultimately involved over 6,000 Marines, soldiers, and Special Forces over the course of six days. Rigid rules of engagement severely limited the use of airpower to support troops on the ground. Artillery was likewise limited to reduce collateral damage and minimize civilian casualties. Nineteen American servicemen were killed in the operation, while at least 50 soldiers of Cuba's and Grenada's armed forces died. Although the American military personnel performed well under such extenuating circumstances, the conduct of the operation was hardly "joint," exposing serious planning, coordination, and communication problems that had plagued the armed services in previous operations.

The apparent poor performance of the American military since Vietnam—the botched operation to rescue the American hostages in Tehran, the Marine barracks tragedy, and now the Grenada operation—convinced many in the military and in Congress that something had to be done. The problems seemed to emanate from a convoluted command structure, service rivalry, and ineffective Joint Chiefs of Staff. Under the leadership of Senator Barry Goldwater and Congressman Bill Nichols, Congress passed the Goldwater-Nichols Defense Reorganization Act in 1986 to address these issues.

Perhaps the most important defense legislation since the 1947 National Security Act, Goldwater-Nichols achieved several things. It made the Chairman of the Joint Chiefs of Staff the principal military advisor to the president. Whereas previously the chairman operated somewhat like a general manager for the service chiefs, he now could voice his own opinion directly to the president. The chairman was also included in the operational chain of command, which now ran from theater commanders to the chairman and then to the president. Theater commanders were also given complete command over all assets, regardless of service, under their authority. Operational command had been streamlined and made more efficient—truly "joint." In addition, the chairman now oversaw his own joint staff, made up of officers from each service. Joint billets were no longer a hindrance to promotion; rather, they were now mandatory for promotion to general officer.

The overall objective of Goldwater-Nichols was twofold. First was to make the American military "joint" in its operational doctrine. Second was to give the chairman of the Joint Chiefs of Staff direct access to the president, who is commander-in-chief. Critics charged that loyalty to one's service would always undermine jointness and that giving the chairman of the Joint Chiefs of Staff so much power lessened the influence of the service chiefs and eroded civilian control of the military. Changing decades of service primacy in favor of joint command would take time, and the role of the Chairman of the Joint Chiefs of Staff would depend a great deal on the personality and command style of the individual holding that position. Coming military operations, however, would show that Goldwater-Nichols had been the correct approach to remake the American military.

◆ "NO MORE VIETNAMS"

By the time Reagan left office in 1989, the American military establishment was well on its way to rejuvenation. Reagan's successor, George H. W. Bush, took office only months before the Berlin Wall fell, a harbinger of the full collapse of the Soviet Union that left the United States as the world's sole superpower. Like Reagan, Bush looked forward to a world in which freedom and democracy were the norm; also like his predecessor, Bush was determined to protect freedom, world stability, and American dominance.

Just six weeks after the fall of the Berlin Wall, the United States invaded Panama to remove the narco-militarist dictator Manuel Antonio Noriega. Although the United States had often intervened in Latin America, it had typically been to prevent the spread of Communist influence into a region that held great strategic significance to America. By 1989, however, conditions had changed. The Soviet Union was no longer the threat it had once been, and the Panama Canal would soon be returned to Panamanian control. The Panamanian dictator Noriega was heavily involved with trafficking drugs into the United States, and he frequently violated American-Panamanian treaties. Panama was also a center for arms smuggling and money laundering.

In 1988, the United States declared its "war on drugs," and a Florida court issued indictments against Noriega for drug trafficking and money laundering. The United States determined to remove him from power. Both the Reagan and Bush administrations attempted to foment coups d'état, and supported political opposition to Noriega. When these measures failed to topple his regime, the United States tried economic sanctions and issued military threats. For Noriega, open defiance of the world's only superpower only enhanced his authority. On December 15, 1989, Noriega's handpicked legislature declared him the winner in a rigged presidential election. Noriega's thugs harassed and beat opposition candidates. The Bush administration had seen enough.

Four days later, on December 19, the United States launched Operation JUST CAUSE, a carefully planned invasion designed to simultaneously strike a number of strategic objectives and capture Noriega while limiting civilian casualties and keeping American residents in Panama safe. At the time of the invasion there were already 13,000 American troops in Panama as part of Southern Command; another 14,000 were airlifted into the country for the initial assault. Despite efforts to keep the invasion secret, the heavy show of American force around the Canal Zone alerted Noriega that American military action was imminent.

JUST CAUSE was the first instance of the so-called Powell Doctrine. Named for then newly appointed Chairman of the Joint Chiefs of Staff, Army General Colin Powell, the Powell Doctrine was actually a corollary to the Weinberger Doctrine, named for Reagan's Secretary of Defense Casper Weinberger. Weinberger had created a list of six prerequisites for the United States to commit to military force. These were a direct response to the disaster in Lebanon and the earlier failed attempt to rescue the

American hostages in Tehran, if not the Vietnam War. First, the United States should not commit forces to combat unless vital national interests of the United States or its allies are involved. Second, American troops should be committed only unreservedly and with the clear intention of winning. Otherwise, American forces should not be committed. Third, American combat troops should be committed only with clearly defined political and military objectives and be given the capacity to accomplish those objectives. Fourth, the relationship between the objectives and the size and composition of the forces committed should be continually reassessed and adjusted to assure victory. Fifth, American troops should not be committed to battle without the support of American public opinion and Congress. Last, the use of force should be considered only as a last resort, after diplomacy and other means have failed. To this Powell added an emphasis on the use of overwhelming force to ensure American military victory. During the 1950s and 1960s, use of force had essentially replaced diplomacy as the primary tool in American national security policy. Now, use of force would ideally take a back seat to diplomacy and economic sanctions. Under the Weinberger-Powell Doctrine, there theoretically would be no more Vietnams and no more Lebanons.

In the predawn hours of December 20, the invasion began with the operational debut of the new F-117 Stealth bomber, which bombed a Panamanian Defense Force barracks. Infantry and armor forces stationed in the Canal Zone moved in to support airborne troops, who had flown all the way from the United States. Special Forces, including Delta Force and Navy Seals, were charged with finding and securing Noriega, which they did on December 24. The operation had been a success, due mainly to the superb integration of the various services into a single joint plan. In an operation that involved over 23,000 service members from all services, only 23 were killed and 324 wounded. At least 314 Panamanian Defense Force troops were killed and perhaps as many as 300 Panamanian civilians unfortunately lost their lives in the crossfire and bombing.

JUST CAUSE had shown that joint planning and joint operations could work. It also confirmed that if the local population is supportive of intervention, things will proceed much more smoothly than if it is not. The American military seemed to have recovered and rebuilt from its Vietnam experience. The all-volunteer American military had become a lethal and efficient fighting force.

The greatest test of the all-volunteer force and the advent of "jointness" was the Gulf War of 1991 that ousted Iraqi leader Saddam Hussein's military forces from Kuwait. The total joint commitment to planning, buildup, and execution, integrating air, land, and naval forces, was a stunning success of American combat arms.

The long Iran Iraq War of the 1980s had left Hussein's Iraq with over $90 billion in debts and a less-than-full treasury. To compensate, Hussein ordered the invasion of his wealthy southern neighbor Kuwait in August 1990, where he hoped to secure Kuwaiti oil fields and production facilities as well as access to deepwater ports. Kuwait's army was no match for the large, well-equipped, experienced Iraqi military. When three armored divisions of Iraq's elite Republican Guard invaded, the Kuwaiti military was already off-balance from pre-invasion probes by Saddam's army. The invasion began on August 2, and within only a few days eleven Iraqi divisions had occupied the small country and were threatening the Kuwaiti border with Saudi Arabia. Iraqi control of Kuwaiti oil fields had already shaken the global oil market; a worldwide economic disaster would follow if Saddam also gained control of Saudi Arabian oil production.

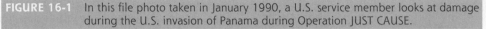

FIGURE 16-1 In this file photo taken in January 1990, a U.S. service member looks at damage during the U.S. invasion of Panama during Operation JUST CAUSE.

Source: U.S. Navy photo/Released.

On August 7, at President Bush's direction, the U.S. Central Command, or CENTCOM, began deploying forces to protect Saudi Arabia. CENTCOM was, and remains, one of several Unified Combatant Commands enhanced by the Goldwater-Nichols Defense Reorganization Act and given operational control over all American forces in specified geographic regions. At the time of the Gulf War, Army General Norman H. Schwarzkopf commanded CENTCOM. Because Bush and his military advisors wanted to project the impression that American actions were strictly defensive, the initial military deployment under CENTCOM's Operations Plan 1002–90 was code-named Operation DESERT SHIELD. The operational plan for the combat phase of the Iraq crisis was called DESERT STORM.

Navy battle groups that regularly patrolled the Mediterranean Sea and Indian Ocean immediately diverted to patrol the Gulf of Oman and the Red Sea. Formed around the aircraft carriers *Independence* and *Dwight D. Eisenhower*, the two battle groups were the first American forces to arrive on station. A third carrier battle group joined the naval force the following month. In addition, *Missouri* and *Wisconsin*, battleships that had been recommissioned during the Reagan administration, were sent to the Persian Gulf. On August 8, two F-15 squadrons arrived from Langley Air Force Base, Virginia. Within a month there were approximately 800 aircraft in the Persian Gulf, including Marine and Army air assets. Also on August 8, the first ground forces joined DESERT SHIELD when a brigade from the 82nd Airborne Division, part of the XVIII Airborne Corps, deployed in Saudi Arabia.

No one expected a single brigade to turn back the Iraqi invasion of Kuwait; rather, the paratroopers comprised a task force intended to deter an Iraqi attack against Saudi Arabian oil fields. Most of the oil fields lay along the Saudi gulf coast, directly south of Kuwait. By the end of August, most of the XVIII Airborne Corps had arrived in Saudi Arabia. More heavily armed units followed, until by December American troops numbered approximately 500,000. It took almost two months, however, before troop strength was sufficient to stop an Iraqi attack against Saudi Arabia, in part because the military buildup of the 1980s ignored logistical concerns in favor of high-tech weapons systems and manpower issues. As a result, military transport, especially sealift, was at a premium, and units were often initially deployed without spare parts or adequate ammunition. At the very least, Schwarzkopf reasoned, the presence of such a large American army would make Saddam think twice before moving against Saudi Arabia.

At the same time that the United States was deploying forces to the Gulf region, it was engaged in diplomatic efforts to politically isolate Iraq. Both the United Nations Security Council and the Arab League passed numerous resolutions condemning the invasion of Kuwait and demanding that Iraq withdraw. The most important United Nations measures were Resolutions 660 and 678. Passed on August 2, Resolution 660 demanded that Iraq leave Kuwait and declared United Nations determination to ensure Iraqi compliance. Hoping to avoid war, diplomats attempted negotiations with an ultimately intransigent Iraq for a peaceful settlement. Its collective patience nearly exhausted, on November 29, the United Nations Security Council passed Resolution 678, which set the withdrawal deadline for January 15, 1991, and authorized the use of all necessary means to restore order and peace to the region. Military action against Iraq now had United Nations sanction.

While the United Nations and the Arab League pursued a diplomatic resolution, the United States continued military preparations, including the formation of a world-wide coalition against Iraq. Although a number of nations were less than enthusiastic toward non-Arab interference, Secretary of State James Baker eventually convinced thirty-three nations from Europe, Asia, Africa, and North and South America to join the American-led coalition. President Bush also had to convince the American public that intervention in the Iraq-Kuwait crisis was justified. Since the war in Vietnam, Americans had generally been wary of foreign military adventures. Moreover, a vocal minority of Americans against the war was convinced that the administration's true purpose was to assert greater influence over Middle Eastern oil production, which was admittedly a vital American interest. Bush administration arguments in favor of intervention, however, emphasized Saddam's human rights abuses, his "naked aggression" against Kuwait, and the long-standing Saudi-American friendship.

As military preparations neared completion, negotiations for a peaceful settlement continued. Neither Iraq nor the United States, however, were in the end willing to compromise on Kuwait. The United States demanded Saddam's unconditional withdrawal. In an attempt to rally Arab support by linking his invasion of Kuwait to Arab nationalism, the Iraqi dictator refused to leave Kuwait unless Syria withdrew from Lebanon and Israeli troops left the West Bank and other areas contested by the Palestine Liberation Organization. Arbitration having failed, on January 12, 1991, Congress authorized military intervention after three days of intense debate. Coalition nations quickly fell into line in support of using military force.

AMERICAN OBJECTIVES IN THE GULF WAR

On January 15, 1991, President Bush issued National Security Directive 54, outlining the reasons for taking military action against Iraq as well as the military and political objectives of Operation DESERT STORM. Significantly, Bush did not include the overthrow of Saddam Hussein among these objectives unless Hussein used chemical, biological, or nuclear weapons, or if he tried to destroy the Kuwaiti oil fields. The president also specified the prerequisites for war termination. Bush would end hostilities when he determined that the objectives had been met. Note also that Bush specifically mentions Israel and wants to ensure that Israel will not enter the conflict even if attacked by Iraq.

> National Security Directive 54
> January 15, 1991
> Subject: Responding to Iraqi Aggression in the Gulf

1. Access to Persian Gulf oil and the security of key friendly states in the area are vital to U.S. national security. Consistent with National Security Directive 26 of October 2, 1989, and National Security Directive 45 of August 20, 1990, and as a matter of long-standing policy, the United States remains committed to defending its vital interests in the region, if necessary through the use of military force, against any power with interests inimical to our own. Iraq, by virtue of its unprovoked invasion of Kuwait on August 2, 1990, and its subsequent brutal occupation, is clearly a power with interests inimical to our own. Economic sanctions mandated by the UN Security Council Resolution 661 have had measurable impact upon Iraq's economy but have not accomplished the intended objective of ending Iraq's occupation of Kuwait. There is no persuasive evidence that they will do so in a timely manner. Moreover, prolonging the current situation would be detrimental to the United States in that it would increase the costs of eventual military action, threaten the political cohesion of the coalition of countries arrayed against Iraq, allow for continued brutalization of the Kuwaiti people and destruction of their country, and cause added damage to the U.S. and world economies. This directive sets forth guidelines for the defense of vital U.S. interests in the face of unacceptable Iraqi aggression and its consequences.

2. Pursuant to my responsibilities and authority under the Constitution as President and Commander-in-Chief, and under the laws and treaties of the United States, and pursuant to House Joint Resolution 77 (1991), and in accordance with the rights and obligations of the United States under international law, including UN Security Council Resolutions 660, 661, 662, 664, 665, 666, 667, 669, 670, 674, 677, and 678, and consistent with the inherent right of collective self-defense affirmed in Article 51 of the United Nations Charter,

I hereby authorize military actions designed to bring about Iraq's withdrawal from Kuwait. These actions are to be conducted against Iraq and Iraqi forces in Kuwait by U.S. air, sea, and land conventional military forces, in coordination with the forces of our coalition partners, at a date and time I shall determine and communicate through National Command Authority channels. This authorization is for the following purposes:

    a. to effect the immediate, complete, and unconditional withdrawal of all Iraqi forces from Kuwait;

    b. to restore Kuwait's legitimate government;

    c. to protect the lives of American citizens abroad;

    d. to promote the security and the stability of the Persian Gulf.

3. To achieve the above purposes, U.S. and coalition forces should seek to:

    a. defend Saudi Arabia and other GCC states against attack;

    b. preclude Iraqi launch of ballistic missiles against neighboring states and friendly forces;

    c. destroy Iraq's chemical, biological, and nuclear capabilities;

    d. destroy Iraq's command, control, and communications capabilities;

    e. eliminate the Republican Guards as an effective fighting force; and

    f. conduct operations designed to drive Iraq's forces from Kuwait, break the will of Iraqi forces, discourage Iraqi use of chemical, biological, or nuclear weapons, encourage defection of Iraqi forces, and weaken Iraqi popular support for the current government.

4. While acting to achieve the purposes in paragraph 2 above and carry out the missions in paragraph 3 above, every reasonable effort should be taken to:

    a. minimize U.S. and coalition casualties and

    b. reduce collateral damage incident to military attacks, taking special precautions to minimize civilian casualties and damage to non-military economic infrastructure, energy-related facilities, and religious sites.

5. The United States shall seek the maximum participation of its coalition partners in all aspects of operations conducted in either Kuwait or Iraq.

6. The United States will encourage Iraq's neighbors Syria and Turkey to increase their forces along their borders with Iraq so as to draw off Iraqi forces from, and resources devoted to, the Kuwait theater of operations.

7. The United States will discourage the government of Israel from participating in any military action. In particular, we will seek to discourage any preemptive actions by Israel. Should Israel be threatened with imminent attack or be attacked by Iraq, the United States will

respond with force against Iraq and will discourage Israeli participation in hostilities.

8. The United States will discourage any participation in hostilities by Jordan. Similarly, the United States will discourage any Jordanian facilitation of, or support for Iraqi military efforts. The United States will also discourage violation of Jordanian territory or airspace.

9. The United States recognizes the territorial integrity of Iraq and will not support efforts to change current boundaries.

10. Should Iraq resort to using chemical, biological, or nuclear weapons, be found supporting terrorist acts against the U.S. or coalition partners anywhere in the world, or destroy Kuwait's oil fields, it shall become an explicit objective of the United States to replace the current leadership of Iraq. I also want to preserve the option of authorizing additional punitive actions against Iraq.

11. All appropriate U.S. government departments and agencies are to prepare and present to me for decision those measures necessary to stabilizing to the extent possible energy supplies and prices during hostilities.

12. Military operations will come to an end only when I have determined that the objectives set forth in paragraph 2 above have been met.

George Bush

Source: George Bush Library and Museum.

In advance of the ground attack, Schwarzkopf ordered an air campaign directed against strategic targets within Iraq. Civilian targets were off-limits, but that did not completely eliminate civilian casualties or "collateral damage" because objectives marked for destruction were sometimes surrounded by civilian structures. Nevertheless, the Air Force designed a carefully controlled campaign intended to immediately acquire air superiority and then to inflict as much damage as possible, as quickly as possible on Iraqi command and control as well as advance Iraqi ground forces while keeping civilian casualties to a minimum. Purposely contrasting the Gulf War plan against the ROLLING THUNDER air campaign against North Vietnam, the Air Force dubbed their concept INSTANT THUNDER. It seemed that the spirit of Billy Mitchell had returned, as Air Force planners believed that INSTANT THUNDER had the potential to force Saddam's surrender before the ground war ever began.

Beginning on January 16, 1991, the air phase of Operation DESERT STORM began with strikes against the Iraqi capital city of Baghdad and Iraqi air capabilities. During the first day of DESERT STORM, American Air Force, Navy, and Marine aircraft along with coalition air assets flew over 1,300 missions and met with only halfhearted attempts at air combat by the Iraqi Air Force. On the second day of the war, air attacks began against Iraq's military and governmental infrastructure and against Iraqi ground forces. Desperate to break up the coalition allied against him, Hussein fired Scud surface-to-surface missiles against Israel and Saudi Arabia. If Israel entered the war, Arab members of the coalition would leave the anti-Iraq alliance, and attacks against Saudi targets might convince the royal family that its friendship with the United States was too dangerous. Equally intent on keeping the coalition together, the United States hurried Patriot antiair and antimissile missiles to Israel and Saudi Arabia. Thwarted by delivery of the Patriots, which had mixed success in knocking incoming Scuds out of the sky, Saddam began dumping crude oil into the Persian Gulf. This gambit wasted oil and caused substantial environmental damage, but had no effect on the war.

Over the following month, near-constant air strikes repeatedly hit military and naval facilities, power stations, communication centers, transportation networks, and Scud missile launchers. Of these targets, the Scud missile launchers perhaps represented the greatest waste of Allied air assets, as the mobile launching units were difficult to locate and target in what became known as the Great Scud Hunt. When the ground war began on February 24, the Iraqi military was in disarray; its command and logistics system had broken down, and much of its frontline equipment was destroyed. Although the Republican Guard retained cohesion, discipline, and fighting morale, most of the Iraqi conscript army was badly shaken and demoralized.

Iraq launched its only organized offensive of the war during the night of January 29. Late in the evening, Air Force surveillance aircraft registered troop movement in southern Kuwait. Two Iraqi divisions were preparing to attack the evacuated Saudi Arabian city of Khafji. Iraqi forces quickly overran the nearly deserted city, as well as several American outposts along the Kuwait–Saudi Arabia border. Two Marine reconnaissance teams became trapped inside Khafji during the battle to retake the city. Although their positions were precarious, the Marines directed artillery and air strikes on enemy forces. Within forty-eight hours a pan-Arab force recaptured Khafji, taking minimal casualties in the process. By February 1, the Battle of Khafji was over. As many as 2,000 Iraqis had died, over 400 Iraqi soldiers had been taken prisoner, and the rest of the invading force had expeditiously withdrawn to Kuwait.

Although the Battle of Khafji received little media attention at the time, the poor Iraqi showing prompted Schwarzkopf to reconsider the professionalism of the Iraqi military. After Khafji, Hussein's forces seemed less formidable. Moreover, in the American military's most intense combat since Vietnam, the Marines had performed admirably. Unfortunately, Khafji also resulted in the worst incidence among American forces of deaths caused by friendly fire.

Most significantly, Khafji later gave airpower proponents an opportunity to argue that air forces could subdue ground forces. At Schwarzkopf's direction, the Air Force took the lead in repelling the invasion, permitting attacks deep into Iraqi-held territory and eliminating the need to redeploy American forces to respond to the offensive. Air attacks destroyed Iraqi transport columns, disrupting the flow of troops and supplies and making it impossible for them to unfold the attack as planned. According to an Air Force study conducted a few years after the war, Khafji was conclusive proof that airpower could control the battlefield. The dominance of airpower is still debated, but the American armed forces have dramatically increased the number of airplanes purchased.

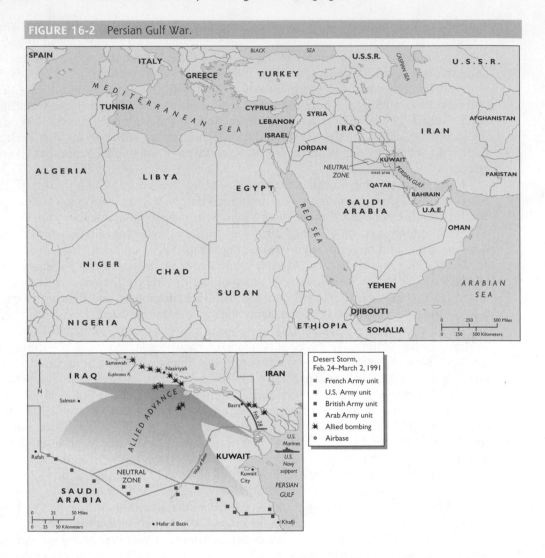

FIGURE 16-2   Persian Gulf War.

Plans for the ground campaign fully exploited Iraqi anxieties and weaknesses. Although Iraq's coastline is relatively short, extending less than forty miles along the Persian Gulf, it offered an entry into Iraq and threatened the nation's two deepwater ports. A disinformation campaign deceived the Iraqi military into believing that an invasion would begin with an amphibious assault by the 5th Marine Expeditionary Brigade. Saddam also expected an attack through Wadi al Batin (a *wadi* is a seasonal riverbed) that runs along the Kuwaiti border and into Saudi Arabia. In response to the 4th Marine Expeditionary Brigade's apparent preparations, Iraq deployed eight divisions in defensive positions. Combined with the extensive defenses Iraq positioned along the wadi, approximately 20 percent of Saddam's military strength was unavailable to deflect the actual ground assault. In contrast, the Marines landed in friendly

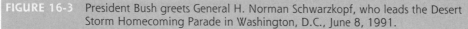

FIGURE 16-3 President Bush greets General H. Norman Schwarzkopf, who leads the Desert Storm Homecoming Parade in Washington, D.C., June 8, 1991.

Source: George Bush Presidential Library and Museum.

territory and the 1st Cavalry Division conducted only a short feint up Wadi al Batin before withdrawing, freeing the units for their roles as reserves for the supporting attack launched by the 1st Marine Expeditionary Force and for the sweeping main attack spearheaded by VII Corps, a combined American British formation.

Positioned along the Saudi-Kuwait border, 1st Marine Expeditionary Force had to attack into Kuwait across two heavily defended, heavily mined areas. Engineers and tanks fitted with mine plows quickly breached the minefields, eventually clearing twenty lanes through which the Marines could advance toward the capital, Kuwait City. Along the way they took 10,000 Iraqi prisoners and seized control of Al Jaber Airfield. By the third day, the Marines had repulsed an Iraqi counterattack and isolated Kuwait City.

The nearly 150,000 soldiers of the VII Corps faced the vaunted Republican Guard as they made their great sweep across the desert north of the Kuwaiti border. Like the 1st Marine Expeditionary Force, VII Corps quickly breached Iraqi-built obstacles and eliminated the first manned line of defense while opening lanes of advance. Other units enveloped Iraqi positions to the west. In short order, one British and three American divisions launched an armored assault against the reinforced Republican Guard. M1A1 Abrams tanks and M2 Bradley fighting vehicles made quick work of the Iraqi force. Enemy targets were either destroyed or surrendered. From the air, Air Force A-10 Warthogs struck Iraqi armor up and down the battlefront. Although VII Corps thoroughly defeated the Republican Guard units and took thousands of prisoners, large numbers of Republican Guardsmen escaped and continued to serve as the core of a weakened but still troublesome Iraqi military.

By February 27, Kuwaiti forces made their way back into Kuwait City, which the Iraqis had abandoned. By February 28, the remaining Iraqis, including the vaunted Republican Guard, were in full retreat toward Baghdad. Ground combat in Operation DESERT STORM lasted a mere 100 hours. Early casualty predictions for American and coalition forces had been high, in the thousands. Army and Marine Corps units suffered only 122 combat deaths, including 35 from friendly fire, and 131 noncombat deaths. The Air Force lost 20 killed in combat and 6 dead from accidents. The Navy had only 6 combat and 8 noncombat deaths. These numbers include 15 American servicewomen killed during DESERT SHIELD and DESERT STORM. Twenty-one Americans, including one woman, were captured and later released by the Iraqi military. Melissa Rathbun-Nealy was the first American woman taken prisoner of war since World War II. One Navy F/A-18 pilot remains missing. Lieutenant Commander Michael Scott Speicher was shot down on the first day of the air war; it is not yet known whether he survived, since neither he nor his body has been recovered. Only 278 Americans were wounded in the war. Coalition casualties included 92 dead and 318 wounded. Iraqi casualties amounted to at least 10,000 military and 2,000 civilian dead.

Although the United States had confronted a larger but inferior army, success in the Gulf War convinced many in military and civilian circles that the American military had banished the shadows of Vietnam. The Gulf War had been the largest mobilization of American military power since the Korean War, and had been fought according to standards set by decades of planning for a similar type of conflict against the Soviet Army in Western Europe. American troops returned home to much fanfare, including a ticker-tape parade in New York City and a presidential review in Washington. It is indeed ironic that this war was fought at the end of the Cold War, for it did not represent the conflict that the American military would face in the future.

◆ PEACEKEEPING AND NATION BUILDING

As the United States basked in the glory of victory in the Gulf War and contemplated the peace dividend of the end of the Cold War, the power vacuum created by the end of forty-plus years of Soviet-American conflict contributed to a variety of wars and conflicts around the world. Some were admittedly peripheral to American interests, while others were more vital. During the 1970s and into the Reagan administration of the 1980s, the American military had conducted brief operations, such as bombing Libya in retaliation for that state's support of terrorism and providing escort for shipping in the Persian Gulf during the Iran-Iraq War. In the 1990s, the military found itself involved in rather complex peacekeeping and nation-building missions in places like Somalia, Bosnia, Haiti, and Kosovo. One of the influences in these missions was the new president, William Jefferson Clinton, who exhibited a mix of Wilson's idealism and Carter's humanitarianism that held that the role of the United States as the sole superpower should be to improve places where chaos still reigned.

American involvement in Somalia actually began in the last years of the Bush administration. Warlords who controlled humanitarian aid and food distribution had wracked Somalia since 1989. In what amounted to a large-scale gang war, heavily armed gangs ruled Somalia, especially the capital city of Mogadishu. In early January 1991, American Marine and Naval units evacuated over 400 Americans from Mogadishu in a very complex operation called EASTERN EXIT. Using twenty-year-old maps, the rescue force had difficulty even locating the American embassy compound but was able to secure the area—amid violent looting—to complete the evacuation. Over the course of the next two years, the situation in Somalia deteriorated even more, finally forcing the United Nations to step in with a large peacekeeping force. Hundreds of thousands of Somalis had died from starvation and disease as rival warlords battled for control of this town or that. Even in Mogadishu, warlord Mohammed Farrah Aidid waged relentless gang warfare on his rivals.

In April 1992, the United Nations sent in a small security detail to protect relief workers and guard aid warehouses and transport. This token force had no effect on the warlords. In July, two United Nations relief aircraft were basically stopped at gunpoint at the Mogadishu airport and looted. Red Cross relief flights began arriving in August 1992; to protect them, Army helicopters sent from Mombassa hovered above the airport. The Red Cross had at first forbidden any ground security; but when a 500-man Pakistani infantry unit arrived, the Red Cross relented and allowed the airport to be secured. Not long after, the first of 3,000 United Nations peacekeepers began arriving.

By December, the United Nations authorized an American-led peacekeeping force representing a variety of nations. With warlords hijacking relief trucks as they left the safe confines of the airport, little aid was actually reaching the population that so desperately needed it. President Bush authorized American forces to provide for the safe distribution of relief, while the United Nations hoped the Americans would actually disarm the rival gangs.

By the spring of 1993, Aidid and other gang leaders increased their attacks on United Nations and American personnel. A new United Nations Quick Reaction Force began conducting offensive operations to wipe out the warlords. Aidid was its chief target. In July, a multinational force attacked Aidid's compound without success, while angry Somalis violently protested against the United Nations, including one instance where a mob killed four foreign journalists. A car bomb killed several American soldiers in August. In late August, Secretary of Defense Les Aspin ordered the Joint Special Operations Force to Somalia to remove Aidid from power. Task Force Ranger, as it was called, was not under United Nations command, but rather remained directly under CENTCOM at its headquarters in Florida.

The nadir of American involvement in Somalia occurred in October, when American Special Forces got hard intelligence of Aidid's exact location. As troops took off in Blackhawk assault helicopters and moved into Mogadishu by road in several Humvees, the assault began. Things went awry when Somalis shot down one of the Blackhawks. The remaining force became pinned down in the city center, surrounded by thousands of armed Somalis. After 17 hours of fierce combat that cost the lives of 18 American soldiers and perhaps over 1,000 Somalis, the Americans were extracted. Subsequent television news footage of dead American servicemen being dragged through the streets of Mogadishu helped cause public support for the operation to evaporate almost overnight.

President Clinton, who took office in January 1993, ordered the American force to withdraw from Somalia by March 1994. Also in March, Clinton signed Presidential

Directive 25, which stated that American participation in peacekeeping operations must be contingent upon the conflict's threat to international security or upon whether participation directly serves American interests. Arguably, the sad and tragic events in Somalia had done neither.

A 1991 military coup that exiled Haitian President Jean-Bertrand Aristide provided the United States with reason enough to intervene in Haiti in 1994, continuing a long tradition of intervention in the Caribbean island nation's affairs. United Nations embargoes and other sanctions against the military government of Haiti failed to bring about the return of legitimately elected government. In the face of congressional, public, and international disapproval, the Clinton administration nonetheless ordered over 5,000 American troops and Marines to occupy Haiti in September 1994. In Operation UPHOLD DEMOCRACY, American and international forces met next to no resistance in gaining control of the country. President Aristide was returned to power in October after the military junta agreed to a general amnesty passed by the restored Haitian assembly, though most of the junta leadership left Haiti. Token American and international forces remained in Haiti through 1998, maintaining order and conducting nation-building tasks.

The United States became involved in peacekeeping operations in the Balkans in the 1990s, where decades of authoritarian rule had given way to ethnic-based governments and civil war. The most horrific aspect of these conflicts was the widespread use of ethnic cleansing among rival peoples in the former Yugoslavia. In Bosnia, United Nations peacekeepers entered the fray in 1992 to protect relief workers. Their impact was negligible, as the Serbs continued slaughtering Bosnian Croats, sometimes murdering the entire population of a village. The United Nations peacekeepers struggled simply to protect themselves, much as the Marines had needed to do in Lebanon in 1983.

The United States stayed out of the conflict in Bosnia until 1995, when President Clinton ordered tactical air strikes against the Serb capital of Belgrade to stop the bloodshed. Wanting to avoid a ground war in the Balkans, the Defense Department testified before a wary Congress that such a force might require more than 400,000 American troops fielded against well-armed and experienced armies in Serbia, Croatia, and Bosnia. Chairman of the Joint Chiefs General Colin Powell was adamantly opposed to intervening in a conflict that, though fraught with human tragedy, was in his mind militarily untenable and peripheral to American interests.

Fortunately, NATO had taken the lead in offering some air patrol and aid protection in the beleaguered region. Beginning in 1993, American Air Force planes assisted in patrolling over the Adriatic Sea and Bosnia, while the U.S. Navy kept a carrier battle group in the Adriatic Sea to monitor merchant ships for arms smuggling into the former Yugoslavia. What followed were two years of escalating violence between NATO and Serb forces. Finally, in August 1995, NATO air bombardment hit Serb targets around Sarajevo and other locations, forcing the Serbs to the peace table. The Dayton Peace Accords of November 1995 ended the fighting in Bosnia and put in place a NATO peacekeeping force of over 60,000 troops.

Meanwhile, in Kosovo, armed nationalists began threatening Serbians living in Kosovo. Serbia responded, beginning an even more horrific ethnic cleansing than had occurred in Bosnia. By 1999, the situation was completely out of hand. In March, Clinton approved NATO air bombardment of Serb targets in Kosovo and Serbia.

This initial bombing only intensified the fighting on the ground, where Serb forces decimated Kosovar villages. Horrified, Clinton nonetheless refused to send in ground forces to stop the fighting. Airpower would have to do what it had promised it could do since the 1920s—break the political will of a people and bring a government to its knees. NATO bombing began to focus on Belgrade itself, the Serb capital, hitting command and control targets, electric plants, bridges, and other vital infrastructure. Some said the scene in Serbia recalled the height of strategic bombing in World War II.

After enduring seventy-eight days of bombing, Serb leader Slobodan Milosevic agreed to a peace settlement wherein Kosovo was divided into occupation zones. The United States had used NATO for the first time in a major campaign and had significantly shied away from United Nations involvement. The tragedy in the former Yugoslavia was immensely complex and thus made the United States and much of Europe hesitant to get deeply involved. However, humanitarian and security concerns finally motivated NATO to take action that arguably had been needed years before, finally ending the bloodshed.

◆ CONCLUSION

American troops remain a part of the NATO peacekeeping force in the Bosnia-Serbia-Kosovo region. Nation building has become the new focus of their mission, as American forces assist in establishing law enforcement and government administration. American forces conducted similar operations in Haiti in 1994 to ensure fair elections. After the Gulf War, American pilots patrolled the southern and northern thirds of Iraq, occasionally destroying antiair missile batteries and radar stations. It seemed that the great American military establishment, made so by decades of Cold War, was now relegated to dealing with so-called small wars. With such a future in mind, successive Secretaries of Defense began looking at reconfiguring force structure, procuring different weapons systems, and downsizing personnel. The new American military would have to be leaner, faster, and more lethal in order to deal effectively with these conflicts. Such a force, however, was ineffectual if the United States lacked the political will to use it. After being eager to flex American military muscle, the American political as well as military leadership had been convinced by the unpleasant experiences of the 1990s to be ever more cautious in using force in the post-Cold War world order.

Further Reading ·

Adkin, Mark. *Urgent Fury: The Battle for Grenada*. Lexington, Massachusetts: Lexington Books, 1989.

Atkinson, Rick. *Crusade: The Untold Story of the Persian Gulf War*. Boston: Houghton Mifflin, 1993.

Bacevich, Andrew J., and Efraim Embar, eds. *The Gulf War of 1991 Reconsidered*. London: Taylor & Francis, 2003.

Beckwith, Charlie A., and Donald Knox. *Delta Force: The U.S. Counter Terrorist Unit and the Iran Rescue Mission*. New York: Harcourt Brace Jovanovich, 1983.

Benis, Frank M. *U.S. Marines in Lebanon, 1982–1983*. Washington, D.C.: U.S. Government Printing Office, 1987.

Bolger, Daniel P. *Savage Peace: Americans at War in the 1990s*. Novato, California: Presidio Press, 1995.

Bowden, Mark. *Blackhawk Down: A Story of Modern War*. New York: Atlantic, 1999.

Burg, Steven L., and Paul S. Shoup. *The War in Bosnia-Herzegovina: Ethnic Conflict and International Intervention*. Armonk, New York: M. E. Sharpe, 1999.

Freedman, Lawrence, and Efraim Karsh. *The Gulf Conflict 1990–1991*. Princeton: Princeton University Press, 1993.

Hillen, John. *Blue Helmets: The Struggle of U.N. Military Operations*. Washington, D.C.: Brassey's, 1998.

Hutchthausen, Peter. *America's Splendid Little Wars: A Short History of U.S. Military Engagements: 1975–2000*. New York: Viking Press, 2003.

Lederman, Gordon Nathaniel. *Reorganizing the Joint Chiefs of Staff: The Goldwater-Nichols Act of 1986*. Westport, Connecticut: Greenwood Publishers, 1999.

Locher, James R. *Victory on the Potomac: The Goldwater-Nichols Act Unifies the Pentagon*. College Station: Texas A&M University Press, 2002.

Olsen, John A., and Edward N. Luttwak. *Strategic Air Power in Desert Storm*. London: Taylor & Francis, 2003.

Record, Jeffrey. *Hollow Victory: A Contrary View of the Gulf War*. Washington, D.C.: Brassey's, 1993.

Stevenson, Jonathon. *Losing Mogadishu: Testing U.S. Policy in Somalia*. Annapolis: Naval Institute Press, 1995.

mysearchlab Connections: Sources Online • • • • • • • • • •

READ AND REVIEW

Review this chapter by using the study aids and these related documents available on MySearchLab.

Study Plan

Chapter Test

Essay Test

Documents

Jimmy Carter, The "Malaise" Speech (1979)

In 1979, President Jimmy Carter gave this speech to the American people, in which he warned of crisis in American confidence as the nation faced new security threats, specifically in energy dependence.

George Bush, Allied Military Action in the Persian Gulf (1991)

In January 1991, President Bush went before the American people on primetime television to announce the beginning of the air campaign against Iraq, which was soon followed by a land offensive to liberate Kuwait from Iraqi occupation.

Bill Chappell, Speech to the American Security Council Foundation (1985)

In this document, Bill Chappell explained then President Ronald Reagan's Strategic Defense Initiative concept in a speech to the Security Council Foundation.

RESEARCH AND EXPLORE

Explore the following review questions using the research tools available on www. mysearchlab.com.

1. What challenges confronted the U.S. military in the aftermath of the Vietnam War?
2. What role did technology play in the revival of U.S. military capabilities?
3. What were the limitations on the exercise of American power in this period?

CHAPTER 17

Into the Twenty-First Century

◆ INTRODUCTION

At the close of the twentieth century, the United States enjoyed unrivaled power in the world; it was the center of an informal global empire unique in history. The collapse of the Soviet Union and the end of the Cold War with an unambiguous victory for the liberal-capitalist West left the United States unchallenged militarily. To a considerable extent, the globalizing world economy was driven by the American economy, while American popular culture reached around the world. In many parts of the globe, especially in the developing world, American and Western interests were considered synonymous and indistinguishable.

The 2000 presidential election brought George W. Bush to office with an administration whose senior members had, in many cases, spent the previous two decades defining and honing the neoconservative position on American power and its use in the world. The most influential among them—Vice President Dick Cheney and Secretary of Defense Donald Rumsfeld—believed implicitly in the need to use American power to further reinforce American global dominance and check potential rivals and threats. Latent and potential threats certainly existed. Secretary Rumsfeld also believed strongly in the need to rebuild the American military in order to reflect American strengths in technology and global reach while at the same time directing defense spending into areas other than conventional military capability, such as space-based missile defense. Rumsfeld called this program to make the American military lighter, leaner, and more lethal "transformation." The major loser in this process was ultimately the U.S. Army. At one early stage, there was discussion of reducing the

Army's order of battle still further, from 10 divisions to 8, although all of the services stood to lose specific projects and capabilities.

Vice President Cheney, on the other hand, appears to have come to office already convinced that the regime of Saddam Hussein in Iraq continued to pose a compelling threat to American interests. There is evidence that from the beginning of his first term in office, President Bush was being asked to actively consider the renewal of offensive action against Iraq.

◆ **A NEW WAR**

The terrorist attacks on the World Trade Center in New York City and the Pentagon in Washington, D.C. on September 11, 2001, shattered post-Cold War assumptions of domestic security that accompanied the Bush administration into office. The new administration had all but completed the Quadrennial Review (QDR) of national security policy and had to hastily rewrite the review document in light of dramatically changed strategic circumstances. Many of the features of American military superiority were challenged by the attacks: The vaunted air defense system that had been fashioned to counter Soviet air and missile attacks in the Cold War was impotent in the face of hijackers flying fully laden passenger aircraft into buildings, while the fundamental premises of the Revolution in Military Affairs (RMA) lay in tatters. There had been massive failures in intelligence, as the most devastating attack on American soil since Pearl Harbor had been carried out by only nineteen men armed with nothing more than inexpensive box-cutters.

Although the impact of the destruction of the World Trade Center was immense, the attacks represented a culmination in developments going back a decade or more. Terrorism was not new, even on American soil. The deadly bombing of the Alfred P. Murrah Federal Building in Oklahoma City and the 1993 attempt to bomb the World Trade Center had both suggested the vulnerability of American society, while many of America's allies in Europe and Asia had battled domestic and transnational terrorism for decades.

Moreover, anti-Americanism had been on the rise for years, especially, but by no means exclusively, in the developing world and in parts of Western Europe. Militant fundamentalism had also been a growing problem for many governments in the Muslim world for decades; in theological and intellectual terms, fundamentalism was grounded in Wahabbism and took its political inspiration from radical movements such as the Muslim Brotherhood, which had been active since the 1950s. Al Qaeda and its leader, Osama bin Laden, were both consequences of American policy that had fostered the anti-Soviet mujahidin in Afghanistan during the protracted Soviet occupation of that country in the 1980s, while the radical fundamentalist turn in Afghan politics that saw the Taliban come to power was, again in part, a result of meddling in the internal politics of Afghanistan by Pakistani intelligence services over several decades.

On September 11, 2001, all of these disparate elements finally successfully came together with devastating effect. Characterized by one early analysis as a meeting of "Saudi money and Egyptian brains," the attacks set in motion a series of responses culminating in the war in Iraq—Operation IRAQI FREEDOM—which, like so much else surrounding the "War on Terror," was already under active consideration when the destruction of the Twin Towers gave it an impetus that it had hitherto lacked.

The damage from the attacks was far more psychological and financial than it was physical—it tends to be overlooked that the actual number of casualties inflicted that day was many times fewer than it might have been, and that tens of thousands of people successfully evacuated the World Trade Center before it collapsed. In fact, for the first time in American history, local law enforcement and firefighting units were arguably on the front lines of an attack on the United States. The impact, nonetheless, was global. President Bush had little trouble persuading the international community that the attacks had been planned in Afghanistan, that the chief perpetrators of the outrage remained there protected by the Taliban, and that it was just and appropriate for the United States and its coalition allies to launch a major offensive—Operation ENDURING FREEDOM—into Afghanistan to kill or capture those responsible and remove the Taliban from power. Strategically, in this most unusual conflict, the forbidding mountains of Afghanistan represented an exploitable center of gravity. (It should be noted, in passing, that while ENDURING FREEDOM was originally confined to Afghanistan, it subsequently spawned a number of subsidiary operations in the Philippines, Horn of Africa, trans-Sahara, and Kyrgyzstan as part of the "Global War on Terror.")

The campaign to remove the Taliban illustrates both the strengths and weaknesses of the American military and the American way of war at that point in its development. American capacity to project and maintain combat power at great distances from the continental United States was seemingly effortless. The absence of existing advance bases and airfields either in Afghanistan itself or in surrounding countries was quickly negated through swift diplomacy with small and impoverished neighboring countries eager to become clients of the United States and through the use of carrier battle groups and the strike aviation capabilities they deployed. Advances in precision-guided munitions, combined with improved targeting systems deployed by Special Forces elements on the ground, greatly increased lethality and helped minimize casualties to civilians and friendly forces (although these can never be eradicated entirely). The transport and logistic effort was vast and highly successful, as it had been during Operation DESERT SHIELD/DESERT STORM in the early 1990s and, indeed, consistently since World War II.

The campaign was orchestrated and commanded through Central Command (CENTCOM), based in Florida under the command of Army General Tommy Franks. The initial attack began on October 7, 2001, with concentrated strikes against a wide range of targets mounted by B1, B2, and B52 bombers; tactical strike aircraft; and Tomahawk cruise missiles launched from American and British submarines. The Taliban controlled around 80 percent of the country, its authority contested principally by the Northern Alliance under the capable leadership of Ahmed Shah Masood, who was murdered by Al Qaeda members on September 7. Taking advantage of the chaotic, tribalized politics of Afghanistan was an important factor in American success.

Contrary to subsequent claims, there was considerable heavy ground fighting against Al Qaeda and Taliban forces. But much of this was done by the Northern Alliance aided by Special Forces and CIA teams rather than American regular forces, allowing the impression to form in some quarters that American airpower had been the overwhelming and decisive factor in the success of the war. In fact, the United States was able to field only relatively small ground elements (initially from the Army's 101st Airborne and 10th Mountain Divisions and Marine Expeditionary Units) precisely because the anti-Taliban forces inside the country were ready and willing to fight. Coalition allies, principally the United Kingdom, also supplemented American forces. Ultimately, contributions of various kinds from 68 nations, of whom 27 supplied military capabilities of one form or another, aided this initial campaign in the War on Terror.

The provincial center of Mazar-al-Sharif fell on November 9, the old capital of Kabul on November 13, and the Taliban capital of Kandahar on December 13. The Taliban's positions unraveled quickly in the face of concerted pressure on the ground and from the air, aided by the fact that the regime's only reliable fighters—Al Qaeda members known locally as "Afghan Arabs"—were widely hated by the local population. Remaining resistance was quickly driven to the rugged and inhospitable south-eastern fringes of the country along the porous border with Pakistan, and coalition operations, such as ANACONDA in February 2002, contained and then eliminated many die-hard groups of fighters.

An interim government was established on December 22, 2001, and the American command element was replaced by the International Security Assistance Force (ISAF), which covered all coalition elements deployed but still relied heavily on American forces. Casualties to December 2005 reflect this: 252 American personnel killed and 393 wounded with 127 coalition troops killed and 381 wounded. Afghan casualties, military and civilian combined, probably ranged in the vicinity of 40,000.

The early operations in Afghanistan were in many respects so successful that they perhaps served to disguise the fact that no absolute solution had been obtained. The Taliban was seriously damaged, although small groups loyal to the former regime continued to operate in the country. Al Qaeda's senior command structure was partially destroyed and its remaining capability seriously degraded, but bin Laden remained at liberty, and the nature of the organization was such that the removal of its leaders in Afghanistan did little to impair its effectiveness elsewhere—as subsequent events in Iraq and terrorist attacks in Western Europe and Southeast Asia demonstrated.

The operations in Afghanistan suffered from the switch in focus to Iraq and the rapidly increasing difficulties that U.S. and allied forces encountered there. The criticism of the Bush administration—that it embarked on a large and uncertain enterprise in the Middle East before completing the task in Central Asia—is undoubtedly correct and meant that the gains made in Afghanistan were quickly eroded, the Taliban was able to rebuild and greatly increase the extent and intensity of its operations, and the task that the allied forces then faced after the withdrawal from Iraq was far more difficult than perhaps it need have been. The balance between the two theaters gradually shifted, marked by a surge in Afghanistan that corresponded (roughly) to the troop withdrawals in Iraq: The number of U.S. troops increased from 26,000 in January 2008 to 48,000 in June, an 80 percent increase. British troop numbers also increased while they, the Canadians and, of the non-NATO allies, the Australians continued to make significant combat contributions in the southern provinces.

The war spilled into Pakistan in September 2008, a response to the ease with which Taliban groups maintained sanctuaries in the tribal border regions. The Taliban likewise intensified operations here, making attacks upon NATO convoys running between Peshawar and Kabul. The United States subsequently intensified its operations against targets in Pakistan, especially through drone strikes against leadership assets located there and, most importantly in a symbolic sense, an assault team launched against a compound in Abbottabad on May 2, 2011, that killed Osama bin Laden, who had been living, quite brazenly, under the eyes of the Pakistani authorities. U.S. troop numbers continued to increase to a high of 90,000 (from an ISAF total of 132,000), and in July 2010 General David Petraeus assumed command after the relief of General Stanley McChrystal for unwise and insubordinate public comments critical of the Obama administration. It was assumed that Petraeus would achieve the sort of significant short-term success that would justify a partial troop withdrawal from Afghanistan, and although President Obama signaled in June 2011 that troop withdrawals would commence with the aim to be gone by 2014, the security situation remained problematic when Petraeus departed in August 2011 to assume the directorship of the Central Intelligence Agency.

Despite considerable effort in recent years, the weak link in the Afghan security environment remains the Afghan forces themselves. Considerable gains were made in improving and expanding the Afghan National Army, but much less attention was paid to the quality and training of the Afghan National Police, and this remains one of several weak elements in the attempt to build a viable nation-state with a functioning civil society. Corruption and nepotism remain widespread, and these, along with popular resentment at the presence of foreign forces and the inflicting of civilian casualties by ISAF operations, provide a steady stream of recruits for the Taliban.

◆ OPERATION IRAQI FREEDOM

It is much harder to be definitive about the outcomes of Operation IRAQI FREEDOM at any but the most obvious level. The justifications for waging renewed war on Iraq—the elimination of weapons of mass destruction and the threat that Saddam Hussein allegedly posed to the United States—were much less clear-cut and compelling than those that justified the war in Afghanistan. There is no question that Saddam's Iraq had used chemical weapons against both the Kurds and Shiites within the country and against Iranian forces during the Iran-Iraq War of the 1980s, and there is equally no question that the regime had expressed the intention to acquire nuclear and biological weapons in the future. But Iraq did not possess them in 2003, and as the existence of such weapons became increasingly more difficult to verify, the international coalition of opinion that the Bush administration sought to build rapidly fell apart. In marked contrast to the international support for military action in Afghanistan, the "coalition of the willing" for Iraq consisted essentially of American and British forces with minor additions from Australia and a handful of other countries such as Canada, Poland, and Spain. Relations with many European nations, notably France, reached new lows.

The war in Iraq also offered a test for Secretary of Defense Donald Rumsfeld's much-vaunted (and only partially implemented) transformation policies, and this occasioned heated arguments within the Pentagon and elsewhere. Operation DESERT STORM had been fought successfully by a very large force that had taken months to build up and an enormous logistic effort to sustain; central to Rumsfeld's idea of transformation, in contrast, was a belief that American objectives in the wider world should be pursued with a greater emphasis on the technological superiorities that the United States could deploy, and a corresponding lessening of reliance on manpower, which is easily the largest single expense on the defense budget.

Although the total size of the American forces deployed in Operation IRAQI FREEDOM topped 460,000, the numbers actually deployed forward for combat and the war on the ground in Iraq itself were very much smaller. This size discrepancy was the hub of the argument between Rumsfeld and the U.S. Army, including Army Chief of Staff General Eric K. Shinseki. Along with Secretary of the Army Thomas White, Shinseki testified before the Senate Armed Services Committee that the deployment in Iraq was far too low to handle combat and postcombat operations. For this break with Rumsfeld, Shinseki was ultimately sidelined and publicly humiliated by the Secretary of Defense before his term of appointment ended, while White was forced to resign.

Drawing on the experience of recent operations in Kosovo and elsewhere, Shinseki and others argued that the forces deployed on the ground would be insufficient to deal with the demands of occupation and reconstruction that would inevitably follow even a short and successful campaign. In line with "transformational" thinking, however, and reflecting the infatuation with technological solutions to military problems, General Franks' war plan called for an initial decapitation strike—dubbed "shock and awe"—that would destroy the Iraqi command authority, including Saddam, and make full-scale ground operations either unnecessary or less central to the campaign that might follow. The promise, drawing on flawed premises concerning the efficacy of precision operations from the air in the former Yugoslavia in the 1990s, was not realized. The attacks did have the effect of destroying much of the civilian infrastructure of the country—notably the electric power grid—without any plan for quickly rebuilding it early in the occupation phase that would follow. It was one of a number of decisions that in hindsight would have been better not made.

One way of viewing the conflict between the United States and Iraq involves two short but intense periods of open warfare, in 1990–1991 and 2003, separated by a decade of low-level conflict involving sanctions; weapons inspections; the enforcement of "no-fly" zones in the north and southeast of the country, dubbed Operations NORTHERN and SOUTHERN WATCH; and an increasingly tense diplomatic standoff. American aircraft also regularly targeted the Iraqi command and air defense networks, routinely bombing these in response to Iraqi provocations and attempts to violate the no-fly status of Kurdish and Shiite areas within the country. The sanctions program, largely enforced at sea by a multinational naval force, aroused considerable controversy internationally with claims about the effect on the civilian population—especially women and children, whom Saddam's regime ruthlessly but effectively exploited for propaganda purposes.

The inconclusive outcome of the shock-and-awe strike was followed, inevitably, by the opening of a coalition ground offensive into Iraq staged from Kuwait. An intended simultaneous northern invasion using the American 4th Infantry Division had to be abandoned when the Turkish government refused Washington permission to stage it in Turkish territory; the division had to be rerouted through the Gulf states and took no part in the initial invasion or subsequent operations until close to the

FIGURE 17-1 The Iraq War.

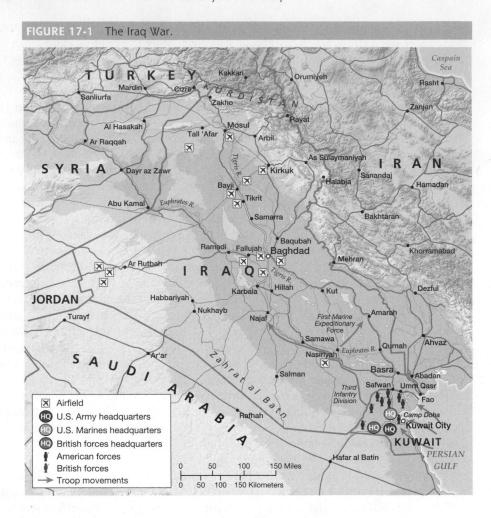

end of hostilities. British forces in conjunction with the Marines seized the oil fields, the port of Um Qasr, and the city of Basra in the south, while the American Army's 3rd Infantry Division moved to envelop Baghdad and the 1st Marine Division secured the Rumaylah oilfields and the key city of Nasariyah. The 82nd and 101st Airborne Divisions and the 1st Armored Division were also fed into the operations, securing cities and facilities that consolidated and extended the advance while pinning and diverting Iraqi forces that might otherwise have interfered with the move on Baghdad. On April 5 and for several days thereafter, American forces staged "Thunder Runs" into parts of the Iraqi capital, using Abrams tanks and Bradley infantry vehicles to test the defenses and draw out the defenders. Control of the airport and a strong foothold inside the city were established in this way, with the city finally secured on April 9. Saddam fled into hiding, and his regime was declared at an end.

The collapse of Saddam's authority was rapid, aided by a careful campaign to exploit disaffection at senior levels of the military involving bribes and various deals.

This should not obscure the absolute mastery that coalition forces quickly acquired over their opponents, especially those in the vaunted Republican Guard divisions that were expected to fight hardest in defense of the regime. The superiority exercised over the Iraqi forces was generally one-sided, moreover; the Iraqi air force, for example, took no part in operations at all, while morale among many Iraqi troops was low and declined rapidly, with soldiers refusing to fight or surrendering to the advancing coalition forces. On a positive note, all this helped to ensure the success of a conventional campaign that lasted just 21 days and involved remarkably low coalition casualties (American 138 dead, UK 42 dead) while also avoiding inflicting heavy losses among the civilian population (figures are contested, but range from 1,200 to 5,000 dead) and even among the Iraqi armed forces (figures again are contested, and range from 2,300 to as high as 20,000).

President Bush dramatically declared an end to "major combat" on May 1 by landing aboard the carrier *Lincoln* in a Navy S-3B Viking to make the announcement to cheering sailors and network news cameras. This was certainly premature. The vacuum created by the rapid collapse of the regime was clearly not anticipated, as demonstrated by the widespread looting and disorder that quickly followed across the country and that coalition forces were powerless to stop. A leaner and transformed

FIGURE 17-2 U.S. Soldiers of Alpha Battery 2/32 Field Artillery in support of 4th Infantry Brigade Combat Team, 1st Infantry Division from Fort Riley, Kansas, secure the area and rush U.S. civilians back to the convoy of ambush-protected vehicles after receiving small arms fire during a routine security mission in rural Tikrit, Iraq. Alpha Battery troops are trained to counter all threats to their company and their mission.

Source: Sgt. Jason Stewart/U.S. Department of Defense.

"Rumsfeldian" military might have been sufficient to win the conventional operations of the opening phases of the war, but it was incapable of successfully reestablishing order and security, rebuilding infrastructure and central authority, and engaging in the range of national reconstruction tasks that now presented themselves.

The critics were correct—perhaps in hindsight—that there simply were insufficient forces on the ground to deal with the rapidly growing insurgency that now faced occupation authorities and that both helped create the chaos in civilian society and then profited from it. The United States made serious mistakes early in the occupation, and these compounded structural deficiencies in United States forces and in United States policy more generally. After decades of Baathist repression, the Iraqis saw no reason that they should now be an occupied country, and even those who detested the former regime and had no truck with the radical jihadists felt little love for the coalition forces that remained in their country. Paradoxically, like many in the developing world, ordinary Iraqis had been sold on the idea and image of American bounty and the American dream, and they were frustrated when none of it seemed to quickly come their way. The complete lack of preparation for military government on such an extensive scale and the needs of national reconstruction, together with the wrong-headed insistence that rebuilding would be undertaken by the private sector on a for-profit basis underwritten by Iraqi oil revenue, brought inordinate delays and mismanagement and increased suspicion about American intentions.

FIGURE 17-3 President George W. Bush walks between rows of saluting Side Boy Honor Guard members in front of an S-3B Viking jet aircraft on the deck of the USS Abraham Lincoln aircraft carrier.

Source: U.S. Navy.

The gravest error was the wholesale disbandment of the Iraqi military and the initial refusal to have any engagement with former Baathists. Disbanding the military threw tens of thousands of trained men into idleness and made them unable to provide for their families, thus creating a source of recruits and other support for the growing insurgency. De-Baathification also robbed the occupation authority of a priceless security resource—men who possessed local knowledge, knew the language, and were able, at least in theory, to soften the image of the occupation. While there were real monsters in the ranks of the Baath party, many of these were already dead, like Saddam's sons, or in American captivity. Lumping all former party members into one category suggested how much the Americans had to learn about the country for which they now exercised responsibility—and about the best ways in which to combat a modern insurgency.

The extended nature of the reconstruction task, and the declining security situation that, in turn, made reconstruction more difficult (not least by frightening off many of the civilian contractors who had been expected to rebuild the infrastructure) led to an urgent need for more American troops on the ground. The failure of the Bush administration to build a wide-based coalition before the war now made itself felt, with the majority of American allies refusing to become involved in a war they had thought ill-advised and unnecessary (although it is only fair to add that some made additional force contributions to the coalition effort in Afghanistan in order to relieve the pressure on American resources globally). The increasing shortfall in manpower had to be made good from American resources, and this entailed the widespread mobilization of the National Guard and the Reserves for extended tours of duty in Iraq.

The Reserves would have been called forward in any case, and here again history came round to demonstrate the law of unintended consequences. As part of the rebuilding of the military following the defeat in Vietnam, the armed forces made the decision to locate many combat support and combat service support functions in the Reserves. The theory was that to do so would mean that no president could take the military into a major war again without taking the country with it as well, since protracted operations now would be unsustainable without at least a partial mobilization. The downsizing of the active-duty military in the 1990s meant increasing reliance on National Guard units to provide personnel for duty in Iraq, and elsewhere, with unfortunate consequences. Casualties mounted, deployments were extended with little warning, and guardsmen began failing to reenlist while both recruitment and retention in the active-duty military experienced significant problems due to casualties and a growing perception in parts of the American population that the task in Iraq was thankless and possibly unsustainable. In 2004 there was even some talk about the possible reintroduction of the draft, although by the end of 2005 this had come to nothing and was probably politically impossible in any case. In the same year, senior officers within the National Guard and Army Reserve publicly commented that the continuing war in Iraq had seriously damaged both organizations to the point that it might take a generation to recover. The impact on the existing stocks of ground-force equipment, from individual items to major combat vehicles, also placed sustained pressure on equipment refurbishment and replacement systems, in the Army and Marine Corps especially.

By December 2005, American forces in Iraq had suffered 2,182 killed and 16,155 wounded. Iraqi civilian deaths had climbed to around 30,000, while numbers of foreign journalists, aid workers, and contractors were killed in shootings or car bombs, or kidnapped and gruesomely murdered at the hands of jihadists with the proceedings filmed and broadcast, often over the Internet. The nature of the insurgency was complex, involving both radical fighters external to Iraq (who accounted for most of the suicide fighters), former Baathists increasingly drawn from the disaffected Sunni population, and other Iraqis angered by the continuing occupation.

The operational tempo to some extent belied the label of insurgency, and its defining characteristic in 2004–2005 was sustained close combat on a protracted scale. The new Iraqi army, manned largely by members of the old Iraqi army, gradually improved in size and capability but remained for the most part unready for independent operations. National elections were successfully held in 2005, and the trend to sectarian violence and civil war intensified, with Iraqi soldiers and especially civilians incurring heavy casualties in the ensuing fighting. In June 2006, Abu Musab al-Zarqawi, the leader of Al Qaida in Iraq, was killed while the Iraqi government proceeded with the execution of Saddam Hussein and a number of his key lieutenants. Meanwhile, President Bush received the report of the Iraq Study Group, which he had tasked with advising on a way forward in (to be read, ultimately, as a way out of) the growing mess in that country; by the end of 2006, insurgent attacks had intensified to 960 per week.

The result was the deployment of some 20,000 additional combat troops in a "surge" under the command of the newly appointed General David Petraeus. Coupled with a change in emphasis in operations and, crucially, the emergence of the "Anbar awakening," which saw a move by Sunni Arab tribes towards active cooperation against Al Qaida, this "surge" brought about some decline in civilian deaths and sectarian violence, although "ethnic cleansing" of urban districts by both Sunni and Shia forces also may have contributed to this. At the same time, Petraeus placed a renewed emphasis on training and upgrading the Iraqi National Army (INA). Relative success was reflected in the INA operations in Basra and against the Shia stronghold of Sadr City in Baghdad in March 2008. Although the Iraqi forces sustained heavy casualties, the Shia militias opposing them were forced to accept negotiated settlements (though the durability of these was open to question).

Domestic pressure in the United States for a withdrawal from Iraq was matched by similar pressure within Iraq for the U.S. forces to leave. In December 2008, the U.S. and Iraqi governments negotiated a status of forces agreement, and in the following month control of the Green Zone was transferred to the Iraqis. That month's nationwide provincial elections were characterized by assassinations and intimidation, but there was a strong sense that the U.S. phases of the war were winding down, and in June 2009 U.S. forces withdrew from Baghdad altogether followed by the final withdrawal of combat forces in August 2010. A robust advisory and training effort remained in place, however.

The Iraq War was controversial and divisive, and the costs of the Bush administration's decision to widen the "war on terror" in that manner will take many years to calculate. U.S. forces lost 4,476 dead and more than 32,000 wounded; Iraqi losses are set at 26,000 insurgents killed, with civilian losses anywhere between 125,000 and 654,000. The total cost to the U.S. economy alone is estimated at $3 trillion, with some critics pointing to the additional strains it placed on the U.S. economy as contributing to the severity of the global financial crisis that emerged in 2008–2009. The impact on the U.S. armed forces and the Veterans' Administration will prove to be profound.

◆ CHALLENGES FOR THE FUTURE

The American military had thus found a clear and pressing role in the world, but one that again threatened to place it under severe stress as an organization. The 1990s had offered a confusing mix of messages as to likely future roles for the armed forces: peacekeeping, counterterrorism, the front line of the drug wars in Central and South America; none of these roles accorded with the military's own view of its traditional and expected role in national security. The U.S. Army, in particular, has never been comfortable with peacekeeping as a mission; and indeed, Americans are often regarded as lacking the temperament for either peacekeeping or counterinsurgency, each of which requires patience, a long-term view, and an understanding that armed force is only one part, and usually the lesser part, of the security function involved.

Counterterrorism has become a bread-and-butter issue for the variety of special forces organizations within the various armed services, but in the War on Terror, again, much of the fight belongs to police and intelligence agencies and only secondarily to the active-duty military. Military involvement in the War on Drugs during the Reagan presidency was often seen as a misuse of capabilities, and in any case raised some difficult constitutional and civil-military relations issues when transferred to American soil.

The operations in Afghanistan and Iraq demonstrate both the potential and the limitations of advanced technology as applied to the battlefield. Despite increased spending on sensors, satellites, and other mechanisms of electronic intelligence, after an intense hunt lasting months, Saddam was captured in December 2003 by a foot patrol from the 4th Infantry Division acting on local knowledge and human intelligence. As Secretary of Defense, Rumsfeld emphasized the need to wean the services from expensive, high-technology systems designed for a Cold War environment that no longer exists—the Army's Crusader 155 mm self-propelled artillery system, canceled in 2002, is a good example. But other systems and platforms, such as the F-22 Raptor and the Joint Strike Fighter (JSF), have derailed the acquisitions budgets of the armed forces, and as per-unit costs climb and initial orders are scaled back to fit within projected expenditure limits, new platforms may appear in such limited numbers as to undercut their intended roles and missions.

The potential job losses and local and regional economic impact of program cancellations and scale-downs make these highly sensitive political issues. The same has proved true of attempts to rationalize force structure and deployments through the base closure program begun in the 1990s. In addition, as American forces outstrip even their closest allies—such as the British—in terms of technological and cutting-edge capabilities, their ability to cooperate satisfactorily on, around, and over the battlefield becomes increasingly compromised, thus making coalition warfare all the more difficult.

The demands of operations since 2001 have brought into sharp relief several issues that were already present, if less starkly delineated. The all-volunteer military always faces problems in recruiting and retaining the best-quality personnel whenever the domestic economy is booming, jobs are plentiful, and salaries are healthy. Without compromising the quality of either enlisted or commissioned personnel, the armed forces must work harder to broaden the demographics of those to whom they seek to appeal. As happened with the racial integration of the military from the Korean War onward, women have found increasing opportunities within the military as more specializations and musterings have opened to them in the absence of sufficient numbers of skilled males.

This has led to an ongoing argument about the involvement of women in combat, a function that officially remains closed to them despite female combat casualties in Iraq and Afghanistan. Political and social conservatives maintain that the involvement of women in combat (by which they often mean combat units) will fatally undermine capability and commitment on the part of their male counterparts. Proponents of the role of women in combat (by which they, too, often mean combat units) point to the increasing combat role of some female personnel in Iraq. Women often made up as much as 50 percent of the logistic and other support units deployed in Iraq, which, especially in 2003–2004, were regular targets for jihadist ambushes increasingly wary of engaging regular Marine and Army combat units.

Women did not serve in actual combat units in Iraq, but a portion of them certainly served in combat, and some acquitted themselves well. In June 2005, Sergeant Leigh Ann Hester, serving with the 617th Military Police Company of the Kentucky National Guard, became the first woman since World War II to be awarded the Silver Star for her part in fighting off an ambush on a supply convoy in March of that year. Women are neither as congenitally incapable of combat as opponents maintain, nor are they as widely and regularly exposed to close combat as proponents suggest.

Another sociopolitical flash point concerning service relates to homosexuals. President Clinton famously fell afoul of traditional opposition to acknowledged gay service in the military at the beginning of his first term. The "don't ask, don't tell" policy theoretically protected homosexual personnel so long as they adhered closely to its strictures. But the policy was clear that "homosexual conduct is not compatible with military service" and that openly gay service members will promptly be discharged, and the mechanism clearly was open to abuse. The issue had both civil rights implications and very pragmatic operational capability implications, with well-publicized instances of soldiers with much-needed language skills in Arabic, for example, being discharged because of sexual orientation. President Obama came to office with a clear policy of opening service to homosexuals, which was signed into law in December 2010 and enacted when the Congress repealed the earlier legislative restrictions in September 2011. The Chairman of the Joint Chiefs, Admiral Mike Mullen, personally endorsed the changes, and extensive training and orientation efforts were undertaken within the services to ensure compliance.

Another issue that has arisen is the role of the military in responding to national disasters, such as Hurricane Katrina in 2005. While states can call out their respective Guard units for emergency response, natural disasters, such as Katrina, encompass such scale and destruction that a larger, better-equipped federal agency is needed to coordinate search and rescue, recovery, and rebuilding operations. The American military is really the only federal agency that can undertake such a large operation. States, however, do not wish to relinquish control over their Guard units while conducting operations within their borders. The debate over the old tradition of state control and *posse comitatus* was again brought to the fore because state and federal civilian agencies failed to respond effectively to Katrina, after which the military finally came in and seemingly restored order, bringing much-needed aid to people in desperate situations. The American military's role and capacity to provide relief in international disasters, as evidenced in the 2004 tsunami in Indonesia and the 2010 earthquake in Haiti, also remains a critical asset to American security interests.

The wider military organization faces some pressing challenges in the early twenty-first century. It remains heavily committed across the world in operations, and it is smaller than at any time since the Vietnam War. Because of downsizing in the 1990s, the Army alone declined from 780,000 to 480,000, and the senior levels of the Pentagon expressed strong opposition in 2004 to congressional attempts to increase the strengths of the services. The National Guard is a finite resource, while regular repeat deployments for active-duty personnel to Iraq, Afghanistan, or elsewhere will inevitably have an impact upon service families and raise various quality-of-life issues that in turn will significantly impact retention rates. The much-debated and familiar questions of who serves, and why, are likely to come into sharper focus in the ensuing years. The continuing weakness of the U.S. economy in the aftermath of the financial melt-down of 2008–2009 has significant medium-term implications for the U.S. military across the board.

◆ CONCLUSION

As the United States in the next several decades approaches a multifaceted security environment, it faces immense military challenges. While U.S. Navy Seals killed Osama bin Laden in Pakistan in May 2011, the threat presented by terrorism remains, as do threats from piracy, rogue states, emergent nuclear powers, and conventional powers. Moreover, new threats to American national security, such as global climate change, financial crises, and increased competition over energy resources offer unique and unprecedented challenges to the American military. The American military's past shows that this democratic nation has somehow managed to overcome security challenges in part by building an adequate military establishment to meet them. This has not been done without cost or mistakes, however. Civil-military relations, funding priorities, force structure, weapons procurement, doctrinal debates, incorporating cutting-edge technology, and a focus on having an all-volunteer force, be it militia or regulars, have always tested American military effectiveness.

A standing military in a democracy remains a delicate thing, and will perhaps remain so for the United States due to the very nature of its governing system and political principles. Challenges abound. What security threats will the United States face over the next century? How will the United States procure weapons systems, adapt its force structure, and fund the increasingly expensive and diverse mission to provide not only for its own security but also that of others? And how will it do these things without resorting to politically unpopular conscription, increased taxation, and base consolidation—and without alienating allies? These are most difficult questions.

The American military has evolved, dramatically, from what was originally intended. Its history has been storied and gallant, but also littered with tragedy and troublesome issues. Nonetheless, it has defended the United States successfully for over 230 years, and it will most likely continue to do so.

Further Reading •

Atkinson, Rick. *In the Company of Soldiers: A Chronicle of Combat*. New York: 2004.

Bacevich, Andrew J. *The New American Militarism: How Americans are Seduced by War*. New York: Oxford University Press, 2005.

Cordesman, Anthony H. *The Iraq War: Strategy, Tactics, and Military Lessons*. Westport, Connecticut: Praeger, 2003.

Friedman, Norman. *Terrorism, Afghanistan, and America's New Way of War*. Annapolis: Naval Institute Press, 2003.

Herek, Gregory M., Jared B. Jobe, and Ralph M. Carney, eds. *Out in Force: Sexual Orientation and the Military*. Chicago: University of Chicago Press, 1996.

Herspring, Dale R. *Rumsfeld's Wars: The Arrogance of Power*. Lawrence: University Press of Kansas, 2008.

Katzenstein, Mary Fainsod, and Judith Reppy, eds. *Beyond Zero Tolerance: Discrimination in Military Culture*. Lanham, Maryland: Rowman & Littlefield, 1999.

Mullaney, Craig M. *The Unforgiving Minute: A Soldier's Education*. New York: Penguin Press, 2009.

Murray, Williamson, and Robert H. Scales, Jr. *The Iraq War: A Military History*. Cambridge: Cambridge University Press, 2003.

Record, Jeffrey. *Dark Victory: America's Second War against Iraq*. Annapolis: Naval Institute Press, 2004.

Ricks, Thomas E. *Fiasco: The American Military Adventure in Iraq*. New York: Penguin Press, 2006.

Ricks, Thomas E. *The Gamble: General David Petraeus and the American Military Adventure in Iraq, 2006–2008*. New York: Penguin Press, 2009.

Smith, Ray L., and Bing West. *The March Up: Taking Baghdad with the 1st Marine Division*. New York: Bantam, 2003.

The 9–11 Commission Report: Final Report of the National Commission on Terrorist Attacks Upon the United States. Official Government Edition. Washington D.C.: U.S. Government Printing Office, 2004.

mysearchlab Connections: Sources Online • • • • • • • • • •

READ AND REVIEW

Review this chapter by using the study aids and these related documents available on MySearchLab.

Study Plan

Chapter Test

Essay Test

Documents

George W. Bush, Address to the Nation (2001)

On September 11, 2001, the president addressed the nation, as had previous presidents during the Cuban Missile Crisis, the Pearl Harbor Attack, and other national disasters, to prepare the nation for possible war.

Notes from Donald Rumsfeld on Iraq War planning (2001)

This brief document includes Secretary of Defense Donald Rumsfeld's personal notes on the initial planning for the invasion of Iraq.

Oral History of Colonel Terry L. Sellers (2007)

Army Colonel Terry L. Sellers details his combat, pacification, and nation-building experiences during his tour in Ghanzi Province, Afghanistan, in 2004–2005, to Army historian Christopher N. Koontz.

RESEARCH AND EXPLORE

Explore the following review questions using the research tools available on www. mysearchlab.com.

1. What was the U.S. response to the attacks of September 11, both at home and abroad?
2. How effective was this response?
3. What has been the impact of the wars in Iraq and Afghanistan on the U.S. military?

Index